This Land Was Theirs

This Land

second edition

Was Theirs

A Study of the
North American Indian

Wendell H. Oswalt
University of California, Los Angeles

John Wiley & Sons
New York   London   Sydney   Toronto

Library of Congress Cataloging in Publication Data
Oswalt, Wendell H.
  This land was theirs.

  Bibliography: p.
  1. Indians of North America. I. Title.
E77.08   1973   970.1   72–11973
ISBN 0–471–65717–4

Printed in the United States of America

10 9 8 7 6 5 4 3 2

to Edward H. Spicer

*. . . so long as the waters shall flow
and the sun shall shine . . .*

Also by Wendell H. Oswalt

Mission of Change in Alaska
Napaskiak: An Alaskan Eskimo Community
Alaskan Eskimos
Understanding Our Culture
Other Peoples, Other Customs
Habitat and Technology

Preface to the Second Edition

Preparation of a second edition of *This Land Was Theirs* has been a very satisfying experience. An editor once told me that publishing a book is the nearest approach to childbirth for a male in academia. At the time I believed him, and still do in a sense, but in preparing the text to follow I came to realize that writing a revision is even better than first-time book birth. The reason is that in this revision I am able to offer a partially new creation which hopefully is superior to the last.

In the preparation of the second edition I have weighed the criticisms by general readers, college students, and reviewers. It seems quite appropriate to consider the changes and why they have been made. All my critics felt that a revision must include illustrations, and I have obliged with hopefully adequate coverage. Some persons, especially students, objected to what they considered to be excessive historical detail in the presentations, and when my conscience permitted, some history has been deleted. The chapter on the Beothuk appears to have been satisfying only to me and thus has been omitted; the last chapter, often labeled unsatisfactory because of its perspective, has been changed a great deal; and the opening chapter, which is new, has been included in an effort to answer the types of questions initially asked by persons interested in American Indians. The Caribou Eskimo and Yurok chapters were added as counterpoints for the existing chapters about the Kuskokwim Eskimos and the Tlingit. Furthermore it seemed essential to include a chapter about the Eastern Cherokee since they are the major group of Indians in the eastern United States at the present time. The final chapter attempts to convey an overview of the emergence of contemporary Indian life, a general perspective which could not be presented in the chapters about individual tribes.

vii

Acknowledgements

The manuscript for the first edition chapter about the Cahuilla was read by Dr. Lowell J. Bean, and the one for the Chipewyan was reviewed by Dr. James VanStone. Since comparatively minor changes have been made in these chapters for the second edition, their positive aid remains appreciated. I also am most grateful to Mrs. Joyce Giaquinta, Librarian, State Historical Society of Iowa, for help in locating Fox photographs and to Ms. Sharlotte N. Williams for Eastern Cherokee sources. Mrs. Helen Taylor Oswalt served again as critic, copyeditor and proofreader of this edition, and my debt to her is vast.

Los Angeles, California   *Wendell H. Oswalt*

viii

Preface to the First Edition

The writer of every book reasons, or feels, that he is able to offer something that exists nowhere in published form. No matter what the topic may be, it is likely that an author somewhere aspires to present old information in a new form or a new interpretive point of view. It may seem that far too much already has been written about North American Indians, and even a casual survey of the literature is staggering. There are, for example, the accounts of explorers, missionary records, biographies and autobiographies, fiction, poetry, histories, vehement crusades, and anthropological studies. Also, books published in recent years have attempted to bring some order to these voluminous writings. Still, in spite of all that has been written, I feel or know, depending on my frame of mind at the moment, that yet another book on the American Indian is both desirable and needed. This book is designed to present descriptive accounts of various tribes free, it is hoped, of highly technical terminology, and to trace their diverse ways of life from historic contact to their extinction or to modern times. Additionally, because I am concerned with the concept of the Indian in modern society, I have in a final chapter summarized the position of Indians in modern Canadian and American life.

In the presentation of the ten chapters devoted to geographically representative tribes I have attempted to deal with the same range of topics as far as this has been possible. In general, the topics are presented in the same subject sequence. I sometimes have departed from this general plan because sections organized in an identical manner are boring to write as well as to read. By varying the topical order I had an opportunity to elaborate on diverse subjects in different contexts. Although the subjects are, in general, the same, the emphasis varies considerably from chapter to chapter. This variation is in part due to the nature of the archaeological, ethnographic, and historical literature. When a relatively complete study of a tribe's history exists, the historical dimension is stressed. In other instances stress

ix

has been placed on continuities or discontinuities with the past or on a particular dimension, social or cultural. In making the tribal selections a number of factors were considered. Since the culture area approach, as described in the introduction, has been the organizational point of departure, it was deemed essential to obtain a broad geographical sampling of North American tribes; as far as possible, a diversified representation in terms of culture, society, and languages was also sought.

The attentive or casual reader will find that the chapters are free from any particular theoretical orientation. This approach was decided on only after pondering the problem of presentation at length. Rather than include an analysis of sociocultural change, an obvious theoretical approach, I considered it more appropriate to offer straightforward descriptions of representative Indian tribes.

Comments on the use of some words might be appropriate since I have attempted to follow a patterning. When generalizations are made about American Indians, they should be considered to encompass Eskimos as well. This approach is justified on the grounds that the cultural and linguistic differences separating Indians and Eskimos are no greater than those separating many Indian tribes. Additional justification is found in the fact that the United States government, although not the Canadian government, has for many years considered Alaskan Eskimos and Indians as one for administrative purposes. It will be noted that maize has been used most often rather than corn, except for cornmeal and green corn, whereas bison is employed instead of buffalo; these usages offer a modicum of exactness. The reader with an eye for terminology will note that I have sometimes applied the proper noun "Sioux." The word is imprecise because there was no such Indian tribe. There were, however, diverse tribes which spoke Siouan languages. The only justification I have for using Sioux is that often historical records refer to the Sioux as an ethnic group and do not specify the particular tribe of Siouan speaker involved. Throughout the book the terminology that has come to be accepted in anthropological usage has been kept to a minimum. When a technical word has been employed, it is defined in context, which should present the reader with little difficulty. It will be noted that the term *clan* does not occur, for this is a word with many meanings; I have preferred to use in its place the partial substitute *sib*. One final comment on words is my usage of tribe or ethnic group. These are not exact terms but refer to a population which considers itself, or is considered by others, to be different from other similarly conceived units.

Whenever possible, in writing about a people, I have attempted to limit my descriptions to a particular segment of a tribe. This was desirable in order to present as nearly as possible an actual culture-carrying unit. For example, in writing of the aboriginal Chipewyan, I found it necessary to draw together information about diverse segments of the population, and even then the descriptions are far from complete. When dealing with modern Chipewyan life, however, the descriptions have been limited to one community. While the chapters were being assembled, I made an effort to consult works both lengthy and authoritative. I did not attempt to survey all of the literature on most tribes. At the end of each chapter is appended a list of the references consulted; the key items are marked with a single asterisk and annotated. A brief bibliography of references employed in many if not all chapters appears at the end of the book.

LOS ANGELES, CALIFORNIA   *Wendell H. Oswalt*
March 1966

Contents

xiii

List of Illustrations

Maps

Kinship Diagrams

xvii

Plates

Introductory Perspectives

What is our greatest debt to American Indians? The initial response is abundantly clear: We are indebted to them first and foremost for our country because this land was theirs. Far too often we conveniently ignore this most salient fact. Instead, the inclination is to cite the material contributions of American Indians to our way of life, which are indeed worthy of consideration. An inventory of material borrowings from aboriginal Americans who lived north of Mexico includes moccasins, parkas, birchbark canoes, kayaks, snowshoes, and toboggans, and possibly one domestic plant, the sunflower. This list is perhaps surprisingly short, and if so, it serves to reflect the vast differences between Americans today and aboriginal Americans. Our modern materialism is of such great complexity that North American Indians could not be expected to have contributed a great deal to it. We have freed ourselves from those intimate associations with the environment which characterized American Indian cultures.

Our feelings of guilt about the manner in which we have considered the American Indian in the past gnaws increasingly on our collective social conscience, and the Indian is "in," at least temporarily. Motion picture stars rally to the cause of a tribe, Indians are the subjects of depressing television documentaries, and Indians sometimes are depicted now as heroes in other celluloid dramas. An Indian folk singer in her balladry records old and new injustices, and we listen. Legislators in Congress less often give speeches about how the Indians must be assimilated into the American "melting pot." VISTA workers on reservations become outspoken critics of Federal administrators. Alaskan Eskimos flex their political muscles as the "ice block" in the statehouse, and the Iroquois want their wampum back from museums. Who would have listened to them a few short years ago?

The American Indian has a place in our cultural heritage which may be minimized but never denied. It is doubtful, however, that the thoughts of most persons in the United States ever linger very long on Indians. We have taken them for granted, which is in itself a clear indication that they are a part of our world. We learn about their ways in grade school and something of their history in high school. We may visit Indian reservations and read novels about Indians on occasion. It is in these ways that Indians most often intrude on our thinking, but there exists another dimension to their presence which is worthy of at least a moment's consideration. Indians are our challenge because they represent a homegrown experiment in tolerance, understanding, and compassion.

In historical perspective one enormously important borrowing by white

2

Americans occurred first along the eastern seaboard during colonial times. The early European settlers, who were established only precariously, borrowed the entire maize complex from local Indians. They did not absorb the social or religious associations but were taught by Indians how to cultivate corn, process the harvest, and how to prepare it as a food. The event may not seem of great importance today, but in the context of the time at which it took place it was immensely significant.

If we were to include Indian discoveries or inventions for all of the Americas, the list of contributions would be greater, because American Indian cultures climaxed in Central and South America rather than in North America. To the list would be added potatoes, beans, tomatoes, tobacco, and various drugs, as well as a few material items such as pipes, hammocks, and the rubber syringe. Again, this list is not long, but some of the plants are economically very important around the world today. It still may be asked if American Indians in general were not woefully unimaginative in devising complex items, and the answer would be an obvious yes. To the question of why, the answer seems to stem not from any lack of intelligence on the part of the Indians but rather from their total environmental setting and its potential for the development of civilization. The New World was devoid of such animals as the horse, cow, and pig which had great potential as domestics, and neither were there grains such as wheat and barley. More important, in the New World the animals and plants which had potential as domestics were not concentrated in one restricted geographical area. A contrary situation existed in the Old World, for in the Near East, about 8000 B.C., there emerged the basis for all Old World civilizations. New World developments, however, are not to be cast aside as failures if one considers the complex societies that emerged in aboriginal Mexico and Peru.

Words and phrases derived from a background of Indian contacts continue to be a part of American English. Examples such as Indian summer, happy hunting ground, wild Indian, Indian giver, and "to bury the hatchet" are known widely. When place names are added, the number with an Indian origin is staggering, not only for lakes and rivers but also for states and cities. Indian trails were to become important not only for their names but as roadbeds for the later highways of white Americans.

Indians played a major role in shaping the belief system of one of the few large and lasting religions originating in the United States, the Church of Jesus Christ of Latter-Day Saints or Mormons. The Book of Mormon relates that Indians originated from a segment of the Jewish population which came to the New World before Christian times. According to the Mormon belief system, the Indians descended from the Lamanites; although these were thought to be a degenerate people, the Mormons have been inordinately kind in their dealings with Indians. As noted by A. Irving Hallowell (1958, 461) the inclusion of population theory in a religious dogma "could hardly have occurred anywhere but in early 19th-century America." It might be added further that the nondoctrinal part of the Book of Mormon most likely originated from a novel written, but not published, by Solomon Spaulding.

In early American literature no subject had greater appeal than the Indian, but his literary image has been far from uniform through time. The Indian's entry into American literature was direct via speeches recorded during treaty-making. The oratorical skills of Indians were appreciated, and the texts were printed for general circulation in the eighteenth century. Because Indians were close at hand in the eastern United States and were in the way when the whites began coveting more lands, they soon were looked on as foes. As the frontier drifted westward in the first half of the nineteenth century, the image of the Indian reverted to a nonantagonist, in fact to a romantic figure. Drawing on Indian ethnographic accounts, James F. Cooper wrote his great novels and produced the character of Leatherstocking, a white Indian with no literary equal. Then, too, Henry W. Longfellow's *Hiawatha* is a literary monument of this era. One of the most popular nineteenth-century American plays was "Metamora," and playwrights have continued to build plots around Indians. In the first American opera, "Tammany," performed in 1794, there was a Cherokee melody, and the Indian exists in such American folk songs as Charles Cadman's "From the Land of Sky Blue Waters" and Thurland Chattaway's and Kerry Mills' "Red Wing." Other Indian contributions are now a part of American history; these include the Wild West show, the Indian medicine show, the cigar store Indian, and the romantic appeal of the Indian as a subject for painters.

In the western frontier the Indian assumed a different cast for those white Americans who quested for Indian lands. The Indian was now a sort of vermin to be exterminated since he impeded progress. When the Indian wars and skirmishes had been won and the remnant Indian population confined to reservations, these people again could be viewed romantically; but even before the West was seized, the Indian was a standard figure in nearly half the 320 dime novels that originated in the 1860's. The Indian theme never died but was recast in different mediums with the introduction of motion pictures and radio. Needless to say, American television owes a great debt to the Indian, nor is he forgotten in contemporary novels.

Who Is an Indian?

In the sixteenth century when ever-increasing numbers of European maritime explorers ventured to the Americas, there was no difficulty in establishing who was an Indian. The racial, linguistic, and cultural differences separating Europeans and Indians were apparent to all observers. Indians belonged to the Mongoloid racial stock in obvious contrast with the Caucasian racial background of the intruders. Indians spoke languages which differed widely from one tribe to another, but none could be understood by the explorers. Indians dressed in an unaccustomed manner, and their bodily adornments were different, if not bizarre, to a traveler from Spain, England, or France. Then, too, the major crops that Indians raised, maize and beans, were not cultivated in Europe. Thus the New World clearly was inhabited by peoples who stood in striking contrast to Europeans and their ways.

The problem of classifying a person as an Indian became more complex after the exposure of the American aborigines to European fishermen, adventurers, traders, trappers, settlers, and missionaries. Three sets of conditions resulting from these contacts were important: First, white men mated with Indian women and produced individuals of mixed blood; second, Indians captured whites and sometimes made "Indians" of the captives; and third, some Indians lost their identity by becoming at least partly assimilated into white society. To identify an Indian with clarity after the period of early historic contact we are forced to deal with two primary sets of factors—racial and sociocultural. It can be imagined that whites who were assimilated into an Indian tribe would be considered "Indians," in spite of their racial identity. Likewise there were Indians who disassociated themselves from other Indians and came to be judged as "whites." Situations like these are rather straightforward, but for individuals of mixed Indian and white ancestry, the distinctions are not so clear. Such persons may be Indian in one context and white in another, Indian or white exclusively throughout their lives, or Indian at one time in life and white at another. The identification of an Indian has become a matter of definition and is most reasonably considered in a legal sense.

Before considering Indian identity further, one point of potential confusion should be noted. For all practical purposes Eskimos may be considered Indians. Eskimos were classed by Europeans as separate because their physical appearance was distinctive and because their way of life in the arctic contrasted rather strikingly with the customs of other Indians. In racial terms Eskimos are the most Mongoloid of indigenous New World peoples, and their subsistence adaptations to the arctic littoral do stand apart from the economies of most other Indians. However, the linguistic and cultural differences separating some Indian tribes from each other are greater than those which separate Eskimos from many Indians. Thus, Eskimos and Indians may reasonably be referred to simply as Indians.

In the history of Indian law in the United States there has not been a precise and uniform definition of an Indian. In general, however, precedent has established that if a person is considered an Indian by other individuals in his community, he is legally an Indian. The degree of Indian blood in an individual may be important, but under most circumstances this is secondary to his sociocultural standing in the community in which he lives. Examples will illustrate why there is so much confusion. If an individual is on the roll of a Federally recognized Indian group, then he is an Indian; his degree of Indian blood is of no real consequence, although usually he has at least some Indian blood. In *Federal Indian Law* it is stated that a person may, on some reservations, be considered an Indian even if records show that fifteen of his sixteen immediate ancestors were not Indian. However, the real need for defining an Indian is with reference to a piece of legislation at a particular time. A person who is on the roll of a tribe and lives on a reservation clearly is an Indian; if he moves from a reservation but remains on the roll, he continues to be an Indian. If he receives a clear title to allotted reservation land, he may or may not subsequently remain an Indian, depending on the circumstances. It would appear that one's status as an Indian is lost by disassociating oneself voluntarily from other Indians and becoming identified with some other social segment of society.

In the United States all Indians did not become citizens until 1924 when the Citizenship Act was passed by Congress. Previous to this time about 250,000 Indians had become citizens by other means; the act itself made citizens of about 125,000 persons. As early as 1817 individuals were granted citizenship under treaty arrangements if they met certain provisions, such as the acceptance of title to individual lands in contrast to living on tribal lands. It was for many years the prevailing opinion of the Federal government that when Indians followed tribal customs and were not under the control of the state or territory in which they lived they could not be citizens. Becoming a citizen was given a different basis with the passage of the Dawes Act of 1887. This act was designed to break up reservation lands into personal holdings of individuals and families. After an individual received a clear title to his land, he became a citizen, or if he adopted civilized ways and lived apart from any tribe he also became a citizen. Because he was an Indian he might still retain a special status and receive treaty or other benefits. Thus he was a citizen, but one with special privileges not granted to other citizens. In 1888 a law was passed making Indian women citizens if they married citizens, the assumption being that these women were following the path of civilization. Indians were not inducted into the armed services during World War I since they were not citizens. However, those who volunteered were made citizens by Congressional action. It is noteworthy that by 1938 seven states still refused to allow Indians to vote, and only in 1948 were voting rights granted to Indians in Arizona and New Mexico. Opposition to Indian suffrage was based on the fact that they still retained a special relationship to the Federal government.

One of the provisions of the Canadian Indian Act of 1876 was that any Indian who had a university education or its equivalent thereby became a citizen. In other instances, the individual or the band by majority vote initiated enfranchisement proceedings; this method required a probationary period before becoming effective. When a man with a wife and minor, unmarried children became enfranchised, his family was granted the same legal status. These provisions did not in general apply to the Indians of British Columbia, Manitoba or the Northwest Territories. In 1880 the mandatory enfranchisement was made voluntary. Prior to 1895 an enfranchised Indian received a land allotment by the band; after this time he received land as well as his share of funds belonging to the band. In 1920 it became possible for officers of the Superintendent General to enfranchise an Indian, male or female, without a prior request from the Indian for full citizenship. Such a person still received land and his share of tribal funds. In 1922 the involuntary process leading to citizenship was repealed, and it again was necessary for an individual or a band, by vote of its majority, to apply for enfranchisement. Again in 1933 involuntary enfranchisement was made possible by a new amendment to the Act. Consideration was given in 1917 and 1948 to granting full citizenship to Canadian Indians in general, but no legislation to this effect was passed. Canadian Indians, as a result of the Indian Act of 1951, became subject to the same general laws that applied to other Canadians. They could vote in national elections and in most local elections, and for the first time, they could consume intoxicants legally.

Eskimo-white relations throughout the history of Greenland stand in striking contrast with the policies of the United States and Canada toward aboriginal peoples within their borders. The modern history of Greenland began in 1721 when the Norwegian Lutheran missionary Hans Egede left Denmark to found a trade and mission settlement at Godthaab, the modern capital of Greenland. The trading enterprise was not a success initially, but the mission slowly began to prosper. For the first fifty years Danish traders and missionaries dictated in an autocratic manner to the Eskimos along the western coast of Greenland. When it became apparent that the vast island could not be self-supporting, it was closed to outsiders. The Noble Savage concept of Jean-Jacques Rousseau made a great impact on a number of influential politicians at the Danish royal court, and the king was persuaded not to destroy Greenland's Eskimo culture. In the *Instructions* issued in 1782 concerning trade, the welfare of the Eskimos was to have priority over the trade itself. Relations with whites were controlled rigidly, and the introduction of potentially harmful items, such as alcoholic beverages and tea, was prohibited. Furthermore, the Royal Greenland Trade was made responsible for the welfare of the poor, and it set prices for all goods bought and sold. Thus the Eskimos were sheltered from the outside world and the ills of civilization. As Diamond Jenness (1967, 32) remarked, Denmark set out "to create in her arctic colony a Garden of Eden." By 1840 all the profits from the trade were used for the welfare of the Eskimos, an almost unheard-of policy for a colonial government. Yet Greenlanders suffered greatly because their major export, blubber, could not be obtained in quantity at this time since whales had been over-hunted. About the same time the waters around western Greenland became slightly warmer, and great numbers of cod began to migrate northward to serve as a major new economic focus. Population aggregates at salteries became increasingly dependent on imported foods and manufactures. The skin-covered kayaks and umiaks were displaced by the fishing boat of plank construction. Slightly later sheep began to be raised in increasing numbers and emerged finally as an important source of income and local meat.

With an ecclesiastical reorganization in 1905, an effort was made to replace Danish missionaries with Eskimos trained as Lutheran clergy and soon the "Church of Greenland" was created in which Greenlanders came to dominate the ranks, although higher positions still were held by Danes. In 1906-1907, educational opportunities were expanded to include the high school level of training, but education remained under the control of clergy. This move was followed by a decision to grant the people more control of local affairs; this change occurred in 1908. Municipal Councils comprised only of Greenlanders maintained public order, settled civil disputes, administered relief funds, and elected representatives to a higher advisory council which reported to the local Danish administrators. One major change was introduced in 1925: Danes became eligible for election to the Municipal Councils. The following year the social welfare program was expanded broadly to provide pensions for all persons over fifty-five years of age who could not provide for themselves and their families. Eskimo had always been the official language; Danish was a second language, the one of instruction in the schools, which remained under church control.

During World War II when Denmark was occupied by the Germans, Greenland was administered by the Danish representatives to the colony, and its economic ties were with Canada and the United States. It was during this era that Greenlanders first learned to cope with the world at large. The most far-reaching change was initiated in 1950 when the elected Greenland Provincial Council was created as the governing body for most of Greenland, and the island was incorporated as a province of Denmark.

Indian Origins

To determine the region of the world from which the American Indian population originated is intriguing and has had lasting romantic appeal. To probe the origins of anything is a legitimate concern of scientists, humanists, or laymen alike, and persons in each of these categories have long puzzled over the original home of Indians in the Americas. It is fascinating that each of the major theories advanced to explain the derivation and spread of Indians involves something that is lost to modern times. The Lost Tribes of Israel, the lost continents of Atlantis and Lemuria (Mu) and the sunken land bridge across Bering Strait—each stands as a candidate for consideration. They share the common characteristic that supporting data must be indirect because fully conclusive evidence has vanished.

The earliest theory of Indian origins must be the one involving a lost continent, reportedly in the Atlantic Ocean and called Atlantis; speculation about it predates the discovery of the Americas. Once aboriginal Americans became known to Europeans, the island of Atlantis became the logical stepping stone for these migrants from the Old to the New World. Plato reported that Atlantis was a vast island beyond Gibralter, where a complex civilization had existed until it was destroyed by a cataclysm. The idea seemingly lingered among the Romans and was accepted by some persons in medieval Europe, but before the Atlantic Ocean was explored no one could be certain whether or not the island existed. Christopher Columbus appears to have sailed toward its presumed position, and some thought that the land he discovered was Atlantis. The thesis that indigenous Americans were derived from Atlantis crystallized in sixteenth-century Spain and first emerged with clarity in the writings of Francisco Lopez de Gomara, which appeared in 1552. He proposed, for example, that "atl," which was the word for water among Indians in one sector of Mexico, was a lingering remembrance of their homeland called Atlantis. By the 1880's the island's disappearance still was attributed to a major cataclysm which had occurred after the people destined to become American Indians had left its shores, and the theory was advocated by some more staunchly than ever. Each author who supported the theory of this lost island was struck by the cultural similarities between American Indians, usually those in Mexico, with some early Old World civilization, usually from Egypt.

A second lost continent theory involves the prehistoric presence of a great Pacific island called Lemuria or Mu. This thesis has found considerable support among some laymen. Its proponent was James Churchward, and his last book on the subject appeared in 1931. He reportedly traveled in India, and he met a priest who saw him attempting to decipher some old inscriptions. The priest befriended Churchward and spent two years teaching him what was said to be the original language of man. Later Churchward was shown some secret inscribed tablets which recorded the original creation story with Lemuria detailed as the place of human origins. The mystical nature of this theme, the failure of anyone else to be aware of this original language, and an inability to produce the original or similar inscriptions, seriously weaken the entire argument.

Rivaling these lost continent theories is another which contends that Indians are descendants of the Lost Tribes of Israel. Samuel F. Haven long ago summarized the supporting evidence. Ten tribes of Israelites, defeated by the Assyrians, were removed to the northeastern sector of the Assyrian empire. Here they became lost by wandering into Asia, and they ventured on to a point nearest the Americas, where they crossed the waters to another land. This was the New World, and evidence to support the Hebrew ancestry of the Indians was to be found in certain of their customs, words, and idioms. The theory long has been popular and continues to find particularly active support among members of the Church of Jesus Christ of Latter-Day Saints. Although the Book of Mormon is not concerned with the lost tribes, the Mormons persistently have sent archaeological parties to Middle America to find support for a Hebrew migration to the New World which in turn gave rise to Indian civilizations.

A host of other conjectures have been advanced to explain the origins of American Indians. Some speculators have singled out seafaring peoples such as the Carthaginians or Phoenicians as being responsible for the original occupation. Others felt that the Tartars, sometimes viewed as remnants of the Lost Tribes of Israel, were the earliest occupants of the Americas; they were relatively near the New World in geographical terms and were a far-ranging people. The Chinese, Ethiopians, Scandinavians, Polynesians, and Welsh similarly have attracted speculative attention. It was Cotton Mather in colonial America who advanced one of the most unique explanations for Indian origins. He wrote that "probably the *Devil* decoyed those miserable salvages hither, in hopes that the gospel of the Lord Jesus Christ would never come here to destroy or disturb his absolute empire over them" (Drake, 1837, 9).

In 1570 the Jesuit missionary Father Joseph de Acosta went to Peru, and about 1580 he began to write his *Historia natural y moral de las Indias*. The book appeared in its first Spanish edition in 1590, three years after he returned to Spain. Acosta reasoned that since Adam was the original ancestor of mankind and since Indians were people, then they must have come from the Old World which Adam's descendants had peopled. He rejected the ideas of Atlantis or Hebrew origins for Indians, and he did not think there could have been a second ark or that angels accounted for aboriginal man's presence in the New World. He reasoned that the New World and the Old World were connected, or separated by a narrow strait, because certain land mammals were the same in the respective hemispheres. He felt that men and animals alike had traveled along the same route. The human entry was visualized as having taken place slowly and as having been caused by overpopulation, famines, or the loss of their former living areas. Thus, Acosta was the first to advance a land bridge theory and to offer an explanation of why peoples entered the New World. He theorized too that these original occupants were hunters who later developed a more complex way of life. Therefore any comparisons between New and Old World civilizations could not be very meaningful.

Contemporary anthropologists second and support the thesis of Indian origins advanced first by Acosta. It is abundantly clear that man did not evolve in the New World; instead he was a migrant to it. This conclusion is reached in part because the nearest living relatives to man all are found in the Old World. Furthermore, no bones have been recovered in the Americas which represent early stages of man's physical emergence. By contrast, in the Old World, especially in Africa, bones repeatedly have been recovered which are clear markers along man's evolutionary trail. In the same context, the earliest human remains in the New World date about 10,000 B.C. and belonged to individuals who were essentially modern in their physical appearance. Thus from the fossil record we must conclude that man entered the Western Hemisphere in the not-too-distant past.

After increasingly sophisticated research, no geological evidence exists to suggest the presence of any former continents in either the Atlantic or Pacific oceans. Thus, the lost continents of Atlantis and Mu could not have served as stepping stones to the New World. Neither does it seem likely that the first men entered the Western Hemisphere by traveling from one known island to another, across either the Atlantic or Pacific oceans. If such had been the case we would expect to find their remains on at least one of the possible islands involved. However, no archaeological finds ever reported from Iceland, Greenland, the Aleutian Islands, the islands of Polynesia, or any others, have suggested that they were way stations for the first entrants to the New World. Furthermore, at the time when man is presumed to have entered the Americas first, he did not possess vessels which as a standard activity could be used to cross sizeable bodies of open water.

The weight of current evidence is that the first people to arrive in the New World entered over a land bridge in the Bering Strait area. They probably lingered in Alaska for a considerable length of time and eventually followed western mountains southward into Canada, ventured on into the western United States and Mexico, and finally continued southward into South America. The economic lives of the earliest migrants must have been based on hunting methods adapted to subarctic conditions. The Bering Strait entryway appears to have served as a cultural filter through which only hunters could pass. Their way of life must have been comparatively unelaborated, and most, if not all, of the later complexities in their cultures must have developed in the Americas. In much later times, but long before the arrival of Columbus, new groups of people from the Old World continued to enter the Americas along the Bering Strait route and possibly via a number of other passages.

Indian Antiquity

The accepted theory of American Indian origins points to the northeastern sector of Siberia as the most probable point of departure. The next question is precisely how long have they occupied the Western Hemisphere. Before considering current thoughts on the subject it is relevant to consider, in brief, historical thoughts about the problem.

In 1590, Acosta felt that Indians had inhabited the Americas about 2000 years or even less, and in the context of his times this was a reasonable supposition. Theologians then presumed that the world and men had been formed by God in the very recent past. It generally was agreed that man had been created about 4000 B.C., a figure established by calculating the generations represented in biblical genealogies. The date, which a revisionist specified as 9:00 a.m., October 23, 4004 B.C., was not called into serious question until the science of geology emerged. Two Englishmen above all others contributed the most to the first empirical understanding of the earth's history; they were James Hutton and Charles Lyell. Hutton reasoned that the same principles of geological changes which were observed in his time had prevailed in past times, and Lyell expanded broadly on this thesis. The most important conclusion was that the earth was changing very slowly in physical terms and that therefore it must be very old. Before long a French civil servant, Boucher de Perthes, established as a result of archaeological studies that men once lived among animals now extinct. Boucher's conclusions were a direct challenge to the idea that God in his wisdom had created a perfect world and that all the creatures which existed originally still lived. In the 1840's the thoughts of Charles Darwin were crystallizing and soon would produce the evolution revolution. Not until the knowledge gained by investigators in the first half of the nineteenth century had been sorted, ordered, and broadly accepted could a synthesis of American Indian prehistory be advanced in reasonable terms. Not unexpectedly it was an Englishman, John Lubbock, who guided the way. Although his primary interest was not in aboriginal Americans, he was the first to suggest a sequential patterning for Indian cultural development. In *Pre-Historic Times* (1865) he suggested that the first people were barbarians, which presumably meant Indians who lived mainly by hunting. The next stage was that of the mound builders, and it was followed by farmers; by the time of historic contact, however, the Indians had retrogressed to a partial state of barbarism.

During the 1860's it was thought that the earliest stone tools in Europe had been made 100,000 to 240,000 years ago, and those from the Somme Valley in France were termed Paleolithic by Lubbock. Since the men living in Europe at that time hunted animals now extinct, it was anticipated that similar associations would be found in the New World. As a result of searches for these early remains, tools found in gravels near Trenton, New Jersey, were attributed to the Paleolithic, and a human skull from a California gold mine was considered of Pliocene age. This dating was not to endure, and by the turn of the present century a reaction had developed against assuming a great antiquity for New World man. Aleš Hrdlička, a physical anthropologist and archaeologist, spearheaded the attack. From a detailed study of all the reportedly ancient finds he concluded that man had been here only in postglacial times. In terms of what now is known of this chronology, this would have meant about 11,000 years ago at the earliest. Although Hrdlička was dogmatic and overemphasized the conclusions which could be drawn from the morphology of human bones, he also pointed up the poor field methodology which had led to much of the confusion.

By the second decade of this century anthropology had expanded rapidly as an academic discipline, and archaeologists were not only more numerous but were far better trained than ever before. Their excavation techniques became increasingly sophisticated, and they were much more careful to document their finds. The problem of Indian antiquity now was being studied by skilled professionals utilizing precise methodology. In spite of all that is known about the subject, at present we still must pause and heed the reminder of Alex D. Krieger (1964, 25): "Scholars simply do not know how much material there is on both American continents that bears on the earliest cultures. . . ."

The antiquity of New World man remained largely speculative until the year 1926. It was then that a party of paleontologists working in northern New Mexico unearthed the bones of a species of bison considered to be long extinct. In dirt from the excavation were found two pieces of flaked flint points. Before long another point fragment was found embedded in clay near the rib of an animal. It later was realized that one of the first two pieces found had been broken from the fragment recovered near the rib and that when they were combined the two sections formed part of a projectile point. It seemed that here was clear evidence of early Americans hunting ancient animals during the Pleistocene, but archaeologists were reluctant to accept the validity of the association. Nonetheless J. D. Figgins, the director of the Colorado Museum of Natural History, from which the field party emanated, ordered a continuation of the excavations the following year. After four broken flint points were found near bison bones but free from the matrix, a fifth was observed in place. Work was stopped, and leading anthropological institutions were telegraphed to send representatives to the site. Those who responded accepted the validity of the association. The projectile points were named Folsom after the type site, and the bison bones came to be known as *Bison antiquus figginsi*.

Plate 1 *Folsom point and associated fossil bison bones embedded in matrix from near Folsom, New Mexico* (Courtesy of the Denver Museum of Natural History).

At first the Folsom points and extinct bison remains were thought to be of Pleistocene age, but it is now known that these flints and bones date approximately 8000 B.C. It further has emerged with considerable clarity that the Folsom point makers were specialized bison hunters who occupied much of the Great Plains for a comparatively brief span of time. We know too that earlier, around 10,000 B.C., Americans hunted mammoths using flint spear points now termed Clovis. The distinctive Folsom and Clovis flints left by Paleo-Americans may have served as knives as well as projectile points. Very little is known about the lives of these hunters apart from their stone technologies, which are unrelated to specific developments in any other area of the world. This general stage of development often has been termed Paleo-Indian, and a most intriguing question is whether any remains of man which have greater antiquity exist in the New World.

The most tantalizing find in this respect was made near Lewisville in northeastern Texas, where charred plant remains found in hearths were dated by the radiocarbon technique as having been alive about 35,000 B.C. It is most unfortunate that someone "planted" a Clovis point in this deposit so that it would be found and considered as a valid association. The Clovis point was indeed recovered, but eventually the hoax was revealed. Because of it, the entire site has a tainted quality to many, perhaps most commentators. In spite of this fact it is worthwhile to consider the evidence in brief. Some twenty feet beneath the ground surface at the site the remains of twenty-one hearths were uncovered at varying levels. One hearth was an irregular circle about eight feet across and included the plant remains which were dated as well as the bones of birds, deer, horses, prairie dogs, rats, snails, terrapin, and wolves; a short distance away a flint scraper was found. Near a group of four other hearths was found a crude quartzite chopper, and a quartzite cobble used as a hammerstone was recovered on a nearby erosion surface. These three stone tools, the hearths, and the scattered bones, some of which were burnt, seemingly are a valid triumvirate. Suggestively the site was a camping place for hunters who killed and ate diverse species.

The Tule Springs site in southern Nevada dates around 30,000 B.C. and has yielded what may be hearths along with associated split and burned bones of camels, horses, and mammoths as well as stone choppers and flakes seemingly produced by man. Yet a huge excavation there in recent years uncovered virtually nothing more. Another intriguing site is on Santa Rosa Island off the coast of southern California. In the late Pleistocene when the sea level was much lower than now there probably was only a narrow channel of water separating this island from the mainland, whereas today Santa Rosa Island is forty-five miles offshore. On the island about 27,000

B.C. there lived a species of dwarf mammoth; the skeletons of some have been found disarticulated, with vertebrae and skulls often missing, an indication that they might have been butchered. Skulls were recovered that had been smashed, apparently to remove the brains, and some bones had been burned. Added to these finds was a piece of chipped stone which was recovered among the bones. Finally large abalone shells were found in the locality, possibly carried there by man.

Some archaeologists, perhaps even a majority, would not accept the Lewisville, Tule Springs, or Santa Rosa remains as clear evidence of man in the New World around 30,000 B.C. and somewhat earlier. However, a recent symposium organized by Richard Shutler and devoted to early man in North America indicates that there is a growing body of evidence that man has been in the New World for at least 35,000 years.

Influences from across the Seas

The subject of voyages to the New World before the arrival of Columbus has almost boundless imaginary appeal. To conceive of brave men in small boats setting off for they know not where is spine-tingling, and the romance of the idea has led numerous men to visualize a wide variety of voyages. Even when we set imagination aside, the realities of what might have occurred are in themselves most inviting.

The only pre-Columbian voyages beyond reasonable dispute must be cited first, and these involve the Vikings. Iceland was settled in the ninth century by Scandinavians, and within a hundred years Greenland had been discovered as well. Eric the Red (he had red hair) was exiled from southern to northern Iceland for homicide, and when he again murdered a number of persons he was forced to leave for three years. He spent his exile, A.D. 981-984, exploring southwestern Greenland, and on his return he organized a colonizing expedition. It left for southwest Greenland the following year, and over the years other settlers were attracted there. The Greenland colony was occupied by the Vikings until about 1500 and had a maximum population of about 3000 persons. Given the turbulent weather in the north Atlantic Ocean, many ships heading toward Greenland were lost or blown off course. One vessel strayed to the coast of North America, in 986, but did not land. Later, the son of Eric the Red, Leif Ericson, purposefully sailed for Vinland or North America about the year 1000; the first document mentioning Vinland is dated 1073. In the centuries to follow numerous purposeful trips were made to Vinland from Greenland, especially to obtain building timber. The Vikings also founded a settlement at L'Anse aux Meadows in Newfoundland, which was discovered and partially excavated by Helge Ingstad. Radiocarbon dates demonstrate that the community was occupied about A.D. 1000. Artifacts of Norse manufacture and the presence of wrought iron in the site leave no doubt that the remains were those of Norse colonists. At the same time there is no present evidence that this Viking settlement, or any other that may have existed, had any impact on the cultural ways of the aboriginal Americans.

If voyagers from the Old World, apart from the Vikings, did arrive in the New World during pre-Columbian times, we would expect to find artifacts that they brought with them. Conversely, if travelers ventured in the opposite direction, we would expect to recover in the eastern hemisphere objects which were made in the Americas. In spite of the thousands of excavations in which millions of artifacts have been recovered, not one such artifact has been found in clearly valid context. Admittedly such objects may exist in unexplored sites, and if any are found, our thinking must be revised or even reversed. The fact remains that currently there is no reason to think, on the basis of the specific artifact forms discovered, that any pre-Columbian voyagers other than the Norse reached the New World.

Another perspective is gained by comparing Old and New World languages. If there were contacts of a substantial nature, we might expect to find clear or vague linguistic ties. Evidence for relationships between languages cannot be based on the occurrence of a small cluster of isolated words with the same form and meaning because such parallels may be accounted for on the basis of chance alone. In order to demonstrate the presence of historical ties between languages, there must be clear phonemic and grammatical similarities as well as numerous parallels among morphemes. Is there any evidence of this nature to link pre-Columbian peoples of the two hemispheres? The answer is "yes," but it only occurs in the Bering Strait area. The Eskimo-Aleut language family which spans the American arctic and the Chukchi-Kamchatkan family of northeastern Siberia are related closely and belong to the American Arctic-Paleosiberian linguistic phylum. Thus the New and Old Worlds are joined in linguistic terms but not in the manner most speculators might assume.

We realize that it is asking a great deal to expect to find Old World artifacts in New World sites, if only because very few might survive long ocean voyages. Similarly we may suggest that the bearers of Old World languages could have arrived and their languages might have passed out of existence when the original migrants died. This raises the question of whether or not there are direct *influences* from Old World sources to reach the Americas? In order to consider the question it first is necessary to make one critical observation. There are innumerable examples of the people in one part of the world originating an artifact form which was quite similar to those independently conceived and produced by other peoples. Thus, we must be cautious when deducing that a form was invented independently in different parts of the world or that a form had a single place of origin and spread from there to other peoples. Furthermore, if complexes or configurations of Old and New World forms are identified as similar, such evidence is of greater potential significance than are similarities between particular artifact types or design motifs.

One of the persistent, but cautious, advocates of transpacific contacts has been Gordon F. Ekholm. He suggests that wheeled "toys" from Mexico and Asia might have common origins and wonders too whether pottery-making in the Americas is not from an Old World source. The iron pyrite mirrors of Mesoamerica and the copper axes used as currency in Mexico during the Aztec period suggest the bronze mirrors and ax money in China. The Olmec people of Mesoamerica exhibited the earliest complex culture in this region, and in its first known stages it is already quite sophisticated but without any local basis. The great Olmec stress on the tiger motif in art recalls a similar stress in the early bronze age Shang dynasty of China in the latter part of the second millennium B.C. Around the time of Christ the cylindrical, tripod pottery vessels found in parts of Mexico recall similar shapes in pottery and bronze from the Han period in China. Furthermore, in certain Maya sites of the Late Classic and Postclassic periods, are some suggestive similarities with Hindu-Buddhist developments in India and Southeast Asia; included are lotus panels, phallic sculptures, tiger thrones, and the "tree of life" motif.

Possibly of greater conclusiveness is the occurrence of certain artifacts in sites along coastal Ecuador, dating about 200 B.C., which are Asian-like. As Emilio Estrada and Betty J. Meggers have noted, the cluster of types is largely restricted in distribution to Ecuador in the New World. Included are pottery models of houses with saddle-shaped roofs and columns, figurines with one leg folded above the other, and the coolie yoke. They have suggested that a seagoing vessel from Asia arrived and the migrants successfully introduced these and other novelties.

The evidence for Old-New World culture contacts based on linguistics and artifacts is conclusive only with reference to language ties across Bering Strait and Norse artifacts in northeastern North America. Hints and suggestions that bonds reached tenuously across the Pacific Ocean exist but are not as yet entirely convincing. Another approach to the problem centers on evidence of another nature: domestic plants and animals transported by pre-Columbian man to the New World. In a symposium organized by

Carroll L. Riley, he and his associates stressed a consideration of just such cultigens. I can do no better than quote their summary remarks in this regard (Riley, et al., 1971, 452-453). "The consensus of botanical evidence given in this symposium seems to be that *there is no hard and fast evidence for any pre-Columbian human introduction of any single plant or animal* across the ocean from the Old World to the New World, or vice-versa. This is emphatically *not* to say that it could not have occurred." Thus, the case rests on a largely negative note.

Indian Studies

No matter where Europeans settled in North America, it soon became apparent that Indians had arrived at an earlier time and that a great deal of diversity existed among them. In physical appearance the members of some groups differed greatly from those found elsewhere, and even within a community there might be considerable variation. Then too some Indians primarily were fishermen as others farmed and still others hunted to make a living. They spoke many highly diverse languages, and they organized themselves in many different ways, ranging from small, mobile, autonomous communities to large, stable confederations. In order to begin to understand this diversity it is necessary to define some of the concepts which have proven useful in ordering information accumulated about Indians along spatial and temporal dimensions.

Any reasonably systematic descriptive account about the customs of a people is called an ethnography. Their manufactures, language, social and political organization, art, knowledge and myths, all are ethnographic dimensions. An ethnography is overwhelmingly descriptive, and it pertains to a brief period of time. In more exacting terms, an *ethnography* is a descriptive framework for behavioral information about a population for a particular point in time. The peoples considered by an ethnographer usually are aboriginal or are derived from an aboriginal base, and the time coverage is a typical calendar year. It should be noted that ethnographic data are collected as systematically as possible and are checked for internal consistency; for these reasons, most accounts by explorers, travelers, or journalists would not qualify fully. There are two general categories of ethnographies: baseline studies made about life at the time of historic contact and others made about Indian life for later points in time. A *baseline ethnography* describes a people before they had any significant degree of contact with representatives of literate or civilized societies. Thus the data represent conditions before the subjects for study were influenced or disrupted by Europeans, Euro-Americans, or the members of other more complex societies. In a strict sense, a baseline ethnography should be compiled before contact even with European trade goods or diseases of European origins. Yet it is seldom that a capable observer was present to record a broad range of information about an American Indian population in a systematic manner before their customs were altered by agents of Western civilization. The first comprehensive ethnography of an American Indian tribe, or of any aboriginal people for that matter, which made a significant impact on anthropology was written in 1851. The author was Lewis H. Morgan, and his study was of the Iroquois Indians in New York state. Thus, ethnography as a separate and distinct intellectual pursuit is of comparatively recent origins.

Trained investigators did not begin making reasonably thorough studies of American Indian life until shortly before the turn of the present century. Usually they attempted to collect verbal information about the way of life the Indians had followed at the time of historic contact, or at least for a period as far back in time as an informant could recall. An ethnographer visited Indians and talked with them about their past; he also consulted written sources; and by utilizing both forms of information, he compiled an ethnographic account about aboriginal life, or a reconstructed baseline ethnography. The primary difficulty in such an enterprise was to obtain reliable information pertaining to the early historic period. Most ethnographies written by anthropologists about American Indians were reconstructions made long after the first historic contacts of the groups studied. One of the major difficulties was validating statements by informants, especially when documentary sources had not been studied thoroughly, a typical failing of most early ethnographers. The time factor could not be held constant at the early historic period, and as a result the accounts which they wrote were composites of past customs at various points in time.

As the lives of Indians changed following prolonged firsthand contact with exotic complex societies, the Indians were said to be undergoing the process of acculturation; the end product was either stabilized pluralism or assimilation into the dominant society. Thus we may consider *acculturative ethnographies* as the second type of study. They present a description of life relating to a brief span of historic time and may be assembled from documents or by observations and interviews.

Another ethnographic approach, one with a broader scope in terms of time covered, is the study of a people through all of their history in order to plot the changes in their lifeway; this type of presentation is called *ethnohistory*. The sources consulted are standard ethnographies, the Indians themselves if possible, and diverse writings ranging from early to late in their history and in type from diaries to newspapers. *Ethnoarchaeology* is the employment of archaeological techniques to acquire ethnographic data about a particular population. The time range represented by the excavated remains is immaterial in classifying it as a study of this type; the major consideration is that the archaeology must be identified with a particular people. If broad or narrow generalizations are drawn from ethnographic information, the study is termed *ethnology*, which is the comparative study of ethnographic data.

To this point the units for study have been termed "peoples" or "populations," but a greater distinction is required. Different groups of Indians usually are termed "tribes," yet no general agreement concerning the criteria for a tribe will accommodate all North American Indians comfortably. The difficulties in deriving a concept which encompasses the diversity of social norms and cultural forms may be illustrated by considering a rather typical definition. Alfred L. Kroeber (1925, 474) stated that a true tribe "has a name, a dialect, and a territory." Yet among the nearly fifty major Indian groups in California, only the Yokuts of the San Joaquin valley had all three characteristics; most California Indians did not have a distinct name, identifying themselves only as the residents of a particular community. Efforts to define a tribe on the basis of political cohesiveness have proved to be equally unrewarding. As John R. Swanton (1953, 1-2) has pointed out, the reported variability seems to defy the use of a single label. The Creeks confederated dominant with subordinate tribes; the term Powhatan embraced about thirty tribes or subtribes united by conquest; the Chippewa (Ojibwa) label included small groups of people who had little if any political unity, while each Pueblo village governed its own affairs, and was in a sense a tribe.

Kroeber (1955, 303-314) later attempted to bring some order into the terminological maze. He wrote, "What are generally denominated tribes really are small nationalities, possessing essentially uniform speech and customs and therefore an accompanying sense of likeness and likemindedness, which in turn tended to prevent serious dissensions or internal conflicts." Within such nationalities were smaller sovereign states usually termed "bands" or "villages" which were in fact economically self-sufficient and had a recognized territory and political independence. Kroeber reasoned that a "tribe" was rather like one of the numerous German states before their consolidation in 1871; each state functioned independently although they shared a common language, culture, and ideology. In the United States these units more properly were designated nations in the seventeenth and eighteenth centuries. Actually the concept "tribe" or nation most often was a product of white contact as government officials grouped bands or villages so they could more conveniently negotiate treaties, arrange resettlements, and so on. Aboriginal decision making most often was at the band or village level, although among some peoples these were consolidated into larger political aggregates. For the chapters to follow, the difficulties in defining a tribe are not overwhelmingly important, but the reader should be aware that a tribe is not consistently a "tribe." Those interested in pursuing the topic further are referred to a volume devoted to the subject which was edited by June Helm (1968).

Formulation of an adequate definition of the concept tribe has not been the only persistent problem. Another is that the time of historic contact differed widely from one region of North America to another. Many tribes in the eastern United States had been destroyed by disease and homicide or displaced from their lands before others to the north and west had ever heard of a white man or knew of the diseases which he carried. Historic contact began about A.D. 1000 in one sector of Newfoundland, while in the Southwest it was 1540 and was 1885 in one sector of central Alaska. Thus no single decade or even century represents the "contact" period. This means that there is a *sliding historical baseline* for the beginnings of Indian history on a regional basis. Swanton (1953, 3-6) suggested that if A.D. 1650 is taken as a base date, it is possible to establish the indigenous Indian boundaries for the southern and eastern United States as well as for eastern Canada. In the northwestern sector of the continent there appear to have been no major relocations of peoples between 1650 and the time of actual historic contact, which makes it possible to tentatively include them under this date as well. For the balance of the continent north of Mexico, the date of 1650 is probably less satisfactory. An adjustment backward in time to around A.D. 1540 might be more accurate to accommodate the peoples of the Southwest. The plains area would require several dates over a considerable time span. The most important conclusion to be drawn is that the boundaries and positioning of many tribes on standard ethnographic maps, including the ones in this volume, are not entirely accurate for any single time period. Instead they attempt to represent the area of any particular tribe at the moment in history when it was surveyed and located on a map.

Languages

It has been estimated that from 1,000,000 to 1,500,000 Indians lived north of Mexico when they first were contacted, and they spoke about 300 different languages. In some sectors, such as among Eskimos along the arctic rim, one language was spoken over a great lineal expanse. In other regions, as in northwestern Canada, were found a large block of different but closely related languages. Elsewhere several highly distinct languages would be spoken in a limited area. In California, for example, there was far greater linguistic diversity than is found in all of modern Europe.

European settlers could ignore Indian customs if they wished since they lived in separate communities, but they could not ignore Indian languages if they hoped to communicate with them. Since typical colonists felt superior to Indians, they seldom attempted to learn an Indian language; it was most often Indians or persons of mixed-blood who became bilingual. Yet for missionaries intent on converting Indians to Christianity it was virtually essential to learn the languages of peoples among whom they worked in order to convey the complexities of their dogma. The first landmark in American Indian linguistics was the publication in 1663 of a Bible which had been translated into Massachuset, an Algonkian language, by the missionary John Eliot; in 1666 he published an Algonkian grammar.

The most prominent person from a relatively early period who was interested in Indian linguistics was Thomas Jefferson. He was concerned that these languages were disappearing rapidly, and before he became president in 1801 he had collected both vocabularies and grammatical information about diverse languages. Jefferson's interest in the subject spanned thirty years, and he hoped to publish information about fifty languages. However, in 1809 a trunk containing his linguistic materials was stolen, the papers were scattered, and only a small portion were ever recovered. Jefferson (1801, 149) reasoned that by collecting linguistic data about Indians in the Americas it eventually would be possible to trace the relationships among these peoples. The first comparative linguist of stature in the United States was Peter S. Du Ponceau. Born in France, he came to America and served in the Revolutionary War. He later practiced law in Philadelphia, where he became a member of the American Philosophical Society in 1791. In 1815 the American Philosophical Society, quite possibly influenced by Jefferson and Du Ponceau, founded a Historical and Literary Committee with the combined purpose of collecting historical documents and materials about Indian languages. Among the notable conclusions drawn by Du Ponceau in his study of languages was that a relationship existed between the Chukchi of Siberia and Eskimos in arctic America. However, no Asian language was identified as having been spoken in North America, and he further suggested tentatively that no south Pacific area languages were spoken along coastal America.

The next person of note is Albert Gallatin because he was the first to analyze and classify systematically many diverse Indian languages of North

America. His scholarly interest in linguistics began in 1823 and was but one of the many achievements of this Swiss-born language teacher who became a businessman, later the Secretary of the Treasury, and finally a minister to France and then to England. In 1836, Gallatin published a classification of all languages in that part of North America north of Mexico and east of the Rocky Mountains. In later years he also supported Du Ponceau's conclusion about the essential homogeneity of American Indian languages when compared with those found elsewhere in the world. When John W. Powell published his definitive study of American Indian linguistic families in 1891, he credited Gallatin as the person who previously had contributed the most to the subject. The essence of Powell's classification has withstood the test of time, but he deserves credit primarily for assembling sources rather than for making a highly original contribution. A map was prepared and fifty-eight language families were recognized; it was revised slightly in 1907 and has been reproduced on innumerable occasions. The classification which prevails at present is based on the studies by Gallatin and Powell. Compiled by C. F. and F. M. Voegelin, it was released in 1966 and appears in simplified form as Map 1.

In conclusion, it should be noted that of the approximately 300 aboriginal languages spoken during the early historical period, about half of them now are extinct. Wallace L. Chafe estimates that about half of the surviving languages are not spoken by children of the tribes involved, and it seems unlikely that these languages will endure beyond the present century. The languages which seem likely to last the longest are Cree, Chippewa, Eskimo, and Navajo; Chafe doubts, however, that they will be spoken 150 years from now.

Culture Areas

Linguists were the first to establish the relationships among tribes on a sound conceptual basis. They identified families of related languages, whose speakers unquestionably were derived from a common background. When the Powell linguistic map became available, it was possible to group some 300 tribes into fifty-eight units which reflected meaningful relationships and thus reduce tribal diversity to an almost manageable whole. At the World's Columbian Exposition held at Chicago in 1893, the Indian collections appear to have been arranged by Otis T. Mason according to the linguistic groups on the Powell map. By 1896, Mason had formulated another means for grouping ethnographic information, this time on the basis of environments or culture areas. The idea of describing Indians in terms of geographical clusters was relatively well-accepted at this time, but Mason was the first to describe the characteristics of each area in detail. A *culture area* is a geographical sector of the world whose occupants exhibited more similarities with each other than with peoples in other such areas. Culture areas were in theory determined on the basis of baseline ethnographies and by taking the sliding historical baseline into consideration. The concept was applied to information about American Indians most systematically by Clark Wissler and has served as the organizational basis for most continent-wide discussions of Indians. The system has the distinct advantage of making it possible to cluster all the tribes into a relatively small number of comparatively meaningful groups. Its main disadvantages are that it refers to a single point in time and tends to stress material culture. We find too that a single area might include peoples with rather different ways of life and that tribes along boundaries may represent a blending of the characteristics for two areas. Finally, no two classifiers can agree on the same number of areas, which is at least in part a result of the fact that the divisions are based on impressionistic evaluations of traits and their importance.

The peoples described in the twelve chapters to follow were selected partially on the basis of representation by culture area; however, this organizational method was not the primary determinant. Since the culture area approach does provide a helpful ethnographic overview, a table has been included listing and annotating ten areas. In this presentation I have attempted to reduce the number of culture areas to the smallest reasonable number.

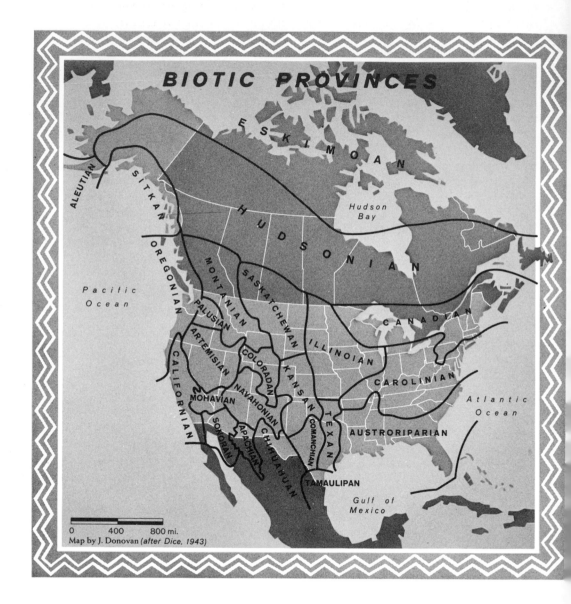

BIOTIC PROVINCES

Map by J. Donovan (after Dice, 1943)

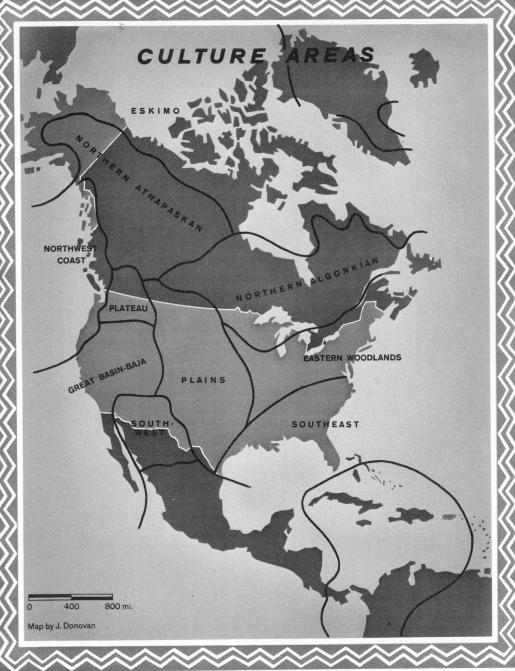

CULTURE AREAS

ESKIMO

NORTHERN ATHAPASKAN

NORTHWEST
COAST

PLATEAU

NORTHERN ALGONKIAN

GREAT BASIN-BAJA

PLAINS

EASTERN WOODLANDS

SOUTH-
WEST

SOUTHEAST

0   400   800 mi.

Map by J. Donovan

(From Other Peoples, Other Customs: World Ethnography and Its History by Wendell H. Oswalt.
Copyright (c) 1972 by Holt, Rinehart and Winston, Inc. Reprinted by permission of Holt, Rinehart and Winston, Inc.)

Culture Area	Language	Subsistence	Descent
Eskimo	Eskimo-Aleut	sea mammals caribou fish	bilateral
Northern Athapaskan	Na-Dene	caribou salmon in west whitefish in east	bilateral matrilineal
Northern Algonkian	Algonkian	caribou moose fish	bilateral patrilineal
Great Basin-Baja	highly varied	acorns pine nuts mesquite beans game	bilateral
Plateau	Salish	salmon hunting collecting	bilateral
Plains	Macro-Siouan	bison in west hunting & maize in east	bilateral patrilineal
Northwest Coast	Na-Dene in north Wakashan in south	salmon land mammals sea mammals	matrilineal, in north patrilineal, in south
Eastern Woodlands	Macro-Algonkian Macro-Siouan	maize, beans, squash hunting fishing	matrilineal
Southwest	Hokan Aztec-Tanoan	maize, beans, squash hunting	matrilineal bilateral
Southeast	Macro-Algonkian Macro-Siouan	maize, beans, cane hunting, fishing	matrilineal

Political Organization	Religion	Housing	Manufactures & Other
charismatic leaders bands	shamans good & evil spirits ceremonies in west	wood, stone, sod in east & west snowhouse in central area	tailored clothing elaborate harpoons umiaks, kayaks, dog sleds sinew-backed bow feuds over women; infanticide
charismatic leaders bands	shamans Nakani	double lean-to or rectangular log-frame	semi-tailored clothing spruce root & birch bark baskets toboggans, snowshoes, bark canoes deadfalls & snares cannibalism during famines
charismatic leaders bands	shamans shaking tent divination	conical tent	semi-tailored clothing toboggans, snowshoes, bark canoes deadfalls & snares hunting dogs
bands	elaborate female puberty ceremonies shamans diverse spirits	impermanent brush, bark, grass	developed basketry seed grinding stones sinew-backed bow nets for land mammals
villages	shamans diverse spirits	semisubterranean winter reed- or mat-covered summer	basketry important bark fiber clothing
bands band alliances military societies warfare important	vision quest guardian spirits emerging ceremonialism	skin tepee	developed bone & skin working dog-drawn travois game surrounds hide shields
village	potlatch elaborate ceremonial round complex masks	rectangular, plank multifamily	elaborate wood-working dugout canoes social classes, slaves
tribes confederations	developed ceremonial round; harvest stress secret societies dogs eaten ceremonially	dome-shaped wigwam multifamily palisades	hide clothing bark canoe
village	elaborate ceremonial round kiva masked dancers	pueblo-type	developed pottery & basketry cotton garments fermented beverages domestic turkey irrigated farmland
tribes confederations warfare important	complex ceremonies sun worship priests	rectangular multifamily fortified	feathers over netting for clothing house-like storage facilities "black drink" emetic

Labels on map: Wakashan, Chimakuan, Salish, Yuki

Legend:

AMERICAN ARCTIC-PALEOSIBERIAN
NA-DENE
MACRO-ALGONKIAN
PENUTIAN
AZTEC-TANOAN
MACRO-SIOUAN
HOKAN

Kutenai
Beothuk
Keres
Timucua
Karankawa

Major linguistic groups for aboriginal North America north of Mexico. The widespread phyla are designated in capital letters; the phyla for which there is a single representative language are in italics, and the families for which there are no established phyla are underlined (After Voegelin and Voegelin, 1966: Courtesy of the American Ethnological Society).

References

Chafe, Wallace L. "A Challenge for Linguistics Today," in *The Philadelphia Anthropological Society,* Jacob W. Gruber, ed., 125-131. New York. 1967.

Churchward, James. *The Lost Continent of Mu.* New York. 1931.

Crook, Wilson W., and R. K. Harris. "A Pleistocene Campsite near Lewisville, Texas," *American Antiquity,* v. 23, 233-246. 1958.

Drake, Samuel G. *Biography and History of the Indians of North America.* Boston. 1837.

Driver, Harold E., and William C. Massey. "Comparative Studies of North American Indians," *Transactions of the American Philosophical Society,* n.s., v. 47, pt. 2. 1957.

Ekholm, Gordon F. "Transpacific Contacts," in *Prehistoric Man in the New World,* Jesse D. Jennings and Edward Norbeck, eds., 489-510. Chicago. 1964.

Estrada, Emilio, and Betty J. Meggers. "A Complex of Traits of Probable Transpacific Origin on the Coast of Ecuador," *American Anthropologist,* n.s., v. 63, 913-939. 1961.

Federal Indian Law. U. S. Department of the Interior. 1958.

Gallatin, Albert. "A Synopsis of the Indians within the United States east of the Rocky Mountains and in the British and Russian Possessions in North America," *American Antiquarian Society Transactions and Collections,* v. 2, 1-422. 1836.

Hagan, William T. *American Indians.* Chicago. 1961.

Hallowell, A. Irving. "The Impact of the American Indian on American Culture," *American Anthropologist,* v. 59, 201–217. 1957.

Hallowell, A. Irving. "The Backwash of the Frontier: The Impact of the Indian on American Culture," *Annual Report of the Smithsonian Institution, 1957-58,* 447-472. 1958.

Hallowell, A. Irving. "American Indians, White and Black: The Phenomenon of Transculturalization," *Current Anthropology,* v. 4, 519-531. 1963.

Haven, Samuel F. "Archaeology of the United States," *Smithsonian Contributions to Knowledge,* v. 8, 1-159. 1856.

Helm, June. *Essays on the Problem of Tribe.* American Ethnological Society. Seattle. 1968.

Holmes, William H. "The World's Fair Congress of Anthropology," *American Anthropologist,* v. 6, 423-434. 1893.

Huddleston, Lee E. *Origins of the American Indians.* Austin. 1967.

Hutton, James. *Theory of the Earth, with Proofs and Illustrations.* London. 1899 (original ed. 1795).

Jefferson, Thomas. *Notes on the State of Virginia.* New York. 1801.

Jenness, Diamond. *Eskimo Administration: IV. Greenland.* Arctic Institute of North America Technical Paper No. 19. 1967.

Krieger, Alex D. "Early Man in the New World," in *Prehistoric Man in the New World,* Jesse D. Jennings and Edward Norbeck, eds., 23-81. Chicago. 1964.

Kroeber, Alfred L. "Handbook of the Indians of California," *Bureau of American Ethnology Bulletin 78.* Washington, D.C. 1925.

Kroeber, Alfred L. "Nature of the Land-Holding Group," *Ethnohistory,* v. 2, 303-314. 1955.

Lyell, Charles. *Principles of Geology.* v. 1. London. 1830.

Mason, Otis T. "Influence of Environment upon Human Industries or Arts," *Annual Report of the Board of Regents of the Smithsonian Institution, 1895,* 639-665. Washington, D.C. 1896.

Mason, Ronald J. "The Paleo-Indian Tradition in Eastern North America," *Current Anthropology,* v. 3, 227-246. 1962.

Oswalt, Wendell H. *Other Peoples, Other Customs.* New York. 1972.

Powell, John W. "Indian Linguistic Families North of Mexico," *Seventh Annual Report of the Bureau of Ethnology, 1885-'86.* 1-142. 1891.

Riley, Carroll L., ed. and others, *Men across the Sea.* Austin. 1971.

Shutler, Richard, ed. "Papers from a Symposium on Early Man in North America, New Developments: 1960-1970," *Arctic Anthropology,* v. 7, no. 2, 1-91. 1971.

Swanton, John R. *The Indian Tribes of North America.* Smithsonian Institution, Bureau of American Ethnology, Bulletin 145. 1953.

Voegelin, C. F and F. M. *Map of North American Indian Languages.* American Ethnological Society. 1966.

Wauchope, Robert. *Lost Tribes & Sunken Continents.* Chicago. 1962.

Wilmsen, Edwin N. "An Outline of Early Man Studies in the United States," *American Antiquity,* v. 31, 172-192. 1965.

Wissler, Clark. *The American Indian.* New York. 1938.

Wissler, Clark. "The American Indian and the American Philosophical Society," *Proceedings of the American Philosophical Society,* v. 86, 189-204. 1942.

Wormington, H. H. *Ancient Man in North America.* The Denver Museum of Natural History. Denver. 1957.

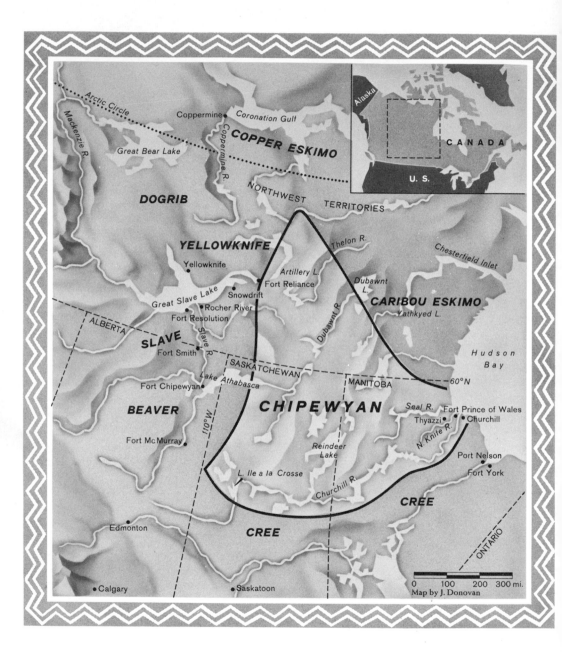

Arctic Circle

Mackenzie R.

Coppermine • Coronation Gulf

Great Bear Lake

Coppermine R.

COPPER ESKIMO

DOGRIB

NORTHWEST TERRITORIES

YELLOWKNIFE

Yellowknife •

Thelon R.

Chesterfield Inlet

Artillery L.

Fort Reliance •

Dubawnt L.

CARIBOU ESKIMO

Great Slave Lake

Snowdrift •

Rocher River •

Fort Resolution •

Dubawnt R.

Yathkyed L.

ALBERTA

SLAVE

Slave R.

Hudson Bay

Fort Smith •

SASKATCHEWAN

MANITOBA

60°N

Lake Athabasca

Fort Chipewyan •

BEAVER

CHIPEWYAN

Seal R.

Fort Prince of Wales

Thyazzi • • Churchill

N. Knife R.

Fort McMurray •

Reindeer Lake

Port Nelson •

• Fort York

L. Ile a la Crosse

Churchill R.

CREE

Edmonton •

CREE

Alaska

CANADA

U. S.

• Calgary

• Saskatoon

0   100   200   300 mi.

Map by J. Donovan

101°W

The Chipewyan:

hunters and fishermen of the subarctic

The territory of the Chipewyan was a great expanse of subarctic tundra and forest, extending some 500 miles from east to west and up to 600 miles from north to south. This area is a part of the vast Canadian shield and lies within the Hudsonian biotic province. The climate is continental; its winters are long and cold and the summers short but relatively warm. Everywhere there are interlaced networks of waterways, foaming as well as hesitant streams and rivers, great lakes, and countless scattered smaller lakes. The barren rocks show obvious signs of glacial wear on their smoothed or striated surfaces. The glaciated nature of the country is particularly evident in the north, where rolling masses of bedrock give way to boulder-strewn valleys. The highland areas support thin layers of lichens or nothing at all, whereas the valleys are covered with mosses and lichens. This area is known to the Chipewyan as the Barren Grounds, a fitting appellation which has been incorporated into the geographical literature. As one moves southward over the Barrens, gnarled spruce appear as outriders of their species, and farther south the spruce form small stands in sheltered draws. This is a taiga environment, where the tundra meets the northern forest, and the area in which the Chipewyan were most at home. Still farther south the spruce become dense, and juniper, aspen, and birch stands are fringed by marshy bogs and upland tundras. The land was forbidding to an outsider, and to the aboriginal peoples living there it offered little. Yet it was and still is in part the land of the Chipewyan.

The Chipewyan have been referred to by three terms in ethnographic accounts. In early reports they were called the Northern Indians, reflecting their geographical relationship with the Hudson's Bay Company traders who introduced the term. The easternmost bands have been called Caribou Eaters, indicating their dietary staple. The name Chipewyan is now the accepted designation for the entire group, and in casual conversation they are often called "Chips." The word Chipewyan is taken from Cree and means "pointed skins," a graphic reference to the dangling points on the front and back of the caribou-skin, poncho-like garments of the men. These people term themselves "Dene," which means "humans." They never were numerous, and at the time of contact with Europeans their population is estimated at 3500. If one considers the vast extent of the country which they occupied, their population density was one of the lowest for a North American Indian tribe.

It may be asked why these Indians are described as representative of the subarctic. The reasons are linguistic, ecological, historical, and sociocultural. The Chipewyan represent one of the aboriginal variants of northern Athapaskan Indians in language and culture. Since Athapaskans

36

spread over interior Alaska and western Canada, it is desirable that one people of this aggregate be included in any description of the major variants of North American Indian culture. Most subarctic peoples utilized two major subsistence sources, fish and caribou, and the Chipewyan were typical in this respect. We know more about them than most other northern Athapaskans, largely because of historical chance. They were reasonably well described by Europeans soon after initial historic contact, and they are mentioned in a number of subsequent accounts; furthermore, in 1960 a thorough study of one modern community was undertaken. We do not have this much documentation through time for any other northern Athapaskan tribe, yet the information available about them is not as plentiful nor as detailed as that for many American Indians. The sociocultural reasons for describing the Chipewyan are equally significant, for in complexity of life-way they were among the simplest of Indians. They illustrate a family-based social type in which there was a minimum of extrafamilial contact or feeling of community cohesion. They also were a people among whom women were oppressed to an inordinate degree.

The Chipewyan speak a language that belongs to the Na-Dene linguistic phylum and the Athapaskan family. The Na-Dene ranged from near Bering Strait to the western shore of Hudson Bay and were scattered southward to the Mexican border. One group of Athapaskan speakers lived in the Pacific northwest of the United States, and another, which included the Apache and Navajo, was in the American southwest. The Na-Dene were essentially an inland people and relatively recent migrants into the New World. The major dispersal of the Athapaskan family took place during the Christian era, and at present it appears on the basis of lexicostatistics that they consisted of one closely related group of Indians in northwestern Canada around A.D. 700. Some of these people spread south to form the Pacific group, and another cluster went on to the southwest. These internal splits were not completed until about 1800. Diversification in the northern Athapaskans took place between 900 and 1400, with the Chipewyan completing its divergence at the later date.

The span of human occupancy in historic Chipewyan country may not be stated with even superficial exactness. It is possible only to interpolate a tentative statement from the scattered archaeological finds. One site, near the extreme eastern sector of the early historic Chipewyan range, is adjacent to North Knife River and is called Thyazzi. It is an inland site, of unknown age, at which the artifacts are blowing out of sand hills. The recovered lithic products fall within the range of a tool tradition most commonly associated with Eskimos and called the Denbigh Flint Complex, after the type site on Cape Denbigh in western Alaska occupied around

1000 B.C. The tools recovered give no clear clues to their makers, but in form they are unlike Athapaskan artifacts. Furthermore, aboriginal Athapaskan stoneworking does not appear to have been derived from this base. At another series of sites, along the Thelon River in an area of seasonal penetration by the Chipewyan in historic times, are archaeological remains assigned to an era shortly after 3000 B.C. These sites reflect an Indian type of hunting economy. There is evidence of some continuity for this general tool complex and eventual identification with the Chipewyan.

The Chipewyan received their earliest historical notice in connection with the Hudson's Bay Company efforts to expand the trade in furs to the west of Hudson Bay. The company administrators at the trading center of York Fort, founded in 1684 and located along southern Hudson Bay, were anxious to bring Northern Indians to their post. This was difficult because the Cree Indians had pushed the Chipewyan to the west from their Churchill River territory. In 1715 William Stewart set out with a Chipewyan woman to induce her people to settle their differences with the Cree and to trade at York Fort. Accompanied by a small party of Cree, they sought out the various Chipewyan bands. In a year's time their purpose had been accomplished. Peace was made, and ten young Chipewyans went to York Fort to learn to speak Cree and become interpreters. Through the efforts of Stewart the country to the south of Great Slave Lake was opened for trading. The next move for the Hudson's Bay Company was to establish a trading center at the margin of Chipewyan country along the western shore of the bay. The selected site was the former whaling station at Churchill, where earlier still the Danish exploring party under Jens Munch had wintered in 1619–1620. Before the establishment of the Hudson's Bay Company post at Churchill, Eskimos occupied the area. In fact, the point of land on which Fort Prince of Wales was constructed was called "Eskimo Point." However, when the Indians, presumably Chipewyan, received guns from the traders, the Eskimos were forced northward. The post was constructed in 1717, while the great stone fort named Fort Prince of Wales was built between the years 1732 and 1771.

Still the heart of the Chipewyan area had not been brought under any realistic control. It appears that in 1720 James Knight traded with Yellowknife Indians, and in 1766 three Dogrib Indians traded at Churchill. Thus there was some knowledge of the great area to the north and west. Moses Norton, governor at Fort Prince of Wales, was anxious to open trade relations in this area and at the same time settle the exact whereabouts of a reported copper deposit. The problem of a proposed overland expedition to the "Far Indian" country was that the Chipewyan, who were making tremendous profits as middlemen in the trade with more distant tribes, were reluctant to guide the Hudson's Bay Company explorers. Company support for a land expedition was forthcoming, and at this point the name Samuel Hearne becomes intimately associated with the Chipewyan, copper, and explorations in northwestern Canada.

Samuel Hearne was born in London in 1745. His response to formal education was indifferent, and he went to sea as a captain's servant before he was in his teens. He served on two different frigates during the Seven Years' War. His service with the Royal Navy was terminated in 1763, and in 1766 he became a seaman on a small Hudson's Bay Company vessel engaged in trading and whaling along the western shore of Hudson Bay. He continued this work until 1768, when his fortunes came under the influence of Moses Norton. In 1768 Norton consulted with Company officials in England and convinced them that a search for the copper deposits known to exist somewhere to the north and west of Fort Prince of Wales would be an important enterprise. Once official sanction was forthcoming, Norton organized the trip. The small party of whites and Indians under Hearne's direction was to be guided by a Chipewyan named Chawchinahaw. This trip of 1769 was unsuccessful, partly because the Indian guide was a fraud who hindered rather than aided the endeavor and also because the Chipewyan hunters refused to supply the whites with game. The trip, although a total failure in terms of their purpose, did teach Hearne that the average Chipewyan was not reliable in his dealings with Europeans and could not be led if he did not choose. Again Hearne set off for the copper deposits in early 1770, this time under the guidance of Conneequeese, but this Indian leader was also a poor choice. He had no authority among his people and to compound the confusion, he did not know where the copper was located. He led the party north to the Dubawnt and Yathkyed lake area. At this point Hearne broke his quadrant and could no longer take the necessary readings for accurate mapping, and so he returned to the fort late in 1770. The third attempt, organized within two weeks after his second failure, was planned differently. The ultimate success of this venture hinged on the Chipewyan guide, Matonabbee, who had his own opinions about how to succeed. The key to his plan was to take women along to relieve the men of the many burdensome chores of traveling. To make matters even better, Matonabbee had six wives of his own at that time. The trip to the Coppermine River and Coronation Gulf had been completed successfully by mid-1772, and it was one of the most noteworthy feats of individual exploration anywhere at any time. Hearne's maps were not accurate, and for this he has received criticism periodically. It is far more important that Hearne's book is a classic in exploration literature, the first balanced account of the Chipewyan, and that no one has since duplicated his journey. The manuscript was accepted by the publisher in October of 1792, and its author died the following month.

The map prepared by Hearne and the knowledge he gained about the country through which he passed facilitated further expansion to the northwest. The first trader to settle in the midst of Chipewyan country was Peter Pond, who settled near Athabasca Lake in 1778. The organization of the North West Company in 1783 introduced an era of fierce competition with the Hudson's Bay Company, and not until their amalgamation in 1821 did trading conditions become stabilized. In 1789 Alexander Mackenzie explored the river that bears his name and reached the Arctic Ocean. His account is one of disappointment, for he had hoped to reach the Pacific Ocean. The travels of Mackenzie wrote finis to speculations about a northwest water passage to the Pacific. The entire history of the Chipewyan country centered about the quest for mineral wealth, the expanding northern fur trade, and disappointing searches for a water passage to the Pacific Ocean. Later the search for souls was begun. In 1846 Roman Catholic missionaries founded a permanent mission at Lake Ile a la Crosse, and the Anglicans located at Churchill in 1912. Even today it is fur and souls that attract most outsiders into the Chipewyan country.

Most peoples in the world have at least a passing concern about their origins and seek some rationale for their existence. In the absence of systematic knowledge concerning the past and a scientific view of the world, they most often explain their presence in a supernatural context. The creation myth of a people becomes a meaningful explanation for their very being. The Chipewyan regarded the primordial world as centering about a woman who lived in a cave and subsisted on berries. In time a dog-like creature followed her into the cave and lived with her. She thought that she dreamed this animal turned into a handsome young man who had sexual intercourse with her, but it was no dream, and the woman became pregnant. At this juncture a giant man approached; he was so tall that his head reached nearly to the clouds. With a stick he outlined the bodies of water and caused them to fill. The giant then tore the dog-like being to shreds and threw its internal organs into the water, creating various fish. The flesh was tossed on the land in bits and became land animals, and the skin was torn and thrown into the sky to become birds. The giant then told the woman that her offspring would have the ability to kill as many of these creatures as they required and that she need not worry about the animals' abundance, since it was his command that they multiply. The giant then returned from whence he came and was never seen again. In this way order in the world emerged, and the abundance of game was assured. This tale was a rationale for the indiscriminate killing of game and also served as a supernatural association with dogs, since the woman's human offspring were descended from this creature related to the dog. The creation myth was not only taught to children but also formed a guide to thoughts about the adult world.

Chipewyan clothing was made from caribou skins taken from animals killed in the early fall when the skins were strong and light and the fur dense but not extremely long. In general, eight to ten skins were necessary to outfit one individual for the winter. The upper garment of a man consisted of a loose-fitting, sleeved poncho with the fur side out. It was not hooded and it extended to the thighs with the skins cut to a point in front and back. At least two skins were required for such a garment, and the seams along the sides were sewn with an awl, not an eyed needle. A fur boa sometimes was worn when the temperature was low, and the ears might be covered by a fur band or cap. Leggings reaching from the thighs to the ankles were of dehaired caribou skin, and moccasins were sewn on at the bottom. In severe weather a caribou skin cape was draped over the shoulders. The garb of a woman included a sleeved dress, again made from two skins and sewn at the sides. This garment reached to the woman's knees or even to her ankles. In order to hold the dress up from the ground a belt girdled the waist. Vanity was not unknown to Chipewyan women. According to Hearne, on one extremely cold February day, one woman held her dress high with her belt so she could "shew a clean heel and good leg," and managed at the same time to freeze her buttocks and thighs so badly that huge blisters developed as a result. It was a joke to all except her. The leggings of the women reached from below the knee to the ankle and may not have had attached moccasins. The women also wore capes, and both sexes used mittens of double thickness. They could slip their hands out of the mittens without the chance of losing them because each was attached to a leather harness that hung about the neck.

These fur-clad people were described in less than glowing terms by the Europeans with whom they first had contact. First there was the haughty attitude that these Indians assumed with Europeans. The Chipewyan firmly believed that they were more intelligent than the whites. This, of course, could not have endeared them to the English. The men are described further as being patient and persevering but morose and covetous. Still they were peaceful insofar as this meant not shedding the blood of another Chipewyan male. When angry with one another, they wrestled, pulled their opponent's hair or ears, or twisted his neck. In a scale of honesty for the eastern tribes of the northern Athapaskans, the Chipewyan were ranked as superior to all others; they abhorred a thief. It would appear, however, that because the Indians thought of whites as not quite human, taking their property was not considered thievery.

No description of these people could be complete without commenting on the status of women. Females were subordinated to men in every way. They were treated cruelly and were held in gross contempt by the men. Female infants were on occasion permitted to die, a practice viewed by adult women as kindly. In fact, they are said to have wished their mothers had done it for them. Women were beaten frequently, and although it was an odious crime to kill a Chipewyan man, if a wife died from a beating by her husband, it was no crime.

The settlements in which these Indians lived ranged from an individual family dwelling isolated from others to clusters of as many as seventy separate households. The size of any community was a function of the time of the year and the availability of food resources. In general, aggregates which included more than a few families were rare or of brief duration. The dwelling in which the people lived was a subarctic variety of the tepee, which is best known from the plains of western America. The Chipewyan tent consisted of a framework of poles set in a circle and bound together at the top. The cone was covered with sewn caribou skins and measured a few feet to more than twenty feet across at its base. A large tent required as many as seventy caribou skins for the cover. At the apex of the poles was an opening which allowed the smoke from the central fireplace to filter upward. If spruce boughs were available, they were placed around the fire, which was lighted with sparks struck from iron pyrites. Over these boughs caribou skins were spread, and it was on these that residents reclined and slept.

In and around the tents one would expect to see most of their manufactures. Among the possessions of the women were cooking and storage containers of birchbark or skin. A basket of folded and sewn bark commonly was used for cooking by filling it with preheated stones, water, and raw meat. The women probably had skin bags in which they kept sewing awls and thread of caribou sinew. The men's tool kits included wedges of antler or wood for splitting planks from logs; a crooked knife with a copper blade and antler handle, the most important form of knife; a curved, wooden-handled knife with a beaver incisor for a blade, another highly useful tool for cutting small sections of wood; and a hand drill with a copper bit and an antler handle, the only drill form known. There were also awls of copper, and a copper ax head hafted on a wooden or antler handle. All of these uses of copper, in addition to its further utilization in ice-pick points, arrow-points, spearheads, and spoons, reflect a reliance on this metal. The copper tools were made by pounding a raw lump of the metal into shape. These people never treated copper as a metal by heating or smelting it, but processed it in the same manner as they would stone.

The preparation of food in a Chipewyan household was a major reason for the household's existence. The favorite items were primarily caribou products: the head and fat from the back, a fetus either raw or cooked, and grubs from under the caribou's skin. They did not consider steaks and chops as luxuries. Food, which most often meant caribou meat in the east and bison in the west, or fish if these animals were not to be found, could be eaten raw or cooked. In addition to being boiled in a birchbark container, flesh could be roasted over an open fire. One might cook by using the stomach of a caribou as a container and the contents as food. To the fermenting lichens in a stomach were added shredded fat, blood, tender meat, and cut-up heart and lungs. The caribou stomach was hung over a low fire for roasting and then served. Their diet rarely included plant products, although a moss soup is reported and moss also could be added to meat soup as seasoning. At a winter camp a compact lump of snow was skewered on a stick, which was tilted toward the fire so that it would melt into a birchbark container. The meals at camp were prepared by women, but it was the men who ate first. The women received only what the men had not consumed, which might at times amount to nothing. One other food was pemmican, which usually is thought of as characteristic of the Plains Indians. Pemmican, from a Cree word meaning "manufactured grease," was made from lean meat that had been cut into strips and dried by the sun or near a fire. It was then pounded into a powder, mixed with fat, and stuffed into caribou intestines. It was a highly concentrated and portable food and a particular favorite of travelers.

Scattered around the camp would be other items of the material culture inventory. A well-supplied camp would have tripods of poles from which caribou skin bags filled with dried meat were hung. On the ground would be a canoe, but not of the form made famous by the Algonkian Indians and carried over into modern types. The Chipewyan variety was about thirteen feet in length and some twenty inches at its greatest width, which was toward the stern. The cover of birchbark was supported by ribs of spruce, and it was decked over the forward third. The seams were caulked with pitch for summer, and fat was added to the pitch as the weather turned cold. Such a canoe, propelled with a single-bladed paddle, was used for hunting caribou as they swam across streams or lakes and to pursue molting birds in the water. A canoe was carried by summer travelers so that they could hunt from it and also ferry across rivers or lakes. Another item of transportation was the toboggan, which ranged in length from eight to fourteen feet and was some fourteen inches wide. It was made from thin juniper planks which were steamed at the front and bent upward. The planks were bound together with crosspieces probably fixed in place by means of thongs passed through holes made with a hand drill. Chipewyan women, not dogs, pulled the toboggans. If wooden toboggans could not be constructed because of a scarcity of wood, caribou leg skins sewn together provided a temporary substitute. The cariole, which is a more complex toboggan with sides and a back, was a European introduction.

If a summer camp was in a region where caribou or bison were unavailable, it would be located near a lake or stream known to contain fish. The principal fishing device was the gill net made from strips of caribou skin. These nets had wooden floats attached along the top and heavy stone sinkers at the lower corners. They were set across narrow streams or at favored spots on lakes. The species of fish taken most commonly were whitefish and pike. There was a supernatural involvement in netting fish. The Chipewyan felt that each net had its own personality. For example, one net was not joined to another for fear that they would be jealous of one another, with the result that no fish would be caught. Other precautions included the attachment of charms to the four corners of a net; without them it was believed that no fish would be taken. These magical associations point to a supernatural concern for fish, in contrast to any similar involvement with caribou. The wooden, bone, or antler fishhooks often had charms attached. The first fish caught with a new net or hook was boiled and the articulated bones removed intact and burned in a fire. Other fishing implements included dip nets used in association with weirs, which were brush fences across shallow stretches of water. Barbed fish arrows were shot from bows, and leisters were hurled from canoes. It is probable that the hooks and fish arrows were most important for travelers, for the take with these devices would be limited.

In camp women prepared meals and cared for children, as would their counterparts throughout most of the world. To these obligations may be added the task of processing raw skins, particularly those of caribou. This was one of their most important activities. After a caribou had been killed by a man and retrieved by his wife, it was skinned with a copper- or stone-bladed knife. During the skinning, bits of flesh and fat clung to the cutaneous layer. This matter was scraped away by drawing a caribou leg bone toward the user. If the hair on the skin was to be removed, the woman first set a wooden beam obliquely into the ground and then draped the skin over the beam with the hair side up. She scraped against the grain of the hair, holding with both hands a scraper made from a caribou leg bone cut longitudinally along a medial surface. A dehaired skin often was smoke-cured by hanging it over a pole framework under which decayed wood smoldered. A skin to be used with the hair intact was scraped with a one-handed scraper, softened in water, wrung out and dried, and rubbed on the inner surface with a paste of partly decayed caribou brains. Afterward it was permitted to dry once again and finally scraped with a copper-bladed end scraper with an antler handle. The skin probably was rubbed by hand to make it pliable and relatively soft. This process of skin preparation is detailed because it was an important complex of technological knowledge among a people who relied on skins not only for clothing but for bedding, dwelling covers, containers, and ropes. It should be added that American Indians did not tan skins in the technical sense of the word.

In the early spring the easternmost bands ranged into or along the Barren Grounds to hunt caribou. A hunting party first assembled in a birch grove at the northern edge of the forest. Here they cut poles to be carried to the north or west, and canoes were made for crossing deep or swift water. Two hundred persons gathered at one such spot in the time of Hearne. Women were taken along on these trips to carry most of the camping equipment. Hearne records that a strong woman could carry 140 pounds, which is an impressive burden, considering the nature of the terrain. While traveling, the men hunted on both sides of the trail taken by the women and young girls as they pulled the heavily loaded toboggans along the most direct route. Dogs, laden with parcels of tent skins, containers, and poles, accompanied the women. In the early spring when snow was still abundant, snowshoes were essential for travelers. The snowshoes were made of birchwood frames laced with babiche (thin, dehaired caribou skin strips) through holes in the frames. Five wooden crosspieces supported each frame. These snowshoes had slightly turned-up tips and were asymmetrical in outline; the outer edge flared, but the inner edge was relatively straight. The men prepared the frames, and the women laced the babiche into place with eyed needles. When traveling on snowshoes, the men jogged along at a pace that was faster than a walk, and they traveled in this manner for hours at a time.

If a party needed food, they selected a camping place near a lake thought to contain fish. They unloaded the tent poles, which were carried along when they went beyond the range of timber, and cleared the snow away to ground level by using a snowshoe as a shovel. The pole frameworks were erected and the skins lashed into place. Afterward caribou skins were placed on the ground, and snow was shoveled over the structures and packed into place. As the hunting party ranged beyond the tree line, where the snow had melted, they discarded their snowshoes and toboggans. They were then forced to backpack the camping equipment. Hunting as they moved, the men paused only when food was plentiful. Ducks, geese, and swans were killed on their flight northward; musk oxen were hunted in open country; caribou were lanced from canoes as they crossed a river or lake; and fish were taken with set nets or spears.

Once they had arrived at a well-known caribou crossing, they were joined by other hunting parties, so that there might be as many as 600 persons in the same locality at one time and an average of nine individuals per tent. Families or groups of families who were seeing each other for the first time in months or years followed an established procedure at their reunion. They sat some thirty yards apart saying nothing at first. Then an old person of one party would recount all the disasters that had transpired in their lives since their last meeting, and the women of the other group would wail on hearing of their misfortune. The second party's fate was then unfolded in the same manner until all had been told. The men would then greet the men, and the women joined the women to exchange presents and good news.

When the Barren Ground caribou arrived, their number truly was fantastic. Sometimes so many were killed that only the skins, long bones, fat, and tongues were taken, and the carcasses were left to rot. As the caribou ranged along the northern forest border, the Indians followed, drying as much meat as they could carry conveniently. The caribou were killed at this time with arrows shot from bows or by spearing them from canoes. The bow employed in hunting was the self-bow strung with babiche. Arrow shafts were vaned with three split feathers attached by sinew. The caribou arrowpoint was unbarbed and of bone or stone, whereas bird arrows were tipped with blunted points simply to stun the bird or hare. Arrows used for fishing were barbed but did not detach from the shaft.

It might appear that summer treks into the Barrens served little purpose except to provide a temporary food supply, which was essentially the case. However, the westernmost bands were able to exploit the bison that ranged along the southern shore of Great Slave Lake, and the northern forest dwellers could take the woodland caribou. Both the bison and woodland caribou were slain by essentially the same hunting methods used among the Barren Ground caribou.

During the caribou rutting season in October a man sometimes attached lengths of caribou antler to his belt so that they clashed together as he walked. A bull caribou in the vicinity thought he heard two other bulls fighting over a female and would lose his habitual caution at the prospect of leading off the female. A bull could be killed more readily this way than by the usual method of stalking against the wind.

In the eastern sector winter and early spring camps were established on promontories along the forest edge, in a locality frequented by caribou and near lakes known to contain fish. If a camp were situated ideally, the people would be obliged to move only once or twice during a winter. Such camps were accessible to lakes or wide rivers along which the caribou normally passed, and there surrounds were constructed. Converging lines of brushy poles were erected, with poles at about twenty-yard intervals. When the caribou approached the wider end of the funnel, they were unaware of the poles, which sometimes extended over a three-mile span. As animals entered the surround, the women, boys, and some men appeared from behind to herd them. The caribou were driven into a trap, which was a large enclosure of branches at the end of the funnel, with snares set at narrow exits. After the entrance was blocked with trees, the confused caribou were killed by hunters who shot arrows at the loose animals and speared those caught in snares.

When the snow was deep and soft, the caribou were sometimes tracked on snowshoes, but this technique necessitated following a single animal until it was exhausted from floundering in the snow. It was easier to track and kill a moose in this manner, but moose were not common. In the winter, the men might set gill nets beneath the ice of lakes or jig for fish through a hole in the ice with a hook. In the western area of Chipewyan country fishing was more important than among the eastern bands.

Other significant, but secondary, methods for taking game included the erection of deadfalls for bear, wolverine, marten, and squirrels. Nets were used for taking beaver in summer, but in winter their lodges were broken into and demolished. The animals were then taken from retreats beneath the ice along the banks of a stream or lake. Babiche snares were made to entangle hares or ptarmigan. Even though these Indians reached the sea at Churchill, they did not hunt sea mammals, which were locally abundant at certain seasons.

Additional facts of Chipewyan hunting and fishing activities could be detailed, but enough has been said to make it obvious that caribou and fish were the primary staples. Relying as they did on very few species, there were often periods when food was scarce and people starved. Famine was probably more common among the northern Athapaskans than among any other block of American Indians. At these times the people would collect berries, mosses, or rose hips, and after the more edible plant products were consumed, they turned to the most appetizing items of clothing and finally, under extreme conditions, to cannibalism.

Social life exhibits a general organizational simplicity which has come to be associated with many peoples at a subsistence level. In this environment each household was self-sufficient and could exist in isolation from all other such units until it was time for a member to find a wife. Hence it is not surprising that individualism was well developed. Each man assumed complete responsibility for himself and his family, and every woman was responsible totally to her husband. Feelings of group identity hardly existed, and the concept of community cohesion was unknown. Neither were family units restricted in their utilization of the environment to particular geographical localities; thus the concept of family hunting territories did not exist. What we do recognize in the structure of their social lives beyond the family level are reactions to threats from outside the tribe and more rarely from within the tribe, plus the occasional emergence of an outstanding individual within the group.

External threats came from the neighboring Algonkian-speaking Cree or the Inuit-speaking Eskimos. The hostility stemmed primarily from the belief that the shamans of these people could and did send evil by supernatural means to cause illness among the Chipewyan. The Chipewyan believed that no death or disease occurred from natural causes except among the aged. Thus, in theory, each physical disorder resulted from the hostile activities of a shaman. The shamans of the Chipewyan attempted to negate the effects of such evil. They controlled personal spirits and performed feats of magic. When someone fell sick, a shaman sang and danced to summon his supernatural aids or "shadows," who were animal, bird or imaginative supernatural familiars. He then sucked and tried to blow the intrusive disease substance from the patient. If the case became extremely serious, the people erected a small square tent with no opening at the top, and in it the shaman treated the patient in the usual fashion and followed it with a sword-swallowing performance. Death and lingering disease were causes of constant hostility between these people and their non-Athapaskan neighbors. This knowledge united all the Chipewyan and sent their men on sporadic forays into the lands of their tormentors. A raid on Eskimos was described by Hearne, who was with the Athapaskans. The participating individuals carried wooden shields on which they had painted different designs, which represented individual guardian spirits. After the encounter the Indians were obligated to observe numerous taboos in order to placate the spirits of those they had killed. A raid of this nature united the participants against a common enemy, but at the same time it did not require elaborate organization. Raids were bizarre melees for individual prestige, plunder, potential glory, and tribal security.

Diverse families could be joined through the aegis of a charismatic leader. An individual of this nature seems to have been an outstanding provider, a man with inordinate ability to take game and fish. Thus the leader Matonabbee supported his six wives, himself, his seven biological children, and two adopted children. Such a person probably would be thought to have supernaturals working in his behalf. Once a reputation of this nature was established, a man with marriageable daughters sought him as a son-in-law. A potential father-in-law saw a personal advantage in having the younger man attached to his household, the pattern of marriage residence being for a husband to join his wife's natal household (matrilocal residence). Subsequent wives could be a sister or sisters of the first, but other women could also be chosen. Such a man was physically strong, for he was forced to validate his claim to any particular wife, especially a young one, by successfully wrestling to keep her. A leader attracted to his camp less successful hunters, relatives, and nonrelatives, who cast their lot with him in an effort to find greater security. An important characteristic of this form of leadership was that it was very transient. A man could keep his wives and other followers only so long as his powers of persuasion, hunting skills, and physical strength endured. As he began to fail physically, he sometimes could retain his position of authority through craft and intrigue, but this would be only a temporary respite before he slipped into obscurity.

These people calculated their ancestry through both their male and female relatives (bilateral descent), the same general type of descent pattern as found in the United States today. When a man married he attached himself to the household of his father-in-law, and his ideal mate was his father's sister's daughter (patrilateral cross-cousin). In *recent* times at least some Chipewyan termed a father's sister's daughters and mother's brother's daughters (cross-cousins) the same as they would a "sweetheart," a convention that gives strength to the possibility of cross-cousin marriage. As the anthropologist Fred Eggan has pointed out, a man would rely on his son-

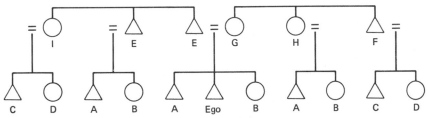

Aboriginal Chipewyan kin terms. Each letter represents a different term. Note: In this and all of the other kinship charts relationships are determined with Ego as the point of reference. Triangles indicate males and circles are for females; horizontal lines join siblings and vertical lines join parents and offspring; an equal sign indicates marriage.

in-law for support, and the son-in-law in turn would be aided by his wife's brother's son. It appears that in the aboriginal system of kinship terminology the cousin terms were of the Iroquois type. Father's brother's children and mother's sister's children were termed the same as siblings, but different terms were employed for a father's sister's children and mother's brother's children. This terminology would be compatible with cross-cousin marriage. For the generation above Ego the kinship terms for father and father's brother are alike, and mother's brother is distinct. Mother, mother's sister, and father's sister are all termed differently. Thus the terminology on the first ascending generational level was bifurcate collateral for females and bifurcate merging for males. This terminology indicates that probably siblings and parallel cousins of the same sex (who were terminological siblings), particularly if they were males, extended mutual aid to one another and regarded their cross-cousins as possible mates. With the further presence of wife exchange, we find an integrated network of blood relatives on Ego's generational level. On the parent's generation the same social distance separated aunts and uncles from one another as from parents. The inference is that these individuals were not as important socially or economically as near relatives of one's own generation.

The number of games and amusements was small, and dancing was unknown except for one step borrowed from the Dogrib Indians. The widespread hand game was known and was popular. This was a guessing game in which two opponents sat opposite each other with ten to twenty counters beside them. One man hid an object in one hand and, behind a skin, shifted it. His opponent then guessed the hand that contained the gaming piece. A correct guess gave the winner one counter, and the game was won when one man had all of the counters.

A composite sketch of an individual's life cycle, from birth to death, provides insight into the operation of the Chipewyan sociocultural system. Yet the information available about pertinent aboriginal conditions is neither balanced nor reasonably complete. It does, however, permit a sketch in broad outline of key events and behaviors. It is a virtual certainty that these Indians, as all others in North America, realized that conception resulted from sexual intercourse. As the time for delivery approached, a small tent or brush-covered structure was erected for a pregnant woman away from the main camp. Here she bore her offspring and remained apart from normal camp routine for about a month. Her isolation was enforced whether the group was traveling or at a relatively permanent camp. The mother was cared for by other women, but she had no contact with men. The father did not see his infant until the period of isolation ended. Physical isolation of this nature was also the norm for a menstruating woman and for a girl at her menarche. It was the blood associated with those persons that was considered potentially harmful if it came into contact with male hunters, because game and fish were thought to dislike any contamination of this nature. Apparently the women were successful in keeping the true nature of the menstrual cycle a secret from the men. When a woman sought to avoid her husband, which might be several times in one month, she simply crawled out of the tent beneath a side and went to the menstrual hut.

During the first year of its life the naked infant was carried on its mother's back next to her skin. The infant was held in place by a belt which passed from the middle of the woman's back over her shoulders and breasts, and it wore only a diaper padded with moss in this secondary "womb." The conventions surrounding the naming of an infant were such that a female was named after a form or characteristic of a marten. Examples are White Marten, Summer Marten, and Marten's Heart. The names for males were taken from the seasons, a place, or an animal. Unfortunately, little is known concerning the social environment of these children. It has been reported that in at least some households considerable affection was shown them. Males occupied a favored position in comparison with their sisters, but children in general were treated as adults. Conversations in the presence of children were as free and frank as though they were not there.

Childhood betrothal was practiced, and parents were careful to prevent a girl from participating in sexual intercourse before she married. Matches were made by the parents or relatives, and a girl had no choice. The usual marriage was between a pubescent girl of about twelve and a man who was about twice her age or older. Since there was no marriage ceremony, the man simply attached himself to the household of his wife. The marriage assumed a stability only after an infant was born to the couple. Offspring seldom were born during the early years of marriage, and from this it may be presumed that the young brides were passing through adolescent sterility, which tended to delay conception. The nuclear family (a man, his wife, and children) was neither a stable nor a long-lasting social unit. The possibilities of death by accident, disease, or starvation always existed, and life expectancy was probably less than thirty years for the average individual. These factors, plus a growing dislike for a spouse, could rupture a household. Furthermore, wrestling to retain one's wife whenever challenged did not lead to familial stability. Skill in wrestling was developed during youth, and the rule was that the man first thrown to the ground was the loser. An opponent could be downed most readily by grabbing his hair—thus it was cut short—or by seizing his ears—so they were greased. The woman being fought over had no voice in these matters but was expected to follow the winner dutifully. Sometimes, however, a newly won wife had to be taken by physical force. In one instance a group of Chipewyan chanced upon an enterprising Dogrib woman who had lived alone for seven months after having escaped from her captors and was attempting to find her way back home. The Indians who found her considered her as a fair and desirable prize; she was won and lost in some six wrestling matches during a single evening. It is noted also that the Chipewyan were not averse to the group rape of women belonging to their own tribe but not known to them previously.

A wrestling match for a wife did not always end well. One case is recorded in which the husband killed a potential rival. He and his wife then were forced to live in isolation, and whenever other Chipewyan happened on the couple, they would take everything they owned except their clothing. Women did desert their husbands, but because of the physical isolation of most camps this was a dangerous undertaking. The woman might be caught and beaten by her husband or seized by another man before she found refuge with a man she desired. Men guarded their wives jealously, not allowing them out of their sight if the opportunity for adultery existed. Wives generally were faithful to their husbands, even though a particular wife sometimes shared her husband with as many as seven other co-wives. The exchange of wives for a night perhaps helped temper any urge to seize a woman for sexual purposes alone. These exchange arrangements were made between two men and had implications that were more economic than sexual. The bonds between the men were those of continuing friendship and mutual aid. Then, too, if one man died, his partner in a wife exchange would at least temporarily assume the responsibility of caring for the surviving wife and her children.

As an individual aged and became less capable of supporting himself, he was regarded as an unwanted burden. The aged had the poorest of tattered clothing, and their meals consisted of the least desirable foods. Their abandonment usually took place when the camp was moved. A shelter was constructed for them, and the travelers would say, "They were dead; they appeared alive, but they were dead," and leave them to starve alone. A person dying in isolation was not buried subsequently, and even the corpse of one who died in camp was simply placed on the ground. In either case, the bodies were consumed by animals. The personal property of the deceased was destroyed, and the immediate relatives also destroyed their own property. A mourning widow cut her hair short as an overt sign of her bereavement, and some of her shorn hair might be placed beside the deceased. For a dead husband a woman wailed about camp, stripped of her clothing and other possessions, to be aided and soothed by relatives and friends but not to remarry for a year.

The supernatural world of the Chipewyan included animistic spirits which hovered about constantly. Some were more potent than others. The spirits of wolves and wolverine were dangerous, and for that reason these animals usually were not hunted or killed. The bear, too, was dangerous; when one was killed, its skin might be burned and the large bones scattered in the four recognized directions. A woman could not touch or step over a bearskin; thus one placed before a door was a means of keeping women out of a tent. The spirits of a shaman were powerful, and even the spirit of an ordinary person sometimes was feared. There was only a vague notion of a future life, which was like that on earth but free from cares, according to one observer. Not all accounts agree, however. One states that the soul of the deceased crosses a river, and if the individual has been good on earth he reaches an island on which life is free from worry. If he was evil, he struggles up to the neck in the river forever.

The foregoing descriptions were recorded by explorers or reconstructed by anthropologists. This manner of living changed as a result of the fur trade and through the efforts of missionaries. The era of change, from about 1770 to 1960, is little known, but it is possible to note that life moved in new directions.

The exact geographical range of these Indians at the time of historic contact is uncertain, but they did control the Barren Grounds by early historic times. Likewise, they occupied the northern forest border from the upper Churchill River to Hudson Bay. Probably by 1820 they controlled Lake Athabasca once again, after temporarily giving it up to the Cree, who subsequently became decimated by disease. In the 1890's some Chipewyan bands ranged along the western edge of the Barrens. In the winter they trapped principally marten, which they traded at Lake Athabasca, Reindeer Lake, or Churchill. In summer they lived off fish and in the fall no doubt took caribou. By 1913 some Chipewyan were concentrated near Churchill on Hudson Bay, along the western sector of their aboriginal territory, and westward around the settlements of Fort McMurray, Fort Chipewyan, and Fort Resolution. The move westward by the Chipewyan probably was brought about by Caribou Eskimo reoccupancy of the Barren Grounds and also coincided with their commitment to the fur trade since the principal fur animals, the beaver, river otter, and marten, are boreal animals.

It is probable that during the first stages of historic contact the Chipewyan lost much of their vitality as a group because of exposure to diseases that previously had been unknown. The most destructive epidemic was that of smallpox in 1781-1782. Hearne estimated that only 10 percent of the population survived, but he referred to only a portion of the total Chipewyan population. In 1819 there was another epidemic of smallpox (Simpson, 1938, 81) which "carried away whole bands." Thus, the Chipewyan were a remnant people near the beginning of their history. It is likely that because they were weakened by disease they were less able to support themselves, and there were associated famines. Another momentous change took place as a direct result of the fur trade. When they began to trap intensively, they spent less time hunting caribou and fishing, and lived within a more tenuous economic system. They desired trade goods and trapped to obtain them, but at the same time they deprived themselves of the opportunity to acquire their basic foods. Thus, if they did not take large numbers of fish and caribou at certain seasons, they faced starvation. Famines made devastating inroads into the vitality of the society; although famines were not new, they now occurred more often. It is reported (Back, 1836, 209) that at Fort Resolution in 1833 some "forty of the choicest hunters" died in a famine, and between 1879 and 1881 "many died in hunger and misery."

In aboriginal times the charismatic leader was respected because of his unique abilities, and a number of such individuals, among whom Matonabbee was an outstanding example, are reported. This leadership did not embody the qualities of power and authority however. With the advent of the fur trade and intermittent contact with traders, a different form of leadership developed. The traders desired to deal with a group representative and not with individuals; from this stimulus emerged the role of the trading chief. The traders furthered the trading chief's standing by deferring to him and presenting him with clothing, medals, and a formal reception on his arrival at a post. By the late 1800's it is noted that the "chief" distributed the meat of caribou and moose to whomever he chose, irrespective of the wishes of the man who killed the game, although the hunter personally kept the skins and the pelts of animals. If this was the norm, we are forced to conclude that the position of chief carried not only the quality of influence but of authority and some form of power. By 1908 the chief represented the group in their dealings with officials of the Federal Indian Affairs Branch, but, as we would expect, he was not an effective representative.

It is insightful to consider the changing status of dogs over the years. It will be recalled that a dog-like creature was thought to have fathered these people, and the dog, along with wolves and wolverine, had strong supernatural associations. In the 1820's the people were convinced by a powerful man that they should not use such closely related animals to do their work, and consequently they destroyed all of their dogs. It was for this reason that during the early period of contact the people had very few dogs or none at all. It would appear that dogs were not widely used as beasts of burden, nor did they pull toboggans, until some time in the mid-1800's. Yet Hearne mentioned that in his time dogs hauled birch poles as hunters moved into the Barrens. Certain taboos still surrounded dogs in the early 1930's. For example, dogs were not shot, and to feed a dog a moose head or bear intestines brought ill fortune.

The unformalized supernatural system of the aboriginal population came to assimilate Cree concepts, and by the early 1800's they had borrowed the concept of manitou. An evil manitou was blamed for sickness, disease, or bad luck. The Chipewyan, by 1908, had learned many of the Cree folk-tales, including the trickster-hero complex.

Dependence on fish and caribou continued, but interestingly enough the prohibitions surrounding the treatment of these creatures were far from balanced. It has been noted that there were precautions needed in setting fishnets or using fishhooks, yet early references to taboos surrounding caribou hunting are rare. The implication is that this animal could be taken adequately by existing means so that any supernatural appeals were unnecessary. By the early 1940's taboos surrounding caribou were recorded for the Chipewyan living along the eastern sector of the Great Slave Lake. For example, if a woman's skirt were to pass over a hunting knife, there was fear that the caribou would not migrate in that direction during that year. Again a woman must pierce the caribou's eyeball before she butchered the carcass to prevent the spirit of the deceased animal from reporting its fate to others. The implication might be that the caribou-hunting emphasis among the Chipewyan took place quite recently, perhaps even in early historic times, and the network of taboos did not develop until very recently.

By the early 1900's the caribou skin tent was rare; it had been replaced by a similar but cotton-cloth form. The cotton was said to be superior because the dogs would not eat it as they did the skins. The apex of a cotton tent was still made from caribou skin, for it was less likely to burn than a cloth top. This blending of the old with the new to arrive at something better is what we often find in aboriginal adjustments to Western technology.

Plate 2
Chipewyan carrying a canoe
(From Hearne, 1796).

Plate 3 *Chipewyan dwellings and a canoe in 1913*
(Courtesy of the National Museums of Canada neg. no. 26068).

Plate 4
The Chipewyan chief named Squirrel in 1913
(Courtesy of the National Museums of Canada neg. no. 26092).

Plate 5
Chipewyan Indians at Churchill in 1923
(Courtesy of the Danish National Museum).

Plate 6 *The Chipewyan community of Snowdrift in 1971* (Courtesy of L. M. Walsh).

Plate 7 *Houses at Snowdrift in 1971* (Courtesy of L. M. Walsh).

Plate 8 *Snowdrift women scraping a moose hide in 1971* (Courtesy of L. M. Walsh).

One of the points of disagreement about peoples in the subarctic of Canada has been whether they possessed family hunting territories that were the exclusive domain of a particular household or group of related households. Family trapping territories are reported among the Chipewyan by Jean M. Penard for the period around 1900, and they are likewise recorded by Ernest T. Seton for the same period. When the owner of a trapline died, his most capable son inherited the trapline. However, the weight of evidence is that family trapping areas did not exist among the aboriginal Chipewyan.

In the year 1908 the anthropologist Robert H. Lowie visited the Chipewyan in an effort to record their way of life. It is significant to note that Lowie was able to gather only superficial information about these people. As he stated (1959, 40), "Scientifically, it was the least fruitful trip I ever made." Athapaskans have no reputation among anthropologists of being ideal subjects for study. Lowie did record that the Indians were receiving $5 a year per person from the Federal government for ammunition and twine for nets. The Chipewyan were, of course, drawn deeply into fur-trade economy, for the Hudson's Bay Company gave them trade goods in exchange for pelts. By this time the entire population around Fort Chipewyan wore trade clothing. Although their social life had undergone change as a result of contacts with Roman Catholic and Anglican missionaries, they retained a few old customs, such as naming girls after marten.

In 1923 the Danish ethnographer Kaj Birket-Smith visited Churchill to study the Chipewyan of that region. At this time he recorded an annual subsistence cycle which was undoubtedly stabilized. The people shifted from the forest in winter to the tundra in summer. Late in summer they ascended the Seal River to known caribou crossings, where they met other Chipewyan. After caribou hunting was concluded in the fall, they moved southward to the edge of timber, where they fished and hunted on snowshoes. They began trapping in November, and in late December, as well as again in February, they returned to Churchill to trade pelts, caribou meat, and skins. In the summer they reassembled at Churchill, where they fished and collected their treaty money, of which more is said later.

Most knowledge of modern Chipewyan life is a result of the anthropological studies of James W. VanStone at the community of Snowdrift on the southeastern shore of Great Slave Lake. From these data it is possible to observe a continuity with the old and also the new elements which gave a different cast to Chipewyan culture and society. This information is presented organizationally in much the same sequence as the aboriginal descriptions, and interpretive comments are incorporated in the descriptions.

Snowdrift is located along one of the many indentations of the southeastern shore of Great Slave Lake. It occupies a subarctic forest setting with tree line 100 miles east of the village. In terms of aboriginal Chipewyan territory, Snowdrift is beyond the western margin. Most people of this area traded at Fort Resolution, which was founded in 1786. After the Hudson's Bay Company post at Snowdrift was built in 1925, families from the eastern sector of Great Slave Lake, Lake Athabasca, and along the Slave River traded at Snowdrift in order to avoid traveling to more distant stores. It was not, however, until 1954 that the majority of the current residents made their home at Snowdrift. They created the permanent village in response to urging by the Federal Indian Affairs Branch agent at Yellowknife. In 1960 the settlement consisted of twenty-six houses, most of which were constructed of logs; the Hudson's Bay Company and Northern Affairs and National Resources physical plants, centering about the store and school respectively; an Indian Affairs Branch freezing and cold-storage buildings; cabins of sport fishing and mining entrepreneurs who are white and do not live permanently in the community; a Roman Catholic church and residence for the transient priest; and small cabins for visiting administrators of the Department of Forestry, the Department of Fisheries, and the Royal Canadian Mounted Police.

The commitment to settled village life was a radical change with far-reaching implications. Before their arrival here the people had lived in scattered temporary campsites from which they ranged to hunt, fish, and trap. Their settlement in Snowdrift was a response to governmental pressure and the presence of the store. The move radically changed the nature of social contacts, and subsistence activities were maligned. Many people were clustered together, exploiting the same resources, and it became increasingly difficult to maintain their previous standard of living. Furthermore, the Indians were under the control of Federal agents, whereas previously these ties were tenuous or absent. In studying this process of change, it is essential to recognize the importance of Federal intervention, which led to the new circumstances.

Modern clothing was quite unlike aboriginal forms although a few men still wore hooded and sleeved caribou skin ponchos in preference to manufactured parkas. Most persons depended almost entirely on the Hudson's Bay Company inventory for their apparel needs. Men wore long underwear, shirts, trousers, sweaters, and skin moccasins. Women wore petticoats, briefs, skirts and sweaters or dresses, and heavy cotton stockings, plus footwear of skin slippers in summer or shoes in winter. Young girls wore clothing like that of the women, with the addition of slacks, colorful lightweight jackets, and commercial shoes. Young girls often curled their hair, and young women as well as girls wore lipstick. The girls used commercial perfumes and set off their appearance with brooches, earrings, and finger rings. The young men were particularly fond of wide leather belts with large buckles and short, ornamented, black leather jackets. Sweatshirts with "Snowdrift, N.W.T." printed across the front likewise were popular among younger males. Men wore billed caps, often with decorative buttons, while women and girls were partial to colorful cotton kerchiefs. The implication of the modern clothing styles is at once obvious; most items were obtained from the store, and it was necessary to have something that the outside world valued for their purchase.

The houses had an air of permanence unknown in the past. About 1912 the first ridged commercial canvas tent was bought locally, and soon this style replaced the conical tents of old. After 1950 most families began to construct more substantial dwellings. The Indian agent obtained Federal support for the construction or renovation of the cabins at Snowdrift. The Indians at first were reluctant to participate in the program since they were hesitant to commit themselves permanently to the village. Most of the dwellings were one-room log cabins with board floors. The furnishings included homemade beds, chairs, a table, and shelves. Light was supplied by kerosene lamps, and heat furnished by wood-burning sheet-iron stoves. A household inventory included trunks or bags for extra clothing and bedding, a battery-powered radio, a hand-operated sewing machine, and utensils. In nearby log storage sheds were frozen or dried fish, dog harnesses, outboard motor parts, traps, snowshoes, rifles and fishnets. The accumulation of these and other material goods indicated that families were becoming increasingly sedentary.

Each established family owned a large, square-ended, commercially manufactured canoe, an outboard motor, and a small canvas-covered canoe of modified aboriginal design. Although a form of toboggan existed, it was purchased from the Hudson's Bay Company store and was more correctly a cariole, for it had a rear panel and canvas sides. Dogs, not women, pulled the cariole. Each family owned about five dogs, which were chained near the houses of their owners. The use of dog teams and outboard motors as sources of power unquestionably had greatly increased their mobility.

Their foods included those of aboriginal times plus additions from modern Euro-Canadian inventories. The Indians preferred meat or fish with each meal, but since these often were unavailable, bannock had become an important staple. Bannock, the standard fare of poor Eskimos and Indians throughout Alaska and Canada, is made of white flour and baking powder mixed with water into a paste and spread in a greased skillet to be fried. Often this was the only food at a meal; bannock and tea are the bread and water of depressed subarctic living. The dominant method of cooking was by boiling; after a food was well cooked, it was allowed to cool and then eaten. When families were able, they purchased prepared foods from the store. The imported items most desired were flour, sugar, tea, coffee, crackers, peanut butter, canned meats and fruits, evaporated milk, and seasonings.

Traditionally the economic lives of these people centered about obtaining caribou and fish, and these foci persisted but with the addition of trapping fur animals. Most men did not hesitate to abandon their traplines if caribou appeared in the vicinity. The lure of the hunt remained very strong, and as recently as 1930 hunting was more important to these Chipewyan than trapping. A trapper was obliged to hunt for food while on a trapline and was likely to take only spruce hens, ptarmigan, or hares. Likewise he fished through the ice with a gill net for dog food. A trapline was reached after one to three days travel by dog team, and commercial steel traps or wire snares were set for mink, marten, white fox, lynx, and wolverine. Red, silver, or cross fox were not trapped intentionally since their market value was very low. Trapping was a difficult pursuit which was surrounded by many uncertainties. Enough food had to be obtained for oneself and the dog team; wolverine sometimes ate the animals caught in sets or might spring a line of sets and remove the bait; a Canada jay, ermine, or other creature might spring a trap, and in addition, the working conditions on a trapline were difficult. A canvas trapping tent was small and impossible to heat adequately, and the men found it difficult to work alone for weeks on end. The increasing tendency was to range out from the village for only short periods during November and December when the pelts of most fur animals were in their prime.

Trapping activities were linked to the Hudson's Bay Company, for it was only at their store that a man could exchange his furs for trade items. The descriptions by Hearne of the Indians' relationship with traders were in many ways similar to those of VanStone for the modern Chipewyan. The Indians attempted to outwit the trader and resorted to diverse subterfuges to obtain credit. In Indian eyes the only good traders were those concerned with Indian welfare. In spite of their opposing goals, the Indians and the Hudson's Bay Company were linked within one economic system. The price of pelts was not very high; in 1959-1960 the average take per trapper was worth about $320. Since white fox prices were relatively high, they were trapped conscientiously in the winter. The most important fur animal taken in the spring was beaver, and there were Federal limits to an individual's take. In theory no man could take more than five animals, and each pelt was tagged before being exchanged at the store. Energetic trappers, however, bought unused tags issued to others and increased their catch in this manner. When an Indian agent proposed the registration of traplines, the people opposed the suggestion because they felt it would restrict their mobility.

It appears that while all men trapped, the pattern was declining in importance, and most men did not think it had a great deal of future potential. There was a time in the recent past when entire families accompanied a man on trapping ventures, but this was no longer possible if there were school-aged children who were obligated to attend classes. Furthermore, the income from trapping was not sufficient to meet subsistence needs. For these reasons, the area trapped and the intensity of trapping were declining steadily.

Other economic pursuits were highly significant, and of prime importance was the late summer caribou hunt. A household head felt that he required about one hundred caribou per year, of which about twenty should be obtained in the fall. Yet harvests of this magnitude had not been realized in recent years. To hunt caribou the people traveled by large canoes to the Fort Reliance area. If there were no animals at the eastern end of Great Slave Lake, the hunters portaged eastward to the vicinity of Artillery Lake. Burdened by their families, large amounts of equipment, and big canoes, they were unable to reach the best hunting grounds. As a result they were not likely to kill many animals. The meat which was obtained was smoked and brought back to the village to be stored in the Indian Affairs Branch cold-storage unit. In 1960 nearly half of the households were unrepresented in the fall caribou hunt, although some families shared in the take of others because they had provided a hunting party with equipment.

In the late fall nylon or cotton gill nets were set in the lake or along nearby rivers; they were fitted with stone sinkers, wooden floats, and large anchor stones at each end as in aboriginal times. Lake trout and whitefish were caught most frequently, and these fish were hung out to dry partially and then were stored as winter food for dogs and people.

Fishing, trapping, or hunting caribou had come to be considered less desirable pursuits than wage labor, but opportunities for such labor were limited and temporary. Construction jobs were few and of brief duration; work on commercial fishing vessels was unpredictable and physically demanding; fire fighting was seasonal and sporadic; and serving as guides for tourist fishermen was just beginning to become important. Clearing brush and trees from the right-of-way for a road was a steady form of employment, but it too was seasonal. Thus making a living by wage labor was as uncertain as the subsistence pattern of old.

The Snowdrift Chipewyan were included in Treaty Number 11, which was signed by the Indians in 1921 and provided them with direct monetary and other benefits. The Indians gave up their aboriginal rights to the land but at the same time were protected in their exploitation of local resources. In exchange, the Indians received certain tangible benefits such as formal education, health services, and material goods. Each year a band member received a cash payment of $5; the band chief received $25, and counselors, $15 each, and in recent years the Indian Affairs Branch had provided fishnets, ammunition, and items such as roofing and doors for house construction. Furthermore, families in need, as defined by the Indian agent, received a "ration" from the Indian Affairs Branch through the Hudson's Bay Company store. Persons eligible for aid included those with physical disabilities, families who raised foster children, families of hospitalized men, or households in which the family head was absent permanently. A national program of old-age assistance provided for the welfare of persons sixty-five years of age or older. Even more important was the "baby bonus," which was a national program. The Family Allowance, as it was called, was paid to each family every month; $6 was received for each child under ten and $8 for those ten through sixteen. The program was designed to improve child care, and it probably served this end at Snowdrift.

With subsistence activities and material culture changing so much from an aboriginal base-line, we would expect and do find equally significant differences in other aspects of living. There was no remnant of the old attitudes toward women and their harsh treatment. Although VanStone was not explicit on the subject, he conveyed the impression that domestic harmony existed. Certain activities, such as food preparation and child rearing, remained as female obligations, but men performed these tasks when the need arose. A further indication of the improved status of women was reflected in the fact that they profited monetarily from their labors. A woman who processed a moose or caribou hide or sewed skin garments for someone outside her family was paid directly and retained the profits. The much more favorable position of women at Snowdrift may have resulted from the fact that they were in the minority, and as a scarce item they were handled with care.

In terms of their formal social structure, these Indians traced their descent along both the male and female lines (bilateral descent), as was true of their early historic ancestors. The cousin terminology, however, was the Eskimo type (similar to the cousin terms which prevail in the United

States). At the same time preferential cousin marriage no longer existed; in fact it was not recalled by informants to have been an aboriginal practice. It may be that during the one hundred years of contact with Roman Catholic missionaries, the church prohibition of cousin marriage had influenced the change. At the same time, premarital fornication between cousins existed.

When a person married, he was most likely to select a mate within the community (village endogamy), and immediately after marriage the couple lived with the in-laws who were best able to receive them (temporary bilocal residence). As soon as possible the couple built a separate dwelling and lived alone (neolocal residence). In 1961 most households were nuclear or nuclear core families, the latter being comprised of a nuclear family to which were added a near relative or two of the husband or wife. Plural marriages no longer existed, and capable providers did not attract followers who lived with them. The overall impression is that the nuclear family was still the most important social unit, but it was no longer as independent in social relations as before.

Social bonds beyond those based on kinship were new and of expanding importance. Living in one settlement had led the people to feelings of unity, and the village inhabitants thought of themselves as physically, economically, and morally superior to persons in adjacent settlements. Other evidence of village cohesion is the widespread sharing of locally available foods. By the time a hunter who had killed a moose beached his boat he had given away most of the meat, and the same applied to a catch of fish. Food was shared in aboriginal times, but seemingly not in as pervasive or egalitarian a manner. Furthermore, an intensive pattern of reciprocal borrowing had developed, and this included major as well as minor items of material culture. These attitudes and their behavioral manifestations clearly were means to integrate the community on a social as well as a physical basis.

One result of living in a stable community was the intensified contact with the Indian agent stationed at Yellowknife. The agent visited Snowdrift every two months and sometimes more often. When there was a matter of community-wide concern to be presented, the agent called a meeting, but attendance usually was poor. It was difficult for him to guide the meeting, for each Indian was inclined to raise issues of personal concern, usually in the form of a specific request for aid. Thus the process of democratic group action failed. Unity, when it was manifest, consisted of a stand against a proposal rather than any positive approach. The Indians preferred to deal with the agent on a private, almost secret basis, concerning specific requests. The Chipewyan felt that an agent was in a position to grant favors, and for him not to do so was regarded as pure stubbornness.

In 1960 the bands were reorganized to make allowance for the physical movements of people from one band to another. Under the reorganized system the Snowdrift Indians had their own chief and two counselors. The Indians clearly had formulated what they considered to be ideal behavior for a chief. In theory, he did not interfere in the affairs of villagers, but he adopted a stern attitude toward Euro-Canadians in general and toward the Indian agent in particular. The whites, by contrast, expected a chief to be cooperative; if he was not, they bypassed him and acted through the trader or teacher. This pattern of the whites for accomplishing their purposes undermined Indian authority and contradicted the purpose of having a chief, counselors, and recognized Indian authorities.

Visits to the village by the Royal Canadian Mounted Police (R.C.M.P.) were more a show of power than the result of actual need. Crimes as defined in the Canadian legal system were rare, and the most important cause for arrest was the manufacture of home brew. Since everyone was secretive when making home brew and avoided being seen intoxicated when the police were present, few arrests were made for this, the most prevalent offense. The Indians felt also that it was wrong to appeal to Canadian legal authorities for the settlement of personal disputes, and they rarely did so, although they might threaten such action.

Political life for the Snowdrift Chipewyan was organized formally along the lines of national Canadian ideals, but the results were not what Euro-Canadians had hoped. The same was true in the sphere of religion. Everyone was a participating but nominal Roman Catholic. The priest serving the village was stationed at Fort Resolution and visited the settlement frequently throughout the year. He sometimes stayed two months at a time, and he always was present during the Christmas and Easter seasons. Church dogma and belief were understood poorly by the people, but participation in formal ceremonies was high. In general, the Church was regarded as something beyond the context of daily living. The Indians felt that the Church was wealthy and that people should be paid for any labor performed on its behalf. Thus the feeling of belonging to a church and strengthening its purposes was not understood by these members. Interestingly enough, it was in the supernatural sphere that Indians admitted openly that they were different from whites. The concept of a "bush man" prevailed here as it did among other northern Athapaskans. This creature was a man who wore manufactured shoes and appeared at a distance during the summer. He kidnapped children, but apparently he did not harm adults so long as they remained beyond his reach. The Indians believed that certain supernatural beings could harm them but did not affect whites. There also were beliefs about trapping practices, but these were of unknown dimensions. The curing of physical illness had passed out of the hands of a shaman, who no longer existed, into the domain of the Indian and Northern Health Services and a lay dispenser, usually the Hudson's Bay Company manager. If a case was considered serious, the nurse at Yellowknife was telegraphed, and she decided what course of action was to be followed. This nurse, sometimes accompanied by a medical doctor, visited the village at intervals. These Indians were concerned about their health but did not use patent medicines or turn freely to Euro-Canadians for aid. They seemed to enjoy talking about their aches and pains, but they sought treatment only if they were quite ill.

New political institutions had arisen, and perhaps the most important of these surrounded the annual payment of treaty money. The payment was made ceremonially to each individual by the Indian superintendent, who was accompanied by the Indian agent and an R.C.M.P. constable. The evening of the same day a "tea dance" was held to the accompaniment of large tambourine-like drums. Roast moose meat and other foods were served at a feast the following day. Another highlight was Christmas Eve, which featured a church service, the consumption of home brew, and card games which lasted long into the night. Christmas Day was one of rest and recuperation.

A popular form of entertainment was square dancing. The steps probably had been learned from commercial fishermen who docked periodically at Snowdrift for a few days of relaxation during the summer fishing season. Accompaniment was provided by men, who played guitars or violins. They learned dance music by listening to records played on one of the four village phonographs or broadcast by the Yellowknife radio station. The square dances were called expertly by village men, and participation at dances was good. Less formal entertainment included nightly card games, which were extremely popular, particularly blackjack and gin rummy. Men and women often played together, and the stakes ranged from small change and ammunition to $3 hands in gin rummy games if the men temporarily were affluent. While adults were playing cards, children sometimes gambled by pitching coins to a line. The hand game of old was known but seldom played; card games were considered more interesting and exciting.

The consumption of alcohol was as much a ritual as a form of entertainment, and prescribed drinking patterns rarely were ignored. The only alcoholic beverage regularly consumed was home brew, produced from yeast, raisins, sugar, and water. It was made in secret by two or three men and allowed to age for about twenty-four hours. It was thought better if it aged longer, but anticipation negated the possibility. The brew was drunk in the home of one of the makers or in the brush during the summer.

The object of drinking was to become intoxicated, and into the three-gallon pail a cup was dipped, the beverage drunk, and the cup passed to the next participant. Normally some brew was stored in bottles, to be consumed after the brew pail had been drained. When participants became reasonably intoxicated, they visited one house after another, regardless of the time, and drank as they chatted with their reluctant hosts. Sometimes they offered their hosts a drink, but this was not consistent. The conversations of intoxicated men were about village life, and they became more outgoing during such sprees than at any other time of their adult lives. Younger men talked about sexual activities but did not discuss individual experiences. Eventually, if their bottles were not emptied first, the drinkers became boisterous, and fist fights, usually over women, resulted. Drinking was reasonably common, and most men became intoxicated about once a month. There was no "dry" faction in the community, but neither were there any alcoholics.

Time and circumstances had added new dimensions to the individual life cycle, yet these new customs were not simply borrowings and blends of the Chipewyan and Euro-Canadian ones. Conception was understood, and modern techniques of birth control were known but not employed. If female infanticide existed, the practice was covert, and informants said that infants of either sex were desired. Yet there was a disproportionate number of males, and male infants were looked on as a means of economic support in one's old age. For a pregnant woman there were no food taboos or prohibitions, and it was increasingly common for women to deliver at the Yellowknife hospital. A neonate was greeted with affection, and as an infant it was played with and enjoyed by both parents. Diapers from cotton cloth were changed frequently, and babies were breast-fed whenever they were discontent. An infant slept and rested in a hammock or crib, and at least some were swaddled in a blanket. Infants were dressed in baby clothes purchased from the store, and were not, incidentally, the frequent charges of their older siblings. Between the ages of one and two children were encouraged to walk. Babies were noticeably fat, perhaps because milk was considered the only normal food for them, and exercise was not a part of their routine. Weaning began at about two years, although it was earlier if the mother became pregnant again or took the nurse's advice and weaned the baby after a year.

As in many, if not most, contemporary Indian communities in North America, there were more children than any other age group. In a population of some 150, half were under fifteen years of age. Until a child was about six, he was treated with warmth and affection by both parents. Men took small children with them on walks and were demonstratively affectionate, kissing and hugging their offspring. Like an infant, a child was permitted to play with almost anything that drew his attention, save those objects which obviously were dangerous. At the same time, a small child sometimes was permitted to cry and scream with vigor if the parents were busy. After the age of ten a child was treated differently. He was regarded as an adult, and the quality of independence was encouraged, especially among males. A father proudly referred to a small boy as "my son who is almost a man," when a boy displayed skill or intelligence.

The young child in Snowdrift had few restrictions placed on his wanderings so long as he was home for meals and by the time it was dark. Children had chores to perform, but parents were not demanding if a task was forgotten or avoided. Until they were about ten years old, boys and girls played together freely, but after this age there was a division of play groups along sexual lines. By the time a boy was thirteen he had a regular routine of duties which he was obligated to perform. He fed the dogs, hauled the water, and disposed of the garbage. By the time he was eighteen, he had more demands on his time than any other household member. He released his father from many subsistence activities, such as checking fishnets, running the outboard motor on trips, and maintaining the household equipment. The responsibilities of a teen-aged girl had been increasing in intensity since she was about eight years old. She had many household duties, and the care of younger siblings became important. Thus enculturation at home was a cumulative process, in which few actual demands were made but in which the number of responsibilities increased as a child grew older. There was more obvious continuity in the rearing of a daughter than of a son. A boy's adult responsibilities were thrust on him more abruptly.

A new and different enculturative force resulted from the introduction of formal education for children. There was no village school until the fall of 1960; before that time children were sent to a government boarding school at Fort Smith or Fort Resolution, but the new Northern Affairs and National Resources school had eliminated this practice. The Snowdrift school provided instruction for grades one through eight, and attendance was compulsory between the ages of six and sixteen. Children spoke only Chipewyan at home and thus had no proficiency in English when they entered school, which was a serious handicap in their formal education. The curriculum was not adapted to Indian needs but included the usual round of arithmetic, language skills, social studies, art, and music. One anticipated result of better educational facilities was that increasing numbers of children would continue their formal education beyond the elementary level. The majority of persons going away to high school were not likely to return permanently to Snowdrift, and if they did it seems probable that their formal education would hinder, not help, them. They would not have learned the subsistence skills in the manner of their stay-at-home cousins, and they would be less prepared psychologically to settle down to village life.

Sexual activities were commonly observed by children from a tender age and did not emerge as a subject of conversation among young people. Fornication occurred between teen-agers, with males of sixteen and females of thirteen having had at least some experience. One difficulty in arranging such affairs was to find an isolated spot to carry them out. The rather pervasive fornication of young men may have resulted from the fact that most of them were not married and could not find a wife in the village. There were fifteen unmarried males between the ages of eighteen and thirty-one; only three males in this age group were married. By .contrast there were no unmarried females over twenty and only three who had reached sixteen. This posed a dilemma for males, and they saw no solution to the problem. Ideally females married at about nineteen, and males when about twenty-eight. A few influential old women made the formal arrangements between the families of a potential couple who may or may not have had a voice in the decision. A wedding ceremony took place in the Roman Catholic church, and afterwards there was a feast and sometimes a dance. Divorces did not exist, and adultery was reasonably common.

It was assumed that soon after marriage a couple would adjust to adult responsibilities, especially once they had set up their own independent household and had begun to raise children. The couple then was expected to participate in community life as it has been described. A family picnicked together, visited friends and neighbors frequently, and the parents played cards with other couples. A husband and wife discussed family matters and shared common interests in daily life. This generalized ideal did not prevail always, but it did apply to most couples.

As an individual aged, he faced the traditional Chipewyan rejection of the aged, which still was apparent. Old people were unwanted, scorned, and ridiculed. Tempering these feelings, however, was the fact that old people received aid from the Federal government, and thus they were a potential source of economic gain. Exploitation by their children had led some old persons to establish independent households. Old age and impending death were accepted with the philosophical calm that has come to be expected of the Indian stereotype. After death the body was wrapped in a blanket, then sewn into a shroud by old women, and placed in a plywood coffin. The funeral service was Roman Catholic, and afterward the body was transported by cariole or boat to the cemetery a few miles away. If the burial took place in the summer, the mourners had a picnic before returning to the village.

In a study of folktales Ronald Cohen and VanStone explored the nature of self-sufficiency and dependency among the Chipewyan. They analyzed the early twentieth-century folktales recorded for these people and compared them with original stories by Chipewyan children which were recorded in 1961, as well as with a sample of Grimm's fairy tales as control material. As a basis of analysis the authors assumed that "taken broadly, self-sufficiency and dependency refer to a basic and universal quality of all human social experience, namely, action by ego which affects his environment, i.e., self-assertiveness or self-sufficiency, and action directed towards ego over which he has no control, i.e., dependency." Different social systems would be expected to exhibit both qualities in varying proportions. An analysis of Grimm's fairy tales reflected the Protestant ethic and exhibited a high degree of self-sufficiency. The folktales of the Chipewyan exhibited about equal proportions of self-sufficiency and dependency, suggesting that a balance had been established by these people in their relationship with the environment. An increase in dependency, reflected in the children's stories, suggested to the authors either that Federal welfare programs had made the Chipewyan less capable and less desirous of caring for themselves or that the contact situation had caused them to feel that their efforts to affect the environment were more likely to fail than to succeed.

VanStone characterized the Snowdrift Chipewyan as moving toward the stagnation of deculturation. The people had lost most of their old design for living and were not able to replace it with a comparable design along Euro-Canadian models. It was particularly in the economic sphere that this trend was evident, since trapping had only partly replaced the subsistence-based economy; the resulting mixture did not provide a satisfactory standard of living. This led VanStone to use such terms as "poor white" and "lower class" for the scene in 1960. The depressed standard of living at Snowdrift indicated that these people were at the fringes of modern developments in the Canadian north. They not only lacked technical skills and formal education, but they had not made the changes necessary in their values which would lead to an improved living standard. Therefore the more rewarding jobs in the north went to white Canadians from the south. These Indians may, as Jacob Fried has suggested, become an increasingly depressed economic class within Canadian society.

By 1972 many far-reaching changes had taken place at Snowdrift, largely as a direct result of governmental programs. The information about changes since 1960 was made available through the kindness of L. M. Walsh, principal of the Snowdrift school. The Indian population had grown from about 150 to some 220 persons and included a few Dogrib families new to the community. As is true of so many contemporary Indian settlements, the population had a youthful cast, since nearly 120 individuals were under seventeen years of age. In 1960 there had been a far larger percentage of marriageable males than females, and the same situation prevailed in 1972, with twenty unmarried men and only four marriageable girls or women.

In 1969 the administrative responsibilities for the area had shifted from the Federal government to that of the Yukon Territory. As a result of this change there was an attempt to have community members assume the responsibilities for local government, but without initial success. The impact of governmental programs was well reflected in the number of whites at Snowdrift. An R.C.M.P. constable was stationed there as well as three teachers, two adult educators, and a nurse. A second store had been opened by a fishing outfitter, and there were still fishing lodges nearby. In terms of the physical community all of the houses had electric lighting, electric stoves, and oil furnaces. Oil delivery was provided as well as garbage service, but when contracts were signed by persons for certain goods and services, payments were not generally met.

Comparatively few men trapped, and their mobility was more often provided by snowmobile than by dog team as in the recent past. Fighting fires still provided some cash income, and there were local construction jobs as well as service types of employment. By and large, however, welfare aid loomed large and important in economic life.

The long-range effects of changes begun during the 1960's are unclear, but it is significant that much of the governmental effort has been channeled into the improvement of physical living conditions. Given the economic base it is quite understandable that the people cannot pay for the housing and services provided for them. In this sense their dependency relationship has expanded abruptly. At the same time efforts to integrate the community into the broader national milieu through education have met with comparatively little success. Less than 10 percent of the children had completed the eighth grade, and all five of the high school graduates had settled elsewhere. Two persons were attending college but seemed unlikely to return to Snowdrift. The pattern seems to be that those individuals who succeed in educational terms choose not to return to the community of their childhood.

Starvation and poverty have disappeared from Snowdrift Chipewyan life. This community is now comfortable if not commodious compared with conditions in the not-too-distant past. Yet in the absence of a sound local economic basis, life in this northern frontier loses much of its purpose.

References

Back, George. *Narrative of the Arctic Land Expedition.* London. 1836.

*Birket-Smith, Kaj. *Contributions to Chipewyan Ethnology.* Report of the Fifth Thule Expedition, v. 6, no. 3. 1930. The bulk of the information in this volume applies only to the Churchill area Chipewyan as they were in 1923 and as the past was reconstructed with the aid of informants. The descriptive emphasis is on material culture; other aspects of culture and society are incompletely described. In spite of its shortcomings this study is second only to Hearne's work in importance.

Blanchet, Guy H. "Emporium of the North," *Beaver,* Outfit 276, 32-35. 1946.

Bryce, George. *The Remarkable History of the Hudson's Bay Company.* Toronto. 1904.

Campbell, Marjorie W. *The North West Company.* Toronto. 1957.

Cohen, Ronald, and James W. VanStone. "Dependency and Self-Sufficiency in Chipewyan Stories," *National Museum of Canada, Bulletin 194,* 29-55. 1963.

Curtis, E. S. *The North American Indian.* v. 18. Norwood. 1928.

Eggan, Fred, ed. *Social Anthropology of North American Tribes.* Chicago. 1937.

Fidler, Peter. "Journal of a Journey with the Chepawyans or Northern Indians, to the Slave Lake, & to the East & West of the Slave River, in 1791 & 2," *Publications of the Champlain Society,* v. 21, 493-555. 1934.

Franklin, John. *Narrative of a Journey to the Shores of the Polar Sea.* London. 1823.

Fried, Jacob. "Settlement Types and Community Organization in Northern Canada," *Arctic,* v. 16, 93-100. 1963.

Giddings, James L., Jr. "A Flint Site in Northernmost Manitoba," *American Antiquity,* v. 21, 255-268. 1956.

Harp, Elmer, Jr. *The Archaeology of the Lower and Middle Thelon, Northwest Territories.* Arctic Institute of North America Technical Paper no. 8. 1961.

*Hearne, Samuel. *A Journey from Prince of Wale's Fort in Hudson's Bay to the Northern Ocean.* London. 1795: Dublin. 1796. (Two more recent, noteworthy editions of this work have appeared. The earlier was edited by Joseph B. Tyrrell and published by The Champlain Society in 1911, and the second was edited by Richard Glover and published by the Macmillan Company of Canada in 1958.) Hearne's book is the standard source on the Chipewyan as they lived soon after historic contact. It is indispensable reading for any serious attempt to understand the culture of these Indians.

Hoijer, Harry. "The Chronology of the Athapaskan Languages," *International Journal of American Linguistics*, v. 22, 219-232. 1956.

*Jenness, Diamond. *The Indians of Canada*. National Museum of Canada, Bulletin 65. 1963. A reading of the chapter on the peoples of the Mackenzie and Yukon river basins provides a view of the Chipewyan in their relationship to other Canadian Athapaskans.

*Jenness, Diamond, ed. "The Chipewyan Indians: An Account by an Early Explorer," *Anthropologica*, v. 3, 15-33. 1956. This article contains abstracts of the Chipewyan information from a previously unpublished manuscript probably written by John Macdonell in the early 1800's. The descriptions are very good and provide a supplement to Hearne.

King, Richard. *Narrative of a Journey to the Shores of the Arctic Ocean*. 2 v. London. 1836.

Lowie, Robert H. "The Chipewyans of Canada," *Southern Workman*, v. 38, 278-283. 1909.

Lowie, Robert H. "An Ethnological Trip to Lake Athabasca," *American Museum Journal*, v. 9, 10-15. 1909.

Lowie, Robert H. *Robert H. Lowie, Ethnologist, A Personal Record*. Berkeley and Los Angeles. 1959.

*MacNeish, June H. "Leadership Among the Northeastern Athabascans," *Anthropologica*, v. 2, 131-163. 1956. Historical sources are evaluated and the Chipewyan discussed along with other Canadian Athapaskans. The major contribution of this paper is a classification of leadership patterns in aboriginal and historic times.

MacNeish, June H. "Kin Terms of Arctic Drainage Dene: Hare, Slavey, Chipewyan," *American Anthropologist*, v. 62, 279-295. 1960.

Mason, John A. "Notes on the Indians of the Great Slave Lake Area," *Yale University Publications in Anthropology*, no. 34. 1946.

Munsterhjelm, Erik. *The Wind and the Caribou*. London. 1953.

Penard, Jean M. "Land Ownership and Chieftaincy among the Chippewayan and Caribou-Eaters," *Primitive Man*, v. 2, 20-24. 1929.

Petitot, Emile. "On the Athabasca District of the Northwest," *Canadian Record of Science*, v. 1, 27-53. 1884.

Rich, Edwin E. *Hudson's Bay Company, 1670–1870*. 3 v. Toronto. 1960.

Richardson, Richard. *Arctic Searching Expedition*. New York. 1854.

Robinson, J. "Among the Caribou-Eaters," *Beaver*, Outfit 275, 38-41. 1944.

Robson, Joseph. *An Account of Six Years Residence in Hudson's Bay*. London. 1752.

Ross, Bernard. "Notes on the Tinneh or Chepewyan Indians of British and Russian America: The Eastern Tinneh," *Smithsonian Institution Annual Report, 1866*. 304-311. 1867.

Russell, Frank. *Explorations in the Far North*. University of Iowa. 1898.

Seton, Ernest T. *The Arctic Prairies*. New York. 1911.

Simpson, George. "Journal of Occurrences in the Athabasca Department, 1820 and 1821," *Publications of the Champlain Society. Hudson's Bay Company Series,* 1. 1938.

Tache, Alexander A. *Sketch of the North-West of America.* Montreal. 1870.

Tyrrell, Joseph B., ed. "David Thompson's Narrative," *Publications of the Champlain Society,* v. 12. 1916.

VanStone, James W. *The Economy of a Frontier Community.* Northern Coordination and Research Centre, Department of Northern Affairs and National Resources. 1961.

*VanStone, James W. *The Snowdrift Chipewyan.* Northern Co-ordination and Research Centre, Department of Northern Affairs and National Resources. 1963. This report and the preceding one contain virtually all of the reliable information on the modern Chipewyan. Although the data are limited in scope to the community of Snowdrift, the generalizations most probably have wider applicability for other Chipewyan populations.

*VanStone, James W. "Changing Patterns of Indian Trapping in the Canadian Subarctic," *Arctic,* v. 16, 159-174. 1963.

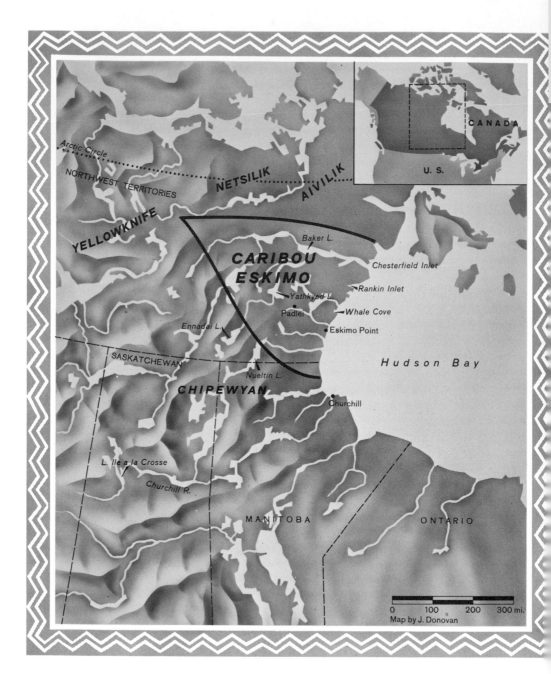

CANADA

U.S.

Arctic Circle

NORTHWEST TERRITORIES

NETSILIK

AIVILIK

YELLOWKNIFE

CARIBOU
ESKIMO

Baker L.

Chesterfield Inlet

Rankin Inlet

Yathkyed L.

Whale Cove

Padlei

Eskimo Point

Ennadai L.

Hudson Bay

SASKATCHEWAN

Nueltin L.

CHIPEWYAN

Churchill

L. Ile a la Crosse

Churchill R.

MANITOBA

ONTARIO

0   100   200   300 mi.

Map by J. Donovan

The
Caribou Eskimos:
hunters of the tundra

Only the Caribou Eskimos may be regarded as truly at home on the Barren Grounds of Canada. The Chipewyan intruded into the area during their summer hunting excursions and may even have wintered there on occasion, but they were above all else a people of the northern forest border. The Caribou Eskimos on the other hand feared the scrawny spruce forests to the south and hesitated to camp there even briefly. Most of them likewise shunned the waters of Hudson Bay as another dangerous unknown. Their primary homeland until the very recent past was a majestic, rock-strewn inland region where lichens grew in the open country and dwarf willows were established in sheltered localities. Yet even the Caribou Eskimos did not occupy all of the Barren Grounds, for parts of it did not offer even the barest possibility of sustaining human life. Collectively these Eskimos referred to themselves by a word which translated "real people". They were labeled the Caribou Eskimos by Danish anthropologists, who were the first to study them systematically; these Eskimos also have been called by the somewhat inaccurate but pleasing name "People of the Deer" by Farley Mowat. The names which link these Eskimos of the Barrens with caribou and deer are anthropological and popular artifices, but each is highly appropriate since these people were above all else specialized inland hunters of caribou.

It may seem strange that these Eskimos should be selected for detailed presentation, particularly since we usually associate Eskimos with the arctic seas and sea mammal hunting. The reasons for their inclusion are both scientific and humanistic. In terms of cultural complexity there were no more primitive Eskimos than the Caribou Eskimos, and in terms of environment, no other inhabited area of arctic America had more limited economic potential. These two factors make the Caribou Eskimos stand out as one of the finest examples of man's conquest of nature. Furthermore, these people have figured prominently in most theoretical reconstructions about the origins and development of Eskimo culture. Then too although the literature about northern peoples includes numerous firsthand accounts of Indians or Eskimos as they lived soon after their initial contact with Europeans, seldom are these by anthropologists. The Caribou Eskimo study, however, was written by Kaj Birket-Smith, a Danish anthropologist, who lived with them in 1922-1923 as they were becoming enmeshed in a trapping and trading economy. Thus, we have a description of an essentially aboriginal people by a leading twentieth-century ethnographer. Following Birket-Smith's fieldwork there is a hiatus of some twenty years before the Caribou Eskimos again attracted widespread attention. The person most responsible for a renewed interest was the prominent Canadian writer Farley Mowat. He wrote a touching plea to the outside world about the plight of the Caribou Eskimos as reflected in their devastating starvations and sought drastic changes in their administration. His verbal pictures were supplemented with graphic ones by Richard Harrington, and as a result these Eskimos received widespread attention from within Canada and beyond. In the summer of 1955 the Dutch anthropologist Geert van den Steenhoven studied Caribou Eskimo political organization and wrote a systematic account of their customary law. These data, supplemented with more recent descriptions, make it possible to plot the changes in Caribou Eskimo life in recent times with considerable accuracy.

Aboriginally the Caribou Eskimos occupied the core of the Barren Grounds, but they ranged along the southern fringes leading to the taiga with caution in order to avoid their traditional enemies, the Chipewyan. Neither did they wander near the northern Athapaskan Indians to the west, the Slave, Dogrib, and Yellowknife tribes, for they too were enemy peoples. In the north they ranged to watersheds leading to the Arctic Ocean and around Chesterfield Inlet on Hudson Bay. Their area was about 400 miles from north to south and 300 miles from east to west, but over this broad region in 1922-1923, the population total was somewhat less than 500 individuals.

Eskimoan languages belong to the American Arctic-Paleosiberian linguistic phylum, which includes Eskimos in northern North America and a small area of eastern Siberia, as well as other peoples in northeastern Siberia. Thus there are clear linguistic ties between the Old and New Worlds in the vicinity of Bering Strait. This particular phylum includes two language families: the Chukchi-Kamchatkan in Siberia and the Eskimo-Aleut in the American north. The latter spanned the north from the Aleutian Islands to Greenland and Labrador and included three major subdivisions, or subfamilies: Alaskan Eskimo, Aleut, and Central-Greenland Eskimo, whose representative languages are not mutually intelligible. The Caribou Eskimos belong to the latter subfamily; their dialect was very similar to that spoken by Eskimos along adjacent coastal areas, which suggests that the coastal and inland Eskimo populations of central Canada were a single people in the not-too-distant past.

According to Birket-Smith, the earliest people whom we now call Eskimos originally were inland hunters and fishermen who lived near timberline from Alaska to Hudson Bay; these people he termed Proto-Eskimos. When they adapted to the sea but retained an older inland orientation, they became Paleo-Eskimos. As these people became increasingly adept at sea mammal hunting and proficiently hunted large whales, we find that Neo-Eskimo culture emerged. According to this thesis some Eskimos continued to follow an old inland way of life and only recently adapted to sea mammal hunting, and some failed to make this adaptation altogether. These are the Eschato-Eskimos, and the Caribou Eskimos are the best example of the inland way of life surviving down to modern times. This well-conceived theory of Eskimo origins and development was built as an ethnographic reconstruction without the aid of a sound archaeological basis, and it is archaeological excavations which have made the theory less plausible. The excavations of Elmer Harp, Jr., in the northern sector of historic Caribou Eskimo occupancy, are crucial. It was found that the Caribou Eskimos do not represent a very archaic form of Eskimo culture, and the primary reason for this conclusion is that none of the sites associated with these people have appreciable time depth. At present the most likely course of events seems to have been that some whale hunters in central Canada, of Birket-Smith's Neo-Eskimo level, were forced to abandon their orientation to the sea. This was because of an uplifting of the earth's crust about 1400 A.D. which made the seas shallower and impossible for large whales to frequent. It was then that some Eskimos became divorced from the sea, built an economy on hunting caribou, and became the Caribou Eskimos. The shift was not difficult to make because they had retained some aspects of their early inland hunting economy, and there were no doubt large if not vast caribou herds on the Barren Grounds. The decision to move inland permanently was not a choice of convenience but one of necessity. Not all coastal Eskimos could remain at sealing grounds, and those with more of an inland hunting orientation settled in the Barrens. Caribou Eskimo culture emerged as one of material poverty and regression toward greater simplicity. As Harp has noted, and as I too have observed, the abandoned Caribou Eskimo camp sites contain amazingly few artifacts because there was little to leave behind except immense piles of broken caribou bones.

History in the making has nibbled away at the fringes of the Barren Grounds for hundreds of years, but to this day, intrusions into the Barrens by outsiders always are temporary. The exploration of Hudson Bay and the establishment of trading centers along its western shore first brought some Caribou Eskimos into contact with explorers and traders of the Hudson's Bay Company. The early exploration and settlement of the Churchill River mouth has been outlined in discussing European penetration of the Chipewyan country. Little of pertinence may be added regarding any special relationships with the Caribou Eskimos. We know that they went to Fort Prince of Wales to trade and that trading vessels contacted some groups along the coast, but such intercourse did not directly affect most Caribou Eskimos. It was not until the great adventures of Samuel Hearne that we learn about the Barren Grounds, but on his travels he met no Caribou

Eskimos. As strange as it may seem, it was not until the trip across the northern Barrens by Frederick Schwatka and his party in 1878-1880 that we first learn about the Caribou Eskimos. After this time travelers to the area have been more numerous, but their contributions to our knowledge of the Caribou Eskimos were comparatively minor until 1922. It is with gratitude and relief that we turn to Birket-Smith, and then to Knud Rasmussen, of the Fifth Thule Expedition, for our base-line study of these people.

These Eskimos smelled of rancid fat and wood smoke, for they never bathed. The exposed areas of their bodies were dark from weathering and from the smoke of their dwarf birch fires. Some men cut their hair so that it was short all over or hung as long bangs around their heads. Others left their hair long and parted it in the middle, holding each segment in place with a browband. Whichever form was adopted, the crown often was tonsured. The faces of women were darker and grimier than those of the men, for it was the women who squatted before the smoky cooking fires. The faces of many women had been tattooed, either by threading a needle with a soot-covered human hair and sewing designs into the skin or by pricking the skin and rubbing the wounds with soot. Usually lines from the bridge of the nose to the hairline were made as a spreading V. From the outer edge of each nostril to the middle of each ear were paired double lines, often with dots between, while from the lower lip over the chin and on the sides of the lower face again were paired double lines with dots between. Some women parted their hair in the middle, braided the segments, and rolled one over each ear, binding them in place with strips of skin. Other women bound locks of hair around oblong wooden sticks and often wound these with strips of skin.

Of all the material culture needs, clothing was extremely important, particularly since sub-zero temperatures were common most of the year and winter dwellings not only were built of snow but were unheated. It is not surprising that Caribou Eskimo clothing was among the warmest reported anywhere in the world. The preferred material for the outer winter parka was fall caribou skin. Thin-haired skins were used to make summer parkas and other garments. Winter clothing for a man consisted of two pairs of trousers which reached from the hips to above the knees and were held in place with draw cords. The inner trousers had the hair facing the body, while the outer ones had the hair facing in the opposite direction. The hooded inner parka, with the hair turned inside, reached to the thigh and was split up each side to form front and rear flaps. Since this parka also was worn in warmer weather, it was trimmed along the cuffs and hood with strips of short-haired skin and with a fringe along the bottom. The outer winter parka was loose-fitting, with side slits and flaps edged in caribou skin strips. In severe weather men wore belts about their waists to keep cold air from circulating beneath their parkas. Men wore knee-length skin stockings with sewn-in feet and the hair side inward; over these sometimes were worn short socks with the hair side inward. The winter boots of caribou leg skins reached to the knees or below and had attached soles with the hair side inside. On his hands a man wore caribou skin mittens with the hair on the outside. Additional items of male apparel included amulets sewn on the inner parka, long-legged dehaired boots for spring wear, and short dehaired stockings with sewn-in soles for wear around the tent.

The clothing of women took the same general form as that for men. The principal difference was in the proportions of the female garments. The parkas were baggier and could accommodate an infant inside. These garments had long hoods, broad shoulders, a short rounded flap in front, and a wide long back panel which was rounded at the corners and extended to the ankles. The trousers of the women reached from the waist to below the knees, and they wore only a single pair, with the hair side out. Women's winter traveling boots bagged grossly above the knees and covered the lower part of the trousers. One item of clothing with no counterpart among males was a cloak of processed caribou skin which was not modified in any other manner. The people were not careful about keeping their skin garments in good repair, but they did attempt to keep them as dry as possible. This was difficult, especially when living in an unheated snowhouse. The parkas were made in such a manner that they fitted loosely, which cut down the amount of moisture which would accumulate from perspiration. Additionally, the snow was removed from a garment with a wooden or antler snowbeater which had a handle and an oblong blade. To facilitate drying, small items of clothing were placed beneath the skin blankets, but this was largely ineffective.

Both men and women had small skin bags in which to store small items since all of their garments were pocketless. A skin bag was suspended from a cord passed around the neck and over one shoulder. Infants were carried in the backs of their mothers' inner parkas, not in the hoods, and a belt from the small of a woman's back to over her breasts held the infant in place. The only clothing worn by the offspring was a caribou skin bonnet. From the time a child was able to crawl and until he was about six years old, he wore a hoodless combination suit with a split up the back. Children also wore boots, mittens, and a larger bonnet as well as a scarf of caribou skin strips.

Caribou Eskimos, like all Eskimos, were extremely sociable. They enjoyed not only the company of relatives and friends but almost anyone except Indians. They liked to talk about their clothing, hunting, or what was stored in their meat caches. Whenever possible, meaning when food was available, families were likely to concentrate, if not next door to one another then at least within a few miles. Families clustered most often in the fall at locations along rivers where caribou preferred to cross on their migration southward. If numerous animals were killed and the meat was cached nearby, a camp assumed a degree of permanence. At the same time it was not unusual for a family to strike out on its own in search of better hunting grounds and later rejoin the camp from which they came or join another. The settlement pattern was one of unstable concentrations of people in aggregates which never were very large. If a family thought it unlikely that they would take any more caribou during a particular fall and if their meat caches were low, they moved to lakes known to contain fish. In the spring of 1922 the largest camp contained forty-six persons. The members of an individual household included a man, his wife, their children (nuclear family), and the occasional addition of a second wife or an old person related to the couple.

When Eskimos are called to mind, most persons envision a fur-clad people living in dome-shaped houses of snow blocks. It is certainly accurate that all Eskimos wear fur garments of one sort or another, but most Eskimos have never lived in snowhouses or "igloos." The snowhouse was limited in its distribution to much of central Canada and northwestern Greenland. The Caribou Eskimos were among those who made their winter homes of snow blocks. The snowhouse has a romantic appeal to dwellers of temperate regions, but the realities of igloo dwelling would tend to destroy this image. The first essential in building a snowhouse was to locate snow of the proper texture, and until this was possible the people lived in skin tents which afforded little protection from the cold and the winds of the late fall. Before the end of October the preferred type of snow, firm but not densely packed, usually was to be found. The snow at the particular spot where the igloo was to be built was probed with an antler shaft which had been steamed straight. After snow with the proper consistency had been located, a snow knife was used to cut the blocks. These knives probably were made from antler and edged with ice for sharpness. The blocks were about thirty inches long, twenty inches high, and eight inches thick; preferably they were cut by one man and fitted into place by another. The blocks were cut from the floor area, over an area thirteen or more feet in diameter. After the first row of blocks was in place, each one was trimmed to slope inward. The succeeding blocks were trimmed also and pushed firmly into place. When the dome was completed and the last block fitted, the builder, who was encased in the house, cut an opening which became the entryway. The gaps in ill-fitted blocks were chinked with snow, and finally the women piled loose snow against the lowest part of the wall with wooden shovels edged with an antler strip. Over the entrance a block of clear ice replaced a block of snow and served as the window. Next an entrance passage was built with its floor at a somewhat lower level than the house floor in order to prevent outside air from entering the house directly. Storage rooms were built off the tunnel, and blocks of snow were piled outside the tunnel entrance as a windbreak. A small room then was added to the side of the house, and it was here that the woman of a household cooked on flat stones with twigs as fuel.

At the back of a snowhouse was a snow platform about seven feet deep at its widest spot. On top of the snow was placed a mat of willows and then thick-haired caribou skins. Additional caribou skins for sleeping were rolled up against the rear of the platform during the day. It was here that the family slept, ate, lounged, and in short lived. A man stretched out on the platform with his back against rolled sleeping skins; women customarily sat with their legs tucked beneath them, and children were everywhere.

Cooking on the flat stones in the kitchen, which had a conical roof to create an adequate draft for the fire, the women burned the twigs from small plants, dry moss or lichens, but never oil. A fire was lighted by striking pieces of iron pyrite together or was kindled with a strap drill. Meat and fish were cut up with a semilunar slate-bladed knife hafted in a wooden handle; this was the well-known woman's knife or *ulu*. Food was cooked in rectangular soapstone vessels, with lugs at either end for their removal from the fireplace. Most of the meat consumed in the summer was cut into pieces and simmered in water. Sometimes fresh fish and meat were eaten raw, especially during the winter when fuel was scarce. Popular food included raw caribou kidneys, liver, marrow, and fat from the back of an animal taken in the fall. Most parts of a caribou were considered edible; the eyes were eaten raw, as were the contents of the stomach and the fly larvae in the skin; the hoofs were boiled, as were the brains and intestines. Excrement was not eaten purposefully, but if it found its way into the cooking pot it was not avoided. Meat was served on oblong wooden trays, where it cooled, and men ate before women. A man took a piece of meat by hand, stuffed as much as possible into his mouth, and cut off the surplus with a knife. Marrow was removed by cracking one bone with another and extracting it with a long bone probe. Soup was removed from a cooking pot with a musk-ox horn ladle and passed from one person to the next to sip. Water was stored in skin pails and ladled out with a dipper. In the spring water was drunk from a bird bone tube to prevent one's lips from cracking in the dry air. After a meal was completed, each person wiped his fingers on a bird skin.

One important household item was the lamp, which was made from a flat stone or a hollowed-out piece of soapstone fashioned into a saucer shape. The fuel was most often caribou fat which burned at the end of a cone-shaped moss wick. It is significant that even when seal oil was available it was not used as fuel and that these Eskimos did not cook over lamps, using them solely to provide light. A snowhouse was not purposefully heated, and yet it was relatively warm. The interior temperature rose to about twenty-five degrees F. and remained at about this level in spite of the fact that it might be from twenty to fifty degrees below zero outside. The insulation provided by the snow, the absence of a direct entryway to the outside, and the body heat of the occupants warmed the dwelling.

The dogs belonging to a family slept outside the igloo to the lee or within the house passageway. Most families had about three dogs, for it was difficult to feed more. Dogs were fed once a day or less often during the winter; they were left to roam unfed in the summer, at which time they hunted small animals and ate human feces to survive. In all likelihood some dogs had a strain of wolf blood, and while they were not vicious neither were they friendly. The Eskimo attitude toward dogs was one of detached interest. A man would whip a dog that did not pull his share of a load, but he would not kill a dog nor utilize its skin in any manner. Individual dogs were named, often with the names of persons. Each team had its lead dog, chosen for its knowledge, as well as a "boss" dog who dominated the other members of the team but was not necessarily the lead dog. When not in use a sled was placed on pillars of snow blocks above the reach of the perennially hungry dogs; it looked like a ladder more than anything else. The parallel, spruce runners were as much as thirty feet in length, with about seventeen inches distance separating them. Nearly a quarter of the distance from the front, the first of some twenty crosspieces was lashed with thongs through holes drilled in the runners beneath. In front of the first crosspiece was a rawhide line, and onto it the traces to individual dogs were attached.

A settlement consisting of four or five igloos was the winter-long residence if the families had caches of caribou meat in the vicinity. Yet the men did not rely solely on their meat reserves, but hunted caribou throughout the winter since there often were small scattered herds which remained on the Barrens. For a winter hunting excursion a man used a shorter form of the ladder sled, on which he placed his bow and quivered arrows. The bow was fashioned from a shaft of wood, and along the length of the front were strips of sinew held into place with half-hitches; this sinew backing served to strengthen the bow, which was strung with a sinew cord. The wooden arrow shafts were tipped with barbless antler points and vaned with two to four feathers. The effective range of an arrow was up to about sixty-five feet which meant that a hunter stalked an animal or waited until it wandered extremely near; either technique was difficult since caribou normally were wary prey during the winter months.

That caribou hunting was the focus of subsistence activities is obvious; without caribou even the precarious Caribou Eskimo existence would have been impossible. Thus, by describing the ways in which caribou molded the lives of these people, we may begin to understand the essence of their living system. It was said by knowing elders that once there was a time when caribou did not exist on earth, but then a man cut a great hole in the earth because he wished for caribou. From this opening so many caribou emerged that the earth was almost covered with them, and then the man covered the hole. This was the origin of caribou which enabled men to live on the Barrens. Since caribou were creatures of the earth, from out of the earth, they existed independently of direct human or supernatural control. Still in all, there were many rules which men followed in order not to offend their guiding spirit or *Pinga,* "The One up in the Sky" who influenced the affairs of man and animals, especially man's relationship to caribou. Pinga was offended when men were careless or wasteful in handling caribou that they had killed; therefore, it was necessary to cover all evidence that a kill had taken place. It was essential, too, for the killer of a caribou to leave a piece of meat and fat beneath a nearby stone to appease the animal's soul. Dogs were prohibited from eating the muzzle of a caribou or chewing its bones or antler. No matter how attentive a man was to these and the other rules pertaining to caribou, he had no hope of controlling their migrations; it was the caribou who controlled themselves.

In order to be at the right place at the proper time to intercept migrating herds of caribou a man trusted his judgment and past experience. Life was in greatest jeopardy during the spring when starvation and death were most expectable. In the early spring before the caribou began to arrive, people hunted ptarmigan to tide them over this very lean period. At times these birds were stunned with rocks, but more often they were shot with blunted arrows. The people anxiously awaited the first sighting of caribou moving northward on a migration route that was eight hundred miles long. In the spring the cows with their year-old calves came first, then all other young cows, and finally the young bulls. Even when caribou were only a short distance away the hunters did not rush to the kill but waited until animals wandered near. To a people who encountered privation so often, it mattered little if one suffered hunger for a few more days. In the late spring when the herds came within easy reach they were hunted but not with persistence. After numerous animals had been killed, the people became unrestrained gluttons until the supply of meat was exhausted. Only then did they once again worry about the problem of food. Female caribou calved in June, and in August the grown bulls arrived in great herds. The herds lingered only briefly before they ranged on farther to the north, but in the fall they turned southward, and it was this time of the year that the hunters most anticipated. The animals then were fat, their skins prime, and they moved in vast herds. It was the success or failure of the fall hunt which predicted whether the members of a camp would thrive, barely survive, or starve during the winter to come.

If meat supplies became low and additional animals could not be located, the only alternative was to fish through the ice. Winter settlements were established with this alternative in mind. Ice fishing did not appeal to these Eskimos, for the rewards often were few and the effort was tedious. Winter fishing meant picking an oblong hole in the ice at a spot where fish were likely to have congregated along a river or more often in a lake. The antler ice pick was lashed with a thong to a wooden handle and newly-forming ice was dipped from a fishing hole with an antler ice scoop attached to a wooden handle. A lure was fashioned from the skin of a fish, which inflated as it faced the flow of water, or from strips of trout skin, which were attached to a sinew line and weighted with a stone. The lure line was raised and lowered in the water as a fisherman stood poised above with a fish spear (leister). This particular weapon consisted of a wooden shaft to which two lateral antler prongs were attached; each prong had a barb facing the shaft, while a central prong was inserted into the end of the shaft. A fish attempting to take the lure was impaled on the central prong and held in place by the lateral barbs. A second ice fishing method involved the use of a barbless hook on a bone shank which was attached to a sinew line and was paid out from a bow-shaped antler reel. Fishing for whitefish, tullibee, and trout could be rewarding or very unprofitable. Without caribou meat, however, the choice was to starve or to fish.

When the spring thaw rendered a snowhouse unlivable, the residents erected a tent. The conical caribou skin tent (tepee), with the hair side out, was built around a frame of about eight poles some thirteen feet in length; a flap of caribou skin served as the door. The family slept and lounged at the rear of a tent on caribou skins. To the left of the entrance was a stone-lined fireplace. A summer tent, just as a snowhouse, was occupied by one family or less often by small, related families. Once the winter's snows had left, making it possible to camp at a higher level, families moved their tents to ridges where the mosquitoes were less bothersome and where they could watch for caribou and Indians. When a camp was abandoned, the family's possessions were carried to the next camp across the tundra. They did not make the large, open skin boats (umiaks) so common among most Eskimos, due probably to the nature of the drainage systems and the fast water. All of the people and dogs, except for infants, the aged, and puppies, carried something. Dogs dragged tent poles or else carried two small packs of caribou skin, one on either side of their backs. The men and women were loaded with bundles of equipment carried on their backs and supported by ropes. During the summer families were generally dispersed, but whenever game was plentiful in one locality, they camped near one another. When the weather was warm and pleasant, the women cooked and scraped skins outside the tent and behind a windbreak of brush. If hunting had been productive, men lounged about the tent, but when they were in need of meat, they ranged far from camp to hunt alone. If a man were unable to return home the same day, he slept in the open, drawing his arms inside his parka for warmth.

In the summer, migratory waterfowl as well as fish provided a change in the normal diet of caribou meat. Molting birds were pursued by kayak and killed by hand when they were exhausted. They also were taken with bird-spears, which had two barbed prongs attached to the end of a wooden shaft; these spears were hurled with the aid of throwing-boards. In the summer arctic char ascended certain rivers to spawn, and with the approach of fall they returned to the sea. In river shallows dam and weir combinations were built of stone to trap these fish in small basins, from which they were taken with leisters. These fish barriers belonged to the persons that made them, but they could be used by anyone. Fish also were taken in shallow waters with gorge sets. This technique involved sharpening a short piece of caribou leg bone at each end and placing a piece of fish skin over the bone. The center section was tied to a line with a float attached and then placed in the water. A fish seized and swallowed the skin-covered gorge which toggled in its stomach to hold the fish fast.

The crucial autumn migration of caribou southward was anticipated by moving camp to a locality where these animals were likely to pass, such as where a lake narrowed. One method of fall caribou hunting involved the use of converging lines of stone cairns. The cairns technically were owned by their builders but might be used by anyone. The women and children slipped behind a herd, driving it by shouting toward the cairns, which were hidden by a ridge. Passing over the crest of the ridge and seeing the cairns the caribou assumed that they were men and nervously kept within the boundaries while converging on the spot where the hunters were hiding with their bows and arrows. Cairns also were used to guide caribou into a lake or river where the hunters were waiting in their kayaks. Once the animals were in the water the hunters approached the caribou rapidly using double-bladed paddles. T⟩ ⎯nimals were dispatched with spears which probably were tipped with ground stone points. In this manner large numbers of caribou could be taken in a short period of time. In the late fall when a thin layer of ice had formed on lakes, caribou were driven onto the ice where they broke through and were killed easily. According to custom if two men shot the same animal the arrow which struck the most vital organ gave its owner the right of possession. If one man wounded a caribou but another succeeded in killing it, the animal belonged to the person who made the initial strike. When two or three men hunted together and an animal was killed, they shared it, while if more than three persons participated in a hunt, then the killer was obligated to provide the day's meat for the community.

When caribou mated in October, mature bulls jealously guarded the females in their company and attempted to keep other males away by force. At this time of the year a hunter sometimes held a set of caribou antlers over his head and imitated the grunting of a bull. A bull caribou protecting his females would approach the disguised man much nearer than normal and could be shot with an arrow. When there was a reasonably heavy snow-fall so that it covered the ground in scattered fields, a snow cairn was built and curiosity attracted the caribou to it. On the path to the cairn a pit was dug in the snow and snow blocks added so that the depth of the pit was about ten feet. The pit was covered with a thin roof of snow, and any animal which walked up the slope to the pit fell into it and was trapped. Such a method was successful only when caribou were numerous; otherwise they would be cautious. A second form of pit dug into the snow was baited with dog or wolf urine to which the caribou were attracted because of its salt content. With these fall hunting techniques more animals usually were killed than could serve the immediate needs of the family and the hunter cached his surpluses. Boulders were cleared from an area, and a layer of old bones was placed on the ground to form a rack for air to circulate beneath. The meat was laid on top of the bones, and boulders were placed over the meat to prevent marauding foxes from eating it. Scattered about the camp of a successful hunter were many such caches, and often they were topped with a caribou's head.

The only other large land mammal hunted was the musk ox, but it did not range widely over the Barrens and does not appear to have been very plentiful. When a herd was discovered, the usual pattern was to release dogs to bring the musk oxen to bay. These shaggy monsters formed a defensive circle with their heads facing outward. In this fighting position they were killed readily with spears or arrows. An entire herd could be taken since any live animal stood guard over its fallen companions.

The most elaborate body of technological knowledge was that associated with the processing of caribou skins. After an animal was skinned, the hide was dried and stored for future use. When a woman was ready to prepare a hide further, she slept with the skin side next to her body for a night to soften it. She then scraped the inner surface with a caribou scapula to remove the subcutaneous fibers and fat, and after draping the skin over one thigh, she went over it vigorously again with a piece of sandstone. The skin was wrung by hand after being moistened and was scraped again the following day. In order to dehair a skin which might be used for a kayak cover or summer boots, it was placed on the house platform and was softened by being sat and slept on. The next step was to soak it in water for a few days, after which the hair could be scraped free with ease. Skins were sewn with an eyed needle made of caribou bone, and thread was made of sinew removed from a caribou's back. A woman's thimble was an oval of skin with a slit at one end through which her finger passed. Her sewing equipment was kept in a bag made from a section of caribou skin, a bird's head, or a split bird's foot.

Apart from the items of material culture mentioned already, little more would have been seen around a Caribou Eskimo camp. There were knives with ground slate end blades and antler handles, whetstones, soapstone pipes, and a bow drill of wood with a caribou astragalus mouthpiece, a wooden shaft, and probably a ground stone bit. A bow drill collected by Birket-Smith was engraved along one surface with representations of bearded seals and bears. Engraved objects of this nature are so rare that some people maintained that they did not exist. One example only is known of a realistic painting by a Caribou Eskimo; this was a caribou figure painted on a kayak and was assumed to have had magical associations.

The fondness of Eskimos for the company of relatives, friends, neighbors, and anyone else who was not a threat is legendary. Their genuine and infectious warmth led families to camp together whenever food was abundant, but large camps could not be maintained for very long. Therefore, social life was organized around the nuclear family. In this as in all human societies there was a division of labor based on sex and age. The duties of women and men were divided, but neither was unwilling to aid the other sex. The work activities of men required hard physical effort, but these were interspersed with periods of comparative leisure; the working pattern of women was one of sustained but less strenuous activity. Men built snow-houses; women caulked the holes and shoveled snow around the base. It usually was women who pitched the tents. Men hunted, and both men and women dressed skins. Both sexes fished, but men did so more often. Women were responsible for raising the children, sewing, and cooking, whereas men drove the dog teams and manufactured artifacts. Since the family's welfare was largely in the hands of the male as the hunter and provider, his decisions guided family life, but a woman had a significant voice in family affairs.

The daily routine of social life was not punctuated with seasonal social or religious highlights. In a tent or igloo the people went to bed early and began the next day's activities early except during the long days of summer. Then they sometimes went to bed late and might not rise until the early afternoon. It was customary to have a light meal during the morning and to eat a large evening meal in the dwelling of the day's most successful hunter. At communal meals the men ate separately from the women and children, but when a family was isolated all the members ate together.

Social control was not a major consideration in daily living, but occasions did arise when it was necessary to take some decisive action concerning the behavior of someone who was not adhering to the traditional norms of the society. The difficulty in dealing with any behavior that was not standard stemmed from the fact that social expectations were defined only vaguely and no individual had any real authority over his fellowmen. According to Birket-Smith, certain guidelines, while not precisely conceived by the people, did constitute grounds for community action. There were rules for the division of game, and each man was expected to hunt unless he was physically ill or aged. Also, no one could settle at a camp without the consent of the established residents. Obviously the distribution of food was a matter of primary concern in their system of customary law. As mentioned earlier the animals killed during a hunt were divided among the hunters, but when starvation threatened, any food belonged equally to all of the persons in a community. Another person's meat caches could be opened with impunity. A man who was lazy and did not provide food for his family soon would be deserted by his wife and children. Such an individual did not starve because someone always would feed him, but he was considered a worthless person. If as sometimes happened an individual was a good hunter but refused to share his catch with others, he was consi-dered antisocial. Mild ridicule probably would be followed by a derisive song, and if that did not have the desired effect, he would be ostracized as socially undesirable.

The social conventions arising from custom and tradition granted the individual a great deal of freedom; he literally was responsible to no man in the ordinary course of life. Situations did arise, however, which brought the actions of an individual into open conflict with the rights of another. Since no one was vested with any authority or power to control others, the means to induce conformity was to turn to subtle solutions which did not require force. Songs of derision were an important means to bring problems into the open and reduce tensions. After any bountiful evening meal, someone was likely to sing. A drum was found for accompaniment, and the course of the evening was set. Songs were sung by men as women formed the chorus. A man usually sang and danced at the same time; he moved his feet very little but swayed back and forward from the waist as the drum was struck in a series of single beats. The songs frequently were about hunting caribou or musk oxen; they might be remembrances by old men of great hunts in the past. Some songs exposed the behavior of others to public scrutiny; these were biting and very much to the point. Usually the victim took the criticism in stride, although fist fights did sometimes result. Such songs included as their subject matter a man hiding food from his wife; illicit sexual relations; a man leaving his family to starve; and a man losing an argument to his wife. In each instance the actions of the offender were not punished except by exposure to ridicule.

Derisive songs sufficed in most instances to make an offender change his behavior, but songs were not enough when a murder had been committed. In theory, each murder required blood revenge against the offender or his immediate family, but after it had been exacted no further retaliation was sanctioned, which avoided blood feuds. It was possible for murders to go unavenged under unusual conditions. An instance of this nature was recorded by Knud Rasmussen. A man planned to marry a girl, but her family arranged her marriage to another man since they did not care for her suitor. The rejected individual went to the igloo of the girl he hoped to marry and killed her father, mother, two brothers, and their wives; afterwards he took the girl as his wife. The man who committed this mass murder was no ordinary individual. Rasmussen (1930, 33) met him when he was older and wrote that the man was "wise, independent, intelligent and exercised great authority over his fellow-villagers." Thus, even murder was tempered by the individual's personality and the circumstances. Geert van den Steenhoven (1962, 104), who investigated the nature of traditional Caribou Eskimo law in the 1950's, recorded that a highly respected man said that "In case of dispute, I rather would run away than fight." In order to rid themselves of "one for whom we do not care" they would move camp suddenly without notifying the offender, simply to avoid his distasteful behavior in the future.

The only other hostile forms of behavior against one's fellowmen were thievery and witchcraft, but neither was a source of great anxiety. In a society such as this, where possessions were few and what each person owned was known to everyone, thefts could not go undetected. A man owned his weapons, clothing, kayak, and tools, while a woman owned her lamp, cooking pot, and household items; both a man and women might own dogs. If someone borrowed an item and it broke or became unreturnable for some other reason, the original owner would not object normally; by releasing the item in the first place, he demonstrated that he had no absolute need for it. However, if something was taken without the owner's permission, this was theft, and the owner probably would ask for the item back. A person who stole repeatedly was looked upon simply as a strange person. Just as the thief was best regarded as abnormal, so it was with a witch. Witches were rare; they usually were old women who knew some magic spell which they repeated in association with the name of the person they sought to harm.

Since cooperation was not the norm in daily subsistence pursuits, we find that leadership was vague and ill-defined. A man could and did attain a position of influence among his fellowmen by being an able person and a capable hunter. Such an individual never attracted a great following but simply was respected by all. Another type of gifted individual was the shaman. He or she clearly was a charismatic leader with inordinate abilities. A shaman became powerful through his cleverness and effective control of spirits, but there were able as well as inefficient practitioners. A shaman healed people of natural and supernatural diseases and performed acts of magic. Rasmussen recorded an account of one shaman's training, which is an enlightening document. This individual chose to gain his power through enduring hunger and suffering from cold, although he could have elected to be "drowned" or "killed" in order to become a wise man. This man, the same individual who committed the mass murder related earlier, was instructed by his father-in-law, not the man he killed but the father of another wife. The instructor took the novice away from all the beaten paths and built a tiny snowhouse for him. The novice shaman sat alone in the unheated igloo for five days and then was brought a little warm water. Fifteen days later he was again given warm water, and finally after ten more days he was permitted to eat. All during his isolation he concentrated on the fact that he hoped to become a shaman so that Pinga would "own" him. A helping spirit appeared to him after about thirty days. He then was taken back to the village by his father-in-law and slowly regained his strength. Only after a year could he sleep with his wife and eat normally. To diagnose a case or see into the future he isolated himself by wandering about the countryside for two or three days, during which time he ate little and rested infrequently. He reported his progress to the camp each morning and then returned to his search for answers in solitude. It was not only Pinga who aided this man but Hila as well. The latter was in many ways confused with Pinga. Pinga's special charge was caribou, while Hila was everything to be feared existing in the air, the cold when the sun was gone, and the storms which brought enforced inactivity with the possibility of starvation.

A shaman wore a special belt to which were attached amulets presented to him by diverse individuals, and a special wooden shaft was part of his equipment. The shaft was tied to his belt and served as an entry path for spirit aids from the ground. The shaft also was used for divining; questions were asked and the answers judged by presumed differences in the shaft's weight. It was believed that all disease was of supernatural origin, but at the same time there were a few, very few, secular cures for illness. For example, fat from a wolf and burnt moss from a lamp were applied to frostbite, broken limbs were splinted, and wounds were bandaged with animal membrane. In most other instances of sickness a shaman held a seance to establish what a patient must do to insure recovery.

During leisure time probably the most common form of diversion was to lounge and chat, but games were a part of evening activities. The day after a shaman had held a seance no one hunted, but adults played a variant of the ring and pin game. A thong was suspended from the ceiling with a strip of antler tied to it; it was anchored at the bottom with another thong to which a stone weight was attached. A hole had been drilled through a mid-point of the antler section, and the object of the game was for the assembled men and women to penetrate the hole with any pointed object thrust at the moving antler. Since it was not unlikely that when others missed the hole, one's hand would be pierced by their probes, a mitten was worn for protection. A stake was put up, and the winner then offered the next prize. The stake was sometimes an item of little value, but it could also be very valuable. The Caribou Eskimos were avid gamblers, playing different games for stakes. A form of roulette was played with a soup ladle. The ladle was spun in the center of a circle of players, and the winner was the individual whom the handle faced when it stopped spinning. They had a hand game, in which one's hands were placed behind his back and a stone shifted from one palm to another; the object was to guess the hand that concealed the stone when they were both placed in front again. The intensity with which a man gambled sometimes resulted in the loss of many possessions, even one's sled, dogs, or wife. Pastimes engaged in for pleasure alone included making cat's cradles, playing ball games, and testing one's strength by pulling an opponent.

On the whole the system for designating kin consisted of distinct terms for nearly every close category of kin. For individuals on the generational level above Ego there were different words for father, mother, maternal aunts and uncles, as well as paternal aunts and uncles (bifurcate collateral terms). On Ego's generational level there were distinctive words for older brothers, younger ones, older sisters, and younger ones. Maternal cousins were termed differently from paternal cousins, but there was no differentiation by sex for cousins; the cousin terms do not fit into any common type. Most Eskimos have "Eskimo" cousin terms, which are of the same type as found in the United States today, but the Caribou Eskimos are an exception, as are most Alaskan Eskimos. The terms alone suggest a highly fragmented set of role expectations from kin. Close relatives were conceived separately except for the terminological grouping of cousins. Likewise the terms for wife and temporary wife were different; nearly a quarter of the men had two wives. Relatives were traced along both the male and female lines (bilateral descent), which provided a widespread network of kinship obligations.

Thus far mention of the few Caribou Eskimos who visited the coast as a part of their economic activities has been avoided to eliminate confusion, but this is not to deny that some of these people utilized maritime resources. By the early 1920's only two families remained at the coast throughout the year, and the members of one particular band visited the coast each summer to hunt seals and walrus. It should be emphasized, however, that seal blubber was rarely burned in lamps and seal meat was considered more fit for dogs than for people. Furthermore, kayak covers were made of dehaired caribou skin but not of the superior sealskin. Thus it appears that the coastal side of their economic life was relatively unimportant.

While a woman was pregnant and when she gave birth, she was obligated to follow particular conventions surrounding the event. As her time approached, for example, she untied her hair as a sympathetic means for facilitating delivery. An offspring was born in the family residence, and the mother was aided by two experienced women. One held her hands as the second applied downward pressure to hasten the delivery. The neonate was wiped with bird skins, and the umbilical cord was severed with a piece of quartz. The afterbirth was hidden to prevent dogs from finding and eating it. For the next month the mother was restricted to the dwelling and could not sleep with her husband. In addition she cooked and ate from containers which were separate from those of the other family members. Following her confinement she threw away all the skins and clothing which had touched her body. Infanticide rarely was practiced, probably because the infant mortality rate was high.

Names were not associated with a particular sex. Before an offspring was born, it was named after a recently deceased individual, and individuals with the same name were prohibited from marrying. The widespread Eskimo aversion to stating one's own name was not a custom. As soon after an infant's birth as possible, it began to acquire amulets. These usually were bird or animal skins or insects which had been caught unharmed. The particular species which served a person in this manner could not be killed by him. These skins or insects were sewn into skin bags and attached to the inner parka of the individual.

As an infant passed into childhood, he led a life free from "do's" and "don'ts" and was not punished physically until about seven years of age when he began to understand adult values. If a child misbehaved, he was threatened with the hare as a "bogey man," and if this ruse failed, the parents simply allowed the child to have his own way. Children played games which were imitations of adult pursuits, using small sleds, kayaks, and snow knives. They also had toys designed for entertainment alone. A buzz was made from a piece of sinew looped through two holes in a circular piece of skin. An oblong piece of wood with notched edges was attached to a sinew cord and made a whistling sound as it was twirled; this was a bullroarer, which to some peoples was a sacred object. Popguns were made from bird bone tubes which had a piece of chewed lichen inserted into one end; a rod forced into the opposite end of the tube propelled the ammunition. Girls owned dolls dressed in skin clothing to resemble men or women. They might entertain each other by flipping their fingernails against their teeth, to produce a variety of different tones. They enjoyed swinging around until they became dizzy, and they also did the "cossack" step for fun.

At the onset of a girl's menarche she changed to an adult style parka, and she was subject to the food taboos for a menstruating woman. When boys passed into adolescence, there was no formal recognition of their change in status. When a boy actively hunted caribou, he was on the path to manhood. The first caribou killed was butchered inside a dwelling, which normally was forbidden, and the meat was eaten by all except women and children. Infant betrothals were the rule, and marriage, which was without ceremony, took place as soon as the man was able to support a wife. Although there were no clearly established prohibitions against marrying a near relative, it seems unlikely that couples were more closely related than second cousins. It was customary for a man to present his father-in-law with material goods as compensation for the loss of a daughter. The newly wedded couple most often attached themselves to the household of the husband (patrilocal residence), but this arrangement was flexible. It is probable, too, that the couple set up their own separate household as soon as they were able. It was not at all unusual for the partners to separate and remarry someone else. When there were children in a family, they accompanied the mother; however, the presence of children tended to keep a couple together. Apparently a man married his deceased brother's wife (levirate) if the occasion arose. A man left his wife in the care of his brother if she could not accompany him when he traveled. Men also exchanged wives for short or long periods of time, which led to binding friendships between the men involved. However, a woman was not free to make such an arrangement since to have done so would be an infringement on her husband's rights.

The physical hardships, starvations, and discomforts of life limited the productive years of an adult, and as a result few persons attained old age. When an individual was old or became infirm, he or she remained as active as possible but realized that death was not far off. The Caribou Eskimos did not as a rule kill old people (senilicide). Individuals sometimes were abandoned to die alone, but this was not a common practice such as encountered among certain other Eskimos. It was more customary for an old or ill person to commit suicide by hanging, often aided by a dutiful relative. More taboos surrounded handling the dead than any other facet of social life. When someone died, the survivors were obligated to behave in a precise manner in order to avoid further deaths in the settlement. The body of a person who died during the day was removed from the snowhouse or tent as soon as possible. If the death was at night, a man's body remained at the back of the dwelling for three days and a woman's body for five days. The settlement, however, was not abandoned because of a death. Mourning women loosened their hair, and the survivors wailed while the corpse was in the house. Although men continued to hunt caribou, no one could drive a sled and many food taboos were observed. In order to insure that the soul of the deceased would not harm the living during this period, each person slept with a knife beneath his head. During these three or five days, the household possessions were placed outside to air. Only old women and young girls handled the body, and they wore mittens to flex the corpse and shroud it in a skin. The body was removed through an opening made at the back of a snowhouse or tent and was taken to the place of burial by near relatives who plugged their nostrils with caribou

Plate 9 *Caribou Eskimo women and a child cooking behind a brush shelter at Eskimo Point in 1923* (Courtesy of the Danish National Museum).

Plate 10 *(Right) Caribou Eskimo Women in 1923* (Courtesy of the Danish National Museum).

Plate 11 *A Caribou Eskimo woman with a child in the back of her parka, at Eskimo Point in 1959* (Photograph by the author).

Plate 12 *The permanent dwelling of a Caribou Eskimo family at Eskimo Point in 1959* (Photograph by the author).

Plate 13 *The community of Eskimo Point in 1969*
(Courtesy of Valene Smith).

Plate 14 *A Caribou Eskimo man making a soapstone carving in 1969* (Courtesy of Valene Smith).

hair. Some graves were ringed with stones, and other bodies were covered with a pile of stones. A long pole was set obliquely in the ground at one end of a grave. Grave goods were included in the burial, but some property of the deceased was divided among the survivors. Numerous food and behavioral prohibitions were required of surviving housemates, but these usually were of brief duration, except that bone and wood could not be cut with a knife for a year. Souls of the dead traveled off to Pinga, who returned them to earth as another person or in animal form.

The Caribou Eskimo lifeway as it has been described prevailed into the early 1920's, but by this time their future had become quite uncertain. It was no longer simply a matter of successfully intercepting caribou herds in order to obtain the necessities for life in the Barren Grounds. How to procure the marvelous things seen at trading posts became an increasingly important goal. There was a market for caribou skins, but it was insignificant compared with a trader's desire for white fox pelts. The white fox was the only item of economic importance to persons beyond the Barrens. With these furs the people could obtain the goods that traders brought into their country. Exotic manufactures long had been known; perhaps the first iron was obtained from the vessel and structures left by Jens Munch when he wintered at the mouth of the Churchill River in 1619-1620. With the establishment of the English at Fort Prince of Wales in the early 1700's trading sloops occasionally were sent northward along the coast, and some Caribou Eskimos began to obtain imported goods locally. These trips were highly irregular, but by the end of the century some of the more southerly bands traded at Fort Prince of Wales. Then the trading sloops began to frequent the western shore of Hudson Bay more often, and in the late 1800's commercial whalers often wintered there, which intensified contacts with Europeans. In the 1920's there were Hudson's Bay Company stores at Chesterfield Inlet, Baker Lake, Eskimo Point and elsewhere; by this time the pattern for the future had become ominously apparent.

The commitment of fashionable European and American women to fur coats, coupled with the presence of white fox on the Barrens and the Eskimos' desire for trade goods, joined two disparate sociocultural systems. The only means that the people had to obtain material items was by trapping fox. Their decision to do so caused a chain reaction in their culture. The Hudson's Bay Company traders induced the people to trap fox, which had virtually no worth in their aboriginal economy. In order to encourage trapping the traders furnished men with traps, other equipment, and food on credit against their potential catch. One of the first purchases by a hunter was a rifle and ammunition, for in theory a man with a gun could hunt caribou much more efficiently. At this point the picture seemed bright. An individual could even obtain goods from a store, trade it to more distant peoples who did not have access to European goods, and thereby reap a great profit. However, the Eskimos had no foresight concerning the future, and the Hudson's Bay Company was more concerned with immediate profits than with what was happening to the people.

As strange as it might seem, the rifle worked to the detriment of the Caribou Eskimos. Shooting caribou at their traditional crossing places apparently led to shifts in their migration routes. They no longer could be intercepted as of old, and it was impossible for hunters to seek out these unsettled paths. Then too Indians to the south also traded for rifles, and they not only killed more animals but disturbed the caribou's wintering grounds. Although caribou were increasingly scarce, fox usually were abundant, and the Caribou Eskimos had the reputation of being among the best trappers. Taking fox was not an easy way of life, for a man was obligated to feed his family and at the same time range from a base camp to tend traps. This required food from a store; although credit was obtainable, adequate amounts could be charged by only the best trappers. In some years fox were more abundant than in others, and when the prices for pelts were high, the people could obtain great quantities of material wealth and large quantities of food from traders. When a trapper took his catch to a trader, he was given trade goods immediately; he did not handle money nor was he encouraged to have something on the credit side of his account. It was economically desirable for a trader always to have a trapper in debt to him. Thus the Eskimos bought canned meats and other imported foods at astoundingly high prices, and a few even purchased such items as harmoniums. Success in trapping drastically reduced the physical mobility of a family since they acquired more material goods than could be moved readily. Even more unfair or more incomprehensible from the Eskimo's point of view was that the fox prices fluctuated widely from year to year. A great stack of pelts one year meant wealth, while another year the same sized stack bought only enough to survive. Always, however, the trader would buy the pelts, for the company could store the skins against the day that the world market price would rise, and the traders strongly desired to keep the Eskimos trapping. Gambling with fox, caribou, and rifles under these conditions was fatal for the Caribou Eskimos. In years when caribou could not be intercepted and fox prices were low, a man might be unable to obtain enough food from the trader, and his family would go hungry or even starve. Even when the price of fox pelts was high, if caribou could not be located and killed for food during the trapping season, a family's survival hung in doubt. It often is said, and probably is true, that men have been found who starved to death with hundreds and even thousands of dollars' worth of fox pelts in their possession.

In 1919 one-fifth of the Caribou Eskimos died of starvation.

As stores were built locally, the people acquired such manufactured items as weapons, matches, knives, bowls and spoons, steel needles and thimbles, axes, and wood planes. The most popular new clothing was the shawl for women, and the second was ready-made summer garb. The people retained their own style of boot, and they allowed their shirttails to hang out just as their skin parkas had hung over their trousers. New ornaments included browbands of brass for women as well as hair combs. The introduction of trade beads made it possible to create designs in beads on the outer parka. Floral motifs were worked into various patterns, which probably were learned from Indians to the south as also was true of triangular designs, zigzags, disks, and simple curved lines. Small cloth bags for sewing equipment or bags for other possessions were similarly decorated, as were the beaded cloth bands wrapped around locks of hair.

The most important weapons and devices for hunting and trapping were the rifle and steel trap respectively, but binoculars and telescopes also were useful aids. Additional ways to take game resulted from the use of new equipment, and the most famous of these was the blood knife. A sharp steel knife was covered with a coating of blood and set in the snow with the blade upward. A wolf smelled out the blood and licked the blade to obtain it, cutting his tongue in the process and eventually bleeding to death. One change in the hunting pattern of old was the Canadian government's prohibition upon the taking of musk oxen. Since the musk ox was never very important, this restriction was not critical. Traders introduced gill nets which greatly increased the fish catch, but since there arose also the prohibition against eating fish which had died in the net, some of the value of the innovation was negated. Commercially manufactured canoes made it possible to carry heavy loads by water, but the weight of the vessels and the large number of rapids in the rivers tended to minimize their importance. Whale-boats were advantageous for coastal travel, but the people did not become confident sailors along Hudson Bay.

By the early 1920's canvas tents with ridgepoles began to make their appearance, and the ubiquitous primus stove was used for cooking. New dietary items included bannock made from flour and baking powder; this was the staple when nothing else was available. Tea had become a very popular beverage, and the people drank it in great quantities. The Caribou Eskimos were inveterate smokers from a very tender age. They mixed tobacco with dried and cut whortleberry leaves which they smoked in a monitor type pipe. The bowl was made from soapstone mounted above an opened cartridge which had been fitted into a wooden stem.

The relationship between the traders and the Eskimos modified the seasonal subsistence round and introduced trapping as a new form of livelihood, but this was not the only influence from the world beyond the Barrens. Missionaries began to concern themselves with the Caribou Eskimos, but like the traders they did not arrive until comparatively recent times. The most active mission group in this sector of Canada was the Oblate order, founded in 1816, of the Roman Catholic Church. They had a mission among the Chipewyan in 1846 on Lake Ile a la Crosse, but it was not until much later that their priests ranged north into the Barren Grounds. In 1906 Father Arsene Turquetil visited the Caribou Eskimos along the southern frontier and spent five months among them. In 1912 both the Hudson's Bay Company and the Roman Catholics established themselves at Chesterfield Inlet among the more northerly segment of the Caribou Eskimo population. It was to the distinct advantage of the priests to build a mission station where a trading post existed. Eskimos had to come to the stores to exchange pelts for trade goods, and the priests could contact them there.

In his study of the Caribou Eskimos, Birket-Smith barely mentioned the influence of Christian missionaries. This is not to say that Christianity had no effect but rather that it had not become an important force in their lives. The first mass held by the Oblates at Chesterfield Inlet was regarded by the Eskimos as a striking example of sorcery, but the missionaries were unaware of this impression made on the people. Missionaries were regarded as shamans capable of killing Eskimos who offended them, and thus it was necessary to tolerate their presence. It became apparent to the priests that in order to convey any meaningful understanding of their purpose they must learn the language of the people. By 1915 Father Turquetil preached a sermon in Eskimo, but the people remained unconvinced of his sincerity, especially since the trader told them he did not believe in Christian teachings. Furthermore the trader maintained that the priests were insane and had come to preach their madness to the Eskimos. This description of the Hudson's Bay Company trader was written by an Oblate priest in a history of their northern mission. While it may come as a surprise, there is no reason to question its validity. This example points up the type of problem faced by the missionaries in dealing not only with the people whom they hoped to convert but with the other whites. It is no wonder that not until 1917 were the first Eskimos baptized.

It is worthwhile to consider some of the differences between the supernatural systems of the aboriginal Caribou Eskimos and the Roman Catholic missionaries. The gulf between Western and Eskimo culture was indeed wide. Initially there was the problem that many complex core ideas about Christian concepts had no counterparts in the range of experience of the Eskimos. This symbolic barrier, even though the priests spoke Eskimo, was a formidable obstruction, for new means of expression had to be created for new concepts. The priests were full-time specialists in dealing with the supernatural, which was unheard-of among Eskimos, and they did things no rational being would do. They handled the dead without fear and were sympathetic and helpful to people whom the Eskimos regarded as beyond social worth. The success of the missionaries was due largely to their deep devotion to what they considered their duty and to the Eskimos' final realization that these truly were good men.

The next locality of Caribou Eskimo occupancy to be settled by the Hudson's Bay Company and Roman Catholic missionaries was Eskimo Point. The Hudson's Bay Company had sent trading vessels to this spot during the summer for many years, and the Eskimos were accustomed to assembling there as well as at Sentry Island. In 1923 a store was built, and the following year a Roman Catholic mission was constructed near Eskimo Point; the entire settlement was moved to its present location at Eskimo Point in 1928. The mission was founded by the Oblate priest, Lionel Ducharme, who had served earlier at the Chesterfield Inlet mission. In 1926 an Anglican Church mission was constructed at Eskimo Point. Although this settlement emerged as an important trading, mission, and administrative center, for Eskimos it was a place to be visited from the interior and not an Eskimo community. The people remained inland as caribou hunters and fox trappers through the 1940's. Then new and unprecedented influences came into the lives of the people when they were visited by the young Canadian writer Farley Mowat and a gifted photographer Richard Harrington.

Mowat was a wanderer who had visited the edge of the Barrens in 1935 when he was fifteen years old. After World War II he was determined to return to the Barren Grounds, but to the interior rather than just the fringes. He flew to the northern edge of Nueltin Lake in the spring of 1947, where he visited the camp of a southern band briefly; the next year he spent the summer in the same locality. Mowat first wrote a series of articles about these Eskimos, and in 1952 he published a book about them titled *People of the Deer*. It included descriptions of the country and the caribou, but most of all it is about the Caribou Eskimo band called the Ahearmiut (Ihalmiut) who lived to the north and west of Nueltin Lake. The book described the decline of the people as a result of disastrous famines, which were related as stories and biographical sketches. There is no question about the literary abilities of Mowat, but the details of his descriptions, the accuracy of his statements, and the depth of his under-standing of the people is open to doubt. Perhaps these criticisms are rather unimportant, for Mowat did what no one before him could accomplish. He vividly conveyed the plight of these people. Mowat hoped to convince Cana-dian and American readers that these people were being destroyed by star-vation through bungling governmental policies and greedy traders. He could see that the same process was taking place elsewhere in the Canadian arctic, and he hoped that he could avert a repeating of the tragic results.

In the winter of 1950 the photographer and writer Richard Harrington traveled by dog team from Eskimo Point to the Hudson's Bay Company store at Padlei and visited the surrounding Eskimo camps. The inland area was one of desolation where starvation loomed. At the Padlei post a fox pelt was worth $3.75, caribou were rare in the vicinity and had been scarce on their fall migration, while fish could not provide a sustaining diet. The thirty Eskimos around the post were receiving Destitute Rations of flour or rolled oats. This was a poor substitute for caribou meat, and yet it kept the people from starving. Their dogs, however, had starved, and without the mobility provided by a dog team, fox could not be trapped in numbers nor could caribou be hunted efficiently. The pictures that Harrington took were printed, along with his stories of the starvation, and the ensuing atten-tion directed to the Barrens and its people brought temporary relief from the outside world. In the spring of 1950 an effort was made to introduce commercial fishing on Nueltin Lake, but this enterprise failed as might be expected since it was contrary to the lifeway of these Eskimos.

In 1955 the Dutch anthropologist Van den Steenhoven visited the Ahear-miut, who then were living along the northeastern fringe of Ennadai Lake and ranged southward to Nueltin Lake. In 1949 a government weather station was built along Ennadai Lake, and the people were attracted to it. By 1955 the official in charge of the station handled their Family Allow-ance payments and their fox pelts which were forwarded to Churchill. These people had not been Christianized, and their contacts with weather station personnel constituted their link with civilization. In 1955 there were fifty of these Caribou Eskimos divided into three camps, the largest of which included twenty persons. Above all, they were still caribou hunters who would eat nothing else if caribou meat were available. Observations by Van den Steenhoven add to our ethnographic knowledge and supplement the earlier descriptions of Birket-Smith. Van den Steenhoven was most concerned with customary law, and from his interviews at Eskimo Point and Ennadai Lake we have valuable new and supplementary information.

The observations by Birket-Smith about the division of game, meaning caribou, were verified, but it was noted further that once food was brought into a dwelling it came under the control of the woman of the household. The significance of this rule was that women distributed the food which their husbands had obtained. The rationale behind this arrangement was that since a wife was responsible for the welfare of her children, she could best judge how much meat could and should be shared.

The mid-1950's brought nothing but disease and disaster. In the fall of 1955 the Eskimos who had been attracted to the coast to work on a proposed Distant Early Warning radar site at Eskimo Point were dismissed and the project terminated. Then came the measles epidemic during 1956-1957. In the fall of 1956 many caribou migrated southward along the coast, but they were not hunted intensively due to the adverse effects of the epidemic on the hunters. In 1957-1958 caribou were scarce, and the few families around Ennadai Lake migrated toward Padlei, with starvations and murders taking place along the way.

In the late 1950's and early 1960's the remnant Caribou Eskimo population was concentrated largely at Eskimo Point, for here among the trader, missionaries, and governmental representatives they knew that they would not be permitted to starve. Eskimo Point is a windswept, boulder-strewn point of land which supports a few species of vascular plants and mosses. In the summer of 1959 the largest segment of the population consisted of 165 Caribou Eskimos, although this figure fluctuated seasonally. Thirty other Eskimos from more northerly settlements lived there along with thirteen Euro-Canadians attached to mission or government establishments. The physical settlement was organized around Euro-Canadian institutions; the Hudson's Bay Company, the Roman Catholic and Anglican missions, the Royal Canadian Mounted Police, and the Northern Affairs and National Resources each had frame or log buildings for its representatives. It might be expected that the Eskimo residents had lived there as long as the other residents, but this was not the case. Through the early 1950's there were no year-round Eskimo residents. The Eskimos arrived to trade and then returned to the interior. It would seem that it was the starvations of the late 1940's and early 1950's that first led some families to make Eskimo Point the central base from which they ranged to hunt and fish. While at the community most people occupied canvas wall tents from late spring through the fall. The spot where a family erected its canvas tent, or more rarely a cone-shaped skin and canvas tent, depended both on where the ground was first free of snow and the religious affiliations of the family. The Christian Eskimos tended to cluster near the mission with which they were identified, but non-Christians lived away from church-controlled property. The same general pattern of residence prevailed during the winter months when most Eskimos occupied snowhouses. The Eskimos who were special constables of the Royal Canadian Mounted Police lived in frame dwellings provided by the government, and the school janitor occupied a government-owned log house. Additionally in the late 1950's three Eskimo families lived throughout the year in jerry-built rectangular dwellings of wood, cardboard, and canvas. Four frame houses owned by Caribou Eskimos dated from a period of high fox prices; these were rarely occupied by their owners but served primarily as caches for equipment. The members of all these households were nuclear families, although one or more relatives of a husband or wife might have joined such a household. Closely related families tended to live in adjacent tents or igloos with a common entrance passage.

Canadian style clothing, as represented in the Hudson's Bay Company store inventory, prevailed by 1959. For men there were trousers, shirts, socks, sweaters, and jackets. For younger women and girls, slacks, blouses, and sweaters prevailed, but older women preferred dresses of cotton print. Colorful shawls were owned by all the women, and kerchiefs were popular among them. Light canvas was sewn into parka covers, and duffel was made into footwear. Skin boots, shoes, and shoepacs were worn as well. Caribou skins were so scarce that few individuals owned a complete winter outfit of skin clothing, but families attempted to make and maintain a set of skin garments for each hunter.

With increased physical stability, the Caribou Eskimos accumulated more material property than ever before. Everyone had a one-burner primus stove for cooking and heating. Likewise most families built bed frames, which they put at the rear of their room and cushioned with caribou skins, blankets, and an occasional sleeping bag. Along the walls and beneath the bed were small trunks and cardboard boxes containing clothing and skins or cloth for the manufacture and repair of clothing. An inventory of household goods included trade items almost exclusively. The pots, pans, eating utensils, and sewing equipment of the women were all purchased, as were the woodworking tools of the men. The women still used the ulu form of old as their most important cutting implement, but it had an iron blade made from an old saw blade. Accordions and windup phonographs were popular items and were found in many households. A family possessed a sled, a few dogs, very few traps, and perhaps a canoe and outboard motor, all of which were cached near the dwelling.

The ties binding these Eskimos to Eskimo Point and the greater sphere of Canadian national life all funneled through whites in the community. The wife of the Hudson's Bay Company store manager was the nurse and local representative of the Indian and Northern Health Services. Anyone who was sick went to her, and she treated them or arranged for transportation to the hospital at Churchill. In 1959, seven persons were hospitalized in the south with tuberculosis, and four were in hospitals with other disorders. Once a year a medical party arrived to X-ray the people in a rather vigorous effort to control tuberculosis. When the Hudson's Bay Company supply ship arrived, many men were employed to unload supplies, and there was monthly commercial air service to the community. A Royal Canadian Mounted Police aircraft often landed at Eskimo Point on official government business. To the Caribou Eskimos most of these activities had very little meaning and simply represented part of the white world. It is true that being sent to a hospital opened new vistas of experience, but these were simply impressions about another world, one which had no direct relationship with the realities of living at Eskimo Point.

The Caribou Eskimos of this community had not abandoned hope for once again making caribou the focal point of their economic lives. They still hunted, but it was with less conviction and less ability. In the fall of the year shortly before caribou were expected to move southward, about half of the families obtained flour, tea, sugar, and ammunition on credit. The amount of ammunition which could be purchased was limited by the trader to one hundred shells for each high-powered rifle and the same number of .22 caliber rifle shells, under the theory that if caribou were intercepted in great numbers there would be no needless slaughter. The families traveled inland by canoe, using outboard motors for power, up the Maguse or McConnell river drainages or else set off on foot for the inland area. In the lakes known to contain fish they set out gill nets in the early fall, and as ice formed on the lakes they reset the nets beneath the ice and also jigged for fish. If it happened that numerous caribou were killed, then fishing was unimportant. If it happened that caribou did not pass the place where hunters had stationed themselves, they returned temporarily to the coast and hunted seals. As fall turned into winter, they moved into a snowhouse and began trapping fox. Each man maintained his own trapline, and an energetic person had as many as a hundred sets in a three-day traveling radius from his camp. Mobility was a direct function of the diligence of the trapper, the number of dogs he owned, and the food available to feed the team. In 1957-1958 many dogs had starved to death, and so most trappers had only limited mobility in the following years. The trappers returned periodically to Eskimo Point with their fox pelts in order to settle their accounts and obtain additional supplies for themselves and their families.

A highly successful trapper might take 200 fox during a winter and earn as much as $4000.00 in trade goods for his efforts. Since it required about $700.00 a year to support a family of four with the essentials of life, some trappers were periodically affluent. Fluctuations in the number of fox taken as well as the prices paid for pelts, however, varied widely. For example in 1950-1951 the store at Eskimo Point received nearly 750 white fox pelts, whereas in 1953-1954 the number was about 5500. In 1950-1951 the average price per pelt was about $9.20, while in 1958-1959 pelts averaged nearly $17.00 each. The only other major sources of income were from Family Allotment, Old Age Assistance, and Special Relief funds with a combined total of $9000.00 for the entire settlement in 1959. It should be stressed that none of these funds were paid in check or cash nor were the pelts sold for cash. The government aid was in the form of supplies provided through the Royal Canadian Mounted Police, and the trade in pelts was for goods on the shelves in the store.

At the end of the trapping season in mid-April the scattered families returned to Eskimo Point, hauling the boats and camping equipment by dogsled. The people erected their tents along the point, and the men began to hunt seals, particularly the bearded seal, at the edge of the ice some seven miles from the shore. The Caribou Eskimos persisted in considering seal meat and fat as food for dogs. After the ice melted from the shore and drifted away, gill nets were set by some persons for arctic char, but only enough were caught to provide food on a day-to-day basis. Beluga also were hunted by some persons, but the meat was used mainly as dog food.

Opportunities for summer employment existed but usually for only a few individuals. The best prospect was to go to Churchill and work as a laborer, but some men found work locally on the construction of the Northern Affairs and National Resources school which was completed in 1959. Of the people who lived year-round at Eskimo Point, a few had steady employment with the government agencies or the store, but most men ranged from the settlement to hunt caribou and trap fox without any outstanding success. A few families consistently were unable to support themselves and relied on Destitute Rations or informal relief provided by the missions. In 1957 the number of people at Eskimo Point was greater by nearly 100 individuals than in 1959. The ones who left in the late 1950's did so to work at the nickel mine along Rankin Inlet. These persons received a steady wage for their efforts, and it was said by persons familiar with the Eskimo Point economy that the mine attracted the most able individuals, who were accompanied by their families to their new jobs. The mine closed in 1962. Some of the people appear to have moved to Whale Cove, and others returned to Eskimo Point.

In 1959 the social life of these people reflected much the same patterning which it exhibited when observed by Birket-Smith. The nuclear family remained the unit around which individuals built their social lives. The family head was a hunter and trapper, and his abilities alone set the standard of living for a family. As of old there was no cohesion to bind diverse families together into larger economic units; each remained self-sufficient, although this basic attitude was tempered by the needs of near relatives as it must have been in aboriginal times. Families belonging to the same Christian church, whether it was Roman Catholic or Anglican, tended to live near one another, with Roman Catholic family integration apparently stronger. The cohesiveness along religious lines was reinforced in the social halls maintained by the missions, which attracted members during their leisure. The Roman Catholic social hall was better equipped, better lighted and more attractive than the one of the Anglicans, and Roman Catholic services were held daily. The Anglicans held services for their members only on Sunday. It is not surprising that the Roman Catholics were more successful in developing stronger feelings of identity among their membership. The fact that there was no resident Anglican missionary between 1946 and 1957 led some families to abandon the Anglican Church. The religious and national factionalism which was such an important divider between Canadians to the south clearly had penetrated the north. Religion as a focal point for social life was such that Roman Catholic and Anglican Eskimos tended not to marry each other, and until the Federal school began to function in 1959, each of the missions maintained its own parochial school. The non-Christian Eskimos seemed to fall into one of two groups. Either they were not interested in Christianity and were successful materialists, or else they were unsuccessful providers of the type known as "tea and tobacco natives," meaning that their attitude toward religion was to consider either church as their own if they could gain materially from the identification.

One aspect of Caribou Eskimo social life had eroded away completely. This was the charismatic leader, "the one who is thinking," of aboriginal times. Such an individual was an outstanding hunter who through his skill and insight was able to locate and kill vast numbers of caribou. He usually had more than one wife, and less successful families gravitated to his camp. He was a man of influence to whom everyone paid attention because experience had proved him to be wise. In this new setting caribou hunting skill was not nearly as important; hunting failed to keep the people from starving and good hunters could not solve the problems of the day. The Hudson's Bay Company trader more than anyone else controlled the economic future of a family. The trader judged a man's worth to be his abilities as a trapper and on this basis alone extended credit for food and equipment. A trader was powerful and usually handled his clientele in an authoritarian manner.

A trader's success, in the eyes of the company, was measured in terms of the inventory of furs which he assembled, not in terms of his kindness to Eskimos or the future of these people. As the trader was a leader, so were the police, for they controlled Family Allotment and Destitute Ration funds. The police could and did at times intimidate the people. The same applied to the missionaries but not to as great an extent as to the trader and police. Thus, all economic matters, except for bringing in the fox pelts, were in the hands of white Canadians.

In 1959 the inland Caribou Eskimo population consisted of sixty persons around Yathkyed Lake and sixty-eight within the vicinity of the Padlei post; these bands were the most traditionally oriented People of the Deer. When the Padlei post was closed in 1960, the Eskimos moved from that area to Eskimo Point, and the Yathkyed area population began to move to the coast. By 1963 all of the inland Eskimos had relocated along Hudson Bay either voluntarily or as a result of direct governmental intervention. Many families hoped to return permanently to the interior of the Barren Grounds, but it is unlikely that they will be able to realize this end. What then does the future offer?

An intensive two-year economic study of the Keewatin mainland, which includes all the traditional Caribou Eskimo area, was made in 1961-1962 under the auspices of the Department of Northern Affairs and National Resources (subsequently Department of Indian Affairs and Northern Development). The report by D.M. Brack and D. McIntosh is an insightful compendium about not only the problems, but the potentialities, for Eskimos along the western shore of Hudson Bay. In a foreword to this study, Donald Snowden observed that with the current population increase the Federal government must offer either direct relief or provide "make-work" programs, and even by following the latter alternative the people could not be expected to become self-sufficient in the foreseeable future. The area had no mineral prospects that could support the population, and communities could not maintain themselves adequately by following traditional Eskimo subsistence activities.

In determining why this situation had developed, it seems rather clear that the wasteful hunting practices initiated by the Eskimos and Indians were a major factor contributing to the scarcity of caribou. It was not the wolf which destroyed the caribou, but man. There had been great slaughters of far more animals than possibly could be consumed; many animals were wounded but not tracked and killed; caribou were not utilized fully when they were killed, and often cached meat was allowed to spoil. Furthermore, fish as a potential source of food never was utilized fully, and the seals and white whales of Hudson Bay were not exploited effectively. If the situation was as it has been summarized, then what steps could be taken to once again make the people economically self-sufficient? One possibility was to move these Eskimos to the south and integrate them into white Canadian society, since the Barrens appeared to offer nothing which might lead to a stabilized economy in the near future. Mass relocation would have been a solution, but the Canadian government did not seriously entertain the possibility. Statements about Eskimo policies stressed the government's desire to bring these people into the greater sphere of Canadian national life while at the same time respecting their cultural integrity as Eskimos. It was maintained further that political institutions should be developed at the local level and every effort made to develop an economic base to support their way of life in the north. This might seem to be noble idealism, especially considering prior statements of the economic potential of the area, but such a policy could keep the people viable if there was a firm and enduring commitment of Federal support.

An anthropological field study was carried out at Eskimo Point in 1959 by James W. VanStone and Wendell H. Oswalt. It was financed in part by the Department of Northern Affairs and National Resources, and its purpose was to make recommendations about possible administrative innovations. It was recommended that since each of the white Canadian institutions represented in the settlement had its own plot of ground with obvious boundary markers, it would be fitting to have a similar plot of ground set aside specifically for the Eskimos. In this way the Eskimos clearly would be recognized as a part of Eskimo Point. After living in a tent all summer at Eskimo Point and being confronted with some of the environmental difficulties which faced the Eskimos, the authors felt that some sort of adequate permanent housing should be provided. Precisely what type of structure was not suggested, but the houses should be clustered in the Eskimo sector of the community. In order to develop a sense of community cohesion and leadership among the Eskimos, it was considered desirable to foster a council organization which would have the power to control certain facets of community life then under police supervision, such as the control of loose dogs, thefts, and similar minor problems of community life. Furthermore, the council should be provided with a physical locus, a building which could serve the Eskimos for meetings, social events, and working. This would help foster group identity among Eskimos apart from any direct involvement with the government or the missions. The school which opened in 1959 could and should become a focal point of community life for adults as well as for children. In the school the concepts of national identity could be conveyed, and instruction in such practical matters as boat building and sea mammal hunting could be carried out. A community cooperative store was suggested for obvious reasons, but the likelihood of such a project being undertaken was highly doubtful. A more realistic aim would be to open a post office at Eskimo Point so that the people could be sent their Family Allotment checks directly. A post office also would open the potential for purchases from large mail-order houses, which would make comparison shopping possible. The value of relocation was explored briefly, but very little emphasis was given to this approach because of its negative connotations.

During the latter half of the 1960's the Canadian government made a major commitment to the development of Eskimo Point, and the variety of goods and services provided by the end of the decade was phenomenal. In 1969, Valene L. Smith made a detailed study of conditions at Eskimo Point and was kind enough to make available a copy of the resulting manuscript; it is from this work that most of the following information has been drawn.

By 1969 there were about 550 permanent residents at Eskimo Point, and almost half of the population was under fifteen years of age. Most people lived in one of the nearly 150 prefabricated houses provided by the government. These dwellings, which had up to three bedrooms and were furnished, were rented by the Eskimos with fees scaled according to income; an aged person or family on welfare paid $2 a month. The rental cost included electricity, water, and fuel delivery as well as sewage disposal service. The community also included three missions, the Alliance, Anglican, and Roman Catholic, and a Hudson's Bay Company store which carried a five million dollar inventory. Government buildings and services included street lights, street clearance, a snowmobile repair garage, jail, R.C.M.P. Post, school for kindergarten and the first seven grades, a nursing station, adult education and craft centers, bathhouse and laundromat, and post office. The government investment in buildings and equipment was in excess of two and a half million dollars.

It is little short of astounding to contrast the living conditions in this period with those a decade earlier. In the recent past the only Eskimos with adequate dwellings were a few government employees; all others lived in jerry-built structures of canvas, cardboard, and planks, or else in tents during the summer and snowhouses in the winter. Furnishings of the earlier period included mainly homemade beds and a box for a table. The government housing in 1969 included beds with mattresses, tables, chairs, cookstoves and heaters. Some people owned freezers and motorscooters, and a few even maintained automobiles.

Within the 1950's and 1960's Eskimos were attracted to Eskimo Point because caribou hunting was no longer a viable economic base and as a result of governmental pressures. Yet the economic offerings at their almost luxurious new community were far from favorable. Only twenty-seven Eskimos were employed on a permanent basis; this meant an average of one wage earner for each six households and an average annual income of $445 per person. Most men were able to find only temporary, seasonal employment, and it was generally felt that a minimum of $600 cash a year was necessary to "get by" even with critical services provided. Thus some men enjoyed job security and were reliable employees, but many of the men remained hunters at heart and still attempted to live off the land. Yet to be a hunter and trapper was no longer as feasible as in the recent past. Caribou were scarce, and even before they could be hunted a considerable cash investment was necessary. In order to maintain a dog team for hunting and trapping, a man required a boat and outboard motor to obtain the seals and fish to feed his dogs. If he depended largely on a snowmobile for hunting mobility, he had an expensive investment originally and repairs also were costly. Thus to range far enough from the community to find caribou involved a major commitment of time and money with no assurances of a positive return.

Stable economic alternatives to hunting must be found if the lives of most residents are to be imbued with meaning. Experimental whale hunting yielded such a slight return that it was discontinued. Mink ranching or reindeer herding are possible, but the potential for economic success through such enterprises, based on experience elsewhere in the far north, seems tenuous. Since white fox were plentiful along the coast and Caribou Eskimos were superior trappers, it might appear that trapping could provide much-needed cash. The steady decline in popularity of long-hair pelts has had an adverse effect on the market for fox pelts. A skin brought about $11, which was less than the investment required for a trapper. Polar bear pelts were valued at as much as $450, but the government set a limit of four per year to be taken locally. Hunting skill did not guarantee this catch since the licenses were obtained by lottery. Seal skins were worth as much as or more than fox pelts, but they could be obtained only during a brief period and only about ten men were skilled enough to hunt safely among the ice floes. Fish were not plentiful, nets were expensive, and these people lacked a commitment to fishing.

Smith observed, "As the 1970's begin, the economic picture is not rosy, but neither is it alarming." Welfare payments had begun to decline, largely as a result of the creation of an Arts and Crafts Center which enabled individuals to earn cash. The program was initiated in 1965, and a large building was built as a workshop, although individuals were encouraged to work at home. The most successful efforts have been in stone sculptures, which previously had become a well-established craft enterprise in the Canadian arctic. The Caribou Eskimos had no aboriginal craft tradition of this nature, yet about seventy persons were soon able to earn about $75 each per month. Thirty others produced stone sculptures to supplement their earnings from other sources. In order to promote the growth of the craft, the governmental representative purchased each item produced regardless of its quality.

Social life centered in nuclear family households which typically included a couple with two or three children. Most of the residents of Eskimo Point belonged to the Padleimiut band, but a distinction existed between those whose ties to the coast were old and others who had migrated there from the interior only recently. The interior people were considered inferior by their more-established neighbors, but the differences between them were not of great significance. Another segment of the population consisted of coastal families who had long been associated with whites (Kabloona). They were termed "Kabloonarmiut" by other Eskimos and identified more with whites than with the remainder of the Padleimiut. The social interaction between Eskimos as a whole and the thirty adult whites tended to be formal but sincerely friendly; they did not visit in each other's homes, however. Whites referred to Eskimos by their Eskimo names, which included no surname; whites virtually always were called by their family names.

The social side of living at Eskimo Point developed along new lines. The laundromat and bathhouse emerged as a place to chat and gossip; although there was talk of constructing a community hall, none was built. Motion pictures were shown twice a week, and numerous individuals were interested in curling, for which a facility was constructed. Intoxicants were not sold locally, and there was no problem of excessive drinking, nor any desire to have alcoholic beverages sold locally. The residents appeared to have developed some feelings of identity with their community. Nothing reflected this community spirit so much as the construction of an adequate airstrip. A government employee during his off hours prepared a rough airstrip with a bulldozer, but the large rocks and stones which remained on the field were dangerous for aircraft. "Stone-picking bees" were organized, and participation was intensive. This cooperation eventually led to the completion of a 4000 foot runway with an apron and an airstrip which was serviceable throughout the year.

Major and many minor political and economic decisions at Eskimo Point were made by the Area Administrator stationed there. His decisions were binding, but in an effort to develop local leadership an Eskimo Council, Residents' Association, and Eskimo Housing Council were organized. These bodies were developed in order to foster local leadership and participation in governmental institutions. A more far-reaching effort by the government to cultivate political autonomy was embodied in the Hamlet Ordinance enacted by the legislature of the Northwest Territories in 1969. It provided for the establishment of local elected councils to govern small communities such as Eskimo Point, and this experience was designed to prepare the people for a transfer to provincial status. Most administrators appear to have felt that at Eskimo Point a community council would be ill-prepared to assume control of local affairs until the members had broader administrative experience.

Smith found that among Eskimo males their heritage as hunters was deeply ingrained in their value system. To be an able provider whose family prospered because of one's hunting prowess brought self-esteem and prestige. The mobility and freedom of a hunter contrasted strikingly with the sedentary life of a part-time wage earner. The attitudes of women about life at Eskimo Point appear to have differed rather sharply from those of men. Women enjoyed sedentary village life with its relative economic security, comfortable physical accommodations, and the intensity of social contacts which contrasted with living in an isolated hunting camp. They had more leisure time, and some women were beginning to emerge as energetic leaders. An interesting and possibly not unimportant effort was initiated by males to perpetuate their roles as hunters and trappers. They organized a school for boys to learn survival skills at the subsistence level. The program included field trips led by adults and was to be expanded with the formation of partnerships between experienced hunters and youths. It was very favorably received by the Area Administrator as well as by the Eskimos in general. Obviously the idea of going back into the Barrens as caribou hunters still lingered as a hope, if not for fathers, possibly for their sons. Although dog teams are being phased out of existence, skin clothing is old fashioned, and the construction of snowhouses is a dying skill, the new way of life is an uncertain hope.

References

Baird, P. D. "Expeditions to the Canadian Arctic," *Beaver,* Outfit 279, March, 44-46; Outfit 280, June, 41-47; September, 44-48. 1949.

*Birket-Smith, Kaj. *The Caribou Eskimos*. Report of the Fifth Thule Expedition, v.5, pts.1, 2. 1929.

This work constitutes the standard ethnography for the Caribou Eskimos and is the basic source. The author was among these people in 1922-23 at the time that they were just coming into intensive contact with Europeans.

Brack, D.M., and D. McIntosh. *Keewatin Mainland, Area Economic Survey and Regional Appraisal*. Northern Affairs and National Resources. 1963.

Eskimo Point, Northwest Territories. n.d. Eskimo Point Residents' Association.

Harp, Elmer, Jr. *The Archaeology of the Lower and Middle Thelon, Northwest Territories*. Arctic Institute of North America Technical Paper no. 8. 1961.

Harrington, Richard. *The Face of the Arctic*. New York. 1952.

Hirsch, David I. "Glottochronology and Eskimo and Eskimo-Aleut Prehistory," *American Anthropologist*, v.56, 825-838. 1954.

Lotz, James R., Northern Research Officer, Northern Affairs and National Resources. Personal communication, May 13, 1963.

Morice, Adrian. *Thawing Out the Eskimo*. Boston. 1943.

Mowat, Farley. *People of the Deer*. London. 1954.

Mowat, Farley. *The Desperate People*. London. 1960.

Pruitt, William O., Jr. "Behavior of the Barren-Ground Caribou." *Biological Papers of the University of Alaska*, no. 3. 1960.

*Rasmussen, Knud. *Intellectual Culture of the Caribou Eskimos*. Report of the Fifth Thule Expedition, v.7, no.2. 1930.

No other anthropologist understood Eskimos as well as Knud Rasmussen. His conversations with Caribou Eskimos and observations about their way of life add an essential dimension to a reconstruction of the culture and society of these people. However, when the information provided by Rasmussen contradicts that of Birket-Smith, the latter source has been used since Birket-Smith spent more time with these Eskimos than did Rasmussen.

Smith, Valene L. Eskimos and Caribou: The Padlimiuts of Hudson Bay. Manuscript.

*Van den Steenhoven, Geert. *Leadership and Law Among the Eskimos of the Keewatin District, Northwest Territories*. Rijswijk. 1962.

In 1955 and 1957 the author collected information in the field on Eskimo social life with particular emphasis on political organization. The case studies are very revealing, and there is considerable information provided on the culture of the people.

*VanStone, James W., and Wendell H. Oswalt. *The Caribou Eskimos of Eskimo Point*. Northern Affairs and National Resources. 1960.

The 1959 field study of these authors focused on the modern cultural and social scene with particular emphasis on the deteriorating economic position of the people.

Map by J. Donovan

The
Kuskowagamiut:
riverine eskimos

In descriptive accounts Eskimos most frequently are described as a happy, fur-clad people who live in snowhouses, munch on raw meat, and lack the refinements of taste and manners noted among many of the world's peoples. Stereotypes such as these arise easily and for good reasons. The first ethnographies about Eskimos described those in Greenland and Canada, and these peoples did possess most if not all of the characteristics mentioned, although even among them there were significant differences. Later, when southwestern Alaskan Eskimos were encountered, it was learned that they differed greatly from those to the north and east. There was essential linguistic homogeneity among all Eskimos, but vast differences in other respects became increasingly apparent with each new study. The "typical" Eskimos lived in northern Alaska, along the northern coasts of Canada, and in Greenland; their cultures represented extreme adaptations to the arctic littoral and they numbered about 28,000. Yet there were at least 20,000 other Eskimos who lived in southwestern Alaska and pursued a very different way of life. The Caribou Eskimos have been described to represent one varient of northern Eskimo culture, while the Kuskowagamiut have been singled out to stand for the more southerly population segment.

The Kuskowagamiut numbered possibly 7000 in aboriginal times and lived along the Kuskokwim River, which flows into the Bering Sea from southwestern Alaska. This particular riverine Eskimo population is presented because there is more information about them than about any other Eskimos in this general region. The authoritative but brief account compiled by the Russian explorer Lavrentiy A. Zagoskin in 1843-1844 provides a general description of aboriginal life soon after the beginnings of local history. These data are supplemented by excavated finds at the historic Kuskowagamiut site of Crow Village. There is, furthermore, an ethnographic reconstruction compiled largely from Moravian Church missionary records for the period around 1900. An account of life at one village, Napaskiak, in 1955-1956 provides a glimpse into the recent past. The amount of information available about these Eskimos is not nearly so full and illuminating as might be suggested by this outline, but it does offer an intermittent record of what occurred in one Alaskan Eskimo population. By describing the Kuskowagamiut a neglected but major variant of Eskimo culture is revealed. These people subsisted primarily on salmon, they lived in relatively large and permanent settlements, and their ceremonial life was far more elaborate than usually is anticipated among Eskimos.

The Eskimos with whom we are concerned live along the central and lower Kuskokwim River, which is broad and gently flowing as far inland as they ranged during aboriginal times. The current in the lower river

124

flows slowly over a mile-wide riverbed, and tides from the sea carry water into the river and draw it out again. The lower river and estuary land is low and laced with diverging waterways, lakes, and ponds. In unprotected areas a tundra vegetation flourishes, but in depressions sheltered from the wind dense willow thickets, rare stands of birch trees, and dwarfed spruce form tongues of dark green vegetation into the tundra. This is a transitional zone between the coastal Eskimoan biotic province and the Hudsonian biotic province of the interior. On such land the animal species of economic importance were caribou, muskrat, mink, hare, and an occasional river otter. Stands of trees grew near most riverine settlements, but away from the banks of the lower river there is tundra. Farther upstream the tundra is less common, and spruce growths become denser, although at higher elevations tundra vegetation reappears. As the central sector is reached, higher hills are encountered, and soon hills and low mountains front the river. Animals along the central river include black bear in addition to the species known from the lower river. Migratory birds pass through the country in the spring and again in the fall, while spruce hens and ptarmigan live in the vicinity throughout the year. Salmon contribute the most to the stability of Kuskokwim Eskimo economy and are the most important anadromous fish; there are annual runs of king, red, dog (chum), and silver salmon. In the main river, lakes, and sloughs, depending on the time of the year, whitefish, burbot, pike, and blackfish abound. The only other fish of importance is the smelt, which ascends the lower river to spawn early each spring.

A great many competing theories based on archaeological evidence, ethnographic data, or a combination of the two have been advanced to explain the origins of Eskimo culture. At present it is most reasonable to presume that the distant ancestors of modern Eskimos and Aleuts ventured into Alaska from northeastern Asia. By about 3000 B.C., maritime sea mammal hunting economies had been developed by Eskimos in Alaska. At the time of historic contact the greatest linguistic diversity among Eskimos was in southwestern Alaska, and presumably it is in this area that the roots of Eskimo culture are deepest. From excavations along the Kobuk River in northern Alaska it appears that Eskimos repeatedly surged inland during prehistoric times only to be replaced by Indians. It is quite reasonable that the same sequence could have taken place along the Kuskokwim River, but there is no archaeological information either to support or deny this possibility. It does seem, however, that the Kuskowagamiut moved into the river system in comparatively recent times, possibly about 500 years ago.

The first contacts with outsiders were those with the Russians, who came into the area in order to trade. They founded Alexander Redoubt (modern Nushagak) as their first settlement along a Bering Sea river drainage in 1818. From here the Russian-American Company hoped to expand their trade in beaver and river otter farther to the north. Eskimos from inland areas north of the redoubt brought many pelts to the Nushagak station. During the summer of 1830, Ivan F. Vasilev, an ensign in the Pilot's Corps, led a small party up a Nushagak River tributary and over a divide to the Holitna River, which they descended to the Kuskokwim. They made their way downstream to the river mouth without undue difficulties and from there returned to Alexander Redoubt. Because Vasilev reported favorably on the fur resources of the Kuskokwim, the company dispatched parties to the area to obtain furs during 1832-1833 and 1833-1834, and they also founded two different odinochkas, an odinochka being the smallest unit in the network of Russian trading stations. Finally in 1841 with the founding of Kolmakov Redoubt the company opened a year-round post along the central Kuskokwim. The redoubt was abandoned in 1866 as the Russian-American Company prepared for the purchase of Alaska by the United States.

No known traditions account for Eskimo movements into the Kuskokwim River system. The myths which seek to explain the origins of these people cite Raven as a creator in primeval times. Raven also was a culture hero and a trickster as well; in recent times Raven is regarded as just another bird, one with sometimes strange behavior and no usefulness. Versions of the creation myth vary with the locality, but all stress a supernatural relationship between man and the ravens of old.

These people are relatively short in stature and tend to be long-trunked and short-legged. The men are lean and muscular, and the women may be plump. Neither men nor women are fat, as is true of most Eskimos, in spite of numerous reports to the contrary. The long keel-shaped head of classic Eskimo description is not typical here; instead, the people tend to be roundheaded and lack the distinctive keel. Eskimos, as the most mongoloid of New World aboriginal populations, have extremely high cheekbones, distinct epicanthic folds, and shovel-shaped incisor teeth, all reflections of a clear racial affinity with Asian populations. The people are darkskinned only on their faces and hands where they color deeply from weathering. Many of the men have rather heavy beards, but in aboriginal times they plucked all facial hair. They wore their hair in two styles, either long over the shoulders or tonsured and had bangs falling over the eyes. The women permitted their hair to grow long, and when they concerned themselves about their appearance, they gathered it back into a lock or braid. Facial adornment for women included small blue glass beads strung on sinew and hung from a hole in the nasal septum. The beads were obtained in trade from Siberia even before direct contact was made with the Russians. The women usually had pierced ears, in which earrings were worn or strings of beads suspended. Likewise, their faces from lower lip to chin were tattooed, and they are reported to have worn a lateral labret at each outer corner of the lower lip. Men wore either paired lateral labrets or a single large medial labret just beneath the lower lip, but they were not tattooed.

The most typical winter garment for both sexes was a loose-fitting, sleeved garment reaching to the calves or ankles. This type of parka most often was made from the skins of ground squirrels, with the claws and tails still attached. Some parkas were manufactured from marmot, musk-rat, or caribou skin, depending on local fashions and the skins available. The parkas of women were hooded and had splits up the sides, but a man's parka was hoodless, and the sides were not split. When an individual of either sex found the length of his parka to be an impediment, he attached a belt about the hips and gathered the excess length above the belt. The parkas were trimmed elaborately, particularly those of the women. White caribou hair was added to the cuffs and lower border, and strips of animal fur dangled at the breast and from the middle of the back. The parkas of men had similar but less elaborate border trim. A man protected his neck from the cold with a bearskin collar sewn about the opening in the parka and wore a head covering of skin or fur. Some men wore headpieces made from a complete goose skin split open at the breast. Men apparently wore short caribou-skin undertrousers, over which were added trousers fitted to just below the knees. Their boots were knee-length and were made from caribou leg skins, with sealskin soles attached. Inside the boots socks of caribou skin or woven grass were worn, and grass insoles cushioned the feet. Women preferred to wear sealskin boots which reached to the hips, although other skins were substituted, particularly along the central river. The only other major clothing item was mittens. These were of caribou skin and were worn in winter by persons of both sexes. Items intended for summer use included rain parkas made from sewn strips of intestine or from fish skins. These garments were hooded and probably reached just below the knees. During rainy summer weather people also wore fish-skin boots of varying lengths and fish-skin socks.

The Kuskowagamiut population was scattered along the river in settle-ments located on both banks. The number of persons occupying any par-ticular settlement varied from ten living in an isolated house to villages of about three hundred. The isolated household-community was not uncommon, but people usually occupied larger settlements. Judging from the settlement pattern about 1900, few families lived away from the riverbanks. The most detailed information available about the village dwellings is from Crow Village, where a rectangular anteroom usually was constructed in a shallow excavated pit. The roof style is uncertain, but the sidewalls probably were supported by vertical poles set into the ground. Entrance was gained through an oval opening in a vertical wall plank. Inside the room was a fireplace where meals were cooked, and smoke from the fire drifted out through a hole in the roof. Stored in this anteroom were various wooden dishes, ladles, baskets, and pottery containers, all of which were associated with domestic activities. Some houses had short ground-level passages which led into the living room, and others had long subterranean tunnels. In either case the passage prevented cold air from penetrating the living area. Usually during cold weather and even at other times of the year the family's dogs slept in the tunnel and were a minor hazard to anyone entering. The living room, which tended to be square, with walls measuring about fifteen feet in length, was separated from the tunnel with a woven grass mat or skin curtain. Inside the house, which was built in an excavation, were either vertical or horizontal planks or logs which formed the walls. Two stout posts were set into the front wall and two into the rear wall; across these were the main roof beams. Split logs extended from the edge of the wall excavations to rest against these beams. The center of the roof was covered with short, split logs, but allowance was made for an opening over which was placed a framework covered with sewn fish skins or animal intestines to serve as a window. The entire structure except the window was covered with sheets of birchbark (in houses along the central river) or bundles of grass (along the lower river). Above this protective layer earth or sod was added to complete the construction. The house floor consisted of packed earth, which often if not always was moist and soggy. Near the center of the floor in houses along the central river was a fireplace, but some houses along the lower river appear to have lacked this feature. Benches usually paralleled the sidewalls, and in some houses they also paralleled the rear wall. It was on these benches that people lounged during the day and slept at night. On top of the benches were planks, slabs of birchbark, or layers of grass. Animal skins were used for mattresses and blankets.

To a non-Eskimo the odor inside a house would have been its most striking feature. The smells of stale urine, skin clothing which had never been cleaned, and dried salmon must have been an impressive combination. The interiors were relatively dark because of the accumulation of soot on the walls, but some light penetrated the translucent window. This covering could be set aside during warm days for still more light from outside. Artificial light came from the fireplace or from bowl-shaped clay lamps. The lamps were placed on stands in front of the rear bench or at the edge of a sidewall bench. Oil, preferably seal oil, burned on a wick of moss. The central floor space was filled with wooden food trays, deep water buckets with sides of bent spruce root fitted into a flat bottom, and cups made in a similar manner but on a smaller scale. The pottery cooking vessels were situla shaped. If there was any surface treatment, it consisted usually of horizontal bands of dots and lines which had been incised into the moist clay just below the rim. In the central river houses round stones were kept near the fireplace. These were heated and dropped into birchbark vessels for cooking food. Furnishings would also include a woman's sewing equipment in a neat, folded leather container, her semilunar slate-bladed knife, or *uluak,* wooden cutting boards, chipped and ground stone scrapers for processing skins, and awls, to mention some of the more important items. Such a dwelling was occupied by a woman, her daughters, and her young sons.

The residence of men and older boys, bathhouse, workshop, and ceremonial room were combined in one structure which was called a *kashgee* and served as a men's house. A building such as this typically measured thirty feet on each side and was the largest building of a community. The walls were made of vertical planks or split logs, and the roof was cribbed. Access was through a tunnel either at ground level or beneath it, and some men's houses had both varieties of entrance. The floor of a kashgee was covered with planks except for an area some four feet square at the center of the room. Here there was a fire pit which could be planked over when not in use, and above the fire pit was a window. Kashgee furnishings included two or three tiers of benches around the walls, and there were at least two large bowl-shaped oil-burning lamps to provide light.

Inside a kashgee were all of the typical tools and equipment used by men. Conspicuously absent were cooking vessels and eating containers, for these were brought in by females at mealtime and removed after the men and boys had eaten. The woodworking tools included wedges; wooden mauls or hammerstones for driving the wedges; slate-bladed adzes; whetstones of various grades of fineness; paint mortars; engraving tools; and the ubiquitous crooked knife, to cite a few of the most important tools. Other belongings of a personal nature would include snuffboxes, tobacco pouches, pipes, and quid boxes. Near each man's assigned position on a bench were his sinew-backed bow and arrows, spears, and other weapons. Hanging from the ceiling were the bladders of animals and the skins of birds and small animals which would play an important part in certain ceremonies.

Scattered about the settlements were excavated pits which served as storage containers. Along the lower river these pits might be lined with grass. They usually contained the silver salmon taken too late in the season for sun drying, or fish heads being made into headcheese. Most processed fish were placed in caches built on four elevated posts. Above an overhanging wooden platform was the cache itself, a rectangular wooden structure with a gabled bark- or plank-covered roof and an oval entrance at the front. Inside a cache were stored not only dried but frozen fish, herbs, and equipment such as snowshoes and nets which were not in current use. Sleds often were stored on the cache platform, where they would be out of reach of the dogs.

Pulled up above the riverbank were boats of several types. Along the lower river each man owned a kayak made by covering a driftwood frame with dehaired sealskins. An extended family as a unit owned the larger open type of skin boat or umiak. Along the Kuskokwim the large skin boat was called a *baydara* and the smaller one a *baydarka*. Both types were used along the central river, as was a small type of birchbark-covered canoe built around ribs of birch and decked a short distance fore and aft. The only other vessel was an improvised form wider and shorter than a baydara. It had a rough wooden frame and was covered with the skins of freshly killed large animals. Such a vessel was used to carry meat to a village from distant hunting camps.

The ordinary winter conveyances were wooden sleds with built-up beds which were suspended on stanchions mortised and bound with babiche through lashing holes. Sleds with low flat beds were used to carry baydaras over the snow to camps where they would be used after the spring thaw. Smaller but similar sleds were carried on the aft section of a baydarka or canoe to be used in portaging the vessel from one lake or slough to another. Snowshoes were another essential item for traveling overland at certain times of the year. Along the lower river snowshoes were required only when traveling in timbered country where the snow was loose, for the snow on the lakes and tundra soon crusted from the action of the wind. When the crusted snow began to melt on the tundra in the spring, a man wore short and crude wooden snowshoes. Along the central river, where powdery snow was often encountered, snowshoes were used more often and were made with long light birch frames with babiche webbing.

All of these riverine Eskimos depended on fish as their primary staple, and for them the salmon catch was most critical. After the winter's ice had broken up on the main river and the high water accompanying the breakup had subsided, all the people moved from their scattered spring hunting camps to riverbank residences where they prepared their summer fishing equipment. Along the lower river any man who was in his village just after breakup made certain that his long-handled, small-meshed dip net was in good repair for use during the coming run of smelt. These small fish were dipped from the river's edge at certain spots where they swam near the bank. Smelt were taken by the thousands, but only over a period of a few days, for the run was of brief duration. The smelt were strung through the gills on willow branches and hung to dry on racks placed in the sun. After they were thoroughly dry, they were cached for winter, at which time they would be dipped in seal oil and eaten whole. Following the smelt run, the gill nets were readied for use. These were made of the knotted inner bark of willows or of rawhide thongs and probably were about thirty feet long and six feet deep. They were set in river eddies and were tended daily from a canoe or baydarka. These nets had oblong bark or wooden floats strung along the top, and sinkers of bone or antler along the bottom. The eddy in which a man set his net was the one he had used the year before; the right to an eddy was lost, however, if it was not claimed each year. Since the river channel shifted frequently, there was no real permanence for any eddy. The first species likely to be caught was the sheefish, a large whitefish. Few of these were taken, and as a result they were likely to be boiled and eaten rather than preserved for winter consumption. A fisherman was most anxious to take king salmon, and after a number had been caught he took up his set net and joined it to all the king salmon netting he might have. He then placed the net in a wooden bucket or birchbark basket in his baydarka and paddled to a straight stretch of river where the current flowed evenly and where there were no obstructions beneath the water. Here he threw out a large wooden float attached to a line leading to the gill net which he then paid into the water. After the net was set, the end nearest the baydarka was tied to the vessel, and the fisherman paddled so that the net floated at right angles to the current. When he saw a float bob violently, he knew a fish had struck the net, and he detached the net rope from his vessel, tied a large wooden float to the end, and threw it overboard. After paddling to the spot where the fish had thrashed, he gently lifted the net from the water and either clubbed the salmon to death or stuck a bone bodkin into the base of its head. The fish was killed as efficiently as possible, for if it thrashed violently a section of the net was likely to be destroyed. The fish was put in the vessel and the net straightened into an even drifting pattern with the current. After a drift of about two miles the net was hauled in and the process repeated

if the take had been small. This technique is called drift netting and probably was the most important means of taking salmon among all the riverine
Eskimos. Not only were king salmon caught in this manner, but with small-
meshed gill nets, red, dog, and silver salmon were entangled.

When a man finished his drift, he returned to his fish camp or village,
put the fish in a wooden bin and covered them with a mat of grass. His
wife or daughter processed the fish for immediate consumption or for storage. Salmon to be eaten during the summer were cut into chunks and
boiled in water or partly dried and later boiled. Most of the fish taken
were dried for winter. The heads were cut off first; these were cooked for
human or dog food, dried and split, or buried in the ground to make
headcheese. The body cavity was split with an uluak and the contents,
except for the roe, kept for dog food. The roe was mashed and eaten mixed
with oil or dried and later mixed into soups or *agutuk*. Better known as
Eskimo ice cream agutuk consists mainly of rendered fat of any type mixed
with berries, greens, fish, or roe; when the mixture has been chilled, the
fat turns white. The body of the fish being prepared for drying was split
through to the backbone and detached as far as the tail. After the flesh
was sliced, the fish was hung by the tail over a drying rack made from
poles. It was covered during rainy and damp weather with grass matting.
Beneath the rack a small fire of alder wood was sometimes built to prevent
flies from laying their eggs on the fish and to smoke-cure the salmon. After
the fish had dried, they were bundled together and stored in caches. Any
fish not prepared for drying were placed whole in the ground. Here they
decayed slowly and became "stink fish," as later whites termed them. It
would seem from late nineteenth-century ethnographic reports that families
did not fish intensively throughout the salmon season. They fished only
until they felt that they had enough to last them through the winter. If
a man took a large number of king salmon, he was desultory about fishing
for other smaller species. Although salmon always ascended the river to
spawn in the small adjacent streams, high water made it difficult to net
them during certain years. However, starvation from a failure of the salmon
run apparently did not exist.

Along the lower river, small white whales (beluga) ascended the river,
particularly when the smelt appeared. Seals, too, swam into the lower river
in the spring. These sea mammals were hunted from skin boats with toggle-
headed harpoons or harpoon darts. As one was struck repeatedly with harpoon heads, it was forced to surface frequently for air, until finally it could
be dispatched with a slate-bladed lance. The meat and skin of a whale
were divided according to a pattern, with the man who embedded the first

harpoon receiving the greatest share. Lesser portions went to the other men whose harpoons or lances had struck, but every family in the settlement received at least a small portion of the kill. The division of a seal probably was similar to that for a whale, except that the first man to harpoon the animal received the sealskin.

Some, or perhaps even most, families did not remain at the village to fish for salmon but scattered to small fishing camps along the banks of the river or sloughs. On the central river some families remained in the winter villages but moved into temporary structures. These were round in outline, about ten feet across, and had a pole framework covered with slabs of spruce bark, birchbark, or even bundles of grass. Inside was a fireplace, and smoke drifted out a hole left in the roof. Along the lower river the summer dwelling was a small, winter-type house without a tunnel or anteroom. Some central river Eskimos located their fish camps away from the villages along a stretch of the river where shallow water ran over a gravel bottom. Here weirs were built across the channel, and funnel-shaped fish traps of spruce splints were set at intervals, with the mouths of the traps facing downstream. In these traps salmon, whitefish and pike were taken. More ambitious individuals along the river set and maintained similar traps in the narrow streams leading from lakes into sloughs and rivers. With the end of the salmon fishing season the families who were away from their winter settlement moved back, taking with them their winter supply of dried fish.

The lower river families either went to their fall camps by baydara before the lakes and flowing waters froze or waited until after freeze-up and traveled by dog sled. To pull the sleds, dogs were harnessed to individual towlines attached to stanchions at the sides. In all likelihood, a man pushed at the rear of a sled while women and children pulled in front. It was not until about twenty years after the Russian arrival that dogs were hitched tandem at the front of a sled in the manner of peoples in Siberia.

During the early winter the men moved out to tundra camps, where they set fish traps in small streams leading from the lakes. Their primary purpose was to take the small blackfish which left the lakes via small streams during the fall. These fish were caught in great quantities and stored frozen in woven grass bags. Later in the winter they served as food for both people and dogs. Another fall activity of the men was to take squirrels, hares, and marmot with snares; mink and river otter were caught in fish traps or in smaller traps of the same type but made with heavier splints so that they could not break away. Ptarmigan snares were set in clusters around willow thickets. If beaver were in the area, they were taken with nets set beneath the ice. If caribou were about, they were hunted with bows and arrows; in the late fall their skins were prime, the animals fat, and their meat at its best.

By midwinter, the people were in their riverbank settlements with their food caches well stocked. As the season wore on and grew colder, there was less and less subsistence activity. Fish traps were set through river ice in association with weirs, and hooks baited with live blackfish were set for burbot. As the ice thickened, these fishing techniques ceased. It was now the ceremonial season; one settlement hosted another for major ceremonies and they held lesser celebrations among themselves. When supplies of fish were plentiful, there were few cares to disturb the tranquillity of winter.

With the approach of spring, the villagers became restless and were eager to return to their tundra camps. They traveled there by dog team before the trails became free of snow and before the sloughs and rivers were covered with melt water. Here, as the last snows were melting, ptarmigan were hunted and early migratory birds were snared or shot with arrows. The women gathered berries, particularly highbush cranberries, which still clung to the dried bushes from the year before; the men refurbished fish traps to take blackfish, as they once again ascended the small streams to their summer habitat in the lakes. Gill nets were set in larger sloughs and streams for pike and whitefish; the surplus fish were cleaned and dried for later use. Men traveled widely by baydarka once there was open water, hunting and snaring fur animals. When they judged that their take was sufficient or when they simply wearied of the tundra camps, they returned to their riverbank communities. They would do so, however, only when reasonably certain that the river ice had broken up and the flood waters had subsided.

Men lived with their families only at the tundra camps or at fish camps away from the village. By piecing together various reports it would seem that houses generally were occupied by a line of females. A woman raised her daughters in the house, but her young sons would move into the kashgee. Ideally, daughters would remain with their mothers after they had married and would raise the next generation of children in the same house. Only when the number of females overcrowded a dwelling or when a house became uninhabitable did they move. Through female infanticide the number of girls to grow up in any family was limited artificially. The surviving females lived in a lifelong intimacy, whereas males were more closely associated with others of their own sex. Under social conditions of this nature we would not expect, nor do we find, a closeknit domestic unit in Kuskowagamiut society.

In an early but brief description of the Kuskokwim Eskimos by Ferdinand von Wrangell, which was drawn, at least in part, from observations by Vasilev, the activities in the village are recounted. Early in the morning, a designated boy lit the bowl-shaped lamp in each house, and the women rose to prepare the morning meal. In the meantime, the kashgee residents dressed, and the shaman with his assistants went there and performed a ritual, which included the use of the tambourine drum. Women then took food to the males in their families. Following the meal, the women and children collected the day's supply of wood for the kashgee and houses. The men then went out on their subsistence activities by dog team or baydarka, depending on the season. After being away for the day, the men returned to the settlement and went directly to the men's house. It was the duty of a close female relative to unload the catch and put away the equipment of each man. Afterward women prepared the evening meal and dried the men's clothing. Village life gravitated around what happened in the kashgee, especially since it was here that decisions of village-wide concern were made by the men, and here too, ceremonial life found its focus. Furthermore, the kashgee was the village bathhouse, but only for males. The procedure for a bath began with building a great fire in the fire pit; after the wood was reduced to an ash bed, the men stripped off their clothing, covered the skylight with the gut window, and sat absorbing the intense heat, after which they washed in urine. When the bath was over, some men sat in the snow or had water from a hole in the river ice ladled over their heads.

The normal workload of women included the preparation and processing of food, caring for the children, manufacturing and repairing clothing, picking berries and a few other plant products, and collecting firewood. The men were obligated to provide fish and land mammals for food and clothing, but their duties did not extend beyond bringing the subsistence items to the settlement. This arrangement probably was not completely rigid; it is likely that the men sometimes processed food for storage or cooked a meal and women fished or hunted. Still it would have been difficult for an unmarried adult to lead a normal life. The same applied to an orphan; such an individual was dependent entirely on the kindness of other persons. In terms of specialization the only part-time specialists were the shamans and dance leaders. A shaman lived in part on his earnings as a specialist in supernatural matters and did not hunt or fish with the same intensity as other men, but the dance leader received no material rewards for his efforts.

Information about aboriginal Kuskowagamiut marriage and residence patterns is nonexistent, and the reconstruction from much later historical sources is of questionable validity. In any event, these people appear to have attempted to arrange marriages within a community (village endogamy). Since households were associated with lines of women, this meant that a man would become associated with his wife's natal unit (matrilocal residence) whether he had been raised in her settlement or elsewhere. Sometimes men, especially shamans, had more than one wife (polygyny), and if so the women seem to have been sisters (sororal polygyny). Persons traced their relatives along both their father's and mother's line (bilateral or nonunilineal descent) to a given degree of collaterality; this meant that each person, except for brothers and sisters, was a member of a different bilateral kin group (personal kindred). In their kinship terminology a mother's sister's children and father's brother's children (parallel cousins) were called by the same terms as brother and sister (siblings). However, mother's brother's children and father's sister's children (cross-cousins) were termed "cousin." On the parental generation the word for mother was different from that for mother's sister, but the latter term was the same as for father's sister; the same patterning applied to father, father's brother, and mother's brother (lineal avuncular terms). We would expect that since parallel cousins were termed brother and sister their parents would be called "mother" and "father," but such was not the case. Thus, we would be led to conclude that this terminology was in the process of radical change at the time it was described first.

With villagers together in a settlement for at least half of each year, we might expect a degree of political unity, but group decisions which affected the entire community seem to have been rare. This condition is at least in part a reflection of subsistence activities based largely on individual, not community, endeavors. Most likely a man supervised the hunting and fishing activities of his sons, and an older brother, in the absence of a father, directed the economic life of a younger brother. It is likely, too, that older men informally resolved the routine problems of community life, such as disputes over property or hunting and fishing rights. Possibly a wider range of opinion was sought concerning differences with persons in other settlements or the formalities of arranging ceremonies. If any one individual had a prominent voice in the decision making, it probably was the shaman because of his supernatural affiliations. The nonconformity of any individual would lead first to gossip and then to mild ridicule, which was usually sufficient to bring deviant behavior into line with community expectations. If a father was annoyed with the behavior of a son, he would express his dissatisfaction to his best friend during a sweat bath, and this person would make known the father's feelings to the son. Ridicule songs appear to have been sung as a more forceful and face-to-face means of pointing up the failings of an individual. Witchcraft was the most serious form of antisocial behavior of which one could be accused. If the witch lived in a distant village, its malevolence could be counteracted by a powerful local shaman. If the witch lived in one's own settlement, this was much more dangerous. Examples of witches using their powers within their own community are rare, but one instance was recorded. In this case an old woman reportedly killed several of her own children, and the accuser was her husband. The man clubbed her to death and then severed all of her joints. Afterwards her remains were burned with oil.

The most serious rupture of social harmony was the murder of an individual by an outsider, but such an occurrence appears to have been rare. If it did happen, an influential relative of the deceased assembled the men from his and adjacent communities. He entertained them, presented each man with a gift, recounted the offense, and requested them to exact blood revenge. The situation became balanced if someone in the family of the murderer were killed and there were no additional murders. Sometimes revenge flared out of hand, and a family feud erupted. This would cease only with the displacement or murder of one faction. Formalized warfare did not exist.

Shamans were more powerful among these Eskimos than among most others, and in general they tended to recur in particular family lines. Although women might become shamans, they normally were not as powerful as males. A young male with a predilection toward shamanism was apprenticed to a successful shaman, and later in adult life he would practice independently. Among other things, his training necessitated acquiring supernatural aids and learning tricks, songs, and drumming. Shamanistic performances were held to diagnose, to predict, to cure by supernatural means, and to demonstrate the power of the shaman. Shamans likewise knew of cures that did not require the aid of spirit helpers; thus they also were secular curers. The shaman also saw to it that people observed the sociocultural prohibitions. A settlement sometimes had more than one shaman, but a single individual would be considered more capable than the others. It was he to whom the villagers turned in the most critical circumstances.

When a person was taken ill and there was no obvious cause for the disability, a shaman's help was enlisted. If the patient did not improve or died, the shaman stood the chance of being accused of witchcraft, which could lead to his murder. A curing session involved the use of assistants who drummed and sang the shaman's songs while the shaman summoned his spiritual helpers, who often took the form of an animal. Once his body was host to this force he behaved strangely, reflecting the motions and sounds of the helping spirit involved. The disease substance was then driven from the person's body by sucking or brushing it away. It happened, too, that while a shaman was possessed by a spirit he sometimes learned that a villager had caused the illness by breaking a taboo. When the offender confessed, harmony was restored to the universe. When a shaman performed during a traditional ceremony in the established round of rituals, he did so as an actor and trickster showing off his skills before an audience. His legerdemain and vanishing acts are legendary. So long as no one knew the key to his trickery the people were impressed, but it is most likely that they knew it for what it was. Shamans also interpreted unusual events. An eclipse of the moon was expected to usher in illness and death; it was an ominous sign when the earth quaked, and comets foretold starvation, to list a few examples of the folk beliefs. Not only the shaman but other persons, especially the old, knew of particular cures for nonsupernatural ailments.

It is unlikely that a clear record of the kashgee ceremonial round ever will be assembled. All we have is incomplete and fragmentary information about particular rituals and certain generalizing statements. Common features included ceremonies that spanned a four-day period, during which time the people of one or more adjacent settlements were guests. The host villagers prepared for the celebration by storing large quantities of food, composing songs, and manufacturing dance masks, along with practicing their parts until they were perfected. The general supervision, at least along the lower river, was in the hands of a dance leader whose duty it was to act as host and make certain that the activities were carried out in the traditional manner. This office tended to be passed down a particular male line from father to son. The dance leader appears to have had little if any power but was respected as an authority on the rituals. The most important ceremonial event was the Great Ceremony for the Dead, which was performed every four to ten years, depending on the number of deaths and the time required to assemble the necessary assets for holding the event. On alternate years reciprocating villages held a Sending a Messenger Ceremony, which was the climax to yearly ceremonials. Along the central river the annual Doll Ceremony was important, but whether it was held along the lower river is not certain, although it is likely.

The Great Ceremony for the Dead was designed to free the souls of the dead so that they could rest forever in a world in the sky. The Sending a Messenger Ceremony was in honor of the recently deceased and included the institutionalized giving of gifts. The person or persons hosting the celebration were relatives of the deceased and had accumulated food and property in large quantities. Messengers were sent to the guest community with a mnemonic stick on which symbols were carved or appended. The announcement was made formally, and the signs on the stick were to convey the details of the invitation. When the guests arrived, they were greeted ceremonially, and during the evenings of the festivities dances and songs were performed to commemorate the dead and his merits. If the deceased was not a noble individual about whom any good could be recounted, the praises of his ancestors were sung. The climax of the ceremony came a few days later when gifts were distributed to the guests in honor of the deceased; there was no obligation to make a return gift.

Along the central river the Doll Ceremony involved retrieving from their hiding places three small human figurines of wood dressed in skin clothing. When they were unwrapped from their container, the clothing was inspected for a piece of animal hair, fur, or fish scales which would indicate the species to be taken in abundance during the forthcoming year. In this area there apparently existed more complex staging effects than on the lower river. These included curtains before a stage, dramatic entrances of the performers, and the extensive use of stuffed birds, fish, or animals which moved across the stage in the context of certain songs. Evidently ceremonial life was quite complex along the Kuskokwim, suggesting that the rather rich environment afforded opportunities for more elaborate group ceremonies than were possible among most Eskimos.

From the writings of Wrangell we learn that a year was divided into eleven months which took their names from the conditions of animals, fish, or birds or from climatic conditions at that particular time. The months corresponded to the current Western calendar except that December and January apparently were combined. They were able to predict the equinox, and certain constellations and planets were known and named.

The prospects of survival were not equal for all infants born into a Kuskokwim Eskimo household. The pregnant woman gave birth at home and was aided by her mother or another female relative. Delivery was in a squatting position, and downward pressure was applied to a woman's abdomen if the process was delayed. The birth of a female offspring was not a particularly joyous occasion, except for the woman who desired a daughter. If there were daughters already in the family, or if it was a lean time of the year, female infanticide was likely to be practiced. Infanticide was not restricted to the newborn but might take place at any time during the first two or three years of life. The attitude was that since one portion of the soul of any deceased individual returned to the body of the next one born, this was no real destruction of life. The name of a baby was that of the person who had died most recently in the local area, and the relatives of the deceased behaved toward the namesake as they had toward the deceased. Names obviously were not associated with a particular sex, and they were changed if their bearer was plagued with misfortune. Infants and small children growing up in a household dominated by older females were pampered and catered to; this treatment was based on supernatural beliefs as much as, or more than, natural affection. Since an infant had the soul of a recently deceased individual, he mirrored the feelings of the deceased and was appeased in order not to offend the watching spirits. This association decreased in importance as the individual grew older and acquired a distinctive personality of his own.

A growing girl soon was integrated into the household routine of the older females. Her toys were facsimiles of the artifacts used by her mother, and by the time she was eight or ten years old she was a reasonably capable housekeeper. One set of household roles of fascinating dimensions was that existing between a grandmother and her granddaughter. The grand-daughter's activities and world view seem to have been molded largely by this older woman who occupied the rear platform in a large household. The reason for considering the grandmother so important stems from a study of stories told by contemporary Eskimo girls. These stories, or story-knife tales as they are known, were illustrated with stylized representations of people, houses, and other physical forms. The illustrations were made on a mud or snow surface with an oblong-bladed implement known as a storyknife. It has been deduced that grandmothers originally made up the stories and illustrated them for their granddaughters. There is no evidence whatever of either men or boys telling or listening to storyknife tales. The tales of a grandmother served to entertain and to instruct, and the main characters most frequently were a grandmother and her granddaughter. Some of the significant ideas repeated in stories are that one should offer food to people when they come to visit, that nonrational behavior is to be expected from males, and that if a granddaughter disobeys her grand-mother it is likely that the grandmother will suffer for the girl's transgressions.

By the time boys were ten years old they had left their natal home and moved into the kashgee. Here they came under the supervision of the older males in their families and under the indirect control of all the older men who were kashgee residents. The boys were no longer regarded as children; more and more was expected of them, even though their activities were supervised casually. The steps toward adulthood were achieved by an adolescent as he increased his hunting skills. The birds and small animals killed by each boy were skinned and stuffed by his mother and then were hung from strings in the kashgee. In the fall or early winter ceremonial recognition was given to the boys' accomplishments. The boys were feasted, and they danced in places of honor. At the completion of the rituals the skins were secreted away to a safe location. After a male had killed one of each species of animal, he was considered to be marriageable. Ceremonial recognition was given a girl when she picked the first of each species of berries, but a more important event was the ceremonial acknowledgment of her menarche. At this time she probably was restricted to one corner of the dwelling, wore old clothing, and observed food as well as behavioral taboos. Possibly it was about this time that a girl had sexual intercourse with a male shaman, which was essential for a maiden before she could be admitted to kashgee ceremonies.

A female was nubile at about the age of fourteen, but a male was likely to be at least four years older and perhaps as much as twenty years her senior. The marriage itself was without ceremony and was arranged by the families of the couple or by an older man and the girl's family. Thereafter the man slept with the girl; she was responsible for preparing his meals, caring for his clothing, and processing the subsistence items he obtained. In the event either of the couple became dissatisfied with the other they ceased cooperating and cohabiting. A marriage might also be terminated with a wrestling match. Any man was free to challenge any other man to wrestle, and the man thrown to the ground was obligated to give up his wife. Usually it was only young women without children for whom one wrestled. No stigma was attached to divorce, and most individuals had at least two partners during their lifetimes. Marriages tended to stabilize after the woman bore a child, particularly if it was a male.

As adults, the activities of a man and his wife were complementary, and although marriages may have been brittle, an adult did not willfully remain unmarried for long. In the early years of marriage the partners might remain cool toward one another, but as time passed they were more likely to become outgoing when together. The personality of an adult Eskimo manifested a phlegmatic realism, and an even-tempered, jovial person was the ideal. Verbal aggression or physical dominance was abhorred, and to be withdrawn or caustic was symptomatic of the sick or diseased. As people aged, they were not killed but often came to be respected for their knowledge. Some old men were great storytellers and passed the traditions of their fathers on to the men and boys of the next generation. Old women held forth from the rear platforms of their dwellings with advice and criticism, both of which were offered freely.

A dead or even an expiring person's body was flexed with the knees bound up to the chest. The women wailed, and the men killed the dogs of the deceased. His clothing and other property save those items that were kept as mementos were destroyed or deposited on the grave. The body was removed through a hole made in the wall of the kashgee or dwelling so that the spirit of the deceased could not find its way back into the structure after the opening was closed. The body was placed in a small plank coffin with mortised corners, and it was raised above the ground on four short poles. The cemetery was usually located on an adjacent hill or a rise near the settlement. Over the coffin sheets of birchbark were placed, and on this were deposited those possessions that had not been destroyed. At the head of the coffin a board might be placed between two poles; on it were pegged wooden carvings of human faces. Sometimes, too, the coffins of men were painted with animal representations of the species taken by the man during his lifetime. Were a person to die and be buried away from the settlement, poles decorated with feathers would be erected and animal figures of wood attached.

Between the beginning of sustained Russian contacts in the 1830's until their withdrawal in 1866, two Russian institutions had a major influence on the lives of local Eskimos. These were the Russian-American Company and the Russian Orthodox Greek Catholic Church. The trading organization was by far the more immediately important, but Orthodox Church influence was more enduring. The Russians were searching for new sources of furs, and by the 1820's they had turned to the region north of the Alaska Peninsula. Of the earliest traders we know comparatively little except that two men, Fedor Kolmakov and Semen Lukin, were most instrumental in opening the inland fur trade. Kolmakov was of aboriginal Siberian and Russian ancestry, while Lukin appears to have been of Eskimo or mixed Russian and Eskimo ancestry. Both men traveled widely, exploring the Kuskokwim River drainage and adjacent areas in their quest for furs. Initially the Russians most desired the pelts of beaver, which were to be found along the central and upper reaches of the river; thus, at the earliest stage of their penetration the lower river region held little attraction to them. In 1853, however, white fox pelts began to be traded, which indicates that by this time the Russians had initiated trading ties with Eskimos along the lower river, since white fox could be obtained only from areas near the coast.

The most permanent and important inland trading center of the Russian-American Company was Kolmakov Redoubt along the central Kuskokwim. The physical plant originally was what we have come to expect of frontier outposts. A stockade surrounded the main settlement, two small cannons were the primary means of defense, and there was a blockhouse with gun ports. The station also included a store, quarters for transients and others for employees, a chapel, bathhouse, and outbuildings. Lukin was the first manager, and he held this position throughout most of the Russian era. He was a religious man authorized by the Orthodox Church to baptize converts, and even before a chapel was constructed he led weekly church services in the store. He was well-regarded by the local Eskimos, and while there were intermittent rumors of pending attacks on the settlement, none ever materialized.

Kolmakov Redoubt never was a bastion in the north; in fact, it usually was staffed with about a dozen employees of Russian, Eskimo, or mixed blood, and a military garrison never was stationed there. The post never really thrived, yet this was the community where local Eskimos first were exposed intensively to European ways. Two major reasons were behind the failure of the post to expand during the Russian era. The first and more important consideration is that the worldwide demand for beaver pelts was in a decline at the time the redoubt was founded, and thus the company was not motivated to expand the station. Second, this was the most inaccessible of all redoubts. It was necessary to supply the station by boats in the summer, and these were necessarily small ones because of the portages along the established routes. Winter access by dog team was even more difficult because of the need to carry enough food to feed the dogs and the risks involved in traversing trailless country. As a result, the trade goods available usually were small, highly portable, and not readily destructible. Items such as tea, beads, knives, metal containers, needles, copper ornaments, and similar goods were stocked; even so the post often was without these imported goods and then dealt only in local products such as oil and dried fish. The overall impression is that the Russians adapted to Eskimo ways and made very few radical changes in the traditional patterns. Even the trading complex was not a radical innovation, for the Eskimos had obtained goods of Western manufacture before the arrival of the Russians on the Kuskokwim. Barter with the Russians followed the pattern already established in trade between various Eskimos and Indians.

The first Orthodox missionary to consider the spiritual welfare of the aboriginal peoples north of the Alaska Peninsula was the illustrious Father Veniaminov, who was later to become the leader of the Russian church. In 1829 he baptized individuals at Nushagak, and in 1832 he returned there and held church services for seventy persons. It was Veniaminov who gave Kolmakov and Lukin the authority to baptize the heathen. The first Orthodox priest to visit the Kuskokwim was A. Petelin, who traveled there from the Nushagak station in the 1840's, but we have no knowledge of an Orthodox missionary stationed along the river until the arrival of Hieromonk Illarion in 1861. He visited Kolmakov Redoubt intermittently until his departure from the area in 1866. It would seem that by the end of the Russian era many if not most of the Kuskokwim Eskimos along the central river considered themselves to be Christians. They were baptized and were given Russian names, but the core of Christian dogma was certainly poorly understood. What is important about the effects of the early Orthodox missionaries is that they did convey to the Eskimos the essential elements of Christianity, and the church as an institution became an established part of their lives.

Yet another complex of Russian origin must be mentioned briefly, and this is the Russian steam bath. A bathhouse was constructed by Lukin at Kolmakov Redoubt. The Eskimos trading into these posts were familiar already with bathing in intense heat, but the Russian bath was somewhat different from the sweat bath in the kashgee. It was taken in a small structure, and stones were heated above a stove or in an open fire and water poured over them. Bathers sat back and enjoyed the hot air moistened by the steam from the rocks. Initial Eskimo reaction probably was unfavorable, but as time passed the Russian type of bath was to assume more importance.

During the initial period of contact with the Russians, Kuskokwim Eskimos seldom were hostile; in fact, they appear to have welcomed the Russians for the trade goods which they made available locally. However, this harmony was tested severely in 1838-1839. During these years there was a local smallpox epidemic in which possibly as many as half of the riverine Eskimos perished. The survivors thought that the Russians purposefully plagued them with the disease, and some Eskimos from the Kuskokwim massacred the Russians at a post on the Yukon River. The epidemic destroyed the fabric of aboriginal social life, and the distrust engendered probably never completely passed during the Russian period.

From the excavation of the five houses and midden debris at Crow Village, a central river settlement visited by Zagoskin in 1843 and 1844, we would expect tangible evidence of Russian influence. In spite of the fact that this community was occupied throughout all or at least most of the Russian era no remains were identified positively as having been brought by Russians. A few artifacts such as a copper bracelet and certain bead types are most likely of Russian derivation, but this is all that may be said to have resulted materially from a span of more than twenty years of direct contact. The logical conclusion is that Russian material culture did not make a significant impact on the Crow Village Eskimos, despite the fact that the settlement was only a short distance downstream from Kolmakov Redoubt.

Crow Village was occupied into the American period and was abandoned about 1910. Material items left at the site and dating from the time of American traders include a woman's high-laced shoe, a man's square-toed shoe, a man's wide-brimmed felt hat, kerchief, metal pendant, assortment of metal containers, metal axes, a strike-a-light, cartridge cases and musket balls, and American-made pottery. Another important category of artifacts includes items that reflect traditional craft skills applied to new mediums. For example, mending holes were drilled in a broken sherd of imported pottery so that sinew could be laced through to bind the break; the same technique had been employed in aboriginal times when a vessel of local manufacture cracked. These Eskimos also attempted to make uluak blades by recutting tin-can metal into blade form. However, the softness of the metal must have produced a blade of very limited utility, and slate uluak blades continued to be manufactured and used. The people folded sheets of tin-can metal to make small metal containers, just as they folded birchbark to make vessels. One salmon harpoon dart head had been cut from metal, although the traditional outline of the antler type was retained. These and other items reflect a flexibility in dealing with new material media.

For nearly twenty years following the purchase of Alaska by the United States the only interest in the Kuskokwim was of a commercial nature. Hutchinson, Kohl & Company of San Francisco bought all the assets of the Russian-American Company, which had held a monopoly on the Alaskan trade since 1799. Hutchinson, Kohl & Company became the Alaska Commercial Company in 1868. Kolmakov Redoubt continued as a trading center, but the main post was located at Mumtrekhlagamiut Station closer to the mouth of the river. Supplies were brought in from a transfer point along the south shore of the estuary. The most important observation to be made about Russian and early American trading along the Kuskokwim is that neither developed a major commercial enterprise. The stores were not a great source of profit, and consequently their inventories were quite limited. In the change from the Russian to the American period there was no abrupt break in trading pattern; in fact, two of the three traders during the early American period were Russian or of Russian-Eskimo extraction.

Then, in 1883, a series of events occurred in Bethlehem, Pennsylvania, which were to have a major influence on the Kuskowagamiut. During this year the Presbyterian missionary and Federal agent for education in Alaska, Sheldon Jackson, spoke to an audience of Moravians at the Moravian College and Theological Seminary in Bethlehem. He convinced the officials of the church that they should take an active interest in the

Eskimos of Alaska. Inasmuch as the Moravians had long maintained missions to Eskimos in Greenland and Labrador, it is not surprising that they responded favorably to this request. In 1884 an experienced Moravian missionary from Canada, Henry Hartmann, accompanied by a seminary student, William H. Weinland, set off for Alaska to find a site where a mission could be located. They traveled to Nushagak and found that this area was dominated by the Orthodox, but were led by the local priest to believe that the Kuskokwim Eskimos were heathens. They ventured on to the Kuskokwim and traveled as far as the vicinity of Kolmakov Redoubt in their search for a site at which to found a mission. Finally they concluded that the small, lower river community of Mumtrekhlagamiut Station (modern Bethel) was best suited to their purpose. The following year Weinland graduated from the seminary, and he, along with another graduate, John H. Kilbuck, and their brides, set off for the Kuskokwim. They were accompanied by a lay minister, Hans Torgersen, who was also a skilled carpenter.

The establishment of the mission center, which came to be known as Bethel, was delayed because of the drowning of Torgersen before the buildings were constructed. With the aid of Eskimos, the missionaries were able to construct a small dwelling, and when winter arrived they were reasonably well prepared. Weinland and his family stayed at the station for two years and then left for the United States. He was to spend most of the remainder of his life as a missionary among the Indians of southern California. Kilbuck remained at Bethel until 1898 when he left the service of the church, but in 1921 he again became a missionary and went to Akiak, where he died the next year. There has been an unbroken line of missionaries at Bethel since the founding of the mission, and although some stayed for very brief periods, others devoted the greater part of their lives to working with Eskimos. The Moravians opened an orphanage near Kwethluk in 1925; both it and the Bethel mission have endured.

The feverish search for gold in northwestern North America around the turn of the twentieth century profoundly changed the history of many areas of Alaska, but this was not the case along the Kuskokwim. Men searched for Kuskokwim gold during the Russian period, and a small number of Americans prospected in the 1880's. It was not, however, until 1907 that a significant deposit was discovered along the upper Tuluksak River. This operation has been productive through the years, but it is far from any Eskimo settlement and has not been a major influence on the local economy. One material innovation of miners did make a change, however; it was the fish wheel. This device is a log raft with a large opening at the center over which is mounted a horizontal axle hung with large baskets and paddles. The river current propels the paddles and baskets which rotate in the direction of the current. Fish swimming upstream within reach of the baskets are lifted from the water into them and then slide down a chute into a box at the side of the raft. The fish wheel is an extremely effective method of taking fish, for it does not require constant tending. However, it can be used successfully only under certain circumstances. The water must be opaque and must flow rather fast, and the fish must swim relatively close to the shore. This means that only in regions above tidewater would this device be practical. Brought to Alaska around the turn of the century, the fish wheel had been employed only for a relatively short time in the northwestern United States, but it was known earlier in the eastern states.

Through Moravian efforts a small number of reindeer were brought to the lower Kuskokwim in 1901. The successful introduction of reindeer herding among Alaskan Eskimos in 1892 had been another of Sheldon Jackson's accomplishments. The Kuskokwim herds increased until in the 1930's there were about 40,000 head being grazed along the river system. Then in the early 1940's the herds decreased rapidly so that by the end of the decade they were no longer in existence. Thus the early hope of creating a new basis for the economy was a failure. As time passed, the herds owned by the Moravian mission became an economic liability, and it was the rare Eskimo who owned a profitable herd. The deer came to be concentrated in the hands of whites and Lapps, who had been brought to Alaska originally to teach herding to the Eskimos. It was the vacillating Federal policies that finally wrote finis to the local reindeer industry.

Bethel has emerged as the most important town along the Kuskokwim. One of the most significant factors in its early growth was the discovery in 1908 that a deep channel reached from the estuary as far as Bethel. Before this time all imported goods had been transferred from large ships to small riverboats at the coast. The channel was adequately charted in 1914, and an oceangoing vessel anchored at Bethel the following year. Shortly after the turn of the century, too, there was an increase in fur prices which encouraged independent traders to open posts. The Moravian Church also operated trading establishments in order to offset the mounting cost of its Alaskan missions.

In terms of education and health it is again Bethel that led the field. The first formal school opened at Kolmakov Redoubt during 1861-1862 under Hieromonk Illarion, but it functioned only briefly. It was not until 1886, when the Moravians opened a mission school at Bethel, that Eskimo children first became formally exposed to American education. This school received Federal aid until the U.S. Bureau of Education opened another in 1913. In 1923 a territorial school was built for white children. The first doctor, a medical missionary for the Moravian Church, practiced at Bethel

Plate 15 *(Top left)   Lower Kuskokwim River Eskimos photographed in 1907* (Courtesy of the University Museum, Philadelphia).

Plate 16 *(Bottom left)   Lower Kuskokwim River Eskimos in front of a cache photographed in 1907. Smelt are drying on the pole* (Courtesy of the University Museum, Philadelphia).

Plate 17 *(Below)   Kuskowagamiut hunters in their kayaks (baydarkas), photographed in 1907* (Courtesy of the University Museum, Philadelphia).

Plate 18
*A Kuskowagamiut man with labrets
and earrings, photographed in 1907*
(From Gordon, 1917).

Plate 19
A Kuskowagamiut girl in 1907
(From Gordon, 1917).

Plate 20 *Grave goods above Kuskowagamiut burials photographed in 1907* (Courtesy of the University Museum, Philadelphia).

Plate 21 *Kuskowagamiut community photographed in 1884* (Courtesy of the Archives of the Moravian Church: Original in the Archives of the Moravian Church, Bethlehem, Pennsylvania. Further reproduction may not be made without the written permission of the Archives Committee).

Plate 23 *A Kuskowagamiut woman cutting up salmon in 1956* (Photograph by the author).

Plate 24 *A Kuskowagamiut family on an outing to gather greens in the summer of 1962* (Photograph by the author).

Plate 22 *A view of the Kuskowagamiut community of Napaskiak in 1956* (Photograph by the author).

Plate 25 *A Kuskowagamiut house with a storage shed in the foreground at Napaskiak in 1970* (Photograph by the author).

from 1896 to 1905. In 1918 a small hospital was built at Akiak, but in 1937 another was constructed at Bethel and the earlier one was abandoned. Since that time the hospital at Bethel has served the entire river and adjacent areas.

Before turning to more recent happenings among the Kuskowagamiut, two major events with long-range effects should be discussed briefly. The first was a severe epidemic which took place in 1900-1901. During these years influenza accompanied by whooping cough, measles, and pneumonia devastated the riverine population. One estimate, made by a medical doctor who was there at the time, is that half the population, including all of the babies, perished. Some villages were deserted completely, and there is every reason to believe that the people were seriously demoralized. Their continuity with the past was interrupted or perhaps even broken in most settlements. The cultural and social effects must have been great, particularly since this was the gold rush period in which many Anglo-Americans were entering or passing through the area. The Eskimos seem to have reacted by giving up many of their old ways and rapidly adopting American customs.

The second change, which began after the smallpox epidemic of 1838-1839 and was accelerated by the epidemic of 1900-1901 involved the movement of Eskimos farther and farther up the Kuskokwim. The country which they came to occupy belonged to Athapaskan Indians, and by the early 1840's they had gone far enough inland to share a village across the river from Kolmakov Redoubt with Indians. The traditional hostility between most Indians and Eskimos cannot be said to have existed along the central river. By 1960 Eskimos occupied the banks of the main river as far inland as the Stony River junction, and by 1970 individual Eskimos were to be found living at the trading center of McGrath as well as the Indian villages of Nikolai and Medfra. Eskimo genealogies along the central river indicate that the pattern is for Indians to marry Eskimos and adopt Eskimo ways. Thus we see the continuing adaptability of Eskimos in their deep penetration of interior Alaska.

Shifting the descriptive emphasis to one particular village makes it possible to see the direction in which Kuskokwim Eskimo culture has moved on the community level. For a few days short of a year during 1955-1956, I lived at Napaskiak and collected information about life at that time. The oldest villagers reported that the settlement had been occupied for many generations and that before its establishment their ancestors had lived at nearby settlements which now are abandoned. They have no traditions of movement into the area at an earlier time. The modern village stretches along the southeastern bank of the river at the lower end of a slough. The twenty-seven frame and seven log houses at Napaskiak are occupied by 141 persons. The most imposing structures are the Bureau of Indian Affairs school, with attached teacher's residence, and the Russian Orthodox Church. Across the river at Oscarville live forty-two persons in twelve log, frame, or sod houses. Here also the store and trader's residence are located. Oscarville and Napaskiak are considered as one community since they use the same school, store, and church and maintain close social ties. Scattered around the houses were drying racks and smokehouses for fish, caches, steam baths, and privies.

The earliest known reference to Napaskiak is on a map dating 1867, and the settlement is listed in the Federal Census of 1880. The Moravian missionaries Weinland and Kilbuck visited there repeatedly in the 1880's. Napaskiak has always represented a failure in the Moravian mission program, for the settlement is only about seven miles downstream from Bethel, yet few of its residents ever became Moravian converts. As early as 1886 an effort was made to found a local mission school, and Eskimo lay preachers for the Moravian Church wintered there in 1897-1898 but made little progress with the people. In the 1950's virtually all residents were members of the Russian Orthodox faith. The small settlement of Oscarville began about 1912 as the home of Oscar Samuelson, who maintained a trading post until his death in 1953. Over the years a few families have elected to live near the store, which has continued to function under the management of the founder's daughter and her husband. For a brief span in the mid-1950's, another store served the people at Napaskiak, but it soon failed. At this time the residents of Oscarville attended the Napaskiak church, which was constructed in 1931, and all the children went to school in Napaskiak. The school was opened in 1939 and has held classes continuously except for a brief period during World War II.

The most intensive contacts outside the community were with the urban settlement of Bethel. The five large stores, the U.S. Public Health Service hospital, pool halls, restaurants, and theaters were among the greatest attractions in Bethel for the villagers. Here, too, they met friends and relatives from other settlements, and ordered intoxicants to be brought in by air from Anchorage. Thus Bethel was the center of diverse forms of socializing. Contacts with adjacent villages were largely social or religious in nature. A family traveled to visit relatives, attend a funeral, or arrange church business. The only other local trips were taken downriver by men in the spring to hunt seals and upriver in the fall to hunt moose. A few men worked at distant urban centers in Alaska, but this practice was not common. Many of the men, however, were members of the local U.S.

National Guard unit and attended an encampment near Anchorage each spring. The only other contact with the outside world was through hospitalization at Anchorage, Seward, or in the state of Washington.

Not all exotic contacts necessitated leaving the community, for one could listen to a battery radio, which was found in most houses, and learn what was happening beyond the local area. One program broadcast from Fairbanks and called "Tundra Topics" was particularly popular, for it presented news about isolated settlements. Then, too, there were people who came to the village from urban areas in connection with some form of governmental work. The only outsider to reside in the community was the Bureau of Indian Affairs teacher, but the Bureau also sent supervisors and maintenance men to the settlement on occasion. U.S. Public Health Service field nurses and those working with the special program for the control of tuberculosis made regular visits. Scientists were rather frequent callers; their work usually had to do with some aspect of public health. An occasional U.S. National Guard officer or enlisted man from the Bethel headquarters visited on official business, and the same applied to the U. S. Deputy Marshal from Bethel; sometimes there was even a stray tourist seen in the village.

The clothing of men consisted of trousers, shirts, underwear, and shoes which were purchased from a store or mail-order house. An exceptional man, particularly one who was old, wore sealskin boots, but these were passing out of style. The most popular outer winter garment was a surplus U. S. Army parka, but in fashion among some of the younger men were tight-fitting, light-weight cloth jackets. Conservative women, young and old, wore cotton bloomers and petticoats, both of which usually were made by hand. More cosmopolitan older girls and women wore ready-made underwear. Women usually preferred cotton dresses of the housedress style, but some wore knit sweaters and slacks. Older women wore sealskin boots, but most of the younger ones wore shoes or short rubber boots. Many women, especially the middle-aged and older, still had squirrel-skin parkas adorned elaborately with calfskin trimmings, but skin parkas were passing out of fashion, being replaced by readymade jackets. In summer, particularly when cleaning fish, a woman wore a hooded cloth parka over her dress. A male child had the same general type of clothing as his father but was more likely to wear skin boots, and a girl's garments were similar to those of the more conservative women.

In this community were forty physically separate households, with closely related families tending to live in adjacent structures. Twenty homes were occupied by nuclear families, and in seven others one person lived alone. In the remaining houses the residents were related to one another by an

extension of nuclear family ties. The larger families usually had houses
with two or three rooms, but smaller households consisted of a single room.
If there was a second room, it served primarily for sleeping and storage.
Each house had an anteroom or storage shed attached which contained
a jumble of objects. A gasoline washing machine was often the largest item;
others included food brought from a cache but not yet consumed, winter
parkas, a chamber pot, and an assortment of axes and other woodworking
tools. The houses usually were rectangular in floor plan and had at least
one curtained window on each side. The floors were planked, and the walls
as well as the ceiling usually were covered with painted wallboard. The
furnishings included a cast-iron woodburning stove with a drying rack
above it. A teakettle rested on top of the stove, and a pair of sadirons
often were off to one side. A homemade wooden cupboard contained the
dishes, pots, and pans, and on top of an adjacent washstand was an
enameled basin. Above the stand was a small mirror, and to one side a
five-gallon gasoline can with its top cut out contained waste water. A
wooden table, frequently with an oilcloth cover, was along one wall, and
around the table were either locally made or imported wooden chairs or
boxes for seats. On the table were knives, forks, and spoons in one or more
drinking glasses, along with salt and pepper shakers and a bowl of sugar.
Overhead hung a gasoline lantern which supplied the only light in most
households; two families owned gasoline-powered generators to supply their
houses and those of near relatives with electricity. The largest items were
the metal-framed beds with mattresses, blankets, and bedspreads. Beneath
a bed were cardboard boxes filled with clothing, cloth, and sections of pelts.
Each house also contained trunks or suitcases piled somewhere and filled
with clothing not then in use. On the walls there was always an Orthodox
Church calendar around which hung prints of icons and a container of
holy water. It is striking that none of these household objects were aboriginal in form. In most dwellings the only object of traditional Eskimo material
culture was an uluak, which now had a blade cut from an old wood-saw
blade and mounted on an ivory or antler handle.

A village-wide search for material items associated with Eskimo
technology in the past produced very few forms. The most obvious examples
were the baydarka and canoe styles, but both were now covered with canvas
and the frames lashed together with cords. The large plank boat made
of spruce and powered with an outboard motor had long since replaced
the baydara. Raised caches retained their form of old, as did the dip and
gill nets, although the netting was made from cotton, linen, or nylon twine.
Hunting weapons included rifles and shotguns; a few boys used bows and
arrows, but preferred slingshots or air rifles. Most of the equipment neces-

sary for living off the country was purchased ready-made from nearby stores, and even the items of local manufacture, such as plank boats, sleds, or fish traps were constructed of imported materials.

Food habits reflected far greater continuity with the past than did the material inventory. This was because salmon continued to be the most important staple in nearly all households. The aboriginal processing techniques persisted; that is, fish were dried and smoked and salmon also were buried whole. Smokehouses were used, but such may not have been the case in aboriginal times. The principal method of cooking salmon was still by boiling, and dried salmon continued to be stripped from the skin in pieces and dipped into seal oil before eating. However, these people had come to consider that a meal of salmon alone was one of poverty. They made unleavened bread to eat for breakfast with coffee or tea; coffee was preferred by most, but tea was substituted when a family's resources were low. The Russians had introduced tea, which was most likely traded in brick form; bread, too, probably was a Russian innovation. From an analysis of the tin-can remains from Crow Village it appears that the most popular imported foods at the turn of the century were fruit, meat, and fish, as well as syrup, salt, lard and baking powder, with flour inferred. In the 1950's every family regarded sugar, flour, salt, canned milk, tea, coffee, tobacco, and cooking oils as necessities. They also bought canned meats and fish, crackers, candy, and canned fruits, depending on their resources.

For a family to thrive it was essential for the male head to possess diverse skills. Each man had to be a salmon fisherman, and to vary the diet, fish traps, nets, or hooks were set for other species. A man needed to be a good trapper to obtain those pelts which could be traded for imported foods and manufactured goods. In theory, a man worked for wages whenever possible in order to buy items from stores and mail-order houses. Then, too, he should be a capable carpenter and hunter. If he possessed all these skills, he could always compensate for a poor season of trapping, an inadequate harvest of fish, or poor wages by emphasizing an alternative activity. A high degree of flexibility was required since it was almost impossible to fall back on gains from the previous year. As a result, any deficiency in a man's subsistence abilities led to a rapid deterioration in his family's living standard.

Before the sloughs and lakes froze in the late fall, some of the men traveled by plank boat and outboard motor to their tundra camps, where from one to three nuclear-family heads lived in a single camp. The principal activities before freeze-up were to haul firewood and shoot migratory birds as the last of them flew southward. After the small streams leading from lakes froze, the men set traps for blackfish. They harvested these fish by the thousand and froze them in burlap sacks for dog food later in the winter. When it was safe to travel by dog team, they returned to the village with meat and fish for their families. The majority of men no longer went to fall trapping camps; they set blackfish traps within about half a day's journey from the village by dog sled. It is important to note that fall trapping camps were no longer family abodes. The people were torn in two directions. A man had to obtain furs with which to purchase manufactured goods, but he disliked remaining at a camp alone. The women and children remained in the village because the children were obligated to attend school and also because most women no longer accepted the primitive living conditions at camp.

With the approach of winter men fished for burbot through the ice in front of the village by setting hooks through the ice baited with live blackfish. About three fish were caught each day, and these were boiled for immediate consumption. Late in the fall men and boys traveled to nearby stands of alders where they cut firewood. Men who were concerned about keeping their homes warm for their families when they were away at trapping camps had large woodpiles; others had no reserve wood at all. With the beginning of the mink trapping season in November, men traveled by dog team to their tundra camps. Most camps were about four hours' traveling time from the village, and the particular trapping area might have been in a male line for a number of generations. One to two dozen steel traps were set for mink and were visited every few days. When checking a line of traps, a .22 caliber rifle was carried on the sled for shooting ptarmigan, the only edible creatures likely to be about at this season.

The distance between a man's camp and his village showed a correlation with the number of mink that he was likely to take. When he ventured a long distance, he was less likely to return often to the village and was more likely to spend his time setting and checking traps. In 1956 most mink pelts brought $20 to $25 from local traders, and an average catch totaled $300 for the season. Most of the men ceased trapping about a week before Christmas, when it often was quite cold, but the primary reason for gathering up their traps was to be at the village during Christmas festivities.

During the extended celebrations of American and Russian Christmas, the families relied on surpluses for their food. There was very little that anyone could do in the way of subsistence activities from then until early spring. In March ptarmigan became plentiful in the willows along sloughs, and hares became active and thus more easily snared in their trails. Again the blackfish began to ascend small streams and could be trapped through the ice. In the middle of winter, when there was little other activity in the village the U. S. National Guard unit held most of its drill sessions. For the seventeen members these earnings were a small but welcome addition to their families' incomes.

When the snow began to melt, burbot hooks again were set beneath the river ice, and women jigged for pike through holes in the ice. As the days lengthened and the snow melted on southern exposures, preparations were made for the spring move to tundra camps, usually the same ones as those used in the fall. If a family head had not gone to his camp by boat the previous fall, it was necessary to haul a plank boat on their dog sled at this time in order to have a means of returning to the village after breakup. By late April most families had settled in their tents or small wood and sod houses at camps, and while classes still were held in the village school there were few children in attendance. A spring camp bustled with diverse subsistence activities. The first concern of the men was to kill as many ducks and geese as possible to satisfy their hunger for fresh meat. The girls and women gathered last year's berries, and the men set small-meshed gill nets in sloughs for pike and whitefish. The men and boys hunted muskrats, the real rationale for going to spring camp. They traveled by canvas-covered canoe and baydarka from one lake to the next, hunting along the way. In 1956, a relatively poor year for muskrats, a pelt was worth up to 85 cents, and the value of the take per man ranged from $20 to $200. As the number of muskrats shot diminished and the ice cleared from the lakes, people returned to the village by boat, arriving just after the Kuskokwim broke up.

Not all families went to spring camp in 1956; in fact, the same trend as that observed for fall camp seemed to be emerging. A dozen families remained in the village; some of the men were sick, another did not have the equipment necessary for making the trip, one worked at the Bureau of Indian Affairs school, and a few men were just not inclined to make the trip. Those who did stay and a few who returned from spring camp before the breakup were on hand when the ice swept from the river. The principal activity at this time was to snake logs out of the high water which carried vast quantities of driftwood downriver. These logs were used later for construction purposes or more often as firewood. When the river waters dropped into their normal channel, smelt were dipnetted from anchored boats or from the banks of the main channel. They were strung and dried just as in aboriginal times and stored in raised caches for winter consumption. About this time, too, some men hunted seals in the estuary. Four or five men made the trip, and about half a dozen seals were killed. Only rarely did a seal or beluga whale ascend the Kuskokwim as far as the village. By the beginning of June large-meshed gill nets were set in the river eddies, and a few sheefish were taken. Soon the first king salmon of the year were caught in set nets, and these nets then were used for drift netting salmon. The technique differed from the aboriginal pattern in the use of long commercial nets, a plank boat, and clubs for killing the fish. As in the past, the catch was placed in a wooden bin for women to prepare for drying; they followed the same techniques as had their grandmothers. Salmon were sun dried on pole racks and then smoked in a large pole-framed structure covered with planks or sheets of metal. The intensity with which other species of salmon were netted later in the season depended on how many king salmon had been taken. The last salmon of the season, the silvers, were buried whole in oil drums and served as dog food for winter. Because of their Orthodox beliefs men did not fish on Saturday afternoon or night, so that the women would not be obligated to process fish on Sunday, and men did not normally fish on Sunday.

Salmon fishing was largely village-based. The shift from scattered family fish camps of old to the new pattern largely was a function of the mobility afforded by plank boats and outboard motors. Efficient boats and motors also made it possible for men to travel to the mouth of the Johnson River, some nine miles downstream, to gillnet whitefish when they concentrated there in the fall or to travel about a hundred miles up the Kuskokwim and its tributaries to hunt moose.

The traditional importance of salmon fishing was declining, for men considered wage labor during the summer as essential. As many as twenty men earned about $100 each unloading supply vessels docked near Bethel. About the same number also were flown to the Bristol Bay salmon canneries where they earned $300 to $600 each for the season. A few others had summer jobs working for visiting scientists, for the U. S. Public Health Service hospital at Bethel, or with the Oscarville trader. Only one man in the village, the general assistant at the Bureau of Indian Affairs school, had a permanent job; he earned about $3000 a year. Family excursions were made in the summer to gather berries, particularly salmon-berries, which were placed in small barrels and stored for winter use in agutuk.

A form of income unassociated with the immediate environment was the money received from Territorial (in 1956) and Federal agencies. Thirteen persons received monthly checks from the Alaska Department of Welfare because they were more than sixty-five years of age and without means of support. Two men received Aid to the Blind, and eight families were helped by Aid to Dependent Children funds. Social Security earnings were received by two men over sixty-five and by three heirs of men who qualified. The total community income from these sources was about $18,000 a year.

In Napaskiak only the persistence and good fortune of a male family head made it possible for a household to prosper, and the relationship between a father and his son was of key importance. A son learned subsistence-directed skills largely through informal instruction from his father. When in the company of his father, a son was withdrawn; although he might covertly disagree with the older man, a son never overtly expressed his dissatisfaction in a face-to-face situation. The pelts that a son trapped and the wages that he earned were at the disposal of his father even if the son were married but living at home. It was the father, too, who had first call on the use of the dog team or boat and outboard motor. Ideally, as a father aged, he was cared for by his son, but in all likelihood the elder man had begun receiving Old Age Assistance. Because of this cash income, a father sometimes continued to dominate the economic activities of the household. The relationship between a father and his daughter was much cooler and more distant than the close ties between father and son. Girls were expected to marry and move into their husband's household (patrilocal residence); thus they offered a father few comforts in his old age. In times of stress a father might defend his daughter with vigor, but the need for this seldom arose.

The bonds between a mother and her daughter were close and overtly warm. After bearing a son, every mother hoped for a daughter to help her with household activities, and a certain degree of affection bound the pair. A conscientious mother sought to find a spouse for her daughter in the community in order to keep her daughter near, and she vigorously defended the girl from real or imagined abuse from her husband or his family. Mothers also were the most outspoken defenders of their sons, but there was not the same warmth expressed toward a son. The relationship between siblings, which extended to parallel cousins, was one of friendship and mutual aid. Married male siblings might live in the same household, draw their food from a common cache, and share equipment. An older male managed the subsistence affairs of the household in the absence of the father. Siblings of the opposite sex were not socially close during their adult lives, but they could be depended on in times of crises. The ties between cross-cousins were looser, and the degree of closeness was largely dependent on the personalities of the persons involved. It was these individuals with whom one joked and, if called on, they would render assistance to each other.

In this community the nuclear family clearly was developing into the most important social unit. Cooperation beyond it was desirable but was not essential for subsistence welfare. The abilities of the man were critical, for he was the provider of his family's material needs. He helped his wife with the cooking and the care of their children, but he rarely processed fish. A woman prepared foods for storage and consumption, and performed diverse other domestic duties, but no longer was charged with hauling wood.

The sexual division of labor was rather sharply drawn, and to be without a spouse was a stressful condition which hopefully was temporary.

The kinship terminology had separate terms for father and mother, as well as uncle and aunt terms for the brothers and sisters of one's parents (lineal type). For cousins, however, cross-cousins were "cousins," whereas parallel cousins were grouped with siblings (Iroquois cousin terms). However, some terms existed for older and younger biological siblings which were not normally extended to parallel cousins. The most important set of relationships seems to have been between males who were classificatory or biological siblings, as previously mentioned.

From as long ago as anyone could recall until 1950 Napaskiak had a kashgee, which served the same functions as in other aboriginal Kuskowagamiut settlements. In the kashgee, two or three older men who were respected for their wisdom constituted an informal council of elders. Their judgment in any situation was not likely to be challenged nor would the opinions of an important shaman be disregarded. In rare instances of irreconcilable differences between families, the weaker family and its allies would leave the settlement. In 1906 a Russian Orthodox priest visited the community and appointed a representative, who became the first "chief." He appears to have been the head of a large extended family and soon was replaced by his son, for he was an old man at the time of the appointment. The original duty of a chief was to arrange matters pertaining to church affairs, and this obligation has remained one of his most important functions. In 1947 the first elected chief took office. His duties had come to include secular as well as sacred obligations and were confused in the minds of most villagers. Some said that he was the head of the village, but others regarded the Orthodox Church Brotherhood as the collective head of local affairs. The authority of any particular chief seemed to be dependent on his personality. Part of the role confusion resulted from the efforts of the Bureau of Indian Affairs officials to introduce an elected council organization into the village. In 1939, when the first teacher arrived, the Indian Reorganization Act, as extended to Alaska in 1936, was being promoted by the local Indian Affairs personnel. The teacher at Napaskiak attempted to induce the villagers to organize under the terms of the act but never was successful. The villagers did organize an elected council in 1945 but did not request Federal recognition. The ineffectiveness of the council was in part because its members were reluctant to take any overt action against other persons. The major problem dealt with by them was the intoxication of villagers. The usual course of action was to warn the guilty party; on rare occasions, a warrant for the arrest of someone was sworn out with the U.S. Deputy Marshal at Bethel. Meetings also were called to collect funds for village medical needs, to establish a curfew for school children, or to request that the airline offices in Bethel refuse to accept orders for intoxicants from villagers. However, there usually was very little reason for council meetings since little community cohesion existed along secular lines.

One reason for the ineffectiveness of the village council was that the Orthodox Church Brotherhood long had cared for the crisis needs of the community and held monthly meetings to deal with ongoing problems. The general purpose of this organization was to coordinate church activities and to provide welfare aid for members. Because all of the families participated in at least some Orthodox Church functions, and only one family and one other man claimed membership in another church, the welfare provision embraced everyone. The Brotherhood had elected officers with established duties. The specific obligations of its members were to prepare coffins when they were required and to bury the dead; to arrange for the annual trip of the bishop to the area; to aid the aged by providing services, such as obtaining firewood for old men; to maintain the church structure; and to perform certain ceremonial obligations. From the time of its organization in 1931 until just after World War II, the Brotherhood provided food and funds to families without means of support, but this function subsequently was assumed by the Alaska Department of Welfare and the Bureau of Indian Affairs and was no longer a Brotherhood duty in the 1950's.

Warfare was not a part of village life except as it was imposed through the political control of the United States. Early in World War II the Alaska Territorial Guard was organized as a scouting unit for the U. S. Army at a time when an invasion of the mainland of Alaska seemed likely. In the village unit older men were appointed as officers, and the younger ones became enlisted men. There was little military discipline, but there was the wholesale issuance of military equipment which the men were permitted to use daily. Thus real material advantages were to be gained from Alaska Territorial Guard membership. After the war ended, this organization was replaced by the U. S. National Guard, and the policies changed drastically. The older men were not encouraged to re-enlist, especially if they spoke no English. Promising younger men were sent to special training schools, and regular drill sessions became a routine part of membership. The village unit came to reflect military norms and emerged as a disruptive institution in village life, particularly since it encouraged the overt authority of young aggressive men, an unprecedented innovation in village social structure. Younger men regarded the National Guard as romantic, and the yearly two-week encampment near Anchorage was a great adventure.

The older men who remained in the unit did so because of the monetary rewards.

As explained earlier, Christianity was introduced to the Kuskokwim in its Russian Orthodox form, but there is no evidence that any of the priests lingered among the people of the lower river in Russian times. The attempts of the Moravian missionaries to win converts have failed, although they did at one time number among their members a few village families. An Orthodox priest baptized some persons during a visit in 1905, and in the following year a priest and a songleader held services in the kashgee and appointed a village chief. Everyone in the community considered himself to be a Christian, including an old man who was a practicing shaman. Still, the dogma of Orthodoxy was not understood except in a superficial manner. Among the villagers there was considerable variation in what was regarded as proper Christian behavior, but most agreed that helping other people when in need was an important Christian ideal. After an individual died, his soul automatically went to hell if he had not been baptized or if the death resulted from suicide. Otherwise God evaluated a person's deeds during his life, and the spirit was admitted to heaven or hell. At times the ghost of a dead person returned to the community, and to decrease the likelihood of a visitation the windows were opened after death and closed after burial. An icon was hung on the door to prevent the spirit from returning through the doorway. Although a ghost might return if it disapproved of the behavior of someone in its former house, this was not usual, and ghosts were not a great concern to the people.

The cycle of ceremonials duplicated the Orthodox calendar elsewhere in the world. Along with regular church services, special observances were held at Russian Christmas and New Year, the Epiphany, the Easter season, and during the annual church conference. Of far greater importance than any other ceremonial event was the celebration held at Russian Christmas. This time of the year was one of forced inactivity because of the cold weather, and the season was ideal for prolonged ceremonies. The preparations were elaborate, by village standards. The choir practiced Russian Christmas songs in both Russian and Eskimo; the men hauled and chopped enough wood to heat their houses during the holiday season, wine was ordered through an airline, the ceremonial equipment was made ready, and special foods were prepared. Finally, visitors arrived from surrounding communities. The central theme of the three days of processions was to announce the birth of Christ in each household by singing Christmas songs while carrying a guiding star made of metal. Since the performers and the crowd of observers were fed at each house, most of the three nights were taken up with eating vast quantities of food. The Russian New Year was celebrated by putting lighted kerosene lanterns on the graves of the dead, as was done also at Russian Christmas. At about midnight, the Christmas trees which had decorated the houses for the season were burned in front of the village, as fireworks and guns were shot off. The climax of the event was a short service in church; this was mainly a sermon about the ideals of behavior for the coming year.

A woman was expected to conceive soon after she married, and children usually were born when the mother was between the ages of eighteen and forty. It was not uncommon for a wife to have conceived eight to eleven times, but families averaged three children because of the high infant mortality rate. Every couple hoped that their firstborn would be a son; ideally, a woman had two sons who lived and then a daughter or two. Because no effective method of birth control was known, family size was not regulated except by giving males up for adoption if the parents felt that they had enough boys; no one would have considered adopting a girl. In an effort to insure a safe delivery women followed certain rules during a pregnancy. For example, chewing gum was thought to result in a difficult birth, as was standing in a doorway. Women not only obeyed these rules, but they also sought out prenatal care at the Bethel hospital. Delivery took place at home or at the hospital, with hospital births becoming more common each year. About two weeks after birth the newborn was baptized and given an Eskimo and an English name, both of which usually were those of a dead relative but not necessarily the same one. An infant was nursed whenever it cried. Weaning was begun at about six months by more acculturated mothers, but among conservative women it was delayed until the child was three. The first solid foods usually were chewed by the mother, but commercial baby foods were becoming popular. Early toilet training was attempted by some mothers, but not until a child was about two years old were its elimination habits controlled reasonably well. A child walked at about a year but was not expected to talk until it was about two. Village children unquestionably were spoiled by contemporary American standards. They were mildly scolded at times, but it was more common to hold, feed, divert, or simply give in to a small but unhappy child.

Young children most frequently played with individuals of the same sex and age, and favored games were imitations of adult pursuits. There were few toys, but little girls had dolls or jacks while boys had toy guns and trucks. A favorite and almost obsessive pastime of small girls was to tell and illustrate stories. It was more common to see a metal tableknife used for illustrating the stories than the old form of storyknife. Likewise, the stories with plots involving a grandmother and her granddaughter were being replaced by reworked European children's stories which the girls had learned in school. Some effort was made by adults to instill the values of the community into the minds of the children, but the attempts were not systematic. An old person often told stories to informal gatherings of children, and occasionally a church official called the children together and lectured them about proper behavior. One recurring theme was that children should obey their parents. The compulsory school law made it necessary for all children between the ages of six and sixteen to attend school, but progress through the grades was slow because most beginners did not understand English. Commonly, by the time a sixteen-year-old child left school he or she was in the third or fourth grade. The classroom instruction was much the same as that found in elementary schools in the United States, and no attempt was made to adapt the curriculum to Eskimo needs. As a part of school activities special celebrations were held at Halloween, Thanksgiving, and Christmas. At Christmas one pupil dressed as Santa Claus and distributed presents, most of which the students had made, to the assembled villagers.

Adolescents were expected to contribute directly to family welfare by assuming some of the more simple but strenuous physical chores. A young person who worked hard at chopping wood or caring for a younger child was praised, whereas avoiding such responsibilities brought the disapproval of parents. By the time a girl was thirteen she usually was courted by boys who were at least four years older, but since marriages were still arranged by old women and parents, courtship did not lead directly to marital ties. A girl usually was regarded as ready for marriage when she was thirteen or fourteen, but territorial and then state law prohibited marriage before the age of sixteen. Because of school birth records, it was impossible to falsify a girl's age. A girl was expected to accept her parents' decision about whom she married, but a young man voiced his preferences or at least was able to reject someone whom he disliked. If at all possible, parents found mates for their children in the village; when this was impossible it was the girl who moved to another village or, very rarely, to Bethel. A marriage license was obtained from the U. S. Commissioner at Bethel and the ceremony performed in the Russian Orthodox Church. For an initial period after marriage the couple was most likely to live with the husband's parents, and the girl became subordinated to her mother-in-law. The older woman was never very patient with the bride, and some made life most difficult for the young girls. There was no discontinuity in the groom's life; he was likely to continue lounging in a steam bath for many hours with friends and taking frequent trips to Bethel, as he did before marriage. Within a year or two he was expected to be more diligent in providing for the welfare of the household. Sexual freedom before marriage made settling down with one person difficult for both members of the unit, and adultery was the norm during early married life. After a number of children had been born to a couple, they eventually slipped into the routine of adult life, and then the man usually constructed a separate residence near the home of his parents.

The round of subsistence activities at times kept adult males away from the village for as long as six weeks and partly as a result, wives frequently were responsible for household management for extended periods. If a husband prepared for his absences by providing adequate supplies of wood and fish at home and credit at the store, his family was not deprived of what were considered necessities. Some men did not make these provisions, and in cases of deprivation relatives of the couple aided the woman. The comparative freedom of a man was expressed also in the time he devoted to baths. Nearly all men took steam baths, and for most men these lasted hours on end, four or more times a week. The small Russian-style bathhouse had an outer dressing room and an inner steam room; each could accommodate about a dozen persons. There were nine such bathhouses in the community, and certain men bathed together frequently. These structures had in one sense replaced the kashgee as the place in which men relaxed in each other's company. Unlike the kashgees of old, however, women were permitted to bathe in these bathhouses. Sometimes a woman bathed with her husband; only in rare instances would one bathe with any other man. It seemed that the old sexual dichotomy existed still; a woman was primarily responsible for the home, and her husband was something of an outsider. Thus there was a subdued but pervasive individualism which dominated social life. It likewise was reflected in the behavior of old people, both men and women, who frequently lived alone in houses of their own, a pattern facilitated by old age assistance funds.

The village problem considered most critical by the people and government officials alike was health, and tuberculosis was the most dangerous disease by far. Among the 180 permanent residents in 1956, forty-five had active cases of tuberculosis, and unquestionably there were additional cases. Villagers had vague notions about the germ theory of disease but recognized that no one cure was invariably successful. Therefore, in an effort to increase their chance of recovery, they attempted diverse cures for this or any other serious illness. They turned first to patent medicines and the traditional pharmacopoeia, then might take steam baths, consult a shaman, drink holy water or pray in church, and finally turn to the scientific medicine dispensed by the teacher and the Bethel hospital. A major program of tuberculosis control was being implemented largely through a chemotherapy program at the village level by the U. S. Public Health Service.

The most common forms of diversion were steam bathing for males and visiting for females. More formal entertainment with village-wide appeal consisted of motion pictures; these were shown at the Napaskiak school during the winter and at the Oscarville Trading Post during the summer. The favorite motion picture themes were Tarzan, cowboys, and war. Another form of socializing was the consumption of intoxicants, and at one time or another each of the village men had drunk rather heavily. By the 1950's, however, some such persons had become outspoken advocates of abstinence. The nondrinkers usually were outstanding church leaders, but this was not consistently the case. The favorite alcoholic beverages were port or muscatel wine, vodka, and gin. Beer was preferred by some men, but it was expensive to ship in by air and therefore seldom ordered. Men usually drank alone or with a few male friends. About eight individuals became intoxicated every month or two, and a dozen others drank heavily from one to four times a year. Although consumption of alcohol was a concern to some villagers, it did not appear to be a major disruptive force in community life, partially because the drinking most often took place in Bethel. It did result in some deaths by drowning, however.

With the approach of old age, villagers became increasingly independent in their attitudes. They were fond of talking about the past and enjoyed pointing out that the younger generation lacked the vigor of their parents and grandparents. Older persons willingly conceded, however, that life had become much easier and more secure for everyone than when they were young. Old people realized that they might die at any time, and they wanted only to die at home where they knew they would receive a good burial and would always be near their village.

By 1970 Napaskiak had grown considerably as a physical settlement, and yet in many respects it appeared to be much the same as in 1955. The church and National Guard armory were unchanged, but the physical plant of the Bureau of Indian Affairs school had been enlarged. Although a few houses had been torn down and rooms had been added to others, most of them looked as they had fifteen years before. Although the village continued to occupy the same area, the number of houses had increased greatly, which created the most striking contrast with the recent past. Then too there was a new community hall and another building which housed a community well and water storage tank. The old bathhouses had been torn down and replaced with new ones. There were no longer a few decrepit outhouses; behind most houses were new ones of like design but painted white. Fifteen years earlier numerous dogs were tied out behind the houses, and this was still true in 1970 but with the addition of numerous snowmobiles. Other physical changes were more subtle and yet important. Few canvas-covered canoes were to be seen, and most kayaks were falling to pieces from obvious disuse. The people had more plank boats and far more high-powered outboard motors than previously. Within the houses certain changes were quite notable such as the quality of the imported tables and chairs, the factory-made beds, the presence of oil-burning space heaters, as well as the number of expensive radios and clocks. Household inventories were far larger than before and reflected far greater capital investment.

By 1970 the population had grown to 260, and this figure includes only a handful of migrants to the village. The very striking population increase is explained in part by the decline in infant mortality which has enabled more individuals to survive into adulthood. These young people who came from large families have begun to raise large families of their own. In addition, tuberculosis, which was a pervasive killer and crippler in the past, had been eradicated as a result of U. S. Public Health Service efforts. It truly is astounding that the death rate from tuberculosis, which among native Alaskans in 1950 was 653 per 100,000 (compared to 22.5 for all races in the United States), had declined to 3.7 in 1969, and was nonexistent in 1970.

The dramatic population increase was accompanied by greater affluence among the residents. This resulted from two changes: an expanding economic base and more comprehensive welfare programs. The local incomes from trapping, National Guard membership, and work at Bristol Bay area salmon canneries continued, but in addition the wage labor opportunities at Bethel had increased so greatly that numerous persons commuted there to work. Furthermore, by 1970 the Alaska Department of Fish and Game permitted salmon fishing along the lower river. The partial displacement of dogs by snowmobiles meant that fewer salmon were required as dog food, and as a result men sold much of their catch to commercial buyers. Unearned income from government sources continued in 1970, but because of liberalization of welfare aid requirements and the availability of more funds this income was significantly increased. Furthermore, and of real importance, the food stamp program had enabled families to obtain far more adequate food supplies than ever before.

Another change of dramatic dimensions centered around intoxicants; the scope and intensity of drinking had mushroomed. More money was available to buy alcoholic beverages, and they were available from a liquor store and a bar in Bethel. In the 1950's intoxicant consumption was not a major disruptive force in community life, but the same was not true in 1970.

Deaths, usually by drowning, directly attributable to drunkenness were common; by village standards a number of men were alcoholics; and most younger men drank heavily. In the 1950's doors to houses had simple interior locks or just a piece of cord wrapped around a pair of nails on either side of the jam. In 1970 each house had a substantial lock and sometimes solid, and paired, locked doors. In a very real sense houses were familial defensive positions against roaming drunks.

In this general region a number of trends are evidenced. The increasing commitment to a wage labor economy is clear, as is the expanded dependence on unearned income. The Eskimos in this area also have a growing awareness of their political power through regional and statewide organizations of their own creation. The settlement of native Alaskan claims by the U. S. Congress, involving great expanses of land and large sums of money, clearly will improve economic conditions and strengthen the political influence of village Eskimos. These are broadscale changes, but others of importance also are notable. Dog teams are being displaced by the "iron dog" to such an extent that in some settlements there was not a single dog team in 1970. Educational opportunities have expanded greatly, and it is not unusual for a youth to complete high school and attend college. The expectations of younger people contrast with the relative contentment of most parents. For Napaskiakers the lure of Bethel is great, and a growing number of young persons have moved there. Yet most of them hesitate to settle in larger urban centers in Alaska and elsewhere. Their commitment to the village remains, yet it is lessening as their awareness of what lies beyond Napaskiak expands.

References

Anderson, Eva G. *Dog-Team Doctor*. Caldwell. 1940.

Gordon, George B. *In the Alaskan Wilderness*. Philadelphia. 1917.

Johnson, M. Walter. "Tuberculosis in Alaska" (paper presented at the Second International Symposium on Circumpolar Health, Oulu, Finland, 1971).

Nelson, Edward W. *The Eskimo about Bering Strait*. Bureau of American Ethnology, 18th Annual Report, pt. 1. 1899.

*Oswalt, Wendell H. *Napaskiak: An Alaskan Eskimo Community*. Tucson. 1963a. This 1955-1956 study of one Kuskokwim Eskimo community supplies virtually all that we know of contemporary riverine Eskimo life in southwestern Alaska.

*Oswalt, Wendell H. *Mission of Change in Alaska*. San Marino. 1963b. A historical reconstruction, supplemented by the author's field notes, of Kuskokwim Eskimo life, with concentration on the period from 1884 to 1925. Additional summary information is provided on the Russian era and events subsequent to 1925.

Oswalt, Wendell H. "Traditional Storyknife Tales of Yuk Girls," *Proceedings of the American Philosophical Society*, v. 108, no. 4, 310-336. 1964.

*Oswalt, Wendell H., and James W. VanStone. "The Ethnoarcheology of Crow Village, Alaska," *Smithsonian Institution, Bureau of American Ethnology*, Bulletin 199. 1967. The excavation of the Crow Village site, which was occupied by Eskimos from ca. 1830 to 1912, provides insight into the material changes which took place during the Russian and early Anglo-American periods.

Petroff, Ivan. *Report on the Population, Industries, and Resources of Alaska.* United States Department of Interior, Census Office. 1884.

Schwalbe, Anna B. *Dayspring on the Kuskokwim.* Bethlehem. 1951.

Weinland Collection. The William Henry Weinland collection of manuscripts, letters, and diaries. Henry E. Huntington Library, San Marino, California.

Wrangell, Ferdinand von. *Statistical and Ethnographic Data Concerning the Russian Possessions on the Northwest Coast of America.* St. Petersburg. 1839 (in German).

*Zagoskin, Lavrentiy A. *Lieutenant Zagoskin's Travels in Russian America, 1842-1844.* Henry N. Michael, ed., Arctic Institute of North America, Anthropology of the North: Translations from Russian Sources/ No. 7. Toronto. 1967. This early historic Russian traveler's account is the primary source for aboriginal Eskimo life along the Kuskokwim River.

Mojave Desert

PAIUTE

San Gabriel Mts.

SERRANO

San Bernardino Mts.

San Bernardino

San Gabriel
Mission

Los
Angeles

Morongo Res.

San Gorgonio Pass

Cabazon

Palm Springs

CAHUILLA

Long Beach

LUISENO

San Jacinto
Mts.

Palm Springs Res.

Coachella Valley

Santa Rosa Mts.

Chocolate

Santa Rosa Res.

Torres
Martinez
Res.

Santa Rosa Res.

Borrego Valley

Salton Sea

Mts.

Colorado Desert

Colorado R.

ARIZONA

DIEGUENO

Laguna Mts.

KAMIA

Imperial Valley

San Diego

CALIFORNIA

MEXICO

CANADA

U. S.

MEXICO

0   25   50 mi.

Map by J. Donovan

The Cahuilla:
gatherers in the desert

In the beginning, there was no earth or sky or anything or anybody; only a dense darkness in space. This darkness seemed alive. Something like lightnings seemed to pass through it and meet each other once in a while. Two substances which looked like the white of an egg came from these lightnings. They lay side by side in the stomach of the darkness, which resembled a spider web. These substances disappeared. They were then produced again, and again they disappeared. This was called the miscarriage of the darkness. The third time they appeared, they remained, hanging there in this web in the darkness. The substances began to grow and soon were two very large eggs. When they began to hatch, they broke at the top first. Two heads came out, then shoulders, hips, knees, ankles, toes; then the shell was all gone. Two boys had emerged: Mukat and Tamaioit. They were grown men from the first, and could talk right away. As they lay there, both at the same time heard a noise like a bee buzzing. It was the song of their mother Darkness (Hooper, 1920, 317).

With this great event the natural world began to emerge as an orderly system; at least this was said to be so by the Iviatim, the descendants of Mukat and Tamaioit who have come to be known in the ethnographic literature as the Cahuilla (Coahuillas, Kawia).

Once the twin creators existed, Mukat reached into his mouth and then into his heart to remove a cricket, another insect, a lizard, and a person. These creatures were charged with driving away the darkness, but they failed. From their hearts the creators removed tobacco, pipes, and a coal to light one pipe. Mukat and Tamaioit argued over which one was born first and which was the more intelligent. Mukat became associated with making things black, and Tamaioit made forms that were white. Together they created the earth, ocean, sun, moon, people, and some plants and animals. Finally Mukat and Tamaioit disagreed so violently that Tamaioit disappeared beneath the ground, taking with him many of his creations. It was then that mountains emerged, the earth quaked, and water from the ocean overflowed, forming streams and rivers. After this Mukat lived in a big house with people and animals who had human qualities. The moon was there as a lovely female who instructed women about marriage, child rearing, and both menstrual and pregnancy taboos. Mukat, who had created her, desired to make the moon his wife. She knew this but said nothing. Since she could not marry him because he was her father, she traveled to her present home in the sky. When she was asked to return, she said nothing; she only smiled. One day, while in a humorous mood, Mukat caused the people to speak different languages. As the sun grew hot, some of these people sought shelter and were transformed into different plants and animals. Those who had stayed with Mukat remained human. He told the people how to make bows and arrows and how to shoot at each other, which led to the first deaths. It was about this time, too, that the sun turned people different colors. Those people who were nearest the sun's rays became Negroes, those that were far away stayed white, and the Indians turned brown because they were in between.

The people became angry with Mukat after he had caused a rattlesnake to bite a friendly little man, the moon woman to leave, and people to kill one another. They decided to kill Mukat but did not know how to do it. Mukat lived in the middle of the big house and only went outside to defecate when everyone was asleep; this a white lizard discovered. One night a frog caught the feces of Mukat in his mouth, and Mukat grew ill. The shamans pretended to try to cure him, but Mukat became sicker. As he was dying, he sang songs and told the people how to conduct a mourning ceremony in memory of the dead each year. After his death, Mukat was cremated, the big house was burned, and the essence of the world was established.

The Cahuilla lived, and continue to live, in an interior region of southern California. They possibly numbered about 2500 at the time of early historic contact. By 1885 their number had declined to about 800, and it remained at this level for some sixty years. In the early 1960's the 530 who retained their identity as Cahuilla were divided into three groups: the Desert Cahuilla of the Torres-Martinez Reservation, about 225, and Palm Springs Reservation, 100; the Pass Cahuilla of the Morongo Reservation, 120; and the Mountain Cahuilla of the Cahuilla and Santa Rosa reservations, 85. Not all of these people lived on their respective reservations in the 1960's, but they were on the tribal roles and claimed Cahuilla affinities. A sense of tribal identity probably did not exist in aboriginal times but emerged later under Mexican-American and Anglo-American influences. There did exist among the Cahuilla in the early period of contact a sense of local identity which was reflected in the Pass, Mountain, and Desert groupings. Their region is within the Sonoran biotic province, but there is considerable ecological diversity among these sectors. According to tradition their original homeland was in the desert, but they were forced into the San Jacinto and Santa Rosa mountains by a great flood. This is a region of steep granite ridges and barren tablelands at the medium elevations, but at higher elevations are streams, open meadows, and forests of oak and pine. The Desert Cahuilla moved into the Coachella basin after the flood, according to tradition. The flood probably formed the sea which covered much of the present desert lowland until some 500 years ago. The desert area supports arid vegetation, which includes various forms of cacti, mesquite, agave, and screw beans as economically important plants. This is a region with very little precipitation, and settlements were located around excavated wells, water holes, or streams at the base of the San Jacinto Mountains. The desert in the summertime is extremely hot, with temperatures as high as 120°F. Although it seldom rains, precipitation, when it comes, is often torrential and causes widespread erosion. Furthermore, severe duststorms may whip across the valley. Some sectors, particularly in the eastern part of the Desert Cahuilla range, are devoid of vegetation. The Pass Cahuilla occupied the country surrounding San Gorgonio Pass, where open grassland and some oak groves were found as well as desert areas.

The Desert subtribe is a striking example of adaptation to an extremely arid sector of America. For these people we have the fine ethnobotany by David P. Barrows and additional ethnographic information collected around the turn of the present century by Alfred L. Kroeber and Lucile Hooper. There was virtually no anthropological interest in these people from 1925 until 1959 when Lowell J. Bean began working among them. Bean has emerged as a ranking authority on the Cahuilla. However, not only anthropologists have a vested interest in these people; they have become significant to journalists, lawyers, farmers, land speculators, Bureau of Indian Affairs employees, congressmen, and municipal officials, particularly those in and around the resort center of Palm Springs. The concern is for the most part clearly neither philanthropic nor humanistic but monetary, for certain reservation lands are of fantastic value. The situation is ironic because so few Indians are involved. Thus a study of the Desert Cahuilla affords an excellent opportunity to consider in detail the relations of a now-prosperous Indian group with the greater Anglo-American society which surrounds them. It is customary to think that the old policy of grabbing Indian lands is a chapter in American history that is not only past but best forgotten; however, the Cahuilla example clearly demonstrates that Anglo-Americans have not changed their course of action, simply their methods. All of this is particularly interesting when it is realized that among the Palm Springs Cahuilla it was the women who dealt most efficiently with land problems. These people had until recently the only Indian tribal council composed exclusively of women. The Cahuilla manifest many other characteristics that make them appropriate for consideration, not the least of which is their thoroughgoing romantic appeal. The once fabulously popular novel *Ramona* was about the life of a Cahuilla woman, and its writer, Helen H. Jackson, was to play a significant role in the lives of southern Californian Indians just before the turn of the century.

In the following discussion of the Cahuilla the major stress is on the aboriginal lifeway of the Desert and Palm Springs (Agua Caliente) Cahuilla. In drawing from ethnographic sources it was not always possible to establish the specific group of Cahuilla discussed, however. Like the vast majority of ethnographic reconstructions, the descriptions to follow do not apply in every detail to any single community but rather represent the people in a general area.

The Aztec-Tanoan linguistic phylum, which is represented widely in the western United States and Mexico, includes Cahuilla. These Indians belong to the Uto-Aztecan language family. The emergence of the Cahuilla as a separate people is revealed through linguistic rather than archaeological researches. Unfortunately, no archaeological sites have been excavated and published on to provide clues to their past. Linguists, however, do offer some insight into the past affinities of these people. Kenneth Hale, after analyzing the vocabularies of certain Aztec-Tanoan languages, concluded on lexicostatistical grounds that the Cahuilla became a separate linguistic group about 1000 B.C.

In aboriginal times clothing seems to have been nonexistent, although it is possible that the women wore short skirts of plant fiber and the men wore breechclouts. A more certain item of apparel was their footwear, which consisted of sandals made from mescal fiber pads. Women sometimes wore ill-fitting, flat-topped caps made of coiled basketry. Women were tattooed on the chin, and certain men, most likely leaders, had their nasal septums pierced and inserted a deer bone in the opening. Both males and females wore strings of beads in their pierced earlobes. The beads were thin curved and circular pieces of shell received in trade from the coastal regions of southern California.

The settlements of the Desert Cahuilla were clustered around hand-dug wells and water holes, whereas the Palm Springs people lived near the permanently flowing streams in Andreas, Palm, and Murray canyons at the base of the San Jacinto Mountains. Communities were permanent so long as the local water supply was lasting. At each corner of their rectangular houses were forked posts of mesquite on which roof beams rested. Along the sides, except at the entrance, and on the top of the beam were placed lengths of brush which were held in place with horizontal poles. On some houses the brush was smeared with a covering of mud, and a layer of dirt was added to the roof. Attached to the front of a house was a ramada which was constructed like a house but with open sides in all but the windward direction. Another structure found in a community was a rectangular sweathouse built in a shallow excavated area. Two vertical forked posts were set toward the middle along the longer sides and a beam was fitted into the crotch of the forks. On this frame poles were laid from the beam to the ground level, with a space left for an entry on one of the longer sides. Over the structure probably was placed brush and then earth. The fireplace was between the posts, and the smoke escaped out the doorway. In each settlement there also were caches of a distinctive form for the storage of plant products. These usually were raised above the ground on a pole platform topped by small branches intertwined in successively smaller circles. The finished product looked very much like a bird's nest some two to four feet in height. The only other structures were a brush enclosure used for certain ceremonies and a large enclosure, walled on three sides and attached to the house of a sib leader. Among the Palm Springs Cahuilla the *net*, or social and ceremonial leader, occupied his sib's dance house, which in 1925 was about forty feet in diameter with walls of fitted boards and a palm-thatched roof. At the back was a room in which the sacred sib bundle was kept; in front of the structure was a fenced enclosure.

Artifacts made from plant fibers were the most numerous manufactured items. Basketry was constructed by using one species of grass for the warp and either reedgrass or sumac for the weft. If a design was to be woven into a basket, the most common color employed was black. The dye was made by soaking the stems of elders in water. A basket usually was coiled around a multiple foundation, and a wide variety of forms were produced for diverse purposes. Apart from the hats made for women there were flat circular trays and one for food or seeds which had a flat bottom and slightly flaring sides about eight inches in height; a larger variety of the preceding type was used with a carrying net. Small globular baskets served as receptacles for utensils and diverse small items. The designs woven into all the basket types except the globular form included encircling bands or zigzags, a series of short stripes, rectangles, triangles, or stepped elements. If the design was in two colors, black usually was combined with red or dull yellow. The small globular baskets, which always seem to have been decorated, had vertically patterned designs. Furthermore, these baskets were coiled counterclockwise, whereas all other forms were coiled clockwise. In addition to coiled baskets the Cahuilla made twined baskets, but these vessels were of little importance. One such form was a shallow, rounded basket with an unspecified use. A jug-shaped twined basket, covered with asphaltum, may have been made, but it is not certain that this was an item of Cahuilla manufacture. A net for carrying baskets was like a small hammock and was made from the mescal fiber. At each end was a loop, and from one loop was attached a cinching cord. The cord passed over the forehead of the woman carrying it and rested against her basket hat.

The next major cluster of artifacts were made from stone, but in comparison with basketry, stonework was less elaborate. Peoples the world over who collect plant products usually employ a set of stones to prepare seeds which in unprocessed form would be indigestible. A flat or slightly concave stone on which seeds were spread is called a milling stone, quern, or metate; the smaller pulverizing or grinding stone is called a hand stone or mano. A second means for preparing seeds was to crush them with a stone pestle as the seeds rested in a stone mortar. At least some women had one or more bedrock mortars at an oak grove where they collected and processed acorns. Another object of stone was a block of soapstone (steatite) with a groove along one surface. Apparently the stone was heated, and a cane arrow shaft was straightened by fitting it into the groove. One additional type made of stone and owned by certain Desert Cahuilla sibs, was a sacred pipe, but the details of its form are unrecorded.

Indians of California normally were not pottery makers, but the Cahuilla are among the exceptional peoples in the southern part of the state who made it. Pottery was not extremely important, for basketry served most of the functions pottery fulfilled elsewhere. The vessels were constructed by building up the sides from rope-shaped bands of moist clay. The inside of a damp vessel was smoothed with a stone, and the outside was flattened with a wooden paddle. The vessels were fired in an oxidizing atmosphere, and the finished product was a thin, rather brittle, red ware. Only red paint, probably hematite, was used for making surface designs, which were similar to styles known among the Mohave. The vessel forms included round-bottomed pots with narrow necks for water, a widemouthed, round-bottomed type for cooking, and dishes with flat bottoms.

Entering an aboriginal house, an observer would have been impressed with its relative coolness even in the hottest weather. The inside was dark from the soot on the walls, and natural light filtered in only through the doorway. On one side of the entrance stood the woman's food grinding stones, covered with a mat when they were not in use. On the other side of the doorway was a pottery water container which was filled each morning. Toward the center of the room fire-blackened cooking pots encircled the fireplace; at the back of the house were blankets and animal skins which served as mattresses. Attached to the roof beams or in the thatch were bundles of plants or dry meat for future use.

Somewhere near every house a section of log was set vertically into the ground; the top was flat and the center was hollowed out a foot or more in depth. A smooth pole some two feet in length served as the pestle for this mortar. This combination was designed to pulverize mesquite beans, which were an important item in the diet. Other manufactures of wood included a bow made from a shaft some four feet in length (self bow); the bowstring was made from plant fiber or sinew. The arrows were about three feet in length and were vaned with two split and twisted feathers. One form of arrow shaft, made from wormwood, simply was sharpened to a point and probably was used against small game. The second form had a cane shaft and a wooden arrowpoint bound in place with sinew. Apparently the latter type arrow was used against large game and enemies. Another weapon of wood was the nonreturning boomerang, commonly called a throwing stick when reported in western North America. It was a flat, curved piece of wood thrown at small game such as birds or rabbits.

The economy was based much more on plant collecting than on any other form of subsistence activity. The hunting practices which did exist, however, were surrounded by numerous restrictions. For example, among the Desert Cahuilla the mountain lion and grizzly bear were considered as shamans. If at all possible the people avoided killing these animals. In one recorded instance in which a mountain lion was killed, the claws were made into a dog collar and the skin kept to decorate images used in the Mourning Ceremony. It was said that only young men hunted, and before a hunt they observed food taboos and restricted their consumption of water. When a mule deer was killed, the usual custom was to take it to the dwelling of the net; here the people gathered to sing all night and eat the deer the following morning. In general, a man or boy did not consume any of the animals that he killed. Rabbits, squirrels, and other small game taken by a young boy in a communal hunt usually were given to his mother's family. The kills of an adult male were given alternately to his own family and to his wife's family.

The only domestic animal, the dog, does not appear to have been important as an aid in hunting, but served as a pet and a watchdog. The dog was not an ordinary pet, for it possessed certain supernatural powers. Dogs could understand human conversation but could not speak, and like people, they had souls. At the time of Mukat's death, the people had only one dog, and among some twentieth-century Desert Cahuilla, dogs still were named after the first dog. Other dog names referred to their appearance or to some behavioral characteristic.

These people recognized three major seasons: the budding of trees, hot days, and cold days. Some persons divided the year into eight more specific seasons, each of which was associated with the development of mesquite beans. Another calendar based on thirteen months was lunar, but probably was less important than the one marking mesquite development. In order to predict the beginning of a season, old men gathered in a dance house and discussed when a particular star would appear. When the star was seen, they rejoiced and prepared for the collecting activities to follow. These observations were particularly important in the spring when stores of food were low and edible plants were ripening in the mountains.

The most important food plant of the Desert Cahuilla was the mesquite tree, which grew in groves found anywhere between the desert floor and heights of up to 3500 feet in better-watered areas. Stands were particularly numerous near springs or streams and in washes. In the early summer the blossoms were picked, roasted in a pit of heated stones, formed into balls, and stored in pottery containers; later the balls were boiled in water and eaten. Mesquite beans ripened from June through August, depending on the locality. At this time, or even earlier if unripe pods were to be artificially ripened in the sun, they were picked by entire families. Children helped by climbing the trees to dislodge pods from high branches. The pods were not gathered indiscriminately, for the beans of some trees were regarded as more palatable than those from others. The pods could be stored from one year to the next, which may have been necessary on occasion, since the trees of a particular grove were not necessarily as productive each year. The ripened pods were crushed in an upright wooden mortar with a stone or wooden pestle, and the juice was made into a beverage. The pods might be ripened artificially, picked ripe, or gathered after they had fallen from the trees. The dried pods, either complete or broken into small sections, were stored in raised caches made of brush on top of a raised pole framework. Further processing included grinding the pods in a mortar or on a milling stone. The meal then could be placed in pottery or basketry containers and moistened; when it had dried, the cake of meal was removed and stored in the rafters of a house. Sections of the cakes were broken off and eaten as a snack or carried by travelers as food. The meal could also be made into a gruel or soaked in water to make the mesquite juice beverage. Loose ground meal was stored in pottery or basketry containers to be made into gruel later.

The mesquite bean was the most important staple, but the people of the desert areas also ate screw beans. The screw bean or tornillo grew under the same general conditions as the mesquite and was processed in the same manner as mesquite pods. In ethnographic studies of Californian Indians acorns are often specified as an important staple. This clearly was the case over much of the state, but the acorn was not as important among the Cahuilla as among many other aboriginal groups. Of the four varieties available, the acorn from the Kellogs oak was preferred for its taste and consistency. As was true with the mesquite beans, when the first acorns were collected, they were eaten ceremonially in the home of the net. If an individual collected acorns prior to this ceremony, he was expected to become ill or to die. In the sib-controlled groves, each family owned particular trees, and from October to November, families visited their trees, which the men climbed to knock ripe acorns to the ground. Women removed the shells after cracking the acorns between two stones; they spread the kernels out to dry for several weeks and then pulverized them in stone mortars. In order to remove the bitter tannic acid from the meal it was spread out on a loosely woven basket or in a depression in the sand. In either case grass or leaves were placed in the leaching basin to prevent the meal from washing away. Then water, either cold or warm, was poured over the meal several times; during this process the mixture was stirred. The capabilities of a woman were measured by her skill in leaching and grinding acorn meal. Finely ground meal was made into cakes and baked in hot coals, while coarse meal was made into a gruel. Acorns which were not ground at the time they were gathered were stored in raised platform caches.

David P. Barrows recorded the use of over sixty plants for subsistence, with the mesquite and screw bean serving as the most important staples. In well-watered localities grew a species of *Chenopodium* which locally was called careless weed. The seeds from this plant were collected, ground, and baked in cakes. One of the most important seed-producing grasses was chia, a member of the sage family. Its seeds were dislodged from the whorls with a seed beater onto a flat basket. They were parched and ground to be baked into cakes or mixed with water to make a nourishing drink. When the century plants or agave of the canyons produced stalks, the stalks and "cabbages" were roasted in sand pits heated with stones. The hillsides and sandy canyons were visited when yucca produced fruit, which was picked while green and roasted among coals. Fruit which had ripened on the stalk was consumed raw. The ocotillo, which grows near the base of the San Jacinto Mountains, is a desert shrub with thorny branches and bright red flowers produced in clusters. After the flowers had wilted, oblong capsules remained filled with seeds. The blossoms as well as the seed pods were eaten. The wild plum trees growing along the canyons produced fruit with little pulp but a large pit. Plums were dried in the sun, and then the pits were broken open. The kernels were removed, crushed, leached, and cooked as gruel. The berries of elders were collected and dried. Before being consumed the berries were cooked into a thick sauce. To this listing could be added many other plants, but the enumerated species and their utilization provide a gauge to the range of plants collected and the varied methods of food preparation.

Desert Cahuilla social life was sustained by water, for it was only around wells and water holes that communities could develop. A typical settlement was socially conceived around a group of males who traced their descent to a known common ancestor (patrilineage). Closely related patrilineages with a presumed common ancestor comprised a larger unit (patrisib), which was the most important social and ceremonial grouping. Thus these people traced their descent along the male line (patrilineal), and a married couple resided with or near the husband's family (patrilocal residence). In 1924-1925 the anthropologist William D. Strong attempted with the aid of an old Desert Cahuilla informant to reconstruct the disposition of the sibs for the period around 1870. This era, although not aboriginal, possibly reflected the patterning of settlements before the creation of reservations.

In primeval times Mukat was associated with the wildcat and Tamaioit with the coyote. These became moiety divisions, and each sib was identified with either the wildcat or the coyote moiety. The Wildcat moiety contained eight or perhaps nine named sibs, and two of these included separate named patrilineages. The sibs of the Coyote moiety numbered ten, and two contained separate named patrilineages. Theoretically, in aboriginal times each sib occupied a single settlement, but with the passage of time and an increase in numbers some sibs moved to other villages where they emerged as named lineages. These might eventually acquire the standing of a separate sib, but full identification as a sib was achieved only when the group had its own leader or net. The Desert Cahuilla community of Touched by the River, for example, existed before 1880 at an artificial well with a nearby mesquite grove. The village took its name from the name of the first sib to settle there. These people were of the Coyote moiety and traced their earlier residence to the Santa Rosa Mountains. The next sib to settle by the well, the Dogs, belonged to the Wildcat moiety and also came from the Santa Rosa Mountains. With the Dogs came the Wantcinakiktum people, who derived their name from a Santa Rosa mountain. These people were subordinate to the Dogs, for they had no net of their own. The Wantcinakiktum was once an independent sib, but apparently the members decreased in number or moved apart.

In the Touched by the River village the members of the original sib occupied seven small nuclear family households. When the leader of the sib died, presumably his elder son did not possess the necessary qualities to serve as leader, and a younger son was chosen by the sib members to succeed the father as the net. The house of the net, unlike all the others of the sib, had a dance house attached to it. The living arrangements of the Dogs were different, for they occupied two large houses containing extended families. The eldest son succeeded his father as net in the one known instance; this was the ideal form of succession. Like the Touched by the River sib the Dog net had a dance house appended to his residence.

The Wantcinakiktum lived in four nuclear family households and were very poor, seemingly quite dependent on the Dogs for much of their food. Since they had no net of their own, they were responsible to the net of the Dogs. Each sib ranged out of the relatively permanent community to collect on its own lands; for example, the Touched by the River sib owned a nearby foothill area where there were groves of mesquite and cacti in the canyons. The Dogs collected on their ancestral lands in the Santa Rosa Mountains over an area shared with another sib. Each spring when they moved with the other sib to the mountains, they did so under the leadership of the oldest net of the two sibs. The Dogs additionally collected from scattered groves of mesquite which were near a village they had occupied on the desert. The Wantcinakiktum collected in the desert area used by the Dogs and also in a canyon area in the Santa Rosa Mountains. The people of any sib were free to hunt mountain sheep, mule deer, rabbits, or other game on the collecting territory of any other sib.

The major social division among the Desert Cahuilla was along moiety lines. The Coyotes and Wildcats were prohibited from marrying each other (moiety exogamy). It is interesting to note that all animals were regarded as having a moiety affinity in the same manner as human beings. When the songs of a sib were sung, birds were mentioned which belonged to the moiety of that sib, and this established the singers' affiliations. The evidence of whether or not members of the opposite moiety aided in certain ceremonies for the dead is contradictory, but this problem will be discussed later. The members of the moieties did, however, joke with one another in a friendly, not malicious, relationship.

Hereditary leadership among the Desert Cahuilla did not extend above the sib level, and in instances where the activities of one sib impinged on those of another the differences were resolved by the nets in council. Decisions of a sib as a collectivity were made by the net, who ideally was a man of exceptional abilities. A net was required to know the boundaries of all sib lands, all sib traditions, and a broad range of esoteric facts important to the sib's viability; he also was expected to be a good orator and fair minded. He did not possess more material property than anyone else, but families presented him with the first fruit of any plant harvest, which was partial compensation for the time he devoted to sib activities. At the rear of the net's house was a small room, and here in a rolled mat of tules were kept sacred objects and ceremonial paraphernalia of the sib. Included in at least some of the sibs' sacred bundles were stone pipes, and in the bundles of all were eagle feathers. One particular bundle held eagle feathers, part of an eagle skin, and an eagle feather kilt. Clearly the net, as guardian of the most sacred sib objects, which collectively were termed the "heart" of the sib, was the most important ceremonial specialist. This led to his importance as a social leader as well. The theory of passing the office from eldest son to eldest son (primogeniture) had obvious advantages, for a potential net was required to acquire a great deal of knowledge about his sib.

A woman retained the names of the sib of her birth and that of her patrilineage as well if the sib were divided into a number of lineages. In time, however, she became associated ceremonially with the sib of her husband. The strength of her ceremonial ties with her personal sib depended on how far she was from its community center. She appears to have been excluded from the more esoteric ceremonial activities of her husband's sib, yet older women participated in at least some such activities.

Other more specialized officeholders among the Desert Cahuilla included the *paha*. His role existed only in certain localities, and his functions are obscure and of uncertain dimensions. When the office was known, however, the individual who filled it was powerful and feared. His prime duty was to make the preparations for ceremonies and to maintain order on such occasions. It seems that he may have performed his duties for a sib of the opposite moiety. Upon his death he was replaced by his son or another near male relative. The only other leader of importance was the shaman. This status was not hereditary among the Desert people, nor was there any limit on the number of shamans in a particular sib. Shamans often had been ill a great deal as children and had required the treatment of a medicine man, who became aware of the child's potential as a curer, magician, and seer. As a young man a novice dreamed of a song which became a tangible manifestation of his inordinate powers. It was Mukat, one of the twin creators and culture heroes, who conveyed the dreams and the association with a guardian spirit. Next the youth danced before the people of his sib in the dance house for three nights; after this he was known as a shaman. In time he learned other songs, dances, feats of magic, and bewitching methods, all through his dreams. In his dreams, too, a shaman learned of specific herbal cures for particular ailments, while at other times "spells" which were harmful or curative were revealed to him. When not drawing from his pharmacopoeia, he attempted a cure by sucking on the afflicted part of a patient's body. Reputedly he removed the disease object without breaking the skin. When plant products were employed, they usually were applied externally, such as putting golderino weed on a snake bite or an unspecified plant product on the bite of a poisonous spider. Only a few plants were recorded as having been used in curing, which is in contrast with the extensive knowledge of them and their diverse uses as foods. Certain animals, birds, and insects, such as the coyote, fox, owl, hummingbird, and fly, were messengers for shamans; they brought warnings of impending illness. As a shaman succeeded in his calling, his reputation increased. While a youth, he did not accept material rewards for his cures, but as he grew older he charged for his services. If a shaman became malevolent in the use of his spirit powers, he was a threat to the security of the community, and in some instances such individuals were killed by common agreement.

A net in the Palm Springs area had greater power by far than in surrounding localities. People obeyed his decisions because they feared his abilities to cause illness or even death by manipulation of the objects in the sacred sib bundles. The paha, as an important official, was known from the beginning of the world according to the Palm Springs area people, and he served as an assistant to the net in all of the latter's activities. A paha kept order at sib functions, saw to it that each family provided food enough for ceremonies, and was the net's messenger. The manner in which the Palm Springs Cahuilla differed from the others is cited in order to stress that behavioral differences of considerable significance may exist among the segments of a "tribe."

The major religious activity which did not have to do with the life cycle of an individual was the Eagle Killing Ceremony. The mountainous lands of some sibs included locations favored by eagles, and their nests were watched carefully. A guard was posted to observe the nest from a vantage point, and when eggs were laid the sib was notified and a feast was held. When the eaglets were well-feathered, the sib net, regarded as their owner, sent men to retrieve one or more of the nestlings. A captured eaglet was caged in the net's house and fed by his family. When it attained full plumage, the neighboring sib or sibs were notified and the ceremony planned. When all had assembled, the members of a guest sib sang special songs throughout the night concerning the death of eagles. They were joined in their song and the accompanying dances by the entire audience. Next the eagle was removed from its cage and rolled into the sib's ceremonial mat, and it was held by the net's nuclear family members as they danced in a circle. With the dawn the eagle screeched and died, probably from being squeezed gradually. The body of the bird was placed by the fire, and the people wailed to lament its death. After the sun had risen, the eagle was skinned. The net kept the feathered skin; the body most likely was burned. The skin was rubbed soft and placed in the sacred bundle. Some feathers might be made into a ceremonial skirt, and others were set aside for adorning images in the Mourning Ceremony.

When the members of different sibs assembled, especially when a girl was to be tattooed or a boy's nasal septum was to be pierced, songs known as "enemy songs" might be sung. Between certain sibs, usually those which were geographically distant from one another, there was a rivalry of unknown origins. Members of the competing sibs originated songs into which they incorporated the names of persons in the rival sibs. These names were the personal ones bestowed by a net ceremonially and secretly. The fact that they had been learned by members of other sibs was shameful, and the songs into which they were incorporated were derisive. The performance was by first one sib and then the other, and the dubious victory went either to the side mentioning the most names of rivals and heaping the greatest abuse or else to the sib whose members were physically able to sing longer than the other side.

The enemy songs were an obvious means for giving vent to aggressive behavior in a socially approved manner. The joking relationship between moiety members served the same function in a friendlier atmosphere. From the literature it is evident that serious, overt ingroup hostility was rare, but petty quarrels were rather common. It would seem that the nets had rather firm control over those persons responsible to them, and quarrels between members of different sibs were handled by the nets of the sibs involved. On occasion an individual did emerge who was a threat to ingroup harmony. Such a person usually was a malevolent shaman. One example illustrates the course of events and action in such a situation. In the latter part of the nineteenth century one old man was considered to be the world's most powerful shaman. This was proved by the fact that when the shamans gave an exhibition of their abilities, he always performed last and challenged the others to kill him. None was able to do so because he was protected by spirits on all sides. Finally the old shaman was told by a man of a different sib to stop killing people. The man who gave the warning was soon struck by a "pain" which none of the shamans consulted could remove, and he died. Everyone knew that the old shaman was responsible. A man from the shaman's sib and men from other sibs met and decided that he must be killed. It was decided that the net of another sib should be the executioner since he was both strong and brave. This man and a shaman from yet another sib visited the old shaman and were invited to spend the night. They did so, and after everyone else was asleep, the net crushed the old man's skull with a stone pestle. At the head of the victim's bed were found a variety of small feathers and the skin of a gopher snake. It was these items that the old man had made into pains. As they were trampled into the ground, a thunder-like sound was heard. In the morning people came to view the body, and later the same morning the body and the house were burned. This case is one of the rare recorded instances in which collective sib action was taken for the good of all the people.

Formalized warfare or even feuds with neighboring ethnic groups were rare. To the east was a desert area with no permanent occupants until the Colorado River was reached, where the aggressive and warlike Yuma lived. The Cahuilla feared the Yuma, but the intervening desert was an effective barrier to intensive contact. The Chemehuevi who lived to the east along the Colorado River and into the deserts of California were quite friendly with the Desert Cahuilla. The southern neighbors of the Desert Cahuilla were the Yuman-speaking Kamia, but the dimension of intercourse with these people has not been reported upon and is assumed to have been relatively unimportant.

In the kinship terminology a male Ego distinguished among his older and younger male and female siblings, and in the first ascending generation he made similar distinctions between his father's brothers and mother's sisters. He employed still other terms for his father's sisters and mother's brothers; these did not take relative age into consideration. A male Ego referred to his father's older brother's and his mother's older sister's son and daughter by the same term as his older brothers and sisters. Similarly, the son and daughter of his father's younger brother and mother's younger sister were referred to by the same terms as his younger brothers and sisters. In essence parallel cousins (father's brother's and mother's sister's children) were termed the same as siblings, with the same age distinction as for siblings. For cross-cousins (father's sister's and mother's brother's children) the male-female kin terms were the same but different from those for siblings or parallel cousins. This cousin terminology is of the Iroquois

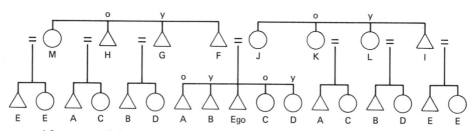

Aboriginal Cahuilla kin terms. Each capital letter represents a different term; o indicates older than Ego or Ego's parents and y indicates younger than Ego or Ego's parents.

type, while the terms on the first ascending generation are bifurcate collateral. The Iroquois cousin terms make particular sense since moiety exogamy existed. Thus certain near relatives, such as father's brother's

children and mother's sister's children, were of one's own moiety and reasonably called brother and sister. Parallel cousins on the other hand were
of a different moiety and termed differently, but in spite of the terminological difference one could not marry such a person.

Of all the forms of diversion probably the most important was the game
of *peon*. It was played avidly at the Mourning Ceremony, at other ceremonial events, and at secular gatherings. George H. Shinn, who knew the
Cahuilla rather well in the late 1880's, described the game as he saw it
played among the Desert people. A team from one village played against
one from another settlement; perhaps it was one sib against another. Shamans aided their respective sides, while women sat behind the men of their
team and sang at certain times during the game. One person was assigned
the role of mediator, and it was his duty to keep a fire burning by which
the game was played, to hold the stakes, settle disputes, and take charge
of the tally sticks. The game was played by eight men, four to a side, who
knelt or sat cross-legged with a blanket between them. Lots were drawn
to determine which side would first have the peons in hand. A peon was
a small bone tied to a string about two feet long; at the opposite end of
the string was a small piece of wood. Each man on the starting team held
a stick in one hand and a peon in the other and crossed his arms with
his fists beneath his armpits. These men then took the blanket, probably
a skin in aboriginal times, in their teeth to hide the manipulation of their
hands from view. They swayed from side to side in time with the singing
of the women on their side, switched the peons back and forth, and then
suddenly dropped the blanket from their teeth, revealing their arms still
crossed and fists beneath their armpits. They continued swaying, and their
opposites attempted to guess which hand held the peon. For every correct
guess the second team took the peon, but with each incorrect guess the
first team received one of the fifteen tallies. A particular game ended when
one side had lost all four peons or had won all of the tallies. Then a new
game was started and new stakes put up. Peon was played frequently
throughout the night, and as one player tired he was replaced by another.

Other games included races between two groups of men. A wooden ball
was kicked for several miles and then back again to the starting point.
The men on each team took turns kicking the ball, and the team which
finished first was the winner. Another race took place on the night of a
new moon. The first boy to see the moon would call the others, and they
would race to water where they could swim. After swimming they then
raced home, and by so doing they would bring good luck in the coming
month. Cat's cradles were made by persons of both sexes. This skill had

supernatural implications since before a person's spirit could pass into the world of other spirits, it was required to demonstrate ability to make string figures.

The course of an individual's life from womb to tomb was surrounded at critical times with numerous prohibitions. One of these periods was pregnancy. The potential mother refrained from eating any more than necessary; she drank only warm water, ate very little meat, and consumed no salt. If a pregnant woman ate fruit pecked by a bird, her infant would have sores; if she ate meat from the legs of game, a breech presentation would result; but if she was industrious when pregnant, her offspring would be energetic. These are but three of the specific rules to insure a safe delivery and a normal offspring. When a woman gave birth, she was in a sitting position. As soon as she had dispelled the placenta, she lay in a specially prepared trough dug into the floor of the house. This depression was lined with sand which had been heated with stones, and after the woman stretched out, additional hot sand was piled over her body. Here she remained for about ten days, leaving the trough only to urinate and defecate, to have the sand reheated, and to be bathed with hot water each morning. During the month following parturition the mother remained subject to food taboos, and the father could eat no foods containing salt. A nursing mother did not have sexual intercourse with her husband, for to do so was thought to spoil the mother's milk, and a woman was teased if she weaned her infant early.

An offspring was not named formally until several children had been born into the sib and each child's parents had accumulated an abundance of food and wealth for a feast. This meant that a child was between the ages of four and twelve before it received its name. If a child had not been named formally by the time he was thirteen, he would have only nicknames throughout his life. The naming ceremony was held in the sib dance house, and the members of the father's and the mother's sibs were invited. The participating children received traditional sib names of deceased ancestors selected by the sib net. The names for males tended to be those of animals, birds, or insects, and those for females were most often from plants or household artifacts. The climax of the ceremonial dancing and singing occurred when the net held each child up and shouted its name three times, after which the name was repeated by the audience. Sometimes a net would not state the real name for fear an "enemy" sib would learn of it and incorporate it into their songs. In this case the correct name was revealed in secret. The father also might acquire a new name at this ceremony and in the process gain additional standing. Following the naming ritual, presents such as food, baskets, a deerskin, and even ceremonial equipment were distributed to the guests. With the presentation of gifts the ceremony was concluded.

As a Desert girl approached adolescence, she was tattooed by her mother's sister, and other persons in the operator's sib came as guests. The tattoos were made by using a cactus thorn to prick straight or angled lines from the lower lip to the chin of the girl. Into the openings was rubbed a black paint obtained in trade from the Yuma Indians. At this time the earlobes of the girl were pierced. When a girl menstruated for the first time, the net summoned the sib of the girl's mother to a ceremony which began that evening. A fire was built before the net's house to heat the ground. After it was hot a trough was dug, the girl was placed in it, and her body was covered with hot sand. Throughout the night the members of the girl's sib danced and sang around the pit. In the morning the girl was removed, bathed in warm water, and her head covered with a white paint or a powdered mineral. For the next three weeks she was subject to food taboos very much like those surrounding pregnancy. The girl stayed in or near the house, and she scratched her head with a special implement, not with her fingernails, in order to prevent her hair from dropping out. Subsequent menstrual periods were surrounded by the same taboos, and in addition, a married woman must never touch her husband when she was menstruating. The good health of a couple depended on how well the woman obeyed these rules.

Strong records that his informants denied the existence of an initiation ceremony for Desert Cahuilla males, but Hooper described male initiation for the Palm Springs group. Boys between the ages of ten and eighteen were selected by elders for initiation and taken to a brush enclosure outside the dance house. The boys were secluded there for five days and saw only those persons who brought them special foods. During three nights the old people danced until morning. The climax came on the fourth night when the initiates were brought out and given a drink of cooked jimsonweed, or toloache as it is known in Spanish. After taking it, the boys danced briefly, but they became dizzy and were placed in a corner while the older people continued to dance. The following evening the effects of the jimsonweed had worn off, and for the next five nights the boys were taught how to dance, sing particular songs, and otherwise instructed concerning correct adult behavior. The function of this ceremony seems to have been to symbolize the death of the initiates as children and their rebirth as knowledgeable adults. The only forms of body mutilation among males were piercing the ears and piercing the nasal septum. The latter operation was not common and was said to have been performed only on young boys with promise as leaders. Into the opening at the base of the nose were inserted pieces of deer bone.

Desert Cahuilla marriage patterns included moiety exogamy and a prohibition against seeking a spouse from known relatives on either side of the family. Since genealogies were not remembered over many generations, it was possible to marry a distant cousin so long as that person was in the opposite moiety. Instances of infant betrothal were known, with the prospective in-laws frequently exchanging gifts to bind the agreement. A person was most likely to marry someone from a nearby community. Most commonly a girl was about thirteen years old and the male about eighteen at the time of marriage. The match was arranged by the parents, and the proper procedure was for the mother of the boy to ask the girl's parents if the girl would help her collect mesquite beans. The girl's family delayed responding until they considered the match; if they judged it desirable, the girl's father notified the boy's father. Presents were taken to the bride's home by a relative, who returned with the girl. She was led into the house by the boy's mother and seated facing a corner, with her back to the assembled relatives of the groom. The groom then sat next to the girl, and the couple was given food as the boy's relatives ate. After the feasting was over, the couple was considered married, and that night the newlyweds were given a single blanket with the theory that if affection did not bring them together the cold desert night would. A girl who was unhappy in the home of her in-laws might return to her mother's home, but if she did this repeatedly, the presents which had been given were returned and the marriage considered dissolved. The groom and his parents had the right to expect the bride to bear an infant within two or three years. Failure to do so might annul the marriage and again mean a return of the wedding presents. A man could, if the woman's parents agreed, receive a younger sister of his wife if the latter died (sororate). It was less common for a woman to marry her deceased husband's brother (levirate). Among these people monogamy was the prevailing form of marriage, and familial relationships appear to have been quite stable.

In the routine of adult life a woman was the outsider in the extended family household of her husband. The husband and wife were expected to be reserved with one another in the presence of others, and the wife generally was retiring when with her in-laws or around men. Ideally, younger persons were thoughtful and unselfish in their dealings with older persons; these values were instilled in children when they were still quite young. Young boys who hunted or collected the first plant products of the season were expected to take them to the aged. The most virtuous adults were those men who hunted best and those women who could work most efficiently.

Death brought destruction to a Cahuilla household in the distant past. It was recalled that on the morning following the death of a person, the house in which the death had occurred was burned, and the body of the deceased was likewise burned. More recently, however, this pattern was modified. When an individual died, the members of his and other sibs assembled, bringing presents. The body was washed, dressed, and taken to the sib dance house of the deceased. Here the assembled mourners sang over the body throughout the night. If a man had died, the creation narrative was sung; for a woman, a song about the moon was sung, since it was the moon who had originally instructed women. The body was burned the morning following death, and within a week the person's house and possessions were likewise burned. Within a month of the cremation the Pass Cahuilla held a ceremony to prevent the spirit of the deceased from returning. The members of the dead person's sib took food to the dance house and sent for the members of neighboring sibs. Bolts of calico—probably reed mats in aboriginal times—were dragged about the dance floor to destroy the tracks of the dead, and songs were sung to propitiate the deceased. Relatives of the deceased threw out gifts which were gathered up by the guests, and any possessions of the dead person which had not been burned previously now were destroyed in a fire.

During the fall or winter of every year, a Mourning Ceremony extending over seven days was held for those sib members who had died since the last such ceremony was held. This was the most complex of all Cahuilla ceremonials, and an essential feature was a narration of the creation myth. Mukat described the proper rituals before he died, and the ceremony was conducted for the first time after his death. The sib net, with the aid of the paha and others, was the director and organizer. Arrangements were made months in advance. Guests were people from other sibs who were related by marriage to the deceased members as well as persons who had brought gifts after a death. Each sib was invited to arrive on a specific night so that the assembled group would not be too large. The first three nights the shamans of the host sib or other sibs performed tricks and danced. They attempted to communicate with the spirits of the dead in the process. One shaman's performance at such a Mourning Ceremony has been described thus: he tied a band about his head and inserted three clusters of owl feathers in it, and then another cluster of owl feathers was attached to a stick about eight inches in length which the shaman held in his hand.

Plates 26 & 27   *The Cahuilla woman Ramona Lubo at her home,
probably photographed around the turn of the century.
Her life was fictionalized in the novel* Ramona *by Helen Hunt Jackson*
(Courtesy of the Southwest Museum; inset photo courtesy of
the San Bernardino County Museum).

Plate 28 *(Left)   A Cahuilla woman grinding a food product in a metate* (Courtesy of the Southwest Museum).

Plate 29 *(Below)   The Palm Springs Tribal Council in 1959.*
From left to right are Elizabeth Monk, Le Vern Saubel, Eileen Miguel,
Doro Joyce Prieto, and Priscella Gonzales
(Courtesy of *The Desert Sun*, Palm Springs, California).

He sang and shuffled around a fire and began to tremble violently. He then pushed the stick down his throat three different times, and the third time he brought up a small black object said to have been a lizard. After the "lizard" was removed from his heart, he stopped shaking. A favored performance upon such an occasion was for the shaman to place live coals in his mouth and swallow them. Throughout the three nights to follow, different sibs sang all night long. Those individuals singing the last night aided the relatives of the deceased in making images of each person who had died and for whom the ceremony was being held. The images were nearly life-sized and were constructed from reed matting and clothed with deerskins. The male images had bows and arrows and eagle-feather head-dresses; the female images had baskets decorated with eagle feathers. They were further adorned with ornaments, or a decorative skin such as that of the wildcat, and eagle feathers. At sunrise on the final day of the Mourning Ceremony the assembled guests were presented with food or artifacts. Then the host net led a procession around the inside and outside of the dance house. He was followed by women, each carrying the image of a near relative. Then came the throng of participants and attendants. The people gathered in a circle in front of the dance house, and the images were placed in the center of the circle as the people danced, sang, and wailed. Objects of wealth were thrown over the images to show respect for the dead. These items could be retrieved but not by members of the sib hosting the ceremony. Next, the images were carried to a designated place and burned. The sib members who had been invited to the ceremony were presented by the net with strings of beads made of small round shell disks, and then the people left for their homes. The souls of the dead were now released, further mourning was unnecessary, and their names were no longer mentioned.

The presence of a soul in a living person was considered a reality, for when people fainted or dreamed their souls seemed to wander. Spirits also left the bodies of persons months before they died. A spirit might wander unknown to its possessor, or else the individual might become ill and a shaman be summoned to retrieve it. When the soul of a person was beyond recall, it went to a place created in the east by Mukat. Here stood two mountains which clapped together and then separated. The souls found their way to these mountains, and once there a deathless guardian spirit questioned and tested them. After passing the tests, which included making cat's cradles and answering questions, the soul attempted to go between the clapping mountains. Only those who had lived according to the rules of Mukat were able to pass untouched. Otherwise they were crushed by the mountains and became butterflies, bats, trees, or rocks nearby.

The Cahuilla often have been grouped under the general category of Mission Indians, but this designation is not accurate. They were not subject to the mission environment associated with the Indians of the coastal region of southern California, nor did most Cahuilla have more than indirect contact with the Roman Catholic priests of the missions. The first European to skirt the fringes of Cahuilla country probably was Pedro Fages. In 1772 he followed deserting soldiers from San Diego into the Colorado desert, went northward to the Borrego Valley and then on to the vicinity of the San Gabriel mission. About this time too the Spanish were intent on establishing a land access route to Alta California from Mexico. Supplying the new Spanish colony by sea was precarious, and it was hoped that an overland link could be developed. Juan Bautista de Anza was selected to pioneer the trail. He set out with a small party from Arizona in early 1774, wending his way from one water hole to the next without any expectation of difficulties until he met the Yuma Indians along the Colorado River. The aggressive and bellicose Yuma were in a position to contest his crossing of the Colorado River. De Anza, however, gained the support of their chief, Palma, and made the crossing without incident. The desert beyond was more of a challenge. The first attempt to cross failed because of a lack of forage and water for the horses and mules. This forced them back to the Colorado River. A smaller party was organized to attempt a crossing, and the second push into the unknown was successful. They passed through a portion of Cahuilla country, crossed the San Jacinto Mountains, and finally arrived at the San Gabriel mission, which had been founded in 1771. De Anza traveled on to Monterey, returned across the desert to the Colorado River, and went on to Tubac. In September of that year he again set out for Alta California, but this time with settlers and large herds of livestock. The route taken was a more northerly one than before. Although the Colorado River crossing was difficult, it was negotiated, and the party reached the San Gabriel mission. In 1780 a Spanish settlement was established as a belated attempt to secure the Colorado River crossing and to give the Yuma Indians the mission they had requested, but the Yuma in 1781 destroyed the outpost and killed the settlers, missionaries, and soldiers. This negated the usefulness of de Anza's efforts and his hopes for an overland trail. Following the War for Independence in Mexico, attention again was turned inland, especially as the Mohave Indians, linguistic and cultural neighbors of the Yuma, were raiding ranchos and settlements from the east. In 1819 the Indians in the San Bernardino area requested a mission, and an outpost or rancho was established among them. In 1823 Jose Romero left Tucson with a small party to reestablish the overland route, and he traveled westward without serious difficulties. On the unsuccessful return trip it was noted in the diary of Jose Maria Estudillo that the most eastern rancho passed was at San Gorgonio. Shortly after this the party met some "Cohahahuilla" Indians traveling to San Gabriel.

From the 1823-1824 diary of Jose Estudillo and its annotations by Bean and William M. Mason it is apparent that the Desert Cahuilla, at least those as far south and west as Palm Springs, were in rather close contact with the San Bernardino mission rancho. Surprisingly, some of the people of the Coachella Valley were raising maize and pumpkins by this time, crops which they no doubt had acquired from Colorado River area Indians who were aboriginal farmers. The Cahuilla of the desert also were growing watermelon, which is an Old World domestic plant introduced by Europeans.

Before 1834 the California missions were under the control of Roman Catholic clerics, and the setting maintained by these Franciscans had been the primary acculturative influence upon the Indians. After this date some missions, including the one at San Gabriel, passed through the administrative process of secularization, and the missionaries lost their control. In the year 1834, the San Bernardino rancho was sacked and burned by Indians. With secularization the rancho passed into private hands, but there were serious difficulties in keeping the herds of livestock out of the hands of marauding Indians. The Mountain Cahuilla leader, "Captain" Juan Antonio, and his small band were retained to stop the raids, which they did with great success. In 1846 the United States acquired California, and a few years later, in 1852, the San Bernardino rancho was purchased by Mormon settlers. Juan Antonio's followers then moved to the western end of San Gorgonio Pass. All during the late Mexican and early American periods the raids by Indians for livestock, particularly horses, contributed to the hostile feelings of the whites toward most Indians in southern California. The combative Mohave, Yuma, and Paiute were the greatest villains; it seems unlikely that the Cahuilla took a significant part in these raids. The sequence of events in the early American period did not lead to serious militant resistance by the Cahuilla, for they were not by nature combative and were not obstructing the interests of any major segment of the white population. Thus they were left very much to their own devices.

As early as 1847 the military governor of California, General Stephen W. Kearny, appointed Indian agents, including one for the southern part of California. Apparently they did nothing of importance, however. In 1850 the U. S. Congress sent three commissioners to California to negotiate treaties with the Indians and assign lands to them. O. M. Wozencraft was the commissioner who arranged the Cahuilla treaty of 1852. This treaty set aside lands from San Gorgonio to Warner's ranch, an area about forty miles in length and thirty miles in width. The U. S. Senate, however, refused to ratify any of the eighteen treaties with Californian Indians. Congressional resistance stemmed from a number of facts: the commissioners had committed the government to expend a great deal of money, the white citizens of California were vigorously opposed to the treaties, and possibly it was thought that some of these lands might contain gold.

In the fall of 1852 a Superintendent of Indian Affairs in California, Edward F. Beale, was appointed. He was the colorful and extremely capable administrator who selected Benjamin D. Wilson as the subagent for the southern part of the state. Wilson was a former mayor of Los Angeles, a landowner who had married a Spanish-American, and a leading merchant. In a report possibly, if not probably, written by Wilson's friend Benjamin Hayes, we have some comments on the Cahuilla as they were in 1852 and a good account of conditions among the Indians of southern California in general. The Wilson Report was twice rescued from oblivion, once by its publication in the Los Angeles *Star* in 1868, and again in 1952 with the annotated re-publication by John W. Caughey. The Wilson Report noted that by 1852 old ethnic groupings had been disrupted, for among the Desert Cahuilla there were Luisenos, Dieguenos, and a leader who was a Yuma. The elders and many others spoke Spanish, and claimed to be Christian, but the last Christian ties with the San Bernardino rancho had been severed with its destruction in 1834. In general the Indians worked as laborers and domestics on the ranchos of whites. They were paid at a much lower rate than white laborers and frequently were intoxicated. One of the major problems concerned the rights of Indians to lands. Wilson, or Hayes, pointed out that under Spanish law the Indians had rights to their settlements and pasture lands, and in theory the state of California recognized Indian landrights. A number of recommendations were made in the report concerning the future, including the suggestion that a subagent and skilled artisans such as farmers and carpenters be located at principal settlements. At the beginning at least, missionaries would be recruited to teach the Indians about American ways. It was pointed out that the state laws were "*All* punishment. *No* reform!" It was proposed further that lands be set aside for the Indians and that administrative centers be established in different areas, including one among the Cahuilla. The people would be encouraged to concentrate in these towns and would be regulated largely by a legal code derived from the Spanish administration of Indians. These and other proposals sound very much like a re-creation of a mission type of environment.

The Wilson Report stands as a perceptive document on southern Californian Indians, but it made no recognized impact on policy during the early

American period. Probably the principal reason for inaction was the rejection by the U. S. Senate of the treaties. In late 1852 Beale had recommended that lands be reserved for Indians. These lands would be military reservations as well as areas in which the Indians could be instructed in farming and other skills. Soldiers were to be in their midst to maintain order, and the military would be supported from the surplus Indian crops. He successfully convinced his superiors of the advantages of this plan, and the first such reserve began operating at Tejon in 1853. This was the beginning of the modern reservation system in the United States. Initially, the Tejon Reservation was strikingly successful; however, in 1854 the political enemies of Beale brought against him the charge that he was making a personal profit from the reservation. He was fully vindicated, but the system lost impetus and did not become a vital force in the lives of most Californian Indians. Wilson passed into politics and Beale out of Indian affairs in California; the scope and importance of the reservation were never fully developed in the area where it was conceived.

In the mid-1850's the Cahuilla reportedly numbered about 3500 males, of whom 1500 were of fighting age. These figures unquestionably include many non-Cahuilla, but in any event they far outnumbered the local white settlers. The Indians were discontented after the government's failure to live up to the treaty negotiated by Wozencraft, and the Cahuilla leader Juan Antonio attempted to form an alliance with the Yuma and Mohave to force their demands. Formal agreement among the Indians could not be reached, and it became obvious to Antonio that the whites would resist in force. The Indian complaints included not receiving farming implements as promised in the treaty and the trespassing and squatting of whites on traditional Indian lands, from which they took water and wood. Then in 1862 an epidemic of smallpox spread inland from Los Angeles, and among those who died was Juan Antonio. How many others perished is not recorded, but this epidemic probably was another significant factor in eroding away the people and their way of life.

Throughout the latter part of the nineteenth century some Cahuilla worked on the ranches of whites, the men as laborers and the women as domestics. The men worked also in orchards and vineyards; they cut mesquite wood and labored at salt works. Still they continued to collect products of the desert, and some of the better-watered localities were cultivated. Likewise they worked as laborers when the Southern Pacific Railroad was being built through the area in the 1870's. The effects of increasingly intensive contacts with whites went largely unrecorded; we have some information about the changing scene, but very little. For example, by about the turn of the century pottery was fired with dung, which is a nonaboriginal method, and some of the milling stones used were the three-legged variety made from lava and obtained from Mexicans. There is also the fact that bowstrings were of wire instead of sinew or fiber. Then too the women made baskets for sale to whites. The designs included figures of lizards, snakes, men, animals, and birds, none of which were of aboriginal provenience. By 1925 economic changes included the possession of farm lands by sibs, but this probably had been the case for about a hundred years previously. The amount of arable land was small because water was scarce. Changes were notable in dwelling forms and the nature of settlements. A frame house was no longer burned after a household member died but rather after three deaths had occurred there. Among the Desert Cahuilla a sib dance house still was occupied by a net and his family, but it had assumed a new form. Although it was rectangular as of old and still was covered with cane and palm fronds, the roof was now pitched like a shed. By the late 1950's few aboriginal traits remained. Although acorns still were processed, they were consumed only on special social and ceremonial occasions.

The sociopolitical life moved in new directions, for the rule of moiety exogamy was no longer observed with care. In aboriginal times gifts were presented to a bride's family, but during the early American period money was substituted. The girl's family received $30 around the turn of the century. By 1925, however, a female infant was termed scornfully "a paper," meaning a marriage license which no longer brought a gift. The pattern of leadership long had been impinged on by diverse outside influences. Suprasib leaders did not exist in aboriginal times, although one outstanding charismatic leader, Juan Antonio, emerged in the mid-1800's. In order to exercise effective control over the Cahuilla, whites appointed "chiefs" or "captains" through whom they dealt. It was said by informants that one such person was appointed as the leader of the Desert Cahuilla and was given "papers" and a horse by the Mexicans as symbols of his authority. When he died, the office passed to his son. These leaders, even as late as the 1920's, were not effective spokesmen for their groups.

Ceremonial life reflected reintegration and disintegration in the early part of the present century. The major shift was toward combining unrelated ceremonies with the Mourning Ceremony into a "fiesta" week. For example, among the Pass Cahuilla in the late 1880's, the Eagle Killing Ceremony was integrated into the Mourning Ceremony; the eagle feathers were used to decorate the images which were burned two days later. In aboriginal times the people had cremated their dead; under Spanish, Mexican, and Anglo-American stimulus, they began to bury the dead. Interment sometimes included placing food, clothing, and bedding with the body in the hope that these things would be useful to the spirit if it did not soon find a permanent resting place. Changes in the Mourning Ceremony included dressing the images in manufactured clothing, even hats and veils. Coins and buttons replaced shells for the eyes of the images, while the nose and ears were appliqued pieces of cloth. Coins were thrown on these images near the end of the ceremony. Indian-owned lunch counters sold food and coffee to participants and observers. In 1931 it was recorded that at Palm Springs the Mourning Ceremony was biennial and was held by alternating sibs for the dead of the two previous years. Among the Desert Cahuilla one of the last nets died in 1958. He had directed local ceremonial life, but when he died, the ceremonial structure, his house, and all of the ceremonial equipment were burned; this was the end of the end.

Returning to the course of Desert and Palm Springs Cahuilla history from the late 1860's, we see that the dominant theme running through the record concerns land and Indian rights to it. In 1869 the Superintendent of Indian Affairs for California hoped to be able to set aside lands for Indians before whites encroached further, and he succeeded the following year in establishing small reservations in San Diego County. Then in 1875 President Ulysses S. Grant authorized the establishment of the Agua Caliente and Cahuilla reservations. A Mission Indian agency began to function out of San Bernardino in 1879. Now for the first time slight but realistic efforts were being made to recognize the needs of southern Californian Indians. In 1881 Helen H. Jackson published a book called *A Century of Dishonor*, which was a scathing indictment of the manner in which American Indians had been treated. Because of her crusading interest in Indians, she was retained to make a report to the Commissioner of Indian Affairs on the Indians of southern California. A study was conducted with Abbott Kinney and a report submitted in 1883. It is in part a chronicle of wrongs against the Indians, particularly by Anglo-Americans, and partly a series of recommendations. Suggestions were that honest boundary surveys of Indian lands should be made and monuments erected to indicate the limits, that white settlers on such lands be removed, and that in some instances additional lands be purchased for the Indians. Then, too, Indian communities on lands which had been granted to whites should have the support of the Federal government in their claim for prior occupancy and ownership, particularly because the Indians were in no position to press their own claims. Furthermore, Indian lands should be held under a trust patent by the Federal government for twenty-five years and then turned over to the Indians. The desirability of additional schools was stressed plus the need to have a government agent visit the Indians at least twice a year to settle disputes. A law firm or lawyer should be retained to protect the Indians from the numerous forms of injustices now suffered. Direct economic needs were acknowledged in the suggestion that farming implements be distributed and some provision made for the needs of old and infirm individuals. The report of Jackson and Kinney did not make a strong impact, and this led Jackson to write a novel about the plight of these Indians. As a novel, *Ramona* was highly successful, but it did not lead to the reforms desired by the author.

The problems of the Palm Springs Indians over the legal rights to their land have followed a confused and meandering course. The original reservation was set aside in 1875, but subsequent Executive orders changed the scope of this grant. The modern reservation was formed in 1896 under the authority of the 1891 Mission Indian Relief Act. It consisted of approximately 32,000 acres of land in essentially a checkerboard pattern around the town of Palm Springs in Riverside County. The attitude which guided the formulation of the Mission Indian Relief Act grew out of the General Allotment Act of 1887. The keystone of this legislation was to allot reservation lands to family heads. After a period of twenty-five years the allottee could, with the sanction of the Secretary of the Interior, receive a fee patent title whereby he would be the legal owner and could do whatever he might choose with the land. Allotments were issued in 1923 as a result of a Federal act in 1917. The allotted land per family was to be limited to a total of 160 acres, and a Federal agent went to Palm Springs to make allotment selections for the band members irrespective of any particular Indian's attitude toward the program. Many persons were dissatisfied, and in 1927 an agent made allotments only to Indians who requested them; nearly half of the members made requests. These allotments consisted not of 160 acres but of five acres of irrigable land, forty acres of dry land, and two-acre lots in the town of Palm Springs. None of the 1927 selections were approved by the Federal government, and legal action was taken by the Indians in the late 1930's to force approval. Meanwhile, the Indian Reorganization Act of 1934 had been passed, bringing a basic change in Indian policy. First and foremost in the context of the Palm Springs land dispute, further allotments were prohibited unless the Indian group had voted against coming under this act. The Palm Springs band voted against it, and thus allotments were still possible. The attitude of the Bureau of Indian Affairs officials was very much against allotments, however, and they obstructed the granting of allotted lands at Palm Springs as elsewhere. The courts held that the Secretary of the Interior could not be forced to make allotments, which brought the litigation down to 1940. New action was taken the following year to have the allotments approved. The U. S. Supreme Court required a review of the litigation; the result was the 1946 verdict that the allotments were valid. Some allotments were approved in 1949; the ones which were unapproved involved conflicting claims, but finally selections were approved for the entire band.

One of the suits involving allotment selections resulted in a 1950 court decision that the allotted lands should be of approximately equal value for each individual since this was the original intent of the allotment law. This brought an awareness of the disparity among the values of the allotments. Based on 1949 estimates, the allotment values ranged from approximately $17,000 to $165,000, with a total value of lands allotted and pending allotment being about $7.4 million. In order to equalize the allotments it was proposed that the Secretary of the Interior organize a tribal corporation and convey to it all of the tribal assets. This organization would be empowered to issue equalization stock redeemable from the sale of or income from the lands managed by the tribal corporation. Persons who held equalized allotments would receive only membership stock until the equalization process was complete. Then all members would receive dividends equally.

The U. S. Senate Bill 2396 of the Eighty-fifth Congress, first session, 1957, was to provide equalization of allotments along these general lines, but the Indians objected and sent tribal representatives to Washington, D. C., to attempt modifications. The Bureau of Indian Affairs representatives refused to make any changes and stated that if this legislation were not passed, the tribal reserves would be used to equalize the allotments. These reserves, the cemeteries, hot springs, and particularly the canyons, were the prime centers of tribal identity. To allot them would be to destroy the tribe as a social and political unit. The Bureau of Indian Affairs forwarded the bill to the Committee on Interior and Insular Affairs of the House of Representatives, and since the bill involved persons from his district, Dalip S. Saund was given the privilege of introducing it. Saund studied the bill and stated later, "I came to the conclusion that under no circumstances would I be a party in introducing the bill." He was instrumental in having the bill set aside until a hearing could be held in Palm Springs. During the hearing held in October 1957, it became evident that the bill was not in the best interest of the Indians nor could it be conceived of as just. Probably the most dangerous provision was that a tribal corporation was to be established and given title to all unallotted land. It would issue equalization stock to bring each individual's allotment to the value of the most valuable allotment and would redeem the stock from income or from disposal of the land. This was in fact a liquidation corporation, and it is highly questionable that either legal or moral justification could be offered in its defense by the Bureau of Indian Affairs.

At the hearing, diverse issues were aired, including the problems of the control of the proposed tribal corporation and the status of the reserve lands. The city attorney for Palm Springs favored the bill with certain changes to enable the city to tax Indian lands to aid in the support of the city government. The subcommittee was outspoken in its condemnation of this stand. Another problem involving taxation was whether or not the State of California might tax the tribal corporation if the bill were passed. Federal immunity against taxation was to be provided, but such assurances were not forthcoming from the state officials. Further evidence was given concerning the inadequacy of the leasing laws.

As a result of the 1957 hearing Congressman Saund in 1959 submitted two new bills before the Eighty-sixth Congress, and these became law. The major provisions of the equalization bill, Public Law 86-339, follow. Allotments would be made to all band members who had not received them, but no future-born members would receive allotments. Equalizations would be made on the basis of 1957-1958 appraised land values. The cemeteries, Roman Catholic church, hot springs, and certain canyons were to remain tribal reserves not subject to allotment, but all other lands were to be allotted regardless of prior acreage limitations and in proportion to the highest monetary value of the prior allotments. The second bill, Public Law 86-326, provided that reservation lands could be leased for a period not exceeding ninety-nine years except for grazing land which could be leased for not more than ten years. The 1957-1958 allotment appraisals ranged from approximately $75,000 to $630,000, in contrast with the 1949 appraisal range of $17,000 to $165,000 cited previously. Obviously the land was rapidly becoming fantastically valuable. Even with the passage of the first bill mentioned above, it was impossible to equalize the allotments fully. Some 80 percent of the band obtained allotments valued at not less than $335,000; the remaining 20 percent of the allotments had values in excess of $335,000. Most of the land was still in trust status by 1962, and thus was not producing income. However, with the changes in leasing laws, it was likely that over the next ten years individuals would derive considerable profit from it. The first major leasing enterprise was the Palm Springs Spa complex at the hot springs. The Spa was completed in 1960 at a cost of $1.8 million, and an adjacent hotel, also on Indian land, was completed in 1963. In 1961 the city of Palm Springs purchased lands allotted to eight adults and twenty-two children for $2,979,000 which was shared by the allottees. Without the honesty and integrity of the "Congressman from India," Dalip S. Saund, the future which now looked so bright for these people would have been clouded and dismal.

The most remarkable aspect of all the Palm Springs land problems is the leadership role assumed successfully by women. When the issues were coming to a climax in 1957, the band included only thirty-two adults and sixty-four minors. At that time there were ten adult males and twenty-two females; of the males two were in the U. S. Navy, two were over seventy years of age, and two were incapable of handling their own affairs. At this point one of two courses of action was possible: either the band could trust the Bureau of Indian Affairs and its lawyer to handle their business affairs completely, or the women could assume the roles of leaders. The latter alternative was pursued. In aboriginal sociopolitical life there was no precedent for female leadership except that a woman did occasionally hold an office in trust for a son and old women sometimes were very active in sib ceremonies. The net was always a man, and in the early historic period whites appointed Indian men to act as intermediaries and later as reservation leaders. These persons seem to have been sib leaders. From 1900 to 1945 Palm Springs band affairs were managed by a three-man elected business committee. During the same period the aboriginal pattern of leadership and ceremonial life almost had faded away, and band integration came to center on their rights to land. In Cahuilla acculturation there is evidence to suggest differential rates for males and females. The men continued to follow a "collecting" pattern in their economic activities; they worked only sporadically as grape pickers, ranch hands, woodcutters, or railroad laborers. In their jobs they interacted most often with other Indians, not whites. Women by contrast often worked as domestics in the homes of whites and therefore became much more familiar with their ways. Possibly this was a major reason that women could become the stable core around which the society was reorganized. From 1935 to 1939 a woman was the secretary for the band business committee, and in 1939 two members of the committee were women. In 1945 the business committee was accused of graft, and band business was handled in town meetings. In 1954 an all-woman tribal council was elected, with Mrs. Vyola Olinger as its chairman. Mrs. Olinger, who was an active member of the band, was an apt choice, for she was not only intelligent and articulate but willing to work constructively with the Bureau of Indian Affairs officials. The men had by this time come to distrust virtually all proposals by the bureau. It was under the tribal council of women that the major land disputes were resolved. In 1961 a young male was elected to the council, and this brought an end to the era of all-female political dominance, but it was the women who had handled the major issue.

Thus by the early 1960's this small group of determined Indians had gained a settlement, and surely the avarice of whites had become just another episode in our blemished past; justice had prevailed. Alas, it was not to remain. In 1967, George Ringwald, a reporter for the *Daily Enterprise* of Riverside, California, wrote a series of articles about the administration of Palm Springs Cahuilla lands and funds. He demonstrated beyond any doubt that greedy whites still were taking grossly unfair advantage of Indians. Among the individuals involved in the immoral and often illegal handling of Palm Springs Cahuilla affairs were:

> Bureau of Indian Affairs personnel;
> a Superior Court judge;
> a municipal judge;
> a former mayor of Palm Springs;
> a Palm Springs real estate broker;
> a host of attorneys-at-law.

As a result of Ringwald's journalism the Bureau of Indian Affairs was forced to conduct an investigation into the system of court-appointed guardians and conservators. It was demonstrated, for example, that a municipal judge and one attorney had, over a seven-year period, collected $485,000 in fees. From 1956 to 1967, approximately 40% of the $10.8 million received by eighty-four estates went to conservators, guardians, or their attorneys under the supervision of the Riverside County Superior Court.

Will the Palm Springs Cahuilla Indians ever receive real justice in the white man's jungle called "law"?

References

Ames, Walter. "Palm Springs Indians Still Protest Land Split," *Los Angeles Times*, November 12, 1961.

Bancroft, Hubert H. *History of California*. 7 v. San Francisco. 1890.

*Barrows, David P. *The Ethno-Botany of the Coahuilla Indians of Southern California*. Chicago. 1900. A general history of the Cahuilla precedes a description of the local geography. These sections are followed by a discussion of houses, baskets, and the utilization of plants. The botanical information in particular is quite comprehensive and serves as a standard source.

Bean, Lowell J. Verbal communications.

*Bean, Lowell J., and William M. Mason. *Diaries & Accounts of the Romero Expeditions in Arizona and California*. Los Angeles. 1962. The publication of these records offers a previously unknown historical dimension to the Cahuilla. Their primary value is in conveying certain details of Cahuilla acculturation by Spanish-Americans.

Bean, Lowell J., and Katherine S. Saubel. "Cahuilla Ethnobotanical Notes: The Aboriginal Uses of the Oak," *Archaeological Survey, Annual Report 1960-1961*,

Department of Anthropology & Sociology, University of California, Los Angeles, 237-249. 1961.

Bean, Lowell J., "Cahuilla Ethnobotanical Notes: The Aboriginal Uses of the Mesquite and Screwbean," *Archaeological Survey, Annual Report 1962-1963,* Department of Anthropology & Sociology, University of California, Los Angeles, 55-76. 1963.

Beattie, George W., and Helen P. Beattie. *Heritage of the Valley.* Oakland. 1951.

Bolton, Herbert E. "In the South San Joaquin Ahead of Garces," *Quarterly of the California Historical Society,* v. 10, 211-219. 1931.

Bourne, A. R. Some Major Aspects of the Historical Development of Palm Springs between 1880 and 1938. (Occidental College, Master of Arts thesis.)

Caughey, John W. *California.* New York. 1940. (See also Wilson, Benjamin D.)

Ellison, William H. "The Federal Indian Policy in California, 1846-1860," *Mississippi Valley Historical Review,* v. 9, 37-67. 1922-1923.

Gifford, Edward W. *California Kinship Terminologies,* University of California Publications in American Archaeology and Ethnology, v. 18. 1922.

Hale, Kenneth. "Internal Diversity in Uto-Aztecan: 1," *International Journal of American Linguistics,* v. 24, 101-107. 1958.

*Hooper, Lucile. *The Cahuilla Indians.* University of California Publications in American Archaeology and Ethnology, v. 16, no. 6. 1920. Most of what is known about the aboriginal Cahuilla will be found in this ethnographic reconstruction, a similar reconstruction by Alfred L. Kroeber, or the analysis of social life and settlement patterns by William D. Strong.

Jackson, Helen H. *A Century of Dishonor.* New York. 1881 (an 1890 edition contains the Report on the Conditions and Needs of the Mission Indians of California).

James, Harry C. *The Cahuilla Indians.* Los Angeles. 1960.

*Kroeber, Alfred L. *Ethnography of the Cahuilla Indians.* University of California Publications in American Archaeology and Ethnology, v. 8, no. 2. 1908. A brief but valuable ethnography which concentrates on material culture. It supplements the reconstructions by Lucile Hooper and William D. Strong.

Land Allotments on Agua Caliente Reservation, Calif. Hearing before a Special Subcommittee of the Committee on Interior and Insular Affairs, House of Representatives, 85th Congress, 1st session. Serial No. 17. 1958.

Ringwald, George. *Riverside Press-Enterprise and Riverside Daily Press* articles, 1967.

Rush, Emmy M. "The Indians of the Coachella Valley Celebrate," *El Palacio,* v. 32, 1-19. 1932.

Saund, Dalip S. *Congressman from India.* New York. 1960.

Shinn, George H. *Shoshonean Days.* Glendale. 1941.

*Strong, William D. *Aboriginal Society in Southern California.* University of California Publications in American Archaeology and Ethnology, v. 26. 1929. The best information about aboriginal social structure, the movements of people, and settlement patterns.

Transmitting Report by Subcommittee on Indian Affairs. State of California, Senate Committee on Rules Resolution No. 8. Sacramento. 1961.

Wilson, Benjamin D. *The Indians of Southern California in 1852*. John W. Caughey, ed. San Marino. 1952.

1962 Progress Report, Agua Caliente Band of Mission Indians. Long Beach. No date.

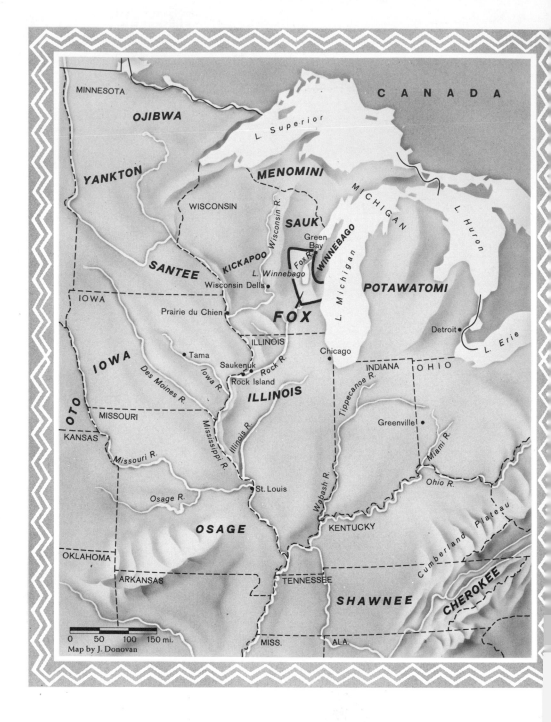

Map by J. Donovan

The Fox:
fighters and farmers of the woodland fringe

Most Algonkian tribes in the east-central United States disappeared long ago, but the Fox still survive as a small ethnic group. In colonial times the French had set out to destroy them completely and nearly were successful. The Fox contested the settlement of their lands by whites and harassed the pioneers involved until the turmoil climaxed in an Indian war. Afterwards the surviving Indians were displaced, and their number was depleted further. The Fox possessed a haughty independence, their warriors were brave men guided by very capable leaders, and they manifested a nobility and purpose which made them stand out as exceptional. A striking illustration of their resilience occurred in 1854. After having been defeated and displaced a generation earlier by whites, they began to leave their reservation in Kansas and to settle on land they once had owned, but now purchased from whites in Iowa. The intriguing questions are why and how the Fox managed to survive in the face of the hostility expressed against them by most people with whom they had contact.

The Fox know themselves as the Mesquakie, which is translated "red-earth people." This name stems from their creation myth which recorded that they were made from red earth. According to one account they received the name Fox when some members of the Fox sib met a party of French. When the Indians were asked who they were, they responded Fox, meaning of the Fox sib and Mesquakie tribe. It is estimated that the Fox and Sauk (Sac) numbered about 6500 individuals at the time of historic contact, of whom possibly 2000 were Fox. An estimate for 1728 gives 200 warriors, and an estimate for 1805 is for 300 warriors in a total population of 1200 persons. In the 1950's nearly 1000 Fox lived in Oklahoma, 500 in Iowa, and 125 in Nebraska. By 1970 there were 500 in the vicinity of Tama, Iowa.

The Fox, Sauk, and Kickapoo lived near one another and spoke closely related languages in the Algonkian (Algonquian) linguistic family, one of the nine families comprising the Macro-Algonkian phylum. Algonkian speakers occupied a vast sector of eastern Canada and a smaller area in the eastern United States. Remarkably, the other groups with whom they are clearly affiliated linguistically include two small northern Californian tribes, the Yurok and Wiyot. The earliest historical records locate the Fox along the Fox River of eastern Wisconsin. In this general area were three different types of environmental settings: deciduous forests, mixed forests, and prairie country.

Two major difficulties are encountered in the presentation of a balanced description of aboriginal life among the Fox. First, the information about these people does not date from the period of early historic contact. Thus,

216

it is not possible to establish with authority an aboriginal base-line account; the Fox way of life had been modified as a result of the fur trade before it was described. However, the Fox have been considered by most observers to be highly conservative, and except for superficial changes, we might expect that recent ethnographic accounts about them reflect the past more accurately than would be the case for many American Indian groups. A second difficulty in dealing with the Fox is their intimate association with the Sauk throughout most of their history. It is difficult if not impossible in some instances to separate the Fox historically from the Sauk. Although the descriptions will be confined to the Fox insofar as it is possible, frequent reference will be made to the Sauk. The Fox have been singled out for analysis for many specific reasons. First of all, they are a people who lived in an eastern woodland environment but maintained a way of life that had affinities with the Indians of the prairies. The Sauk occupied a similar position, but the ethnographic information about them is not nearly so comprehensive. Additionally, the Fox historical and ethnographic data have more continuity than those of the Sauk or other adjacent people. There are ethnographic accounts by an anthropologist, William Jones, who was part Fox, and by the anthropologist Truman Michelson, as well as William T. Hagan's history of the Fox and Sauk. The Fox Project of the University of Chicago, Department of Anthropology, under the direction of Sol Tax, is an invaluable source of information for the period from 1948 to 1959. In addition, the information published by Tax, Natalie F. Joffee, and Frederick O. Gearing supplement the earlier accounts of Jones and Michelson.

In the Great Lakes region the earliest human occupants were unsettled hunters, Paleo-Indians whose general way of life is reflected in scattered assemblages of stone tools. Their lithic traditions often included fluted projectile points of the Clovis type as a recurring and distinctive form. It is clear that these mobile mastodon hunters came to occupy the Great Lakes region by 10,000 B.C. and that they continued hunting these huge beasts until about 7000 B.C. when the climatic picture changed and mastodons became less common. Indians characterized as being of the Aqua-Plano group dominated the area from about 7000 to 4500 B.C. The people involved in this chipped stone industry must have hunted deer, caribou, and elk as important species of large game animals. By the end of the era there emerged two other patterns of culture, termed Boreal Archaic and Old Copper. Each was adapted to a forest environment and possessed woodworking tools, such as the ax, adz, and gouge, which were not present in the earlier periods. The methods of working stone shifted from flaking to grinding; some of the copper tools were annealed. The bearers of these traditions were hunters, fishermen, and collectors, with hunting possibly of the great-

est importance. Their principal weapon was not the bow and arrow but
the spear used with the spear-thrower (atlatl). The technologies of these
Indians gradually increased in efficiency until about 500 B.C., when two
radical innovations appeared, artificial burial mounds and pottery, which
may have spread into the area from Asia. Still the basic economy appears
to have remained much the same until the era of the Hopewell culture
of the Early Woodland tradition. The Hopewell people, centered in the Ohio
River valley, built great earthworks upon which they must have expended
an inordinate amount of time and energy; they had elaborate manufactures
in stone and organic materials; they used great care in producing grave
goods for the important dead; and their economy, although still dependent
on hunting, had a firm foundation in the domestic crops they raised, maize,
beans, and squash. The Hopewell Indians pushed into the Great Lakes
region and reached a climax in complexity around A.D. 400. During the
Late Woodland period, from about A.D. 800 until historic contact, there
was an essential continuity with the past but a wide local variation in
the cultures, indicating no overall unity. In the Lake Winnebago area the
Indians of this period planted maize, beans, squash, and tobacco. They
hunted small and large game and collected nuts, berries, and mussels. Their
material culture is of the type which we associate with early historic Indians
of the area. The bow and arrow was the principal weapon; fish were taken
with hooks, leisters, and nets, and their stone manufactures were of both
the chipped and ground varieties. The basic continuity with the previous
Woodland traditions is apparent and stands in contrast with the earlier
Paleo-Indian and Archaic developments.

The earliest known reference to the Fox occurs on a Jesuit map which
was drawn in 1640. At this time they lived near Green Bay, Wisconsin,
and according to their traditions they arrived in this area after being driven
westward by other Algonkian tribes. Historically, the first direct contacts
between Fox and Europeans were in 1665 when French traders and
explorers pushed into the western sector of the Great Lakes region. In the
year 1670 a mission was founded among them by the famous Father Claude
Jean Allouez, but he was able to win converts only among persons who
were ill or dying. The Fox were hostile toward the French during the period
of initial contact, and yet they appreciated European trade goods. Some
Fox who went to Montreal in 1671 were ill-treated by the French, and
they later sought revenge. As the French pushed to the west of Fox country
to trade with the Chippewa (Ojibwa) and Siouan-speaking tribes, the Fox
resisted, since the French were arming their enemies. The Fox began a
systematic plundering of French trading canoes, which brought them into
direct conflict with the French. When Detroit was established in 1699, con-

tact between the French and the Indians in the Great Lakes region intensified. In 1700 the French made a treaty with the Iroquois, and in it the
Iroquois promised not to disrupt the trade to the west. In 1701 many of
the tribes of the western Great Lakes area met at Montreal to make peace
with the French. The Fox were among those tribes, and they along with
the Iroquois and the Siouan speakers to the west were not to interfere
with the French trade. However, the French continued to supply weapons
to Indians who were at war with the Fox. Meanwhile, the British were
anxious to establish themselves in the fur trade in the northwest. They
incited the Fox against the French and offered higher prices for pelts
besides. By 1712 the French and Fox conflict could not be resolved peacefully, and the Siege of Detroit led to heavy Fox losses. The Fox hoped to
eliminate the French, and the French were equally determined to destroy
the Fox. In order to make an efficient resistance against the French, the
Fox invited the Abnaki to settle among them. The Fox also received assurances from the Iroquois that they could live among them if defeated by
the French, and they made peace with the neighboring tribes. They even
ranged southward among the Omaha and the Chickasaw in their search
for allies, but they could not convince the latter tribes to support their
efforts.

A Fox village known as the Bell site appears to have been destroyed
by the French in 1716. It was excavated by Warren L. Wittry and provided
the greatest detail about the early historic technology of these people. The
settlement, which had a spring at the center, was located on a high bank
and was surrounded by three rows of oak palisades. The occupants of the
site raised both maize and squash, and hunted bison, bear, beaver, and
elk. They also fished for sturgeon, suckers, buffalo fish and other species,
and collected plant foods. They lived in rectangular dwellings made by
covering pole frames with mats or sheets of bark or in circular structures
with pole framing covered with bark. Their weaponry included not only
the bow and arrow but muskets as well. Artifacts associated with the aboriginal past and others obtained by trade existed side by side. Awls were
of bone and of iron; brass kettles were found along with others made from
carapaces or local clays. Bracelets were fashioned from bone as well as
from brass wire or pieces of broken brass kettles, and diverse forms of
glass beads supplemented the small bone tubes used as beads. Clay pipes
of European origin existed along with those of local manufacture. Thus,
we find artifacts from competing cultural traditions at this stage in Fox
history.

French and Fox hostility came to a climax in 1728 when nearly 500
whites and 1200 allied Indians moved against the Fox. They demolished

Fox villages but failed to destroy the people. However, with French support the Indian enemies of the Fox succeeded in virtually destroying the tribe by 1730. Over a period of about two years nearly 1200 Fox were killed, and the tribe was no longer an independent entity. However, the Fox consolidated again when the prisoners held by other surrounding peoples were released. In 1731 some 200 remaining Fox took refuge in the Sauk villages. Two years later the French attempted to obtain the Fox from among the Sauk and planned to ship them to the West Indies as slaves, but the Sauk refused to cooperate. The French attempted to take the Fox by force, and a fight developed in which some French were killed. The Sauk fled southward to avoid French reprisals and were joined by the Fox. It was not until the year 1737 that peace was made between the Fox and the French.

Toward the end of French control over the Great Lakes region the Fox once again moved to Wisconsin, but it was not until the British replaced the French at the Green Bay post in 1761 that the Fox felt reasonably secure. Fox and British relationships always were very good. However, they were forced, not by the British but by the Chippewa to abandon their Wisconsin lands permanently about 1780. The Fox were not to remain undisturbed long in their new home in Illinois. Around 1800 increasing contact was made with the Americans in the Northwest Territory. The Indians lived in scattered communities along both banks of the Mississippi River north of the mouth of the Des Moines River. By this time the Fox had become dependent on the fur trade in order to receive goods that they considered necessary to maintain their way of life. They were often in debt to traders for the goods that they obtained against their next year's take. Still the relationship between the Fox and the Sauk and the traders, especially British, seems to have been very good. The Fox expected certain privileges, such as being entertained when they were at the trading post, receiving gifts from the traders, and being cared for in times of stress. At the same time they relied on trusted traders to help guide tribal and village affairs. The traders were important in molding Indian attitudes toward both the British and the American governments. The Fox and Sauk were brought into contact and conflict with the Americans through the actions of William Henry Harrison, governor of the Northwest Territory. The Americans had no reason to consider the Fox and Sauk sympathetic to them, since the British had been aided by these Indians during the American Revolution. With the influx of settlers into the Northwest Territory there was increasing pressure on all Indian groups of the Midwest to sign treaties with the American government and to move westward. In 1804 a small party of Fox and Sauk went to St. Louis, and here they became intoxicated and signed a treaty with the United States for the release of their lands along the Mississippi River. Trade goods worth $2000 were distributed to the Indians plus an annuity of $600 to the Sauk and $400 to the Fox. The treaty authorized further settlement of Illinois lands by settlers from the United States. Not only were the Indians at St. Louis unauthorized to contract the treaty, but the tribes as a whole did not know of it until after the chiefs had arrived back from St. Louis. The Treaty of 1804 was to be a great cause for Fox anger against the Americans. They felt that the Americans had deceived them and that these lands had been taken from them illegally. This treaty was to be the one document to which the Americans referred constantly in asserting their claims to Fox and Sauk lands. The treaty was made, the damage was done, but the bitterness was to linger always in the minds of the Indians involved. The area ceded to the United States included western Illinois north and west of the Illinois River, a small section of southern Wisconsin, and another small section of eastern Missouri.

The Americans found that a major difficulty in their dealing with Indians stemmed from wars between tribes. These not only disrupted trade routes but made settlement of the country difficult. In an effort to end the conflicts all the major tribes in the upper Mississippi River drainage were invited to attend a council held in St. Louis in 1805. The chiefs met with Governor Harrison and the Indian agent for the area, and they signed a treaty of peace. In order to impress upon the Indians the power and strength of the United States it was arranged for selected Indians to visit Washington, D. C. About one third of the group to meet in Washington were Fox or Sauk Indians. The journey east was an impressive one for all involved. However, at the time that some chiefs were in Washington others were on the warpath against the Osage and the Chickasaw. Thus this effort to bring about a peaceful settlement of Indian affairs was unsuccessful. During the winter of 1805-1806 Fox and Sauk war parties roved along the Missouri River to search out Osage camps and right wrongs they felt the Osage had done to them. Because Americans were also killed by these warriors, there was increasing pressure on the government of the Northwest Territory to bring about a more effective settlement of Indian differences. To add to the governor's administrative difficulties additional settlers entered the Northwest Territory between the years 1806 and 1812. They were particularly active in clearing the land and establishing farms in the region between the Ohio and the Mississippi rivers, precisely the region where there was the greatest Indian unrest.

At this point the Fox and Sauk came under the influence of the Shawnee. At historic contact the Shawnee, who were Algonkian speakers and linguistically related to the Fox and Sauk, centered in the Cumberland region of Tennessee. Later many of the tribe moved to Ohio and assisted the British against the colonists during the Revolutionary War. At the treaty of Greenville in 1795 they were forced to give up their lands along the Miami River in Ohio. In 1798 some joined the Delaware who were by now in Indiana, but the ones who were most hostile to the Americans moved to Missouri. In 1806 the half brother of the great Shawnee leader, Tecumseh, rose to prominence. His name was Tenskwatawa, but he is better known as the "Shawnee Prophet." He reportedly died and was reborn; while dead he visited the land of the spirits and was given a view of the future. This messiah saw contentment only for those who gave up white ways and returned to the old Indian way of life. With Greenville, Ohio, as the center of his activities he received tribal representatives from the surrounding region. The movement coalesced into an effort to rid the country of the "Long Knives" or Americans. With the Treaty of 1804 as the rallying point for their grievances against the Americans, the Fox and Sauk were ready and willing to follow this confederation organized by the Shawnee and actively fostered by the British. In the Battle of Tippecanoe Creek of 1811 the Shawnee Prophet's prestige was destroyed by William H. Harrison's stand against the Indians, but the battle was not decisive. Afterwards, however, it was unlikely that an Indian confederation could emerge. In early 1812 an Indian delegation which included Fox and Sauk went to Washington, D. C., and this time they were well received because the War of 1812 had erupted into open conflict. The most the Americans could hope to do was to keep the Indians from joining in the conflict on the side of the British. In order to prevent Fox and Sauk participation the Americans decided to move these Indians to Missouri, where they would be beyond effective contact with the British. They were partially successful, for approximately 1500 members of the combined tribes eventually were moved to these new lands.

Black Hawk was the only major Indian leader who was an active supporter of the British. He was born in 1767 into the Thunder sib of the Sauk tribe. At fifteen he distinguished himself as a warrior, and at seventeen he led a raid on an Osage camp, bringing back the scalp of a warrior. By the time he was nineteen he had led a party of 200 warriors against an equal number of Osage. Nearly half of the Osage were killed, with Black Hawk himself killing five men and one woman. By 1812 his reputation as a leader and warrior made him the most honored and respected man of the combined tribes. At the opening of hostilities in the War of 1812, Black Hawk journeyed to Green Bay, Wisconsin, with 200 warriors and was received heartily by the British. They convinced him that the first task was to secure the Great Lakes region. Black Hawk and his warriors traveled to Detroit to participate in the British siege. Although they arrived after the victory, they remained to fight for the British during the war. At this time many members of the combined tribe were being pressured by the Americans to move on to Missouri, away from potential participation in the conflict.

While Black Hawk was away, there was the threat that American troops would destroy the principal village of Saukenuk near the mouth of the Rock River in the present state of Illinois. The people were ready to flee after deciding to do so in council, but at this juncture Keokuk asked to speak. This man's mother was said to have been half French, but he was an unimportant member of the Sauk tribe and his sib affiliations were not those of a leading political group. He was a fine orator and spoke up at the council meeting to say that the Indians should resist the American invasion. The persuasiveness of his speech convinced the people that they should not abandon their village. When the American force failed to arrive to oust them, he became a hero. By his oration and his convincing stand against the Americans, Keokuk established himself as a leader and was to rival Black Hawk in political importance.

Keokuk was friendly with the Americans, while Black Hawk aided the British. When an American military party attempted to ascend the Mississippi River in force in mid-1814, a party of Sauk, Fox, and Kickapoo, under the leadership of Black Hawk, successfully prevented the American vessels from reaching their goal. Their victory was indecisive, but the British were pleased with the Indian effort, particularly with their aid in preventing the Americans from taking the Rock River country. As time went on, however, there was a marked division among the members of these two tribes. The Missouri faction attempted consistently to be neutral although a few of its members, from time to time, fought for Black Hawk and the British. By the fall of 1814 the course of the War of 1812 in the Northwest Territory had changed. It was obvious that the Indian war was not being successfully managed by the British, and the Americans were consolidating their forces. The Treaty of Ghent brought an end to the War of 1812, but the breach between the Sauk and Fox, brought on by their division during the war, continued over the years.

In order to impress the Indians with the strength of their arms, the Americans founded Fort Armstrong at the lower end of Rock Island, at the mouth of the Rock River. The fort was established primarily to demonstrate that the Americans were prepared to defend the frontier against complete reoccupancy by the Indians. In spite of the fact that the Americans were victorious in the War of 1812, many of the Indians of the Northwest Territory still looked to the British for aid in their struggle against American penetration. The unsettled conditions among the Fox and Sauk from 1815 to 1817 led to sporadic raids against frontier settlements and clashes with other Indians upon whose lands they encroached as they were pushed west. In an effort to end these conflicts, in 1820 a meeting was held among those Indians who lived along the upper Mississippi. The primary American interest was to settle the frontier conflicts among the Indians so that the Indian trade would not be interrupted and settlers would not be harassed. It was during these unsettled years that Keokuk became a powerful instrument of white appeasement in the central prairies. Keokuk was quite willing to abide by American decisions so long as they furthered his own ambitions; meanwhile the effective influence of Black Hawk declined.

In 1824 a tribal delegation again visited Washington, D. C. The meeting was arranged in order to show the chiefs the strength of the United States. Unfortunately, Black Hawk was not among the individuals who were exposed to this power. Finally, in 1825, the Treaty of Prairie du Chien was signed by the Fox, Sauk, and Siouans. It was agreed that the tribal boundaries set up by this treaty were binding for all the members involved. It further was agreed that the Indians were not to seek aid from, nor to be in contact with, the British in Canada. It was apparent at this time that the encroachment of white settlers on the lands ceded by the Fox and Sauk, but still occupied by them, would cause additional hostilities. As the Americans occupied Fox and Sauk country, so these tribes in turn invaded the lands of the Sioux, which caused additional hostilities among the Indians. Once again in 1830 the Fox and the Sauk along with other adjacent tribes gave up their claim to all the lands between the Missouri and the Mississippi rivers. The amount of money received in this settlement could not begin to compensate the Indians for their loss. It also was made clear to the Indians that they could no longer return to Saukenuk; that they were to leave and never come back was an injunction issued by the government in 1830. Black Hawk, however, intended to reoccupy the village as soon as his group had become consolidated. It was difficult now for the Indians to live in their traditional lands because settlers were constantly selling them intoxicants. The Indians did not have enough food to take them through the winter of 1830-1831 because they had sold most of their equipment in order to obtain intoxicants. To complicate conditions further there were heavy snows which made it impossible for the Indians to hunt efficiently. By this time Black Hawk was desperate and appealed to other Indian tribes in order to organize a confederation to resist the whites. He turned to the very unstable Winnebago Prophet, and he sent parties to visit the Creek, Cherokee, and even his old enemies, the Osage. However, the emissaries were not successful in enlisting systematic Indian aid. In the spring of 1831 Black Hawk and his "British Band" returned to Saukenuk, and the women began to plant maize. The 300 warriors in the party were not actively aggressive against the whites, but between the settlers and Black Hawk's band were antagonistic feelings. In an effort to bring about the removal of the Indians, troops were dispatched to the Rock River country. If they had been regular troops, the difficulties which were to arise might not have been nearly as complicated. However, the anxious officials dispatched militiamen in order to put down what was termed an Indian uprising. On the 26th of June in 1831, Saukenuk was bombarded even though the Indians had left, and the village was destroyed. Black Hawk was forced to agree not to return to Saukenuk and to submit to Keokuk as the leader of the combined tribes. This did not mean the end of the Indian raids in the Illinois country, for numerous small parties of warriors went out on the warpath against the will or with the passive approval of their chiefs. There was little that the chiefs, including Black Hawk, could do to stop them. At this point it would seem that resistance against the Americans was no longer feasible, but Black Hawk was told that the Winnebago, Potawatomi, Chippewa, and British would support an attempt to retake Saukenuk. The Indians supposedly had promised to send braves to fight the Americans, and the British had promised to supply the army with guns and ammunition as well as provisions. Unknown to Black Hawk, this report was false and had been misrepresented by one of his own subordinates.

In the spring of 1832 the British Band, including 2000 persons with something more than 500 warriors, crossed the Mississippi River and moved toward Rock Island. By this time the frontier was in turmoil, volunteer militiamen were called out, and troops were moved into the area in an effort to prevent Black Hawk from reoccupying his traditional country. The American military effort was hopelessly confused; at the same time, Black Hawk was unaware that he had been deceived by his lieutenant. The British would not be coming to their support, and neither could they count on any major aid from other tribes. As Black Hawk traveled up the Rock River, he came in contact with the Potawatomi. They told him that they could not possibly give to his people the corn they needed, and they also warned that no British were going to aid the Indians. Under these circumstances, Black Hawk felt that he must surrender before being over-taken by the whites. He sent a party of warriors back to the camp of the whites beneath a flag of truce in order to secure terms for peace. The whites, however, who were not under any realistic military command, misunder-stood the purpose of the warriors. One of the three Indians carrying the flag was killed. The other two and the Indian scouts who had followed them raced back to their encampment. Black Hawk now was forced to fight. He rallied around himself forty warriors to hold off the whites. The Indians ambushed the rush of oncoming whites, and soon the militiamen were fleeing in panic. The rest of the troops were routed, and all were swept along in the retreat. These disorganized volunteers fled to relate exaggerated stories of the Indian numbers and of the defeat they had suffered. After the skirmish Black Hawk and his followers returned to the American camp, looting and mutilating the bodies of the slain whites. Afterward they withdrew to the headwaters of the Rock River. When the regular military contingent reached the battleground, they found there were only eleven individuals who had been killed by the Indians. As the Indians retreated, they massacred a group of whites on a farm and sent scalping parties into the settlements along their path. This caused settlers and the government to demand decisive action. The American forces were reinforced, and by the end of June the United States military operation included 400 regular soldiers, 3000 militia, and 200 to 300 Indian auxiliaries. By this time the campaign had cost the Americans approximately $300,000, and the Indians still were not defeated.

On June 15 Major General Winfield Scott took charge of a large contingent at Chicago with the purpose of trapping the Indians between his forces and the American forces to the west. As conditions grew more desperate for the Indians, not only from losses of individuals in battle but also deaths from exposure and starvation, their few allies began to desert at every opportunity. Black Hawk decided to try a breakthrough. If it was successful, the Indians could move west and rejoin Keokuk or escape on the prairies. The banks of the Wisconsin were reached before the Americans were close enough to attack the entire band. The Indians were driven from the hillside down into the river bottom. In this engagement nearly seventy of Black Hawk's warriors were killed, but the Americans lost only one man. In spite of this loss and the desperate position in which he found himself, Black Hawk successfully crossed the river bottom and maintained his followers as a cohesive group. On the first of August, approximately 500 members of the original British Band arrived along the eastern bank of the Mississippi River. Black Hawk advocated retreating farther to the north, but the majority felt that their best chance for survival was to cross the Mississippi River. Fifty moved northward with Black Hawk, and a hundred escaped across the Mississippi River. Black Hawk eluded capture until he had reached the vicinity of the Wisconsin Dells where he finally was taken by a party of Winnebago who were to receive a reward for delivering him to the military forces.

The price the Indians were to pay for their defeat was to forfeit some 6,000,000 acres of land, except for a small reservation, along the western bank of the Mississippi River in the present state of Iowa. Among the stipulations were that they were to remove themselves from this land and never again return there to "reside, plant, fish, or hunt." In return for the lands that they were to give up, the Indians were to receive a blacksmith, a gunsmith shop, and an annual allotment of tobacco and salt. They also were given winter provisions and $40,000 to pay their debts to the traders. Over the next thirty years they were to receive $660,000 for their cession. Another stipulation in the treaty was that Black Hawk and other chiefs should be taken to Fort Monroe on Chesapeake Bay as prisoners. It was thought necessary to remove the Indian leaders in order to prevent any further violence along the frontier. Black Hawk arrived in Washington, D. C., in late April but was a prisoner at Fort Monroe for only a brief period of time. He was released to the custody of Keokuk in May and was given a tour of the major cities in the eastern United States in order to impress upon him the power of the Americans. He was overwhelmed by the seventy-four gun *Delaware,* amazed by the mobs of people that surrounded him, and awed by the arsenals that the Americans maintained. According to the historian William T. Hagan, if Black Hawk had accompanied one of the earlier Indian parties to Washington, D. C., and had come to realize at that time the power of the Americans, the Black Hawk War in all probability never would have been fought.

In their defeat the Fox and Sauk settled in Iowa where they had a small, inadequate reservation which could not possibly accommodate their needs if they were to follow their old way of life. They attempted still to hunt and plant their crops; however, the lands soon were depleted of game, and they turned to the west to hunt bison. As time passed, this, too, was unprofitable, and they spent more and more time wintering among whites. Here they had contact with unscrupulous traders, dishonest agents, and whites who were hostile toward them. The Indians were plagued with disease, and the consumption of intoxicants became almost a way of life for them. As if these troubles were not enough, there was additional dissension in the combined tribes. There were those individuals who favored Keokuk and supported his policies, and there was a faction that was against him. As if to compound their already tremendous problems, the Fox and Sauk were thrown into closer contact with their traditional enemies, the Sioux. There were raids by parties on both sides, and their embittered attitude toward one another continued. To climax all of this, there was an increase in the number of settlers migrating into this area, and once again, the Fox and Sauk were forced to move. Americans with the interests of these Indians at heart attempted to introduce scientific farming to them, but the Indians would have no part of the program. Neither would they permit schools to be established, and they rejected the efforts of missionaries to convert them to Christianity. What we see is a crystallized hostility against white culture emerging from the nature of their 200 years of direct contact with it. Again, in 1837, the Indians were forced to cede a portion of their land to the United States, and there was the usual monetary compensation. In 1842 the Fox and Sauk were forced to sell all of their land in Iowa, embracing approximately 10,000,000 acres. They moved to western Iowa temporarily and in the fall of 1845 journeyed on to their new home at the headwaters of the Osage River in Kansas.

In Kansas the Fox obtained nearly 400,000 acres of land, but it was prairie country ill-adapted to their horticultural-hunting economy. In order to live the people were forced to depend on annuities from the government. They still continued to hunt bison on the prairie and to seek other game in more sheltered country, but they never were successful in maintaining themselves in this manner. Hunting on the prairies brought them into conflict with additional groups who had not previously been their enemies. The Comanche, Kiowa, and Arapaho all resented the intrusions by the Fox and Sauk. The number of warriors that the Fox and Sauk could assemble always was small, but they were brave and had weapons that were superior to those of the other Indians in the area. However, by the 1860's, with their numbers depleted by disease and by losses in warfare, they could no longer effectively cope with the more populous hostile groups.

The Fox never were reconciled to their Kansas reservation; they were bitterly opposed to the Treaty of 1842 and rallied around the Fox chief Poweshiek who, because of his disgust with the Sauk for ceding the Rock River country, had moved to Iowa with many of the Fox. He later was joined by Keokuk and the other Sauk who were unwilling to aid the British Band in the Black Hawk War. Soon after the Fox removal to Kansas, Poweshiek died under mysterious circumstances. After his death many Fox became more discontented, and during the winter of 1851-1852 nearly a hundred, most of them Mesquakie, returned to Iowa. The Indians purchased eighty acres of land in Tama County and settled again in Iowa. Legal recognition of the Fox in Iowa was given by the state government in 1856, and the land was held in trust by the governor of the state. Then in 1858 other Fox from Kansas defied the Federal government and moved to Iowa. Amazing as it may seem, the Indians were welcomed by the white settlers. Altruism was not their motive; the ease with which the Indians could be separated from their annuity payments was what brought the friendly reception by the whites. In 1862 an additional group of Fox moved back to Iowa after there was a disagreement about annuity payments on the Kansas reservation. Finally, when the Fox and the Sauk were forced to give up their Kansas reservation and move to Oklahoma in 1869, still more

Fox returned to Iowa. By about 1870 there were some 300 Fox Indians in Iowa, and they began to settle down to a new way of life in an old environment.

The history of the Fox and Sauk Indians, with their many moves from lands that were traditionally theirs to new lands they occupied for short periods, is complex. However, it may be summarized briefly. Originally the Fox occupied the Green Bay, Wisconsin, area, and from there they moved into western Illinois. In 1804 they unknowingly ceded their lands in Illinois and a small sector of Missouri and Wisconsin to the United States. They were given lands in Iowa, but their holdings in the eastern section were ceded in 1832, and the remainder of their Iowa land was relinquished in 1842. Next they were forced to move to a reservation in eastern Kansas. Except for those who moved onto land they purchased in Iowa, they remained on the reservation in eastern Kansas until they were resettled on another reservation in northern Oklahoma. The reservation in Oklahoma was procured for the Indians in 1867, and they moved there in 1869. In Oklahoma the Fox and the Sauk retained their identity as an integrated group; however, they always remained aware of their separateness. When the move to Kansas was made in 1842, many of the Fox were dissatisfied there and returned to Iowa. At the time of the move from Kansas to Oklahoma, additional Fox returned to Iowa; thus the Iowa segment of the combined tribes has retained its separate identity much more clearly than that in Oklahoma.

The information which follows about the Fox is very different from that which has been compiled for the other tribes in this book. None of the Fox ethnographic material dates from their early period of historic contact. Most data were collected around the turn of the present century, or shortly thereafter. Fortunately, however, a great deal of this information was compiled by a Fox who also had Welsh and English ancestry and who became a professional anthropologist. This individual, William Jones, was born in 1871 on the Sauk and Fox reservation in Oklahoma. When Jones was nearly a year old his mother died, and he was cared for by his Indian grandmother. However, she died when Jones was nine years of age, and his father sent him away to school. After three years of schooling he returned home and became a cowboy, but in 1889 he went to the Hampton Institute, then to Andover, and finally to Harvard. Jones had planned to study medicine, but financial difficulties and Frederic W. Putnam convinced him that he should become an anthropologist. He graduated from Harvard in 1900 with an A.B. degree and completed his professional training at Columbia where he received a Ph.D. in 1904. Jones worked among Algonkian tribes, but he could not obtain a permanent position in Algonkian research and finally began working at the Field Museum in 1906. He made a field trip to the Philippine Islands, and in 1909 when he was ready to leave, he was murdered by the Ilongots. During the course of his life Jones had compiled a considerable amount of information about the Fox; his notes were edited posthumously and published by Franz Boas, Margaret W. Fisher, and Truman Michelson. It is primarily from these sources that we are able to reconstruct in a reasonably systematic manner the Mesquakie way of life.

At a place which is not on earth and is so far away that no one is able to travel there, a place where it is always winter, lives Wisaka. In the remote past he lived on earth with his younger brother, but the manitous met in council and plotted to kill the brothers. They killed the younger brother, but the older brother, Wisaka, survived their attempts. First they tried to kill him with fire. Then they created a great flood, but Wisaka climbed a tall tree on a mountain top, a canoe appeared at the top of the tree, and he paddled about on the water. A turtledove brought him twigs, and a muskrat brought mud from which he made a ball. He threw it into the water, and it grew into the earth as we know it.

It was Wisaka, too, who created all the things on earth and man as well. The Fox, according to their own traditions, are people with such antiquity that they do not know when they first arrived on earth. They were the first people to dwell on the land made by Wisaka, and they lived by the sea. Out of the sea came a great fish with the head of a man. As this great fish walked on the land, he became fully human, and he was followed by other fish who made the same transformation. These individuals established a community near the Fox, and every aspect of Fox life was copied by the fish-turned-to-men. These were the manitous of the world. When Wisaka formed the Fox they were red, the same color as blood. As time passed, people grew more distant from the manitous, and the world in which they lived changed. In recent times animals and birds have begun to disappear, and the manitous who control the universe are unhappy about this new state of affairs. Sometime in the future the manitous will destroy the earth, the Fox will revert to their original red condition, and then the world will begin again.

Fox tradition records that when they lived along the northern sea they were surrounded by enemies who harassed them constantly. Finally the opposition was so great that they were forced to flee from their homeland. Somewhat later the Fox built a fort which their enemies found but could not take. They traveled on to a place where the seas were joined by narrow waters. It was here that they encountered and defeated the Chippewa, the tribe which had been most active in making war against them. The Fox continued to move westward to settle finally in the vicinity of Green Bay.

Fox men were particularly striking in their appearance, largely because of their hair style, termed *moconi,* which is a variety of the roached head-dress. A man shaved all the hair from his head except for a palm-sized tuft left at the crown. Most of the tuft was approximately two inches in length, but in the center grew a long scalp lock that never was cut and usually was braided. From this braid hung an eagle quill, and along the middle of the tuft were attached lengths of deer hair which very frequently were painted red. The typical clothing of a male included a buckskin breechclout, leggings, and moccasins which reached nearly to the knees. When the weather was cold, a man wore a skin cape. The women dressed their hair by parting it in the middle and drawing it to the back of the neck. Most probably the women wore long buckskin dresses and short leather moccasins. Young children usually wore only a long, loose shirt. As a boy grew older, he wore the same type of clothing as a man; girls followed the clothing styles of their mothers. By the end of the last century most of the Fox had abandoned their old hairdressing and clothing styles. A few men still kept the traditional hair style, but most men allowed their hair to grow down the back of the neck. At the neck the hair was gathered and braided into a small pigtail from which were hung ornaments of silver and beadwork. Store-bought shirts were seen on men except at home where they wore a breechclout and blanket. Moccasins changed from buckskin to cloth, and the skin cape was replaced by a blanket or shawl. Fox males favored a wide variety of jewelry, including earrings, rings, wristlets, and armlets, all preferably made of German silver. The shirts and skirts of women were made from calico; women wore at least two shirts, which were loose at the waist and buttoned at the front. They wore two or more skirts, which hung loosely from the hips to just below the ankles for younger women and girls and reached just above the ankles for older women. The women also were attracted to jewelry made from German silver; other orna-ments included beads around their necks, earrings, and finger rings as well as wristlets. Women wore short leggings of woolen material which reached their knees. They preferred beaded shawls, but those who could not afford shawls wore blankets.

The summer settlements of the Fox were along rivers and streams in lowlands where the women could find adequate ground to clear and plant. The dwellings were oblong, bark-covered structures with pole frameworks and were up to forty feet in length and twenty feet in width. Along each interior sidewall was a bark- and skin-covered platform raised above the ground to serve as seats and beds. In the open space at the center of a house were fires for cooking and heating. Clusters of lodges were occupied from April through much of September, but in the winter small family groups dispersed to follow a wandering life. The winter dwellings were oval structures framed by placing the ends of poles in the ground, bending the poles together, and tying them at the top. Over the framework were placed reeds or mats, and at the doorway hung a bearskin.

The inventory of Fox material culture is incomplete, and most descriptions date from about 1900. Material goods were for the most part portable since much of every year was spent in scattered hunting camps. The principal hunting weapon was the bow and arrow; the bow was sinew-backed, and arrows were placed in a quiver of buckskin. Other items of material culture included wooden mortars for pounding maize and other grains. The people also had digging sticks to prepare the ground, and they made various forms of bark and skin containers, in which they placed not only household goods but products from the hunt and from their farming activities.

By the turn of the century they used the clothing and everyday household equipment which they purchased from whites. During any important religious or social event, however, they wore clothing and adornments which they had come to regard as traditional finery. Anything made from silver was regarded as "good medicine," particularly when made into jewelry on which were executed certain designs. The silver once came in long processed strips from Mexico, but by about 1900 it was obtained from Colorado. A silver hair comb for a woman was a particularly potent charm, for it was inserted near an individual's soul, located just beneath the scalp lock; the teeth of the comb were arranged so that they touched the soul. To wear numerous silver bracelets also was desirable, even if they stretched in an almost continuous band from the wrist to the shoulder, for the bracelets with designs on them represented prayers. On ceremonial occasions girls and women wore a wide variety of decorated, beaded ornaments. Most important among these was the strip of beaded leather which was wrapped around the roll of hair at the back of a woman's head. Furthermore, attached to the hairwrapper were long woven strings which dangled nearly to the ground. These hairstrings were regarded as particularly sacred, and the owner's welfare could be controlled by possession of her hairstring even temporarily. Strings of beads were worn by girls and women; it was felt that four pounds was the most one should wear. A man's most important ornament also was that which protected the scalp lock. Habitually, each chief wore an eagle feather set in a small bone mounting, and at the end of the feather was red dye, which indicated that the man had killed a warrior. The feather also was decorated with golden-winged woodpecker feathers since this bird was important in the supernatural system.

By the time the records about Fox food habits are reasonably complete, we find that an iron kettle hung from a hook above the fire was the usual cooking utensil. When they lived in Wisconsin, they harvested wild rice as an important food, but the only wild rice that they were able to obtain in later years was supplied by the Winnebago and Menominee. The most important food staple for the Fox was maize. The varieties raised were white, red, yellow, and blue. As might be expected, a wide assortment of maize dishes were prepared and consumed. Corn was boiled or made into hominy by leaching the shells away with wood ash and washing away the lye. Corn also was parched in a fire, but most frequently it was ground into a meal and made into gruel, which was consumed after boiling. A wide variety of beans were grown which had reached the Fox from the Southwest. Another domestic plant was squash, which was prepared for future consumption by cutting the fruit into rings, which were placed on a pole and half dried in the sun. The rings then were plaited and placed between two mats, which were pressed by walking over them. The pieces again were dried in the sun and finally stored for winter. Among the wild plants gathered were broad-leafed arrowhead corms, either collected from the plant rootlets or robbed from muskrat caches. These "potatoes" were boiled, sliced and strung on strings which were hung from the rafters of a bark house. A potato-like growth was the groundnut which grew along the plant roots and was as much as three inches in diameter; it was peeled, boiled, sliced, and then dried to be cooked with meat in the winter. A third plant, rootstock from the yellow lotus, was dried for winter; when needed, it was soaked and cooked with meat, corn, or beans. Additionally, the Fox collected sugar-maple sap, which was an important seasoning in cooking, and a few plants were used specifically for seasoning. Hickory nuts, butter-nuts, and walnuts were eaten, and diverse forms of wild fruit were consumed either at the time of collecting or later in the winter after they had been dried.

The subsistence activities of the Fox around 1820, and most likely before, were divided into two phases. In the spring and summer they occupied villages and tilled the lands adjacent to their bark-covered lodges. The women planted and maintained the gardens while the men hunted. The most important game animal was the deer, valued not only for its meat but for its skin and fat. Small game and birds were hunted, as was the bear, which the Fox considered a choice meat. The staples, however, were maize, beans, and squash cultivated by the women and the wild plant foods which they collected. These foods were dried and stored in cache pits, in bark baskets, or in the rafters of a bark house. In mid-September when families left their summer settlement they took a small quantity of corn and their other possessions to a winter hunting area. The scattered families lived in their dome-shaped, mat-covered structures which could be taken down and rebuilt easily by carrying the mats from one camp to the next. As the number of game kills declined in late winter, they assembled in large camps and were not active until they began to trap beaver in the spring. Following the beaver trapping season they traveled back to their villages, planning the trip so that they would arrive simultaneously. This was done to minimize the exposure of small groups to hostile peoples and to prevent any person from illegally taking provisions from another's cache.

According to the able analysis of early historic Fox life by Natalie F. Joffe, the most important social and economic unit was the small extended family. It might include about forty individuals since a man sometimes had two to five wives, and their children sometimes brought their spouses into the household. In addition, there might be household members from other tribes who had been adopted or were considered captives. Female prisoners might marry Fox men, and their offspring were regarded as Fox. A family group also might include individuals adopted to take the place of deceased persons; these individuals did not take up residence in the household but were regarded as members of it.

The Fox traced their most important kinship ties through males (patrilineal descent), and those persons who were presumed to have stemmed from a common but unknown ancestor comprised patrisibs, which were the most important descent groups. The members of one patrisib were obligated by custom to seek their spouses from another sib (sib exogamy). The names of the leading sibs were Bear, Fox, Wolf, Thunder, Swan, Eagle, Sturgeon, and Bear Potato. The largest patrisibs were the first four mentioned, and it is possible that they were among the oldest sibs. From one particular line with a known common ancestor (patrilineage) was derived the line of paramount chiefs. The Fox sib was known also as the War Chiefs and had split into named sub-sibs which in at least one instance formed a lineage. The Fox, Thunder, and Bear sibs contributed most of the chiefs, the leaders of war parties, and council members; the other sibs normally provided only councilmen. The sibs appear to have been grouped into two groups (moieties) which provided reciprocal services in ceremonial activities; the Bear and Wolf reciprocated with the Eagle, Fox, and Thunder sibs. It must be added, however, that the exact nature of these mutual obligations is not known.

A second type of moiety division has been recorded. In this arrangement each person was assigned to one of two groups, the To'kana or Kicko, depending on birth order and the father's affiliation. A firstborn was usually assigned to the division to which his father did not belong, and the second to the group of his father's affiliation. The third belonged to the moiety of the first and so on. Assignment was irrespective of the sex of the person and had nothing to do with marital arrangements. Between the members of the moieties there was a friendly rivalry. They competed in games, and the division was important in certain festivities, hunting arrangements, and the assignment of camp police.

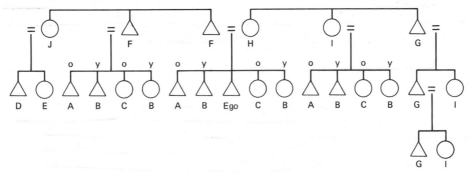

Aboriginal Fox kin terms. Each capital letter represents a different term; o indicates older than Ego and y indicates younger than Ego.

In the Fox kinship terminology collected by Sol Tax in the 1930's we find that on a male Ego's generational level there were specific terms for older brother and older sister, whereas younger brothers and sisters were considered as younger siblings. These terms were extended to father's brother's children and to mother's sister's children. There were additionally distinct and separate terms for father's sister's son and daughter as well as for mother's brother's son and daughter. Furthermore, the terms for father's sister's son and daughter were the same as for sister's son and daughter. This form of cousin terminology is termed Omaha. On the generational level above Ego we find that the word for father was extended to father's brother, but there was a different term for mother's brother. It was extended to all males in the direct line from mother's brother—for example, mother's brother's son, mother's brother's son's son. The terminology for males on the first ascending generation above Ego is bifurcate merging. The most important observation to be made about the terminology is that there was the inclination to group individuals on both sides of one's family into a small number of categories and to ignore generations. In kinship behavior there tended to be egalitarian relationships between sets of individuals. For example, between a father and his son we find the behavior tended to be as between two brothers in the ideals of modern American society. Among the Fox, the mother-son relationship was more like that between sister and brother; restraint was necessary without avoidance. Again between a father and his daughter there was the brother and sister attitude, while the mother and daughter relationship paralleled that of a father and son.

Political life was organized around the tribe and the village. The paramount chief was from a particular lineage in the Bear sib, although most sibs contributed lesser chiefs who, like the tribal chief, must be from a particular patrilineage. In the event that the elder son of a chief could not or would not succeed his father (primogeniture) the title and position were passed to a younger son, a brother, or a nephew of the chief. At the village level it is apparent that the chief was important, for it was the village that organized subsistence activities and raiding or war parties. A village chief was in office for an extended period of time, and his influence was great even though he had little power. He was expected to be nonaggressive, and he served as an arbitrator in collective discussions. The council, which made the decisions affecting the community as a whole, had a required membership from different patrilines but also included other men with outstanding qualities. The village chief listened to discussions and attempted to reconcile conflicting views. From the above descriptions, it may appear that the chief and council were quite powerful, as they in fact were, although it is true that they were most often guided by tradition. The Fox, as Walter B. Miller stresses, were rugged individualists who knew what was expected of them, and in normal activities they strongly resented anyone's attempt to direct their behavior. As the Jesuit missionary Father Allouez (Miller, 1955, 286) wrote long ago, "These people are self-willed beyond anything that can be imagined!"

In order to illustrate how the political system operated, it is instructive to follow what took place when a man killed his wife. She was of course a member of a different sib, and her male relatives summoned the murderer to appear at their main lodge. He did as he was directed and squatted on the floor while the men of the woman's sib seated themselves on the platforms. One man held an ax which would be used to smash the murderer's skull if he were to be executed. When the jury was assembled, a man at one end of the line silently nudged the person next to him; this was a vote to kill the murderer. This man nudged the one sitting on his far side and so on until one man failed to nudge his partner; this indicated that he did not approve of the death penalty. Since a unanimous verdict of guilt was required, the murderer was not doomed to die. Instead, his relatives were permitted to offer gifts as compensation. This example demonstrates that the crime of murder was not judged on the tribal or village level, but was considered an offense against the kin group of the deceased individual. The example also illustrates that alternatives of action, death or compensation, were possible.

One activity at which the Fox excelled was warfare, and it consumed much of their time and energy. Aggression against another Indian group or against whites was organized at either the tribal or raiding party level. A national war such as those fought against the French, the Americans, the Sioux, or Osage met with overall tribal approval, but very rarely involved large numbers of warriors and large-scale battles. Raids were most common, and they were organized by individuals against a particular enemy in order to accomplish a specific purpose. Warriors ventured forth to secure hunting areas against intrusion by others, to acquire new lands upon which to hunt, to avenge the death of a Fox, or to gain prestige and honor. A war leader at any level was able to organize a raid because of prior success and the power he had been granted by a manitou. A war leader supervised the strategy, but he had limited power, for no participating warrior ever was obligated to follow the war leader against his will, and he could return home at any time without the loss of honor. Even though a warrior might submit to the authority of a war leader and follow instructions, the participants were obliged to bend to the war chief's modicum of authority only during the period of the raid. The important point is that the Fox war leader had more authority and power than any other individual at any other time, and yet his prerogatives were very few indeed. As if to emphasize the temporary nature of his position, after returning from a raid he was obligated not to enter his settlement until he had been purified ceremonially. Within Fox society a great deal of honor was heaped upon the successful warrior. To be a great warrior was a value instilled in boys from early childhood. A child was given portions of the eyebrow or heart of a brave but slain enemy so that he might eat them and acquire the qualities of the deceased. A boy attempted to join a war party as soon as possible in order that he might boast of his exploits according to the custom for all warriors. Anyone could attempt to lead a war party; if he dreamed and his dreams were judged propitious by other warriors, they would pledge themselves to join the raid. Before departure, war songs were sung, and men abstained from the company of women. Although a woman might join her husband on a war party, she would not have sexual intercourse with him during the trip. A raiding party advanced slowly, hunting along the route and caching the dry meat for the return trip. If the party numbered twenty or more individuals, a sacred bundle was taken along for supernatural protection; a smaller party relied on the party leader's medicine bundle to secure supernatural aid. Some men served as scouts, and one was designated to cook for the attackers. An attack always was planned to surprise the enemy. If the party were successful, the return was led by the man who made the first kill; in defeat, each warrior returned home as best he could. If scalps were taken and captives secured, the aged often were killed on the way home. A successful raid ended with a scalp dance and feasting at the village of the warriors. A woman could gain important status and rights among men if a male relative permitted her to club the head of an enemy he had killed. For a Fox man to steal horses was honorable; however, such theft did not have the social value reported among most Indians of the plains and prairies. A warrior could and usually did take new names repeatedly if he excelled in warfare. The warfare complex among the Fox was not nearly as elaborate as among many Indians of the plains, but it did nonetheless manifest most of the important features found among them.

Individual experience in supernatural matters centered in the concept of manitou. Manitou was sacred and mysterious, a fickle but necessary power with which an individual must communicate if he were to be successful. As a supernatural, manitou was a pervasive quality in nature. It was approached with humility and apprehension, and yet one was aware of the moment when a personalized manitou had manifested itself simply by the thrill felt and by a sense of feeling different. The normal way in which one sought out a manitou was through prolonged fasting, and yet at a critical or even unanticipated time this force might be heard or seen. The manifestation of a manitou might be conveyed in a song, an object, or a ritual to be performed. In discussing supernatural experience among the Fox, Miller stresses the important point that religious systems are essentially projections from one's social experience and an extension of the manner in which men deal with other men. The central religious concept of manitou was a pervasive supernatural force; it was abstract and impersonal. Yet, it was received by an individual, and it was a personalized manitou that was drawn into the experiences of an individual. The blessing and cooperation of a manitou had no built-in permanence; it could at any time be lost inadvertently or through carelessness. The varieties of manitou were endless and pervasive. The force could be animal, human, organic, inorganic, material, nonmaterial, natural or supernatural, and an individual receiving such power always sought to reinforce it.

Each individual sought rapport with the supernaturals, for personal welfare and success depended on one's relationship with a manitou. To achieve this condition each adolescent boy fasted for four days and four nights or even longer. He darkened his face with ashes and stayed alone in the forest. At the end of his isolation he dreamed of a manitou or received a vision which included instructions. The receipt of a manitou's power was contingent on following certain rules set down by the supernatural. These usually included, among other things, the avoidance of menstruating women and a periodic offering of tobacco to the manitou. In addition, other instructions might be given such as wearing a certain item of clothing, singing a particular song, or owning a particular object which became the basis of a medicine bundle. If a boy conducted himself correctly in his relationship with a manitou, the association would endure, but if the boy failed the manitou withdrew his support. Then the youth would fast again and isolate himself in order to obtain an affiliation with another manitou. A faithful manitou would not only remain with a man during his lifetime but continue to be with him even after death.

The supernatural forces in the religious system were conceived around the idea of manitou; the most important personification was called Gitche Manitou, the great manitou. There was also the creator and culture hero Wisaka who was addressed as "my nephew," which among the Fox implied equality. Other mythological creatures, usually animals, could bestow power on men. Medicine power could be granted by bears and snakes and the deer made one swift of foot. An individual's contact with these creatures served as a basis for sacred bundle rituals, which were the essence of Fox ceremonialism. The founder had learned from one of the supernaturals the essential rituals, and around each bundle a cult developed. Affiliation with sacred bundles and their ceremonies was passed along sib lines, or it could be achieved by learning the ritual and by being invited to participate. Other ceremonial ties did not pass along sib lines; membership was granted through initiation. Although there were differences in the details of sib ceremonies, the rituals of different sibs had much in common. The spring and summer rituals included dancing in a bark house of the sib. In the winter ceremonies were held in the wigwams; these included no dancing. During summer rituals the singers and the drummer consistently sat on the south side of the bark structure. Hoof or gourd rattles were used by certain sibs, and rasps were used by others. The dance directors blew flutes. Participants consistently performed four dances and ate three times, with the main feast following the third dance. Ceremonial attendants often were drawn from particular sibs who reciprocated with one another. An emphasis also was placed on dogs as ceremonial food, seating position according to moiety, the sacrifice of tobacco, and numerous other specific traits and trait complexes which demonstrate the essential homogeneity of the ceremonies, which were conceived of by the Fox as quite diverse in origin and details. A leader of the Fox ceremonies committed to memory the ritual speeches which were punctuated by other episodes. Such a leader followed established tradition in his performances, and the authority he had was limited to the activities involved in the ceremony.

Apart from the manitous, there were other supernatural beings. Probably the most important single category was that of witches, who were envisaged in either male or female human form. It was reported that witches, who often were members of the Bear sib, learned their skills from other witches. They ventured about during the night, flashes of light which illuminated the landscape came from their mouths, and furthermore, they made a hissing sound when passing. The evil created by witches took diverse forms; for example, when a part of a person's body swelled the cause was a witch. Then, too, when someone died for no apparent reason, a witch was thought to be behind the death. If an individual was bewitched, certain techniques could be used to turn the malevolent power against the witch. When a witch entered a house, it turned into a feather if its identity was discovered.

In the Fox concept of the world most natural phenomena were considered within the supernatural sphere. Thus, the sun was a man, a manitou, and the grandfather of the Fox; he was not always considerate of the people. The moon, as their grandmother, had a gentle quality and could be looked upon at any time. The months were named and associated with the arrival of each new moon. The Milky Way was a river of stars, and other stars in the sky either were persons who had died and had gone to live in the sky, or else they were great manitous. The four stars forming the body of the Big Dipper were thought of as a bear; it was followed by three stars who were hunters. They killed the bear in the fall, and its blood fell to earth, turning the leaves of some trees red and fading the color of others. Then the bear came back to life, and the hunters pursued it for another year. The color red symbolized the fall of the year; it also signified hostility and was used for decoration. Black was the color for winter, for fasting, and for mourning. Green was for spring and peace; it was the special color of the chief's sib. Yellow symbolized summer.

Curers among the Mesquakie used plant products and to a far lesser extent animal substances to heal patients. As a plant was collected, it was necessary to follow certain rules. Songs were sung before removing roots, and an offering was placed in the ground where a root had been. This ritual was necessary in order to appease the grandmother earth, for plants were the hairs from her head. The earth was the grandmother of Wisaka and the Fox as well; her name was Mother-of-all-Things-Everywhere. Her hairs, the plants, were alive and the grandparents of the Fox. Plants knew about the behavior of people, and they were able to talk with one another. Their conversation was heard as the sound produced when the wind blew through the trees. Plants could be happy or sad, they mated in the spring, and they bore fruit in the fall. Wisaka was appeased so that plants would be potent cures. Not only was there a proper manner but a proper season in which to collect medicinal plants, and only stipulated amounts were to be taken.

In attempting to effect cures it was possible to mix herbs and roots of diverse plants according to the diagnosis of a disease. Sometimes as many as nine plants were combined in a single medicine. The ethnobotany published by Huron H. Smith for the Fox was compiled largely from a collection made by Jones about 1900. It contained nearly 200 plant substances used in curing, most of which were taken internally although some were applied externally and a few were burned, using the smoke as a cure. More items in the pharmacopoeia were used to cure or ease intestinal disorders than for any illnesses. They comprised nearly a seventh of the known medicines. The next large category consisted of diverse types of poultices, followed by plant products used to treat urinary or bladder ailments and those surrounding some aspect of menstruation or childbearing. At least five different plant medicines were used against colds, snake bites, to stop or impede the flow of blood from wounds, to provide strength, or as love magic. Only rarely were plants used in a diagnosis, or for some psychological illness such as excessive fear. Rarely, too, were botanical cures borrowed from whites. The use of animal products as cures was limited to a few items, and likewise inorganic substances only rarely were employed.

In order for a woman to conceive, the Fox believed that it was essential for her to copulate repeatedly with one man. During the course of her pregnancy many restrictions surrounded her behavior. For example, to ensure a normal birth the woman abstained from eating nuts so that the embryo would not break through the membrane; she could not touch a corpse for fear her baby would die, and to stare at a corpse would make the baby cross-eyed. In childbearing a woman knelt and leaned forward, supported by a rawhide strap. She could not cry out no matter how severe the pain. If the delivery were long and difficult, a shaman or woman sang around the outside of the hut but usually offered no other assistance. Parturition took place in a small hut away from the family dwelling, where the mother was cared for by an old woman. Here she remained for ten days after the birth. For the next twenty days the woman slept in the main house but apart from the other members and ate in the birth lodge.

A baby was placed on a cradleboard and carried by its mother for nearly a year. As children grew older, the parents did not favor one child over the other unless a boy became an outstanding hunter. The ideals of childhood behavior were recorded by Michelson from a Fox text. From it we learn that children were told not to visit other families often, for if they did so people would think that they always were searching for something good to eat. Children were expected to be retiring and honest and, when someone died, to fast and not be noisy. These fastings prepared boys for additional fasts which were an important part of growing up and becoming a man. Abstaining from food also was emphasized for girls, especially as their menarche approached; the purpose was for them to have a long and good life. These ideals may not have been followed exactly, but they did constitute the normal expectations for children. A role assumed for two years by young males of high social standing was that of a "slave" in the service of a chief. After this period the volunteer was freed from the drudgery of menial tasks such as cooking and camp chores throughout his life.

As mentioned earlier, the relationship between a father and his son was somewhat comparable to the behavior between brothers in our society. Hunting instruction began when a boy was about seven, and by the time he was twelve he was given a gun and expected to obtain small game. He was taught not only objective hunting skills but associated magical practices. When a boy killed his first game a feast was held in his honor, a widespread practice among North American Indians. A son who disobeyed was not punished physically but was instructed by his father to fast. To fast and seek solitude was not new to the child, but it became intensified. While the boy was still young, he was expected to seek out a manitou. When he went alone into the forest on his quest, his parents mourned the loss of their son, for after establishing this supernatural relationship he would no longer be a child. To fast and paint one's face with ashes made a manitou approachable and encouraged it to grant the young man success in the hunt and in war, and give him longevity as well.

At about the same age that a boy began to receive hunting instructions, a girl was taught domestic skills by her mother. She learned to sew, to cook, and to care for the garden. About the age of twelve, she began to acquire the more complex skills necessary in making moccasins and house mats. At her first menstruation she was isolated from the settlement in a small hut where she lived for ten days with a blanket over her head. Her companion during this isolation was an old woman, who instructed the girl about adult behavior. At the end of this initial isolation the girl bathed in a stream, and her skin was pierced, especially about the back and sides, until she bled freely. The blood-letting was to ensure that the girl would not menstruate excessively. She then moved within sight of the settlement, living there for twenty days. After this time she took a second bath and finally was permitted in the family dwelling once again. During all subsequent menstrual periods, a woman was isolated in a hut. She was not only potentially dangerous to herself but to men and supernaturals. If she were to touch her hair, it might fall out; if she ate sweet or sour food, she might lose all her teeth. She could kill a tree with her touch, or cause a crop to fail if she ran through a garden. Most importantly manitous abhorred menstruating women, and such women were avoided by men so that they would not jeopardize their special powers.

A girl was considered ready for marriage only after she had acquired the skills of making fine beadwork and ribbon applique. Her behavior was supervised carefully by her mother and her mother's brother, who was a joking relative. He not only joked with her but made certain that she behaved properly since he would be shamed if she misbehaved. She was taught not to be promiscuous nor to giggle, for giggly girls were open to sexual overtures. As a boy became a young man, he was expected to be respectful toward girls, and to have sexual intercourse only with the girl he planned to marry. A young man sometimes courted a girl by playing a flute near her home, which was an attempt to lure the girl outside. The melody of the flute conveyed his desire, but for a girl to accept the lure invited seduction. The parents of a courting couple preferred to have the man visit their home openly to win their daughter in marriage.

The principal means for obtaining a wife was by bride service or elopement, with the former being more common. The suitor usually became friendly with the girl's brother and mentioned the subject of marriage to him, although he could approach the girl directly. The girl was of necessity a member of a different patrisib from the man. If the match was acceptable, the girl's family usually required the services of the groom until the first offspring was born. An alternative was for a man's family to present the girl's family with gifts so that the period of service would be unnecessary. This was attempted especially if the parents of the boy did not want to lose their son as a hunter. If gifts were accepted in lieu of bride service or when the service was completed, the couple was free to establish an independent household or to join either set of in-laws. An elopement occurred when a man convinced a girl to join him on a summer hunt; on their return he presented the parents of the girl with gifts. Another less common arrangement was for a bride to be offered to a warrior by her father. This happened when a man had rendered extraordinary service to the family of the girl. For example, if a warrior prevented the scalping of a man's dead son, gave the son a warrior's interment, or rescued the son from an enemy, he might be offered the sister as a wife.

At least a few Fox appear not to have married but to have lived as transvestites. A dance held annually centered about and emphasized the position of such a person. The *berdache,* as he was termed by the French traders and trappers, was danced around by men who had had a sexual relationship with him. The transvestite wore the clothing of a woman, and because of his unusual role he was regarded as sacred.

The dissolution of a marriage usually resulted from sterility or from an inability of a couple to tolerate one another. Some personality characteristics such as extreme jealousy or ill temper led to divorce. When a marriage was dissolved, any presents which had been exchanged during the marital arrangements were returned, but personal property was retained by each partner. Sometimes a divorce occurred after a few days of marriage, with the husband leaving his wife. Instances such as these were said to have taken place when the bride was not a maiden. Examples of a wife committing adultery are recorded, and in extreme instances the husband might kill the couple; another alternative was to cut off his wife's ears or bite off her nose.

One conspicuous characteristic of adult life was that each individual knew what was expected of him and was resentful of being instructed in any manner. A person's behavior was dictated by tradition; he did as his father had done before him, or as he had done the year before. He communicated with the supernaturals as an individual with no other person standing between him and the manitou. He functioned in the institutions of the society without supervision, and in his personal life, again, he was his own authority. Thus, it is not surprising that individualism was the social norm, and strong resentment was exhibited by any Fox who was told to do anything.

When an adult died, there were three possible forms of interment. In one the body was placed on a scaffold or in a tree. A deceased warrior was interred in honor by placing him in a sitting position above the body of a slain enemy. In these forms the bodies were not covered. Most common perhaps was to excavate a shallow pit and arrange the seated body so that the head was above the ground and rocks or a small shed covered it. Food and water were included with the body, and the feet were faced to the west. Weapons were not placed with the dead for fear that the spirits would use them against the living. A stake was erected at the foot of the grave, and the bark was peeled from it. Among the final acts were sprinkling tobacco on the body and killing a pup or a grown dog on the site of the burial. The spirit of the dog was not only to protect but to guide the dead to the next world. The interment was carried out by an appointed person who was assisted by others. Just before the body of a warrior was abandoned, an old warrior recounted the number of individuals the deceased had killed, which meant that the souls of these persons would serve as his slaves in the land of the spirits. The funeral director distributed to his helpers the property of the deceased, along with items contributed by relatives of the deceased.

Each individual had two souls which served different purposes. A small soul came from a particular manitou and was equated with the individual's life; it left the body at the time of death and through subsequent adoption ceremonies was reborn three times. The larger soul, from Wisaka, had entered the neonate's body at birth and was never to be reborn. In the world of spirits a division was made. In one section lived persons who had been good on earth, and in the other, persons who were evil. Some of these concepts may very well be nonaboriginal, or at least partly inspired by Christian missionaries.

After disposing of the body, the sib to which the deceased belonged held a mourning ceremony. A dog was killed for the event and its hair singed by four firebrands taken from the hearth of the deceased. The dog was cooked, and the sib's mourning songs were sung until about midnight when the participants ate the dog. The ceremony then continued through the night. The principal mourners dressed in tattered clothing and blackened their faces. They remained in this state up to four years, which was the maximum time limit before an adoption ceremony which brought an end to mourning. The adoption ceremony was performed by the relatives of the deceased and served to release permanently the soul of the dead. The soul had left the earth after four days but returned at intervals until the adoption rituals were completed. If this did not happen within four years, the soul became an owl. The adoption was of an unrelated friend of the deceased who was of the same sex and approximate age. This individual assumed the kinship position of the deceased but also retained his own prior kinship ties. If the deceased was a warrior killed by an enemy, the adopted warrior was obligated to kill an enemy in order to release the widow from mourning.

Following the course of Fox history once again, the Indians who struggled back to Iowa beginning in 1851, were miserably poor. Their economy was based on hunting and trapping, gardening, begging, and selling curios. Whenever they obtained surplus money, they purchased additional lands.

Plate 30
Black Hawk, a Sauk chief
(After McKenney and Hall, 1934).

Plate 31 *Fox women
near Tama, Iowa, working on
a platform before a reed-
covered dwelling, ca. 1900*
(Courtesy of the State Historical Society of Iowa).

Plate 32 *A Fox woman with her child, ca. 1900* (Courtesy of the State Historical Society of Iowa).

Plate 33 *Fox Indians from Oklahoma welcomed to the Tama Pow-Wow in 1950* (Courtesy of the State Historical Society of Iowa).

Plates 34 & 35 *Mrs. Willie Johnson, a Fox woman in Iowa, sits with her great grandchildren waiting for a cooking fire to heat. Seated in the foreground of the photo below are the Fox couple Mr. and Mrs. Willie Johnson surrounded by their grandchildren and great grandchildren. Both photos were taken in 1962 (Courtesy of Joan Liffring Zug).*

The Fox remained extremely distrustful of outsiders; for example, in 1876 when a school was built, it was not attended by Indian children. Families as units continued to frequent hunting and trapping areas in the winter. In the late 1880's the Fox still refused to allow their children to attend school, and the men would not learn the skills necessary to become farmers. In 1894, after the sale of land allotments which had been held for them in Oklahoma, they were able to expand their holdings in Iowa to 2800 acres. It apparently was about this time that they began to rent farmlands to whites, lands that did not belong to the core of their holdings, and to use the rent money for the payment of taxes. In 1895 the Secretary of the Interior became the trustee for Fox lands in Iowa, replacing the governor of the state in this capacity, but this change was not actually completed until 1908.

A visitor to the Fox lands in Iowa in 1897 and 1898 reported that the population was about 400, and the winter dwellings were described as oblong, pole-framed structures with mat coverings, just as in aboriginal times. The ground inside such a structure was covered with old blankets, and a fire in a central fireplace provided warmth, light and heat for cooking; the only items seen in one such dwelling were containers and food. The standard fare seems to have been flour, lard, and maize. The flour was fried in lard to make a bannock which was eaten with dried sweet corn. Dogs remained an important source of meat for a festive occasion. A few families, particularly those of younger men, lived in frame dwellings with adjacent outbuildings. One of these residence units was provided with a coal heater, and other furnishings included a table and chairs. In the summer the people lived along the bottomland near the Iowa River in dwellings covered with boards and bark over which mats were placed. Inside, a platform extended along the length of the room on both sides. The structures were supplemented with a hut nearby for menstruating women.

By 1937, Fox landholdings near Tama, Iowa, consisted of one large parcel of 2800 acres on which the people lived, and another 520 acres which were tilled by white farmers on leases, The population of 450 supported themselves either by farming or by wage labor on the family plots which could not be alienated by individual occupants but could be leased to another Fox. A family dwelling consisted of a frame house with usually one or two rooms and adjacent outbuildings such as a barn, corncrib, chicken coop, roofless privy, and a canvas menstrual hut. During their monthly periods or at childbirth the women ate in the menstrual huts but slept in the houses. Another important structure was made of canvas or mats covering a frame of poles. It was rectangular, resembling the summer house of old, and was often attached to an arbor. On the arbor platform the men sat and the children played, and much of the cooking was done by the women over an outdoor fire nearby.

The average family income in 1937 was about $500 per year, which included funds from all sources. The total landholdings were worth about $225,000, and tribal assets held by the Federal government returned $6500 a year. Individuals could draw on the funds held by the Federal government for specific projects if they had tribal and Bureau of Indian Affairs approval. About half of the ninety-one families farmed; the other half supported themselves by wage labor. In 1936, a year of drought, seventy-six families received some form of relief. In the farming activities, women cultivated the garden plots after the land had been prepared by the men, and the men raised the field crops, which were important sources of cash income. Men who did not till the soil labored in nearby towns.

Food habits reflected a certain degree of continuity with the past, for maize was shelled and dried or made into hominy as of old, and sections of squash were dried, grated, and stored for future use. The people still collected local plant products and took small game. New items produced in their gardens and fields included oats, alfalfa, potatoes, beets, and onions. They obtained wheat flour and most meat and dairy products from stores, and their maize was ground at a commercial mill. It might be expected that families would raise dairy cattle or cattle and hogs for sale, but few families were inclined to do so since they apparently disliked the chores associated with stock raising. They did raise chickens, but their success in this enterprise was not striking. Innumerable dogs were kept, and young ones remained an important ceremonial food. About half of the families owned horses for hauling buggies and wagons or for plowing and riding, but it was primarily younger persons who rode horses. The material culture in the late 1930's seemingly was typical of rural Iowa. About half of the families owned automobiles, and most shopping was done in Tama, where some effort was made by the storekeepers to stock goods with an appeal to Indians, including shawls, silk neckerchiefs, and beads. Special items for use on festive or ceremonial occasions, such as seed beads, were purchased from mail-order houses; deerskins were obtained from other Indians.

A residence unit consisted of a man, his wife and their biological children, unmarried relatives, and perhaps children by a former marriage. These nuclear-core households were the economic units as well, although all residents might not contribute equally to the family's support, and the near relatives of the couple often were transient. In general, a new household was established near the home of relatives, and there was a tendency to be more closely linked to a wife's family than to that of a man. Yet relatives on both sides of one's family (kindred) offered the typical individual a widespread network of kin, numbering between fifty and one hundred persons, distributed among about a dozen other households. It is significant that although the Fox were patrilineal, the important social ties in their daily lives were with both sides of the family. Family ties were expanded through adoption, which was of the same nature as in aboriginal times, a deceased relative being replaced by an adopted individual of approximately the same age and sex.

The political life of the Iowa Fox had undergone extensive changes by the 1930's, but it exhibited certain continuities with the aboriginal past. The most marked social continuity was represented by the To'kana-Kicko system. As formerly, the firstborn was of the moiety opposite his father, the second was the same moiety as the father and so on. In the 1930's these groups functioned mainly in games and ceremonies. More meaningful was the political factionalism which was important in daily activities. It appears to have originated from a controversy over reporting individual names for a tribal roll compiled in 1876. The members of a conservative faction refused to tell the Indian agent their names, but the progressives did so, which led to inequities in the annuity payments. In addition, a chief was appointed in 1881 who was not a member of the Bear sib. No issue was made of the fact at the time, but when the chief later led the progressives, the conservatives questioned his right to the leadership. This division continued to be important in the 1930's. Families, but not sibs, tended to act as units in the factionalism, but these differences did not affect ceremonial activities in which sibs were important. Marriages tended to be within a faction, but when they did cut across, it was most often the woman who joined the side of her husband.

In 1916 the last chief appointed a council which functioned until 1929, when a council was elected. The elected members of the contending factions could not agree, however, and they never met. Although elections continued to be held, the council remained inactive, owing to internal differences. Then in 1937 the tribe organized under the Indian Reorganization Act, and the elected members of the council, seven in all, began to work together. However, the details of council operations were not recorded. In their political relationships with the state and Federal governments their lands continued to be held in trust by the Federal government. The land was subject to taxation, eminent domain, and other judicial procedures which applied to any other individually owned land in the state. Differences among themselves were usually settled verbally, although women sometimes fought and one man might strike another on the head. The most common offenses prosecuted were drunkenness and differences over property rights. These legal actions often were brought by Indians, but they did not seek intervention from whites for problems such as theft.

The concept of manitou persisted, and formal religious activities coalesced around the sacred bundles of the patrisibs or voluntary religious associations. Christianity, the use of peyote, and the nonaboriginal Drum Society offered limited opportunities for religious participation. The peyote cult was small in 1937, although ceremonial use of the cactus had been known since around the turn of the present century. Peyote was valued mainly for its reportedly curative properties; a person who tried other cures and then turned to peyote often continued to take it after he had recovered. The Drum Society was a religious organization of comparatively recent origin in 1932 and probably was derived from the Potawatomi. The members were from the progressive faction even though the power of the ceremony was derived from the manitou. The ritual involved the use of four drums, and the ceremonies were held four times a year. The drums were associated with particular leaders, and they had specific functions. The religion still focused on the sacred bundles, which were hereditary either in a patrisib line or else crosscut sib affiliations. Forty sacred bundle groups in eleven major categories existed, and within each category were major and minor bundle groups. It was possible to acquire membership in a sacred bundle group through an invitation, which most often was extended when an individual was a good singer and knew the songs associated with the particular bundle group. Certain reciprocal functions linked the groups into various activities. The bundle affiliations did not regulate marriage although this was apparently an old ideal. The ceremonies were held in summer longhouses and extended from morning until sunset of a single day. Food was prepared by the hosts, and the most important dish was stewed puppies, ceremonially killed with clubs, served by members of another sacred bundle group. The dances were in sets of four, and the sacred bundle was opened and its various items used in the ceremony. The dancers, either male or female, were introduced with flute music played in the four directions or to items in the bundle. Both men and women participated in the summer rituals, but only men were active in the winter festivities. The dog feast was eaten between the third and fourth dances, and after the meal the bones were carefully collected and burned.

Witchcraft and sorcery were still very much a part of Fox life in the 1930's, and malevolent power was obtained in a vision quest. It was in a sorcerer's power to take the form of a bear or a snake. If a potential victim could shoot a gun at the spot where a witch was thought to be, the sorcerer would die within four days. One important use of sorcery was as love magic, and, if properly employed, it led to an uncontrollable attractiveness of the user. The medicine at the same time would drive a nonresponding victim to insanity and eventual suicide. The ability to cure, which came from a vision, was limited to shamans, who employed a variety of techniques. A shaman visited the patient, and if he was compensated enough he accepted the case. The curing procedure entailed singing, administering herbs, and sucking out the disease. Because it was a bear or snake that gave supernatural power to the medicine man, a claw or bone formed the core of his medicine bundle and might be used to suck out the substance causing the illness.

A brief but revealing composite reconstruction of an individual's life cycle in the 1930's may be obtained from the description by Tax and Joffe. As in the aboriginal era, pregnant women were obliged to refrain from certain activities which were considered harmful to the embryo which they carried. One taboo was that a pregnant woman could not eat bologna for fear the embryo would be harmed since it too was covered with skin. The father as well as the mother had restrictions placed on his behavior for the safety of the infant. Parturition took place in a separate structure built for this purpose, and the woman was aided by her female relatives. The mother remained separated from her husband for ten days following the birth.

When a child was six years old, it began to attend school. Only after the turn of the present century did schools become intermittently important in the life of a child. At her menarche a girl lived apart in a hut and was visited only by old female relatives. She lived alone for ten days, and then for another ten days she cooked for herself. No similar ritual existed for a boy, nor was there any longer much of an opportunity to teach him to fast.

Although adult life centered about one's family, many forms of entertainment existed outside the family. Tama provided pool halls frequented by men and boys; a men's baseball team and a girls' softball team were active; and during the winter gambling was an important form of diversion for men and women. The varied ceremonial life also continued to be viable, and the yearly Indian Pow-Wow, organized in 1913, provided entertainment for both Indian participants and white observers.

The Fox of Iowa eventually developed stable relationships with whites and other Indians. Their ties with the Sauk remained warm and friendly. They visited with these Indians in Oklahoma and received products from them that were unavailable locally. A similar attitude was maintained toward the Potawatomi of Kansas and Wisconsin. Old Indian enemies such as the Chippewa and Sioux became friends, but the Winnebago still were considered with hostility. Toward whites the general feelings were divided between Bureau of Indian Affairs employees and others. The former were regarded as persons supported by Fox funds, to whom requests for government help were made freely, and from whom compliance was expected. Toward other whites, whose functions were largely commercial, there existed a warm and friendly relationship.

When a person died, messengers spread the word, and the same evening a ceremony was held. It was supervised by the patrisib to which the individual belonged. The following day a grave was dug at one of the three cemeteries, and the body was taken there by truck after it was washed and dressed. About a year later there was a traditional adoption ceremony with the accompanying ritual and a replacement of the dead by the living.

The changes between the 1930's and 1948-1959 were at times striking, but the general feeling among ethnographers was that continuity had been more important than change. In 1948, when Tax returned to the reservation, he was impressed with how little change had occurred. In 1949 there were eighty-two households and a population of 489. Most of the households were two-room dwellings in which an average of seven persons lived. It is estimated that of all the reservation land, about 1500 acres was farmland. A third was tilled by white tenant farmers and the rent money used to pay taxes. The Mesquakie families residing on the reservation continued to find personal identity in the old kinship structure which retained its vitality. The changes that seemed most striking were in the political structure of the tribe.

The status of warrior once again became an important part of Fox life during World War II. Of the forty-seven veterans, twenty-two became members of a local American Legion post organized in 1949. The Fox post was founded through the efforts of a white legionnaire from a nearby community. Initially, the Fox veterans had joined the Tama post, but when they were refused intoxicants, they resigned. The Federal restriction on selling intoxicants to Indians, which was still in force, had been suspended when the Indians were in the armed services. The distinction at the Tama American Legion post between Indians and non-Indians once again made them aware that they were different from the other residents of Iowa. The Fox Legion post served primarily as a means for members to find greater recognition in white society through the common ground of being a veteran and a legionnaire. The large public meetings, involving both Fox and whites, were attended well by both members and nonmember veterans. The Fox community turned to the veterans for leadership, but this was not forthcoming since veterans were no better able to cope with local problems than any other segment of the population. Initially the leader pre-

served the Fox ideal of unanimity in decision making. He assumed authority only with reluctance, and while the next leader was more assertive,
the group would have foundered except that a white veteran assumed the
organizational responsibilities. When he left, the right to use a government
building for meetings was denied the Indians, for it was learned by Federal
officials that they stored beer in the meeting place. After this episode the
organization passed out of existence. Another attempt by a local white to
organize the Legion in 1959 did not meet with any realistic Indian participation.

One of the most pleasurable and lasting of all new Fox institutions has
been the previously-mentioned Pow-Wow held each August. Probably from
the time the Fox had returned to Iowa, whites had been invited to attend
certain ceremonies. In later years nonreligious attractions were added,
although the religious core of the celebration remained. In 1913, as a
response to white enthusiasm, the Pow-Wow was organized formally as
a four-day affair, primarily intended as entertainment for whites. The committee controlling the Pow-Wow was structured as a tribal council, with
representatives selected from the fifteen major family lines. In 1922 the
group was reformulated as a corporate body in a legal sense, with a constitution, officers, and committee members. By 1951 committee membership had
been expanded, and although the positions were elective, there was a great
deal of continuity among the representatives. In spite of the popular election, the idea of representation by major family groups was preserved. By
the early 1950's the rather elaborate Pow-Wow arrangements were guided
largely by the committee secretary, a person familiar with whites; since
such matters as publicity and the various forms of local arrangements had
to be managed through whites, he served as a link between the Indian
and white communities. Yet there was no real authority to guide the event.
The participants followed traditionally established norms for the celebration, which resembled a county fair but had a strong Indian emphasis.
By 1951 there were twenty-four family souvenir and food concessions; the
old dances and songs were performed, and a guitar group sang cowboy
songs. In good weather it was not unusual for 7000 persons to attend the
event, and most families camped at the Pow-Wow grounds during the event.
All normal routine ceased when the time approached, and this was the
one time of the year that all the people worked together as Fox.

In the 1950's the supernatural system continued to be organized around
the traditional ceremonials. Apart from the yearly Pow-Wow, it was still
the sib-affiliated religious activities which most often brought the people
together. The sib organization was weak and somewhat vaguely defined,
serving primarily as the structure around which the traditional religious

ceremonies were organized. This tentative judgment was made by Charles Callender of the Fox Project, who was inclined to believe that in the past patrisibs served the same general function. The greatest support for the old religious system came from community elders, and they were aided by some middle-aged persons. Younger Fox tended to be nonreligious or seemed on the verge of adopting Christianity if it had not been for pressures from their elders. Four sib-affiliated ceremonial groups continued to function. These were the Bear, Fox, Wolf, and Thunder sib ceremonial organizations. The Drum Society members still tended to be progressive, and participants numbered about forty individuals. In the late 1940's participants in the peyote rituals included about a dozen persons. Membership in the two Christian denominations was limited to about thirty persons. The missions were the United Presbyterian and Open Bible Gospel; both were maintained and encouraged by whites, although some meaningful Fox leadership was beginning to emerge.

By the mid-1950's the Fox supported themselves as skilled and unskilled laborers and artisans in communities surrounding the reservation. Most often they commuted to their homes each day, but in some instances they returned to the reservation only on weekends. The Fox had all the obligations of other United States citizens; they paid all the diverse forms of taxes and had the same rights to vote or to receive relief if they were without economic means. At that time about eight families received relief, paid for by state and Federal governments. At the same time the Federal government provided the Indians with services that were not available to non-Indians. They had a grade school maintained by the government, and a medical doctor held a clinic in the school for Indians. The services provided cost the Federal government approximately $60,000 a year. In spite of the comparatively little aid that the Indians received, the local whites had a stereotyped view of the multitudinous benefits the Indians derived from the Federal government.

The local white and Fox attitudes toward each other were an important factor, since these views formed the background for social interaction. The whites regarded the Fox as lazy, which they were by white standards, and as living off Federal dole, which largely was untrue. They considered Indians as sexually promiscuous and physically dirty. These attitudes probably were reasonable in light of observed Fox behavior; nevertheless, Indians clearly were not as lawless as the whites thought. Furthermore, the whites regarded the Fox as temporary and expected them to be assimilated into the American melting pot; however, this assimilation had not taken place. By contrast the Fox thought that the whites were greedy and aggressive, which they were by Indian standards, and that their behavior was artificial. The Indians also believed that they were dis-criminated against. Both groups agreed that the Fox had been maltreated in the past; this made the whites feel guilty and led to hostility from the Fox.

Some anthropologists in their studies of people conceive their role as that of a scientific observer whose duty it is only to record the diverse ways of different people. This certainly is a valid intellectual stance, but there are other anthropologists who feel that recording the facts of social and cultural behavior is not enough. They feel it a duty, if not a moral obligation, to lend their skills to make life somewhat easier and adjustments smoother for aboriginal peoples. Anthropologists with this point of view are not rare, but for them effectively to make changes is unusual. One satisfying exception is Professor Sol Tax of the University of Chicago, who organized and directed the Fox Project. The work by Tax and his associates is a fine testimonial to what can be accomplished under dynamic and effec-tive leadership. It is therefore fitting to follow the course of this anthropolog-ical project which began in 1948. Tax had studied the Fox in 1932 and 1934, and Joffe had made her study in 1937. With this anthropological background and the course of Fox history available for study a group of anthropology students from the University of Chicago embarked on the Fox Project.

As Fred Gearing has stressed, the stereotyped views held by the Fox and whites were being reinforced constantly. As long as this continued, any hope for constructive change was unrealistic. The Fox Project members, after careful preliminary studies, initiated a campaign to change these attitudes. They contacted the whites through newspaper articles, radio and television presentations, and speeches both to various white organizations and to individuals. The Fox were reached largely through conversations with individuals and during meetings. Some of the attitudes toward Indians which were considered most amenable to change follow: the Fox were tem-porary residents of the state; the Fox lived in poverty; the Fox were not good farmers; the Fox were improvident. These were among the values the Fox Project dealt with in order to help the whites understand Indians. At the same time an effort was made to alter those Fox ideas about whites which were untrue.

The most dynamic and successful of the Fox Project innovations was the college scholarship program for Indians who had completed high school. Initial discussion of the idea took place between Tax and the tribal council in 1954. When the idea moved into the planning stage, the Fox overwhelm-ingly approved. By 1955 the problems of sponsorship were solved, and Fox youth began to attend local colleges under the program. By the early 1970's about twenty-five Fox and Sauk Indians from this area were attending colleges or other institutions of higher learning. Under Fox Project encouragement, a community craft industry was organized to produce tile kits, decorative tiles, greeting cards, and jewelry in quantity as well as individually produced craft items. The Fox reaction to the proposal was enthusiastic, and by 1957 the Indians were actively engaged in the industry. Much of the stimulus came from the local artist Charles Pushetonequa, who was very much an Indian and interested in his own artistic production as well as in devising means for bringing others into the program as participants. The craft project has been successful, and the products are well received by whites.

The Fox Project personnel of the University of Chicago made studies basic to an understanding of Fox society and culture before they launched the program of change. The programs they originated or fostered had succeeded or seemed likely to be on-going when the project was terminated in 1960. It appears that through this interest by anthropologists one American Indian group was made a little more viable. One of the basic assumptions made by Fox Project personnel was that Mesquakie culture need not be assimilated into American culture; rather, it had something to offer the modern world. Therefore, the projects initiated were designed to lend stability and durability to the sociocultural lives of the Fox as Indians.

The question is whether or not the social survival of the Fox will continue. An answer is in part provided in a study by Steven Polgar of the Fox Project in connection with boys' gangs in 1952 and 1953. One group of boys who interacted habitually with one another was a gang as this term is used in American society, but other groups of boys were not gangs in the same context. The members of the first group had a high rate of absenteeism in school, and they were suspected of theft and property damage. The clothing they wore was "Indian" in its type; they preferred bright colored clothing and Navajo jewelry. Most of them were from non-nuclear families, and their relatives were not active in local politics. The members were cold to both white and Indian worlds and were delinquent in both worlds. The second group of boys was oriented toward white society as well as their own in a positive manner. This was especially true of its leader. These boys did not wear flashy clothing, and they were participants in the traditional sib ceremonies. They did not habitually participate in the Pow-Wow or other less traditionally oriented activities, as did the first group. It is from the second gang that Polgar expected the traditionally oriented leaders of the next generation to emerge. The third gang was much more oriented toward the attitudes held by the dominant white society. All the members had spent at least a few years away from the reservation, and they were able to compete successfully for jobs in white society. In addition, there was the fact that three of the eight members later entered college. Six of the eight still danced in the Pow-Wow, however, and most attended the sib ceremonies. These boys had begun to find acceptance in white society and were able to move away from Fox traditions although they did not wish to sever their ties with Fox culture.

From this analysis of Mesquakie boys' gangs, it is apparent that one gang was composed of boys whose behavior was antisocial in the eyes of both the whites and the Fox. The members of the third gang were moving rapidly and successfully toward assimilation in the dominant white society. It was the members of the second gang who seemed to have the greatest potential for the continuity of Fox life. They appeared to be adapting to both societies successfully and exhibited a pattern of biculturation, which means straddling the sociocultural fences. If the Fox are to continue their separate ethnic identity, it is these individuals who provide the greatest hope for the future.

In 1969 the Federal government partially rectified injustices of old. In that year the U.S. Indian Claims Commission awarded the Fox and Sauk of Iowa nearly a million dollars for lands ceded in 1830 for which they did not receive just compensation. Each adult received $500, with a like amount held in trust for each person under eighteen years of age. Sixty percent of the settlement money was held by the Fox Tribal Council for planning and development. Of the nearly 800 persons on the tribal roll, only about 500 lived in or near their lands in Iowa. With an inadequate land base economic conditions had forced some persons to leave their homeland-by-purchase. Yet even for the migrants these lands symbolized their identity as Mesquakie, and the settlement funds brought new hope for a more secure economic future.

References

Bicknell, A. D. "The Tama County Indians," *Annals of Iowa*, (3rd series) v. 4, 196-208. 1899–1901.

Bureau of Indian Affairs. Sac & Fox of Iowa. mimeographed. n.d.

Caldwell, Joseph R. *Trend and Tradition in the Prehistory of the Eastern United States*. American Anthropological Association, memoir no. 88. 1958.

Catlin, George. *North American Indians*. v. 2, 207-217. London. 1844.

English, Emory H. "A Mesquakie Chief's Burial," *Annals of Iowa*, (3rd series) v. 30, 545-550. 1951.

Gearing, Frederick O. *The Face of the Fox*. Chicago. 1970.

*Gearing, Frederick O., et al. *Documentary History of the Fox Project 1948-1959*. Chicago. 1960. The Fox Project of the University of Chicago, Department of Anthropology, was designed to compile information about these Indians and to apply anthropoligical knowledge in the solution of Fox problems. The volume includes documents relative to the project as well as selections of various published and manuscript studies. The information provided is basic to any realistic understanding of the development of modern conditions among the Fox of Iowa.

Green, Orville J. "The Mesquaki Indians, or Sac and Fox in Iowa," *Red Man*, v. 5, 47-52, 104-109. 1912.

*Hagan, William T. *The Sac and Fox Indians*. Norman. 1958. Hagan's definitive history of the Sauk and Fox begins with the early historic period and is carried through in detail to the reservation period in Kansas. There is very little information for the time after 1860.

Jenks, Albert E. "The Wild Rice Gatherers of the Upper Lakes," *Bureau of American Ethnology, 19th Annual Report*, pt. 2, 1013-1137. 1900.

*Joffe, Natalie F. "The Fox of Iowa," in *Acculturation in Seven American Indian Tribes*, Ralph Linton, ed., 259-331. New York. 1940. The 1937 field study of the Fox near Tama, Iowa, by Joffe, when consulted in conjunction with the 1932 and 1934 field data of Sol Tax for the same people, provides an excellent view of the historical background and emerging modern conditions for the group.

Jones, William. "The Algonkin Manitou," *Journal of American Folk-Lore*, v. 18, 183-190. 1905.

Jones, William. "Notes on the Fox Indians," *Journal of American Folk-Lore*, v. 24, 209-237. 1911.

*Jones, William. *Ethnography of the Fox Indians*. Bureau of American Ethnology, Bulletin 125, Margaret Welpley Fisher, ed. 1939. Jones, who was of mixed Fox and white descent and an anthropologist, was killed in the Philippine Islands in 1909. Some of his field data on the Fox were edited and published by Truman Michelson and Franz Boas a few years after his death. About twenty years later his notes were presented to the Smithsonian Institution and were edited for publication by Margaret W. Fisher. This volume is ably annotated and is an essential source on the Fox. In it is provided a rounded view of Fox life for the period just before 1900.

McKenney, Thomas L., and James Hall. *The Indian Tribes of North America*. v. 2. Edinburgh. 1934.

Michelson, Truman. Review of: *Folk-Lore of the Musquakie Indians of North America* by Mary A. Owen, in *Current Anthropological Literature*, v. 2, 233-237. 1913.

Michelson, Truman. "How Meswakie Children Should Be Brought Up," in *American Indian Life*, Elsie C. Parsons, ed., 81-86. New York. 1922.

Michelson, Truman. "The Autobiography of a Fox Indian Woman," *Bureau of American Ethnology, 40th Annual Report*, 291-349. 1925. The Fox woman recounting the story of her life supplies a wide range of ethnographic details concerning her people for what must have been late in the nineteenth century. It is only to be regretted that the autobiography is not longer and more detailed.

Michelson, Truman. "Notes on Fox Mortuary Customs and Beliefs," *Bureau of American Ethnology, 40th Annual Report*, 351-496. 1925.

Michelson, Truman. "Notes on Fox Gens Festivals," *Proceedings of the Twenty-Third International Congress of Americanists*, 545–546. New York. 1930.

Michelson, Truman. "Miss Owen's 'Folk-Lore of the Musquakie Indians,'" *American Anthropologist*, v. 38, 143-145. 1936.

Miller, Walter B. "Two Concepts of Authority," *American Anthropologist*, v. 57, 271-289. 1955.

Owen, Mary Alicia. *Folk-Lore of the Musquakie Indians of North America*. London. 1904. It is difficult to know how much of this volume is reliable in view of the criticisms by Truman Michelson (1913, 1936). In compiling the material on the Fox, only Owen's information on material culture was utilized. This section of the book does not come under fire from Michelson and, in fact, is almost praised.

*Polgar, Steven. "Biculturation of Mesquakie Teenage Boys," *American Anthropologist*, v. 62, 217-235. 1960. During the summers of 1952 and 1953 the field study of teen-age boys was made, and it was established that although some of the boys seemed on their way toward assimilation in white culture, others were delinquent in both Fox and white cultures, and still others were able to participate successfully in both white and Indian cultures. This is a very insightful paper and probably reflects an acculturation patterning for many Indians other than the Fox.

Quimby, George Irving. *Indian Life in the Upper Great Lakes*. Chicago. 1960.

Quimby, George Irving. *Indian Culture and European Trade Goods*. Madison. 1966.

Rideout, Henry M. *William Jones*. New York. 1912.

Smith, Huron H. *Ethnobotany of the Meskwaki Indians*. Bulletin of the Public Museum of the City of Milwaukee, v. 4, 175-326. 1928.

*Tax, Sol. "The Social Organization of the Fox Indians," in *Social Anthropology of North American Tribes*, Fred Eggan, ed., 243-282. Chicago. 1937. The core of this article is devoted to the Fox kinship terms and the social units, but there is additional information provided about conditions among the Tama area Fox as they lived when Tax visited them in 1932 and 1934. The emphasis of the chapter, however, is on a reconstruction of the social system of the past.

White, Leslie, ed. *Lewis Henry Morgan, The Indian Journals*, 1859-62. Ann Arbor. 1959.

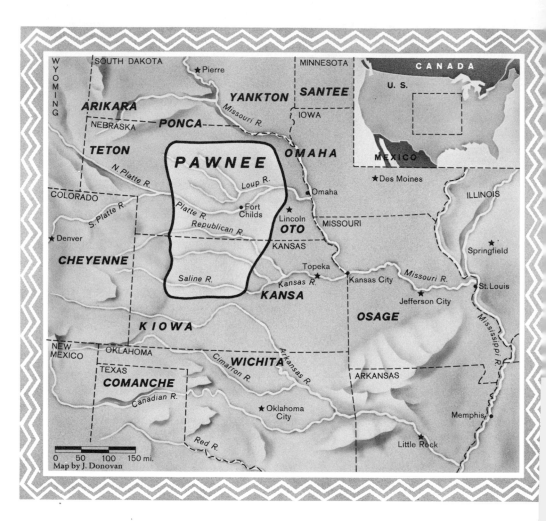

WYOMING

SOUTH DAKOTA

★ Pierre

MINNESOTA

CANADA

U.S.

ARIKARA

YANKTON

SANTEE

PONCA

Missouri R.

IOWA

NEBRASKA

TETON

PAWNEE

OMAHA

MEXICO

N. Platte R.

Loup R.

★ Des Moines

COLORADO

Platte R.

● Fort
Childs

● Omaha

ILLINOIS

S. Platte R.

Republican R.

★ Lincoln
OTO

MISSOURI

★ Denver

KANSAS

Springfield

CHEYENNE

Saline R.

Topeka

Kansas R.

★ Kansas City

Missouri R.

★ St. Louis

KANSA

★ Jefferson City

KIOWA

OSAGE

NEW
MEXICO

OKLAHOMA

WICHITA

Arkansas R.

ARKANSAS

Mississippi R.

TEXAS

COMANCHE

Cimarron R.

★ Oklahoma
City

Canadian R.

Memphis

Red R.

★ Little Rock

0   50   100   150 mi.

Map by J. Donovan

The Pawnee:
horsemen and farmers
of the prairies

In aboriginal and early historic times the border between the prairies and plains of mid-America was occupied largely by small bands of mobile hunters. With historic contact these Indians readily adopted the horse and became equestrian hunters, which increased their mobility but did not change the basis of their economic lives. On the prairies were other Indians who accepted the horse but lived in semipermanent communities; among these were the Pawnee. They farmed, lived in earth lodge communities, and represented a way of life very different from that of the Siouan speakers, Cheyenne, Comanche, or Kiowa, who occupied the plains to the west. The Pawnee in particular typify Indians who utilized the horse as a domestic animal but failed to deal effectively with the rapidly changing historic political environment. The Pawnee suffered a loss of population both from diseases and from their enemies; this is a tribe that barely managed to survive. They represent an Indian tribe buffeted by other Indians and white intruders alike. Their plight and cultural demise was typical rather than unusual among mid-American farmers.

The name Pawnee is of unknown origin and was not employed by these Indians until recent times, after it was in common usage among whites. They knew themselves as the Skidi, Chaui, Kitkehahki, or Pitahauerat, depending on the band to which they belonged. It is probable that they entered Kansas and Nebraska by ascending the Arkansas River and pushing northward to the Kansas River drainages. At this point they separated to occupy two different habitats. One segment settled the plains of southwestern Nebraska, and the other established itself in eastern Nebraska. They lived in small settlements near which they raised domestic plants and hunted. The eastern groups tended to emphasize fishing whereas those to the west stressed bison hunting. In 1837, about 300 years after historic contact, the tribe totaled about 10,000. In 1840, with the first actual count, their number had dropped to about 6200, and by 1881 there were only 1250. In 1940 the population was near a low of 1000, but by 1962 the total had risen to 2000. In linguistic terms they belong to the Macro-Siouan phylum and the Caddoan family; the language Pawnee is very similar to Arikara.

In east-central Nebraska, the historic area of the Pawnee, the prairie environment was primarily open country with a grassland vegetation, but in the alluvial valleys of the easternmost section were well-watered streams, with fertile soil and groves of trees. According to Waldo R. Wedel, who has had an abiding interest in the archaeology of the plains and prairies, the first occupancy of the central plains began around 8000 B.C., and the earliest people were hunters of big game. The Great Plains and

264

adjacent areas were populated initially by hunters who made large, multifluted spearpoints of flintlike material, of the type designated as Clovis. When the elephant population became extinct, the people hunted smaller but more plentiful species, of which the bison was most important. The remains of these bison hunters, who preyed on now extinct forms of the animal, are more widespread and numerous than those of the earlier hunters; kill sites and campsites are not unusual. Among the most important types of spearpoints associated with these people are the famous Folsom points, which are fluted like the Clovis points but are smaller and have only one flute on each face. These technologies were replaced by other lithic industries, and new peoples entered the area around 5000 B.C. As man killed off the herds of large bison, and as new influences from the Great Plains came to bear on the local cultures, different economic patterns emerged. Around 1500 B.C. there developed small populations who favored butte areas for occupancy. Hearths, some of which were lined with stones and were associated with small storage pits, have been found. The bison hunted was the contemporary species, and vegetable foods were collected by these people. The inventory of stone tools was more diverse and complex than previously had been found.

In central Plains prehistory there exists a period of nearly two thousand years just prior to the Christian era about which we have very little information. By about A.D. 200, Indians from the east with Hopewellian traditions had introduced maize and beans as domestic crops along the Missouri River near Kansas City. These people were hunters as well as farmers, and they possessed a technology which included the manufacture of ground as well as chipped stone. The Hopewellian influence, which originally came from the Ohio River valley, brought the first domestic plants and ushered in the potential of a new subsistence base; however, the people themselves never became established on the Plains. Shortly after A.D. 1000 life on the Plains assumed new directions, and although there were regional variations, the most significant changes were as follows: maize, beans, squash, and sunflower cultivation; an inventory of material items far more extensive than that of earlier periods; earth-covered houses with tunnel entrances, central fireplaces, and four posts for supporting the roof; and clusters of houses in small communities. There is good evidence from the nature of certain artifact forms that the people maintained contact with the central Mississippi valley. The relationship of these Indians with the Pawnee is still unknown, although the general similarities with early historic Pawnee culture seem apparent.

Pawnee life was influenced profoundly by the introduction of horses beginning around 1680; they were obtained in raids against tribes to the south and west. At about the same time the old material culture began to be replaced by trade goods from whites. At this time their dwellings were circular earth lodges, and they were clustered in villages. Skin tepees or dome-shaped, brush-covered dwellings were built on hunting trips in the plains. In the nineteenth century some villages were surrounded by sod walls and moats to make them more defendable. In the period just before white traders arrived, pottery was made and utilized, but work in stone, while known, was not elaborate. Manufactures of bone and horn were more complex, as might be expected given their dependency on bison. Wedel was impressed by the similarity between Pawnee productions and the technologies of Indians to the east and southeast. By contrast there were very few borrowings from peoples of the Southwest.

Pawnee history is not a continuous record of events dating from the earliest historic contacts with whites. After initial contacts a virtual blank exists for the next three hundred years before these people again emerge into history. A tradition among the Pawnee records that the Skidi once were a separate people and were conquered by the other Pawnee. Vague tales also record a movement to the north from a southerly direction.

When the Spanish explorers under the command of Hernando de Soto crossed the Mississippi River and moved westward in 1541, they first encountered sedentary Indians, but farther west in the prairie country they came on the Caddoans, who, unlike the Indians along the Mississippi proper, were unsettled and put up fierce resistance. Since the Caddoans were able warriors and the area offered no potential for looting, the Spaniards turned back to the Mississippi River. In 1541 when Francisco Coronado and his party moved to the north and east from New Mexico, they were guided by an Indian whom the Spanish named the Turk because of his appearance. He was to take them to Quivira, which the Spaniards had been led to believe offered untold riches. The exact location of Quivira is not known, but probably it was somewhere in southern Kansas. Quivira offered no riches, and the Turk was murdered by the Spanish, who regarded him as a charlatan. In all probability Quivira was then the homeland of at least some Pawnee. By the late 1600's mounted and armed Apaches were known to be raiding the Caddoan villages for slaves and plunder, and unquestionably the Pawnee were drawn into these hostilities. Those Pawnee who settled on the Republican River, the Skidi branch, probably moved to this area during the seventeenth century. By 1715 the Skidi were grouped into eight villages. It was not long before some of the Pawnee came into contact with French traders who were present along the eastern drainages of the Mississippi River from the period immediately following the Sieur de La Salle expedition of 1679–1682. The traders came to offer more and more goods, including guns, to the tribes in the West. When word of the French intrusion reached the Spanish of the Southwest, the Spaniards became alarmed over potential French penetration of their northern and eastern frontier. In 1720 a Spanish party accompanied by Pueblo and Apache Indians left Santa Fe to investigate the extent of French domination. The guide took the party north of their destination, and in Nebraska, possibly where the Platte River forks, the party was attacked. The Apaches escaped, but most of the Spaniards were killed, along with some of the Pueblo Indians. It was possibly the Pawnee and adjacent tribes who destroyed the invaders; although it was asserted by the survivors that the Indians were aided by French troops, there is no evidence that the French were directly involved. In 1724 the French sent a party from New Orleans to establish peace among the warring tribes in order that French influence could be more firmly entrenched. Surprisingly enough, an enterprising French representative, Etienne V. de Bourgmont, succeeded in establishing peace among the Apache, the Oto, the Skidi Pawnee, and the Iowa, the most important contesting tribes. Two years later French traders pushed into eastern Colorado, but this link was soon broken by Comanche raids. The result was that the Skidi Pawnee came temporarily to dominate the Nebraska country.

A smallpox epidemic plus hostile Indians on almost every quarter reduced the eight large Skidi Pawnee villages of 1725 to a single village during the early 1800's. Through the mid-1700's the Skidi were the only Pawnee to occupy Nebraska in any number; the Black or Southern Pawnee had not yet arrived from the lower Arkansas River. Just after 1770 the Black Pawnee moved north from their location on the tributaries of the Missouri River. These people were to become known as three tribes: the Chaui, or Grand Pawnee; the Kitkehahki, or Republican Pawnee, who were an offshoot of the Chaui; and the most southerly branch, the Pitahauerat or Tapages, who sometimes are designated as the Smoky Hill Pawnee. The arrival of the new Pawnee brought conflict with the Skidi. The disagreements were largely over hunting territory, and the Skidi were defeated in their attempt to remain the exclusive occupants of some key areas. The terms for peace included the stipulation that the Skidi would leave their villages, and they did so temporarily. Although they were forced to recognize the Grand Pawnee as the leaders of the combined tribe, the Skidi never became subordinated as their conquerors had hoped.

The Spanish of New Mexico continued to be anxious to develop regular contacts in Pawnee country and to prevent the spread of French as well as American influence. None of the expeditions sent from Santa Fe were particularly successful in realizing this desire. Countermoves were organized by the Americans, and in 1806 Zebulon M. Pike was sent to visit the Pawnee and then the Comanche to win the support of these tribes and pave the way for the westward advance of the American frontier. Pike's efforts to establish friendly contacts with the Comanche through the Pawnee were not successful because these tribes were at war. At the same time there was a struggle by rival Pawnee factions for internal political control, which erupted as intratribal warfare. When the Pawnee consolidated and moved against the Kansa, they were defeated by them. They were more successful, however, in stealing horses from the Comanche at about this time. In all of these machinations the Skidi Pawnee seem to have remained somewhat apart, and their activities are obscured by scarcity of reference to them.

In 1818 four Pawnee chiefs, one representing each branch of the tribe, went to St. Louis at the request of General William Clark, who was the Indian superintendent of the area. The Pawnee signed a treaty of peace and friendship with the United States and began to be drawn into a new and different type of relationship with foreigners. Unlike the French or Spanish, the Americans were more aggressive in their interest in the Pawnee, and this attitude extended beyond trading relationships. The Indians who went to St. Louis were impressed greatly by American strength, but those remaining at home were not convinced of the power of the Long Knives. The harassment of Americans who were either traders or soldiers led to the withholding of trade goods to the Pawnee area; this induced the Pawnee to return looted items and even to promise a whipping of the Pawnee warriors who had attacked the Americans. As soon as the Americans were out of sight, however, the Pawnee tended to do once again as they thought best. In 1825 the Pawnee signed another treaty of friendship with the United States, agreeing not to interfere with Americans traveling to New Mexico. Pawnee battles at this period were not with whites but with other Indians. The Skidi were defeated badly by the Comanche, but no battle took as many persons as did the smallpox epidemic of 1832, which is said to have killed more than 3000 individuals, including nearly everyone over thirty years of age. In 1837–1838 another smallpox epidemic struck, killing about 2000 persons. In the 1830's the Pawnee were not only fighting local Indians without success, but others who had been moved west of the Mississippi River. To prevent the annihilation of the Pawnee by the diverse tribes bent on their destruction, agents of the United States arranged a treaty in 1833. The negotiations granted hunting rights in western Kansas to most immigrant tribes; in it the Pawnee gave up their exclusive rights to a great area south of the Platte River. They thought this treaty meant sharing hunting rights in return for nonharassment, but it was actually a government attempt to make them settle down as intensive farmers. In 1834 two now famous Presbyterian missionaries, John Dunbar and Samuel Allis, entered the area and wintered with the Pawnee in order to learn the language and to begin their mission activities.

By 1838 the situation among these people was desperate. The smallpox epidemic had destroyed the core of their population, raids of enemy tribes were more and more devastating, and they had no reliable allies. Frequently when they returned from bison hunts in the plains they found their settlements and cached supplies looted and destroyed. At the time they received their annuity payments in 1839, they requested the Indian agent to establish a mission and to teach them American agricultural techniques. When the time came to settle down in one community, however, the Pawnee refused to move to the location the government selected. In 1841 a Presbyterian missionary party of fifteen whites founded a farm and mission to induce the Pawnee to settle down around the Pawnee Mission on Loup Fork in Nance County, Nebraska. Within a few years the government built a blacksmith shop, a school, and an agency center. Some Pawnee began to settle nearby, but a terrible Sioux attack in 1843 on the Pawnee village near the mission led the people to flee south. When they returned, the missionaries Dunbar and Allis, who understood the people best, saw the tribe making slow but steady progress. They encouraged the Indians to settle down, but others of their church group advocated what George E. Hyde has termed "muscular Christianity." They beat the women and children to try to make them conform to Christian standards. An Indian boy was shot in the back for stealing corn, and a Pawnee girl was beaten nearly to death by a missionary's son. To disgrace the scene further the Indian agent, whose background was southern and slaveholding, supported the harsh treatment of the Indians and removed those government employees who worked harmoniously with them. A worse acculturation can hardly be imagined. Finally the Sioux were too much for the government workers and the missionaries, and they were forced in 1846 to withdraw.

In the early 1850's the Pawnee did more begging and stealing from wagon train immigrants than they did raiding and looting. The Skidi attempted to hunt bison in the plains in 1852, but Sioux harrassment made it impossible for them to remain and only a stroke of good fortune kept the party from being completely destroyed. The next year only the organized fighting skills of their allies, the Potawatomi, saved one segment of the Pawnee population from destruction. Finally, there were intruding white settlers who built their homes south of the Platte River, making life unbearable for the Indians there. The Pawnee could not live north of the Platte because of the powerful Sioux. In 1857 the Pawnee accepted a small reservation on the Loup Fork, and Federal aid compensated them for the loss of their land. They received $40,000 per year for five years, and $30,000 a year for every year thereafter, in addition to a promise of active protection against the Sioux and an agency and agent to help them settle down as farmers. Included in the settlement was a trip to Washington, D. C., for some chiefs. In 1859 the Indians took up residence in their new reservation, but during the years immediately following, the Sioux raids continued. Moreover, a good Indian agent was replaced by a greedy one. The villages were exposed to their enemies during the summer hunt of 1862 but were defended with valor by old and young men and even some women. In 1864 the Sioux raids were so devastating to the whites that troops were sent into the region. Although some Pawnee aided the soldiers, ineffective American leadership brought no contact with the hostile Indians. In 1865 a new United States Army commander was appointed, and his military success was due largely to the Pawnee and their cooperation with the Americans. Still, the Pawnee were rovers. They refused to remain on their reservation, and the efforts of corrupt and incompetent Indian agents contributed nothing to their welfare. In 1869 the reservation was put under the administration of Quaker missionaries, which was an attempt by the Indian Service to rid itself of corrupt representatives. The first Quaker missionary found that the Indians could speak no English and although the first school had been established about twenty-five years before, none of them could read or write. Horticulture carried out by the women was still the only type of farming. The Quakers set out to destroy Pawnee customs as rapidly as possible. In 1870 some of the Pawnee chiefs were induced to cultivate fields with a horse and plow; in earlier times it was unheard of for any man to work as a woman. As others followed the example of the chiefs, American farming practices could be introduced for the first time. The missionaries and Indian agents were not satisfied with this progress and hoped to break up the villages and place families on separate plots of farmland. The missionaries pressured the United States Congress to sell fifty thousand acres of Pawnee land to finance the resettlement program. In the summer bison hunt of 1873 some 400 Pawnee were trapped by a force of nearly 1000 Sioux, and almost 100 Pawnee were killed. During the fall of the same year grasshoppers and potato beetles destroyed their crops, while white settlers were taking timber and hay from Indian lands. With all this adversity the people were demoralized, not without good reason. A dissident two-thirds of the population started south, intending to abandon their reservation, but most returned the following spring. Still there existed a deep dispute among the Indians about whether they should move southward to Indian Territory or remain in Nebraska.

With government pressure, removal became a necessity, and in 1874 part of the tribe followed the first group. The land selected for their reservation was to the west of the Arkansas River and north of the Cimarron River, the area occupied by three tribes of the southern Pawnee around 1700. By late 1875 all the Indians had arrived on their new lands. The Quaker ideal of providing 160 acres and a house for each family was fine, but the money to implement the program was not available. There could be no compromises among these Quakers, and the people were destined to live half-starved in canvas tents, with very inadequate clothing and their horses even stolen by whites. The missionaries were delighted when the warriors were forced to trade their weapons for food! The population figures indicate that the misguided idealism of the Quakers became genocide: 1872, 2447 people; 1876, 2026; 1879, 1440; and finally, in 1890, 804. In an effort to force the Pawnee to become more intensive farmers, the government in 1882 cut off the rations provided to the Indians. Some families managed to adjust, but most simply reduced their standards of living and depended on annuities and lease money provided by white cattlemen who grazed their animals on Indian lands. Finally in 1883 the government established a concentration camp for children, euphemistically called a boarding school. Parents were prohibited from visiting their children, and the committed child remained in Federal custody for years on end. All of this was intended to force the Pawnee to give up their Indian ways.

Long ago before the present races of men occupied the earth, there lived a people who were giants. They were so big and powerful that one was able to run a bison down on foot, kill it, and readily carry the carcass over his shoulders. Such men did not believe in Tirawa, as the Pawnee do, but felt that all power rested in their own hands. Finally Tirawa was so angry with the giants that he caused the water level to rise. All the land became soft, and the giants sank into the ground and died. Tirawa next created a man and a woman in the proportions of people today. It was from this couple that the Pawnee were derived.

In their view of the universe, the Skidi, and probably other Pawnee as well, thought that there were two great forces in the sky, the male to the east and the female to the west, while all of life was derived from the zenith. The supernatural power at the zenith where the male and female forces combined was termed Tirawa and even his name was sacred, to be spoken quietly. Men sought aid from him, but he dealt with them through lesser supernatural beings, who were beneath him in strength and power. The first people came to earth upon the winds from the Morning Star, and from each of the seven winds one expected different qualities. The east wind swept in with the dawn, bringing life into a person's body; the west wind brought life and direction to life; the north wind was associated with the North Star; the wind of the spirits drove ghosts from north to south; another sent game, and yet another drove the animals, while the south wind came from the star spirits.

Reports are conflicting concerning the hair style of men; possibly it was roached, with a scalp lock hanging from the back. It is known that women parted their hair in the middle and made two braids, one hanging down on each side of the head behind the ear. Both men and women plucked their pubic and axillary hair, which was considered unclean. Such hair could not be burned but was buried, for to burn something was to offer it to the supernaturals. Likewise, a man plucked the hair from his face. Pawnee males commonly painted their faces and chests with red, white, and yellow pigments; black paint was reserved as a paint for warfare.

A man's clothing included a breechclout, which was a piece of dehaired deerskin which passed between the wearer's legs and overlapped a belt in the front and back. Additionally, men wore moccasins and tight-fitting buckskin leggings, with long fringes at the outer edges sometimes adorned with human hair and beaded designs. A bison-skin or wolf-skin robe was thrown over their shoulders. As adornments a man might wear a necklace of bear claws, beads, or strung sections of bone as well as body paint. The women wore leggings from the knees to the ankles, moccasins, and a wraparound skirt to below the knees. A band of skin was worn about the chest, and it was held in place with shoulder straps. Women also wore bison-skin robes. Young boys went without any clothing whatever, and a small girl wore a loose shirt.

Approaching a Pawnee village in the early part of the nineteenth century, a visitor found well-beaten paths which converged on the settlement. For miles around there were scattered gardens tended by the women, accompanied by their small children and older daughters. When enemies were about, one or more warriors remained with the women as they cultivated the fields. The localities chosen were where the sod was thin and the soil could be worked with a digging stick or hoe. Grazing horses and mules roamed near the village and were tended by small boys or an occasional man. In a settlement were innumerable dogs and children, and many women were busy processing hides. One community of the Grand Pawnee and Tapages in 1820 had 180 earth lodges and 3500 occupants. The lodges with their attached entryways were closely grouped in an irregular pattern. These houses were up to fifty feet across and circular in form. They were log-framed structures, over which were placed layers of grass and then a covering of packed earth. About five families or twenty persons lived in a typical dwelling. Inside an earth lodge, with its entrance to the east, were platform beds along the north and south walls. The area allotted to each family was curtained off from the next with mats, and behind the curtains were the family's possessions. The central area was open, and in the floor were caches for dried vegetable foods. There was also a central fireplace and above it a hole for the smoke to escape. The back and center of a lodge was the place of honor where the household head presided; here there was an altar on which rested a bison skull. Hanging from the west wall of every important man's lodge was a sacred bundle, wrapped in deer-skin and blackened with age. The bundles were surrounded with taboos. They were opened only on special occasions and represented an important link with the past and the supernaturals. Near each home was a log corral for horses and mules. Before each lodge was the homeowner's tripod, on which hung his painted shield and a rawhide case of war supplies. On top of many lodges were scalps on short poles. While in the village during the summer, families slept out-of-doors under arbors; one was constructed for each family lodge.

For the summer or winter ventures into bison country the people traveled in family groups, single file, with each woman and child leading a horse and the men ranging about the column on horseback or on foot. A typical day's march covered between six and eight miles, with three hours required to break or prepare a camp. It was the women who erected the tepees, made of bison skins covering pole frameworks which were as much as eigh-teen feet across at their base. They left an opening at the top and center of the covering for the smoke to pass out from the central fire pit. Reed mats were spread on the ground, and the evening meal prepared over the open fire was the only meal of the day.

Knowledge about the variety of material objects manufactured is derived both from early historic excavations by Wedel and the observations of nineteenth-century travelers. Flaked chert arrowpoints and a few scrapers chipped from quartzite were virtually the only artifacts made from flinty material. The Pawnee apparently pounded meat and berries on boulder anvils into which cup-shaped depressions were worn from repeated use. Pounding, not grinding, seems to have been the accepted way to process food products. For preparing hides, sandstone scrapers were ground and pecked into an elliptical shape; pecking stones were used also to shape grooved stone mauls and axes. Rectangular pieces of sandstone with a groove along one side were used to smooth arrow shafts. Pipes most often were made from catlinite and were of the elbow type with detachable wooden stems.

From bone the people made a variety of objects. A bison rib with a small symmetrical hole cut into it sometimes served to straighten arrow shafts; the shaft was gently bent as it was inserted into the straightener. A most important bone tool was a bison scapula hoe; the distal end of bone had been cut to form a square or rounded blade. The blade was attached to a wooden stick at right angles to the articulation of the bone. The two were lashed together with sinew and then dipped into hot water to shrink the sinew and tighten the binding. Awls and needles of bone were items in the skin-working technology.

Metacarpal bones of ungulates were cut off diagonally above the lower condyle to serve as skin-scraping tools. Sections of antler served as picks, and pieces with a right-angle curve were sharpened to make adz-like skin scrapers. A short section of antler was employed as a flint flaker. Spoons were fashioned from bison horn by cutting the horn in two lengthwise. The people also used the lower jaw of a deer or wolf to remove kernels of maize from a cob.

The dependence of western Indians on the bison and the uses to which the animal was put are well known, yet it is appropriate to cite the many Pawnee usages. The meat from a freshly killed animal could be eaten raw, cooked when fresh, or dried as a winter staple. The summer skins were made into tent covers, ropes, and diverse containers. Winter skins, with the hair intact, served as blankets and robes. The sinew was fashioned into bowstrings or used as thread. The brains of a bison were smeared on skins being processed for use in order to soften the final product and make it more pliable. A hoof became a hammer, and bones were made into scrapers, awls, and other tools. The bladder became a water container, and bison dung was the standard fuel in woodless localities. Bison skins were the major product offered by Plains Indians in exchange for trade goods in historic times.

The early nineteenth century round of economic activities meant abandoning the earth lodge settlements in the summer and again in the early winter. At these times the Indians roamed south and west in search of bison herds. In the summer of 1835 the Grand Pawnee and their close neighbors, the Tapages and Republican Pawnee, traveled westward in three columns, which included 4000 people, thousands of horses and mules, and about 7000 dogs. While on the move to and from the bison country, the orderliness of the hunters contrasted with the medley of women, children, and animals moving with the tents and household equipment. The column traveled at a walking pace, with the chiefs and warriors astride fine horses and poor men walking. The poor permitted their horses to walk along without packs so that they would be fresh in case bison were to be pursued. Docile old horses were employed as pack animals or to draw travois. Such a horse was controlled by tying a strip of leather around its lower jaw; the strip was then held or tied to the saddle. Tent poles were tied to either side of the saddle; these extended from the horse's head to the ground behind the animal. Across these poles might be tied short poles, and on this bed were placed leather containers of dried meat and bison-skin robes. On a travois or litter an ill or wounded person might ride. Tent skins, robes, and household articles were loaded on the saddle, and on top of a load a woman and her children might ride. Colts carried light packs, and young horses were ridden by boys. Horses without loads ran freely about the column.

In order to pursue and kill bison efficiently, a well-organized force of warriors guided the hunt. These were men on whom the chiefs could rely to maintain order and plan the hunt. A column approaching a herd of bison was led by chiefs and shamans. Each man had a particular position in the riding order, and each attempted to have a special horse used only for hunting bison. When the herd was sighted, a crier relayed the decision of how the hunters were to be deployed; once they were in place, at a given signal, all the men descended on the bison together. Preferably they converged on the herd from different directions. The favorite hunting weapon was not the gun, but the bow and arrow, and each hunter rode naked, carrying only his weapons, in the same manner as he prepared for battle. After as many animals as possible had been killed, they were butchered and brought back to camp, where the women cut the meat into thin slabs and dried it on pole frames over a fire in the skin tent. They then pounded the dried meat and packed it into rawhide satchels.

At the end of the summer hunting season the people returned to their villages, where they had planted crops in the spring. This was the most pleasurable season of the year, for food was abundant, with a good harvest of corn, beans, and squash. This was the time for social as well as for religious activities. In the fall and early winter hunting parties returned again to the bison country and made a special effort to obtain bison skins which now were prime. Some skins were exchanged with traders for imported goods, and others were scraped free of the hair, to be used as lodge coverings or folded into rawhide containers. Again in February or March they returned to their villages with the meat and skins. Although in a typical year they might be away from their villages for about eight months, nevertheless the villages represented home for the wanderers.

Spring was the lean period when the Pawnee relied on dried meat and cached maize, beans, or squash. At this time the women began to prepare the garden plots, which seldom were over an acre in extent. The most important crop was maize, which was not only a food staple but was important in ritualistic and mythological terms. The cultivated areas were at the mouths of ravines where the soil was fertile and the sod cover was not extremely thick. After maize was harvested, it was boiled or roasted, then cut from the cob and dried, or stored on the cob in caches. Women likewise cultivated beans and squash; the latter were sun-dried in strips and later were woven together for convenient storage.

The most important uncultivated vegetable food was the wild potato, which was a very important item in times of food scarcity. Berries, wild plums, cherries, and mushrooms were among the more important plant products collected. In general, these were supplements to maize and bison meat. According to one description, an evening meal during a bison hunt consisted of dried bison meat, followed by a combination of maize and beans, then ground parched maize, and corn mush; the meal ended with an ear of roasted corn. Also hunted and eaten were elk, deer, bear, otter, and raccoon, and dogs were eaten on occasion.

The only aboriginally domesticated animal was the dog, and there were huge numbers of these animals, judging from Charles A. Murray's account in the 1830's. The dogs were used as pack animals as well as to drag loaded travois. The first horses possibly were introduced about 1700, judging from the rate of spread of domestic horses out of New Mexico in the late 1600's.

The Skidi Pawnee are best reported by ethnographers, but they were more conservative than the three other bands, and carried out at least some unique ceremonies. Each Pawnee band was divided into village units which were politically and socially distinct. As a tribe they cooperated as a unit only rarely, and the Skidi felt closer to the Arikara than to the other bands. The members of a village traced their descent to a presumed common ancestress (matrilineal descent and matrisib), and they married within the community (village endogamy). A man lived with the family of his wife or was associated intimately with her residence unit (matrilocal residence). At the same time the Pawnee were not completely matrilineal, since the chieftaincy and priestly duties could and did pass down a line of males. Each settlement possessed a sacred bundle, which contained objects of immense religious significance for the villagers; it was assumed to have been passed down a direct male line from the original owner. The village sacred bundle was a supernatural focus leading to a rationale for this social grouping, and village endogamy may have been practiced in order to keep the sacred bundle as a distinct village trust. Village political life was under the direction of a hereditary chief, his subordinates, and a council. Villagers were bound together through participation in joint religious ceremonies and in a joint council.

The activities of each of the thirteen known Skidi villages were supervised by a chief, who among other responsibilities allotted lands to individual users. Most important in terms of village cohesion was the fact that a village chief was the possessor of a sacred bundle which usually was passed down a male line. These bundles were either direct gifts from particular stars or were made by a distant ancestor of a chief under the supervision of a star. The chief owned the bundle; his wife was its keeper, and the associated rituals were conducted by a ritual specialist. The largest earth lodges were the residences of chiefs, and it was here that large audiences attended certain ceremonies.

According to the Presbyterian missionary John Dunbar, the labors of a woman were arduous, and her tasks never seemed to be completed. Besides the processing of skins, cooking and gardening, which might be expected, she was also obliged to saddle and unsaddle her husband's horse, and in the tent she occupied the coldest fringe. As though to compensate for their position, women talked steadily by habit and were very sharp-tongued. By contrast the men seemed devoted to warfare and hunting; they had a great deal of leisure time during which they slept, lounged, talked, sang, feasted, and smoked. A male's social position was based largely on the achievements of his immediate male ancestors; thus there was a certain degree of rigidity in the social structure. At the same time there was the ideal of a poor but ambitious and honorable young man achieving great success. The class system, which molded the lives of most persons, found its sanction in supernatural beliefs, with prerogatives and duties of the leaders similarly derived. One set of divinely instituted obligations directed that a segment of the population must protect the settlement from human enemies; these were the leaders and participants in war. A second group, the priests, took charge of religious obligations, and a third, the shamans, protected the village from disease and famine. These were upper class responsibilities; the lower class consisted of poor people who had little or no influence in village affairs.

Each Skidi village contained a hereditary chief and a particular sacred bundle which represented his authority; the bundle itself and the status of chief was passed on to his eldest son if this individual was capable. The decision about chiefly succession was made by the chief's council, who accepted or rejected the logical successor. If an eldest son was not capable, a younger son or another close male relative of the chief's was chosen. The hereditary chiefs selected warriors of highest rank from each settlement to become nonhereditary chiefs, so that the number totaled thirty-one in the chiefs' council for all of the Skidi. An extremely able warrior was made a chief by being invited to join the hereditary chiefs in their lodge on four occasions. The first three invitations were refused, but the fourth was accepted and gifts presented to the chiefs. The man then became a chief, but he did not pass the title on to his son.

The appearance of chiefs during their council meetings differed from that of ordinary men. A chief wore an eagle feather in his hair, and on his bison robe were representations of stars, the sun, or battle scenes. His leggings were fringed with hair from human scalps and with eagle feathers. His face was painted red; from ear to ear across the forehead was a blue line, along with a forehead design symbolic of the Turkey's Foot constellation.

The most important duties of a hereditary chief were to promote community welfare and be the guardian of the people. A hereditary chief appears also to have been responsible for the allotment and reallocation of farmlands to persons of the village for which he was responsible. A chief was not expected to be an aggressive and constant fighter but was to provide for the general welfare of the community. A chief provided for his family's needs, although he had two retainers to perform more menial tasks. Other men, usually four in number, who were braves, served the hereditary chief. They helped preserve civil order and prepare for religious ceremonies. These braves carried war clubs or tomahawks as symbols of their offices which they held for life and had acquired through an affinity with the Morning Star.

Warriors were men who through their own efforts had risen to positions of authority. Again supernatural sanctions gave rise to this class of individuals. From their group chiefs were chosen, since warriors had by their sacrifices obtained supernatural favor. They were privileged to wear the sacred warrior's costume into battle and to paint three dots on their foreheads, symbolic of an eagle's claw marks.

Decisions of a political nature were made jointly by the hereditary chiefs and the nonhereditary chiefs, but they seemingly could be overruled by the priests. The deliberations of the chiefs in council probably centered most frequently about where and when to hunt or raid, and about relations with other Pawnee groups, enemy tribes, and friendly peoples. In early historic times the principal chief, who apparently took precedence over all others, was from the Chaui subtribe. When the chiefs of a village met in council, they decided issues by a consensus even if the feelings ran against the will of the leading chief. When the chiefs met in council, they seated themselves in an arrangement followed in the Four Pole Ceremony, to be discussed later.

Half or less of the Skidi males were not hereditary chiefs, braves, or warriors, nor were they shamans or priests. Instead they were commoners without authority within the village to which they belonged. These men owned few or perhaps no horses, their lodges were small, and often they received necessities from persons of wealth. Another group was composed of some young men, and occasionally older men, who attached themselves to the households of important men and performed menial tasks for these individuals in return for economic support. At the fringes of a settlement were the outcasts of one type or another, persons who had disregarded tribal customs.

In the kinship terminology of the Skidi Pawnee a male termed his father and his father's brothers alike, whereas his mother's brother was called by a different word. The word for mother was extended to mother's sister and father's sister (bifurcate merging), and the same term was extended

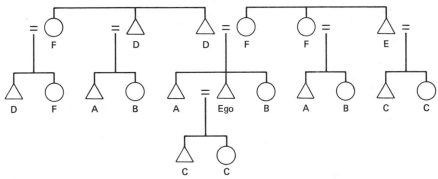

Aboriginal Pawnee kin terms. Each letter represents a different term.

to include father's sister's daughter. The father and father's brother term was applied to a father's sister's son. The patrilateral cross-cousin terms were different from the matrilateral cross-cousin terms; the latter were not distinguished by sex and were the same as for Ego's son and daughter. Parallel cousins on both sides of the family were termed alike but with male-female distinctions. Furthermore, the words for brothers and sisters were extended to parallel cousins, and the latter were Ego's classificatory siblings (Crow cousin terms).

The closest lifelong ties were between siblings, especially brothers; by contrast, deep emotional ties did not exist between a husband and wife.

A warm relationship probably existed between a man and his mother's brother's wife, since this woman, or these women as the case may have been, were sexual partners for the young man from the time he reached puberty until he married. The mother's brother was responsible for the marriage arrangements of both the sons and the daughters of his sister.

Disagreements between individuals or families within a village seem to have been settled without outside interference. The most common dispute appears to have been between men when they gambled. Contestants fought but stopped when blood was drawn. Poor persons were those most often accused of theft, and if the identity of the culprit was established he was punished physically by the victim. In instances of adultery by a woman, the offended husband was irate because he felt his property had been taken from him, and he punished the man by beating or whipping him. Adultery apparently was not uncommon nor particularly serious, but this was not true of rape. Consent or lack of consent by the girl was not the important criterion of rape; her age was the crucial factor. A man who fornicated with a young girl was beaten badly and became an outcast. The unprovoked murder of an individual led his relatives to seek revenge by killing the murderer, who was not defended by his relatives if they considered the case against him to be just. If representatives of each family involved considered its position legitimate, a feud erupted between them.

George B. Grinnell (1961, 303) wrote, "The Pawnees were a race of warriors. War was their pleasure and their business. By war they gained credit, respect, fame. By war they acquired wealth." The emphasis on physical conflict among Indians in mid-America is legendary, and the Pawnee justly are remembered as being among the best warriors. They fought under two different sets of circumstances with contrasting purposes. When they left their settlements seeking an enemy, they were in search of glory, to be displayed in scalps taken and horses captured. The Pawnee fought defensively against enemies who came to their settlements by night to steal horses and to take scalps, or when a large enemy party arrived by day to scalp, to kill, and to loot. Either on offensive raids or in defensive stands the Pawnee warrior was a very brave man. Still the standards of behavior in warfare differed greatly from the norms in Anglo-American society. On a raid the ideal was to slip into an unsuspecting enemy camp, kill as many persons as possible before arousing the populace, and then escape with their best horses. A raid most often was organized to steal horses, and if the opportunity presented itself enemies were slain and scalped. Such raids were most like guerrilla warfare in Western society. The question of a fair fight was not considered, since the primary aim of a raid was to catch the enemy unaware and take full advantage of his vulnerable condition. There was no disgrace in not attacking a well-armed or alert camp, nor did a man lose standing by running away if he was outnumbered.

The Indians living to the south of the Pawnee knew them as the Wolves, possibly a derogatory designation but more likely based on their skill as scouts and horse thiefs. When a group of Pawnee set off on a raid, they organized a temporary association, or Wolf Society, whose origins were traced to mythological times. The supernatural patron of warfare was the wolf, and they patterned themselves after these animals. Items from a sacred bundle or war regalia were covered with a wolfskin and taken along to provide supernatural assistance. A raiding party attempted to move across the landscape in the manner of wolves. One reason for assuming this guise was that prairie wolves were common and often entered Indian camps at night; looking like them, they attracted little attention. All but one of the raiders kept to ravines or river bottoms as they neared the camp of an enemy; the lone individual was disguised as a wolf and scouted from the hilltops. The other raiders covered themselves with wolfskins when they entered the camp of an enemy and imitated the behavior of these animals, thereby hoping not to attract attention to themselves.

A raiding party was organized by any man who could attract a following. He was most likely a successful warrior, but an aspiring youth sometimes could convince others of his abilities. The leader sought supernatural help through prayers to Tirawa, offered while meditating, smoking, or eating. The men selected by a leader to take part in his raid were called together, and the plan was announced. If they wished to accompany the group, they smoked a sacred pipe. If they declined to participate in the raid, they passed the pipe on to the next man without smoking. The leader then secured the aid of a priest, ceremonies were performed, and the priest presented the group with a sacred bundle to take with them. Every man provided himself with as many as twenty moccasins, each stuffed with food for the trip. The food consisted of pounded, cooked corn and pemmican. A warrior also carried sewing awls and sinew to repair his footwear, a bow and arrows, and a robe. The leader carried a sacred pipe and tobacco. They set off on foot, and when they reached country occupied by hostile Indians, they became cautious. If any sign along the way was interpreted as an ill omen, they might turn back. The activities of such a party were under the direction of its organizer, who commanded the warriors. The aspiring warriors who joined the party were assigned menial tasks around the camp, and they learned the tactics of others.

The primary purpose of a raid was to steal horses, but since an enemy kept his best horses near his tepee, often tied just outside the entrance, it required great daring to cut a number of horses loose and escape successfully. The most likely time for a raid to succeed was late at night when one or more men could slip into a camp unnoticed. It was expected that the leader would be the most daring, and if he alone obtained horses, he shared them with other members of the party. He might also give a horse to the priest who had aided them with his prayers. One privilege of a successful war party was for its members to change their names, assuming new names which reflected great deeds.

Success in horse-stealing raids was a rapid road to prestige and riches, to which any daring man could aspire and often succeed. Great bravery was required to steal enemy horses, but it required even greater daring to attempt to make peace with an enemy tribe. To do so it was necessary to expose oneself to great danger by openly entering an enemy camp. Among the greatest chiefs were those who were chiefs of peace.

Battles in defense of a community were organized in a different way. An attacking party might number hundreds of warriors who suddenly would appear one morning on the hills surrounding a village. Each man in the attacking force was mounted on his best horse and wore his most majestic garments, set off with an elaborate feather headdress. They did not ride pell-mell into the settlement, but waited. As soon as the party was sighted, the village men seized their weapons, their best horses, and rode out naked to meet the enemy. The women corralled the remaining horses and climbed on top of the earth lodges to watch the battle. The two long lines of opposing warriors rode slowly toward each other and stopped when about 600 yards separated them. The men on each side chanted war songs and shouted insults to one another. A warrior from one of the lines would then advance before his comrades to make a speech disparaging the enemy, praising his companions in arms, and boasting of his own achievements. When his oration was completed, he galloped toward one of the enemy's flanks, and when within bowshot he rode furiously before the mounted column but in such a manner that little of his body was exposed to enemy fire. He shot arrow after arrow into the line of men. Those that he passed pursued him, and if he or his horse were not struck with arrows, he rode back to his own line and his pursuers returned to their original positions. If, however, he were disabled in any way, his comrades rushed forth to save him. The horsemen were soon at close quarters, fighting with war clubs or anything else at hand. In close conflict men were injured but not usually killed. If the person who made the speech was killed and scalped, his friends withdrew without attempting to recover his body. If he was not scalped, the opponents returned to their original lines and repeated the battle plan again and again until one side withdrew. The Pawnee rarely if ever were routed when making a stand at home, for if they were, their families and the settlement would be destroyed.

If a captive was taken during battle or in a raid, his fate was decided in council. He was most likely turned over to a woman's society which was an amorphous organization functioning only under this particular set of conditions. The women were young, single girls, old maids, or widows, who performed with warbonnets of corn husks, bows made from sticks, and lances of reed stalks. They tortured a captive for four days, during which time every indignity conceivable was heaped upon him before he finally was killed.

The Pawnee fought well but failed to make effective alliances, and this led to their ultimate defeat. They fought with all adjacent Indians, both those indigenous to the area and the late arrivals from the eastern United States. A partial exception might have been the Potawatomi. The established tribes who raided the Pawnee and were in turn raided included the Cheyenne, Kiowa, Kansa, Osage, Comanche, Arapaho, Ute, and Crow. They likewise warred with the Chickasaw, Choctaw, and Cherokee who were displaced from the East. The Pawnee could not even remain peaceful with the Wichita, who were their distant relatives, nor were the Pawnee bands always friendly with each other.

It has been traditional for anthropologists to analyze Plains Indian warfare as an all-consuming game among tribes. Clearly an important value was placed on warfare, but it was more than a game, with lives, loot, and prestige at stake. According to the thoughtful analysis of William W. Newcomb, the conflicts were restricted to small numbers of participants at any one time, with results which usually were indecisive. Newcomb stressed the importance of the horse as leading to the specialized bison hunting methods, and that with the emergence of this pattern, competition over hunting territories led to armed conflicts. There was also the displacement of eastern tribes to the West, and Anglo-American expansion brought yet other forms of competition for land. The eastern tribes, furthermore, possessed guns which aided them significantly in their encroachments. Conflict was particularly fierce at the edges of the Plains, where bison were not as abundant as in the heartland. The erratic seasonal movements of the bison were difficult to follow even when they were numerous. As the herds decreased in size and increased competition developed for the remaining animals, there was bound to be conflict over hunting territories. Additionally, there was the policy of the French, Spanish, British, and Americans of pitting one tribe against another. Thus, it would appear that the fundamental causes of Plains Indian warfare were economic, which is a far more reasonable hypothesis than the supposition that these Indians fought solely for the sake of fighting.

The Pawnee religious system embraced all things in the universe. The supreme deity was Tirawa, and his earthly agents were priests, who supervised the ceremonial round and were guardians of the sacred bundles which linked these people with their gods. For the Skidi the word for a sacred bundle translates "wrapped up rainstorm," a name symbolic of the origins of the supernaturals to the west, whence a bundle's powers came. Such a bundle also might be called "mother," which was a reference to the two ears of maize found in each bundle; these ears were the symbolic mother of the people. One settlement, Center Village, had associations with the Evening Star bundle, which was the greatest of the western powers, the supreme and original authority. Kept in Old Village but belonging to the Skidi in general were four outstanding sacred bundles, the Yellow Star, White Star, Red Star, and Big Black Meteoric Star bundles. It was the power of these bundles, plus that of the Human Skull and North Star bundles, that bound the Skidi together in their dealings with the gods.

The thirteen confederated Skidi communities held the Four Pole Ceremony in an enclosure constructed for the event. At the center was a fire pit, to the west was a bison skull on an altar, and to the east was the entrance. Around the pit were arranged four poles, each associated with a directional color. Within the enclosure the priests and the bundles they possessed were arranged along the north or south sides, depending on whether their community was north or south of the Loup River. If we consider the fire pit as representing the center of a clock, Evening Star (Venus) was located near one o'clock. According to the mythology, she was a powerful and beautiful female deity sought in marriage by all the stars. She married Morning Star (Mars), near three o'clock, who had overcome four powerful stars to obtain his bride. A daughter was born to the couple, and the earth was created as her home. A boy placed on earth was the offspring of Sun and Moon. Then Morning Star required a sacrifice for his efforts, and Evening Star taught a couple to make an Evening Star bundle. Next a man was sent out to tell the people how to perform the Four Pole Ceremony. The details of this ceremony are not recorded, but it obviously was a series of rituals designed to reinforce the unity of the Skidi Pawnee with the supernaturals.

The sacred bundles were gifts from particular stars or else were made under the supervision of a star. They were symbolic of village and band unity. The village bundle ceremonies led by the priest seem to have been for local welfare and the general ones for the success of the entire band. The sacred bundle rituals passed from a priest to his successor, usually a relative, and had nothing to do with the hereditary chiefs. These chiefs, however, were responsible for the physical bundles, and in turn the chiefs obtained their position by virtue of this association. Another feature was that a sacred bundle was not under the physical care of a priest but was kept by a woman, who knew certain facets of the bundle's rituals yet could not take part in the ceremonies.

It would appear that the leadership of each bundle society was hereditary, and membership was open to relatives of deceased members or to other outstanding men by invitation. This generalization applies specifically to the lesser bundles associated with the leading bundles. The well-established leading bundles associated with the Skidi were the Horse, Brave Raven Lance, Reds, Thunderbird, and Those Coming Behind bundle societies. Each member was initiated and underwent tests. Failure in the tests barred one from membership for life, but success led to lifelong association with a particular bundle; one man could be a member of all these societies. Among the Pawnee as a whole the bundle societies were organized for warfare, for hunting, or for both functions. In times of crisis a war society might be selected by the chief to aid in a battle, while a priest would decide which hunting society was to take charge of a bison hunt. These societies served as voluntary associations (sodalities), in which the members found pleasure and other rewards from the social contacts. Each society was divided into two segments, according to their seating in the lodge. Those on the north led the winter ceremonies, and members to the south guided the summer rituals.

Each society performed rituals in order to renew the lances of members. Old lances were set aside for the graves of great warriors, and new ones were fashioned each year. New lances were sanctified with smoke, a feast was held, and the new lances were exhibited by their bearers during a dance. In battle the lance-bearers planted their standards before the enemy and were the last to retreat. A lance stuck in the ground served as the advance rallying point for the warriors. If it appeared that a lance would be carried off by an enemy party, someone who was not a lance bearer could carry it off, and the bearer then could withdraw.

The Red Lance Society of the Skidi had two lances, one associated with the South and another with the North. A pipe was kept by the head of the society and used in the ceremonies as were four rattles and four drums. The Red Lance Society had no duties during the bison hunt; it was a war society that existed only in one settlement. Its function was to police formal raids or repel attacks on hunters. The lances gave protection to the members while fighting, and they were carried in dances of victory. Each year the two lances were disassembled in the fall, to be renewed the next spring.

Another group of societies appear to have been more transient in their nature. These sodalities were organized by men who did not qualify for membership in an established society and were ambitious enough to form their own organization. After having a dream or vision to sanction the organization, the leader sought members and had no difficulty in finding recruits. When they helped out in a crisis, they acquired prestige, but if they failed in battle or during a hunt, or if their leader's persuasive powers failed, they were likely to disband. Among the Skidi we find six such organizations, of which the Crazy Dog Society is an example. It and the other transient sodalities included a ceremonial focus as did the established sodalities. A distinctive feature of the Crazy Dogs was that each member carried a ring-shaped rattle. When they danced, it was in the nude with a cord tied around the penis foreskin and feathers at the end of the cord. Reportedly they had a "no flight" obligation in battle, for the foreskin was tied to a cord attached to a stake in the ground; from this they could not release themselves. The Children of the Iruska was a "contrary" society. The members reversed normal expectations in their behavior. If the camp were attacked, they continued whatever they were doing before the alarm; if someone told them not to go on a raid, they went; and if a mysterious animal which normal persons feared were near the camp, they hunted it. The number of contraries was small, six or seven. They never married and always were painted black, indicating that they were ready to fight. Members were selected by the leader because they were strange, but the society apparently came to an abrupt end when most of its members were killed in a battle.

The priests derived their positions of authority from a star or a planet and were a hereditary group of wise men. The prime prerequisite for becoming a priest was to have an excellent memory, and the second was to be related to a priest. It was a priest who knew the rituals associated with major religious ceremonies designed to ensure community success in farming, the hunt, and warfare. A priest performed as a mediator between men and Tirawa. He was effective when an ordinary man was less so, because he knew more and was more expressive. The sacred bundles were in his charge, and he possessed the necessary esoteric knowledge for handling them. His training was that of a ritual specialist. There were four leading Skidi priests, one each for the Yellow, White, Red, and Big Black Meteoric Star bundles. Each year a different one of the four led the ceremonies and was responsible for the welfare of the band from the first thunder in the spring until after the fall bison hunt. The Red Calf bundle priest was more powerful than the others, but he was called on to perform ceremonies of his own only when the ceremonies of the other four bundles had failed. Although the ceremonies of the bundle societies differed in details, all the bundles were opened at the first thunder of spring and dried bison meat was burned at this time as an offering to the supernaturals to the west.

A priest presided over the name-changing ceremonies for individuals and was the intermediary in marital arrangements. The life of the priest was thought to lengthen if he was most sincere in performing his duties, and his life was shortened if he took his responsibilities casually. The two retainers in each priest's lodge aided in ceremonial activities, and his criers were old and honored men who announced when ceremonies were to be held and recited certain parts of the ritual instructions.

A second major category of supernatural specialists was that of the shamans, who ultimately derived their powers from a time when the deity Tirawa originated certain specific human roles. Shamans controlled spirits of the earth in order to cure people, but they did not command as was customary of a chief. It was from Tirawa that the original shaman received a blue body paint to wear during ceremonies. He also received the wing of a black eagle and a gourd rattle. The powers of a particular shaman were derived from an animal, which in turn had acquired power from a specific star. An emerging shaman might receive power directly from his animal guardian, but more often he became an apprentice to an established practitioner. Shamans were organized into societies of their own in which they performed rituals, usually at the time of the first thunder in the spring and again in the fall. Their activities were designed to purify as well as to renew the power associated with their sacred objects. The rituals involved the use of sacred altars, body paints, rattles, drums, and smoking tobacco as an offering.

Each major subgroup of Pawnee held a Twenty Day Ceremony late in the summer after the harvest and the bundle ceremonies were completed. At this time the shamans held forth for twenty to thirty days; some were aided by one or more assistants and built willow booths in one of the large and important lodges. Among the Skidi a mythological water monster was honored at this time, and an image of it was constructed by the members of all the shaman societies. The head, at the south side of the lodge entrance, was covered with a bison skin, and its teeth, made from willows, showed inside its open mouth. Two long "feelers" were decorated with bright colors, and on top of the head was a down plume. The body was fashioned from willows bent into half circles and covered with mud; the tail was divided like that of a fish. The image of a turtle was fashioned in the fire pit, its head facing the altar to the west. A new fire pit was built on the back of the turtle and represented the sun. Small human figures cut from rawhide were symbolic of stars and hung from the ceiling. A large figure of a man, made of rawhide, was placed on a pole above the lodge; this figure represented the Morning Star. On the floor to the south side there was one additional figure, a life-sized woman, made of clay and clothed to symbolize the Moon. After these objects were in place, the participants paraded around the settlement carrying the sacred animals of the shamans, which were two loons among the Skidi. Shamans were adorned with the species from which they derived their power, and a secret ritual was held in the ceremonial lodge. Afterward the shamans gave a public display of their powers. Examples include having maize mature before the audience or a tree bear fruit miraculously. Likewise, a bear shaman took the liver from a living man and ate it; then the man walked away unharmed. A trick performed unsuccessfully meant expulsion; its success brought permanent membership in the group. During the final days of the celebrations rituals were performed in association with the sacred bundles. Finally, the objects constructed in a lodge for this event were taken to a body of water and placed in a pile, with the mud woman on top.

The sodalities of shamans included the Bear, Bison Doctors, Deer, Blood Doctors, Iruska, and One Horn Dance. The highest ranking shamanistic society was that of the Bear, and in it, as in all the others, the members possessed distinctive rituals, dances, equipment, and taboos. Deer Society members imitated various animals, not only the deer, and received a potion made from mescal beans upon initiation. After the initiate passed into unconsciousness from the narcotic, the leader of the ritual ran the toothed jaw of a garfish down his spine; if the initiate moved he was refused membership. The Deer Society members had control over snakes and were said to be unharmed by snake bites. A unique feature of the Blood Doctors ceremony was for the members to spit up a red substance during their performance and to paint the bodies of those present with the liquid. They likewise painted their otterskins, the otter being their guardian, with the red substance. Men of the Iruska, "The Fire in Me," Society could tolerate great heat, handle hot coals from a fire, and stand barefooted on hot stones during their performances. The member shamans treated the burns of others. The One Horn Dance Society members wore one bison horn as a part of their costume during performances. The membership was drawn from fighting men, and they performed only before an enemy attack. They functioned under the auspices of a deceased warrior who returned at the time of a pending attack.

One of the important ceremonial events in their religious calendar centered about preparations for the summer or early fall bison hunts. The public rituals were preceded by fasting, prayers, and sacrifices by the priests. The ceremony was under the supervision of whichever of the four sacred bundle priests was presiding that year. He also chose the members of one of the sodalities to police the hunt. These police were different from those who supervised the villages and were appointed for the duration of the hunt only. The leader of the camp police was appointed by the chief from the honored old warriors, and he in turn selected three assistants. In a lodge at a village-wide gathering, twelve bison skulls were arranged in a semicircle at the back of the structure. Nearby stood the chiefs and shamans with bison staves, sacred bows and arrows, and other hunting equipment. Invocations were made to Tirawa for success in the hunt, the implements were placed on the ground within the line of skulls, and the prayers were continued. When the appeals to the all-powerful supernatural were completed, a drum was beaten, and a dozen or more warriors formed a circle to perform the bison dance, which continued uninterrupted for the three days prior to the hunt. During the hunt eight carefully selected men carried the bison staves at the head of the moving column. In the 1870's the staves were spruce poles wrapped with beaded red and blue cloths to which hawk and eagle feathers were attached.

The Pawnee looked to the heavens as the source of life and as the dwelling place of the gods. As has been mentioned, the sky with its heavenly bodies was the basis of the supernatural system. Thus it is to be expected that the Pawnee priests studied the heavens. According to Skidi lore there were two great forces in the sky, the male to the east and female to the west. At the zenith was "the silence of the blue sky, above and beyond all clouds" where the supreme supernatural force Tirawa resided. Particular stars or planets were associated with specific events in Pawnee mythology, and an individual acquired supernatural power from a star. A Pawnee star map which was included in a sacred bundle judged to date from precontact times includes stars of five different sizes, each drawn as a four-pointed figure. The largest three were the most important; the others represented the Milky Way or served as fillers. The Milky Way was at the center of the star map, and the stars to one side represented the summer skies while those opposite reflected a view of the winter sky. The constellations recognized are those known to us; the seasonal changes were recorded as well as the presence of double stars. This map demonstrates clearly that the Pawnee had acquired a rather sophisticated knowledge of astronomy.

The Skidi Pawnee sacrifice to the Morning Star is one of the most widely known of American Indian ceremonials. In spite of its bizarre character there was beauty in the accompanying symbolism. The sacrifice was possible only when Mars was the Morning Star and when a man dreamed that the offering should be made. The dreamer obtained from the keeper of the Morning Star bundle the warrior's garb which was part of the bundle. He set out with other men to find a victim from an enemy tribe. The captive, usually a young girl, was dedicated to the Morning Star as soon as she was seized. She was taken to the Skidi chief of the Morning Star village, and rituals which centered about her were performed for four days. The ceremonies began to climax near the end of the fourth day when songs were sung of the Morning Star's quest for the Evening Star, and as each song was completed, a tally stick from the sacred bundle was set aside. Evidently the captor represented the Evening Star, and the sticks symbolized the removal of the victim from this world into the sphere of the supernatural. On the afternoon of the fourth day a rectangular scaffold was erected. The two upright poles represented day and night; the four cross-poles forming the bottom of the frame represented the four directions, and an upper cross-pole represented the sky. The girl, who it was hoped did not know of her fate, was taken to the scaffold the next morning. She was stripped of her clothing, and if she climbed to the upper cross-pole willingly it was regarded as a good omen. Her hands were tied to the upper bar and her feet to the uppermost of the four lower bars. As soon as the Morning Star rose, two men came from the east with flaming torches to touch her armpits and groin. Four other men touched her with war clubs. Her captor shot a sacred arrow through the girl's heart, while another man hit her on the head with the war club from the Morning Star bundle. The priest for the Morning Star bundle cut open her breast with a flint knife and covered his face with her blood. The observers, men, women, and children, shot arrows into the body and then left the scene. The captor of the girl held meat beneath her body so that her blood dripped down to cover it. The blood-covered meat was burned as an offering to the deities. Finally the girl's body was cut down, and the arrows were removed by the priest. The corpse was left to be eaten by animals.

The last sacrifice by the Skidi probably took place in 1838, but the most dramatic moment known to have occurred during the ceremony was in 1817 when the son of a Pawnee chief interrupted the sacrifice. This young man, named Petalesharo, was present when a Comanche woman was to be sacrificed. He cut her free from the scaffold, rode away with her on a horse, and later gave her a horse so that she could return to her people. Petalesharo performed his feat because his father opposed these sacrifices, and he succeeded because of his daring and high standing among the Pawnee. In 1822 Petalesharo visited Washington, D. C., and was presented with an engraved silver medal by the girls of Miss White's Seminary to commemorate his rescue of the Comanche girl. On one side of the medal is depicted the sacrificial scaffold and the surprised leaders of the ritual, and on the opposite side Petalesharo is shown leading the girl away. When Petalesharo died in 1841, the medal was buried with him. In 1884 the medal was taken from his grave, and eventually it was presented to the American Numismatic Society of New York City.

The Pawnee had developed an extremely rich and varied body of folk tales and ritual texts. An example conveys an idea of the richness of their oral traditions. This particular tale was recited by Skidi adults during the

winter for the benefit of children, who were expected to memorize it since
the account reportedly was related by the Evening Star, the first mother.
Like the tales of many people, this example is filled with symbolism meaningful only to the Pawnee, and therefore interpretive comments are offered.
The text was translated by James R. Murie, a Pawnee who collected a
great deal of ethnographic information which was published by the Pawnee
authority George A. Dorsey (1906, 350).

Listen, the girl (1) in distress walks to and fro on top of the mountains.
Listen, the girl's ears tremble, as she runs to and fro, listening.
From the girl is truly descended a fine tribe of people.
There are left behind grass lodges (2).
They rub their backs upon the poles of the lodges.
Many buffalo shall be consecrated, and shall be carried one by one at
the foot of the hill.
Yonder are high hills and low, covered with waving grass.
Now listen, pay attention, they (3) give out their words in their own
tongue.
Yonder on the slopes of the willow-covered hills is a cave.
Turtle (4) shall speak and say, "We will destroy you."
Now I make holy this Comanche (5) who is brought into the lodge.
Meat shall be taken from the back of the buffalo (6).
The rays of the sun (7) shall enter the lodge.
Burnt-offerings of flesh and human beings shall be made.
The earth (8) then shall become a plain.
When this shall happen, people shall see the streams as bows (9).
You shall live under the heavens, and move about over the land as a
tribe.
Then the people shall come together, and all shall live as one people.
The earth shall be fruitful.
The owl (10); the owl.
You shall go to the ravines (11).
The carcass of an animal that has been eaten to the bone.
The spotted rabbit (12) had his way, like a warrior, and he counts coup
upon the enemy.
The mouths shall look round (13).
The noise of sticks (14) and voices shall move to and fro.
May the fathers wave the sticks (15)!

The girl (1) was the first person on earth; she looks and listens for other
people. The grass-covered dwellings (2) reportedly were the first type used
by the Pawnee, and when abandoned lodges of this type were common,

the bison rubbed against the poles. The supernatural powers of animals, they (3), are found in different places. A turtle (4) created a flood to destroy four monsters, and this reference contains the implication that people will destroy one another and particularly that there will be the Morning Star sacrifice. The reference to the Comanche (5) is a further allusion to the sacrifice; the bison meat (6) is for an accompanying feast, and the sun's light (7) consecrates the victim. The earth (8) appears to be flat when shrouded with mist, but as the sun rises the mist disappears and shadows cast by the sun's rays reveal the hills and mountains. The reference to bows (9) is associated with killing animals, dedicating meat to the gods, and offering human sacrifices. Owls (10) are wise; the priests chant their night rituals like the owls. In the ravines (11) are the remains of animals, who like men, die. The Rabbit (12) is a star near the Milky Way who offered a way of life opposed to that of the Evening Star. When the people have an abundance of food, their mouths will be round (13) from singing and shouting. The sticks (14) are a reference to arrows shot at the Morning Star victim, while the sticks (15) next mentioned are associated with a blessing of children by waving pipe sticks.

When a woman became aware that she was pregnant, she and her husband observed certain prohibitions. The most important of these was that the man could hunt and kill only deer and only his wife could eat the meat. A wide range of additional taboos were observed in order to prevent any deformity of the embryo. Each embryo acquired an animal familiar, and its nature later was revealed by the actions of the individual when ill. When the woman began labor, her husband left the dwelling for four days. During this time he continued to observe taboos, and he wore his hair loose, because Tirawa did so while creating. The laboring woman was aided by an old female shaman or the keeper of a sacred bundle. On the dirt floor of the dwelling fresh earth was spread and covered with soft grass to absorb the flow of blood. Birth took place from a kneeling position with the woman leaning forward on a stick. Beforehand she took medicine to ease the process, but if the medicine was not effective, additional women came to her aid. The navel cord was cut and tied by the midwife and was kept to be buried with the mother. The infant was washed, wrapped in a blanket, and placed on a cradleboard. Finally the afterbirth was placed in a tree where it would not be disturbed by birds or animals. The relatives of a child born at night observed the stars and the weather; if the wind did not blow and the following day was clear, they assumed the infant probably would not be ill or plagued with difficulties in his life. The near relatives of the mother cared for the neonate until the umbilical cord dropped off; then the infant was returned to the mother. Now too, the parents' hair was braided, and the midwife was compensated. Were a woman to die in childbirth or the offspring to be stillborn, it was assumed that taboos had been broken. Infanticide was unknown and the possibility was not even imagined. Male shamans were thought to be able to produce an abortion by using herbs, and an unwed woman might attempt to induce an abortion by applying pressure on her abdomen.

From the midwife an individual received a name based on his appearance or behavior just after birth. Examples for the Skidi included Round Eyes, Fatty, and Young Bull. The names White or Black were favorite Pawnee names for boys, and Bright Eyes was a favorite for girls. A small child might receive another name if his father sacrificed a scalp for the occasion in a formal ritual. This name usually was retained by the individual until after marriage. A third name was bestowed by the individual's father after the marriage, and this one might be replaced to insure success in warfare or after a brave deed. Likewise a man might receive the name of an honored relative. So long as a child nursed, it was called by a word comparable to "baby," and the sex was not distinguished. This period lasted for about three years, after which the terms for male and female children were different.

Informal adoption took place when an affluent family raised a child belonging legally to a poor family. It appears to have been somewhat less common to adopt the child formally. Formal adoption took place if a favorite boy or girl died and another was found to resemble it and the parents approved.

A young child was under the direct supervision of his grandmothers, who were severe instructors. Were a child to misbehave, he was reproved verbally, and if he did not obey the rules of childhood behavior, he was whipped. Among the ideals was for children to learn tribal lore from their grandmothers. They were reproved for not being quiet and withdrawn when among adults, for being inattentive during ceremonies or approaching the altar at the rear of a lodge. Older sisters, the mother and father, and the grandparents all served as authoritarian figures for a child. Until a boy was about twelve years of age, he helped his mother with such household tasks as hauling water. Older boys came under the supervision of their grandfathers, and to acquire archery skills was an important part of a boy's life. The favorite game played with a bow and arrows was to shoot at an arrow shot by another boy. Older boys followed their fathers on bison hunts, and as soon as a kill was made, they helped butcher the animal; the horse upon which they had ridden was used to transport the meat to camp.

A girl's training in the essential household skills was under the direction of her grandmother. When a girl menstruated for the first time, no ritual was performed unless the girl's mother was the keeper of a sacred bundle. In such instances the girl was isolated, probably with her maternal grandmother. There were prohibitions on the girl's behavior and restrictions in her diet, with the pattern followed during subsequent menstrual periods. All menstruating women avoided contact with sacred bundles and did not attend the accompanying ceremonies.

A boy who had reached puberty, which was not marked by ceremonial recognition, was placed in a new age group where he remained until he married. He was identified by a word translated "grown" or "straight up." Until this time he went naked except that he wore a robe in cold weather. After puberty he dressed as a man and was linked closely with his mother's brother's wife. When her husband was away, the boy served as a supplementary husband for a few years until acquiring a wife of his own. This form of mating was recorded by Dorsey and Murie in their study edited by Alexander Spoehr, whereas a different form was noted by Alexander Lesser who, although acknowledging the ties between a man and his mother's brother's wife, also stressed that a young unmarried man who had demonstrated his bravery had sexual access to his older brother's wife (fraternal polyandry).

Charles A. Murray, the Scot who passed a summer among the Pawnee, left a delightful account of young men's vanity. When not obliged to hunt, the young braves sought to make themselves handsome and lavished care on their favorite horses, which they groomed and adorned with paint and even a few feathers in the tail. After the rider and the steed were fully presentable, they paraded through the settlement to be admired by all. For a young man to seduce an unmarried girl was disreputable since girls were expected to be virgins when they married. Were a young couple to fornicate and be found out, the parents prevented further meetings. If, however, the girl became pregnant, a hasty wedding was arranged if the man was considered a potentially reputable husband. If not, he might be beaten badly, and no one would defend him, for it was difficult to find another man willing to marry the girl under such circumstances.

In a normal marriage the partners were not to be more closely related than third cousins, if relatives at all, and ideally a mate was from one's own community (village endogamy). A man did not marry until after he had participated in at least one raid, successfully had stolen horses, and had killed bison on a hunt. The woman was about twenty-two years old, and the couple lived with the wife's parents following the marriage (matrilocal residence). When a man married a woman from another settlement, they always resided in the community of the woman, and children were affiliated consistently with the village of their mother.

Marriages usually were arranged by relatives of the couple, with the primary negotiations between a man's mother's brother and the possible bride's mother's brother. If the girl had no maternal uncle, her brothers or grandfathers made the decision. Were the potential groom to object violently to the arrangements he would leave home for a year or two. A girl could attempt to influence her uncle, but she was forced to abide by his decision. The maternal uncle of the man, were he from a leading matrilineage, selected a chaste girl and one with a reputation for hard work. A formal wedding ceremony was performed when leading lineages were involved, but for persons of lesser standing this was not considered necessary. Marriage ceremonies were led by the priest, and formal approval was given by the girl's relatives in a ritual which included smoking and recitations of the young man's merits. Further ceremonial smoking and gifts to the male relatives of the girl followed, and finally the marriage ceremonies were completed when the couple ate and then slept together. Males were referred to by a word meaning "man" and females as "woman" after marriage. After a couple was established, their parents aided them in making a tepee in which they lived alone during the hunts into the open plains; when the man was away on a hunt or with a raiding party, his wife or wives and children moved into the lodge of his parents. Finally, when a man was fully successful in adult activities, his family and his wife's family each built half of the earth lodge which would be the couple's new residence. The lodge was completed when the husband built the altar and the couple made the fireplace.

In theory, a man did not physically punish his wife because it was through two female deities, Evening Star and Moon, that he was able to obtain bison and maize. In fact, it seems that a man rarely abused his wife so much that her relatives intervened on her behalf. Skidi Pawnee divorce seems to have been rare, and when it did occur, the grounds were most likely to be adultery or failure of the husband to be a good provider. Barrenness of the woman was not grounds for divorce. A man could leave his bride on the wedding night if she were not a maiden. Such a woman, along with those who freely fornicated before marriage, or loose widows, lived on the fringes of a community as prostitutes. An adulterous wife was deserted, and an adulterous husband might be ordered to leave by his female in-laws. In cases of divorce the children remained with their mother.

If a married man were to die, his younger brother acquired the widow as a wife (levirate). In instances of plural marriages the first and subsequent wives of a man were sisters (sororal polygyny). A man could obtain the younger sisters or sister of his wife if the girl's family was satisfied with his abilities as a provider. The secondary wives were acquired as they came of age, but there was no accompanying ceremony. One Skidi man had eight wives from two families, which seems to be the record number.

Dunbar and Murray, as well as other early nineteenth-century observers, often remarked at length about the strenuous physical labor of Pawnee women. In spite of the fact that women could not be warriors, priests, shamans, or chiefs, they were recognized in tribal, political and social life. It was the woman who kept the sacred bundles and who sacrificed maize on the lodge altar. Community welfare largely depended upon her successful fulfillment of these duties.

In the daily round of family activities while in the village, all the members bathed in a nearby stream or river in the morning. They then busied themselves around the settlement and ate their first meal around noon. Normally the women sat on the east side of the home during meals and the men opposite them, while the children ate near the women. When a number of families lived in one dwelling, the women of each unit alternated in preparing the meals. A number of food taboos were observed. Shamans and chiefs could not eat fish; the tender meat around a bison's anus was saved for old people; and young people were not to eat the stomach of a bison cow. To break any of these taboos was to court some particular type of disaster. If men were hunting bison, persons remaining in the village were cautioned to keep the lodge clean and to make offerings of maize to the bison skull on the household altar. Likewise, menstruating women were not to approach the skull for fear of angering the bison spirit.

Preparation of a body for burial and the subsequent observances varied depending on the importance of the person during his life and the circumstances of death. For any individual the body was prepared almost immediately for the burial, which took place a few hours later. The body of an old person or one of rank was painted with a sacred red pigment by a priest. The corpse of a man was shrouded in his bison robe, and ceremonial equipment was buried with a person who was a member of a particular voluntary association. For an old man, one who was no longer a hunter or warrior, and a woman after the menopause, both specially designated, there was no prolonged period of mourning; it lasted only the day of the burial. A man who died in middle age from natural causes was not mourned, for such a death reflected the useless nature of the person.

Plate 36
Petalesharo, the Pawnee
who rescued a Comanche girl
from being sacrificed
to the Morning Star
(From McKenney and Hall, 1933).

Plate 37
Medal presented to
Petalesharo by the girls
of Miss White's Seminary and later recovered from his grave
(Courtesy of the American Numismatic Society).

Plate 39
*The Skidi Pawnee
warrior Crooked Hand
who reportedly
died about 1874*
(Courtesy of the
Southwest Museum).

Plate 38 *A Pawnee community of earth lodges photographed in 1871* (Courtesy of the Smithsonian Institution National Anthropological Archives, neg. no. 1245-B).

ate 40   *A Pawnee camp in Oklahoma* (Courtesy of the Southwest Museum).

At the death of an important chief the mourning period lasted months; it was shortened, however, to four days if the death took place just before the bundle renewal ceremonies. If a person of no consequence died, only the family mourned the loss, and then only for three days. If a man died at the hands of an enemy, his close friends and relatives secured an enemy scalp as soon as possible after the death. They consecrated it and tied it to a long stick above the grave. When a man died, it was his brothers and sisters who truly mourned the loss. A surviving brother mutilated himself, while a sister cut her hair. It was said of a wife, however, that she would spit on her hands to pretend tears, simultaneously peering through her fingers in search of another husband. A widow was expected to mourn for a year before remarrying. If she remained in the lodge of her deceased husband, it was expected that she would marry his younger brother or his sister's son at the end of the mourning period. If, however, she returned to her parents' home, these marital arrangements seem less likely to have taken place. A widower was obliged to mourn for at least two years, and frequently he did not remarry. After a man's death, his wife was considered the owner of their lodge and tepee as well as her own utensils and tools; his personal property, such as robes, horses, and riding equipment, was inherited usually by his sister's sons.

The dead almost always were interred in the ground, usually on the top of a hill, and over the body was piled a low mound of earth. A corpse was flexed, covered with matting, and accompanied by grave goods. Items never included as grave goods were those regarded as having their origin in the sky. The most important category of this nature seems to have been meteorites, which were sometimes part of a war bundle. They were from the stars and belonged to the sky. Thus they were placed on hilltops so that they could return to their home.

Information about the Pawnee dating from the recent past is rare, but we do have the detailed study by Alexander Lesser about their participation in the Ghost Dance of 1890. This was the last major effort of the tribe to reaffirm its cultural identity as Indian. The originator of the 1890 Ghost Dance was a Paiute Indian from Nevada named Wovoka (Jack Wilson). He reportedly died during an eclipse of the sun in January, 1889, and went to heaven, where he saw all the dead Indians living in an idyllic state. God reportedly said that if Wovoka returned to earth and taught the people to perform a particular dance, the Ghost Dance, the dead and living would be reunited. Likewise, people were cautioned not to fight with each other nor with the whites, and neither should they lie or steal. If these instructions were obeyed, there would be no more illness, old age, or death. By performing the Ghost Dance this happy new world soon would emerge.

Word of the Ghost Dance spread rapidly, and the doctrine was modified by different tribes. One frequent view was that Wovoka was Christ, who had come to save the Indians. Rumors about the Ghost Dance spread to the Pawnee in 1890, and in 1891 a Pawnee, Frank White, participated in a Ghost Dance in southern Oklahoma. He returned to his people and became their leader of the Ghost Dance. During dances the participants who went into trances revealed that they saw the Messiah and the dead. The leader preached that the world was to change soon and that the whites and persons of mixed Indian and white ancestry would be blown away or destroyed by the wind. Believers, however, would see the dead return and bison again would become plentiful. Dances were held throughout 1891, and by 1892 most Pawnee had accepted the doctrine and were participating in order to hasten the time when a new world would be created. Many persons were so convinced that the present world was coming to an end that they did not plant their crops. Opposition to the dance by the Indian agent and his efforts to break up dances led to their being performed in secret. Finally, the leader of the movement, Frank White, was arrested for holding a Ghost Dance and held for about two weeks. During his hearing the judge sternly warned him against continuing his "insurrection."

At the time when the Ghost Dance movement reached its climax, the Federal government was exerting every effort to induce the Pawnee to change the nature of their landholdings. The Pawnee were living on a reservation, and with the passage by Congress of the General Allotment Act in 1887, reservation Indians were encouraged to select plots of land for which they eventually would receive clear titles. Unallotted reservation lands then were to be sold to whites. The Pawnee resisted the program and viewed it as an attempt to destroy the tribe, which it was. In mid-1892 Federal agents told these Indians that if they accepted individual land allotments, they would pass from Federal control and could then hold their Ghost Dances as often as they wished. This argument apparently was convincing, for by the end of that year the allotment process was completed. The following year the nonallotted lands were opened to white settlers. Over the next few years the Ghost Dance was continued but in a less militant form, and the Indian agents could do little to stop it.

After the death of White in 1893, or possibly somewhat earlier, the Ghost Dance changed to become a more formalized series of four-day ceremonies. The Ghost Dance focused Pawnee attention on being Indian, for one of the doctrines was to give up the goods and ways of whites. This introspection led to a renewal of the importance of sacred bundles, sodalities, and aboriginal games. By 1892 the sacred bundle rituals nearly had ceased to exist, and the elaborate shamans' performances likewise were declining. A number of conditions ran counter to a bundle ceremony revival. Some bundles had been buried with the last priest of a bundle group, and when a bundle did survive the priest in charge of it was not likely to know all of the esoteric lore surrounding it. Lesser (1933, 108) noted that in the late nineteenth century there was a "cultural forgetting" and that the functions of the ceremonies were fading, which made the continuity of ritual knowledge from a priest to his apprentice less likely. Then, too, many persons were dying, and with them went their store of knowledge. The Ghost Dance, with its emphasis on individual vision experience, was one mechanism to revive the nonesoteric aspects of aboriginal life. An individual could acquaint himself with the past through a vision, negating the ritual instructions of old. Such supernatural commands brought a reformulation of Pawnee dances and ceremonies.

In historic times many Indian tribes of the Plains and prairies accepted peyote and integrated its use into their supernatural system. Peyote, a small cactus plant grown in Mexico, has a small "button" appearing above the ground. These buttons were collected and dried for ritual use. They contain nonaddictive stimulants and sedatives which produce a narcotic effect. The first knowledge of peyote was received by the Pawnee from the Quapaw about 1890 when two young men visited the latter tribe. Somewhat later more details concerning its use were learned from Arapaho visitors. When under the influence of peyote, one man learned songs and rituals which became the basis of the Peyote Cult, and this individual emerged as its leader. As is common among American Indian tribes, elements of Christianity were integrated into the belief system, and in part the taking of peyote was associated in the minds of the Pawnee with the Ghost Dance.

As Lesser (1933, 117) has written, "The Ghost Dance proved not only a force for cultural revival, but with a return to the past as an inspirational source and guide, and vision sanctions as immediate drives, the doctrine was an impetus to cultural development." It appeared as though the Pawnee once again could reaffirm their Indian identity. This was not to be the case, however. With the allotment program the reservation was divided into small parcels of land, and whites who purchased unallotted lands lived next door to Indians. The Indians received an $80,000 advance for the lands they had released and a continuing $30,000 a year annuity plus interest from the balance of the sale of Nebraska and Oklahoma lands. These funds were either directly or indirectly available to the approximately 160 families. Furthermore, the Pawnee leased farmlands, grazing lands, and even their houses to white cattlemen and farmers. The result was that by the turn of the century the Indians were well-to-do financially but lived without purpose. There was no positive side to their security, for they lived from day to day, spending their money as rapidly as they received it. The net result was that they became deculturated, they no longer retained their Indian ways, and they adopted only the superficial aspects of the dominant white society.

Fewer than 700 Pawnee survived at the turn of the present century, but by 1962 their number had increased to nearly 2000 persons with one-quarter or more Pawnee blood. Their reservation land in Oklahoma originally comprised about 280,000 acres in 1876. After allotments had been selected by Indians, nearly 170,000 acres were opened up to white settlers by 1893. The sale of allotted lands by Indians reduced their holdings from 110,000 acres in 1893 to about 28,000 acres by 1962. Many of these acres were small plots owned by numerous individuals, and they could not effectively be utilized by families. In 1962 the Pawnee received about seven million dollars from the Federal government through the Court of Claims for lands they had relinquished without receiving just compensation or settlement. Evidence suggests that this money has been used by the recipients to improve their economic conditions. Thus, the Federal government once again has provided money in an effort to buy justice, but the compensation has a hollow ring.

References

Buckstaff, Ralph N. "Stars and Constellations of a Pawnee Sky Map," *American Anthropologist*, v. 29, 279-285. 1927.

Bureau of Indian Affairs. "Pawnee Indians," n.d. (mimeographed).

Catlin, George. *North American Indians*. 2 v. London. 1844.

Dorsey, George A. "Social Organization of the Skidi Pawnee," *Fifteenth International Congress of Americanists*, 71-77. Quebec. 1907.

Dorsey, George A. "A Pawnee Ritual of Instruction," *Anthropological Papers Written in Honor of Franz Boas*, 350-353. New York. 1906.

Dorsey, George A. "The Skidi Rite of Human Sacrifice," *Fifteenth International Congress of Americanists*, 65-70. Quebec. 1907.

*Dorsey, George A., and James R. Murie (edited by Alexander Spoehr). "Notes on Skidi Pawnee Society," *Anthropological Series, Field Museum of Natural History*, v. 27, 67-119. 1940. The definitive study of Skidi social structure with notes on the life cycle of the individual as well as information on certain aspects of political organization.

*Dunbar, John B. "The Pawnee Indians," *Magazine of American History*, v. 4, 241-281, v. 5, 321-342, v. 8, 734-754. 1880-1882 (reprinted, New York, 1883). This is an integrated historical and ethnographic account of the Pawnee by a pioneer missionary.

Fletcher, Alice C. "Pawnee Star Lore," *Journal of American Folk-Lore*, v. 16, 10-15. 1903.

*Grinnell, George B. *Pawnee Hero Stories and Folk-Tales*. Lincoln. 1961 (originally published in New York in 1889). Grinnell describes diverse aspects of Pawnee ethnography, but none in detail. Emphasis is on folk-tales and stories about warfare, but it is still an essential source for a balanced account of these Indians.

Hodge, Frederick W. "Pitalesharu and his Medal," *The Masterkey*, v. 24, 111-119. 1950.

*Hyde, George E. *Pawnee Indians*. Denver. 1951. This book is the definitive history of the Pawnee but has very little to offer about events after 1900.

Irving, John T., Jr. (edited by John F. McDermott). *Indian Sketches*. Norman. 1955.

Lesser, Alexander. "Levirate and Fraternal Polyandry among the Pawnees," *Man*, v. 30, 98-101. 1930.

*Lesser, Alexander. *The Pawnee Ghost Dance Hand Game*. New York. 1933. The focus of this study is on the Ghost Dance and the revival of a game at the time of the Ghost Dance, but the volume also contains a summary of Pawnee history down to about 1900.

"Letters Concerning the Presbyterian Mission in the Pawnee Country, near Bellevue, Neb., 1831-1849." *Collections of the Kansas State Historical Society*, v. 14, 570-784. 1918.

Linton, Ralph. *The Thunder Ceremony of the Pawnee*. Field Museum of Natural History. Leaflet 5. 1922.

Linton, Ralph. "The Origin of the Skidi Pawnee Sacrifice to the Morning Star," *American Anthropologist*, v. 28, 457-466. 1926.

McKenney, Thomas L., and James Hall. *The Indian Tribes of North America*, v. 1. Edinburgh. 1933.

*Murie, James R. *Pawnee Indian Societies*. Anthropological Papers of the American Museum of Natural History, v. 11, pt. 7. New York. 1914. This short monograph is the most complete and readable account of sacred and secular Pawnee societies. It includes also information about other aspects of Pawnee life and is a required source of ethnographic materials.

Murray, Charles A. *Travels in North America*, v. 2. London. 1839.

Newcomb, William W., Jr. "A Re-Examination of the Causes of Plains Warfare," *American Anthropologist*, v. 52, 317-330. 1950.

Roe, Frank G. *The Indian and the Horse*. Norman. 1955.

*Wedel, Waldo R. *An Introduction to Pawnee Archeology*. Bureau of American Ethnology, Bulletin 112. 1936. Not only are the details of Pawnee archaeology presented, but historical and ethnographic data are analyzed into a fine synthesis of sociocultural data.

Wedel, Waldo R. *Prehistoric Man on the Great Plains*. Norman. 1961.
Wissler, Clark, and Herbert J. Spinden. "The Pawnee Human Sacrifice to the Morn-
ingstar," *American Museum Journal*, v. 16, 49-55. 1916.

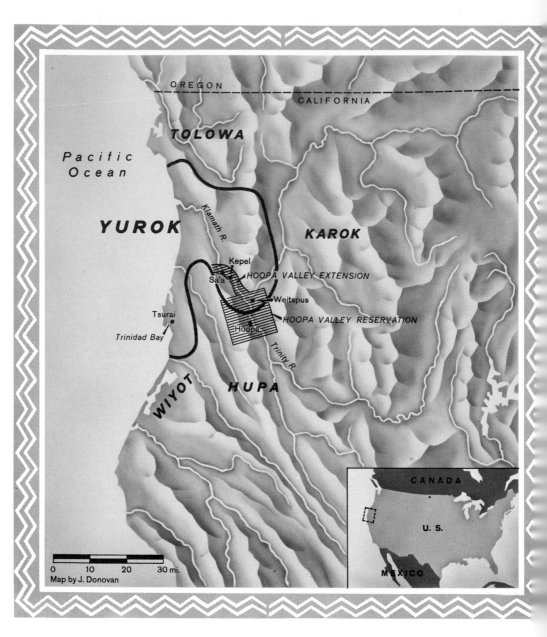

OREGON

CALIFORNIA

*Pacific
Ocean*

TOLOWA

YUROK

KAROK

Klamath R.

Kepel

Sa'a

HOOPA VALLEY EXTENSION

Tsurai

Weitspus

HOOPA VALLEY RESERVATION

Trinidad Bay

Hoopa

Trinity R.

WIYOT

HUPA

0   10   20   30 mi.

Map by J. Donovan

CANADA

U. S.

MEXICO

The Yurok:
salmon fishermen of california

For the aboriginal Yurok the center of the world was near the junction of the Klamath and Trinity rivers in northwestern California, and the earth was thought to extend in a seventy-five mile radius from this spot. Surrounding their forested and mountainous country was an ocean of water and then a sea of pitch. Beyond the water to the west was the home of the Widower across the Ocean, who was a culture hero, and just to the north of his residence lived the salmon, then dentalium shells, and finally another supernatural to the northwest. At the margins of the land to the south was the country of geese; on their migration northward these birds flew through a hole in the sky and disappeared from view. This was the manner in which the world was conceived by these stay-at-home Indians.

The Yurok way of life represented an amalgamation of the Northwest Coast Indian emphasis on wealth and prestige with a simpler material culture typical of northern Californian Indians. The comparatively unelaborated nature of Yurok technology and their rather complex social norms are a combination that attracts attention. Perhaps the most interesting facet of Yurok life was the great stress placed on certain forms of wealth and the accumulation of such objects for personal prestige and honor. The individualistic nature of Yurok society was stressed in another manner, for there was no overall power structure within a community or at the tribal level. The customs of these people are well-documented in descriptions by Erik H. Erikson, Robert F. Heizer and John E. Mills, Alfred L. Kroeber, and the Yurok Indian Lucy Thompson.

The aboriginal population of about 3000 persons lived in a heavily forested area, dominated by Douglas fir and redwoods, which covered nearly 700 square miles of territory, but by 1910 their number had decreased to 700 and their land base was drastically reduced. In 1962 about 450 persons were associated with reserved lands; the total Yurok population had increased to nearly 1000. The largest aboriginal population segment was concentrated along the Klamath River, but there also were scattered settlements along the adjacent coast. At that time coastal and riverine dialect groups existed; they had comparatively little contact with one another, which led also to cultural differences between them. Their language was related most closely to that of their coastal neighbors to the south, the Wiyot. These two small tribes were members of the Macro-Algonkian linguistic phylum but physically were far removed from their linguistic relatives to the east.

The only Yurok area site excavated systematically is Tsurai, located along Trinidad Bay near the southern coastal border with the Wiyot. It was occupied from about A.D. 1620 to 1916, and among the artifacts re-

308

covered from the prehistoric levels were small, tanged triangular arrow-points, drills, and skin scrapers from chipped stone. Ground stone tools included pestles and mortars for pulverizing acorns, as well as adzes with stone handles and blades of stone or shell. A few ornaments and pipe bowls of the tubular variety were manufactured from a local source of soapstone. In addition, artifacts included harpoon dart heads, awls, and ornaments of antler or bone. From an analysis of shell and bone found at the site, it was established that shellfish such as mussels, cockles, clams, and abalone were important items of diet along with rockfish and salmon. The people also took sea lions, seals, and sea otter from the ocean as well as deer and elk from the land. Sea lions appear to have had supernatural associations, since on one offshore rock an estimated thousand skulls were found. Each one had one or more holes in the parietal bones, but no other parts of the skeletons were recovered. The site was not occupied and seems only to have served as a place to deposit the skulls.

Heizer and Mills summarized the history of contacts between the coastal Yurok and whites. They noted that the Portuguese explorer Sebastian Cermeno probably discovered Trinidad Bay in 1595 and that the area was revisited in 1775 by Spanish explorers and by the English explorer George Vancouver in 1793. From 1800 to 1817 the Yurok were involved in the fur trade, for they, like most other Indians along the north Pacific coast, hunted for sea otter whose pelts they exchanged for trade goods. Between 1818 and 1848 there was little known contact with whites, but in 1849 placer gold was mined on the Trinity River, and Trinidad Bay became the most important trans-shipment point for goods and equipment destined for the mining operations. For the Yurok as a whole there was little contact with outsiders prior to 1849, but from that time forward exotic influences expanded greatly, both in scope and intensity.

The Widower across the Ocean made earth, which he kept in a deerskin container, and by spilling it down through space he created firm ground which became the world. Since he could see nothing of his creation, he caused the sun to come into being for light of day and the moon to negate the darkness of night. The earth was without life, and to replace the desolation he created the varied landscape, with streams flowing into rivers and these in turn emptying into the ocean. He made the forests and the animals. The first animal created was a white deer, and then a red eagle was made to command the skies. After the creation of other animals and plants, the first real man was formed of soil, and then a woman was created to keep him company. This couple wandered from their home in the north and finally came to settle in the Klamath River valley.

The Yurok were able to state with exactness the nature of their world:

the land was a flat expanse, circular in its configuration, which rested on water as well as being surrounded by it. They thought they could observe the gentle rise and fall of the land as breakers rolled in from the sea. Localities on the land had specific designations, and a region generally was not referred to as such but was considered in terms of particular localities or spots. Thus the Klamath River was not named but was conceived of in terms of particular locations along it or adjacent streams. It required twelve days' travel by canoe to traverse the land from one side to the other, a distance of approximately 150 miles, according to Yurok thinking. As would be expected, the Yurok were not great travelers; they had contact with their neighbors but apparently never penetrated the depth of territory belonging to other people. Not only did they refuse to travel abroad, but strangers without an introduction, even if arriving from among a friendly people, were regarded as a threat. It was thought that normal people stayed close to home with their relatives and friends. Directions were not conceived of as cardinal points on a compass but in terms of water flow. Thus, there was an upstream and a downstream, and it did not matter if a river meandered in various directions. The analogy of directions with water flow was extended to include the coast, with northward conceived of as downstream. The people normally traveled by boat, but they also used certain overland paths. These trails were conceived of as being "like people" and had designated rest stops along them; to pause at a spot which was not a traditional resting place was to invite ill fortune.

Yurok men wore their hair long, and it hung loose over their shoulders or else was tied in a knot on top of the head. In his hair a man might wear a garland of flowers or feathers. Facial hair was plucked with a hinged mussel shell which served as tweezers. A man's earlobes were pierced, and suspended from a hole in each lobe was an ornamental pin of bone or shell. About his waist and ankles were tied decorative thongs. Men painted their faces with pigments of three colors; white signified mourning, red was for joy, and black for war. The usual designs consisted of three horizontal lines on each cheek, one or two on the forehead, and circles or half circles about the eyes. Several lines were tattooed on the arms of each man to serve as measures for lengths of dentalium shells. Most younger men wore folded skins around their hips, but older males, and some of the younger ones, did not normally wear clothing. When traveling overland a man wore skin moccasins, and when hunting in deep snow knee-length leggings were worn with snowshoes. During cold weather both men and women wore capes of seal, sea otter, or deer skin. Women arranged their hair in two braids, and in these flowers were placed. The women wore caps made of twined basketry, and as young children their chins were tattooed with three parallel bands from beneath the lower lip to the chin. The facial tattoos of women were said to have been made in order that older women would not look like men. Women wore necklaces made from bone, shells, or small pieces of fruit. Their clothing consisted of an inner deerskin apron which was about a foot wide and had shells, nuts, or pieces of obsidian attached to the fringe. A longer skin apron was worn over the first and partly obscured the inner garment. Like the men the women pierced their ears and inserted ornaments in the openings. Males went without clothing, except for furs worn for warmth during winter, until they reached puberty, but girls wore aprons after they were about two years of age. Unlike the adults the hair of children was cut short.

The people built their houses along both banks of the lower Klamath River, on the borders of coastal lagoons, or at points where streams and rivers flowed into the sea. Settlements ranged in size from one to twenty-five dwellings; most villages had from three to seven houses, with an average of six residents per house. Each dwelling was named and was associated with a particular line of males (patrilineage). Settlements appear to have been abandoned rather often; the cause might be a quarrel within or between families, an outbreak of disease, the flooding of a locality, or simply boredom with the setting. A typical settlement included houses, sweathouses, and menstrual huts.

The rectangular houses were about twenty feet across and were built in deep excavated pits. The thick adzed planks, set vertically to form the walls, were as much as ten feet in height at the center of the front and back. At the peaks near the centerline of a house were ridge plates, and at right angles to these were overlapping roof boards which extended from the ridge to beyond the sidewalls; poles were tied over the roof to hold the boards in place. A rectangular opening was left near the center of the roof to permit smoke from the interior fire to escape and sunlight to enter. A house was entered through a round hole in a front wall plank, and the area before the doorway was paved with flat stones. Inside a house, some four feet from the door was a partitioned room piled with driftwood, trash, and assorted equipment such as small round snowshoes made with wooden crosspieces in a grapevine outer frame, large cone-shaped carrying baskets, seed beaters, and disk-shaped trays for collecting seeds. The partition had a large inner door, and beyond it was the main living area. Dominating the room was a large pit in the center; up to five feet in depth and ten feet square, the bottom was reached by climbing down a notched log ladder. Earth at the sides of the pit was retained by a series of logs, and in the center of the pit was a small stone-lined fire pit. Overhead a pole framework was suspended from the ceiling, and from it fish were hung to dry. All the members of a family ate around the fireplace, and women as well as children normally slept there. Scattered about were various items of household utility. There were wooden serving trays for meat, twined cooking baskets with rounded bottoms and vertical sides for preparing acorn meal, and similar but smaller baskets out of which the meal was eaten. Spoons were made from antler, a mussel shell, or the top of a deer skull. Wooden bowls were nearby for washing one's fingers after eating, and small redwood stools served as seats for men. At the side of a house sometimes was a lean-to of planks which served as a menstrual hut; in other cases, the menstrual hut was a separate structure built a short distance from a dwelling.

A bathhouse usually was associated with from one to three dwellings; this building also served as sleeping quarters for men and boys as well as a place where males lounged and gossiped. There was no prohibition against women being in the bathhouses; in fact, they sometimes slept there on cold nights. However, the men did not relish the presence of women in a bathhouse, saying that women had too many fleas. The women in turn maintained that the men talked too much in the bathhouses and they would just as soon not be there. A bathhouse was built in an excavated pit which measured ten by fourteen feet. The vertical sidewall planks, about four feet in length, only reached the ground level, while the vertical end wall planks were cut to form a gabled roof which was spanned with a ridgepole. Roof planks extended from the peak to the sidewalls, and on top of the gable an old dugout canoe was placed facing downward to prevent water from seeping in along the ridge. Before the entrance, in one of the sidewalls, was an area paved with stones. The floor of a bathhouse was paved with stones or covered with planks and was reached by descending a notched log ladder. The stone-lined fire pit was near the center of the structure, and there was a small, round exit hole in one of the end walls, beyond which an excavated area led to the ground level. The only furnishings were pillows made from blocks of redwood. The wood for a bath was collected by men, and as they returned to the bathhouse, they sang songs which were to bring good fortune. To prepare a bath, the wood in the fire pit was allowed to burn down to a bed of coals, after which the men undressed and entered the structure. They placed covers over the entrance and exit and sat in the intense heat for about half an hour. After crawling out the exit, they lounged on the stone platform before the entrance and sang the same songs which they had sung while gathering the firewood. Once they had cooled off, they swam in a stream or river and returned home to their evening meal.

Among the material items of utility around a household baskets of diverse forms were important. The primary method of basketmaking was simple twining, with hazel shoots most often used for the rigid warp elements and split roots of pine, redwood, or spruce for the flexible weft elements. In order to assure a good supply of hazel shoots the bushes were burned, and the new shoots were harvested the following season. Once the shoots were collected and peeled, they were bundled to dry and would be used only after three or four years. Sometimes designs were woven into a basket, using black maidenhair fern stems or weft elements dyed red or yellow. Small baskets for tobacco were globular and sometimes had an attached leather top with a drawstring around the neck. The people also made openwork cradles, another form of basketry, for carrying infants.

The most important subsistence item was salmon, termed "that which is eaten" (Waterman, 1920, 185). Acorns were next in usefulness; far less significant were game and plant products such as roots and berries. Along the seacoast fish were taken from the surf, shellfish were collected, and sea lions were hunted. Kroeber (1925, 87) states, "Acorns were gathered, dried, stored, cracked, pulverized, sifted, leached, and usually boiled with hot stones in a basket." Unshelled acorns were stored in large baskets inside the house and were later processed by removing the nuts from their shells and pounding the meal on a stone slab with a pestle. The bitter acid was removed by placing the ground meal in a sand basin and pouring hot water over it. Acorn meal was cooked by stones which were heated in a fire and transferred with thongs into a basket containing meal and water. The mixture was stirred with a spatula to prevent the stones from burning the woven container. Salmon were split for drying with a knife made by setting a flint blade into the end of a wooden handle, and lampreys were split with a bone awl. These fish were dried and smoked on a rack over the fireplace in a house and then later packed in baskets. Fish taken in the surf were dried whole in the sun. The Yurok attitude toward food was that it should be consumed twice a day, late in the morning and early in the evening.

Among the tools were antler wedges of varying sizes, used for splitting planks from logs. They were pounded with oblong mauls which had flat tops and bottoms. Adz blades of shell or stone were lashed to curved stone handles. The fire-making equipment consisted of a wooden shaft rotated by hand in a flat piece of wood which served as the bearing. Elk antler was used for flakers for chipping flint, gauges for measuring the size of net meshes, and shuttles for an easier handling of netting material. Arrow shaft straighteners consisted of a section of antler with a hole in one end; spoons for men to use in eating acorn mush were made out of antler and had handles carved with various patterns. Antler containers were made to hold dentalium shells; these were about six inches in length and were hollowed out inside. The shells were placed in the tube through a long slit which was covered with a lid held in place by a thong.

Made from wood were money containers, roughly cylindrical sections of redwood up to four feet in length, which tapered toward each end. They were hollowed out inside, and along the top was a separate wooden lid. A wooden flute was made from a hollowed section of elder with three or four stops along the open tube. An ordinary player blew across the mouthpiece of the flute, but the most skilled musicians held the instrument to their nose and sniffed a melody. The most elaborate and time-consuming craft item to produce was the dugout canoe, made from half a driftwood log of redwood. A fire was built along the center of the split log, and by adzing away the charred wood, the vessel was hollowed. A typical canoe was eighteen feet long and fifteen inches wide, with a rounded bottom and sides some forty-five inches high. At the front of the canoe on the inside, a small knob of wood was left, and in its center was a shallow hole. This was the "heart" of the canoe, and without it a vessel was "dead." Pitch from conifers was used to caulk any cracks in the wood, while crosspieces fore and aft prevented the sides from warping. These vessels were propelled by poles or long-bladed paddles employed by men standing in the front; a shorter paddle was used as a rudder by a man seated in the stern. Neither paddle form included a crutch handle. These canoes were designed for river travel, and a fully loaded one drew as much as six inches of water. With a round bottomed vessel of this nature, a man sitting in the stern could quickly change course to avoid obstructions in a rushing river. If traveling in the ocean was necessary, the men sang songs and recited formulas to prevent their boat from capsizing and to keep the water smooth. Considering how ill-adapted such a vessel was to ocean travel, these precautions seem quite reasonable.

Security in subsistence pursuits depended to a large extent on access to areas with exploitative potential. This usually meant individual, family, or community ownership. Places owned included fishing and netting spots along the river, oak groves, seed collecting areas, places to set snares along game trails, stretches of riverbank extending about a mile inland, sections of beach along the seacoast, or offshore rocks where sea lions hauled up. The most important riverine localities were sites where salmon conveniently could be dip-netted. Pools with an eddy where salmon rested while ascending the river to spawn were particularly important spots to own. A platform was erected over the pool, and it was fished with a long-handled dip net lowered into the water. As soon as a fish was taken, the net was jerked from the water and the salmon clubbed over the head. In a single night a fisherman might take as many as a hundred salmon with this technique. The right to use an eddy was owned by an individual or a group of individuals and could be sold for money, inherited, or bartered away. Its worth was calculated on the number of fish which could be taken. As many as ten men might jointly own an excellent dip net site, but these pools were not everlasting, for a shift in the river channel could change the productivity of an eddy. Gill nets were utilized, and these as well as the netting for dip nets were made from iris leaf fibers twisted into two-strand twine. Men manufactured the nets, using both net shuttles and gauges. The nets were weighted with stones, and floats most likely were made from short sections of wood. Salmon also were taken with seines and with toggle-headed harpoons. The harpoon shafts were as much as twenty feet in length, and at the forward end were two slightly diverging foreshafts. To each foreshaft was attached a toggle harpoon head with a line leading from the head to the shaft. When a salmon was struck, a head detached, and it was drawn in with the hand line.

When hunting along the seacoast on rocks where sea lions hauled up, men disguised themselves in animal skins and imitated the behavior of the sea lions until they were near enough to harpoon an animal. The harpoons used were similar to those for taking salmon but were more heavily constructed, and the heads were tipped with flaked stone points. A wounded animal swam seaward and was pursued by boat; the shaft was held in the boat so that the impaled sea lion could not escape and eventually could be killed. There appear to have been two different forms of ownership for sections of the coastline. For surf fishing with hooks and shellfish collecting, beach localities were individually owned, but a community controlled a coastal section with reference to stranded whales. It seems that no matter what section of beach a whale drifted onto, the carcass belonged to the community; however, rights to the meat were based on the ownership of a certain form of strap. Individuals possessing these straps for backpacking were entitled to a section of whale meat equal to the length of the strap. The straps were not manufactured freely, but were inherited and exchanged. A family owning a pack strap of this nature was entitled to a share of whale meat regardless of its place of residence.

Land animals were hunted with a bow and arrows, but the practice does not appear to have been extremely important. The yard-long hunting bow was made from yew wood, strung with a sinew cord, and backed with strips of sinew (sinew-backed bow). The feather vaned wooden arrows had separate wooden foreshafts to which stone arrowpoints were attached. Arrows were carried in a holder consisting of the skin of a small animal, such as a fisher or fox, turned inside out. Deer and elk were chased with the aid of dogs, but probably were more often taken in snares. Dogs were never eaten since their meat, like that of reptiles, was considered poisonous.

A fish or mammal killed for food was not, in Yurok thinking, really destroyed. The spirit for the species continued to exist, leaving only its physical form behind for the hunter or fisherman. A number of restrictions on the taking of salmon will be cited later, but here it is appropriate to mention some of the observances surrounding deer. It was thought that deer had many likes and dislikes which must be considered in order to kill them successfully. Deer did not like a house that seemed unoccupied; they were attracted to the hunters from dwellings where there was smoke. Neither did they care for any association with whales. The reason for washing one's hands in flowing water after eating deer meat was to avoid drowning the deer. Deer meat was eaten from wooden platters, and care was taken during a meal so that none of the meat dropped to the floor. It was by observing these and other taboos that deer could continue to be taken successfully.

The Yurok were not farmers, but they did plant one crop, tobacco. The seeds were sown on hilltops after the ground had been prepared by burning logs on the plots. The plants were cultivated and the crop harvested for use by the grower or for sale to others. The mature leaves were dried in the sun or by a fire, pulverized, and placed in baskets. The cultivated species was seemingly the same as the local wild tobacco, but the latter was not smoked for fear that it might have grown on a grave. Tobacco was smoked in a tubular pipe. Some of these were made entirely from wood. Others had stone inlays in the bowl or else had bowls made of stone. Smoking usually was confined to just before bedtime, but some old Yurok were addicted to smoking. The smoke was inhaled and expelled through the nose. Old female shamans appear to have been the heaviest smokers; other women did not smoke.

The structure and organization of social life reflected a form of contained anarchy. The core members of each community were persons who traced descent along the male line to a known common ancestor (patrilineage); within this unit there were lines of familial authority, with a wealthy old man most likely to have jurisdiction over other members of the unit. A settlement contained one or more patrilineages, each structured as the other; there was no organized system of village-wide authority. An individual also was bound in a network of kinship ties with persons in other settlements through bonds of blood and marriage. Furthermore, there were the riverine and coastal dialect groups, but this dichotomy did not have known political ramifications. Then there were the adjacent Karok,

Hupa, and Wiyot, from whom one might acquire a wife. Relationships with these peoples were structured as with in-laws. Finally, there were strangers, equated with enemies. Thus, any alliances not based on kinship or marriage seem to have been absent. This extreme form of individualism, in which each man was responsible for his own actions, was accompanied by a rigid series of rules which governed interactions with nonkin.

The study of Yurok customary law by Kroeber provides an excellent guide to the legal system. It was based on the idea that any wrong was in terms of an individual against whom the offense was committed, and claims were calculated in terms of material goods, rather than physical punishment. Any deviation from a behavioral norm necessitated a compensatory settlement, and extenuating circumstances rarely were considered. The age, sex, or previous behavior of an offender were unimportant, but his wealth was relevant. Finally, once a dispute had been settled, no further recourse was possible. The major grounds for claims were murder, seduction, adultery, saying the name of a deceased person, trespassing, or a shaman's refusal to treat a person who was ill. All claims were settled with the exchange of specific forms of material property, each with an established value. The property exchanged may be termed money since it was portable, homogeneous in form, durable, and had an assigned value.

Dentalium shells were the most important form of money. These small mollusks had tusk-shaped shells which ranged up to about three inches in length. They were most abundant in the coastal waters off British Columbia and were collected there with a comb-like device which was thrust into the sandy ocean bottom to stab as many dentalia as possible. In western North America the shells were traded from the subarctic on the north to southern California. Among the Yurok, as with most Indians, the shells were graded according to size, with the largest shells having the greatest value. There were six named sizes of dentalia which ranged in length from 2½ to 1⅞ inches. An eleven-shell string, with each shell 2½ inches long, was valued at about $50 during the early American period; a string of the same length with 1⅞ inch shells, which consisted of fifteen shells, was worth only about $2.50. Other monetary units included redheaded woodpecker scalps ranging in value from 10¢ to $1.50 each. Ordinary deerskins, after being prepared for ceremonial use, were worth from $50 to $100; skins of albino deer theoretically were valued at from $250 to $500, although they were never sold. Blades flaked from black obsidian were worth $1.00 for every inch in length until they reached a foot; blades longer than this were worth a great deal more.

Many, if not most, items of material culture were scaled in value against dentalium shells. Around the turn of the present century, a small dugout canoe was worth a thirteen-shell string or three large redheaded wood-pecker scalps; a house was valued at from three to five strings of shells; an oak grove from one to five strings; a fishing spot from one to three strings; a shaman's fee from one to two strings; a slave one string, and a woman's basketry cap filled with tobacco was one small shell. A few items were so valuable that they normally could not be exchanged, but were passed along a patrilineage. These were most important as exhibits during ceremonial occasions. Included were fine albino deerskins with transparent hoofs and the huge obsidian blades which were nearly a yard in length.

The marital arrangements which led to the exchange of money will be considered later, but it is fitting to mention other situations in which wealth exchanged hands. Failure to ferry someone across a river, even an enemy, led to a claim. If someone were on the recognized land of another and injured himself, the owner was responsible for compensation. This was true even of a trespasser, but at the same time, the owner would likely press a claim for trespassing. If a shaman refused to accept the responsibility for treating a patient and the patient died, the shaman was liable. To pass before a village by boat when a family in the village was in mourning for a death due to natural causes was grounds for a claim. Then too, the name of a dead person could not be uttered, and to do so was to invite a claim. If it happened that a person was hopelessly in debt because of some drastically antisocial act, he could in lieu of payment become the slave of the one he had offended. Thus, if a poor person used the name of a deceased individual of wealth or struck the son of a rich man, he could settle his debt through "debt-slavery" for himself or one of his female relatives. "Slaves" were never killed or abused but performed the more laborious subsistence tasks. A slave owner was free to integrate the individual into his household or else maintain his status as a slave. A slave could not escape because no one would receive him. Foreigners or prisoners from raids were never made slaves. The former always were killed if they arrived unannounced, and prisoners were held for ransom.

In the kinship terminology, a man referring to his father used one term; for his father's brother and his mother's brother, he used another term. For the mother's side of the family, the terminology was comparable to that on the father's side (lineal terms). Thus the Yurok employed terms for the parental generation which are of the same type as those used in the United States today. On Ego's generation, the term for sister was extended to all female first cousins, and the word for brother extended to all male first cousins (Hawaiian cousin terms). It would seem that if one were to call cousins "brother" or "sister," the parents of these individuals would be referred to as "mother" and "father," but such was not the case. In the kinship system the most important ties were those along a line of males. It is tempting to regard the descent system as strictly patrilineal, and unquestionably a man was most concerned with his relatives along a male line. Still, there was recognition of a wife and her relatives in calculating social ties. Perhaps it would be best to characterize these people as patrilineal with a distinct and recognized tendency to consider relatives on both sides of a family as important (bilateral or nonunilineal descent).

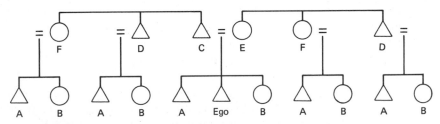

Aboriginal Yurok kin terms. Each letter represents a different term.

Within a patrilineage and beyond it, a person's worth was judged on the basis of his material property, and there were distinctions among rich, well-to-do, and poor families. The nature of Yurok society was such that it was somewhat difficult to become elevated in social position since wealth was retained greedily and more was coveted. However, there existed the ideal of a poor boy acquiring wealth through persistence and supernatural aid. The belief that constant thoughts about money would lead to its acquisition was important. Meditating about wealth when preparing for, taking, or resting after a bath was thought to be most propitious. An ambitious young man was urged to concentrate on dentalium shells for ten days at a time. During these periods he fasted and worked hard. When he gathered wood for the bathhouse, he collected it from the upper branches of trees where he visualized the dentalia to be hanging. As he bathed, he thought of shells, and when peering intensively into the river, he imagined that he saw huge dentalium shells. Such an individual would say to himself, "I want to be rich." He made a tearful invocation for wealth but not to any spirit or supernatural force. The primary earthly force which counteracted the quest for money was women. A young man seeking wealth was warned not to have anything to do with women, while an adult man should not copulate with his wife in the house where his wealth was kept.

As would be expected, formal warfare could not exist in this society where political ties were absent. The conflicts which did erupt were between families and developed into small or great feuds depending on the size of the families involved, their wealth, and how quickly a settlement could be arranged. Fighting was with bows and arrows except that in hand-to-hand combat short stone clubs were employed. Protective armor was made either from elk hide or vertical wooden rods which were bound together, and it seems to have been worn only during prearranged battles. Serious feuds appear to have been caused by murders committed either in the heat of anger or by witchcraft. In either instance the near relatives of the dead person sought revenge. They might approach an enemy village secretly and attack before the defenders could rally, or they might ambush the offending family on the trail. Following a successful raid or ambush the contending parties might negotiate a meeting to attempt settlement of their differences. The two sides would arm themselves, paint their faces black and red, and then line up about a bow-shot distance apart. Songs were sung and a dance of settlement performed; at this point the arrangements sometimes broke down and the sides began fighting. The contesting parties carried with them the full amount of property necessary for a settlement. The side which had killed the most people and destroyed or seized the greatest amount of property was the "winner" but was at the same time required to relinquish the most property. The items to be distributed were placed in baskets and held over a fire as songs were sung and a dance performed. This ritual was to cast away any continuing feelings of hostility and to make any lasting feelings of vengeance the responsibility of the other party. If all went well, the settlement was made, and neither side could make further claims nor hold a grudge.

The ceremonial life of the Yurok was much more integrated than the social or political activities. The major rituals were designed to perpetuate the natural world and its resources as an orderly system. The principal ceremonies were performed in order to prevent disease and cataclysms such as earthquakes and floods. It is important to note, as Kroeber and Edward W. Gifford have stressed, that the world-renewal ceremonies of northwestern California were focused at twelve centers, found among the Karok, Yurok, Wiyot, and Hupa. These Indians represented great linguistic heterogeneity but had similar attitudes toward the world-renewal ceremonies. The principal elements of this ceremonial system were based on precedent set by immortals before the present race of men came to occupy the country. The formulas which were recited concerned these immortals, and the accompanying ceremonies were fixed calendrically as well as localized at particular spots where they reportedly had been enacted the first time. Impressive dances were held as a part of these ceremonies. The dances, and now we are referring specifically to the Yurok, have come to be termed the Deerskin Dance and the Jumping Dance by Anglo-Americans. It was during these performances that men displayed their wealth and greatest treasures.

A somewhat detailed account of the most elaborate Yurok ceremony, the building of the Kepel fishweir, serves to illustrate the manner in which subsistence activities were integrated with religious ceremonies. The community of Kepel was on the south side of the Klamath River a short distance from the junction of the Trinity and Klamath rivers. Nearby at the village of Sa'a was a sacred house and bathhouse associated with the Kepel ceremonies. It was here that the first Kepel fishweir ceremony reportedly was held, although the original boards and posts making up the structures had been replaced from time to time. According to tradition, in the time of *woge* spirits another site was selected first , but the dam actually was built at Kepel. At Kepel the river is wide but shallow, and it was easy to drive stakes into the gravel bottom to support the weir. Before the rituals at Kepel could be held, it was necessary that a ceremony be performed at the mouth of the Klamath River. This ceremony was designed to remove the prohibition on eating salmon which ascended the river that year. For the Kepel ceremonies as for all others there was an individual who might be called a ritual formulist who gained his position by memorizing the essential recitations to accompany the ceremony, in this case the building of the weir. The esoteric knowledge was passed from a father to one of his sons, and he was assisted by another man as well as by a woman.

The Kepel rituals began in July or August of every other year when they were recorded, but in aboriginal times the ritual probably was held each year. The formulist ate at a nearby village, receiving food from different houses, and he was given a deerskin robe to wear throughout the ceremony from another house. He camped at Kepel in a temporary shelter built over a house pit belonging to his family until time to begin the weir. In this structure was a ceremonial door which was closed after initial preparations were made. For ten days the weir chief and his male assistant visited sacred spots that were associated with the Kepel fishweir. The primary duty of the female assistant was to collect wood for a ceremonial fire over which she burned incense. After a series of pilgrimages, ceremonial bathing, and fasting, the weir chief took a sweat bath and unveiled four sacred stones. Each of these crescent-shaped stones had been used by the woge and had been passed on to the present leader of the ceremony. All day he performed rituals involving the stones. Later he made a ritual visit to the spot where the poles for the weir were to be cut as well as to the riverbank locations where the dam was to be anchored. The male assistant went to the adjacent communities and announced that dam construction was to begin on a specified day. When the time arrived, each man who responded to the call was assigned to a work crew, probably made up of ten men each. There were in theory ten such crews, one to work on each of the ten named sections of the weir. The workers returned home for their camping equipment and came back to the site the next evening.

The following morning the crews went to specific stands of pine and began to cut small trees which they limbed, peeled, and split lengthwise. They also gathered long hazel shoots which were split and plaited. Mats were made of the split poles and hazel shoots, and these were rolled up and carried to the dam site. On the fifth day the formulist ceremonially cut three special poles as his male assistant sang and danced in a ritual manner. These poles were for either end and the middle of the weir. The weir chief and his male assistant sweated and slept in the sweat lodge at Sa'a which was used only during the fishweir ceremony. The work teams continued to collect additional material for mats. Each morning the weir chief and his male assistant crossed to the north side of the river. The formulist hid from the workers, while his male assistant gave them any necessary orders. During the night the female assistant burned incense at the sacred rock on the north riverbank; during the day she stayed in a house that was not lived in on other occasions. After the weir chief split the pole for the center of the weir, the workers did the same with the remaining poles, and then joked for the remainder of the day. At this time no offense could be taken against jokes at one's expense, no matter how abusive they were.

On the sixth day actual construction of the weir began. The first pole was driven by the weir chief who used a special and traditional maul weighing some fifty pounds. As he drove the post into the riverbottom, he prayed for salmon. He then gave the maul to others to drive the remaining posts at different angles so that they would not become dislodged by the river current. After the posts were in place, the formulist and his male assistant arranged the first stringer along the tops of the posts, and all of the stringers were then bound in place. The workers then constructed nine or ten traps about twelve feet long and fourteen feet wide, with moveable openings at each end. The traps were placed on the downstream side of the dam, and woven mats were put in to line the pole frameworks. Traps were placed all along the weir except at an opening near the south bank where boats could pass beneath the stringer. Here some salmon were able to escape the traps.

In the meantime, select boys or "novices" fashioned ribbons of bark, imitation pipes, and other carvings which were painted. These were attached to a long pole, and when the dam was nearly completed, about noon on the tenth day, the pole was raised just below the south end of the weir. A little later the female assistant ran from the community of Sa'a to the site with a basket of acorn dough. She placed it on a pile of sand and ran downstream to bathe; when she returned to the spot, girls had assembled there and were dancing. The weir chief and his male assistant along with a novice boy went to the dance ground. The boy carried the basket left by the assistant, which now was filled with water. The girls stopped dancing and covered the female assistant with their bodies. The formulist and his assistant climbed up on the heap of girls, and the boy then threw the basket high into the air, attempting to shower the girls with water. While he did this, the other boys climbed on the pile to protect the female assistant from the spray of water and the poles which were to fall next. The workers, each carrying a pole with ribbons and carved pipes attached, formed a semicircle around the mass of people and let their poles fall simultaneously. Afterwards, the people in the pile rapidly dispersed on all fours.

Following this ritual the three principal participants returned to the weir, and the male assistant removed the first salmon caught. Part of it was taken by the female assistant for her evening meal, but no one else was permitted to eat salmon until the following day. At this time the dance ground was cleared, and a Deerskin Dance was held. Another Deerskin Dance was held some ten miles downstream. The ordinary participants attended one dance or the other, and then returned home, but the weir chief and his ceremonial assistant remained at the site until the weir was destroyed two or three months later.

A Deerskin Dance was an extremely colorful event. The performers were males, and about the waist of each man was the skin of a civet cat or a wraparound deerskin blanket. A performer wore no garment above the waist, but about his neck were hung massive strings of dentalium shells, and on his head was a browband of wolf fur. The dancers all had thin charcoal lines across the cheeks, stripes on the chin, a blackened jaw, or else lines down the shoulders and arms. On a stick attached to a performer's head were eagle or condor feathers arranged to appear as one very long feather. Each dancer carried a pole, and at the top of it was a stuffed deer head, with the remainder of the skin hanging down loosely and swaying back and forth as the pole was moved. In the center of a line of dancers with deerskins were a singer and two assistants. They were dressed as the others except that from their forehead to the shoulders they wore netting fringed at the bottom with feathers. The line of men stamped one foot, which was the standard dance step, and as they danced, two or sometimes four other men, each holding an obsidian blade encased in a deerskin, paraded in front of the dancers in a crouched position, blowing whistles and holding out the blades. The men displaying the blades usually wore a double layer of deerskin wrapped around their bodies and attached over one shoulder. Over a wolfskin browband each man wore another band of leather to which were attached six or more sea lion canine teeth. From the head hung a closely woven netting on which designs such as triangles and diamonds were painted; this entire headpiece was fringed with feathers. The pattern for the Deerskin Dance and for ceremonies in general was for a host community to present its dance first, and then each represented village performed a dance. There were morning and evening performances by each village daily over a twelve-day period. On the final day the performers danced with the finest white deerskins and displayed their most beautiful obsidian blades.

The formal ceremonies which centered about the Kepel fishweir ended with the performance of a two-day Jumping Dance a few miles above Kepel. The performers were males who wore a double layer of deerskin about the hips and many necklaces of dentalium shells. Above the head on a stick was a white plume; the stick was attached to a headband of deerskin which was covered with woodpecker scalps and trimmed with a white band of deerskin. From the sides of this headpiece hung long flaps which swung rapidly as the dancers performed. In one hand a dancer carried a cylindrical basket with an opening along one side. There were two Jumping Dance steps, both of which involved hopping or jumping as the baskets were lowered.

After the Kepel weir was readied for use, three traps were reserved for the principal participants in the ceremony, and the others were designated for particular individuals and his or her relatives. Salmon were removed from traps in the mornings with dip nets; then the weir chief opened the upper ends of the traps for great numbers of unnetted salmon to swim on up the river. Many of the fish were to be kept for future consumption; they were cut up, dried, smoked slightly, and piled in baskets between layers of leaves. The fishing continued for two to three months, always with the weir chief and his assistants nearby. The weir finally was destroyed by the rushing water and the ceremonialists as well as the fishermen returned to their homes.

While the Kepel fishweir ceremonies were the most elaborate, portions of the Yurok population participated in other ceremonies as well. At the junction of the Trinity and Klamath rivers in a community called Weitspus a ceremony was held for renewing the world. It was performed each September and was designed specifically to avert natural disasters and disease. The stated purpose of the ceremony is not unusual, but the configuration of ritual features was. At the site for this particular ceremony there were no sacred structures or equipment associated with the more usual Yurok world-renewal ceremonies. There was a formulist who recited traditional prayers at a secular sweathouse and at specific spots nearby before a ten-day Deerskin Dance was held. Kroeber suspected that this village originally had no ceremony and that as the population grew, the dance and formulas were developed and added but without the usual equipment and complexity. At two coastal villages, a village at the Klamath River mouth, and another a little less than halfway between the Trinity junction and the sea, four other world-renewal ceremonies were held. These were in essence the same; their purpose was not only to renew the world and make its products abundant, but to avert cataclysms and disasters. Each year at the four settlements the ceremonial structures were rebuilt or repaired. These buildings were part bathhouse and part dwelling in their design, and each was used only for this ceremony. In each of the sacred buildings a select group of men and women sang, while in an ordinary dwelling a Jumping Dance was held. Unlike the Kepel complex, the rebuilding or repair of a structure was the most important aspect of the ceremony. There were additional world-renewal ceremonies which probably were as important as those mentioned, but they have not been described systematically by ethnographers. It is apparent that participation in ceremonies was the most important means of unifying the Yurok. Tribal integration clearly was along sacred, not secular, lines.

Another popular celebration, called the Brush Dance by Anglo-Americans, was held to treat an ill child, but it also served as entertainment for most participants. The event was held in a dwelling from which the roof and part of the sidewalls had been removed. On the first night a formula was recited for the ill child, and men danced about the fire holding boughs. Nothing took place the second night, but on the third and fourth nights the Brush Dance continued until dawn. On each night a series of three dances was performed by competing sets of dancers. Furthermore, the sick child was integrated into the performances with the recitation of formulas and the waving of torches above him. Formulas were very important in the Brush Dance as well as in all calendrical ceremonies; they also served individuals' needs under varying circumstances.

Some formulas involved the recitation of a list of sacred spots which someone long ago had visited to accomplish a particular purpose. Others were recitations or prayers, including the spirit responses. Offerings of tobacco and the use of plant products were associated with the formulas.

Shamans who cured by supernatural means were women, and they usually had acquired their power in a sought-after or unanticipated dream about a deceased shaman. It was from a dead curing specialist that a potential shaman obtained a "pain." A pain was regarded as a tangible object which entered her body and became the nexus of power. Once the power had been acquired, however, it was essential to bring it under firm control. This was accomplished by fasting and dancing in a bathhouse for ten days under the supervision of other shamans until the tyro was capable of vomiting her pain and swallowing it again. In a further step toward practicing, the aspirant, accompanied by a male relative, visited a supernatural spot on a mountain for one night during the summer. On the mountain the woman recited a formula, smoked, and danced near a fire. Another ten days in the bathhouse, performing as before, was followed by a dance around a large hot fire to bring the pain fully under the woman's control. This dance was the final step in becoming a shaman. According to Thompson, shamans often were from wealthy families in which the mother was a shaman. Furthermore, Thompson describes a training period which was more extended than was recorded by Kroeber and discussed above; it required as much as from three to ten years. When a female shaman was asked to cure a patient, negotiations were made by the relatives of the sick person and the amount of payment settled before the cure was attempted. A female curer's equipment consisted of a pipe, two strings of feathers in her hair, and a skirt reaching from the waist to the ankles made from shredded inner bark of maple trees. A cure was effected by chanting over the ill person, in addition to smoking and dancing for as long as six hours. A long performance sometimes was necessary in order to see into the body of the ill person and to locate the pains which caused the illness. The pain, or pains, were then removed by sucking. If the shaman was unable to remove the pains, she referred the patient to another curer. Likewise if a patient died, the shaman's fee was returned.

In a second category of curers were males who probably did not acquire their power from supernatural sources but intensified it by supernatural means. They visited mountain tops, recited formulas, bathed ritually, and smoked in order to reinforce their power. These men utilized a pharmacopoeia consisting of plant and mineral products. This knowledge and the position was passed from father to son or to another close male relative. Like a female shaman, the male was paid before he attempted a cure and returned the payment if he was unsuccessful. Among the illnesses treated were wounds, snakebites, and "chronic diseases," as well as other forms of unidentified sickness. It is from Thompson that our knowledge of this type of shaman is derived, and she states that male curers served as a check on the ambitions of female shamans. It is suggestive that the duties of the male and female shamans were essentially separated, with females devoted to psychological ailments and supernatural cures and males to physical disabilities and natural cures.

Some female shamans had the reputation of employing their powers for antisocial purposes. The motivation for witchcraft was material profit; a person was made ill and then a fee collected in order to cure him. Another technique was to leave one of multiple pains in the body of a person who was treated in order to be called back when this pain became troublesome. Other persons were more truly witches; they acquired a malignant object by purchase or special knowledge and used it to kill individuals. If the possessor of such a power went out at night, the power appeared as sparks or as a bluish light. It could be placed on the end of a miniature arrow and shot from a small bow at the home of the victim. The victim died if not treated by a shaman. A person also could be harmed by a poison made of crushed meat from a dog, salamander, frog, or rattlesnake. After this poison was added to a victim's food, the individual remained healthy for a year, but he then became ill and died if not cared for by a very powerful shaman.

When the rights of a person had been violated and just compensation could not be obtained through legal means, the only alternative was to turn to a sorcerer. These usually were men, and they customarily charged as much as a bride price, which meant that their services could be commanded only by aristocrats. A sorcerer was either of high social standing or in the process of achieving such a status. He possessed two to twelve different "poisons" ranging in power on a scale from very mild to lethal, with each strength represented by a different miniature arrow. The most mild form produced a headache, cold, or the combination; the middle level caused breast pains and led to the victim's confinement. From the eighth level upward, all were lethal and were associated with behavior while sleeping. Once the fee and the degree of illness to be induced were agreed on, the sorcerer went outside the victim's house disguised as a dog. Here he shot the mildest arrow from a miniature bow; he returned again and again at specified intervals until he reached the level of illness desired. When the victim showed symptoms of illness, a shaman was called in to extract the "pains," but when lethal arrows had been shot very few shamans had the power to remove them. If a shaman could suck the pain out of a victim, she spit it out of her mouth and the arrow rose into the air and flew back to its maker; only the shaman could see this return. It was essential for a sorcerer to handle the objects of his power with great care. When not in use they were buried in a cache made of stones, and it was necessary for the owner to use the force of the poison at least once a month. If he did not do so the force would harm his children, or himself if he was childless. Quite possibly this form of sorcery may have developed into the complex described during the early historic period when the economic position of aristocratic families was threatened by white intrusions.

According to Kroeber, a year began with the winter solstice and was divided into either twelve or thirteen months, of which the first ten were numbered and the last two or three were named. The eleventh month was the time of the ripening of acorns, and this was the firm reference point for both calendars. Thompson stated, however, that there were only ten months, with adjustments, and four seasons. The Yurok counted with a decimal system and could handle large numbers; this was necessary, according to Thompson, in order for basketry designs to be correctly patterned.

Yurok values invite comparison with contemporary American ethos as these developed in capitalism and the Protestant ethic. Walter Goldschmidt offered a systematic comparison of the northwest Californian tribes, drawn primarily from Yurok sources, with the "protestant ethic." Goldschmidt (1951, 513) summarized the Indian pattern as "a system in which the individual was placed chiefly by personal acquisition of wealth which in theory was freely attainable by all, with both status and power resting upon the ownership of property." There was a basic value placed on hard work, obtaining wealth, self-denial, and the full responsibility of the individual, who was aggressive consistently, for his own behavior.

The first time a woman conceived, her offspring was born after ten months, according to tradition, but later births required only nine-month pregnancies. Kroeber remarked that births were most likely to occur in the spring, but not because there was a mating season as once was suggested. The reason was that a man stored his material wealth in his wife's house, and riches were diametrically opposed to sexual activity. To perform sexual intercourse in the house was to invite poverty. Therefore, a couple was most likely to copulate in the summer when they slept out-of-doors. The people feared the birth of twins of opposite sexes; one, usually the female, was smothered or starved to death. They thought such twins would have an incestuous relationship when grown. Identical twins, however, were raised to maturity. When pregnant a woman worked hard, ate little, and was concerned with the physical actions of the fetus. The fetus was thought to be influenced directly by the woman's activities. A large neonate, for example, was thought to result if the mother ate too much and slept excessively. A pregnant woman bent forward when working in order that the fetus would not "rest against her spine," and as it developed she rubbed her abdomen in the afternoon to prevent the fetus from sleeping at this time of day, which was to invite evil. Furthermore, it was thought that a male fetus was more active than a female fetus. In the birth process a woman rested on her back with her feet braced against a midwife, and her arms were bound with leather straps suspended from the ceiling. During labor she was told by the midwife when to lift herself with the thongs, and she was cautioned to keep her mouth closed in order to ease the birth. The newborn was steamed over wild ginger, and a preparation from ground land snail was applied to the navel. The severed cord was put inside a pine tree branch which had been split to receive it. The Yurok regarded the colostrum from the mother's breast as harmful to the infant's jaws so much as to lead to starvation; as a consequence, a baby was fed hazel nut soup for the first ten days, and then nursed. After twenty days of life, a grandmother, probably most often the paternal grandmother, began to massage the infant's leg muscles to encourage it to crawl when it was very young. Between the time of birth and the healing of the navel, the parents were prohibited from eating deer meat or salmon; their meals were confined to acorn soup. Another prohibition was that they were not to have sexual intercourse until the baby crawled. During this time the infant wore a leather band around one ankle, as though to symbolize its tie to the mother. The cradleboards for male infants were wider at the shoulders than those for females, which were wide at the hips. Near the head of a girl's cradleboard a small dress of shells was hung, while a boy's cradleboard was adorned with a miniature bow and arrow. Cradleboards were manufactured in such a manner that the infant sat, with its legs hanging free. The baby could move its legs at any time, which was in keeping with an emphasis on having it crawl at a tender age. A baby was not permitted to nap between the late afternoon and sunset; for it to do so was considered unhealthy. Many, if not most, aspects of rearing an offspring were designed to encourage self-reliance. This attitude clearly is reflected by the practice of weaning at one year, which is earlier than for most American Indians.

These people distinguished two stages of development for an offspring: a time when it was capable of systematic training, and an earlier stage when it could not be taught in an orderly manner. They judged a child's conceptual readiness to learn on its ability to remember, not on its chronological age. It probably was when it showed this capability, at about eight or nine years of age, that it was named. The names for male children were selected by their father, and female children were named by their mother. Each family seems to have had its own set of personal names which were either male or female. Nicknames of girls often contained some reference to marriage, e.g. Married a Rabbit and Married into Snail's House. Personal names were used in referring to or in addressing individuals, but they were dropped at the time of an individual's marriage.

When a child could remember instructions his formal education began. He was taught to eat slowly, to chew thoroughly, to think of money as he ate, not to seize food greedily, and not to snack. At mealtimes girls sat near their mothers, and boys near their fathers, with the respective parent responsible for instructing them. If a child did not obey mealtime restrictions, the parent removed his food basket, and the offender was expected to leave the house. A child was shown figures in rocks which represented persons who did not follow societal norms. One rock in particular was pointed out as once having been an errant child. There were stories, too, about animals and birds which stressed social norms. One particularly vivid tale concerned the greedy buzzard, who put his entire head in his soup while it was still hot. He scalded the top of his head and henceforth ate only old, rotten food.

Another dominant concern of parents was to insure that a child soon learned not to offend the dead. Any direct statement about the dead or reference to items associated with death was a form of swearing. A rude gesture accompanying swearing was to hold out one's hands with the fingers outstretched and the thumbs together, for this was the manner in which the dead swore. The probable reason for disapproving of such behavior in children or adults was that it led to claims by the relatives of a deceased person. To discourage such words or gestures a mentor placed nettles on a child's lips or hands, a very effective punishment.

Small girls played house in small brush dwellings, using mud dolls, cradles, food, clothing and equipment, as well as imitation money. The toys of boys included canoes, but they were used in artificial bodies of water rather than in the streams or rivers. As children grew older, they were instructed formally by a mature man who taught a group of from five to seven children the norms of adult behavior and technical skills. Boys learned how to handle boats, to fish, and to hunt. For this instruction the teacher received no compensation at the time, but students were expected later to provide their former teachers with food. Not all children accepted formal lessons, and those that did not respond positively were not considered at fault. Their misbehavior resulted from seeing bad spirits of a special kind, and such a child was sent home. More serious problems of childhood misbehavior were thought to have been caused by "wise people." These spirits were thought to be about the size of children and were nonsexual. Unlike a child, a wise person matured at six months and was immortal. A Yurok child who saw a wise person after dark had behaved in an incorrect manner. A grandmother of such a child went to the spot and sang her particular song to counteract the spirits. If this did not succeed, a neighboring grandmother tried, and if she too failed, a female shaman was called in. She treated the patient in the usual manner and went on to probe the affairs of the household. The shaman was likely to establish the fact that in the afflicted child's home an older woman was attempting witchcraft against another, or that a man who prayed for money also had been having sexual intercourse. The accused confessed freely, which normalized the household setting and no doubt led to a more harmonious environment for the child and a cessation of his symptoms. A shaman knew her patients well and from a standard list of transgressions would be likely to predict the faults of family members. The psychoanalyst who recorded these facts, Erik H. Erikson, seemed able to establish rapport easily with an old female shaman, which is not surprising since they had methodological concepts in common.

The most important skill to be acquired by a young girl was to learn basket weaving since a great deal of prestige accrued when a woman made excellent baskets. Usually a girl was about six years old when she attempted to make her first basket. She tried a simple form, and often after completing the first few rows, her mother added others to straighten out the weave. If the girl's interest was sustained, an older woman with acknowledged skills trained her informally. It was thought that there was only one set of techniques for making good baskets, and therefore all superior basket makers produced similar products. The only significant and acceptable variations were in designs.

When a girl menstruated for the first time, she spent most of ten days sitting silently in a corner at home, facing away from the fire. She scratched with a special stick whenever necessary and wore a skirt of inner bark just as a female shaman would wear. The girl moved about as little as possible but brought in a load of firewood each day. For at least the first four days she ate no food, under the assumption that the longer she fasted the more wealth she would accumulate later in life. When she did eat, it was at the bank of a roaring river where she would hear no sound but the water. Each night she bathed the number of times equal to the days of her confinement, except that on the ninth night she bathed ten times. At dusk of the tenth day each small child living nearby washed her back. Finally, her mother or another woman told her she would have ten boys and ten girls. For a boy there were no comparable restrictions at the time of puberty.

A maturing girl of good breeding was watched carefully by her parents to make certain that she did not fornicate. The prohibition was not so much a matter of morality as to prevent the girl from becoming pregnant and thereby decreasing the amount of bridewealth she would bring. A girl who conceived before marriage attempted to abort by placing heated stones on her abdomen; if successful, she threw the fetus in the river. A young man was exhorted to work hard at adult skills, to carry wood for the bathhouse frequently, and to concentrate on money. The only bar to marriage was the prohibition against taking a spouse from among near relatives. An individual in a small settlement was obligated to seek a mate from elsewhere since all the occupants were near relatives, but a partner could be found easily in another village or another tribe. There was no rule concerning the particular unit from which a spouse was derived (agamy). At the same time in large settlements the tendency was to find a mate in one's home community (village endogamy). It has been reported also that men tended to seek their wives from downstream settlements.

Property exchanges at marriage were critical since the social standing of anyone depended on the amount of bridewealth which had been offered at the time of his mother's marriage. The Yurok ranked individuals primarily on this basis. At the bottom of the scale were offspring of nonlegitimate matings; such bastards had no standing whatever. Next was a poor person, whose father had offered little for his wife and could in turn provide his son little wealth for a bride. A third level of prestige was achieved by men who offered wealth but not a great deal of it. Finally, there were rich men who provided far more wealth than was necessary to consummate a marriage. Marital arrangements did not mean simply that the man offered wealth to the bride's family; they also involved various manipulations and compromises. According to the ideal, a man with wealth suggested a suitable amount of material goods to the girl's relatives, had it accepted, and then took the girl to reside in his settlement (patrilocal residence). Such was a "full-marriage," with the formal arrangements made by the relatives of the man. Any particular groom was unlikely to possess enough wealth of his own to satisfy the girl's relatives, but his near male relatives, his father, or his father's brothers, ideally made the young man gifts for the necessary balance. The bride of a wealthy man brought with her a considerable amount of property, which partially offset the outlay of the groom and his relatives. A girl of high social standing might bring ten baskets of dentalia, otter skins, a canoe, deerskins, and other small assorted valuables. It was possible also for a man with a small daughter to be deeply in debt to a man with a young son and to offer the girl in marriage when she was quite young. The girl grew up in the household of her prospective in-laws and married the boy after puberty. Sometimes a father was so covetous of his wealth that he refused to give his son a sufficient amount for a full-marriage. If the son worked hard, sweat often in the bathhouse, cried for wealth, and fasted, after about four years the girl's relatives might feel sorry for him and permit a full-marriage.

Another form of marriage was "half-marriage," which meant usually that the groom could not accumulate the necessary wealth to make a full marriage payment and was forced to be content with lower social standing. He offered his potential father-in-law all the wealth he possessed and went to live in the girl's village, either in the same house or in a nearby house (matrilocal residence). In a typical marriage of this sort, the children of the couple were affiliated with the wife's family, and the bridewealth at the marriage of their daughter went to the wife's kinsmen. Furthermore, the woman in a half-marriage could correct her husband openly and supervise his subsistence activities, while the children were under her direct control even concerning their marital arrangements. A half-marriage sometimes was negotiated quickly if a girl was pregnant in order to prevent the social stigma of bearing a bastard. Half-marriage could later lead to a full marriage if the husband worked diligently for his father-in-law. Instances were known in which a woman bore only daughters, and thus there was no male heir to perpetuate the family line. A man might half-marry a girl from such a family, take up permanent residence with the family, and publicly be declared the male heir by the girl's father. In this instance the groom did not lose class standing. Finally, a greedy father of a daughter who was a successful shaman might force a half-marriage upon her in order to continue his claim on her earnings. In a record of 356 marriages, it was found that 25 percent were half-marriages, indicating that either the number of persons with little wealth was small or that extenuating circumstances often were involved in a marriage. At the same time full-marriages were not all equal, for very rich men would offer far more than the minimum amount of wealth necessary in order to acquire increased prestige for themselves and their children.

Most of the alternatives surrounding marriage were governed by fixed rules. For example, if two men exchanged sisters as wives, the usual exchange of wealth took place; the exchange marriages did not cancel out the bridewealth necessary. If the father of unmarried girls died, it was his sons who received the bridewealth brought in. The wealthiest among the sons received the most, since he would be the most capable of returning large amounts of property if there were a divorce. If such a son or sons did not exist, the father's brother made the arrangements and received the wealth. Were a man's wife to die before she bore three or four offspring the woman's family was obliged to offer one of her sisters or female relatives to replace her (sororate). Under these circumstances the husband was obliged to offer only about half the original bridewealth to the girl's family. If the woman's family could offer the man no substitute wife, they were obligated to return the amount of the original exchange. Conversely, when a married man died, his brother was expected to marry the widow (levirate) and make a payment, possibly equal to half of the original payment. Instances of plural marriages apparently occurred only if the man involved was wealthy. The first wife and her children had the highest social position, which by inference meant that the greatest amount of wealth had been offered at her marriage.

After an individual of either sex married, he changed his name, and the old name never again was employed. A man who owned a house was called by the same name as the house, and even if he moved to another locality, he often retained the old name. For the average person, who was not a houseowner, his name referred to his home village or the one into which he had moved. To this house or village designation was added a suffix to clarify the person's standing. For example, one suffix referred to a woman who after marriage had moved to her husband's house, and the same suffix was used by a half-married man.

Possibly the most common grounds for divorce was failure of the wife to conceive; in such a case it appears that the woman was replaced by a kinswoman or the bridewealth refunded. If a man abused his wife of a full-marriage, she returned to her home, and the husband was obligated to pay the woman's family an additional amount in order to receive her back. If he did not do so, then it was likely that the girl's family would return part, but not all, of the bridewealth, and the couple thereby was divorced. In cases of divorce, if the husband refused to accept a refund of the bridewealth, he retained the children. In an instance such as this, the bridewealth for a daughter went to the father.

The nature and texture of adult life varied widely from one Yurok family to another. There was an almost insurmountable social barrier separating the very rich and aristocratic families from those who were poor. Conditions among the poor were thought to have had a genetic basis which led to their continued inferiority. A man was poor, lazy, and ill—except for instances of sorcery—because such conditions prevailed in his family line. The economic distinction was apparent in various dimensions of life. The speech of aristocrats was different from that of commoners, and the rich were wary and guarded in what they said. Rich people were "high" class and lived "clean" lives. An aristocrat knew the "law" and adhered carefully to its letter, while poor persons were far less familiar with it and also were careless, unclean, and lacked social graces. In order to prevent an ambitious commoner from reaching a position of power, sorcery was practiced to dissipate his wealth or lead to deaths in his family. Thus social distinctions ran deep throughout a Yurok's life, and to change one's status was quite difficult.

Woman and Child.
Jorhs Klamath & Trinity, Oct. 6. 1857

young Weit-spek Chief
Trinity River —

Plate 41 *(Left)*   *A Yurok woman and child sketched by George Gibbs in 1851* (Courtesy of the Smithsonian Institution National Anthropological Archives, neg. no. 2854-F-21).

Plate 42 *(Right)*   *A young Yurok drawn by Seth Eastman from a sketch made by George Gibbs in 1851. The sword-like object in his right hand probably is an obsidian blade* (Courtesy of the Smithsonian Institution National Anthropological Archives, neg. no. 2854-F-27).

Plate 43 *(Above)* *Yurok bathhouse in the foreground and dwellings in the background* (From Thompson, 1916).

Plate 44 *(Top right)* *A Yurok mother with her infant in a cradleboard photographed in 1965* (Courtesy of Dorothy Hosler Runge).

Plate 45 *(Bottom right)* *Yurok clothing kept as heirlooms photographed in 1965* (Courtesy of Cynthia Burski).

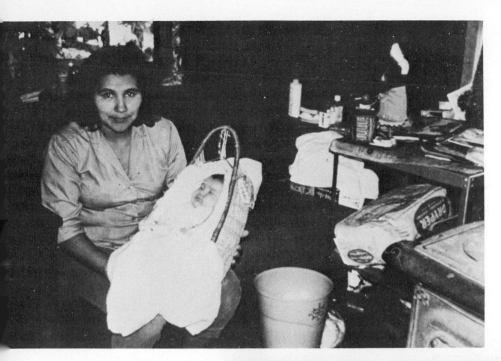

Following a death, the corpse was washed by dipping wormwood branches in water and passing the branches over the body. Precautions were taken to touch the body as little as possible. The corpse was painted, clothed, wrapped in skin, and placed on a wide plank where it remained for twenty-four hours. As mourners wailed before the body, a person in charge of the burial waved flaming stalks of grass over the corpse, permitting the ashes to fall on it. The person's body and his possessions were taken from the house through an opening made in the wall. The body again was bathed after removing the blanket and cutting the clothing down the front. The corpse was rewrapped and then placed in a coffin, over which grass was burned. A cemetery for any settlement was in the midst of the community, or nearby, so that wild animals would not disturb the dead. An excavation about two and a half feet deep was made in the ground, and it was lined with planks. The plank on which the body had been carried was used for the coffin lid. During the burial the mourners wept and sang appropriate songs. They also said good-bye to the deceased and recited their relationship to him. At the head of the grave a stone was placed on the ground, and another was located at the foot. Finally a wide plank was placed across the grave and staked into place. A fence was built around the grave, with posts at the head and the foot. On the posts were fastened crosspieces from which hung deerskins, with the heads and bodies stuffed with grass. Items such as baskets and plates were placed on top of the grave.

The spirit of a person who had been good during his life traveled along a narrow and winding trail to the north. Here it found a ladder, climbed up to the sky, and was rewarded with a peaceful afterlife. The soul of an unworthy individual traveled a broad trail to a river and arrived at a spot where an old woman and a dog lived. Sometimes the dog drove the soul back into the dead person's body, and he came to life again. This was rare, and if it did happen, the person was not happy in life and would meet sudden death. When the old woman had control of the soul, she sent it across the river in a waiting canoe, which was a Yurok type but lacked a "heart," the wooden bulge near the bow. A young man propelled the canoe and landed the soul in a damp, depressing land where the food was unpalatable but plentiful. The fate of souls, taken from Thompson's narrative, sounds suspiciously as though it had Christian origins.

Suicide apparently was rare, for to take one's life would disgrace the surviving children. If a person tired of life, he would hope that an animal would kill him. The wealth of a deceased person was, according to Thompson, divided among his children, with some set aside for the widow so long as she did not remarry. A man also was free to will his wealth to a particular offspring; this procedure automatically would disinherit any other children.

From the artifacts recovered in historic levels of the Tsurai site it is possible to partially reconstruct the transition to modern times among the coastal Yurok. Objects of glass, swords with iron blades, iron wire bracelets, and copper bracelets and rings were recovered or reported. From near the end of the site's occupancy, around 1850 and later, a wide variety of imported manufactured items included iron scraps, broken dishes, and bottles. It also was noted that elk bones became more plentiful, to suggest greater hunting efficiency through the use of firearms. In terms of nonmaterial changes among the Yurok of the Klamath River the most drastic was to accept having foreigners, i.e. whites, in their midst. The primary contacts were with traders, who not only offered useful material goods but intoxicants as well. These Indians not infrequently fought whites when either or both were intoxicated. Another major problem was that of compensation in Indian terms. In one instance a trader hired Indians to transport supplies for his store from the coast, and when the canoemen drowned, the trader was held responsible. Since he would not compensate the relatives of the deceased, they laid siege to his store. He summoned U.S. Army soldiers as protection, and finally a white who had nothing to do with the affair was killed in retaliation by the Indians. Problems such as these during the early period of intensive contact appear to have been relatively common.

Most of the published information about the Yurok pertains to the aboriginal scene; exceptions are the accounts assembled by Heizer and Mills and the book by Thompson. There is in addition an analysis of a nativistic movement by Cora du Bois. The Ghost Dance of 1870 was originated by a Paviotso (Northern Paiute) Indian in 1869. His name was Wodziwob, and he died three or four years after having his most important visions. His disciple, Weneyuga, introduced the Ghost Dance to the Northern Paiute of Oregon. Wodziwob and Weneyuga as well were said to have come back to life after death. They brought from the place of the dead the message that the dead would come back to earth, and they conveyed messages from the dead to the living. A particular dance was performed during the Ghost Dance meetings. By and large the Northern Pauite did not consider the Ghost Dance very important, and as the doctrine diffused through California and Oregon, it was changed from its original form. Yurok reaction to the basic tenets and modifications of the rituals are revealing. The body of beliefs and practices included an end of the present world at which time nonbelievers, including whites, would be turned into stone, and believers would survive to be joined by the dead. Some Yurok, however, thought that all persons would die, and others that all persons would survive the world's end. The wealth of a person was to be exposed during the Ghost

Dance performances or else it would be worthless in the new world. To facilitate the return of the dead, fences were removed from the graves in some localities. The emotional impact of the message appears to have won it support for a short time, with the strongest adherents being the young and the poor. The Ghost Dance of 1870 made no lasting imprint on Yurok society and culture. Du Bois considered that one important reason it was not more widely accepted was that the doctrine had no precedent in the mythology and was without the traditional formulas which formed the core of Yurok supernaturalism.

The state of California never expressed any particular interest in the Yurok until 1953. In that year the U.S. Congress approved House Concurrent Resolution Number 108, which supported the rapid withdrawal of the Federal government from control over Indians. In the same year Congress relinquished to the state of California control of civil and criminal law as it pertained to the Indians. In 1954 it appeared that the Federal government unilaterally was soon going to withdraw most or all of its services to Indians of California. This led the state to form a Senate Interim Committee on California Indian Affairs. It would appear that in spite of earlier and repeated attempts to encourage Federal withdrawal from Indian affairs in the state, the state now feared that the Indians would become a financial burden overnight and held hearings to have existing Federal-State relationships clarified.

A statement issued by the president of the Yurok Tribal Organization to the California Senate committee detailed reservation conditions in the early 1950's and the Indians' response to prospective termination. They disapproved the proposed termination bills without prior fulfillment of diverse Federal obligations. Committee hearings were held at Hoopa, California, in 1954 to clarify the problem areas as viewed by the Indians and the Bureau of Indian Affairs officials. Historically, the Hoopa Valley Reservation was created in 1864, while the Hoopa Extension, a milewide strip of land extending downstream for twenty miles on each side of the river and joining the Hoopa Valley Reservation, was created by an Executive Order in 1891. The Extension included some 14,000 acres of land, most of which was allotted and for which trust patents had been issued. Nearly 3,000 acres of unallotted land were regarded as a tribal holding. This land contained timber having an estimated value of $400,000 in 1954. Of the allotted lands about 8,500 acres were owned under fee patent titles around 1950. On some tribal lands Indians lived on "assignments," which usually were made by a local superintendent to a particular Indian family but had no clear legal justification.

The Hoopa Extension was for many years administered from the Hoopa Valley Reservation, and the extension land was held as a reservation for the people on the rolls of Hoopa Extension, which was not coterminus with the Yurok Tribal Organization. The Federal government had an extremely difficult time negotiating such problems as road rights-of-way, legal sale of timber for Indians from their lands, and the illegal cutting of timber on Indian land as well as establishing the exact southern Hoopa Extension boundary.

Published anthropological information about the present status of the Yurok virtually is nonexistent. Certain insight into modern conditions may be obtained from Federal and State administrative reports, but these provide little information about the people. Fortunately two anthropology students at the University of California, Los Angeles, Cynthia Burski and Dorothy Hosler, visited the Yurok in 1965, and graciously made their field notes available to me. Most of the information which follows is from their work.

During December of 1964 there was a major flood along the Klamath River. The region was designated as a National Disaster Area, and the amount of Yurok property swept away or damaged by the flood was great. Some thirty-five Yurok houses along the Klamath were completely destroyed. The people were appalled by their material losses but were able to receive temporary supplies and clothing through the disaster program. Some Yurok had predicted that disaster would follow the cutting of a road through a sacred mountain by the Division of Highways two years before. Because of this disturbance something "terrible" was anticipated. Other Yurok Indians offered a host of possible causes for the disaster. They cited, for example, that a Deerskin Dance held at Hoopa did not last the traditional number of days. Furthermore, in the fires built during a recent Deerskin Dance driftwood was burned rather than the traditional timber from the mountainsides. Another mistake connected with this dance was that water was sprinkled on the dance area by a truck before the event. Then, too, one man who owned traditional Yurok wealth refused to display it at the dance, which again invited disaster. The people were distressed also because cemeteries had been washed away and the bones of the dead had been exposed by the high waters and rains. The tradition-oriented Yurok explained the continuing rains of January, 1965, as being caused by the exposure of bones of the dead; they thought the rains would continue until the bones once again were covered.

In 1926 the Indian Shaker Church had gained converts among the Yurok, and by the 1930's it had enough adherents to become influential in local life. One result was that sorcery by professionals had almost disappeared although knowledge about it remained widespread. It apparently was not uncommon for a person from an "enemy" family to whistle near one's house at night as a means of frightening the occupants, but this "deviling" was more often mischievous than harmful. Among the Yurok in the late 1960's persons still were suspected of practicing sorcery if they had threatened someone who became ill months or even years later. Individuals also were suspect if they behaved in a suspicious manner, for example, if they wandered alone late at night. Suspected sorcerers, who most often were old, poor, and lived alone, were avoided.

The views of many local whites about these Indians are stereotypic and fall into an expectable pattern. The Indians were considered to be drunkards with little or no respect for the law; dirty, irresponsible employees; and generally unreliable. At the same time the Yurok were somewhat frightening, since their behavior could not always be understood. Unquestionably, there was a certain amount of truth in the opinion of the whites, for the consumption of intoxicants did seem to be important to many individuals, and the attitudes of many Yurok toward wage labor were not shared by whites. The Yurok considered whites to be greedy and felt that they looked down upon Indians. More important and specific complaints by the Yurok were against the Hupa Indians who, they felt, were receiving unjust favoritism by the Bureau of Indian Affairs, and against the Bureau officials for both real and imagined injustices.

Modern Yurok social life is built on the nuclear family residence unit, and one of the rather striking population characteristics is the tendency for Yurok of both sexes to marry whites and for teen-age Indians to court whites. Yurok Indian clothing did not differ from the garments of whites in the area since both men and women wore store-bought clothing exclusively. The Yurok homes were large, rectangular frame dwellings with four or more rooms. One characteristic of households was their cluttered appearance, with a great accumulation of material goods. Household furnishings included the typical range of expected items such as refrigerators, stoves, tables, chairs, and so on, plus many seemingly useless items. The clutter seemed to be compatible with older housekeeping norms. Houses contained collections of baskets, an overt sign of Yurok Indian heritage. Baskets were manufactured primarily for Yurok buyers. Sometimes they were sold to tourists, but production was limited since few women retained the skill to make them. The bathhouses, which once were so extremely important, had ceased to function. The stools, which were one of the few items of aboriginal furniture, were occasionally seen in the dwellings, but they were regarded more as heirlooms than as furnishings. The traditional forms of Yurok wealth, such as elaborate ceremonial costumes, dentalium shells, and white deerskins existed as treasures.

Subsistence fishing for salmon was relatively unimportant although certain family fishing spots were owned and trespassers prosecuted. The timber industry was the primary source of employment, followed by road construction. Furthermore, during the summer months, numerous men served as hunting and fishing guides for tourists. Loggers earned $3.50 an hour, and in a nine-month season they accumulated as much as seven thousand dollars. This was the most lucrative type of employment, especially when wages were supplemented by Unemployment Insurance payments for the balance of the year.

Suggestively, attendance at Christian church services was the most important form of organized religious life. The world-renewal ceremonies died out long ago, but the Deerskin Dance still was held sporadically. One was given in 1955, and the next was held during seven days of August in 1964. Reportedly as a result of the 1955 flood most of the boats were lost, and their destruction made traveling to a dance difficult. The same year much of the ceremonial equipment was destroyed by fire; this caused the long delay between Deerskin dances. The secular Brush Dance continues to be held on the Fourth of July and lasts for three days.

It would appear that the future of the Yurok as an identifiable ethnic group is not very bright. Internal disagreements make effective collective action almost impossible. The old pattern of political anarchy still survives, and the reservation holding, the Hoopa Extension, is not very valuable nor does it include more than a small fraction of former Yurok land. Likewise the Hoopa Extension encompasses only part of the Yurok population, which again is a cause for conflicts. Other significant problems are the high rate of dropouts among high school students and the failure of those students who do remain in school to take advantage of the vocational training and scholastic programs available. The Yurok also exhibit a distinct tendency to court and marry whites, which attenuates their identity. It would appear that the Federal goal of Indian assimilation is succeeding, but the reasons for the success are neither a well-planned program leading to assimilation or the Indian desire for assimilation. The dominant process seems to be one of deculturation, resulting from the cultural background of the people, historical events, and white attitudes.

References

Burski, Cynthia, and Dorothy Hosler. Field notes, January, 1965.

Cooke, Sherburne F. *The Aboriginal Population of the North Coast of California.* Anthropological Records, v. 16, no. 3, 1956.

Du Bois, Cora. *The 1870 Ghost Dance.* Anthropological Records, v. 3, no. 1. 1939.

*Erikson, Erik H. *Observations on the Yurok: Childhood and World Image.* UCPAAE, v. 35, no. 10. 1943. Erikson, a psychoanalyst, visited the Yurok in the 1930's and collected information primarily about children. His field observations and the ethnographic data collected by others are interpreted in terms of psychoanalytic theory to provide a rare dimension in the analysis of ethnographic sources.

Gifford, Edward W. *California Kinship Terminologies.* UCPAAE, v. 18. 1922.

Goldschmidt, Walter. "Ethics and the Structure of Society: An Ethnological Contribution to the Sociology of Knowledge," *American Anthropologist,* v. 53, 506-524. 1951.

Heizer, Robert F. "A Prehistoric Yurok Ceremonial Site (HUM-174)," *Reports of the University of California Archaeological Survey,* no. 11, 1-4. 1951.

*Heizer, Robert F., and John E. Mills. *The Four Ages of Tsurai.* Berkeley and Los Angeles. 1952. The only systematic Yurok archaeology is reported in this history of one coastal settlement. The travelers' accounts presented are an invaluable source on Yurok history.

Hoopa Area News, v. 9, no. 3 (mimeographed). 1964.

Klamath River Indian People. *A Final, Desperate Appeal for Justice to the President and the Congress of the United States by the Klamath River Indian People of the Hoopa Valley Indian Reservation, Humboldt County, California.* (mimeographed) no date.

*Kroeber, Alfred L. *Handbook of the Indians of California.* Berkeley, 1953. The first ninety-seven pages of this volume contain a well-balanced ethnographic description of the Yurok.

Kroeber, Alfred L., and Edward W. Gifford. *World Renewal, A Cult System of Native Northwest California.* Anthropological Records, v. 13, no. 1. 1949.

O'Neale, Lila M. *Yurok-Karok Basket Weavers.* UCPAAE, v. 32, no. 1. 1932.

Progress Report to the Legislature by the Senate Interim Committee on California Indian Affairs. Senate Resolution No. 115. State of California. Sacramento. 1955.

*Spott, Robert, and Alfred L. Kroeber. Yurok Narratives. UCPAAE, v. 35, no. 9. 1942. Robert Spott was an old and well-informed Yurok who related to the recorder, Kroeber, historical accounts, tales of the more distant past, and myths. The historical accounts are particularly enlightening since they provide insight into the functioning of the sociocultural system.

Stearns, Robert E. "A Study of Primitive Money," *Report of the U.S. National Museum, 1887.* 297-334. Washington, D.C. 1889.

*Thompson, Lucy. *To the American Indian.* Eureka. 1916. Written by a Yurok woman, this book is one of the key ethnographic sources and ranks with the studies by Alfred L. Kroeber.

Transmitting Report by Subcommittee on Indian Affairs. Senate Committee on Rules Resolution No. 8. State of California. Sacramento. 1961.

Valory, Dale K. Yurok Doctors and Devils. Ph.D. dissertation, University of California, Berkeley. 1970.

*Waterman, Thomas T. *Yurok Geography*. UCPAAE, v. 16, no. 5. 1920. This monograph is one of the most fascinating specialized studies about the Yurok. The detailed analysis of Yurok geographical concepts and the ways in which the Yurok conceived of the world offer a dimension of culture rarely considered systematically.

Waterman, Thomas T. "All is Trouble Along the Klamath," in *American Indian Life,* Elsie C. Parsons, ed., 289-296. New York. 1922.

Waterman, Thomas T. *The Kepel Fish Dam*. UCPAAE, v. 35, no. 6. 1938.

Waterman, Thomas T., and Alfred L. Kroeber. *Yurok Marriages*. UCPAAE, v. 35, no. 1. 1934.

University of California Publications in American Archaeology and Ethnology, referenced as UCPAAE.*

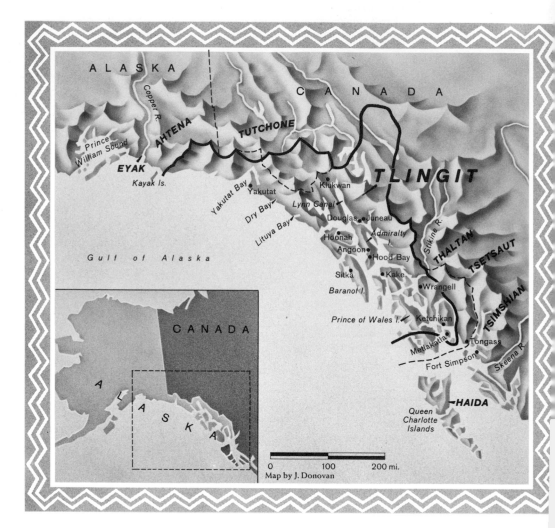

Map by J. Donovan

The Tlingit:
salmon fishermen of the northwest

One day during the summer of 1786 an Indian hunter looked seaward from above the shores of Lituya Bay on the Gulf of Alaska; he imitated the call of a wolf and then ran to a nearby village. The wolf's cry was a sign of important news, and people gathered as the hunter arrived, saying, "Raven is coming." He said that Raven was white and could be seen on the horizon to the west. Everyone knew that long ago Raven had been white, not black, and thus his appearance in this form was not surprising. This was a great moment, for Raven, the creator and culture hero, had said he would return to reward those persons who had obeyed his teachings and to turn the others into stone. Some persons looking seaward peered at the white object through hollow stalks of kelp so that they would not be blinded by Raven's brightness. Then Raven came into the bay and folded his wings. Individuals who expected to be turned into stone stood erect and cut their chests with stone knives; others who were unafraid began painting their faces to receive this great and honored visitor. One wise old man decided to go out to Raven and offer himself to be turned into stone so that other persons might be spared. He paddled a canoe out to Raven and was lifted, canoe and all, out of the water onto Raven. Here the old man saw men with brown hair and blue or gray eyes; their faces were white and they wore strange clothing. The old man began to wonder whether he truly was in the midst of Raven. A man far better clothed than the others appeared, and he was assumed to be Raven. The old man asked for mercy, but the man in the fine clothing sent for food. One of the foods offered to the old man seemed to be a section of a human skull, and something else looked like maggots. Finally he was offered a red liquid which had the appearance of blood; he would eat none of these things. "Raven" then crossed his hands in the air twice, and the old Indian knew that this was not Raven after all since the sign he made was the one people used when they hoped to trade. The old man traded away his hat and garments of sea otter skin for a piece of iron and a small bell. Then, without clothing, he was lowered into the water in his canoe and paddled back to the village. He carried ashore his prizes and told the people of his great experience. This is a modern account by the northern Tlingit recalling the visit to Lituya Bay by Captain Jean de La Perouse of the *Astrolabe* and Paul-Antoine de Langle on the *Boussole*, the first Europeans to explore the area.

Tlingit, which means "people," is the term by which these Indians call themselves. The Russians referred to them as Kolosch, the meaning of which is not known for certain. Their language belongs to the great Na-Dene phylum and is a single language at the family level. Numerically, there possibly were 10,000 of these people around the time of historic contact, and in the 1960's about 8000 Indians in southeastern Alaska were identified as Tlingit. They were divided into named geographical groups, called *kons*, each with a principal village. From north to south the first kon was Yakutat, with its most important settlement along the bay of the same name. The most powerful of all the kons was the Chilkat, whose members lived along the shores of the upper Lynn Canal and occupied four major villages. One of these, Klukwan, had 65 houses and about 600 residents. The only interior groups, the "Inland Tlingit," lived around a series of lakes and occupied the largest area. The other kons, each of which had at least one major village, were the Auk, Taku, Huna, Killisnoo, Sitka, Kake, Kuju, Stikine, Henya, Tongass, and Sanya. Tlingit oral traditions relate that they arrived in their present area from the south, somewhere around the Skeena River, except for the Kake, who came from the interior.

The Tlingit have been selected for discussion as an example of the complex way of life which emerged on the north Pacific coast of North America. They stand as one of the more complex North American sociocultural developments which was not based on a farming economy. An ethnographic study of the Tlingit was compiled in 1881-1882 by two geographers who were brothers, Aurel and Arthur Krause. Their description of Tlingit history, culture, and society, which includes earlier observations of other whites, was published first in 1885. In 1904 the ethnographer John R. Swanton studied the Tlingit, but he was more interested in mythology and language than in an overview of the lifeway. The next significant studies in the era around 1900 were by missionaries, Livingston F. Jones and Samuel H. Young. The unpublished doctoral dissertation by Kalvero Oberg, based mainly on fieldwork at Klukwan in 1931-1932, provides the most valuable factual and interpretive data on aboriginal Tlingit life. Philip Drucker's study of the Alaska Native Brotherhood is an important analysis of a major political and social force in Tlingit life. A monograph by Frederica de Laguna combines archaeological and ethnographic with historical information in an attempt to reconstruct the culture in the area around the modern settlement of Angoon in the Killisnoo kon. Finally, a brief but revealing study of Hoonah, whose inhabitants are in the Huna kon, was made by Seymour Parker in 1961. Thus there are both a relatively complete series of publications about the Tlingit for the American period and satisfactory reconstructions for the aboriginal past.

Tlingit country, of the Sitkan biotic province, is composed of masses of mountains reaching to the sea, islands, deep bays, and glaciers. It is a verdant land, with tranquil and turbulent waters which proffer an environmental richness with great exploitative potential. Along the northern third of the area sheltering bays are rare; it is here that impressive mountains abruptly meet the sea. The southern two thirds of their country contains innumerable large and small islands before a fractured coastline. The channels between the land formations range from deep and wide to shallow, narrow, and rock-strewn. The tides may ebb and flow with a variation of twenty feet in the inlets. The coastal sector is a narrow band of land with mountains a short distance inland; thus, there are very few rivers of any size flowing into the sea, the major exception being the Stikine River.

The most impressive climatic characteristics are the mild temperatures and the heavy precipitation. With the abundance of rain the vegetation is lush and varied. Stands of red cedar and mountain hemlock grow at lower elevations, but Sitka spruce, lodgepole pine, and other varieties of spruce are the most common conifers. The ground cover includes a profusion of smaller plants which form a virtual wall of vegetation. The fallen trees, great ferns, berry bushes, and in some sectors the spiny devil's club, make cross-country travel impossible in the summer except along established trails. In the winter with heavy snow cover it is possible to snowshoe through the forest. Considering the geographical configuration, it is understandable that travel by boat was far more important than walking along overland trails. It was only the trails to the interior at certain passes and along a few rivers that took people inland on trading or raiding trips.

The large variety of terrestrial fauna included both black and grizzly bears, fox, wolves, wolverine, lynx, and deer on some islands. Scattered caribou herds occupied mainland plateaus, and mountain goats as well as mountain sheep frequented the coastal ranges. Smaller species included hare, squirrel, ermine, porcupine, muskrat, and a few beaver. Among the marine mammals were whales, hair and fur seals, sea lions, and sea otter. Of all the fish the most important were the salmon and candlefish (eulachon); halibut, haddock, trout, and herring also were caught. Along the edges of the sea were edible algae, crabs, sea urchins, mussels, and cockles. The avifauna included the bald eagle, raven, owl, and migratory waterfowl which summered in the area.

Tlingit prehistory is little known, owing both to the difficulty in locating and excavating sites and to the fact that few archaeologists have worked in this region. De Laguna's excavations in the Angoon area represent the only systematic work of any consequence. She has classified the remains as village sites, as fortifications, or as localities with petroglyphs or pictographs. However, from the vicinity of rock carvings few cultural remains were recovered. Not only are conditions poor for preservation, but sites are difficult to find because of the rapid growth of vegetation following occupancy. Of the Tlingit artifacts recovered, all probably belong to the early historic period and reveal very little new in terms of the past and their makers.

The history of the Tlingit began with explorations of the Russians who sought to determine whether the Asian and North American landmasses were continuous. It was during the Second Kamchatkan Expedition under the leadership of Vitus Bering that the first contacts were made. The two expedition vessels, the *St. Peter* under Bering and the *St. Paul* under Alexei Chirikov, sailed from Kamchatka in 1741 and soon became separated in the north Pacific Ocean. Chirikov, the first Russian to reach the coast, anchored offshore near the southern limit of Tlingit country. He sent two separate small boats ashore, but neither returned to the ship. Later two canoes were paddled by Indians toward the *St. Paul* and then withdrew. Without another small vessel to put ashore, Chirikov was forced to return to Kamchatka. Shortly after Chirikov's contact the Bering party anchored off Kayak Island at the northern edge of Tlingit country. This island seems to have been occupied by Eskimos, the Chugach. Bering sent a boat ashore for water with orders not to linger. It was not without difficulty that the great German naturalist, Georg W. Steller, persuaded Bering to permit him to accompany the party. No people were seen, but a camp and possessions were found, along with a still-burning fire. The descriptions by Steller of the structure and artifacts he saw are the earliest ethnographic data for the area. On the return voyage the crew of the *St. Peter* was forced to winter on Bering Island off the coast of Kamchatka. Here Bering died, but the surviving members of the crew returned to Kamchatka the next year, bringing with them the pelts of sea mammals. This led to the hasty organization of small trading and hunting expeditions to the Aleutian Islands, and before many years had passed the search for furs had reached the Alaskan mainland.

The Russians were not the first observers of the Tlingit country, however. As early as 1582 the Spanish explorer Francisco Gali saw the northwest coast in the vicinity of Sitka but apparently had no contacts with the people. The Spanish viewed Russian expansions with alarm and in 1774 sent Juan Perez from Mexico northward as far as the Queen Charlotte Islands. The following year a Spanish vessel under Juan de la Bodega landed near Sitka and attempted to take possession of the land. The Spaniards withdrew quickly, however, as a result of Indian hostility. Next, in 1778, it was the English under the command of one of the greatest of all explorers, James Cook, who sailed to the northwest coast. Although Cook saw the Sitka area from the sea, he did not attempt to land. After Cook came the expedition to Lituya Bay by La Perouse in 1786. English expeditions and traders became particularly numerous after word reached England of the profits to be made from selling sea otter pelts in China. Americans also entered the fur trade; the earliest, in 1788, were Robert Gray, commander of the *Washington*, and John Kendrick in command of the *Columbia*. Not until the expedition of George Vancouver in 1792-1794 was the northwest coast mapped with enough accuracy to establish that the legendary Strait of Anian to the Atlantic Ocean truly was a fable.

Throughout the 1780's and 1790's Russian merchants moved to consolidate the Alaskan trade until the Russian-American Company was founded in 1799 and granted a monopoly. The dominant local administrator was Alexander Baranov, who established a permanent base on Kodiak Island in 1791. Baranov's first contacts with the Tlingit occurred along Prince William Sound where he and his party were mistaken by Yakutat Tlingit for Chugach Eskimos and attacked in the middle of the night. The Russians and the Aleuts who were with them fought off the Indians, but each side suffered casualties. This encounter with the Tlingit and all earlier contacts by traders and explorers of all nationalities were hostile. These Indians were haughty, aggressive, thieving, and bellicose, expecially when they outnumbered intruders. A fort and trading post was established at Sitka in 1799, and as long as Baranov was there the Indians did not attack, since they respected his bravery. After he left in 1801, the Indians destroyed the fort and killed the small garrison. In 1804 Baranov returned with about 900 men, 800 of them Aleuts and the balance Russians. At Sitka the Russians hoped to establish a fortress on a steep hill formerly occupied by the Indians. The Tlingit withdrew to a nearby fort, and the Russians founded their hilltop settlement at New Archangel. Anchored before Sitka was the *Neva*, which under the command of Urey Lisiansky was the first vessel to sail to Russian-America from European Russia. The Indians were determined to drive the Russians away if possible, but they could not withstand the bombardment from the *Neva* and withdrew from the fort, which later was destroyed by the Russians.

With the retirement of Baranov in 1818 a succession of administrators controlled the fortunes of the Russian-American Company. Some were extremely capable, while others were poorly fitted for their position. Relationships with the Tlingit fluctuated with the capabilities of the chief administrator. Throughout the latter part of the Russian period, until the purchase in 1867, Sitka was the primary trading center for the Tlingit, but American trading vessels and traders of the Hudson's Bay Company competed successfully for Tlingit pelts. The destructive Indian and Russian hunting techniques led to a rapid decline in the fur trade. Finally when the Russian flag at New Archangel (Sitka) was lowered on October 18,

1867, and the flag of the United States was raised, one era came to an end and another began.

According to Tlingit mythology, the first people simply existed, and no explanation was sought for their ultimate origin. From these people, according to one tale, arose a woman whose sons were killed by her brother. She decided to commit suicide, but an old man whom she met told her to swallow a heated beach pebble. The woman followed his instructions and became pregnant. She bore an offspring, who was Raven in human form. When Raven was older, he visited his uncle in spite of warnings by his mother that his uncle, her brother, had killed his ten older brothers. The uncle attempted to kill Raven, but because of Raven's supernatural powers he was able to save himself. Finally, Raven caused a flood, and all the people perished except for Raven and his mother, who donned bird skins and flew into the air. Raven stuck his beak in the sky and hung there for ten days. After the water subsided, he fell to earth and landed on a heap of seaweed. Raven went to the house of Petrel, a man who had no beginning nor end but always existed. In a small locked box, on which he sat, Petrel kept water, and when Raven was thirsty he was given only a little. Raven tricked Petrel into thinking that he, Petrel, had excreted in his bed. While Petrel was outside cleaning his blanket, Raven drank more than his fill of water and then flew to a tree with pitch in it. Petrel built a fire beneath the tree, and the smoke turned Raven from white to black. Later the trickery of Raven released the stars into the sky, the moon, and finally the sun. Raven was a creator or releaser of forces in the world, a culture hero, and above all else an inordinate trickster.

The Tlingit were medium to tall in height and were lean, with skins no darker than those of many persons from southern Europe. They rubbed their black hair with grease, and it hung loose over the neck. The whiskers of the men were not numerous and usually were plucked. When a male was young, his nasal septum was pierced, and through the opening a small ring was suspended. A man with great achievements might have several small holes made around the outer edge of the ear, and bits of wool or small feathers were stuck in the openings. From the pierced earlobes of men and women were hung ornaments of shell, stone, or teeth. Women wore their hair loose as did the men but parted it in the middle. Body mutilation for adornment was more striking for women; in addition to earrings, each wore a large medial labret inserted through a hole beneath the lower lip. The initial opening was made about the time of puberty or perhaps earlier, and the hole was periodically enlarged until it sometimes stretched four inches; as one observer noted, kissing was impossible for such a person. Female slaves did not wear labrets. Tattooing, if it occurred, probably was restricted to lines beneath the chin among the northern Tlingit, who could have learned the custom from Eskimos. On certain occasions facial paintings were important for both men and women; paint was worn for special ceremonial or subsistence activities, to reflect mourning, or simply to look attractive. One's face was painted also as protection from extreme temperatures as well as from snowblindness in the spring and insects in the summer. Organic and inorganic red and black pigments were mixed with a seal oil base.

Adults of both sexes dressed in long-sleeved shirts of dehaired skin, over which they wore sea otter skin capes with the fur facing outward. Women were described further as having worn undergarments of processed skins which reached from the neck to the ankles. During severe weather they wore moccasins which had been received in trade from interior Indians or had been styled after that type of footwear. Tlingit hats for hunting and ceremonies were woven from root or grass and were shaped like a truncated cone with a flat top. Their clothing hardly seems adequate to an outsider, but these people conditioned themselves to accept extremes in temperature. Bathing in cold or icy water was expected as well as sitting in a scorchingly hot house.

Winter villages were located near good fishing grounds and where canoes could be landed safely. This meant that the Tlingit preferred sheltered bays, inlets, or the lower course of a river for their home sites. If a community was small, all of the houses were built in a line near the beach or riverbank. If the settlement was large, the houses were arranged in rows and grouped according to kinship affiliations. The essentially square, plank dwellings with gabled roofs had entrances facing the water. In the construction of a dwelling four great posts were sunk in the ground, one at each corner; these rose ten feet above the surface. At the middle of the sidewalls were support posts, and on top of these rested plates. Near the center of the front and back walls were higher posts which supported beams reaching the length of the house. Above the secondary roof beams were overlapping horizontal planks, and these short board shingles were held in place with lengthwise poles or stones. Toward the middle of the roof was an opening to let light in and smoke out; a plank covered this skylight in foul weather. A notched pole ladder for reaching the roof was kept against the side of the house. Steps or a platform led to the round or oval doorway which was at the center or off to one side of a house front; entrance was gained after pushing aside a grass mat. The floor inside the smaller dwellings was on one level, but the central area of larger houses was dug down about three feet. Along the sides at ground level were compartments enclosed with matting or boards; these were for sleeping rooms, a sweat bath, or storage. This level was planked, as was the excavated area except near the fireplace. Around the fire pit were stones to be heated in the fire and placed in containers for cooking food. Overhead along the beams were stored various hunting and fishing devices, and fish might be hung from the roof beams to dry. Among the northern Tlingit in particular the house of the leading lineage in a sib was likely to have decorated wall partitions or panels which have been termed heraldic screens. It appears that behind these screens were the apartments of the house chief, and another report notes that behind these panels the ceremonial equipment of the household was stored. Around the entry to a house or even around the entire community were palisades which served to protect the occupants. Included among the other buildings at a winter settlement were bough-covered, cone-shaped structures which sometimes were leaned against the outer wall of a house and were used by women when menstruating or during childbirth. Scattered about a settlement were pole racks for drying fish, and a short distance away, either toward the sea or forest, were clusters of graves.

Among the most important exploited localities were summer fishing grounds where a family obtained its winter supply of fish. The plank structures at these camps were not constructed with care, and some were walled in only on the windward side. The land within a village was owned by particular sibs and was subdivided among house groups. The paths in front of houses were used by anyone, but plots of ground near them were owned by the adjacent households. Trails might be cleared by community members as a group, and the beach was common property. Each of the kons had its geographical boundaries, and each community controlled the sector it exploited. Within the domain of a village, each of the sibs represented had particular localities which they defined as their own. Unclaimed sectors could be exploited by anyone. Each sib, or a portion thereof, owned fishing streams and lands of the stream's drainage which were used for hunting, sealing islands, mountains inhabited by mountain goats, ocean banks, berry patches, and house locations. According to de Laguna the people did not conceive of their ownership in terms of an entire geographical area but rather the specific spots that they utilized.

The craft skills of the Tlingit rank them high among tribal peoples anywhere in the world. Their manufactures in stone, bone, and wood are famous, and their abilities as weavers merit additional comment. In a typical aboriginal household were a wide variety of wooden containers. One form was made from a thin plank of cedar which was steamed and bent into a rectangular form, then overlapped and sewn with root. A wooden bottom was fitted into place and a top sometimes added. Some of these boxes had bulging sides which were painted or carved. The largest and most elaborately decorated boxes were used for the storage of valuables, and others were for cooking or food storage. Another common form of wooden vessel was made from a single piece of wood and ranged from round, to oval, to rectangular in outline. To these basic forms were adapted various animal shapes, such as a beaver lying on its back, with the head at one end, legs on the sides, and tail opposite the head. The rim might be inlaid with the opercula of mollusks or bits of abalone shell, and the eyes of the animal might likewise be inlaid with shell. Other household items included dishes, spoons, and ladles of mountain sheep or goat horn. Oval lamps of pecked and polished stone furnished light from fish oil burning on a moss wick. Stone pestles and mortars which had been pecked and ground into shape were used for mashing berries. Plant fibers were woven into a wide variety of household containers such as trays, bags, or baskets for storing or carrying various items; they also were woven into mats upon which persons lounged. All of these artifacts would have been seen in any typical household, and in each house, too, the family members gathered around the fire to rest, to eat, or to work during the day. The wood for each day's fire was brought in by the younger men and boys on the day it was to be burned. At the fireplace the meals were prepared at irregular times of the day for as many as thirty house occupants. Boiled foods were prepared in wooden or woven containers into which water was placed. Hot stones were dropped in to simmer the meat or fish which was added before the lid was put on. Fish were boiled, roasted before the fire, or dried to serve as the principal dietary items, and were supplemented by flesh from land and sea mammals. Also eaten were shellfish, vegetable products, and fruit, particularly a wide variety of berries, but these foods were relatively unimportant. Boiled foods were dipped from their cooking containers into large spoons, which served as plates, and large quantities of water were consumed at every meal.

The sib crest was carved on any object by a member of the opposite moiety who held a rank equal to that of the individual requesting the carving. By preference this would be a wife's brother; if such an individual was not a capable carver, he could hire someone else of either moiety to make the object. The man who was first asked to do the work paid the craftsman and in turn was paid by his brother-in-law. Carvings produced in this manner fulfilled ritual obligations, and the labor involved was ceremonial.

Two aspects of Northwest Coast Indian life have most attracted the attention of whites: their art and the potlatch system. About these a great deal has been written, and while the potlatch will be discussed later, it is desirable now to summarize briefly Tlingit artistic and craft expressions. As Franz Boas pointed out, there were two basic artistic styles among Northwest Coast Indians. The first was dominated by men; it largely was symbolic and was manifest in sculpture, carving, and painting. The second, or women's style, largely was formal with little or no attendant meaning and was manifest primarily in basketry designs. Although the Chilkat robes contained symbolic designs, the women who wove them reproduced symbolic paintings made on boards by a male designer. The carving skills of men were expressed primarily in wood; red cedar was the favorite medium. The men likewise carved horn and ivory; pounded and incised copper; and further utilized shell, hair, and skin for decorative elements. The women in their artistic crafts utilized animal wool and spruce or cedar root fibers. Their basketry designs usually were geometric, and the specific motifs were named. The baskets had nearly straight sides and were flat-bottomed; the sides were decorated, but rims usually were plain.

Among the common elements in symbolic art were symmetrical, stylized figures. Animals most often were the subject matter, but human figures also appeared. Sometimes these seem to have been portraits of individuals. In general, the art of the Tlingit was not as complex as that of their neighbors to the south; neither was it so monumental, possibly because of the scarcity or absence of great cedar trees in most of the Tlingit area. What the Tlingit did excel in producing was a wide variety of highly imaginative masks, which were used by performing shamans. The human faces might be supplemented with animal figures which were the familiars of shamans. The carvings on utilitarian objects served to enhance their beauty and bring prestige to their owners. Distortion was an important consideration in their creations, since traditional forms were adapted to diverse surfaces. Carving a bear on a totem pole was very different from fitting the bear motif on a rectangular vessel, the handle of a horn spoon, or a flat screen painting. Another characteristic of the artistic symbolism was to emphasize features of an animal as a key to its identification. The beaver was characterized by its incisor teeth and tail, while the killer whale was keyed to its prominent dorsal fin. So it was with other totemic representations. Prominent and recurring characteristics included the skeletal motif, the use of joint markers, and the prominence of stylized eyes. Tlingit craftsmen employing these motifs produced outstanding works in art.

The most important item manufactured for subsistence activities was the canoe. Normally a canoe was constructed during the winter months when unhurried skill led to the production of attractive and sound vessels.

The best canoe wood was from a straight-grained red cedar which was felled by building a fire at the base. A tree which had been blown over by the wind might be utilized, however. With a stone-bladed adz the log was hewn and scraped. In order to spread the sides of the hollowed log the cavity was filled with water, and hot stones were dropped in the water. Pieces of wood were wedged across the gunwales, and as the log softened, the sides were spread and wider pieces of wood inserted until the desired degree of flare was achieved. The height of the sides sometimes was increased by adding planks, and the sides of a vessel might be painted with designs and the bow carved. A small canoe carried two or three persons, whereas larger ones held sixty persons and were forty-five feet in length. Canoes were propelled with paddles, and an extra long paddle was used for steering. When not in use, canoes were protected from the direct sunlight by placing mats or blankets over them and by sprinkling water over the sides. A smaller variety of canoe, made from a cottonwood log, was used for fishing and traveling along rivers.

Snowshoes were essential for winter travel, especially among the Chilkat, who traded with the inland peoples during the winter. The light maple or birch frames were heated over a fire and shaped; the netting was made from rawhide thongs. The shoes were about four feet in length and ten inches wide at their broadest point, with rounded toes which turned up at the front and pointed heels.

The subsistence cycle reached an ebb during the winter months, and even March did not offer reliable weather for fishing. Nonetheless, it was during March that the subsistence year began anew. Canoes were repaired, the fishing gear was readied, and the men waited anxiously. When calm weather arrived, they fished for halibut along the coast fronting the Pacific Ocean. They employed a distinctive form of V-shaped hook which had a tine along the inner side of one prong; on this was baited a piece of fish. The hook was lowered on a long, stone-weighted rope; a wooden floater bobbed on the surface when the bait was taken. Two men fishing from a canoe maintained about fifteen of these lines. When a fish was hooked, they paddled to the bobbing floater, raised the line, and clubbed the fish to death as it was boated. Fishing for trout at this time of the year likewise was important. Several wooden, shanked hooks with bone barbs baited with clam meat or pieces of fish were attached at intervals along a main rope which was anchored at both ends with stones. A second rope was attached to the first and to an inflated seal's bladder, which floated on the surface to mark the spot where the anchored lines had been lowered. The lines were checked after about half a day, and the hooked fish were killed with a club. Following the ice breakup in March women fished with gill nets from canoes; one woman usually paddled as a second handled the drifting net. The nets were made from rawhide or cedar-bark rope, inflated bladders being used as floaters and stones as sinkers. Various species of trout were taken in the gill nets. Clams and mussels were collected in large quantities and either were dried and smoked for future use or else were steamed in a pit by pouring water over hot stones and a covering of leaves. The pelts of fur animals were in excellent condition in March, and wolf, fox, mink, and land (river) and sea otter all were sought. Some of these animals were killed in deadfalls, but sea otter were hunted with darts, marmots dug from their holes, hares snared, and porcupines clubbed to death.

Spring came in April or May, and at this time the plants grew exuberantly. For a brief period in February and again in April candlefish ascended many of the rivers. They were taken mainly with traps and dip nets and were dumped into a canoe which was half-buried in the sand. Water was added to the load of fish, and stones heated in a fire were dropped into the mass of fish. After the stones cooled, they were reheated, and as the oil from the cooked fish came to the surface of the water, it was skimmed off and ladled into wooden containers. The primary use of the oil was as a dip for dried salmon, but it was served also with berries or drunk during feasts. In mid-April herring swarmed into the shallow bays to spawn and were so numerous that they could be impaled on sharp tines set in the side of a pole. A pole was drawn back and forth in the water, and the pierced herring were then shaken off into a canoe. They were either eaten soon after being caught or were strung on ropes to dry for later consumption.

Trading ventures were a means of obtaining unavailable products or those that were scarce locally. In historical documents it has been recorded that in the summer Tlingit men traveled among the interior Athapaskan Indians taking fish oil as their most important item of trade. From these Indians they received caribou skins and sinew as well as lichens for a particular type of dye. It was during the summers too that great canoes were paddled to the Haida and Tsimshian country, with Chilkat blankets being an important trade item. In early historic times the Tlingit are known to have traveled as far as the Puget Sound area of Washington state. Their travels were for diverse purposes, but in each instance the party was organized by a house group under the direction of its leader, the Keeper of the House. Dentalia, haliotis, and shark teeth came from the south, copper from the Copper River to the north, and slaves occasionally from the north but more commonly from the south. The most important trade route seems to have been the one leading into the interior, and it was controlled by the Chilkat.

In the late summer berries were collected and stored with candlefish oil in airtight boxes. Salmon eggs, oil, and berries were similarly mixed and preserved. If large land mammals were killed, their flesh usually was cut into strips and sun-dried or else boiled and stored in oil. Some foods were stored for winter at this time of the year, but it was not until September that the winter food supply became a major concern. Diverse species of salmon were taken during the summer, but no great effort was made to catch and dry quantities of them until September. The species of salmon found in the Tlingit area included the coho (silver), dog (chum), humpback, king, and sockeye, which were taken from July through December. The principal salmon-fishing device was a funnel-shaped trap set with the mouth opening downstream. The stream was blocked with a weir, which opened only at the trap. Fish were cleaned with a semilunar knife with a slate blade. The heads, tails, and internal organs were removed; the fish were then hung on a drying rack with the flesh side up. They were covered during damp weather or smoke-cured in the house, and after being dried, they were bundled and stored. As soon as a house group had obtained enough salmon for the winter, the members left their fishing camp for their village where they settled down for the winter. Very little food was gathered during the winter months, for this was the season of feasting, storytelling, and leisure, which did not end until April. Sometimes in the winter people fished through the ice of the rivers for flounder. A fisherman cut a hole in the ice and squatted over the hole with a blanket covering his head and a long-handled fish spear (leister) poised above the hole. As a flounder swam along, it could be seen through the water and was impaled on the prongs of the spear. Fishing for flounder served only immediate needs.

For hunting sea mammals the harpoon dart was the most important weapon. It consisted of a shaft, at the end of which was fitted a barbed dart head. This head was of bone or antler, with a wedge-shaped tang and a line hole near the base. One end of a cord was attached through the line hole, and the opposite end was attached to the dart shaft. When an animal was struck, the barbed point held beneath its skin, and the shaft was dragged behind as the creature sounded. When the wounded animal surfaced, it either was harpooned again or killed with a spear or club. Among the sea mammals taken by the Tlingit were the seal, sea lion, dolphin, and above all else the sea otter, particularly in historic times. Only the northern Tlingit at Yakutat hunted great whales, and they seem to have done so under stimulus from their Eskimo neighbors. From the ethnographic accounts it would seem that sea mammal hunting was not very important; neither does it appear that inland hunting was important at most settlements. If bears or mountain goats were pursued, they were cornered with the aid of dogs and killed with bone-pointed spears.

The people of each kon were divided into two groups (moieties) which were represented in each of the geographical areas. The moieties were named Raven and Wolf, with the Wolf moiety termed Eagle in the north; these were in turn divided into named sibs. The Tlingit considered that certain personality characteristics were associated with members of the moieties. Raven people were expected to be wise and cautious, but the Wolves were quick-tempered and warlike. According to Oberg, the Raven moiety in the recent past consisted of twenty-seven different groups, each tracing descent through females to presumed common ancestors (matrisibs); members of all groups used the raven on their crests. The Wolves had no similar unity in their crest designations; each sib derived crest symbols from the experiences of its ancestors. According to Krause the Raven sibs included the Raven, Frog, Goose, Sea Lion, *Uhu*, and Salmon. In the Wolf moiety were the Wolf, Bear, Eagle, Whale, Shark, and *Alk* sibs; his list is not complete, however. A person not a member of any sib was thought of as a stranger and was addressed as uncle or son-in-law, reflecting his in-marrying status. At Klukwan the most important sibs were the Wolf and Eagle; these were divided into named subgroups which probably were lineages. Within each sib the lineage with the greatest amount of wealth was most influential. Ideally the leadership of a lineage was passed from a man to his sister's son, but apparently this practice could be bypassed by appointing a new chief while the old one was still alive. Each settlement with a number of sibs would have more than one chief, but one would emerge as dominant in community affairs by virtue of his wealth and personality. An individual in one moiety was obligated to seek a mate from the opposite moiety (moiety exogamy).

Within each moiety the member sibs recognized a particular settlement as the point of their ultimate origins. Although each sib was identified initially with a particular geographical area, by the time of historic contact a number of different sibs were likely to be present in most settlements. If one sib was larger in a particular village, it was divided into lineages represented by house groups. In theory, the sibs of each moiety possessed distinctive titles and associated design motifs which only members could use. These might be lent temporarily or even usurped by a more powerful sib. Again in theory, only members of the Raven moiety had the right to the raven design and those of the Wolf moiety, the wolf design. Furthermore, the animal after whom a sib usually took its name or its tradition was employed in its sib designs. The clarity of design usage became confused when, for example, a sib of the Wolf moiety employed a modified raven design without taking the Raven name for it. A situation of this nature always had as a precedent some mythological, historical, or quasi-historical event. House names usually were derived from a myth of the sib, from the sib's name, or by assuming the name of another sib's house for a legen-

dary or historical reason. The names of individuals were taken also from
sib names. These had either male or female distinctions, but a female could
acquire a male's name if there were no males to carry it on. What we
see are moieties, each divided into a number of matrisibs which in turn
were divided into house groups composed of nuclear families, again related
through females. Nuclear family unity did not exist because the parents
were of different sibs and moieties. The sibs were represented in various
geographical areas, and they would act as a unit only in rare instances
of a feud affecting all sections of the sib. The sib had no common leader
or unified territory, and even crests commonly were identified with localized
lineages rather than with the sib as a whole. Finally, within a sib's membership in a village were persons ranked as nobles, commoners, or slaves,
depending on the social standing of their particular lineage.

In the kinship system we find that a single term embraced all the people
of the grandparent generation. To these persons Ego was attentive and
respectful. The ties between a mother and her son were close even though
the son might leave home to live with his mother's elder brother, who
was for him the most powerful individual in Tlingit society and his authority figure. Fathers were considered too lenient to discipline their sons effectively, and of course a father did not belong to his son's sib or moiety.
Parents especially were concerned about the welfare of a daughter, who
would command a large bride-price only if she was well-mannered and
a maiden; thus she always was watched by someone. A mother's sister
was called by a term for diminutive mother and was treated as one's mother.
The "little mother" term was extended to all the other women of her moiety
in her generation. A mother was aided and advised in raising children

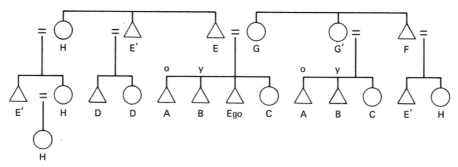

*Aboriginal Tlingit kin terms. Each letter represents a
different term; o indicates older than Ego and y indicates
younger than Ego; E and G prime indicates that these terms
are slight variations on E and G.*

by her sister. A father's sister was termed differently from mother and mother's sister, with the father's sister word extended to all women of her moiety in both her generation and the next descending generation. The father term was unique, but a diminutive word for father was employed for father's brother and again extended to the other men of his moiety of his generation as well as the next lower one. A man treated his father's brother with respect, and a girl on rare occasion married her father's brother. A man ideally would marry his father's sister, and because she was a potential mate, their relationship was always warm. At one's own generational level a man distinguished between older and younger brothers, and these terms were extended to the other men of one's generation and moiety. Older and younger male sibling distinctions were highly important because an older brother had the first rights of inheritance, greater authority, and more ceremonial responsibilities. A woman made the same distinction among sisters. There was also a particular term for a man's sister and one for a woman's brother, which was extended to all the members of that sex of Ego's generation and moiety. Brothers were socially and physically close since they were of the same sib and lived in the same house; with a sister a man must be distant and withdrawn, although he was concerned for her welfare. A mother's sister's children were termed as brother and sister, and the boys were raised in the same household as Ego. The terminology for the first ascending generation was essentially bifurcate merging, and the cousin terminology was of the Crow type. One overriding principle governed the kinship terminology of the Tlingit: to separate blood relatives in one's own moiety from those in the opposite moiety. For persons in the opposite moiety sexual distinctions were important, but generational differences were not considered significant; e.g., father's sister, her daughter and her daughter's daughter were termed alike. The average adult avoided using relationship terms in direct address in everyday conversation for fear of offending someone since there was a great deal of emphasis on an exact ranking of individuals. Thus nicknames and given names were in common usage. Relationship terms were, however, commonly employed on ceremonial occasions.

The most important social and economic unit was the household, which had a significant place in the ceremonial life of the sib and moiety. A house group ideally was composed of Ego and his brothers, as well as his mother's sister's sons who were classificatory brothers, and the sons of the sisters of these individuals, plus the sons of the daughters of these sisters. All were members of one matrilineage, and there were additionally the in-marrying spouses in the household. It was a household of this nature which operated as an economic unit, with the respective members working toward their common welfare. In particular it was brothers, led by the eldest, the Keeper of the House, who aided one another in feuds, potlatches, and other matters of house group concern. The importance of the Keeper of the House in directing house group life cannot be overestimated. He was an individual with very real power and authority. He directed the economic activities of household members and was deferred to by the other men in his residence unit. The house group leader was given choice foods, he allotted items obtained in trade, and was freed from any humble form of household labor. It was this man, the eldest brother, who represented the household in ceremonial activities as well as in sib councils. Furthermore, when he died the rights to his position fell to the next oldest brother, either biological or classificatory. In addition to the position of Keeper of the House the wealthiest of the local household heads in any sib, and thus the ranking Keeper of the House, was designated Rich Man. These men more than any others were responsible for the fortunes of their sib units.

The extensive ceremonial life centered on crucial events in the life cycle of individuals and happenings of important sib or community concern. Thus, birth and death, successful raids, the completion of a new house, or settling disputes required ceremonial acknowledgment. The duration of a ceremony indicated its importance; it might last for one night, several days, or longer if the host could continue providing food. Ceremonies usually included feasting, songs, dances, and the presentation of gifts to honored guests. The most elaborate ceremonies were held in association with the death of an important individual. There was first the cremation ceremony shortly after the death; later there might be an anniversary feast which honored the deceased and established the social position of his successor. The redistribution ceremonies or potlatches of the Northwest Coast Indians are famous, but detailed descriptions of them are rare. The key to Tlingit ceremonial involvement was the emphasis on reciprocity. Whenever a child's ears or lip were pierced, a person initiated into a secret society (a recent Tlingit ritual complex), or the dead buried, someone of the opposite moiety was responsible for carrying out the proper procedures. A house group accumulated food and resources for a year or longer in order to host a ceremony. At the ceremony guests were fed and presented gifts for their labor. There were songs and dances by hosts and guests alike, each of whom was alert to any affront in the words of the other participants or to any mistake in the performance. Any error in a dance or song was grounds for property claims and if breaches of etiquette were flagrant, fights took place.

The institutionalized redistribution of goods played an important part in the economic lives of the Tlingit. Exchanges of gifts linked the various interdependent units of the society in diverse ways. The Tlingit distinguished numerous forms of exchanges, beginning with barter, then gift exchange, food gifts, feasts, the ceremonial exchange of labor, and finally, ceremonial gifts or potlatches. It was through barter that one acquired a needed item, and each person attempted to gain the advantage, tending to ignore any other factors. In gift exchanges those items manufactured by individuals were exchanged for products he or she did not produce well. Such exchanges were made by individuals even within the same house group. The protocol was to work through an intermediary, having him present a gift to the craftsman and make the request. When a major item such as a canoe was desired, a number of gifts were offered to the craftsman at intervals. If the gifts offered did not measure up to the product sought, the craftsman produced an inferior object. Gifts of food, particularly to members of other house groups in the same sib, were offered when a particular house group had a product in abundance. There was no great concern to equalize such gifts, although in time they should balance one another. Feasts were given on private occasions, particularly by a house group when success in hunting, fishing, or trading had been inordinate. Near relatives were invited, and the food not consumed was taken home by the guests. As mentioned elsewhere, the exchange of labor between moieties was socially integrating and economically significant. With the exchange of labor went feasting and reciprocal gifts of property. The most important potlatch goods were slaves, who were killed or more often freed. Second, plates of native copper pounded into shield-like forms, which were a means of concentrating wealth, were exchanged intact, cut into sections as mementos to guests, or thrown into the sea as an ultimate means of validating one's wealth. Finally, blankets, which were not really blankets at all but ceremonial robes, were given as gifts or torn into sections and distributed to guests to commemorate a potlatch. Items offered in a potlatch were borrowed by the house group within its sib, manufactured by the house group, and sometimes borrowed from other sibs in the same moiety. There was the constant effort to give greater potlatches than one's rivals, and as a result emphasis was placed on the production and accumulation of these goods.

The description of a potlatch held in connection with the erection of a new house was recorded by Swanton, and it deserves presentation in summary form since such descriptions of Tlingit ceremonies are rare. This potlatch, which must have occurred around the turn of the present century, probably reflects the aboriginal pattern. In this instance a Raven house builder at Klukwan and a second host sent the former's wife and her friends to Sitka to extend the invitation. When she arrived, she distributed leaf tobacco, fed the people, and told of her mission. The potential guests danced for the visitors and displayed their crests to demonstrate their respect for those extending the invitation. These activities were repeated the following day. The next morning the wife of the Klukwan Raven threw a piece of charcoal outside as a sign that her people, the Wolves, should give property to her. The reason for the request was that the Wolves at Klukwan had helped build her husband's house but that the Sitka Wolves had not. She was given a total of more than $2000 worth of property. After the Wolves of Sitka had prepared all their ceremonial equipment, they set off in boats for Klukwan, followed by the woman and her friends. When they camped, the four dance leaders of the guest party practiced their dances, abstained from women, fasted, and made medicine. As they moved north they plundered towns for provisions, for they were so powerful that no one dared stop them.

When they reached the vicinity of the host village, the hostess had them camp so that she could prepare a final meal. A nearby village chief also feasted them, distributing twenty boxes of candlefish oil; the guests then danced to show their respect. The hosts came to meet their guests and made them presents of candlefish oil, berries, and firewood. They brought crest objects and left them overnight to demonstrate their trust of the guests. When the guests arrived at Klukwan, one of the hosts met them with bow and arrows, pretending to release an arrow. This gesture was to show how brave the host was in the face of the fact that he would be distributing a great deal of wealth. The second host then received the guests, and everyone crowded into one house to dance. The guests, the Sitka Wolves, danced first, after which the Klukwan Eagles danced. Somewhat later the guests were feasted, the main dish being roasted salmon, a favorite dish of the deceased chief in whose honor the potlatch was being held. Another dance was held, followed by a greater feast, and still another dance was given by the guests, competitive with that of the hosts. Food was brought, and a huge platter was set before two men who were guests. They were expected to eat it all but could not quite finish the meal, and the Klukwan people mocked them. Then all of the guests ate, using horn spoons belonging to the dead chief of the Klukwan Ravens, and after they finished the hosts had their meal.

The following morning the Sitka people discussed with those from Klukwan the reburial of the chief's remains. This was the real reason they had been summoned. The guests reburied the bones and erected a carved monument. The following morning the guests were served the best of foods, and the host whose wife had extended the invitation doubled the amount of property she had received and presented it to his guests. As the property was being brought out, the guests were paid to dance and sing, with the most important persons receiving as much as $200 for dancing. It required four days to give out all of the blankets. The host who had sent his wife to Sitka wore a hat which had been used by his uncles and grandmothers; by wearing it, along with distributing so much property, he established his social position as the Raven chief at Klukwan. The two hosts alone distributed about $11,000 worth of property. There was a final feast, and then the guests "left a dance" as a gesture of respect for their hosts. There was a song contest at the end of the potlatch to see who knew the most songs, and after all was over, the overloaded canoes of the Sitka Wolves departed for home.

The pageantry of Tlingit ritual performances brought drama into their ceremonies. The drums, either box or tambourine, provided background music, along with wooden rattles on certain occasions. The ritual dramatizations were derived from the mythology and accompanied by chants as well as songs. The performances took place around the central fireplace of a house. The performers were garbed in their finest apparel, and their typical step was to a two-four beat of the drums. The steps of the dancers were repetitive, with the greatest variations in tense movements of the shoulders, trunk, legs, and arms.

Conflicts between moieties were common, and the modern Tlingit likened these moiety disputes to conflicts between European nations. In order to bring about a settlement of real or supposed injuries it was essential that material goods be exchanged or a life taken. The nature of a settlement was contingent on the ability of the guilty to pay as well as the power of the offended to collect. Any minor conflict was settled eventually at a feast which included a property settlement. When a person was grievously offended, one course open to him was to murder the offender. If this was accomplished, there was bound to be a second murder in retaliation. However, if the persons killed were of unequal rank, there was the further problem of establishing the value of each death, which led to additional complications. Sometimes when an individual felt that he had been wronged and had no means to retaliate, he committed suicide. The relatives of the deceased then demanded compensation for the death. On occasion disagreements between sibs were settled by a duel between warriors representing each group. Murders were from ambush, and the same was true of raids against other tribes or sibs. The only crimes within a sib were incest and witchcraft, both punishable by death. It should be stressed again that there was no overall unity within a moiety, for some of the bloodiest and most bitter feuds took place between sibs of the same moiety.

A warrior conditioned himself for combat by bathing in the sea, even at the coldest time of the year, and being whipped by an older man. The two most important reasons for conducting a raid were to avenge a death and to obtain slaves. The actual preparations for conflict involved abstaining from all contact with women and fasting. As the party traveled, it seized property from camps along the way irrespective of whether the residents were friendly or not. A shaman always accompanied the party and predicted events of the near future. Plans for an attack on an enemy community were kept secret, and the foray was launched at dawn. Rod or skin armor protected a man's body; his face was covered with a mask, and his head with a wooden helmet. All the enemy men who could not flee were killed with daggers; women and children were taken as prisoners. A reprisal attack would be expected to avenge the murders. A copper-bladed dagger, a spear, and possibly a war club, appear to have been the most important weapons. Scalps were taken at times, and the scalped person's head sometimes was impaled on a stick and exhibited. The men in a war party sang of victory as they returned to their village, and the paddle of each warrior killed was stuck up at the spot he had occupied in the boat. In order to bind a peace settlement hostages might be exchanged and kept for a year or longer. Peacemaking followed a pattern of ceremonialism, which climaxed with the exchange of hostages, termed "deer," since they were to behave as timidly as these animals.

Most slaves were persons captured in raids or purchased from peoples to the north or south. Others were the children of indebted men who could find no way out of their dilemma except to offer themselves and as many of their children as necessary to cancel the debt. There was for these persons, in contrast with captives, the possibility that they might be redeemed. There appears to have been considerable variability in the way slaves were treated. In general they seem to have been well cared for by their masters since they were a valuable form of property. Yet there are reports which picture the lot of slaves as extremely difficult since they performed all the odious tasks and might at any time be killed at their owner's fancy. Sometimes slaves were killed to emphasize the importance of their owner, as when he built a new house. In order to gain prestige one man might kill a number of slaves; his rival would be obligated to kill a greater number, and so it went until one contestant had no more slaves. The ownership of slaves apparently was more important for prestige than for any economic gain from their services. The proportion of slaves to free persons is not known, but it is recorded that ten slaves in a house was a large number.

Tlingit shamans were reputed to be more powerful than those found elsewhere along the north Pacific coast; at least they were so judged by Swanton. The effectiveness of a shaman was derived from the spirits he controlled, and these were passed from a man to a sister's son, or rarely to his own son. The usual manner in which a sib acquired a new shaman was for the spirit of a sib shaman to leave his body at death and enter the body of an upstanding sib youth. Nephews who aspired to the position went into trances around the dead man's body, and the individual who remained in a trance the longest was most likely to be named the successor. After this supernatural visitation the novice, accompanied by certain near relatives, went into the forest. They ate little and searched for a sign. The most propitious was to see a bird or an animal drop dead; the spirit of this creature henceforth aided the tyro. After the young man had proved he had his uncle's power, he inherited the ceremonial equipment.

Shamans controlled diverse spirits which were represented on their masks. Most spirits served specific sibs, but some could come under the power of any shaman. The latter category included a spirit associated with the souls of persons who were lost at sea or who died alone in the forest; another was a messenger for shamans. On a mask the primary protecting spirit was represented as the main figure, but helping spirits also might be on the mask. A spirit aid might be posed around the eyes of the mask, thereby increasing the vision of the primary spirit. A shaman neither cut nor combed his hair, and about his neck he wore a bone necklace and a small whetstone, the latter for scratching his head. Upon instructions from a spirit, small bones were inserted through the holes in his nasal septum. A shaman owned rattles which had spirit associations and were used in his performances. Among his charms were the split tongues of animals, especially the land otter, and claws of eagles, which were sources of power. The split tongues, and probably the claws as well, were placed in bundles of cedar bark, grass, and devil's club. After a shaman bathed he rubbed himself with this bundle, and he used it in all his rituals. Among the spirit helpers were those of the land otter, the sun and the sea, and the crest animals of the shaman's sib. After summoning his spirit helpers, a shaman cured an afflicted individual by blowing, sucking, or passing an object over the locus of the affliction, which drew out the cause of the illness. A shaman and his family usually lived in a separate village residence, and in the forest near the house was his shrine. Shamans from time to time retreated to caves for extended periods in order to intensify their spirit relationships.

Witchcraft most often was performed by obtaining some item intimately associated with the victim and then preparing a representation of the victim in the form that the witch desired him to become. When a person was ill, the cause was attributed to witchcraft, and the offender was named by the curing shaman. Persons accused of being witches usually were women, children, or slaves. They were tortured to extract a confession or even killed if a confession was not forthcoming. An accused witch was bound by members of his sib and refused food and water for eight days or even longer. If he did not confess, it was expected that he would die; when a witch did confess, the bewitching substance was scattered in the sea. Other services of the shaman, apart from those mentioned already, were to locate food sources and to predict the future.

A number of charms and their uses were described by Swanton. They appear to have been employed by ordinary persons. Made from parts of plants, they were used in such diverse activities as foreseeing the future, attracting a woman, making one wealthy, or improving hunting abilities. A few additional items seem to have been secular cures, but these were rare and apparently unimportant. In general, it would appear that curing and supernaturalism were shamanistic matters. It is interesting that salmon, which were the all-important subsistence item, were not dealt with in a sacred manner. They simply were accepted as present and were caught and utilized. Even in the mythology salmon play a relatively unimportant role; they seem to have been regarded as a constant part of the environment.

Names for months varied with locality, and one record begins the year with the August moon. The Chilkat appear to have numbered the thirteen lunar months, but at Sitka the months were named, except for two which were numbered. The names referred to seasonal changes in the environment. Knowledge about the natural world was crystallized and integrated into a loosely ordered system. Directions were upriver, which was to the north, and downriver, meaning to the south. The world was thought of as a flat expanse with the sky as a dome above the earth. In all this space everything that existed was alive: on the sun and moon spirits lived; stars were the lights of distant towns or houses; clusters of stars sometimes were named, and Venus was identified. A rainbow was the path of dead souls to the upper world, and the northern lights were human spirits playing. Everything on earth was possessed by a spirit quality, which had subordinates or helpers; each trait, every fire, and everything that one did had its main spirit and helpers.

Childbearing within the mother's home was prohibited because it would have brought ill fortune to the men of the house. Thus a birth took place in a shelter built against the side of a house or nearby, which was never visited by men. In the birth process slaves and a midwife, always a member of the opposite moiety and preferably the woman's husband's sister, aided the woman. Inside the structure a pit was dug and lined with moss, and a stake was driven into the center of the hole. While giving birth, the woman squatted in the pit holding the stake. After a birth the umbilical cord was cut and placed in a bag which hung about the neonate's neck for eight days. The mother was restricted to her shelter for a period of time recorded by different observers as five, ten, or thirty days. To prevent a baby from crying repeatedly, the first cry was caught in a container and apparently buried where many people walked so that it was smothered as the baby grew. The baby was wrapped in skins, with moss for a diaper, and was tied to a board. The mother carried the cradleboard with her or hung it from a roof beam when she was in the house. Among the customs followed in child rearing was to place the umbilical cord of a boy under a tree where an eagle had nested to make him brave as an adult. Likewise, a mother placed woodworm burrowings on her nipples so that as the baby nursed it would swallow the burrowings and would be neat in later life. A child was nursed for three or four years and was given its first solids after about a year. An infant born to a woman without a husband normally was suffocated.

A baby was named after a maternal ancestor; the name itself was taken from an animal associated with the sib. Later in life a child could acquire a name from its father's sib if a potlatch was held for the event. A man who gave his son a second name soon after its birth obligated the offspring to give great potlatches. With the birth of a son the parents referred to themselves by the son's name, as the father or the mother of the son (teknonymy). A family with great wealth could enhance the social standing of all their children by freeing a slave for each child and building a new house. Property was distributed to all those who aided in the construction, and the ceremonial climax occurred when the children had their earlobes pierced by a woman who would then receive many gifts. Such children were termed "of the nobility," and their descendants were referred to similarly. In early childhood children were encouraged to behave in a manner appropriate to adults of the same sex. They were taught to restrain any sign of emotion, to be dignified, and aloof. Physical punishment of children occurred only if they refused to bathe in cold water during the winter; they were expected to take cold baths daily from the time they learned to walk. When boys moved to the household of their mother's brother, they were switched by this man after bathing and were forced to run up and down the beach. After this physical exertion, they were instructed by older men in the customs and history of the sib and learned certain skills by watching the men perform routine tasks. As a boy grew, he came under the increasing influence of his maternal uncle and performed tasks for this older man rather than for his father. A boy tended to gravitate toward a particular uncle whom he wished to emulate in his exceptional skills such as carving, hunting, or those relative to the supernatural. The uncle gave honorific names to his young charges and taught them the lore of their sib, but there were no secret initiations. The most important nephew was the oldest, for he would inherit from his maternal uncle not only material property and wives but titles as well. Even while young, boys were free to use a maternal uncle's tools with permission. If a mother died, the father was obliged to place the offspring in the custody of the mother's siblings.

When a girl first menstruated she was confined to a brush-covered shelter or to a separate compartment in the house behind the heraldic screen, and her face was covered with charcoal. A high-born Tlingit girl was isolated for an entire year, and girls of lesser standing were isolated for at least three months. A girl was attended by close female relatives as well as by a slave during this time. She was obliged to drink water through a bird bone tube, she left the compartment only at night, and she wore a broad-brimmed hat so she would not taint the stars with her gaze. During isolation her mother taught her sib myths, songs, and the behavior considered proper for a woman. It was at the beginning of her isolation that her lip, nasal septum, and perhaps her earlobes were pierced by a woman of the opposite moiety. When she came out of seclusion, she was given new clothing; if her family was wealthy, the slave who attended her was freed. It was expected that the girl would marry soon thereafter, and she must remain chaste. She slept on a shelf above the bed of her parents until she married. The rank of a person was reckoned through both sides of the family and depended largely on the amount of the bride-price paid by one's father for one's mother; thus parents attempted to provide a daughter with all the advantages of careful rearing and wealth.

In marital arrangements there was strict moiety exogamy. A match was initiated by the suitor, who enlisted the aid of a go-between to broach the subject with the girl's family and with the girl. If favorably received, he sent presents to his future father-in-law. The most desirable marriage partners, in decreasing order, were a father's sister, brother's daughter, father's sister's daughter, and finally mother's brother's daughter. In the ideal form of marriage with father's sister, the groom assumed the role of his mother's brother. However, the most common marriage was with a father's sister's daughter, and this was preferred by a young man. These close marriages served two important functions: they kept wealth concentrated and provided mates of nearly equal rank.

A wedding ceremony took place in the house of the bride. The relatives of the groom assembled as he sat in the middle of the floor dressed in his most elaborate ceremonial garb. The bride was concealed in a corner of the house and was lured to sit beside the groom by the singing and dancing of the assembled group. The guests feasted while the couple fasted for two days. Then the bride and groom ate, after which they fasted for another two-day interval. It was only after a month, however, that they were considered married. A wealthy groom gave a potlatch for the girl's family, and marriage residence was either with his or with her family. If the couple moved into a man's household, the bride's relatives presented him with property equal to or exceeding the value of what his relatives had presented to them. Polygyny was practiced by wealthy men; a first wife held a rank superior to that of any subsequent spouses. Five wives seem to have been the maximum number. Polyandry sometimes occurred but only if the second husband was a brother or other close relative of the first husband. The levirate was customary, and if the deceased husband did not have a brother, his sister's son married the widow. If neither category of individual was available, a widow could marry any man of her former husband's sib. If his mother's brother died, a man was obligated to marry the widow even though he might already have a wife, and he inherited his uncle's wealth. In spite of the ideal that a man live in the house of his mother's brother, inherit his wealth, and marry his daughter or another person in this line, his father's sib attempted to lure him into its domain. This especially seems to have been true for a boy who had married into the community. When a married woman was seduced, blood revenge might be exacted by her husband, or the seducer might make a property settlement. If the seduction was by a near relative of the husband, the offender was expected to become the woman's second husband.

An important pastime among adult males was gambling, and some men were so addicted that they sometimes lost prized possessions and even a wife. The most important form of gambling was a hand game in which one man guessed which hand of an opponent held a uniquely marked stick. The game was played by teams, but only one man of each team handled the sticks at any one time. Other adult diversions included dice games and a ball game where the purpose was to drive a ball along the tidal flats to the opponent's goal. Boys played a game which involved throwing a stick at a rolling wad of grass. They also wrestled, hunted, and swam for entertainment. A favorite diversion among little girls was to arrange beach pebbles in the form of figures.

Physicians for the Russian-American Company at Sitka in 1843-1844 described the people as follows (Romanowsky and Frankenhauser, 1962, 35): "The Kolosches are proud, egoistic, revengeful, spiteful, false, intriguing, avaricious, love above all independence and do not submit to force, except the ruling of their elders." To outsiders the Tlingit were not likable. Still adults were patient and persistent; they never seem to have hurried;

and they angered only with provocation. During the fishing season they worked long hours, but for them winter was a time for leisure. During the winter months women made their famous robes and baskets; in general, women appear to have had less free time than the men. The social position and respect that a woman commanded depended on her personality and standing within her sib; a woman with abilities was listened to by the men. Women had well-defined rights and relatives who were willing to come to their defense in case of any injustice from the husband's side of the family. An individual, whether male or female, was expected to behave in accord with his rank in the sib system. Persons were of higher rank if their sib was large, wealthy, and powerful. Still, not all such persons were noble in their behavior, in which case they were treated by others as though they belonged to a lesser sib. Were a person from a high-ranking sib to behave coarsely in the eyes of his fellow sib members he might be killed by them.

As soon as an individual died, relatives began to wail, and the body was arranged in a sitting position at the back of the house, in the place of honor; here it remained for four days or longer. Along the rear wall of the house were placed the greatest treasures of the household. Each night songs were sung, and guests of the opposite moiety were feasted and presented with gifts before the funeral was completed. Near relatives of the deceased singed their hair and blackened their faces during these ceremonies. As the rituals drew to a close, the body was dressed in fine clothing and taken from the house through a hole made by removing a plank from one wall. A dog was thrown through the opening first, a gesture designed to drive evil away from the house. The body was carried to a funeral pyre behind the house and was placed in the midst of heavy logs. A eulogy was delivered, oil was poured over the logs, and slaves might be killed and placed on the pyre of a wealthy man. The fire was lit, but the mourners left before the body was burned completely. Women returned later and retrieved some of the bones from the ashes, wrapped them, and placed them in a small box. The mortuary box was placed on top of a post, which was sometimes adorned with carved figures or paintings. An alternative was to place the ashes in a grave house resting on the ground. After cremation a death potlatch was held and gifts distributed to persons of the opposite moiety who had participated in the ceremonies. All of the major duties connected with the interment were performed by members of the opposite moiety. This included preparation of the body, ritual wailing, and carving a mortuary or memorial pole.

When a shaman died, his body was placed in a different corner of the house each night of the funeral ceremonies, and the house members fasted.

Plate 46
*Tlingit ivory carving,
possibly a shaman's charm*
(Courtesy of The Museum
of Primitive Art, New York).

Plates 47 & 48
*Tlingit shaman's doll (above)
and Tlingit mask (left)*
(Courtesy of The Taylor Museum,
Colorado Springs Fine Arts Center).

Plate 49 *(Top left)   Chilkat woman weaving a dance robe* (From Krause, 1885, v. 1).

Plate 50 *(Bottom left)   A Tlingit lying in state amidst his wealth during the early American period* (From Porter, 1893).

Plate 51 *(Above)   Photograph of a Tlingit house and totem poles taken in 1899* (Courtesy of Smithsonian Institution National Anthropological Archives, neg. no. 43, 548-H).

Plate 52 *(Above)*
*The Juneau Native Band,
ca. 1910*
(From Jones, 1914).

Plate 53 *(Left)*

*The Tlingit totem pole
erected at the town
of Kake in 1971*
(Courtesy of Alaska
Department of
Economic Development,
Fred Belcher
photographer).

For the burial on the fifth day, the shaman was clothed in his best garments. Through his nose was placed a sacred bone which he had used, and another was stuck in his hair. A large basket was placed over his head, and he was buried in a coffin which was raised on four posts and placed on a point of land overlooking the sea. The grave houses of shamans differed from those of ordinary persons by being raised and having steep gabled roofs. If the deceased had been wealthy, the house was decorated elaborately. The body of a slave was not cremated or buried but was thrown into the sea without ceremony. The period of mourning for an ordinary person was one year, and the property of the deceased went to a sister's son. If such an individual did not exist, it was passed to a younger brother; this kept the wealth in the sib of the deceased. If the person's death was not from violence or drowning, his soul traveled along a rainbow to the upper world of the stars, moon, or sun. There existence was a state of happiness. A world above this upper world was inhabited by the souls of persons killed by violence, but one could enter this realm only if his death had been avenged. There was a world beneath the earth to which went the souls of drowned persons.

Sustained contact between the Russians and Tlingit began when the Russians reestablished themselves at Sitka in 1804. From this time until the end of the Russian era in 1867, the administrative center and trading post at Sitka was virtually the only Russian establishment in southeastern Alaska. For Indians the most desired item of trade during the early period of contact was iron. Because the Tlingit were keen traders among themselves and with adjacent peoples, and since they always were ready to accumulate material wealth at the expense of someone else, the foreign traders found them cunning and dangerous hagglers. The fur traders who ventured to deal with the Tlingit all were eager to obtain sea otter skins. Initially, any form of trade goods was accepted, but before long the Indians were highly selective. Woolen blankets were desired because they traded away their animal pelt clothing; they also desired firearms and obtained them from non-Russian sources. Standard early trade items included tobacco; vessels of tin, iron, or copper; axes; glassware; and clothing, especially gaudy uniforms. During the span of Russian contact there never was any effective political control over the Tlingit. The Indians governed themselves, and the Russians did their best to keep violence to a minimum in the vicinity of Sitka.

Russian efforts to Christianize the Tlingit never were very successful because of the strong aboriginal religious system dominated by shamans, the restricted area of Russian penetration, and the scarcity of clergy. The first Russian Orthodox priest arrived at Sitka in 1816, but not until the coming of Father Veniaminov in 1834 did an energetic program of missionizing begin. Veniaminov did not, however, rush into a campaign to make converts of the Tlingit; by 1860 only about 450 were Christians. A school was opened for children at Sitka, but it was not strikingly effective during the Russian period.

For many aboriginal peoples the most devastating effect of contact with Europeans was exposure to previously unknown diseases. These sometimes reduced populations with terrifying rapidity. In 1834 when Veniaminov went to Sitka, he attempted to persuade the Indians to be vaccinated against smallpox, but they resisted the program. Then in 1835 a smallpox epidemic struck. No Russian died, but half of the Tlingit are estimated to have perished. When the Indians realized that their shamans could not cure the disease, they lost faith in these curers and turned to the Russian medical doctor for vaccinations. Europeans introduced syphilis to the area, but according to reports in 1843, it was relatively uncommon.

On the eighteenth of October in 1867 the formal transfer of Alaska from Russian to American ownership took place at Sitka. The Tlingit were not permitted in Sitka for the ceremonies, and in order to observe the ceremony they watched from canoes in the harbor. With American occupancy fortune seekers of almost every variety arrived, and to the Indians this influx must have been shocking. Russian inhabitants had the option of returning to Russia within three years or becoming United States citizens; virtually all of them left within a few weeks of the transfer. For ten years civil government did not exist, and the U.S. military garrisons stationed at Sitka, Tongass, and Wrangell were a primary source of trouble rather than a means for supporting order. The Tlingit clashed repeatedly with the military over Indian deaths that went uncompensated, which led to murders and the destruction or threatened destruction of Tlingit settlements. The most serious difficulties were the failure of the military to understand Indian ways, the wholesale smuggling of intoxicants, and the prevalence of stills among the Indians. After the troops departed, only the U.S. Revenue-Cutter Service vessels and the collector of customs represented legal authority. In 1878 the customs officer at Wrangell stated that within a month he had a thousand complaints from Indians but had no way to deal with them. The difficulty became acute with the influx of miners who wintered that year at Wrangell. In 1880 gold was discovered near the present city of Juneau, which brought more miners and confusion; still it was not until 1884 that a civil government began to function in the more populous areas of Alaska.

Protestant Christianity entered southeastern Alaska in 1876 when a group of Tsimshian Indians from Fort Simpson, B. C., worked at Wrangell.

These Indians had been converted to the Methodist Church of Canada, and one whose English name was Philip McKay remained at Wrangell after the others left in the fall and opened a school. In 1877 the Presbyterian missionary Sheldon Jackson made a survey trip to southeastern Alaska. He was accompanied by Mrs. A. R. McFarland, who formerly had been a missionary among Indians of the western United States. Mrs. McFarland remained at Wrangell and took charge of the school, and during the following year she founded a home for girls. Presbyterian missionaries arrived at Sitka in 1878, and a lasting school was opened there in 1880. In the early 1880's additional schools were established in Tlingit territory with the purpose of educating and missionizing the Indians. It is primarily from the writings of the Presbyterians and the ethnography by Krause that we are able to piece together the major changes in Tlingit life for the forty years surrounding 1900.

The missionaries found the Tlingit women more amenable to the strictures of Christianity than the men. Since in this matrilineal society the women could be quite influential, working through the women became important. Then too the girls attended school more regularly than the boys and became interpreters more frequently than the men, which gave them a certain amount of power and prestige. Certain Biblical messages which the missionaries considered as important could be accepted readily by the Tlingit. For example, the sacrifice of Jesus Christ for the sins of mankind was fully comprehensible in terms of compensation. A Tlingit also considered it much better to give than to receive, which again was a desirable Christian ideal but with a different meaning. The Presbyterian missionary Samuel H. Young was a perceptive person in many ways, and he noted that one of the mistakes made at Wrangell was to give the Indians gifts freely. The people then came to expect gifts as rewards for becoming Christians. When asked to attend church, an old Tlingit was likely to respond, "How much you pay me?" The same compensation was expected by parents when they permitted their children to attend school. The schools were the most important institution for the introduction of systematic change among the Tlingit, and it was through the schools that the missionaries were most successful in winning converts.

Among the diverse problems with which the missionaries concerned themselves was the condition of Tlingit slaves. Except in rare instances slaves were not freed with the purchase of Alaska by the United States, because there was no effective governmental representative to handle Indian affairs. The missionaries also took a firm stand against cremation, shamans, the potlatch system, polygyny, and intoxicants.

In the ethnography of Krause and the writings of the Presbyterians certain specific changes which took place in the late 1870's and early 1880's are reported. The innovations largely were in the realm of material culture. Some items were deleted from the old inventory; women had given up wearing labrets, which had been passing out of fashion even by 1827. Silver jewelry, usually pounded from coins, was made locally. Women wore as many as a dozen bracelets at once, and finger rings for women were popular. Clothing styles shifted from garments of skins to those of cloth, and woolen blankets universally were worn as capes. The women wore loose gowns of calico which were gathered at the top on a yoke. Over these were worn skirts of the same material. For festive occasions women wore jackets that matched their skirts and brightly colored kerchiefs on their heads. Small girls were clothed like their mothers, while a small boy wore only a calico shirt when away from home and nothing at home. The men wore calico shirts and cotton trousers.

House entrances changed from an oval opening to the use of hinged doors, but the lineage house remained the typical residence unit. Changes in food usages included raising vegetables, particularly potatoes, which was a Russian introduction; women were the cultivators. Flour was introduced by the Russians, and it was prepared as a gruel or baked into bread. Coffee and tea were used rarely, and the same was true of eating utensils. Alcoholic drinks were unknown in aboriginal times, and during early contact with the Russians the Indians refused them because of their fear of the Russians. Soon, however, intoxicants became a favorite trade item from roving trading vessels. The governments of Russia and the United States prohibited the sale of intoxicants, but they were smuggled in; also, a discharged American soldier taught the people how to distill their own alcohol. This drink, called hoochinoo, was extremely popular. In aboriginal times the men had chewed a "tobacco-like" plant which they sometimes mixed with lime; now they became smokers. They either carved their own elaborate pipes of wood or stone or else obtained clay pipes from the traders. Imported tobacco was chewed by both men and women. The most important changes in subsistence techniques were the use of iron points to replace those of stone or bone on fishhooks and the use of firearms in hunting; the old methods of fishing were not changed, however.

As Walter R. Goldschmidt and Theodore H. Haas have pointed out, it appears that a consolidation of settlements within a kon had begun prior to historic contact, and the pattern was intensified in historic times. Early in the twentieth century the forces leading to population concentrations included the following: population decline due to wars and diseases; depletion of fish and game in some areas by whites; the availability of better boats which provided mobility from a consolidated settlement; the efforts

of traders, missionaries, and Federal officials to have fewer and larger settlements for more efficient trade, Christianization, and administration; the
desire of the Indians to live in larger communities; and the economic advantages of settling near white communities. During the same era, the early
twentieth century, dwellings of frame construction for individual families
became more popular, but at some villages, such as Hoonah, sib houses
were occupied until quite recently. In 1944 almost all of Hoonah was
destroyed by fire, and only after this time were nuclear family residence
units constructed.

As mentioned earlier the house group was the most functionally integrated social unit in aboriginal Tlingit society. It was likewise the most
important economic and ceremonial unit within a sib. In aboriginal times,
however, within a house group each man supplied pelts for his own nuclear
family. In historic times when trapping became a primary means of livelihood, individual trappers built cabins on sib lands and claimed local areas
for their exclusive exploitation. The major economic focus shifted from the
house group to the individual, and the cohesion of the house group began
to decline. This was one factor which led to the construction of nuclear
family dwellings. The essence of this particular analysis of the shift in
the economy was plotted by Oberg.

Some families had begun to use chairs in their houses around 1900, but
tables were less common. Stoves replaced the fireplaces, and dishes replaced
ladles out of which to eat. Boiling still prevailed as the favored method
of cooking. To wash clothing became a part of household routine, and sewing
machines were bought and used. Although the clothing styles of whites
were well accepted, the ears of persons of both sexes still were pierced
for ornaments, and the nasal septum likewise was pierced to receive a ring.
Jewelry made from silver, which formerly was popular, came to be replaced
by gold jewelry when the value of gold was realized. Facial painting now
was restricted mainly to ceremonial events, but it was used also for protection against mosquitoes and the weather.

The economy continued to be centered on fishing and the sea, but new
skills associated with fishing were beginning to emerge. The halibut hooks
of old were displaced by modern metal hooks. Individuals of both sexes
began to work in canneries, and some men were attracted to jobs in the
gold mines. A few other individuals continued to hunt sea otter until 1911
when the animals clearly were headed for extinction and laws were
introduced to protect them. The skills of the men as woodcarvers and metal-
workers led to the manufacture of craft items for the tourist trade, and
women wove robes and baskets for the same market. Knowing the indepen-

dent nature of the Tlingit, it is understandable that they were not reliable employees. To be ordered about was to be insulted, and as domestic servants or laborers they usually did not satisfy their white employers.

The potlatch system continued to function, and it retained much of the pageantry and drama known in aboriginal times. The predilection for borrowing and imitating the songs, dances, and costumes of foreigners continued. One instance has been recorded of some shipwrecked Japanese arriving at Dry Bay in 1908; in performances by women in 1909 a memorable imitation of Japanese clothing and haircuts was presented. Other changes took place in the form of the potlatch gifts. Blankets from the traders came to be more important gifts than Chilkat robes; silver dollars were a favorite gift item, as was storebought food.

Of all the fascinating subjects connected with the Northwest Coast Indians none has received more attention than totem poles. Their size, complexity, and romantic appeal have long attracted description, comment, and comparison. The poles usually described, however, date only from historic times. The most detailed discussion of Tlingit totem poles has been compiled by Edward L. Keithahn. These monuments are so large and obvious that we would expect even the most casual observer to have made note of them in the earliest historical accounts, that is, if they were present. They are not mentioned by Cook, La Perouse, or Portlock. It was not until John Meares visited the Queen Charlotte Islands in 1788 that "great wooden images" were reported (Keithahn, 1963, 38). In 1791 we have the first good description of a heraldic pole by Etienne Marchand, again for the Queen Charlotte Island people, the Haida. In 1792 there was a description of northern Tlingit mortuary poles at Yakutat by Alexandro Malaspina. When Lisiansky was on the *Neva* at Sitka in 1804, he saw many poles of the mortuary variety. The conclusion drawn by Keithahn is that carved posts in the house interiors and mortuary posts were present among the Tlingit in prehistoric times. Again according to Keithahn, it was not until between 1840 and 1880 that the detached pole standing apart from a house was common along the northwest coast. Even during this era totem poles were not widespread among the Tlingit. Furthermore, Keithahn questions whether the great totem poles could have been carved prior to the general availability of iron-bladed tools. The erection of great totem poles became a means for house groups who became wealthy through the fur trade to record their increased prestige. Some aspiring persons did not have the right to carve the heraldic crests, and so they originated new symbols such as the bull and ship, basing their right to use these forms on the claim that they were the first to see them. When the Krause brothers were among the Tlingit in 1881-1882, it was noted by Aurel that one totem pole was to be found among the Chilkat, none among the Sitka and Killisnoo groups, but that many existed at the Stikine settlement near Wrangell.

Tlingit totem poles were erected to serve diverse purposes. The four main posts inside houses normally were not carved, but they were faced with carved pillars or panels, some of which still stood inside modern Tlingit houses at Klukwan in the early 1960's. The pillar faces were carved with crests of the sib. Often included were abalone shell inlays, and sometimes human hair or ermine fur was attached. A second form was the mortuary pole with a box at the top for the burnt bones and ashes of the dead. In historic times a crest figure was placed on the top of this form, and the ashes were received into a recess at the back of the pole. A later style of mortuary pole had story figures carved on it. A third type was the memorial pole, which most often was raised by a maternal nephew or a younger brother in memory of the former house group leader who had died. These poles were erected within a year of the commemorated person's death and were not habitually raised at the site of interment. Memorial poles not only honored the dead but validated the succession of the new house group leader. Modern forms of memorial and mortuary poles are tombstones made of granite or marble, with crests carved on them by the monument companies. The heraldic type of pole, the fourth form, was erected at the front and center of a house, and an oval opening near the base served as the house entrance. Carved and painted on a pole of this form was a tale associated with the house group. The fifth type, the potlatch pole, is the most recent form of totem pole to develop. These were raised to enhance the prestige of the family group who had accumulated and distributed wealth earned in the fur trade or by working directly for whites. Such poles recorded the holding of an elaborate potlatch. The sixth and final form was the ridicule pole, which usually was raised to force a house group to recognize and compensate for a debt. For example, one ridicule pole is said to have been carved and erected to shame a white trader for not repaying a potlatch that had been given in his honor.

The Tlingit attitude toward totem poles was such that their erection served as an end in itself. A pole was carved and raised for a particular purpose, but it was unimportant as a physical object. As a pole tilted with age or threatened to fall, it was not supported in any manner. Restoration necessitated an outlay of wealth and ceremonial involvements equal to that expended when the original pole was raised. Thus it was more sensible to erect another pole which would bring even greater honor to the house group. Since poles deteriorated rapidly in this damp area and comparatively few new poles were raised after the turn of the present century, most have rotted away. Then too, numerous poles were removed to distant museums and parks. Local parks and national monuments were established beginning in 1890, with the purpose of preserving totem poles. However, a concerted effort to save them was not made until 1938. By 1942 nearly fifty poles had been restored, and about the same number which could not be saved were duplicated. In the early 1970's another effort was launched to once again renovate those poles which had endured. Sophisticated preservation techniques give promise of making the remaining cedar monuments far more lasting than ever before.

The totemic symbols which were exhibited on poles were associated with one or the other of the moieties, with sibs, or with house groups. All of the Raven moiety members employed the Raven design as their primary symbol. The Wolf moiety had the Wolf as its chief totem in the south and the Eagle in the north. Not only the actual crests but the names of animals associated with a sib were important, and their uses were validated through the potlatch system. These honorific names often drawn from the sib or moiety totems tended to pass from great-grandfather to great-grandson. The animals associated with a moiety could be killed and eaten by moiety members, however, and the uniform eating habits of all the tribe indicate no taboo on eating one's totemic species.

No new totem poles appear to have been erected, with the essential accompanying potlatch celebrations, between 1904 and 1971. In the fall of 1971 at the community of Kake a new totem pole was raised, with the proper ritual observances comprising a three-day celebration. In expectable fashion the Tlingit describe this pole as the tallest one ever raised; it is 136 feet in height.

One means of tracing the course of Tlingit acculturation from the turn of the present century to the 1950's is with a discussion of the Alaska Native Brotherhood (A.N.B.). This political institution, studied in detail by Philip Drucker, was founded in 1912 by ten Indian men from southeastern Alaska; nine appear to have been Tlingit and one was a Tsimshian. They shared many characteristics; all were Presbyterian leaders and were committed strongly to the ideal of rapid assimilation into white society. They had personal experience in the structure of Western institutions as reflected in local church organizations. One important and distinctive concept in the formation of the A.N.B. was its nonlocal nature. Chapters, or camps, as they are termed, were organized initially at Sitka, Juneau, and Douglas. By the 1920's chapters had been established in most southeastern

Alaskan Indian villages, and by 1952 there were sixteen active chapters. Within a few years of its organization, a parallel group was formed for women, the Alaska Native Sisterhood, made up mostly of local women's church groups. These organizations held a joint annual convention attended by three delegates of each local chapter in addition to the officers and past presidents of the central organization. Decisions at other times were made by an executive committee composed of past presidents and the Sisterhood president, with the central organization officers as ex officio members.

The initiation fee for membership in the A.N.B. was $10, and the annual dues were $12. Half of this money was retained by the local chapter, and half went to the central organization. Additionally, a yearly assessment of each chapter helped cover the cost of the annual convention. The Sisterhood usually raised most of this money. It often was said that all adults were members of the Brotherhood or Sisterhood, but in fact most were not active. In Ketchikan, there were 85 Indians in 1952 but only fifteen A.N.B. members and twenty-seven in the Sisterhood. At Angoon, during the same year there were twenty-two members of the Brotherhood and fifty-six in the Sisterhood out of a total of 429. In spite of the small village membership, most Indians supported the purposes of the organization, and there was no formal opposition. Each chapter had nine officers and council members; monthly meetings were held, except during the fishing season, to discuss local and general business. Almost every chapter had a building for A.N.B. functions. The one at Hoonah, completed for the 1952 convention, cost nearly $50,000. The better halls had a floor area large enough for a basketball court, a kitchen, restrooms, and a central heating plant. In the halls public meetings and social gatherings were held, and motion pictures were viewed. Thus, much of the social life in a community centered in the Brotherhood structure.

The Brotherhood colors were red for salmon and yellow for gold; these were displayed on ceremonial sashes. The official song was "Onward, Christian Soldiers." The primary goal of the organization was stated clearly in the first article of the constitution: "The purpose of this organization shall be to assist and encourage the Native in his advancement from his native state to his place among the cultivated races of the world, to oppose, discourage, and overcome the narrow injustice of race prejudice, and to aid in the development of the Territory of Alaska, and in making it worthy of a place among the States of North America" (Drucker, 1958, 165). The aim of the Brotherhood clearly was the rapid assimilation of the Tlingit into white society in southeastern Alaska. The Indian's ties with the past had to be broken, and this was attempted in two different ways. First, speaking English was considered to be very important; in fact, eligibility for membership was restricted in Article II to "English speaking members of the Native residents of the Territory of Alaska," and the constitution was printed in English. A second target was to destroy the potlatch system which represented the aboriginal past in the minds of both the missionaries and the Indians.

Brotherhood policy concentrated on gaining citizenship rights for Indians equal to those of whites. The matter of Tlingit citizenship was complicated by the fact that the Russians made no formal recognition of their legal status. In the Russo-American treaty of sale it was stated that the uncivilized tribes, which included most Tlingit and other aboriginal Alaskans, were to be subject to such laws as the United States might pass. With the purchase there was no attempt to negotiate treaties nor to establish Indian reservations, and therefore the citizenship status of aboriginal Alaskans remained unclear. They were not "wards of the government" in the sense of reservation or treaty Indians. They came to consider themselves as citizens, but the whites in Alaska usually regarded them in the same light as Indians in the United States. Until they were declared citizens, the Tlingit could not file on mining claims, and this was a cause of resentment. Indians in Alaska could, under the terms of the General Allotment Act of 1887 or a Territorial Act of 1915, become citizens by demonstrating that they were following a civilized way of life, but few individuals sought to become citizens under these laws. The issue of citizenship was forced in 1922 by a Tlingit lawyer, William Paul. His was the most powerful voice in the A.N.B, and as Drucker (1958, 39) states, "he made a career of the Brotherhood movement." The case in question involved a Tlingit who had voted previously, but whose vote in the 1922 primaries was challenged. Through court action, during which Paul defended him, he was cleared of illegal voting. As a result, Indian voting rights were accepted, even before the Federal Citizenship Act of 1924 gave all Indians the rights of other citizens.

Through the years the A.N.B actively sought to further its ends by diverse forms of institutional action. One campaign was to have Indian children accepted in Territorial schools. Until 1931 the Federal Bureau of Education maintained schools in Indian villages, but in some communities there was both a Bureau of Education school and a Territorial school, with the Indian children attending the former and white children going to the latter. In a 1929 case in which Paul defended the Indian father against the school board, the right of Indian children to attend Territorial schools was established by court action. The Brotherhood moved into the field of organized labor by supporting fishermen's unions. Apparently the local unions were formed, amalgamated, and separated again. Then in 1939 the A.N.B.

became a bargaining agent for the combined unions under the Wagner Act. Soon this group affiliated with the American Federation of Labor as the Alaska Marine Workers' Union. The Brotherhood kept its bargaining power in the A.F.L. merger and thus retained the key function of negotiating wage scales for cannery workers and fish prices for fishermen. In order to be a bargaining agent, the Brotherhood was forced to open its ranks to non-Indians and did so by creating the category of "associate member." One of the recurrent problems dealt with by the Brotherhood was the matter of reservations. The general feeling against the creation of reservations seems to have stemmed from reservation Indian influences on Tlingit children at the Chemawa and Carlisle Indian schools. It was not until the Indian Reorganization Act of 1934, applied to Alaska in 1936, that the matter became a major issue, for it then appeared that the Tlingit would have to request reservations before they could come under the provisions of the Indian Reorganization Act. Over the years some of the more conservative communities favored the formation of reservations in order to secure their landholdings and bring more security. In 1946 the Brotherhood convention took the stand that local communities could form their own policies toward reservations and would have the support of the central organization. The issue of Indian land rights and the fact that land had been taken by whites without compensation led the Tlingit and Alaskan Haida to attempt to obtain compensation through the Court of Claims following the Tlingit and Haida Jurisdictional Claims Act of 1935. The Indians involved sued for $80 million, and the Court of Claims decided that they were entitled to $7.5 million as compensation for lands withdrawn for a national forest, a national monument, and a reservation for Tsimshian Indians from Canada, who settled on Annette Island. Of the 7.4 million acres of public domain in southeastern Alaska during the late 1960's, the Tlingit and Alaskan Haida claimed 2.6 million acres as a result of a Court of Claims decision.

The Brotherhood was active also in fighting discrimination against Indians. The matter came to a climax about 1929 when the Indians openly objected to "For Natives Only" signs in the balconies of motion-picture houses. A boycott organized by the A.N.B. was effective in having theaters desegregated, but it was not until 1946 that an antidiscrimination law was passed by the Territorial Legislature. It is worthy of note that during World War II, the Indians, Aleuts, and Eskimos were organized into Alaska Territorial Guard units composed entirely of natives, but this was not viewed by the people as discriminatory. Finally, in recent years the Brotherhood has attempted to expand its activities into other sectors of Alaska among Athapaskans and Eskimos. Only since about 1962 has the expansion program been implemented seriously. Formation of the Alaska Federation of

Natives in 1966 was an effort to further causes supported by Alaskan Eskimos, Indians, and Aleuts.

In spite of the fact that one of the primary aims of the Brotherhood was to do away with aboriginal customs, their efforts have been only partly successful. The principal target for attack, the potlatch, was regarded as heathen and most deplored; however, as Drucker points out, it actually was primarily social, not religious, in its nature. Certain potlatch customs became incorporated into the Brotherhood structure, such as addressing persons of the opposite moiety in a ceremonial fashion; fining individuals for infractions; making gifts to the organization; and gift giving by the family of a deceased person for burial services provided by the opposite moiety through the Brotherhood. In one sense the A.N.B. served as a new institution through which the moieties reciprocated. Furthermore, although the ideal of speaking English continued, the business meetings of local chapters were sometimes conducted in Tlingit, particularly since the most active members normally were older and were not likely to speak English with ease.

From the ethnographic and historical researches of de Laguna at Angoon, it is possible to note further details of the changing Tlingit sociocultural system. References to the village of Angoon are numerous in 1882 because of a particular chain of events which occurred there. Prior to that date, an 1875 report gives the impression that Angoon was a neat and orderly settlement and mentions that the Indians raised a fine crop of potatoes. In 1882 Angoon nearly was destroyed by a force under the command of a U.S. Navy officer. This event more than any other became a focal point of local Tlingit resentment and hostility against whites. The problem began when a Tlingit employee of the Northwest Trading Company was killed accidentally by the explosion of a whaling bomb. The Indians demanded compensation, but the company refused. The Tlingit seized the two white men who were with them at the time of the accident, along with the boat and other company property. They threatened to kill the whites and destroy the company store because their compensation was denied. The Revenue Cutter *Corwin*, which was at Sitka at the time, went to Angoon to assist the American party. The commander, E.C. Merriman, demanded that the Indians compensate the Americans for the trouble they had caused or else the town would be shelled and their canoes destroyed. When the Indians did not comply and, according to one American account, after it was learned that there were no women or children in the village, the community was bombarded. Many houses and canoes were destroyed, although some houses purposely were spared. Finally, the shelled houses were burned. The white men and the Northwest Trading Company property were recovered. According to one modern Tlingit version of the attack, the Indians had stopped whaling to conduct services for the dead man and did not know why the village was shelled and burned. Furthermore, six children who were in the houses at the time suffocated from the smoke. An analysis of Tlingit and white versions of the event indicates that the stories of neither side are entirely logical and consistent. What is clear, however, is that the Indians did not understand the action of the whites and the whites made no attempt to adjust to the customs of the Indians in this particular instance.

In 1917 the Angoon sib leaders organized as a town with a council under a Territorial law. The government originally seems to have had difficulty in functioning effectively because of rivalries among sib leaders. Furthermore, younger members of the organization, who understood democratic procedures better than their elders, favored more rapid change. A community hall was constructed in 1917 when the town council was founded, and in 1921 local chapters of the Brotherhood and Sisterhood were organized. In 1929 the annual convention was held at Angoon, and the building was improved for the occasion; after that time it was termed the A.N.B. Hall. In 1939 the town organized itself under the terms of the Indian Reorganization Act as the Angoon Community Association. Then in 1948 the council, consisting of seven elected members, established the Angoon Native Village Court, which had jurisdiction over community members. The administration was maintained by a chief judge, three assistants, and a village police force of four men. The court had the authority to try civil cases involving claims up to $200 and cases involving assault, disorderly conduct, adultery, and other crimes of this nature.

In 1918 a Presbyterian church was started at Angoon and was completed the following year. Prior to this time Presbyterian services were held in the house of one particular sib leader who was important in the local organization of this church. A Russian Orthodox Greek Catholic church was constructed in 1928-1929, and although the Presbyterians had a local minister, the Orthodox church did not have a resident priest. At an unrecorded date the Salvation Army built a hall at Angoon, and a local Tlingit leader directed its activities. Membership in the various religious groups in 1950 was one hundred Orthodox, eighty Salvation Army, and seventy Presbyterians who cooperated. Some of the older villagers were educated at the Orthodox or Presbyterian schools at Sitka. A Federal school was not built at Angoon until about 1920; in 1950 some one hundred children attended. Others continued their education at the Bureau of Indian Affairs high school at Mt. Edgecumbe, and two were attending college.

In spite of initial opposition to the Indian Reorganization Act, owing to misunderstandings about its purpose, some provisions of the act benefited the community. The people who were purchasing fishing vessels, which in 1950 cost between $15,000 and $22,000, could finance the boats through the community, which provided more liberal terms than had the fish canneries, the previous mortgage holders. Of more importance was the community purchase in 1947 of the salmon cannery operating at nearby Hood Bay; the cannery first was operated by the community in 1949. The council hired a white manager who in turn hired the remainder of the workers. Most of the men worked as fishermen, and women processed and packed fish in the production line. Union wage scales were paid all the workers, and an additional labor force of Filipinos was hired for the operation. In 1950 the community-owned cannery was on its way to becoming a very successful venture, but by the mid-1960's the project was deeply in debt.

In a brief but revealing study of Hoonah in 1961 the anthropologist Seymour Parker recorded a continuing emphasis on rank in this modern settlement. "High class people" were persons prominent as fishing boat captains or as businessmen. The former also were likely to have prominent positions in their matrisibs. Individuals in this general category were expected to finance potlatches and aid the community in funding various projects. The "common" or "average" people usually were members of fishing boat crews, and while they accepted Federal or state relief they did so with feelings of shame. The lower class was described as "living from day to day." They felt little reluctance in accepting relief funds and had the reputation for heavy drinking of intoxicants. One of the major points made by Parker was the strong sense of individualism which pervaded the value system of the modern Tlingit. Familial, sib, and community ties certainly existed and were on occasion important, but the individual achieved largely on the basis of his own abilities. Previously a man was largely bound to the destiny of his matrilineage, although wealth and prestige were desired by all. With a disintegration of the old sib and moiety system but a continuing emphasis on material wealth and prestige, the modern Tlingit has a strong incentive to compete with other persons in southeastern Alaska.

References

Bancroft, Hubert H. *History of Alaska, 1730-1885. The Works of Hubert Howe Bancroft*, v. 33. San Francisco. 1886.

Boas, Franz. *Primitive Art*. Dover (republication). 1955.

Drucker, Philip. *Culture Element Distributions: XXVI. Northwest Coast*. Anthropological Records, v. 9, no. 3. 1950.

*Drucker, Philip. *The Native Brotherhoods*. Bureau of American Ethnology, Bulletin 168. Washington, D. C. 1958. The Alaska Native Brotherhood, which has been a Tlingit-dominated organization since its founding in 1912, is the subject matter for half of this study. The second half of the volume is devoted to a similar organization in British Columbia. Drucker's largely historical study is a highly significant contribution since it is devoted to one of the organized efforts by the Tlingit to promote assimilation into white Alaskan society.

Drucker, Philip. "Sources of Northwest Coast Culture," in *New Interpretations of Aboriginal American Culture History*. Clifford Evans and Betty Meggers, eds., 59-81. Anthropological Society of Washington, D. C. 1955.

Federal Field Committee for Development Planning in Alaska. *Alaska Natives & the Land*. Washington, D. C. 1968.

Fraser, Douglas. *Primitive Art*. Garden City. 1962.

"From Ketchikan to Barrow." *Alaska*, December, 1971.

Goldschmidt, Walter R. and Theodore H. Haas. *Possessory Rights of the Natives of Southeastern Alaska*. A Report to the Commissioner of Indian Affairs (mimeographed). 1946.

Jackson, Sheldon. *Alaska*. New York. 1880.

Jones, Livingston F. *A Study of the Thlingets of Alaska*. New York. 1914.

Kashavaroff, Andrew P. "How the White Men Came to Lituya and what Happened to Yeahlth-kan who Visited Them," *Alaska Magazine*, v. 1, 151-153. 1927.

*Keithahn, Edward L. *Monuments in Cedar*. Seattle. 1963 (revised edition). This study is particularly useful in any attempt to trace the origins, antiquity, and development of various forms of totem poles.

*Krause, Aurel. *The Tlingit Indians*. 2 v. Jena, 1885; translated edition, Erna Gunther, tr., American Ethnological Society. 1956. The 1881-1882 field study by Aurel and Arthur Krause, written by the former, is the standard Tlingit source. The breadth and balance of the study make it the first to be consulted in any serious study of the Tlingit.

de Laguna, Frederica. "Some Dynamic Forces in Tlingit Society," *Southwestern Journal of Anthropology*, v. 8, 1-12. 1952.

*de Laguna, Frederica. *The Story of a Tlingit Community*. Bureau of American Ethnology, Bulletin 172. Washington, D. C. 1960. Based on archaeological and ethnographic fieldwork in 1949 and 1950, this report concentrates on the Angoon area and its people. The archaeological data are supplemented by historical records and ethnographic field information.

McClellan, Catharine. "The Interrelations of Social Structure with Northern Tlingit Ceremonialism," *Southwestern Journal of Anthropology*, v. 10, 75-96. 1954.

Niblack, Albert P. "The Coast Indians of Southern Alaska and Northern British Columbia," *Annual Report of the Smithsonian Institution, 1887-88*, 225-386. Washington, D. C. 1890.

*Oberg, Kalervo. The Social Economy of the Tlingit Indians. Ph.D. dissertation, Department of Anthropology, University of Chicago. 1937. This unpublished study based on fieldwork in 1931-1932 and conducted primarily at Klukwan stands next to the work by Krause in its merit. Oberg's discussions of the social system and economy are outstanding for their clarity and breadth; it is little short of amazing that this work has never been published.

Parker, Seymour. See Ray, Charles K., et al.

Porter, Robert P. *Report on Population and Resources of Alaska at the Eleventh Census: 1890*. Washington, D. C. 1893.

*Ray, Charles K., et al. *Alaskan Native Secondary School Dropouts*. University of Alaska. 1962. The report in this volume by Seymour Parker on the Tlingit at Hoonah is brief but very good. Parker spent only about a month at Hoonah in 1961, and his emphasis was on values, but considerable additional information is included which is the most up-to-date information in print.

Romanowsky, S., and Frankenhauser. "Five Years of Medical Observations in the Colonies of the Russian-American Company," *Medical Newspaper of Russia*, v. 6, 153-161. St. Petersburg. 1849 (translated from German and reprinted in *Alaska Medicine*, v. 4, 33-37; 62-64. 1962).

*Swanton, John R. "Social Condition, Beliefs, and Linguistic Relationship of the Tlingit Indians," *Bureau of American Ethnology, Twenty-sixth Annual Report*, 391-512. Washington, D. C. 1908. This study based on fieldwork in 1904 at Sitka and Wrangell is not a balanced ethnography, nor does it purport to be, but it does serve as a good supplement to the works of Krause and Oberg.

Wardwell, Allen, compiler. *Yakutat South*. Chicago. 1964.

Willard, (Mrs.) Eugene S. *Life in Alaska*. Philadelphia. 1884.

Young, Samuel H. *Hall Young of Alaska*. Chicago and New York. 1927.

Map by J. Donovan

The Hopi:
farmers of the desert

When Americans think of Indians, their first images are likely to be of Plains warriors with tepees, horses, and eagle feather warbonnets. If they pause and consider again, they are likely to visualize a desert pueblo, fields of maize, painted pottery vessels, and strange katcina dolls. The Hopi of northeastern Arizona represent one such pueblo people, and in many respects they, along with other pueblo dwellers, typify North American Indians better than do the warriors of the plains and prairies. The way of life of equestrian warriors existed for only a brief period in history; it faded away quickly although the glories linger in the memories of a declining number of participants, in verbal traditions, and written records. For the pueblo lifeway the situation is quite different. These desert people continue to live in the same setting as did their ancestors; they still plant maize, produce pottery, and make katcina dolls. Their cultures do not survive in all of their past vitality, but they do exhibit a traditionalism strengthened in part from centuries of outside pressures bent on their destruction. It is striking, for example, that in the 1950's less than 2 percent of the Hopi were practicing Christians. The resiliency of these people and their tenacity in retaining their old ways possibly are unparalleled among other American Indians.

The Hopi have been singled out for discussion because of the vitality of their traditions and because the information about them is of superior quality. They, more than any other pueblo group, display an appealing continuity with the past. Their ancestors settled in northern Arizona at least a thousand years ago, and the Hopi community of Oraibi is one of the oldest, if not the oldest, continuously occupied settlements north of Mexico. Nowhere else are Indians so directly and intimately associated with one locality. Nowhere else among Indians do the past and present blend into a singularly integrated whole. Another reason to write about the Hopi is the wealth of literature describing their way of life. They long have attracted the attention of ethnographers so that studies of the Hopi are diverse and detailed. In the author's opinion the best American Indian ethnography is a monograph about the Hopi; the study by Mischa Titiev titled *Old Oraibi* is monumental. Titiev collected a wealth of facts about these people between 1932 and 1940, and he presented the material in a lucid style with great analytical sophistication. The information on Hopi social and religious life in the present chapter is based primarily on Titiev's study. He offers so much that it is unnecessary to seek other sources except to amplify certain details and to add information on topics which he did not include. The amount of published information about the Hopi is almost staggering. In George P. Murdock's monograph *Ethnographic Bibliography*

398

of North America (1960), there are 381 Hopi entries, representing an impressive amount of material. It compares in volume with the total information available on the Navajo, Iroquois, and Ojibwa.

The word *hopi* is an aboriginal term applied by the people to themselves. Hopi means good, or peaceful, the ideal for all individuals in this society. In linguistic terms the Hopi language is of the Aztec-Tanoan phylum and the Uto-Aztecan family. Their aboriginal population was approximately 2800. After dropping to 2000 in 1907, it has now reached about 5000. Their homeland in northeastern Arizona is part of the Navahonian biotic province. The environment is one of plateaus and, at lower elevations, deserts. This is an area of sporadic and unpredictable rainfall where horticulturalists seemingly could not survive. The only reason the Hopi and their ancestors have been able to farm this area is that rainwater from the upland sandstone region seeps southward above a layer of shale to emerge at the ends of the mesas as seepages and springs. On the higher elevations of the mesas, juniper and scattered pinyon grow. This flora is replaced by grassland nearer the valley floors, and in the lower sections desert vegetation including saltbrush, greasewood, and sagebrush dominate. In damp localities or along irregularly flowing streams cottonwoods and willows grow.

In the Southwest around the time of Christ there lived an Indian population termed Basketmaker. Their remains are known best from findings in dry caves and rock shelters, and along open rock faces, particularly in the San Juan River drainage; burials and living sites alike have been excavated. The houses were round in outline, with walls constructed of horizontally arranged poles and sticks caulked with mud; the roofs probably were cribbed. Inside these substantial structures were food storage pits, "heating pits," and food grinding equipment, manos and metates. Elsewhere in rock shelters were storage pits and human burials accompanied by a variety of grave goods. On the adjacent flood plains of constantly or intermittently flowing streams maize and squash were cultivated with flat-bladed or pointed wooden digging sticks. The people hunted large game such as deer and mountain sheep with a spear and a throwing-board, called an atlatl in the Southwest. A variety of nets and snares were used to take small game. The only domestic animal was the dog, and two different types were found. One was most similar to a short-haired terrier, and the other resembled a collie. The manufactured goods of these people included a wide variety of baskets, usually made by the coiling technique and often decorated with designs in red and black. The people used deep, cone-shaped baskets which were carried with a tumpline. Pottery was just being introduced and was made with organic temper and dried in the sun. The idea of making pottery most likely came from the south. The most important clothing was a blanket woven of rabbit skin strips with the fur left intact and sandals made from woven yucca fiber. The people appreciated ornaments, and necklaces or pendants of stone, seeds, and bone often were found. The Basketmaker burials recovered are from cave sites, usually from pits which had been employed earlier as storage basins. Multiple burials were the rule, but usually without any sign of violent death. The bodies were flexed and wrapped in rabbit-skin blankets. A large basket often was placed over the head of the deceased, and a wide variety of grave goods was included. Frequently cone-shaped pipes were found, along with ornaments, clothing, and weapons.

Around A.D. 500 the Basketmaker culture developed changes of sufficient magnitude to differentiate a new culture, an outgrowth of the earlier period. The people have been termed Modified-Basketmakers. They occupied village communities, and their earliest houses were round. Somewhat later an oval variety was built, and finally by A.D. 700, at the end of this era, the houses were rectangular. Houses were built in pits and sometimes had attached anterooms and entrance passages. Later, the passages became ventilating shafts, and the dwellings were entered through the roof. The roofs of these structures were cone-shaped originally and later were flat; they were supported by posts and crossbeams. The vertical sidewall poles were covered with horizontal poles. On the hard clay floor of such a dwelling was a fire pit; there was also a hole in the floor which probably was a *sipapu*, known in modern pueblo ceremonial structures. With new forms of maize as well as beans added to the diet, manos and metates continued to be used. The weaponry now included the bow and arrow; new tools included grooved mauls and axes. Pottery was manufactured by the coiling process and scraped smooth before it hardened. It was fired by a method which prohibited air from circulating freely about the vessels (reducing atmosphere), producing finished vessels of white or gray color. The earliest fired vessels were decorated with black designs, often modeled after those on baskets. Another category of clay objects was that of stylized female figurines, usually with only the head and trunk represented. In spite of the increasing importance of pottery, baskets continued to be manufactured and frequently were decorated with red and black motifs.

In the same general area between A.D. 700 and 1400 an Indian culture called Pueblo emerged. Three periods, Developmental, Great, and Regressive Pueblo, have been distinguished. Growing out of a Basketmaker background, with new ideas from within and from afar, the Pueblo periods represent a major climax in American Indian cultural developments. The early Pueblo peoples artificially flattened the backs of infants' skulls against cradleboards to produce a new head shape. The garb of the people began to change with the introduction of cotton as a domestic plant. The women may have worn cotton blankets; the men possibly wore kilts as well as breechclouts, and there were new sandal styles. The living unit of the Developmental Pueblo people exhibited direct continuity with the past. The houses evolved gradually into aboveground masonry structures with contiguous units. In the pit house tradition were the round, subterranean ceremonial structures or kivas. The interior arrangements of the kivas included walls of coarse stone with an encircling bench, a fireplace, and a sipapu. The roofs were cribbed, with an opening for an entrance. The economy remained as before, with cotton the only new crop. The only new animal was the domestic turkey, most likely raised for its feathers rather than its meat. In the horticultural system was a new tool, a hoe of flaked stone, which was most often unhafted. Pottery was manufactured with greater skill; the paste was fine, and a thin slip of clay was often placed on a vessel before it was fired. Designs were made with mineral or vegetable pigments, and two-color combinations, black-on-white and red-on-orange, were most prevalent. The designs utilized a wider range of motifs, but still they were most often conceived in geometric patterns.

Southwestern Indian culture came to a climax during the Great Pueblo period, which began around 1050. This was the era of great stonemasonry, with hundreds of residence and storage units in a single multistory pueblo. Mesa Verde was occupied at this time as was Chaco Canyon. The productivity of the cultivated flood plains was great, and irrigated acreage was added. With dependable food surpluses some individuals were freed from tilling the soil, and craft specialization developed. The potters became artists producing individualistic painted vessels, and leisure time fostered an elaboration of the religious system. Quite suddenly, by 1300, there was a virtual abandonment of the area. The exodus probably was related at least indirectly to an extended drought between 1276 and 1299. Arroyo cutting left the flood plains dry and irrigation ditches waterless. It is possible, too, that the nomadic Navajo and Apache raided these settled peoples and contributed to their downfall. The surviving population was to continue its way of life but only in a few pueblos.

The Hopi mesas were one locality in which the Regressive Pueblo period survived in the midst of what must have been drastic population displacements. Here rows of masonry houses were constructed around plazas, and there were small rectangular kivas in which ceremonial activities focused. The striking cultural achievement was in pottery, with the bichrome and polychrome vessels considered among the most pleasing Indian pottery made in North America. The ware was usually black-on-yellow or else red-

and-black-on-yellow. Not only were fine-lined geometric designs executed, but representations from life also appeared. This era ended about 1700, after the first Spanish contacts.

The last year of Hopi prehistory was in 1539; in mid-July of the following year the first Spanish explorers arrived. A small group under Pedro de Tovar traveled from the pueblo of Zuni where Francisco Coronado, the expedition leader, rested. When de Tovar arrived at one of the eastern Hopi settlements, he was met with hostility; he attacked the village and defeated the Indians. De Tovar then peacefully visited the six other Hopi communities, and later a party of the same expedition passed through Hopi country to the Grand Canyon without meeting any resistance. The Spanish search for gold led to the arrival of the next explorers. In the spring of 1583 Antonio de Espejo entered the country. The contacts between the Spanish and the Indians were peaceful; in fact, the five Hopi settlements existing at this time openly welcomed the Spanish. More lasting contact was made by Juan de Onate in 1598 when the Hopi peacefully submitted to the authority of the Spanish king. The Spanish hoped to make these people Christians, but Franciscan missionaries did not settle among them until 1629. Churches soon were completed at three different settlements, and two more missionaries joined the first three. The Franciscans reported they were making great progress, but the poisoning of one of the priests in 1633 suggests that all of the Hopi were not contented charges. The vigorous Franciscan efforts to destroy the old Hopi religion led to cruel punishments for backsliding Indians. In 1655 one of the missionaries caught a man performing an "act of idolatry." The man was beaten severely in public and again beaten inside the church; turpentine was applied to his body and ignited, and he died. The missionary was relieved of his post, but no punitive action was taken against him. In 1650 the Hopi refused to join the other pueblo peoples in a revolt against the Spanish, but they supported fully the Pueblo Revolt of 1680. Their major contribution was to kill the four missionaries stationed among them. Indirectly, too, they aided the insurrection by permitting Indian refugees from the Rio Grande pueblos to live among them when the Spanish struck back; two communities were constructed for these friendly allies. The Hopi did not feel secure in their locality although Santa Fe and the Spanish were far away. They feared Spanish reprisals, and therefore three villages were relocated on mesa tops where they could be defended more easily than in the valley bottoms. The Spanish returned in 1692, and when the Indians willingly swore to support the Spanish king peace again was established. By 1699 the Spanish were in firm control of the Rio Grande pueblos, and this led one Hopi faction to request missionaries from the authorities at Santa Fe. A missionary visited, but after he left, the community was summarily destroyed by the anti-Spanish faction among the Hopi. The men who offered resistance were killed; their wives and children were scattered among the remaining settlements. The pagan Hopi under the leadership of a man from Oraibi went to Santa Fe and told the Spanish governor that the Hopi would make peace if they were permitted to continue their old religion. This, however was unacceptable to the Spanish. In retaliation for the murder of Christian Hopi the Spanish in 1701 attempted to defeat the Hopi in battle, but the smallness of the Spanish force and the adequate defensive positions of the Hopi led the attackers to withdraw. Another attempt to control the Hopi by force occurred in 1706, but it, too, ended in failure. The Hopi retained their freedom not so much by their military skill and determination as by the distance which separated them from Santa Fe and the difficulties the Spanish were having with other Indians. The next major event in Hopi-Spanish contacts was a religious jurisdictional dispute. Both the Jesuits and the Franciscans sought to have the Hopi under their control. The Jesuits won temporary control, which led to a vigorous effort by the Franciscans. The Franciscans did not succeed, however, and neither did the Jesuits permanently. Throughout the 1740's and early 1750's the Hopi thwarted all Spanish efforts to bring them within effective control.

Beginning in 1755 the course of Hopi history was to gravitate more and more toward acceptance of the Spanish. The arid environment in which the Hopi lived led to a major change in Hopi life when a sequence of dry years exhausted their reserve of food. By 1779 many of these Indians had abandoned their homeland and moved among the Zuni in an effort to survive. The next year most Hopi were so scattered that the local population was reduced to about 800 persons. In the midst of this struggle to survive came the smallpox epidemic in 1781. In this same year, however, rain was plentiful and the bountiful crops made it possible for the population to reconsolidate. Pressures by the marauding Navajos forced the Hopi to go to the Spanish in 1818 and request aid, but the Spanish, who were faced with their own survival problems, were by then unable to help. The most striking characteristic of Hopi historical contacts with the Spanish was the ability of these Indians to withstand Spanish pressures toward acculturation, particularly in the religious sphere. It is evident that Hopi resistance toward the Spanish was not consistent, but the pro-Spanish faction seems to have been of minor importance.

The next major problem faced by the Hopi was how to interpret the arrival of another group of non-Indians who began to enter their country as early as 1826. Were these the legendary Bahana who were to come from the east and aid the Hopi? It was thought that the Anglo-Americans might well be the Bahana since their men were successfully preventing the encroaching Navajo from seizing Hopi land.

In primeval times, according to a myth recorded at Oraibi, there was no light or living thing on earth, only a being called Death. Three caves beneath the earth's surface likewise were engulfed in darkness. In the lowest cave people existed in crowded and filthy conditions. Two brothers, The Two, lamented the plight of men and pierced the cave roof; they grew one plant after another trying to reach the second world. A particular type of cane grew tall enough, and the many people and animals reached the second cave world. This setting finally was filled with people, and they ascended to the third cave. Some climbers fell back into the second world, as had also happened in the ascent from the first cave. In the third cave the darkness was dispelled by fire found by the brothers. The people built houses and kivas and traveled from one place to another. Great turmoil developed here when women neglected their duties as wives and mothers, preferring instead to dance in the kivas. Finally the people, along with Coyote, Locust, Spider, Swallow, and Vulture, emerged at the fourth level, which was the earth. They wandered about in the darkness with only torches to light their way. Together the men and the creatures with them attempted to create light. Spider successfully spun a blanket of white cotton which gave off some light. The people then processed a white deerskin which they painted with turquoise paint. This skin was so bright that it lighted the entire world. The painted deerskin became the sun, and the blanket was the moon. The stars were released from a jar by Coyote.

Once the earth was lighted it was realized that the land area was limited by surrounding water. The Vulture fanned the water with its wings, and as the waters flowed away mountains appeared. The Two made channels for the waters through the mountains, and canyons and valleys were formed. The people saw the tracks of Death, Masau'u, and followed them to the east. They caught up with Masau'u, and a girl conspired with him to cause the death of a girl she envied; this was the first death among men. The conspirator was the first witch, and her descendants became the witches of the world. The dead girl was seen living in the cave world below the earth, which had become an idyllic place. Another deity helped the people by making their maize and other seeds ripen in a single day. The witch caused conflicts with people who had emerged on earth before the Hopi, particularly the Navajo and Mexicans. Of the two brothers who led the people from the underworld, the younger brother was the ancestor of the Oraibi people. The older brother went east but promised to return when the Hopi needed him. After many generations and in accordance with this promise the older brother's descendants, the Bahana, were to return when the Hopi were poor and in need. The Bahana would be rich and would bring food and clothing for the Hopi. The Hopi would reject the Bahana, but the latter would treat them kindly.

Men wore bangs over their foreheads, and the remainder of their hair was gathered in a knot behind the neck or else cut off evenly at the nape of the neck. A headband of fur or fiber held their hair in place. Everyday male clothing included a breechclout of deerskin or cotton cloth over which was worn a cotton cloth kilt, belted at the waist. A man also might wear leggings of deerskin as well as moccasins or sandals woven from yucca fiber. In cold weather a cotton shirt was worn, and perhaps a woven rabbit-skin blanket was added. A girl wore her hair long until she passed through the Girls' Adolescent Ceremony; then it was put into two disk-shaped bundles, one over each ear. After she married, her hair was parted in the middle and worn long again. A woman's clothing consisted of a wraparound cotton blanket which passed under her left arm and was fastened together over the right shoulder. This garment extended a short distance below her knees, and she wore leggings as well as moccasins.

At the southern end of Black Mesa, there are three tongues of land. The westernmost section is Third Mesa, and Oraibi is located at the end of it. The pueblo is laid out in a series of eight roughly parallel streets, with a plaza between two streets and kivas scattered about the settlement. In aboriginal times the square houses were made from stones dressed and set in place by men. The roof beams were placed above the uppermost course of stones, and the women for whom a house was built prepared and applied a mud plaster to the inner wall surfaces. A woman and her friends completed the roofing by adding brushwood, grass, and finally mud. A house was windowless, and no doors opened onto the street. The dwellings were owned by women, and a new house usually was constructed next to or near the residence of the woman's mother or another close female relative. The residences often were multistory, and access was through an opening in the roof or the ceiling, beneath which was placed a notched log ladder. The rooms were square, extending about twelve feet along each wall, and floored with stone. Along one side of a room were bin metates of different degrees of coarseness for grinding maize. There were fireplaces in such dwellings but few other furnishings. The rooms without an outside opening often were used for storing feed and material goods. A kiva or ceremonial structure was a rectangular subterranean room with entry gained by descending a ladder from an opening in the roof. The portion of the floor where observers sat was slightly raised, and the remaining portion included a fire pit and sipapu. Along most walls were stone compartments which contained sacred objects. At Oraibi there were about fifteen kivas, and each was owned by a female descent group (sib).

Oraibi land was in theory owned by the Bear sib, and its male head was the Village Chief. He allotted farm land to particular female descent groups (matrisibs), and surplus land could be allotted to any conscientious individual. The result was that no sib was landless although some plots were far more desirable than others. One of the major causes for disputes between sibs was landholdings. In many respects it is remarkable that the Hopi were able to till the soil successfully. The winds, the cold summer nights, the early frosts, baking sun, and very sporadic rainfall all led to an unpredictable harvest.

Their most elaborate manufactures were textiles, usually woven by men. Hopi men prepared their domestic cotton by carding and spinning it into thread, and they wove textiles on looms located either in their homes or in a kiva. The fiber often was colored with vegetable dyes, which turned the cotton yellow, orange, green, black, or various shades of red. Two loom forms were utilized for different purposes. A vertical loom was suspended between the ceiling and the floor for making square and rectangular cloth for blankets. The waist loom was attached to a beam at one end and to the weaver's waist at the other, being held taut by his body. It was used for the manufacture of belts. The only weaving by women was the production of rabbit-skin blankets. These were made on vertical looms. The warp was probably cotton thread spirally wrapped with rabbit-skin strips, with the fur still on; the weft was probably cotton thread. The most important textiles woven by the men for women included wedding robes, belts, dresses, and shawls. For themselves men wove kilts and sashes for ceremonies, as well as kilts, shirts, and blankets for daily use.

Hopi women made both pottery and basketry. The pottery either was undecorated ware for cooking and storage or polished and decorated for other uses. There were sources of gray or yellow clay near all the villages, and it was collected by the women. The dry clay first was soaked and then kneaded into a paste. For cooking and storage vessels quantities of ground sandstone were added to the paste, but little or none was mixed into the paste of other wares. The bottom of a vessel was molded from a single piece of clay, and then coils of moist clay were added spirally to the base. Each coil was pinched to join with the preceding piece, and the junctures of the coils were obliterated by smoothing them with the hand. The complete containers were dried, and any cracked vessels were discarded. Utility ware then was fired without further processing. The vessels were preheated around a fire made from cedar bark and then fired. If a vessel was to be decorated, a piece of sandstone was used to smooth and thin the walls after it was dry. The vessel was moistened and polished with a stone, later to be slipped and painted. The process of slipping involved mixing clay with water to a creamy consistency and applying it to the vessel with a rabbit tail. The mineral pigments were mixed with a vegetable product binder and applied with yucca fiber brushes. Vessels were colored black, yellow, red, white, and shades of orange, and the designs prevalent around the time of early historic contact are essentially the same as those in modern times. This is not an example of long-term stability in the design styles but a revival of old designs. In 1895, Jesse W. Fewkes excavated an abandoned Hopi pueblo at First Mesa. One of his Indian workmen was a man from Hano, a settlement of Rio Grande Indians who arrived to live among the Hopi around 1700. The wife of the man was Nampeyo, widely recognized as one of the best Pueblo potters. Her interest was attracted to the beautifully executed, painted pottery found at the site, and she studied the sherds in order to become familiar with the patterning. Later she developed a style derived from the original but not an exact copy of it and became renowned for the vessels she produced.

Rather surprisingly, the technique of manufacturing basketry varied greatly from one mesa to another. Second Mesa women manufactured coiled baskets, and those of Third Mesa wove wicker baskets. The basketry usually was shaped into shallow trays, and vegetable dyes of greens, yellows, blue, purple, and black were used to produce geometric designs.

Katcina "dolls" form one category of Hopi manufactures which has attracted wide attention among whites. These small painted and adorned wooden images usually were made by men prior to katcina performances. The figures were presented to children by katcinas and were considered by them as gifts from the gods. These katcina images were hung from the rafters of the homes to familiarize the children with the many different forms. Katcina figures frequently are called dolls, but this is a misnomer. They were not played with as dolls but served mainly to instruct uninitiated children about one aspect of the religious system. Harold S. Colton's comprehensive study of Hopi katcina figures noted that there were over 240 different forms. These cluster in six groups: chief katcinas, who were the leaders among katcinas; clowns; runner katcinas; katcinas that appeared in a wide variety of forms at the Powamu Ceremony; those appearing during the one-day katcina performances; and katcina-manas or female katcinas. The images were carved from cottonwood tree roots. A figure was shaped and then was smoothed with a section of sandstone, after which appendages such as ears or horns were pegged into place. A thin layer of white clay was applied, and onto this base were added vivid colors, the same ones used for the body painting of real katcinas. A figure was painted and then adorned with small feathers representing large birds.

The katcina images reflect in a somewhat stylized form the disguises worn by men when portraying katcinas. The head of a katcina impersonator was covered with a mask of leather or basketry. A mask might hide only the upper part of the face, with a beard of hair or feathers hanging beneath to conceal the rest. The most common form of mask was a piece of leather formed into a cylinder, with a circular disk sewn on top. The performer peered through small slits or holes which had no relationship to the eyes on the mask. Noses were highly stylized protuberances, and mouths might be tubular, beak-shaped, or painted in various ways. The top of a mask often was adorned with a wooden tablet, feathers, hair, or wool, A fox-skin boa encircled the neck where the mask met the body. A wide variety of costumes prevailed, with a white cotton shirt, cotton kilt, sash, and green moccasins as common for chief katcinas. Many of the others wore cotton kilts, sashes, a fox skin hanging behind the kilt, and red moccasins. Some might wear breechclouts in addition to skin robes over their shoulders, while a katcina portraying a bride wore a wedding outfit. Other female impersonators wore typical women's clothing. Vivid paints applied to the bodies of the impersonators made them even more striking. Colors symbolized the direction from which the katcina came: yellow stood for north; blue-green, west; red, south; white, east; while red, yellow, white and blue-green in combination indicated the zenith, and black the nadir. The mask, body, and legs were often painted with representations of heavenly phenomena, animal tracks, phallic or vegetable symbols. These vivid colors of the gods offered striking contrast with the drab local desert setting and the bland colors found in the village environment.

The material inventory, in addition to those already-mentioned artifacts, included a rather limited number of objects. The self bows for hunting and warfare were made from oak. Arrows were fashioned from reeds or various species of wood; the reed variety was tipped with a wooden foreshaft. The nonreturning boomerang (rabbit-killing stick) was made from imported oak. It was cut to shape and steamed over a fire to obtain the desired degree of curve. For catching small game, nets and snares were made, probably from yucca fiber twine or cotton thread. In addition to basketry and pottery containers, vessels were made from gourds in aboriginal times. Gourds served as dippers, canteens, spoons, and other containers. Rattles made from hoofs, seeds, and shells were attached to fringed garments or worn in bands about the waist or arms. Rattles also were made by placing seeds in dried gourds. A flute with five stops was manufactured and blown across the end; this instrument was employed by the flute societies. Rasps were made by notching a stick of greasewood and running a stick or animal's scapula back and forth over the notches. The bull-roarer was a sacred object consisting of a wooden tablet attached to a cord. When the cord was whirled about, the wooden piece produced a sound designed to bring rain clouds.

The subsistence year began when crops were planted, for it was farming, not hunting, which sustained these people. The time to plant any particular crop was established by a Sun Watcher; his determination was made on the basis of the sunrise occurring at a particular spot on the horizon. It was habitual for the men of the various matrisibs to plant and harvest their crops as a group. A married man planted the sib land allotted to his wife and her immediate family. The men were considered the owners of crops until they were taken into the wife's house, after which the produce became her property. The farmlands at the foot of Black Mesa derived their moisture from ground seepage or from stream overflow (floodwater farming). The only preparation of a plot for planting was to trample the weeds or cut them with a broad-bladed, spatula-shaped implement and then break the soil with a pointed stick. Maize, the most important crop by far, was planted in holes made a foot deep with a digging stick. Some ten to twenty seeds were dropped in a single hole, and if a planting did not sprout in about ten days it might be reseeded. After plants began to grow, they were weeded and the soil loosened about the roots. Fields, which were about one acre in extent, were not rotated nor was the maize hilled. Beans sometimes were planted among the maize stalks but more often were raised in separate plots. Squash and cotton too appear to have been raised on separate acreage. During planting and harvesting a Masau'u impersonator was usually present, but there were no specific planting and harvest rituals. Most other Hopi subsistence activities also were group endeavors; organized by individuals or societies, they embraced some or all of the community. One of the cooperative communal tasks was to clear sand and debris from the village springs, which were owned by the Village Chief but used by anyone. For such a work party there were sometimes katcinas who served as mock taskmasters.

Hopi knowledge about the flora of their environment probably did not exceed that of many other groups of sedentary Indian farmers. What is unusual is that an extensive ethnobotany has been compiled on their plant usages. Alfred F. Whiting found that there were about forty plants under cultivation among these people in the 1930's. Of this number only five species were aboriginal (kidney and tepary beans, maize, cotton, and squash); four others may have existed prior to Spanish times but more likely represent postcontact domestics (Aztec and lima beans, gourds, and sunflowers). Five species were introduced during the Spanish period (chili peppers, onions, peaches, watermelons, and wheat); all others first were introduced by Mormon farmers or other Anglo-Americans. Ten species of wild plants were cared for by the Hopi, but the seeds apparently were not sown regularly. Seeds from two different species of wild tobacco were sown when necessary to provide sufficient leaves for ceremonial uses. Likewise, wild dock root was used for dye, and the seeds sometimes were planted. Some wild plants such as beeweed were not cleared from a plot; instead, the young plants were collected and cooked. Fifty-four different wild plants were eaten; ten were staples, fifteen were used as greens in the spring, and twelve others were collected when there was a domestic crop failure. The balance were used as snacks or seasonings, or were made into beverages. In the manufacture or decoration of items nearly fifty plant species were utilized; sixty-five were used medicinally and forty ceremonially or for magical purposes. Although there is overlap in the above listings, they indicate that the Hopi made use of a wide variety of plant species. There were about 200 wild flowering plants in the locality, of which half were commonly utilized.

Compared with the rituals for farming, the ceremonial preparations for a hunt were complex. The species most frequently hunted were antelope and rabbits; both jackrabbits and cottontails were considered desirable as food. Rabbits were hunted often in the late summer, when it was not essential to tend the crops. A man organizing a hunt could be of any sib; he made the necessary observances to the God of the Hunt by preparing prayer offerings. The details of when the hunt was to be held were announced by a crier, and the next day further rituals were performed by the organizer. In the actual hunt men formed a surround and moved in until they could kill the encircled animals with boomerangs as well as with hurled clubs. A rabbit killed outright belonged to the killer and a wounded one to the person who caught or killed it. The surround was formed repeatedly, and additional game was taken until the leader called an end to the hunt. When they returned to the village, each man gave his kill to his mother, sister, wife, or father's sister. The recipient "fed" the game cornmeal; later she put some of each animal's gall on a piece of piki (cornmeal bread), added salt and rabbit fur, offered this combination to the dead animal, and then threw the offering into the fire. This ritual was performed in order to restore the game to the God of the Hunt.

Before hunting antelope, deer, and mountain sheep the organizer as well as all the others in the party made prayer offerings, and there was ritual smoking. The surround method was used to capture these animals in aboriginal times. It seems to have been the pattern to run down and suffocate an antelope. A deer apparently was shot with arrows or clubbed to death but not stabbed. Once again there was a ritual propitiation of the deceased animal. Coyote hunts were conducted by kiva members collectively, and as usual the surround technique was employed. After a hunt each coyote was taken to the kiva and given a lighted corn husk cigarette and spoken to as a child before the owner took the animal home.

The primary staple, maize, was the symbol of life to the Hopi. Whiting records that they grew three varieties: flint, flour, and sweet. In early historic times the flint form was quite important, since the hull of each grain was hard and was not easily destroyed by weevils in storage. The flint variety was so difficult to grind, however, that it had declined in importance. The most popular variety of maize in recent times has been the flour type, which was grown by every farmer; the white strain was most important, followed by one which was blue. There were at least twenty different forms of flour maize named and identified. Sweet corn was raised in small quantities, with only two different named strains.

A wide variety of dishes were prepared from maize. The harvested product usually was stored on the cob and shelled as needed. Ground maize was made into gruel, dumplings, soups, and bread. Hominy was prepared by soaking shelled maize in a mixture of juniper wood ash and water, then boiling the grains and washing them to remove the hulls. Maize also was roasted on the ear, parched, or baked in pits. One dish, very much like popcorn, was prepared by soaking the kernels in salt water and parching them in hot sand. Ground cornmeal sometimes was wrapped in corn husks and boiled. One very important food made of maize, piki, was used as bread. It was made from a finely ground cornmeal mixed with water, using ashes as leavening. It was cooked on a special stone slab over a fire. The stone was heated and greased, and the bluish-gray liquid was poured over the stone. After cooking, the piki was folded or rolled into "loaves" for later consumption. It often was eaten by dipping one end into liquid food; the moist portion was bitten off and chewed.

The Hopi knew of no term for household, and yet this was the social unit which dominated and guided the life of each individual. A child was born into this unit and retained a strong emotional identity with it throughout life. The household consisted of a core of women—grandmother, daughters, and daughters' daughters—plus unmarried sons and in-marrying husbands. All of these persons except the husbands belonged to the same female descent group (matrilineage); also members of the lineage were those males born into the unit but now married and living in the houses of their wives. When the members of a matrilocal household outgrew the residence, a room was added on to accommodate the newer members. This adjacent household retained its ties with the parent matrilineage, held farmland in common, and worshipped a common fetish. The lineage fetish (bundle) was in the custody of the oldest female lineage head, and the associated ceremonies were conducted largely by the old woman's brother or son. The ritual obligations were passed down the most direct maternal line. The original lineage residence was the meeting place at which common lineage problems were discussed, and it remained the heart of the matrilineage, sometimes even after it was abandoned as a residence. From a leading matrilineage, with the greatest rights and duties, subordinate (daughter) lineages developed. As a daughter lineage grew in size, it might become socially removed from the original group and lose the underlying ties. The distant lineages would become separate entities if they created new bundles and acquired distinct names. Members of a named group who traced their ties through the same bundle formed a matrisib even though they could not trace connecting genealogical ties.

By 1906 there were about thirty named matrisibs at Oraibi, a number which represented splits as well as the possible settlement there of new sibs. The names, including Bear, Bow, Butterfly, and Lizard, were linked with happenings in mythological times or referred to sib ancestors. These ancestors were termed *wuya* and might or might not be tangibly represented by a sib bundle. A bundle sometimes included more than one wuya; this led to alternative names for the sib and probably represented the consolidation of two sibs. The sibs were grouped into nine nameless groups (phratries). The phratry was associated with the mythological past, and possibly sibs of the same phratry stemmed ultimately from the same lineage base. Members of the same phratry shared common ceremonial and landholding interests, and they could not marry within the group.

Overall village control was in the hands of two individuals: the Village Chief and the War Chief. The Village Chief was from the Bear sib, and a sacred stone in his possession verified his authority. The stone reportedly was brought from the underworld by Matcito, the legendary village founder. Covering the stone were engraved motifs, including human figures, and their interpretation was the basis for a division of lands among the sibs. The stone was inspected as a part of each Soyal Ceremony which the Village Chief headed. The Village Chief had not only the greatest sacred responsibilities at Oraibi but important secular duties as well. He settled land disputes, the most important differences between villagers. His sacred duties, in addition to those dealing with the Soyal Ceremony, included offering prayers for village welfare. It was the Village Chief who remained up late each night smoking and musing about pueblo conditions after most people had gone to sleep. For any critical community matter, his advice was sought, although he could not compel the actions of others. The office of the Village Chief was passed to a brother or to a sister's son after a long period of training. The Village Chief wore no badge of office, but he had a distinctive style of body painting for certain ceremonies and a sacred stick or cane of authority.

The only individual at Oraibi with permanent power and authority was the War Chief, who attained his position by being the most outstanding warrior. He had the right to inflict either verbal or physical punishment for nonconformity. On some occasions, when parties of men were organized for a community project, certain katcinas assembled the workmen and directed their activities. A lazy man might be reprimanded or even in extreme instances beaten by a katcina. The authority and power of the overt leaders never extended beyond the village. There was no means for uniting the Hopi as a tribe; in fact, the only time they clearly joined in a common cause was during the Pueblo Revolt of 1680.

From the point of view of a male Ego the terminology for designating blood relatives often is coextensive with his natal household. Ego termed his mother the same as his mother's sister and would not distinguish between them in normal speaking. Father and father's brother were termed alike, but mother's brother was termed differently. The designations for females in the first ascending generation paralleled those for males since father's sister was distinguished from mother and mother's sister (bifurcate merging terminology). This usage is reasonable since mother and mother's sister were of the same matrisib, and father was in the same matrisib as father's brother. In the cousin terminology parallel cousins were termed as siblings whereas mother's brother's children were termed as one's own children, and a father's sister's daughter was called the same as father's sister. Finally a father's sister's son was termed father (Crow type cousins). The most distinguishing characteristic of the cousin term is the ignoring of certain generational distinctions. The kinship terminology provided the

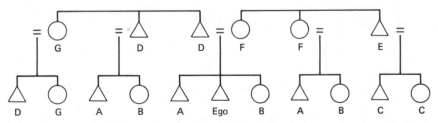

Aboriginal Hopi kin terms. Each letter represents a different term.

framework for lifelong responsibilities, with particular forms of behavior expected in each set of relationships. One of the most bitter overt displays of anger against a relative was to renounce kinship ties.

The Hopi prided themselves on being peaceful people who disliked shedding the blood even of animals, and yet they were organized for armed conflict. They fought to defend their pueblo, and the role of a warrior was recognized as dangerous, important, and necessary. In primeval times, when the Hopi emerged from the underworld, the Kokop and Spider sibs introduced a warrior society. Every man was a member, but not all were of the same rank. Membership was divided into ordinary warriors and stick-swallowers. Boys were trained for warfare with a rigorous program of cold baths, races, archery practice, and rising early. The Warrior Society held a ceremony each year during the late fall. The sacred equipment was held by the Spider and Kokop sibs. The two days of rituals involved the usual pattern of making prayer objects, ritual smoking, offering prayers, and building altars. A war medicine was prepared and drunk, after which there were exhibitions of stick-swallowing by one branch of the membership. For the real warriors, those who acknowledged killing and scalping an enemy, there was a special initiation which involved fasting and secret rituals.

Warfare was said always to have been defensive. Men went into battle clad in ordinary clothing but with the addition of caps made from mountain lion skin to which were attached eagle feathers. A man fought with a bow and arrows, stone club, spear, and boomerang. Before a battle they prayed to the Masau'u and to long-dead warriors; they also sang songs to make them brave. Armed only with a stone club, the War Chief led them into conflict. A slain enemy was scalped to the accompaniment of a scalping song, and scalps were carried into the pueblo on poles. A Navajo scalp was worthless, but one from an Apache or Ute was valued. The permanent resting place for a scalp was in the home of its taker. A scalp was washed with yucca suds and intermittently "fed" by its owner.

To the Hopi, man's relationship with the gods formed a well-conceived and orderly system built around the concept of continuity between life and death. An integrated relationship was maintained between the living and the dead, with the spirits of the dead becoming clouds which brought rain to the living. The katcinas represented generalized ancestors whose activities on earth and in the underworld benefited the living. To the Hopi there was a duality in being human. Man possessed a physical body and a "breath-body," spirit or soul. When an individual died, preparations for burial were in many ways the same as for the newborn, since the corpse was sprinkled with cornmeal, bathed, and given a new name. The breath-body journeyed to the underworld, where its existence was like that of the Hopi on earth, except that when the dead consumed food they took only of its essence. Because of their weightlessness the dead could rise into the sky and become clouds. By bringing rain, the deceased aided the living in a very meaningful manner. The God of Death, Masau'u, logically was a god of fertility since the rain led to fertility and growth. The sun also was a god of fertility, with an intimate association with the dead. The sun spent half of its time in the underworld, the land of the dead, and half of its time on earth. It was by prayers and offerings to the dead and to the sun that blessings on earth were realized.

Dual concepts integrated Hopi society still further. An individual was born to this earth; in death he was born to the underworld, only again to "die" in the underworld and become reborn on earth. Even in death, the breath-bodies were capable of returning to earth. As there was an earthly life cycle of the individual, there was a daily and yearly cycle for the sun. Each morning the sun left its eastern home and at sunset entered its western home; thus it furnished light equally to the earth and the underworld. On a yearly basis, winter began with the summer solstice and ended with the winter solstice, while summer began about mid-December and lasted until about mid-June. During the winter solstice on earth, it was the time of a summer solstice in the underworld, and the reverse also was true. Generalized ancestors, the katcinas, were on earth from the winter solstice until the summer solstice—in the summer season—and in the underworld during the earth's winter. The katcinas seen on earth were impersonations by the living of their dead ancestors. Finally, most ceremonial societies held major and minor rituals separated by six months' time. When a major ceremony was being held on earth, a minor one was celebrated in the underworld by the katcinas. As would be expected, death in theory held no fears to the Hopi, for the living and the dead were one.

The religious system was implemented with a series of annual and biannual ceremonies held by particular religious associations or societies. Each major ceremony was controlled by a different organization which was linked to a different matrisib. An elder male of the leading lineage in each matrisib usually headed the religious association of his sib. In the possession of the matrisib was a bundle called the "mother" or "heart" of the sib, which consisted of an ear of maize, feathers, and coverings as well as other sacred objects. The equipment was owned by the leading lineage, and there was an associated kiva in which services usually were held. Rituals were conducted at particular times determined by phases of the moon, the location of the sun when it rose, or by the number of days since another ritual ended. The general pattern for all the major ceremonies was similar. The rituals extended over nine days, and when kiva members were so occupied, a flag was attached to the kiva ladder to warn off nonmembers. During the rituals there was a prohibition against eating fatty foods, meat, and salt. Sexual activities were restricted before as well as during the time of these celebrations. The first day was a perfunctory beginning; the next eight days were divided into two four-day segments, with the final day devoted usually to a ritual open to the public. The specifics of the ceremonies included the use of altars and associated wooden, stone, or clay tablets. On the tablets were painted motifs symbolic of animals, clouds, maize, and rain. Prayer offerings were left at the proper shrines. Sand paintings and certain fluids with a water base likewise were important. Each secret society was associated with the curing of a particular disease, and to be taken ill with a disease controlled by a society was one means for induction. Initiation rituals usually took place around the midpoint of the ceremony and involved among other things having one's head washed with yucca suds as well as being given a new name by a ritual sponsor who was already a member of the society.

To benefit by all the advantages of being a Hopi in this and the underworld it was essential to participate actively in the affairs of one or more secret societies. At about nine years of age boys and girls were initiated into either the Katcina Society or the Powamu Society, the latter being more restricted in membership. Within the next few years a girl was expected to join one of the four women's societies; boys joined the Antelope, Blue Flute, Gray Flute, or Snake society. Occasionally a woman joined a man's society and vice versa to fulfill a particular role, but by and large the ceremonial societies were divided along sexual lines. When a boy reached adolescence, he was expected to undergo the Tribal Initiation; only then was he free to participate in the most sacred of all ceremonies, the Soyal.

The ritual calendar may arbitrarily be considered to begin with the winter solstice or Soyal Ceremony. The Soyal was conceived around that mysterious moment each year when, in Hopi thinking, the sun rises at the same place for four days, and the days are shortest. The Soyal Ceremony was conducted by men who had completed the Tribal Initiation. At Oraibi the Wuwutcim Society conducted the most sacred of the Soyal rituals, and it was far more popular than the others. This society was composed of Bear sib members and directed by the village chief. The principal purpose of the ceremony was to compel the sun to begin the trip back to its summer home so that it would bring warmth enough for the crops to be planted. The climax of the rituals came when the "Star Priest," called Sun Priest at other times, performed a dance representing the cycle of the sun. The ceremony had the complementary purposes of inducing fertility in both women and plants, and participation was village-wide. Particular men and women dancers, and the katcinas performed. There also was the usual smoking and prayers, plus the manufacture of a large number of diverse prayer offerings of corn husks, feathers, and prayer sticks.

The Powamu Ceremony began when the new moon in February first was seen, and it climaxed in the forced growth of beans in the kiva of the Powamu Society. Fifty to one hundred bean plants were raised by each man in his own kiva. The beans were well watered, and the kiva fires burned hot day and night to force the sprouting. The beans were grown for Eototo and Aholi, those katcina impersonators who planted maize which sprouted at the same time as the beans. If the beans and maize sprouted well and grew heartily until the harvest, it was a good omen for the forthcoming farming season. The sprouted beans were cut and bundled to be presented by katcinas to the grower's uninitiated offspring, his ceremonial children, and favored relatives. A man made small bows and arrows or other gifts for boys and katcina images for girls or women. In each instance the gifts were presented by the katcina impersonators. If a child was to be initiated into the Powamu Society, he saw the sacred rituals for the first time on the fifth day. This new knowledge was not to be revealed, under the threat of punishment by the katcinas. By undergoing the initiation, participants became members of the Powamu Society and were permitted to impersonate katcinas, to participate in katcina rituals, and to become katcina fathers or ceremonial sponsors. Not all children were inducted into the Powamu Society; the remaining children were inducted into the Katcina Society on the sixth day of the Powamu ceremony. Membership carried the right to function as a katcina, but these individuals could not participate in the Powamu ceremony or become katcina fathers. The initiation included revelation of sacred traditions, and the initiated again were cautioned against revealing the secrets they had learned.

In August another high point in the ceremonial round was reached with the performances of the Antelope-Snake or Blue and Gray Flute society ceremonies on alternate years. The Flute societies conducted their most sacred and secret rituals in the home of the leading lineage of the supervising sibs. The pattern of prayers, smoking, and manufactured offerings was climaxed by a ceremonial race, and later the offerings were placed at shrines. The membership assembled also at a spring where one man submerged completely in the water to the accompaniment of singing and dancing. When the man surfaced, he brought up with him gourds filled with water which symbolized water for Oraibi. Another race took place, this time for women, and a ritual similar to the one just described was held at another spring. Then there was a final race to the village by women.

Even though the Flute ceremonies took place after the summer solstice they seem to have been a counterpart of the Soyal, and as with the Soyal, their performance was to bring rain and fertility.

The Antelope and Snake societies were separate organizations, but they combined for their major ceremony. The two societies manufactured prayer offerings jointly, then went to their respective kivas, where they performed secret rituals. At this time the Snake Society members collected snakes in each of the four directions on four different days. As with the Flute ceremony there was a race, but the major event was a public performance in the plaza. Here the Antelope Society men danced with vines dangling from their mouths. The next day the Snake Society members brought the captive snakes from their kiva to the bower and danced with the Antelope performers. The Snake men went in pairs to a previously erected cottonwood booth, where one of each pair received a snake, which he held by his lips or teeth just behind the snake's head. He danced around the plaza several times as his partner brushed his shoulders with a "snake whip," which was a short stick with eagle feathers attached. Another Snake Society member danced along behind the pair. Each snake was danced with and then released on the ground at the plaza. The snakes then were gathered together in a circle and sprinkled with cornmeal by females of the Snake sib. Finally, younger men of the Snake Society picked up as many snakes as they could handle and took them to shrines in each of the four cardinal directions.

The public performances of the Snake Society members have attracted more popular interest among whites than any other American Indian ritual. The reason, of course, is that the snake dancers carried prairie rattlers. in their mouths as often as they carried harmless species such as the bull snake. The Snake Society members handled the poisonous and harmless snakes with equal ease, and yet prairie rattler bites occasionally are fatal. Illness or death from snakebite among the dancers is unreported, and various explanations have been offered concerning the Indians' ability to handle poisonous snakes. There is no evidence that the members have an immunity to snake venom or that the snakes were charmed. Neither is there reason to believe that the snakes were drugged in any manner. Furthermore, the Hopi did not have an effective antidote for venom, which was proven by laboratory tests of their snake medicine. Historically, there appear to have been two different answers to Hopi success in handling rattlesnakes. In 1883 a herpetologist visited a kiva where rattlesnakes were being kept for a dance; he inspected the fangs of one rattler and found them intact. After the dance he sent two of the rattlesnakes which had been used to the United States National Museum, and the venom glands were found to contain poison. Thus it would seem almost certain that the fangs were milked before the public ceremony. The next snake captured after a snake dance was taken in 1932; another herpetologist recovered a rattler from a shrine following a snake dance. The snake's fangs had been cut away rather skillfully. Similar evidence that the fangs were cut out in recent times was obtained in 1951 when another rattlesnake recovered after a ceremony was found to have had its fangs removed. Thus, the limited evidence indicates that the Hopi in aboriginal times and into historic times milked the poison from the fangs of rattlesnakes but that between 1883 and 1932 they shifted to cutting away the fangs. The logical conclusion is that as the Hopi came to understand white attitudes toward rattlesnake bites, they eliminated the risk by a surgical operation on the dangerous snakes.

The final ceremony of major importance was the Tribal Initiation. Controlled by the Agaves Society, it was held only when this society had at least one candidate for initiation. During this ceremony adolescent males were initiated into one of four secret societies, the Agaves, Horns, Singers, or Wuwutcim. It should be recalled that a male could not be a fully participating adult in Hopi society until he had passed through this initiation. The Tribal Initiation was the most complex of the ceremonies and a cornerstone of Hopi religion. It took place in November at a time established by the Sun Watcher. After the announcement that the ceremony was to be held, the four sponsoring societies began their preparations by smoking, fashioning prayer offerings, erecting the kiva flags, and preparing altars. A new fire was made in the Agave kiva by the kiva chief, and some was carried to the other participating kivas. An idol called Dawn Woman was brought from her shrine and exhibited on top of the kivas until the fifth day of the ceremony, when she was returned to her shrine after "delivering" her offspring. The Wuwutcim initiates of the Chicken Hawk sib were considered little chicken hawks, and each was given a poncho-like blanket garment by his ceremonial father which was to represent the feathers of a chicken hawk. The candidates pretended they were little hawks, calling like nestlings for food as they flapped their arms. All candidates slept in their kivas, and on the third and fifth days dances were performed which clearly were associated with fertility, with phallic symbols and simulated pregnancies presented. On the eighth day, dances indicative of germination were held by the Chicken Hawks, and on the ninth day activities climaxed with highly sacred songs, a bonfire, and impersonations of mountain sheep by the Horn Society members. All of these events, along with others which have not been described, symbolized the ritual rebirth of male children into manhood and reaffirmed the connection between the living and the dead.

Once long ago, according to Tawaqwaptiwa, the late Village Chief of Oraibi, after the Hopi had departed from the uppermost level of the underworld they wandered on earth with their gods the katcinas. They were attacked by "Mexicans," and all the gods were killed. The dead returned to the underworld, and the Hopi divided the ceremonial paraphernalia of the dead katcinas in order to impersonate them. It was these impersonations of katcinas which formed the core of Hopi rituals. When a man wore the sacred costume of a katcina, he became a god, and his mask was the most sacred item of his costume. As the masks wore out, became soiled, or broke, they were replaced or repaired; replacement did not detract from their sacredness. The chief katcina masks were the only ones not replaced or duplicated. It was possible also to vary a new katcina mask from the original without impairing its supernatural associations. During each year katcinas were present at Oraibi from the time of the winter solstice until the summer solstice, and then they were in the underworld except for Masau'u Katcina, representing the God of Death, who was about the earth the year long. A Hopi did not deceive himself to the point of believing that an impersonator was a god but rather considered his role as a friend of the gods. Small children by contrast were told that these were the actual gods.

Participation as a katcina was open to all village men under the general sanction of the Village Chief, and the direction of katcina activities was under the control of the Badger and Katcina sibs. The former presided during the early season, and the latter functioned at the end of the season. The first katcina appeared in late November as a tired, bedraggled old man in a worn costume. He performed a dance feebly at the dance plaza, and at the chief kiva he left four prayer sticks, danced and sang, and sprinkled cornmeal in four of the six directions. These activities indicated the kiva was now open for katcinas. Near the end of the Soyal Ceremony in December the sexually aggressive Mastop katcinas arrived. They pretended to copulate with all the women, young and old alike, who gathered to watch their arrival. Ritual sexual intercourse was performed by a katcina when he placed his hands on a woman's shoulders and jumped up and down. This was not a frivolous gesture but a serious fertility rite. The following day, the last of the Soyal, the Qoqoqlom katcinas appeared. Some performed a dance, and others sprinkled cornmeal as though to emphasize the opening of the season. During January nightly performances were given in different kivas, with each kiva head deciding which katcina was to be portrayed. In February in association with the Powamu Ceremony katcinas again appeared. During the time of the Powamu two katcinas in particular served to intimidate uninitiated children who were wayward. These were the So'yoko and Natacka katcinas. Any kiva might supply the katcina actors, and they were instructed by the parents concerning the specific transgressions of particular children. Another performer, Hahai'i, the Katcina Mother, announced the forthcoming event in the kivas. The children were forewarned that something out of the ordinary soon would occur. The Hahai'i left shelled maize at each house in which there were girls and small snares for boys. The girls were warned to prepare ground cornmeal and the boys to trap small mammals for the giants who were coming, or else the giants would take them away. A few days later the awesome giant katcinas arrived, wearing frightening masks and carrying weapons and a basket in which to take away children. The katcinas cited particular transgressions of the children and threatened to seize them. Parents defended their children; the offerings of baked cornmeal by the girls were accepted, but the small animals caught by the boys to appease the katcinas were rejected. Finally, the katcinas left, but only after they had received gifts of meat from the parents. The So'yoko and other katcinas then peered into a kiva and witnessed a dance performed by members. Then the giants hauled the performers from the ceremonial chamber. Intrigued with the dance, the giants began to imitate the performance. Finally all the katcinas and the dancers went into the kiva and ate the accumulated food. The children were told that the katcinas went back into the underworld from the kiva.

The next series of Katcina dances was known as Repeat; included in these was the Water Serpent dance. It could be arranged by any kiva that wished to present it so long as the Village Chief approved. The He'e'e Katcina led other katcinas into the village early one morning. On the evening of the same day the serpents, a male and female with two offspring, were the center of ritual attention. The ceremonial leaders took them to the main spring at Oraibi where prayers were offered, there was ceremonial smoking, and the heads and tails of the serpents were dipped into the spring water. Then the first performance was held in the sponsoring kiva. In the dark, a screen was erected with forced-grown maize plants placed before it. As the kiva was gradually lighted, the serpents appeared out of unseen holes in the screen and, swaying as they emerged full length, finally knocked over the maize in a symbolic harvest. The ceremony then was repeated at the other kivas. The next series of performances was held outdoors by katcinas at irregular intervals prior to the Home Going rituals. Sponsoring kivas impersonated almost any katcina as long as they had the Village Chief's approval. After rehearsals, with prayers and the construction of prayer sticks, the dances were held in the village plaza. An entire series of dances was held during a single day, and clowns might burlesque the dancers or perform independently of the katcinas. Finally the Home Going observances, which lasted about a month, took place just after the summer solstice. The katcina rituals concluded with offerings made at a village shrine; when the shrine lid was closed, the katcina season ended.

The nature of the katcina cult as a whole is expressed well by Titiev (1944, 129). He writes: "The complexities of their Katcina worship are of little moment to the Hopi. They make no effort to systematize or to classify their beliefs, but are content to regard the Katcinas as a host of benevolent spirits who have the best interests of the Hopi ever at heart. To impersonate them is a pleasure, to observe them a delight. Quite apart from its more formal features, the operation of the Katcina cycle brings more warmth and color into the lives of the Hopi than any other aspect of their culture."

Participation in secret societies was not restricted to men. Women controlled three voluntary religious associations, the Lakon, Marau, and Oaqol. Just as the secret societies of men included a few women, so the religious associations of the women included a few males. The organization of women's societies was similar to that of males: they were controlled by a lineage in a particular matrisib, possessed bundles, carried out secret rituals in a kiva, and performed certain ceremonies in public. Each held its major ceremony in the fall, and it appears that the best established of the three was the Marau. Titiev suggested that the Marau may once have been for the initiation of girls and paralleled the Wuwutcim for men. This possibility suggests itself because of similar conceptual and ritual characteristics of the two societies.

The religious dogma of the Hopi was precise, the ceremonial round was exacting, and the katcinas played a major ceremonial role. In order to maintain the balance in nature and to sustain man's relationship with the gods each individual was obligated to contribute to the best of his ability. An individual's contribution was manifest in being *hopi* or good. The anticipated behavior for an individual was spelled out in detail since being hopi involved more than goodness alone. A Hopi ideally was cooperative, self-effacing, and nonaggressive. He had moral as well as physical strength and health. He accepted collective responsibilities and concentrated on good thoughts. Conversely, an evil or bad person was kahope, with personality traits opposite those of the ideals.

Contemplation of the Hopi religious system reveals that it was a finely tuned totality. The katcinas always fulfilled their obligations in the underworld, and if the Hopi on earth did the same, there was no privation or unhappiness. It was the responsibility of each person to fulfill his social and ceremonial obligations by being hopi. Community-wide prosperity indicated that each individual had contributed his utmost, and the ideals of the Hopi Way thus were achieved. But what about failures? Why was it that during some years rain did not fall, winds dried the ground and blew seeds away, and the streams did not flow with water? Obviously, it was essential to be able to explain why it sometimes came to pass that nature did not respond to the complex ceremonies. The burden of failure was said to rest with individuals, persons who were kahopi, thinking evil and doing evil; these persons were witches. The origin of witchcraft was traced to Spider Woman, who caused the first human death. Hopi informants believed that in a typical community there were more witches than ordinary people. Witches might be males or females of any sib; no one was considered to be incapable of witchcraft. A Village Chief or ceremonial leader might be suspect simply because he held an important office. Anyone who was self-assertive was open to the accusation of being a witch because such behavior was not hopi. It was possible to become a witch either by voluntarily practicing sorcery or by unknowingly being inducted into a society of witches as a child. In the latter instance, existing witches reportedly carried off a related child while it slept and inducted it into a secret society which followed the patterning of other Hopi secret societies. The initiate was taught the witches' art of assuming the shape of an animal in order to pursue their nefarious craft by night. The power of a witch was derived from association with an animal familiar, such as a coyote, owl, wolf, or small black ant, from whom the greatest forces of evil emanated; quite logically, a sorcerer possessed "two hearts," his own and that of an animal familiar. Sorcerers worked evil by sending pestilence to the fields, by causing land erosion, or by driving off rain clouds and replacing them with a conjured windstorm. A witch was not content with destroying crops but killed living people as well. Murder probably was the most important activity of a sorcerer since it was by killing one relative each year that the witch extended his life. A relative was killed or his illness caused by shooting stiff deer hairs, ants, a bit of bone, or some other object into his body without breaking the skin.

Just as there were individuals bent on harming and killing people by a supernatural means, there were likewise shamans whose obligation it was to cure the ill. There existed in early historic times a Hopi society of curers, but it passed out of existence before it was reported adequately. In any event, in the more recent past there were curing specialists who relied on pharmacopoeia and massaging techniques. Their knowledge appears to have been secular in nature. Some individuals set broken bones and prepared herbs for patients. They possessed a rather complex body of information which required specialized training, and a secular shaman was likely to pass his knowledge on to a sister's son. In another category were the shamans who performed supernatural cures. These "two hearted" individuals were supposed to employ their powers only for curing illness caused by witches. Obviously such a person would be suspect in a sorcery case and a dangerous individual in any event. He chewed jimsonweed root or some other plant to induce a vision which aided in diagnosing the source of a malady. An ordinary person could best protect himself against a witch, who was most likely a near relative, by wearing arrowpoints of stone, regarded as the ends of lightning flashes associated with the clouds. Another means was to rub ashes from cedar wood on both individuals and objects. The Hopi attitude toward known witches, those persons seen practicing witchcraft, was that such an individual would die or encounter misfortune. His spirit thirsted and hungered for the underworld and approached it by one step a year. Therefore, it was both unnecessary and unwise to interfere with his activities. The sanctions against a witch were not in this world but in the underworld; when his spirit arrived there, it was burned in an oven and became a beetle.

The Hopi emphasis on fertility led to certain forms of expected behavior which were conducive to pregnancy. A woman should pray to the sun at dawn each morning, and she was most likely to conceive if she had sexual intercourse while menstruating. If she did not become pregnant, her husband might make katcina images to be presented to her at the Powamu and Home Going ceremonies; to these images she prayed. A woman recognized her pregnancy by the fact that she failed to menstruate, and if she suspected that she was carrying twins, a shaman's aid was sought to make the twins one. To bear twins was considered difficult, and it was thought that if both lived one parent would die. A pregnant woman prayed to the sun, and she sprinkled cornmeal while she prayed to ease the labor of childbirth. She was active during her pregnancy, and she as well as her husband observed diverse taboos.

A woman bore her offspring in the house of her mother, often the same dwelling in which she had been born. She was unaided and gave birth while squatting over a layer of sand. Most deaths in childbirth were said to result from the woman's failure to expel the afterbirth. The blood, afterbirth, and sand were covered with cornmeal and hidden in a special crevice. If a young person had contact with the blood and afterbirth, he would become ill. Immediately after delivery, the grandmother entered the room, severed the umbilical cord, and took charge. In a short time the father's closest female relative, his mother or sister, arrived to wash the head of the neonate and to direct the activities of the next twenty days, which culminated in a naming ceremony and a feast. It was the father's close female relatives with whom one later in life developed warm social ties. The father was nowhere to be seen during the birth, and usually for forty days thereafter he withdrew to his kiva away from the bustle and confusion in the house of his wife.

Infants were kept contented as much as possible. A baby was nursed whenever it awoke and cried. Furthermore, it was not weaned for two to four years or even longer. To quiet an unhappy child a mentor might rub its sexual organ, and a small child might masturbate without reproof. When a child was able to walk, he was encouraged to urinate and defecate outside the house; if he should defecate inside, he might be scolded or slapped on the head. Matters pertaining to sex were accepted among the Hopi with casual regard. Since a child slept in the same small room with his parents, their sexual activities easily were observable. Children were not instructed concerning sexual matters but came to understand them through observation. It was not unusual for males and sometimes women to urinate before persons of the opposite sex. Furthermore, jokes which we would consider obscene were taught to small boys to be used when they performed as ceremonial clowns. Yet shyness was characteristic of young girls, and a licentious person sometimes was called crazy.

Small children played together or with toys provided by adults. As they grew older, they were expected to rise early and pray to the sun in order to be hopi. They played in water and also bathed each day in a spring. A small boy accompanied his father to the fields and played; in later years he helped with the farming activities. A girl became tied to her home, and the care of her younger siblings or her mother's sister's small children was an important duty.

No formal recognition was given to the onset of puberty for either males or females. It was customary, however, for boys in their early teens to begin sleeping in a kiva rather than at home; this was a distinct break from childhood. There was a ceremony through which a girl had to pass before she married. It was held annually for girls between the ages of sixteen and twenty. The event usually was directed by a young female who had passed through the rituals, and she was aided by two boys in supervising the girls. Most of four days the girls spent morning to night grinding maize in a darkened room in the home of one of the girls' paternal aunts. During this time they observed food taboos and drank liquids only at midday. The boys organized a rabbit hunt on the third day, and the girls spent most of that day baking piki. Afterwards, the girls appeared for the first time with new coiffures termed "butterfly wings" or "squash blossoms." A girl continued to wear her hair in this manner until she married. She was most likely to marry someone from within the community (village endogamy) soon after passing through this ceremony.

Fornication between teenagers was a norm, and it was formalized in the *dumaiya*. After a boy began sleeping in a kiva, he was free to roam the pueblo at night. While doing so, he wrapped himself in a blanket so that his identity would not readily be discerned. As the members of his amourette's household slept, he crept in carefully to the side of the girl, who in a whisper asked who it was. The boy answered, "It is I," and from the sound of his voice, the girl identified her caller. If she were willing, which usually was the case since the boy went only where he thought he would be received, he passed the night with the girl, leaving just before daylight. A dumaiya supposedly was secret, but it could not remain so in a small community like Oraibi. The girl's parents did not interfere with a dumaiya as long as they regarded the boy as a potentially acceptable husband for their daughter. A girl was not likely to have only a single lover, and before long she might become pregnant. If this happened, the girl named the boy she liked best as the father, and the formalities of arranging a marriage were begun. It also was possible for a girl to propose directly to a boy during certain festive or ceremonial occasions. A couple did not court unless they stood in a proper social relationship with one another. A person could not marry another of the same sib or phratry. In the ideal system of marriage, one could not marry a person of his father's sib or phratry, but this rule was not observed with care. Neither was a person who had never married supposed to become the spouse of a divorced or widowed individual, but such marriages did take place. Such individuals, who were more frequently females than males, were termed "basket carriers," indicating that they would be forced to carry heavy baskets from their place of burial to the underworld.

A formal marriage ceremony began after the relatives of a couple approved the match; the girl then went to the boy's home to grind maize for three days. In this trial period the girl demonstrated her abilities as a homemaker, but there was no comparable trial for the groom. When the girl was in the boy's home, his paternal aunts attacked the boy's mother and her sisters with mud and water for permitting the girl to "steal" their "sweetheart." The fight was in an atmosphere of jovial hostility. On the fourth morning the couples' hair was washed in one container by their respective mothers and female relatives. A mingling of their hair symbolized the marital union. Once again the paternal aunts of the boy attempted halfheartedly to disrupt the ritual. After their hair had dried, the couple stood at the mesa edge to pray to the sun and later returned to the groom's home for a wedding breakfast. The couple were now man and wife, but they continued to live in the groom's home until his male relatives and any other men who offered to help, completed the bride's wedding costume. The men prepared the cotton and wove two sets of wedding garments, a small robe and a white-fringed belt; in addition they prepared skins and sewed white moccasins and leggings. During the manufacture of these items the groom's family feasted the workers. After a month or longer, the garments were completed; wearing one set and carrying the second in a reed container, the bride returned home. Her husband informally and unobtrusively took up residence in her household. The wedding garments were very important because they were required for entering the underworld after death.

All Hopi women appear to have married, but such was not the case for men. Indirect pressure was put on a girl by her brothers and her mother's brothers in order to bring another male into their economic unit. A boy was not pressured to marry, for his family then lost him as a productive member. Any form of plural marriage was prohibited, but many unions were not permanent. In a compilation of marriage records for somewhat more than 800 individuals, Titiev found that over 35 percent had from one to eight divorces. The most common grounds for divorce was adultery, followed by what probably would be termed incompatibility in our society. Divorce was a simple matter since it was only necessary for a man to rejoin his natal household or for a woman to order her husband from her household. The primary pressures against a divorce came from a girl's family since they did not relish losing an economically productive male. The mother and her small children continued to reside in their old adobe; an older offspring might join either parent. There was a definitely adverse effect on Hopi society from the sexual laxness and marital instability.

A man tended to be an outsider in his wife's home throughout his life, not only because male activities were distinct from those of females, but because he was bound emotionally to the household of his birth. A man hunted, tilled the lands of his wife's sib, wove cloth, and made moccasins. A wife, her sisters, and her mother owned the house and all the subsistence items deposited there or in their storerooms. A wife prepared the foods for consumption and cared for her children and, at times, her sister's children. A woman was quite free to go her own way, and if she were unhappy with her husband, she could divorce him almost as readily as he could divorce her.

The social core of a household consisted of a line of females. Within this setting the closest bonds were between a mother and her daughters. Daughters were destined to spend their lives in their mother's home or in an adjacent residence, and eventually they assumed their mother's role in the society. From her mother a girl learned domestic skills and the norms of proper behavior. A mother guided the most important decisions in the ceremonial life of a girl and was likely to have a voice in the selection of her mate. As a girl's menarche arrived, she was instructed by her mother about caring for herself. The girl was not isolated at this time, nor at any other menstrual period; neither was she restricted from participating in ceremonies while menstruating. Were a mother to die, the mother's sister, who was called mother, replaced the biological mother in the girl's affection. Between a mother and her son the social bonds were not as close. A mother indulged an offspring of either sex, but a son in his early teens soon found his identity with a kiva group. A man's natal home remained the residence with which he felt most identified, however. He returned there when divorced and was a frequent caller in his mother's house. Like a girl, a man identified closely with his mother's sister, especially if the mother had died. A father was not overtly important in the upbringing of his children. He was, however, interested in having his daughter find a good husband, who by his farming activities could lighten the father's economic labors. A father took comparatively little active interest in a son until the latter's Tribal Initiation. Then the father selected the boy's ceremonial sponsor, which was an important decision. As a boy grew older, his father assumed a major role as his teacher. He imparted farming and ceremonial skills as well as advice about being hopi.

Between siblings of the opposite sex there were bonds of friendship, mutual aid, and affection. Throughout childhood this was true, and there were no restrictions leading to avoidance after the individuals had reached maturity. Girls aided their brothers in farming activities, while boys gave their sisters gifts. Each was pleased by exemplary behavior of the other, and a girl was quick to defend her brother against any slander. Between brothers the social ties were close, with an older brother helping to educate the younger one. There might be indirect competition for ceremonial offices and for girls, but this rarely was disruptive. Often a younger brother married first because the older one was needed to care for their natal household; in marriage, it was ideal for brothers to marry sisters. As would be anticipated, sisters were socially close throughout their lives. When the age difference was great, the older one was the instructor of the younger. They occupied the same household and raised their children together; their solidarity was a foundation stone of Hopi social life.

The maternal uncle of a young boy was the only male of his parents' generation who was of the same lineage and sib as himself. If such an uncle were a ceremonial leader, a boy might follow him in office, which called for systematic training of the youth. A mother's brother was likely to be the most important figure of authority associated with the boy's home, and he did not hesitate to apply discipline. A mother's brother was not all sternness toward his sister's children, however. He often told them myths or tales about their sib and presented them with gifts on occasion. Her mother's brother was influential in the selection of a girl's husband, and he lectured the young couple near the end of the marriage ceremony. A father's sister offered advice, particularly in ceremonial matters, and the relationship included mutual aid. However, the most important function of a father's sister was to assist at the birth of his children. One very warm relationship was between a father's sister and his son. As a small child, a boy soon learned that he was always a welcome guest in this woman's home. Here he received favored foods and frequent demonstrations of love and affection. As he grew older, he took game to his paternal aunt and exhibited his warm feeling toward her. Sexual relations with this aunt and her daughter were possible, and Titiev suspects that in the recent past a youth may have been expected to marry a father's sister's daughter.

As a person approached death, it was said that his body became swollen. Youths as well as most adults left the house because they feared being present at the time of a death. The body and hair of a deceased person was washed, and then he was reclothed. A man was wrapped in a deerskin and a woman in her wedding blankets, and the corpse was flexed into a sitting position. Prayer offerings were fashioned by the father of the deceased or another male in his sib. A prayer feather was placed beneath each foot and in each hand, as well as over the navel, the location of a person's spirit. The face was covered with cotton, symbolic of the time the dead become clouds, while food and water were placed with the body as sustenance on the journey to the underworld. The body was carried to the cemetery by men from the house of the deceased; here a hole had been dug just large enough to receive the bundled corpse. It was placed facing the west, and soil was spread hastily on top. Men who attended the dead purified themselves afterwards by washing in a boiled juniper preparation, and there was a ritual in the household of the deceased to protect members against spirits. The next day the man who had manufactured the prayer offerings took cornmeal and five prayer sticks to the grave. The prayer sticks would help the person on his travels to the land of the dead, and the food was to feed the spirit. A prayer was offered, and the spirit was told not to return for anyone else in the community. Later, each household resident washed his hair and smoked himself over hot coals on which pinyon gum had been placed. All possessions of the deceased were thrown away. A separate cemetery was provided for the stillborn, infants, and children.

Plate 54 *(Above)   The village of Oraibi with melons and peaches drying on the roof in the foreground*
(Courtesy of the Southwest Museum).

Plate 55 *(Top right)   A Hopi woman grinding grain in a bin metate*
(Courtesy of the Southwest Museum).

Plate 56 *(Bottom right)*
Hopi Snake Dance at Oraibi
(Courtesy of the Southwest Museum).

Plate 57 *A 1900 illustration of Water Serpents in a Hopi
kiva being manipulated behind a screen in a symbolic harvest
of small maize plants* (Courtesy of Smithsonian Institution
National Anthropological Archieves, neg. no. 1813-B).

Plate 58
Hopi katcina figures
(Courtesy of the UCLA Museum
of Cultural History).

Plate 59 *Coal mining on Black Mesa in 1971*
(Courtesy of Daniel B. Gridley).

The spirit of an infant did not travel to the underworld but lingered above the house, to be reborn again as an individual of the opposite sex. The death of an adult was surrounded with misgivings and fear in spite of the fact that most dead were to be reborn into a peaceful world which was an intimate part of the Hopi Way.

Among the earliest Hopi and Anglo-American contacts was a conflict which took place in 1834. At this time white trappers raided their gardens and killed about fifteen persons. In 1850 the Hopi attempted to induce the Anglo-American authorities in Santa Fe to control the Navajo depredations, but this was not done until later. Whites who visited the Hopi mesas favorably impressed some of the Indians. They reasoned that perhaps the Anglo-Americans were the Bahanas, or White Gods. Each Hopi knew the origin myth in which an elder brother of the Hopi, a Bahana, departed and promised to return when the Hopi were in need. The problem, debated by the elders, was how to identify the Bahanas when they returned. A more immediate concern, however, was the physical survival of the people, for in the late 1860's a severe drought was followed by a smallpox epidemic. After these depressing events, many of the Indians joined the Zuni temporarily. Anglo-American interest in the Hopi intensified in the 1870's. A Moqui Indian agent was appointed in 1869 and a Moqui Pueblo Agency was established the next year. From a study of the formation of the Hopi Reservation by Volney H. Jones we learn that as early as 1858 the Mormons from Utah had entered the Hopi country, and about 1875 a small Mormon colony was founded in Hopi country. The Moqui Pueblo Reservation was created by an Executive Order in 1882, but the land set aside for Indians was not for the exclusive use of the Hopi. The rectangular area included 3900 square miles, most of it claimed and utilized by the Hopi. It seems not unlikely that the reservation was established as an attempt to prevent increased Mormon settlement locally. A second reason for creating the reservation was the increased Navajo encroachment on Hopi grazing lands. The official reservation name was changed from Moqui to the Hopi Indian Reservation in 1900. It is clear from Jones' study that the United States did not express an earlier interest in the Hopi because of the distance between their land and the administrative center at Santa Fe. Furthermore, the Hopi did not disrupt the activities of incoming whites. On the other hand, Federal officials were occupied with the regional problem of hostile Navajo. After the Navajo confinement to a reservation in 1868, attention was turned to the Hopi. A Bureau of Indian Affairs school and an agency were established for the Hopi in 1874. The first school was administered by missionaries, but in 1887 the Bureau assumed control of the school. The passage of the General Allotment Act by Congress in 1887 resulted in Federal pressures on the Hopi to shift from family and community land-holdings to individual allotments. The Bureau attempted to force the allotment program in 1907 but did not succeed. Conflicts with the Navajo over grazing lands intensified since there had been no boundary survey of the Hopi Reservation at the time of its formation, and Navajo encroachment on Hopi lands has continued. Through a series of executive orders the Navajo Reservation came to surround the Hopi, and about 1937 the Bureau of Indian Affairs reduced the area officially designated as Hopi land to about one-fourth its original size, or 1000 square miles.

After this brief survey of general Hopi contacts with whites, it is time to turn again to the community of Oraibi and to trace what has happened there during the Anglo-American era. In the second quarter of the nineteenth century the killing of some Hopi by American trappers antagonized the Oraibi chief. The next chief also was noted to be unfriendly with visiting Anglo-Americans. When he died about 1865, the succession fell between two young men, Sakhongyoma and Lololoma. Since both were young, their father functioned temporarily in their stead. The Moqui Pueblo Special Agent was well received in 1871 everywhere but at Oraibi. Furthermore, the people of Oraibi were angry with neighboring communities for their acceptance of whites. The younger of the two brothers, Lololoma, was acknowledged as Village Chief at some time prior to 1880, and he continued his father's anti-American policies. Soon after becoming established in his office, Lololoma traveled to Washington, D. C., with a party of Hopi to appeal to the Federal government to contain Navajo encroachments on their land. After the trip, Lololoma reversed his attitude toward Anglo-Americans and became the leader of the progressive, friendly, or pro-Anglo faction. The anti-Anglo faction, called conservatives or hostiles, was led by a male called Uncle Joe by Anglos but actually named Lomahongyoma. It is important to note that he was a leader in the Soyal Society, head of the Blue Flute kiva, and from the same phratry as Lololoma; this made his challenge to the latter's leadership legitimate. The progressives and conservatives grouped behind their able leaders, and the great drama at Oraibi began.

Because a critical issue in the dispute was the precise identity of the Anglo-Americans, each faction drew on sacred myths to validate its stand. Were these Anglos the Bahanas? The hostile faction said no, for a real Bahana would be able to speak the Hopi language and could produce a stone matching the one held by the Village Chief at Oraibi. Obviously these Anglos were not the Bahanas, and by accepting the whites as gods, the progressives were likely to arouse the anger of a supernatural which would send a flood to end the world. The progressives traced Hopi difficulties not to Anglo-Americans but to the underworld and witchcraft. The sides chosen by particular individuals were influenced by a number of factors, among which were their sib and phratry ties as well as the nature of their close kin ties with the outstanding personalities in the conflict.

The attitude of the conservatives was reflected by their categorical rejection of American ways. When they refused to send their children to school at Keams Canyon in 1887, Lololoma identified them to government officials and some were arrested. The remaining hostiles then confined Lololoma to a kiva, from which he was rescued by United States Army soldiers. When in 1891 an attempt was made by Federal representatives to survey Oraibi land, the hostiles disrupted the efforts. When a small group of soldiers came to unseat the leader, they were surrounded. A ceremonial declaration of war was issued with great drama, and the soldiers prudently withdrew. A larger United States military force was sent to Oraibi shortly afterwards and arrested the hostile leaders as well as some of the progressive leaders.

What happened at Oraibi affected the entire tribe, for in 1890 the village contained 1200 of the 2200 Hopi listed on the official census. Laura Thompson points out that behind the rupture at Oraibi was the problem of land. There were Navajo encroachments, but disputes also had arisen between sibs over the lands of an abandoned pueblo. It is to be remembered that successful farming in the past was based on community recognition of sib holdings and sib cooperation in farming. Between 1892 and 1911, however, Federal pressures were great to have the Indians accept individual family land allotments.

By 1891 the friendly and hostile factions were at such bitter odds that they could not be reconciled. Since the hostiles were more numerous, their leader, Lomahongyoma, declared that he was the Village Chief. The fracture became a fissure when attention turned to ceremonial issues. Neither side would cooperate with the other in presenting the sacred ceremonies; nor would either permit the use of its ceremonial equipment by the opposite faction. The progressive leader was refused the right to hold the Soyal Ceremony in the Blue Flute kiva, and the conservative leader decided to hold his own Soyal Ceremony. In 1897 the Soyal Society members were forced to align themselves with one of the two leaders, depending on whether they supported the hostile or the friendly faction. In spite of the bitterness between the factions, each held its own Soyal Ceremony without interference from the other. Each also performed the Powamu and Niman ceremonies, but the progressives did not attempt to hold the Blue Flute-

Snake rituals which belonged to the hostile faction. Between 1899 and 1906 two separate but never fully complete sets of ceremonies were conducted annually. About 1901 there was a change in progressive leadership. Lololoma died, and a younger sister's son replaced him. This young, aggressive man, Tawaqwaptiwa, was selected over his older brother because of his more forceful qualities. In September of 1906 open conflict developed. After some scuffling the conservative leader drew a line on the ground, and a push-of-war was held. Before the pushing began it was decided that the losers would leave the pueblo. The hostile leader was the object to be pushed, with people pushing him from behind or in front. Finally, the hostiles or conservatives lost the struggle. The same evening about 300 persons took their belongings and abandoned the settlement. They founded the new village of Hotevilla, about seven miles to the north of Oraibi. The nature of the split clearly illustrates that the sociopolitical structure of the community could not resolve conflicts of this nature.

The Bureau of Indian Affairs authorities came on the scene soon after the rupture. They sent the conservative leaders to jail and relieved Tawaqwaptiwa temporarily as chief of Oraibi. He was sent to the Indian school at Riverside, California, to learn to speak English and practice American ways. When he returned to Oraibi in 1910, he was extremely anti-American; Titiev (1944, 94) records accounts which describe him as "quarrelsome, stubborn, vindictive, and unusually licentious." Over the next twenty years Tawaqwaptiwa managed to antagonize most of the remaining residents of Oraibi. He forced Mennonite converts and sympathizers, in addition to those who accepted only some American customs, away from the settlement with his constant quarrels. By 1933 only 109 Hopi remained in Oraibi. Some had moved to New Oraibi, on the valley floor beneath Oraibi, and others settled some forty miles to the northwest at Moencopi on the Navajo Reservation. The disintegration of Oraibi, as Thompson has pointed out, relieved the local pressures for land, but social cohesion did not develop in the offshoot communities. In Moencopi two factions emerged, one sympathetic with the Mennonite missionaries and another which retained ceremonial ties with Oraibi. The most conservative community by the 1940's was Hotevilla. The people had a nearly complete ceremonial cycle when they left Oraibi that September night in 1906. Through the years their resistance against whites became almost an end in itself, and the reasons behind it were logical. After the split, most of the Hotevilla men were impounded by the Federal government, and it was very difficult for the women and children to survive until their return. Then too, children were forced by soldiers to attend school, and the people forcefully were dunked in sheep-dip during a 1912 epidemic. These people scorned outside interference and wanted to be left alone.

After 1906 a complete ceremonial round could no longer be held at Oraibi because some sibs were no longer represented, but Chief Tawaqwaptiwa faced the situation calmly as he aged. He maintained that the time would soon come when everyone would abandon him and he alone would carry on the Soyal. Then there would be a great famine, and following it, all of the old ceremonies would be reinstituted at Oraibi. Again the village would thrive in all of its colorful glory. Tawaqwaptiwa waited and waited and died still waiting.

By the beginning of the present century, the Hopi subsistence cycle had undergone major changes. The primary reliance on maize, beans, and squash remained, but new crops and animals became increasingly important. Probably the most important new animal was the sheep, and virtually every man had at least a small flock by 1900. Each animal was owned by an individual, but they were herded cooperatively by men. Most often a man tended a combined flock for a few days, and then his brother, with whom he was a herding partner, took charge. Sheep were held as wealth and were butchered only for ceremonial feasts. Any unconsumed meat was dried in the sun as jerky or dried, pounded, and mixed with fat as pemmican. Cattle were less popular because of their initial cost and because the pattern of allowing them to graze freely led to the destruction of crops, with ensuing disputes over crop damage. The major difficulty in maintaining horses, which were broken to the saddle, was the nuisance of rounding them up each day for pasturing, usually at a considerable distance from the community. Like the sheep, they often were individually owned but tended jointly by men.

It is possible to learn many details of recent Hopi sociocultural change by consulting the admirable works of Thompson. Her field studies were made during 1942-1944 to help solve Bureau of Indian Affairs administrative problems among the Hopi. A vast amount of diverse information was obtained, of which the following is especially pertinent here. In the 1940's about 4000 Hopi were located in fourteen different settlements, including Moencopi, on land which had been set aside for Hopi occupancy adjacent to the Colorado River. The critical problems facing the people were a population increase on a smaller land base and the increasing erosion of the land. The land depletion apparently resulted from a dry climatic phase as well as overgrazing by livestock. Government efforts to remedy the situation were aimed first at a reduction in livestock. The people of the Third Mesa area were required to reduce their holdings by nearly 45 percent, while on the other two mesas reductions were about 20 percent. Thus, the Oraibi area residents were hardest hit by the program. The Federal government had for many years encouraged herding, and sheep had become a very important item in the Hopi economy. Third Mesa people resisted the reduction with vigor but finally succumbed to Federal pressures. Along with stock reduction a program was instituted to encourage better stock management practices, and cooperatives were organized. The farming practices of old remained although the plow was replacing the digging stick. Most of the fields were watered from stream flooding or else were dry land plots. An effort to irrigate Hopi lands has not been overly successful, and even if it were expanded it could include only a maximum of 400 acres. The typical farmer, which meant almost every man, raised a wide variety of crops, but the essentially meatless diet consisted mainly of maize, white flour, beans, potatoes, sugar, and coffee. The nutritive value of the diet was below normal standards for children and just barely sufficient for adults. In 1942 the Hopi economy was based on the following: wage labor, 36 percent; livestock, 34; agriculture, 22; and all other sources, 8 percent. Of the nearly 600 families, more than half had an income of less than $300 in 1942.

All aspects of life at Oraibi underwent tremendous readjustments following the 1906 rupture. When the ceremonial cycle no longer could be held, a man's activities were affected profoundly, and the kiva-centered life of a male was destroyed. There was an accompanying increase in the significance of the nuclear family unit. Tests administered by Thompson and her associates demonstrated that Oraibi children looked to their mothers as the dominant family member, while to children from First Mesa the father and mother both were important. Furthermore, boys from First Mesa were outgoing in their responses, while those of Oraibi were "definitely constricted and are troubled by a vague anxiety," according to Thompson (1950, 97). At the same time the Oraibi children were judged to reflect greater sensitivity than the others tested. In all social units males had suffered more disorganizing influences than the females; if anything, the position of women had been strengthened. The net result was a fostering of previously unheard-of male individualism. Seemingly, about the only course of action remaining for men was to seek to better their position. Since the Oraibi land base was not adaptable to the accumulation of farmlands or even male control of such lands, there was a move toward wage labor by the ambitious males. Another avenue open to individual males was political leadership, but in this role an individual encountered the pervasive Hopi feeling against personal achievements.

A recent problem of the Hopi with whites is more stressful and threatening than any they previously have encountered. In an effort to fulfill the ever-increasing demands for electrical power in southern California, the

Las Vegas area of Nevada, and sectors of Arizona, the Western Energy Supply and Transmission Associates (W.E.S.T.) was formed by municipal, state, and federal power companies. The Mohave plant in eastern Nevada began operations in 1970 and is powered by coal which is strip-mined at Black Mesa in Hopi and Navajo country about 270 miles to the east. Pulverized coal and water are pumped as slurry through a pipeline to the Mohave powerplant. The transport system requires up to 4,500 gallons of water a minute which is drawn from wells some 2,000 feet in depth; during peak operations it is expected that three million gallons of water a day will be pumped from wells on Black Mesa. Ignoring the frightening problem of air pollution, there is the danger that if the deep well casings become cracked or broken, by whatever means, the shallow wells and springs of the Hopi would flow deep into the ground and they could no longer live in the area. An additional danger is posed by the runoff from the ridges of overburden (spoil banks) left by the strip-mining operation. Some of these cut across wash drainages, and if water from them enters cultivated fields the sulfur concentrates probably would ruin the land.

The Hopi theocracy was relatively free from serious disruption by outside political pressures until passage of the Indian Reorganization Act of 1934. Under the terms of this law the Hopi Tribal Council was organized, but the traditionalists or conservatives among them never recognized the legitimacy of this organization and have refused to elect representatives to it. They reason that to acknowledge the existence of authority which supersedes their religious and political institutions would be to break their covenant with the gods. In 1964-1966 through the Department of the Interior, the Peabody Coal Company as a subsidiary of the Kennecott Copper Corporation, negotiated the lease to mine coal on Black Mesa with the Hopi and Navajo tribal councils. The progressive Hopi Tribal Council approved the lease, but the manner in which it was "negotiated" and the legality of the lease are subject to grave doubts.

A great deal of secrecy surrounded the negotiations which led to the entire W.E.S.T. development. No announcements were made before contracts were signed, and no public hearings were held at any level, nor was there any open discussion of what was happening. It is abundantly clear that the Department of the Interior through the Bureau of Indian Affairs worked very closely and quietly with representatives of W.E.S.T. for the benefit of industry at the expense of Indians. In the lease contracts with the Hopi approved by the Bureau of Indian Affairs there were no guarantees about water, reclaiming areas strip-mined, or spoil bank runoff. This appears to be in direct violation of the Hopi constitution. Furthermore, the Peabody Coal Company lease was approved in part by noncertified representatives to the Hopi Tribal Council. Thus, it would appear that the lease is not valid. The Hopi do derive direct and indirect monetary benefits from the mining operation, but they had no idea of what would happen to their lands, nor had they been made aware of the possible spoilage by the Bureau of Indian Affairs.

There is a prophesy among the Hopi that Indian lands will be seized or spoiled and that those of the Hopi will be the last to go. It also is prophesied that when this happens, if the Hopi and their friends cannot prevent these disasters, the world will end by turning over.

References

Beaglehole, Ernest and Pearl. *Hopi of the Second Mesa*. American Anthropological Association, Memoir no. 44. 1935.

Blundell, William E. "Ecological Shootout at Black Mesa," *Wall Street Journal*, April 18, 1971.

*Bunzel, Ruth L. *The Pueblo Potter*. New York, 1929. The discussion of Hopi and other pueblo Indian pottery is one of the finest studies of aboriginal ceramics. The text is particularly noteworthy when dealing with the ways in which designs were conceived and executed.

Colton, Harold S. *Hopi Kachina Dolls*. Albuquerque, 1949.

Colton, Mary-Russel F. "The Arts and Crafts of the Hopi Indians," *Museum Notes, Museum of Northern Arizona*, v. 11, 3-24. 1938.

Cushing, Frank H. "Origin Myth from Oraibi," *Journal of American Folklore*, v. 36, 163-170. 1923.

Forde, Cyril D. *Habitat, Economy and Society*. London. 1934.

Hurbert, Virgil. "An Introduction to Hopi Pottery Design," *Museum Notes, Museum of Northern Arizona*, v. 10, 1-4. 1937.

Josephy, Alvin M. "The Murder of the Southwest," *Audubon*, July, 52-67. 1971.

Jones, Volney H. "The Establishment of the Hopi Reservation, and some later Developments Concerning Hopi Lands," *Plateau*, v. 23, 17-25. 1950.

Oliver, James A. *Snakes in Fact and Fiction*. New York. 1958.

*Simmons, Leo W., ed. *Sun Chief*. New Haven. 1942. This Hopi autobiography is an extremely valuable document, for it offers great insight into the life of one individual.

Spicer, Edward H. *Cycles of Conquest*. Tucson. 1962.

Thompson, Laura, and Alice Joseph. *The Hopi Way*. Chicago. 1944.

*Thompson, Laura. *Culture in Crisis*. New York. 1950. The ethnographic background to Hopi life is provided in summary form, with the addition of the 1942-1944 findings of Thompson, her co-workers and assistants. The volume is devoted in part to Hopi administration by the Bureau of Indian Affairs, but also provides diverse information about Hopi acculturation.

Titiev, Mischa. "Notes on Hopi Witchcraft," *Papers of the Michigan Academy of Science, Arts, and Letters*, v. 28, 549-557. 1943.

*Titiev, Mischa. *Old Oraibi*. Papers of the Peabody Museum of American Archaeology and Ethnology, v. 22, No. 1. 1944. The classic study of a Hopi community through time—a key source.

Whiting, Alfred F. *Ethnobotany of the Hopi*. Museum of Northern Arizona, Bulletin 15. 1950.

Wormington, Marie M. *Prehistoric Indians of the Southwest*. Denver Museum of Natural History. 1951.

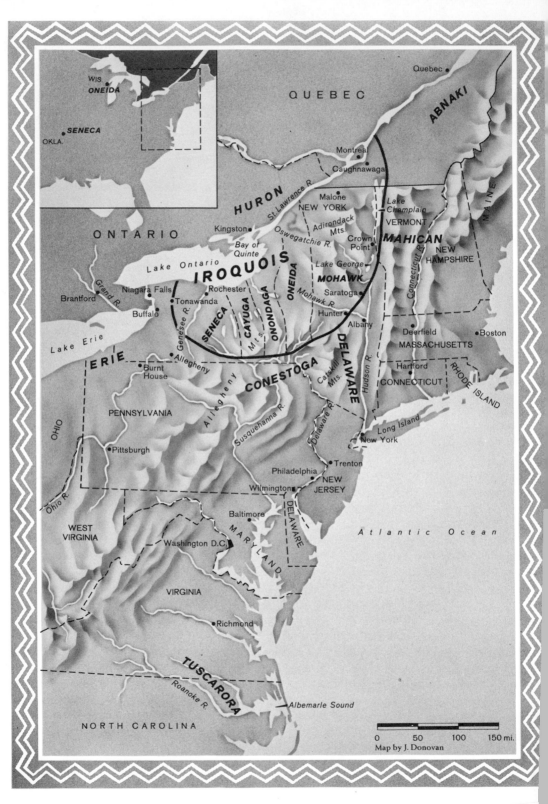

QUEBEC

ABNAKI

WIS.
ONEIDA

SENECA
OKLA.

ONTARIO

HURON

Quebec

Montreal

Caughnawaga

St. Lawrence R.

Malone

NEW YORK

Lake
Champlain

Kingston

Adirondack
Mts.

VERMONT

Oswegatchie R.

Crown
Point

MAHICAN

NEW
HAMPSHIRE

Bay of
Quinte

Lake Ontario

IROQUOIS

Lake George

MAINE

Connecticut R.

ONEIDA

MOHAWK

Niagara Falls

Rochester

Brantford

Tonawanda

Buffalo

Grand R.

SENECA

CAYUGA

ONONDAGA

Mohawk R.

Saratoga

Hunter

Mts.

Albany

Deerfield

Boston

MASSACHUSETTS

Lake Erie

ERIE

Allegheny

Genesee R.

DELAWARE

Hudson R.

Hartford

CONNECTICUT

RHODE ISLAND

Burnt
House

CONESTOGA

Catskill
Mts.

Allegheny R.

Delaware R.

OHIO

PENNSYLVANIA

Susquehanna R.

Long Island

New York

Pittsburgh

Trenton

Philadelphia

Wilmington

**NEW
JERSEY**

Ohio R.

WEST
VIRGINIA

Baltimore

MARYLAND

DELAWARE

Atlantic Ocean

Washington D.C.

VIRGINIA

Richmond

TUSCARORA

Roanoke R.

Albemarle Sound

NORTH CAROLINA

0   50   100   150 mi.

Map by J. Donovan

The Iroquois:

warriors and farmers of the eastern woodlands

Anthropologists long have exhibited a particular fondness for the Iroquois and not without good reason. The first modern ethnography was written by Lewis H. Morgan about these people and published in 1851 under the title of *League of the Ho-de-no-sau-nee or Iroquois*. This work was to set a precedent for modern ethnographic studies and is an anthropological classic. The original Iroquois League consisted of five tribes or nations, the Cayuga, Mohawk, Oneida, Onondaga, and Seneca, and was known also as the Five Nations. These Indians conceived and administered a political bureaucracy of great vitality and justness. In early historic times the League was able to extend its power through conquest and intimidation far beyond its place of origin in present-day western New York State. It was the Iroquois, too, who played a decisive role in shaping the colonial empires of the French and British in northeastern North America. Historians acknowledge also the importance of the League during the American Revolution. From the colonial period to the present the names of outstanding Iroquois have been known to many Americans. During the colonial period there were the warrior and military leader Hendrick, the warrior and politician Joseph Brant, and Red Jacket, the great orator. Kateri Tegaquitha, born about 1656, has been beatified by the Roman Catholic Church and is well on her way to becoming the first American Indian saint. General Ely S. Parker was the secretary to General Ulysses S. Grant and drafted the terms of peace at Appomattox at the end of the Civil War. Finally, there is the contemporary Iroquois, Jay Silverheels, better known as Tonto, of Lone Ranger fame. The Iroquois have continued to retain their clear identity down to the present time with a sociocultural resilience that is rare. Today it is recognized that many Iroquois contribute significant skills within the economies of modern Canada and the United States.

One major difficulty in assembling Iroquois sources is to separate information about the Iroquois in general from that which pertains to a single member tribe or nation. This problem can not be resolved successfully because we do not have parallel information on all the League nations. The descriptions to follow thus represent a broad and composite view of these Indians. In general, the reconstructed aboriginal scene has been drawn from the ethnography by Morgan, whose data came mainly from the Tonawanda Band of the Seneca. Furthermore, Morgan unquestionably presented an idealized Iroquois culture with greater uniformity and nobility than actually existed. For the later period an attempt has been made to follow the fortunes of the Mohawk in particular, and in some respects this does not lead to a balanced reconstruction. The reason is that a major segment of the Mohawk population was Christianized early in its history and

446

has attracted less attention from ethnographers than more conservative and traditionally oriented Iroquois tribes. We will therefore attempt to follow the destiny of the Mohawk and still include the general trends in Iroquois culture and social change.

Consulting the Iroquois sources is an extremely rewarding and at the same time a frustrating experience. It is fascinating to read the studies by Morgan, Horatio Hale, John N. Hewitt, and Frank G. Speck, and it is equally rewarding to study the recent works of Anthony F. C. Wallace. Most of all, however, it has been the continuing contributions of William N. Fenton which are most useful. He has examined a vast amount of historical information and at the same time has made highly original field studies. As Fenton (1951, 305) noted, "the Iroquois and their neighbors cover a time span of three centuries and have had more written about them in the last hundred years than any other American Indian people, including the Navaho.... During three centuries their culture has undergone remarkable change which is abundantly documented; their culture has also demonstrated amazing stability." The frustration in consulting Iroquois materials stems from the failure of any specialist since Morgan to attempt a synthesis of his findings. Considering how few persons are engaged in Iroquois research and the vast number of sources available, this is understandable; nevertheless, a broad, integrative progress report would be invaluable.

The aboriginal Iroquois occupied the area from Lake Champlain and Lake George on the east to the Genesee River drainage and Lake Ontario on the west. The northern boundary was the St. Lawrence River, and Iroquois domain extended southward to the upper reaches of the Susquehanna River. Each nation occupied an oblong strip of country; from east to west, the nations were the Mohawk, Oneida, Onondaga, Cayuga, and Seneca. Population estimates for the period of early historic contact vary widely. James Mooney estimated that the Five Nations in A.D. 1600 numbered about 5500 and the Tuscaroras about 5000. Fenton estimated the Five Nations population at something less than 10,000 for the period of early historic contact. By 1904 the Six Nations (adding the Tuscarora) numbered at least 16,000, including some 3000 persons of mixed blood. In 1962 the Iroquois in the United States who had retained at least some identity as Indians were approximately as follows: New York, with all Six Nations represented, 7700; Oklahoma Cayuga and Seneca, 750; Pennsylvania Seneca, 30; and Wisconsin Oneida, 1400. The total modern Iroquois population, including those in Canada, is estimated at 20,000.

The word Iroquois is derived from the combination of an Algonkian word translated as "real adder" and a French suffix. The Iroquois spoke a language of the Macro-Siouan phylum and the Iroquoian family. The dialects of the Iroquois include Cayuga, Mohawk, Oneida, Onondaga, and Seneca. Cherokee, which is of the same family as Iroquois, separated from Iroquois about 100 B.C. Separations within Iroquois among the member dialects took place about A.D. 700. All of these estimates are based on the results of glottochronology.

The lands of the Iroquois fall into two biotic provinces. The eastern area is in the Canadian province, and the western province is the Carolinian, with an ill-defined boundary between the two. In Iroquois country there are diverse nut-bearing trees such as chestnuts, hickories, oaks, and walnuts, while the conifers are red cedar, white pine, and hemlock. In aboriginal times the area was rich in animal species. The large animals included bear, deer, elk, and moose, and there were also wild turkey, fox, and porcupine. The most important fur-bearing species were the beaver, fisher, marten, mink, and muskrat. Lake fish included bass, smelt, trout, pickerel, pike, and whitefish. From this brief list of the abundant natural resources it is clear that the environment had a great deal of potential for an aboriginal people.

The first inhabitants of the northeastern area of the United States were apparently big game hunters and are known only from scattered lithic finds. These people, who came from the south or west around 9000 B.C., manufactured spearpoints, knives, and scrapers, as well as implements from prepared or polyhedral cores. Following this era, which is relatively unknown, the populations, usually termed Archaic, became more sedentary, possibly representing a settling-down of the big game hunters. The earliest Archaic peoples are not much better delineated than their predecessors, but by some time before 2000 B.C. with the Late Archaic the picture becomes somewhat clearer. The technology came to include ground stone tools. Among the latter forms were adz blades, gouges, grooved stones, and slate points. Sometime soon after 2000 B.C. pottery was manufactured, and such items as bannerstones and semilunar knives were new manufactures. This cultural complex was to be the base out of which developed the Early Woodland, around 1000 B.C., which seems to have been a localized development. Cremations became more important, as did red ocher associations with the dead and an increase in the quantity of grave goods. The climax development was the Adena culture in the Ohio River area before 200 B.C. There were burial mounds and, later in the same culture complex, earthworks, some farming, and a great diversity of artifact forms. The middle period of Woodland is associated mainly with Hopewell cultural developments, which emerged about A.D. 1 from an Adena base influenced by outside contacts. As James B. Griffin (1964, 241) has written, "There is a growing tendency to view Ohio Hopewell as a uniform cultural complex dominated by an elite class that marshaled its manpower for conquest and the establishment of outlying subject groups." He further doubts that Hopewell sociopolitical organization was as advanced as that of the historic Iroquois. Associated with Hopewell are complex earthworks, settled communities, farming, and a highly varied material culture. This cultural period did not dominate the eastern area; instead we find here the Point Peninsula cultural remains which were left by central-based hunters and collectors who perhaps cultivated a few plants. Their technology included chipped as well as polished stone weapon points, knives, and ornaments. The general tradition seems to have developed from an Archaic subsistence pattern based on hunting and fishing. Direct continuity exists into the Lake Woodland culture reflected in the Owasco and associated developments in New York State and adjacent areas. The population was more sedentary than that previously noted for the area, the villages were fortified, and the people depended more on crops which they raised than on gathering activities. Their pipe forms and dwellings were of the Iroquois type, and these Indians have been identified as Iroquoian. Tribes related to the historic Mohawk and Onondaga were in the Montreal region in the early 1500's and moved to New York State about 100 years later. Two conclusions were reached by Griffin concerning the archaeological remains of the Iroquois. Their way of life developed in the northeastern area, and their material culture does not seem out of the ordinary in its complexity for the area in general.

No Indians played a more important role in the growth and development of the British North American colony than the League of the Iroquois. In attempting to follow the history of the League in colonial and later times particular attention will be paid to the Mohawk. The principal historical sources consulted were the pro-British study by John W. Lydekker, the more balanced study of Cadwallader Colden, and the histories of Francis Parkman.

The French entered the St. Lawrence River system in 1534 with the explorations of Jacques Cartier, and they soon established contact with the Algonkians, Hurons, and Montagnais. By the time the imaginative and aggressive French explorer Samuel Champlain was ready to turn his attention from the west to the south he had allied himself with the Algonkians against their enemies, the League tribes. Little did Champlain realize what a powerful adversary he was to confront. As Francis Parkman (1901, v. 1, 9) wrote, the League was "foremost in war, foremost in eloquence, [and] and foremost in their savage arts of policy...." In 1609 Champlain, with a group of Algonkians, canoed to the lake which bears his name and met a party of Iroquois. In the battle which followed, the Iroquois attacked with confidence but were routed after being struck with terror at the appearance of white men clad in strange garb and using exotic weapons. The Iroquois never forgave the French or the Algonkians for the defeat; they soon recovered to raid and terrorize the French and Indian settlements along the St. Lawrence River.

Formal contact between the Mohawk and Europeans led to a treaty with the Dutch in 1644 and one with the Dutch successors, the English, in 1664. The treaty with the English was signed also by the Seneca but not by the other three nations of the League. The following year all but the Mohawk, plus some Cayuga and Seneca, made a treaty with the French; the Mohawk were attacked by the French because of their failure to cooperate. The French attempted to win permanent control over the Iroquois in 1687, but the Iroquois responded to this French pressure by turning to the English for help and acknowledging the sovereignty of James II. The domestic crisis in England and the abdication of James II in 1688 gave the French a fresh opportunity to attempt the destruction of the British colony. However, the Mohawk took the initiative against the French by destroying the community of La Chine, and they went on to successfully attack Montreal. In a conference of the League in 1690 to decide whether to support the French or the English, the Mohawk, Onondaga, and Seneca favored the English. In 1693 the French destroyed the Mohawk settlements and persuaded the Cayuga and Seneca to remain neutral. The French were most effective among the western nations, the Cayuga and Seneca, whereas English influence was strongest among the easternmost member nation, the Mohawk. The French, however, did not give up on the Mohawk. The Jesuit priests were able intermittently to induce Mohawk to settle near Montreal at St. Louis or Caughnawaga. By the early eighteenth century perhaps two thirds of the Mohawk had left their aboriginal home. Divorced from their traditional hunting and farmlands they developed a new means for survival. They served as the transporters of trade goods from English posts in the east to the French traders who were involved in the lucrative trade for beaver pelts from the more distant Great Lakes region tribes.

Hostilities between the French and English erupted anew with Queen Anne's War in 1702, and the outlying New England settlements received the brunt of the attack. The Iroquois remained neutral, but the New England Indians and those in adjacent areas of Canada fought for the French. In the late winter of 1704 the Caughnawaga Mohawk and Abnaki accompanied a French-led party to Deerfield, Massachusetts, where there were about 300 persons at the time. In a predawn attack about 110 persons were taken prisoner and about 50 others killed. During the rapid return to Canada, most of the prisoners who could not keep up with the fast-moving party were killed; only somewhat more than half of them were restored eventually to the English.

When Queen Anne's War ended and the Treaty of Utrecht was signed in 1713, English control over much of eastern America was consolidated. Most importantly, members of the League nations were recognized as British subjects. In 1711, Queen's Fort was founded, but the success of the Church of England missionary who worked there, William Andrews, was questionable. The children soon wearied of attending school, and general conditions among the adults were not what he would have desired. One of his principal complaints was the traffic in intoxicants from Dutch traders to the Indians. The Iroquois passion for intoxicants is well documented, and naturally the missionary attempted to stem its flow. His mission did comparatively little to change the lives of the Indians, and in 1719 he resigned his post in disappointment. The soldiers remained at what was now called Fort Hunter, and it became an administrative center. A mission was opened in Albany in 1727, and the missionary stationed there periodically visited the fort. By 1742 all but two or three Mohawk had been baptized and nominally were Christians. This success was a direct result of the extremely able efforts of Henry Barclay, who became an Anglican missionary in 1735. He seems to have been an ideal choice since he was born in the colonies, graduated from Yale, spoke Dutch and some Mohawk, and was eager to serve. The Mohawk respected him highly, as did the English, and he was able to succeed where his predecessors either had failed or could claim only limited success.

The War of the Austrian Succession, which erupted in 1740 and once again pitted the French against the English, had reverberations on both continents. The French actively sought Iroquois support, and together they raided and burned outlying settlements, bringing turmoil to the Albany area. Since Barclay felt that he no longer could accomplish much in the area, he left the Mohawk without a cleric. For two years the French intruded into the border area, and the English mounted little effective counteraction; they even were forced to withdraw from the border outpost at Saratoga. The English did send raiding parties into French territory under the Mohawk Hendrick in 1747, but the following year peace was concluded. When the next missionary went to Albany and Fort Hunter, he found cause for both joy and anxiety. The Mohawk received him in a friendly fashion and obviously had retained at least some of what they had been taught by Barclay and his predecessors. One Indian had even taken it on himself to spend most of his time preaching and instructing others. The distressing aspects of the scene were that intoxicants had become popular and highly disruptive in Indian domestic life and that the Roman Catholic priests at

Fort Frontenac (Kingston, Ontario) had been successful in inducing more Mohawk to move to Canada. Between 1713 and 1750 the population of Mohawk appears to have dropped from 580 to 418, with the decrease due mainly to Indians moving into French-occupied country.

During the late 1740's and early 1750's the French sought to expand their control by dominating Lake Erie and Lake Ontario as well as by bringing about closer contacts with the Cayuga, Onondaga, and Seneca through building a mission at the junction of the Oswegatchie and St. Lawrence rivers. A major in the militia, George Washington, was sent to induce the French to abandon one post they had seized, but he was unsuccessful. A later attempt by Washington to dislodge the French by force from the upper Ohio River area ended in his defeat and greatly strengthened the position of the French with the local Indians. In the next major conflict, Major General Edward Braddock was killed and his force badly defeated near Fort Duquesne by the French and Indians, including some Caughnawaga, in 1755. The English and French met again in conflict on September 8, 1755, and after a hotly contested battle the English and their allies won the day, thanks in a large part to Hendrick, who was killed, and the Mohawk whom he led. In 1756 a formal war, the French and Indian War, was declared between England and France. The English were defeated soundly until Fort Frontenac fell to them and until the Moravian missionary Frederic Post persuaded the Indians of the upper Ohio River drainage to abandon their French allies. This forced the French to withdraw from Fort Duquesne in 1758, and the site became the English Fort Pitt (Pittsburgh).

In 1759 the English began a two-pronged attack against the French which led to an end of French political power in Canada. In the famous battle for Quebec on the Plains of Abraham the English line met the charging French and did not fire until the advancing army was thirty-five paces away. The French force virtually was destroyed, and a French effort to retake Quebec ended in failure. In the spring of 1760 the English formulated a plan to take Montreal with converging armies. The plan succeeded, and by the end of the year the French had been forced to surrender their principal holdings in North America. Action was taken by the British government in 1763 to license traders to Indians and to prohibit the alienation of Indian lands except with the approval of the Governor-in-Council. These were two extremely important precedents in guiding Indian policies in Canada and the United States.

In 1775 began the final drama in which the Iroquois were to play a significant role in American history. The Iroquois were as a whole loyal to the British, and at best the colonial rebels could hope only to neutralize them. The loyal subjects of the Crown in turn did their utmost to induce the Iroquois to support the cause of the British actively. At the second Continental Congress an Indian Department was created with Northern, Middle, and Southern divisions, and the commissioner of each was charged with rendering the Indians neutral. At a meeting of the Northern Commissioner with the Iroquois a systematic effort was made to insure their neutrality. Joseph Brant, who was loyal to the British, visited England in 1775 in order to clarify the position of the Iroquois whom he represented. While there he was made a captain in His Majesty's Army and pledged Iroquois support. Upon his return he led a force of Mohawk against the American rebels. Joseph Brant, or Thayendanegea, was born in 1742; his father was a full-blooded Mohawk, and his mother was either full-blooded or half-blooded. Brant began his long career as a warrior in 1755 and later was sent to a school in Connecticut where he was reasonably well educated. With the Declaration of Independence in 1776 the political break between rebel colonists and the British was complete, and war began. The policy of unanimity among the League tribes broke down as a result of the conflict. The Mohawk and Onondaga were divided internally, some supporting each side; the Cayuga and Seneca supported the loyalists; the Oneida and Tuscarora were in theory neutral but in fact gave the rebels aid.

After the successful attack of forces under Joseph Brant and Walter Butler to the south of the Mohawk River, the Americans organized an army against these Iroquois. In 1779 the troops of General John Sullivan succeeded well in their task of destroying Iroquois communities, crops, and grain caches. Iroquois effectiveness was ended, and many of them fled to Canada, abandoning their traditional lands forever. In Canada the Mohawk settled temporarily near Montreal where they were given lands and erected a log building to serve as a church and council house. When the treaty of peace was signed in 1783, there was no mention of the Indians and their future status. In recognition of Mohawk aid for the British cause, these Indians were granted land along the northern shore of Lake Ontario and lands along Grand River, which flows into the northeastern sector of Lake Erie. A separate treaty was made between the Six Nations and the United States, in which the Oneida and Tuscarora, who had remained neutral in the conflict, were permitted to retain most of their lands but the other League nations, who had fought for the British, were forced to relinquish claim to most of their land.

Once again Joseph Brant went to England, this time to press for compensation for Mohawk losses. Brant did not obtain all that he had hoped for in the way of compensation from the English government and was somewhat disillusioned by his reception when he returned to Canada. Still he lobbied for a Canadian home for the loyalists of the Six Nations. The Canadian authorities willingly offered an area along the eastern shore of Lake Ontario at the Bay of Quinte, but Brant pushed for a final grant of land in the Grand River country of Lake Erie. Some of his followers preferred the Bay of Quinte site and settled there. In 1784 the Grand River area was purchased from its Indian occupants and granted to the Six Nations. To Brant this meant that the Iroquois who were to occupy the country were granted sovereignty over it and he was the trustee. Thus the land, in Brant's eyes, was subject only to Iroquois national control. The Iroquois began to move to the Grand River drainage in 1784, with approximately 1600 people in the migration. Almost a third of the total were Mohawk, somewhat fewer Cayuga, and the balance mostly Onondaga, Seneca, and Tuscarora, with a few Oneida.

The last time the Six Nations asserted political power in an international dispute was in the War of 1812. The Americans were quick to assure the Six Nations residents that invading forces would not disturb their interest but the Iroquois was rightfully unimpressed; neither were they willing to commit themselves wholeheartedly to the British cause, again for good historical reasons. An initial call to arms brought forth fewer than fifty Iroquois to serve the British cause. Later victories by the Canadians induced some 500 Six Nations warriors to fight, which they did with distinction, but before the end of the war any effective Iroquois cooperation had ceased to exist.

From an Iroquois origin myth recorded by Henry R. Schoolcraft we learn that once there were two worlds. The upper level was inhabited by creatures similar to humans, and the lower level by monsters who lived in water. A female from the upper world descended into the lower realm and onto the back of a turtle. She bore twin boys and then died. The shell of the turtle grew in size and became an island continent, and the offspring of the woman were termed Great Spirit (Ruler) and Evil Spirit. Light was created by Great Spirit by transforming his mother's head into the sun and other parts of her body into the moon and stars. The light from these heavenly bodies drove the monsters deep into the water, and then Great Spirit placed on the expanded turtle shell all the geographical features, animals, and plants useful to man. He created men and women from earth and placed life in their forms. His brother made creatures of evil and geographical barriers to blight the pacific landscape. Thus the brothers were contesting forces, and this led to a fight between them. They fought for two days until finally the Evil Spirit descended into the underworld.

Iroquois clothing was made principally from processed deerskins which were sewn using deer-bone awls and sinew thread. Men wore kilts which reached their knees and were belted at the waist. The kilts were fringed at the bottom and decorated with designs in dyed porcupine quills which had been flattened before being attached with sinew thread. The men wore fringed shirts and long, fringed leggings; on their feet they wore quill-decorated moccasins. Women wore under-skirts which hung from the waist to just above the ankles, with designs in quills along the lower border. Over this garment was a long dress with fringed sleeves and fringe along the bottom. From their knees to their moccasins were short leggings, and in cold weather a skin cape was worn about the shoulders.

Any particular settlement was likely to be built on a hilltop and exist for about ten years. After this period nearby farmlands were relatively unproductive, firewood was scarce, and the dwellings were falling into decay. Twelve or perhaps thirteen villages, each with from three to six hundred inhabitants, are reported shortly before the turn of the eighteenth century. The Mohawk occupied three communities, and a series of major and minor trails connected these with other settlements of the League nations. Villages were not dispersed widely but clustered along an east-west line. Specially trained runners could disseminate information throughout the entire League in about three days.

Around a typical settlement a ditch was excavated, and wooden palisades, up to three rows deep, were imbedded at an angle into the earth from the ditch. A village enclosure might encompass from five to ten acres with fields of as much as several hundred acres adjacent to the fortified community. The dwellings within a settlement were of the well-known longhouse type. A longhouse was between 50 and 130 feet in length and about sixteen feet wide. Such a dwelling was built of seasoned posts, poles, and bark. The bark was stripped in sheets from trees which had been girdled previously, and the sheets were piled on top of each other to flatten as they dried. Four stout posts with forked tops, one at each corner, formed the outline of the structure. Smaller forked poles were spaced between the main posts, and in the crotches of the forks were strung poles, across which other poles were placed as rafters. The arched roof was formed with bent poles, and the entire framework was covered with overlapping sections of bark. The bark slabs were lashed in place and held firm with retaining poles.

The inside of a house was partitioned into two sections, each about twelve feet in length; between the sections were compartments for the storage of maize and other provisions. Along the center of a longhouse were fireplaces, with the families occupying opposite apartments using a single fire. The smoke from the fires drifted through an oblong roof opening which served also to admit light into the structure. In windy or rainy weather slabs of bark were placed over this opening. Each family had an apartment with two platforms, and there might be as many as twenty apartments in a house. An upper platform some five feet above the ground and six feet from front to back was covered with bark, then with mats of reeds, and finally with skins. The lower platform was of similar dimensions and was about a foot above the ground. It was on these platforms that family members lounged or napped during the day and slept at night. At each end of the structure was a doorway leading into storage rooms which opened to the outside. The outer doors were of bark and were hinged at the top; in the winter a second door of skins was added.

For a small family or as a temporary residence, a less permanent dwelling might be constructed. It was triangular in outline, with poles at each corner converging at the top; poles in between served as further framing. Over the frame were placed overlapping bark slabs; an opening was left in one side for the entrance, and one at the top of the structure was for the smoke from the interior fireplace to pass out. In addition to the maize in the house storage compartments and storage rooms, some was placed in underground caches. These excavated pits were lined with bark, the maize was placed inside, bark roofing was added as a waterproofing, and the container was topped with soil. Similar underground caches were lined with deerskins to hold dried meat.

The right to use farmland belonged to the persons who cleared and cultivated the plots, and any uncleared land might be prepared for crops. Beyond the farmlands of an Iroquois settlement were hunting, fishing, and collecting areas belonging to the community. Residents of a settlement joined one another in war and hunting parties, in games, and rendered mutual assistance in times of stress. The landholding unit was conceived in family, village, and national, as well as League, terms. The yearly subsistence round included two distinct periods when people abandoned their villages. From the harvest until midwinter, families scattered to hunt, and again in the spring settlements were abandoned when they collected maple sap, hunted pigeons, and fished.

The most effective means for taking individual deer was with a spring pole snare set in the animal's trail. When a snare peg was tripped, the spring pole righted itself, and the deer was caught by its hind legs and lifted into the air. Herds of deer were driven between converging lines of brush, at the end of which bowmen were concealed. Bears might be snared along their trails; as one tripped a snare, a heavy pole fell on its back and pinned it down. Bears also were hunted by chasing them for long distances until they tired and could be shot with arrows. In the winter if an animal was killed only a short distance from the hunter's settlement, it was placed on an improvised bark toboggan and taken to the village to be dressed. At other times the kill was butchered and the meat prepared for transport by removing the bones, drying it before a fire, and then putting it into bark containers for backpacking.

In the spring men fished and took birds as women planted their crops. A common fishing technique was to make an essentially cone-shaped basket some three feet in length from converging splints of black ash which were bound together with vegetable fiber cords. The fisherman placed the basket beneath the water facing a rapid or ripples over stones. With a stick he guided fish downstream into the trap. Birds were snared with elm bark nooses, and some species, especially quail and pigeons, were taken in nets made from shredded bark. Men spent most of their summer participating in war parties, religious ceremonies, and council meetings, not in subsistence activities.

All farming among the Iroquois was the obligation of women. They seem to have cleared the land, sowed the seeds, cut the weeds, and harvested the crops. The most important domestic plant was maize, of which at least fifteen varieties were recognized. They cultivated some sixty varieties of beans and eight forms of squash. The most important farming tools were the digging stick and a hoe made from a scapula blade. Women also collected plant foods, including over thirty different wild fruits and about fifty plant products varying from roots to leaves. These were collected largely to vary the maize-bean-squash diet and also were important if crops failed.

Summer travelers used overland trails, waterways, or a combination of the two. The canoe was not covered with birchbark since the birch trees were small, but with the bark of red elm or hickory trees. The bark was pried from a tree in a single section if possible, and the canoes ranged in length from twelve to forty feet. The rounded ribs and the gunwales were made of ash, and both ends of a canoe had a slight upturn. They were propelled with single-bladed paddles. For winter travel snowshoes were constructed of hickory frames laced with babiche. Each snowshoe was about three feet long and sixteen inches at its broadest cross section. They were relatively short and broad and well adapted to travel in timber. It is reported by Morgan that a person could travel as far as fifty miles a day on snowshoes.

One rather notable aspect of the Iroquois was that they did not work stone as extensively as might be expected. They knew of stoneworking from their Algonkian neighbors, and stone was locally available; their failure to develop a large inventory of stone artifacts seems to reflect a culture bias. The chipped stone manufactures included triangular and tanged arrowpoints and, more rarely, leaf-shaped knives or spearpoints. Ax blades of chipped stone did not occur among them, and drills were rare. Artifacts which were ground and polished were found more often than the chipped variety. Stone mortars were present, and adz blades were common. They employed a chisel that possibly was of ground stone. The ground stone knives and arrowpoints, long slender points with diamond-shaped cross sections, semilunar knives and gouges known among the Algonkian did not occur normally.

In order to fell a tree they built a fire at the base, chipped away the charred wood with a chisel, and repeated the process as often as was necessary. Fire was kindled with the use of a pump drill, which consisted of a shaft weighted with a wooden spindle near the lower end. The string of a bow drill was wrapped loosely around the shaft. The bottom of the shaft rested on a drill board on which was placed punk. The shaft was rotated in a pumping motion by drawing the drill bow back and forth, and fire soon was created from sparks produced on the punk. A mortar for pulverizing maize was made by the fire-hollowing technique. A section of tree trunk about three feet in height and two feet across was charred and chiseled at one end to form a cavity to receive the maize. The grain was ground by using a wooden pestle some four feet long and cylindrical in shape with a constricted midsection for a hand grip.

The relatively permanent nature of their settlements made it possible for the Iroquois to accumulate a variety of material objects. One major category was bark vessels; these included barrel-shaped storage containers, trays for mixing cornmeal, deep folded trough-like receptacles for maple sap, and bark ladles. Other ladles of wood were deep-bowled, and soup or hominy was consumed from them. The grit-tempered pottery vessels were globular with necks that constricted to collared rims. The most common ornamental surface treatment consisted of lines in triangular patterns on the collar and rim projections. The vessels held from two to six quarts and were used for either cooking or storage. Basketry was limited in variety and included one twined form which was somewhat globular and held salt. Containers from animal skins were used for storage of household items, and a skin bag which hung about the waist of a warrior or hunter contained most of the items he required on a short or extended trip.

Among the diverse manufactures were elbow pipes of fired clay with decorated bowls. It was common to make encircling lines about the bowl and sometimes to decorate a bowl with an animal or human figure. Their tobacco was cultivated but required little attention. Once planted, it seeded itself from year to year and required only thinning. The leaves were picked in the fall after a frost and were dried before use. Tobacco was smoked, never chewed, and often was kept in a weasel skin pouch attached to a man's belt.

When carrying a load a tumpline was passed over the forehead and attached to a basket, cradleboard, or pack frame. A pack frame was made from sections of hickory wood, was fitted to the back, and might be supported by a chest strap alone, a tumpline alone, or a combination of the two. A cradleboard was about two feet long and fifteen inches wide, with the bottom and the lower end made from boards. The outside of the foot of the cradleboard was carved, and at the head was an upright bow-shaped hoop. An infant was swaddled in a blanket and bound to the board with a belt, while a hood covered the hoop. When a cradleboard was carried by a woman, she attached a separate tumpline to it.

For ordinary meals at home, the men ate before the women and children, and the only scheduled meal was in the morning. At other times of day people ate whenever they were hungry. A woman always offered food to her husband when he returned home after any labor and to all visitors. Foods prepared from maize dominated the diet and were prepared in a wide variety. Hominy, cornmeal "bread," succotash, roasted corn, and boiled corn probably were eaten most often. Of these the most important was hominy gruel called sagamite, which is an Algonkian term. The Seneca, according to Morgan, recognized three major varieties of maize: red, white, and white flint, each with a different use. The red variety was roasted and dried for the future; white was preferred for cornmeal bread; and the white flint ripened earliest and was preferred for making hominy. To prepare bread the kernels were taken from the ear, boiled in water with wood ashes to remove the hulls, ground in a tree trunk mortar with a wooden pestle, passed through a sieve, and shaped into loaves which were boiled in water. For roasting, the ears were picked and placed in a line next to a fire. After roasting, the ears were shelled and the grains dried further in the sun and stored. Maize to be stored on the cob had the husks stripped back; these were braided into bundles which held twenty ears each. To the maize diet might be added meats and soups of various types as well as wild vegetable products.

The typical occupants of an Iroquois longhouse were the females of a matrilineage, their children, and the in-marrying husbands. There was thus not only matrilineality but matrilocal residence. The matrilineages were consolidated into fifteen matrisibs with names such as Bear, Wolf, Turtle, Deer, Beaver, and Hawk. Among the Cayuga, Onondaga, Seneca, and Tuscarora the matrisibs were divided into moieties, but the Mohawk and Oneida had no moiety division, only the Bear, Turtle, and Wolf sibs. The matrisibs cut across national identifications so that members of the Wolf sib, for example, were found in each nation, in different villages within a nation, and in one or more households within a village. Where the moiety division existed, it once was said to have formed the exogamous unit; any combination between sibs of opposite moieties was permitted in marriage. By Morgan's time, however, there was simply sib exogamy and continuing matrilineal descent. Thus, the inheritance of rights would pass from a man to his brothers, to his sister's children, or to some other person in his matrisib. The importance of the sib cannot be overestimated in Iroquois society; not only was it the exogamous and property-holding unit, but it was empowered to invest, and remove if necessary, political leaders. Members cooperated with one another in economic and political activities and judged disputes with other sibs. Furthermore, each sib had a common burial ground, could adopt outsiders, and held certain religious ceremonies.

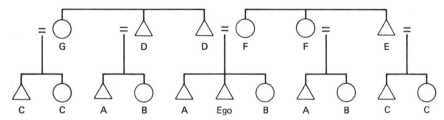

Aboriginal Iroquois kin terms. Each letter represents a different term.

In the kinship terminology a person referred to his father and father's brother by the same word, and mother was termed the same as mother's sister. There were separate and different words for father's sister and mother's brother (bifurcate merging terms). The words for parallel cousins (i.e., father's brother's or mother's sister's children) were the same as for biological brothers and sisters, but cross-cousins (i.e., father's sister's or mother's brother's children) were "cousins." This then is an Iroquois type of cousin terminology. By extension all individuals of one's matrisib, irrespective of their tribal affiliations, were drawn into the system as blood relatives. The basis of Iroquois political life was an extension of household and community kinship ties at the national and League levels.

The League of Hodenosaunee or Iroquois was in its general structure the same when described during the historical period as it was when conceived originally. At least this was so according to tradition, with one important exception. The original League included fifty permanent offices which were filled with individuals from each of the five member nations or tribes. The Onondaga contributed fourteen; Cayuga, ten; Mohawk and Oneida, nine each; and the Seneca, eight. The holder of such an office has been termed a sachem in the literature. This title is derived from a word used by the speakers of diverse Algonkian languages in the eastern United States and refers to the holder of a hereditary office. Among the Iroquois a sachem was called a "Counselor of the People." The sachems were drawn from the sibs of the nations. Using the Mohawk as an example, the three sachems were from each of their three matrisibs. The names these sachems had assumed when they took office were Going with Two Horns, Great Wood Drift, and Puts on the Rattles. The sachems of each nation collectively formed the Council of the League which had legislative, executive, and judicial authority over the entire League. Historically, the first annual League meetings were held at Onondaga in order to invest new sachems, but as League political power increased, more time was devoted to dealing with other tribes and European nations. In theory and seemingly in fact, each of the member tribes of the League was equal in power and authority. The unequal distribution of the sachemships among the nations was not a key to power because any decision made in the name of the League was unanimous.

At some unknown time in prehistory the Tuscarora split from what was later to become the League and settled along the Roanoke and nearby rivers in the present states of North Carolina and Virginia. Hostilities with white settlers erupted in the Tuscarora wars of 1711 and 1712-1713. The second war ended with some Tuscarora moving north to join the League members. They were adopted formally by the Oneida in 1722 as members of the League. The last remnant of the Tuscarora population did not migrate northward, however, until 1802. When the initial group was accepted into the League, it was not accorded rights equal to the other member nations since no sachemships were created for it.

The stated purpose of the League was to avoid the constant wars which occurred before its foundation. League meetings were called to deal with internal and external affairs, to invest new sachems as well as to mourn the ones replaced, or to carry out religious obligations. The influence of any particular sachem depended on his abilities as a speaker, and his primary obligation was to maintain civil order. Occasionally there was conflict between different members of the same sib in different nations. An individual's allegiance was strongest toward his own household, less important toward the sib in general, and least important beyond his nation. Feuds sometimes erupted between the sibs of different League nations, but no doubt these quickly were brought before the League council for settlement.

Sachems did not seek glory as individuals, and except for those deeds performed by the founders of the League, Daganoweda and Hiawatha, and the great shaman and conqueror of the Cayuga and Seneca, Tododaho, their achievements have gone largely unrecorded. The sachems acted collectively so that the achievements of an individual would be reflected only in group decisions. By contrast the outstanding Iroquois leaders known to whites usually were chiefs, a category of leaders who will be discussed shortly.

At a Council of the League the sachems were not free to decide any issue according to their personal feelings. They were obligated to reflect the opinions held by the people they represented. The frequency of interaction among member tribes and the close kinship bonds created a feeling of League unity even when the organization was not in session. The member tribes frequently joined to hunt, fight, and participate in mutual religious ceremonies. If a group of individuals, such as a band of warriors, chiefs, or women, thought a particular matter was important, they met to discuss the issue and then appointed an orator to convey their views to a sachem. If the subject was considered significant it would be introduced by a sachem at the next meeting. If an alien tribe desired to submit a question to the League, the foreign ambassador first went to the Seneca since this nation decided whether a question of foreign origin was important enough for a League meeting. If so, they sent runners to the Cayuga with a wampum belt into which had been "read" the time, place, and purpose of the meeting. Each member nation in turn notified the one to the east. When the topic for consideration was of widespread interest, people came from all over the League territory. A meeting opened with prayers, and the matter at hand was put forth by the envoy, who then withdrew from the meeting. There were discussions, and orators spoke about the issue. When the time to reach a decision arrived, different groups of sachems consulted among themselves until they agreed. The next step was for one from each group to act as a spokesman in consultations with other sachems who were similarly selected. Finally, the varying conclusions were offered. If unanimity could not be reached, the matter was set aside. When a unanimous decision was reached, an orator summarized the proceedings and gave the decision to the envoy. Only once, it appears, was the principle of unanimity set aside; this was when the Oneida sachems refused to agree with the others to side against the colonists during the American Revolution. The conclusion then was to permit each member nation to determine its own position.

In the original League there were fifty permanent sachems. Among the original sachems were Daganoweda and Hiawatha, whose offices were not filled upon their deaths. Although in theory each sachem had the same power as any other, there still were certain sachemships which were more honored than others. The most notable example was the Onondaga sachem titled Tododaho, who had two other sachems as his assistants. The Seneca sachem Donehogaweh was the Keeper of the Door in the council house, and the Onondaga sachem Honowenato was the Keeper of the Wampum for the League.

Certain obligations were attached permanently to a particular nation of the League. The Onondaga, since they were centrally located in the League, were in charge of the council hearth and wampum. In ordinary session the Council of the League met each fall among the Onondaga. Special sessions, however, might be convened among any member nation. The Seneca were the Keepers of the Door because they faced the hostile tribes to the west. Logically too, the two hereditary war chiefs were Seneca, but these individuals were not sachems. When a war was declared by the League in council, these two men were the overall coordinators. The Mohawk, the easternmost of the League tribes, were given the right to receive tribute, suggesting that the non-Iroquois to the east were subject peoples.

It was the accepted custom to validate any important League decision through the medium of wampum. In treaties with whites as well as with other Indians wampum belts were exchanged to bind a contract. The decision of agreement was "talked into" the beads, and the Keeper of the Wampum taught the associated texts to his successor. The wampum beads were spiral-shaped, freshwater shells strung together or made into belts. The word wampum is derived from the Algonkian term which is a condensation of a word meaning "a string of white beads." In general, among the Iroquois white beads were used in a religious context and purple ones as a mnemonic device to recall the details of political decisions.

At the death, or removal from office, of a sachem, his successor was "raised-up" in a council meeting. His former name, the one acquired as an infant, was dropped, and his new name was taken from the one of the office he was to hold. The meeting was held at the council headquarters or capital of the nation involved in the replacement, and the tribe of the sachem to be elevated served as hosts to the League. There were prayers, a mourning rite for the sachem to be replaced, recitations of ancient traditions by reading the wampums, and finally the investiture of the new sachem. The religious ceremonies were punctuated with feasting, games, and social dances which relieved the solemnity of the occasion. A sachemship was passed along matrilineal lines. The office normally passed to a brother or to a sister's son. The ability of possible successors was considered, and the person thought most fitted for the office was invested. If no such individual existed within the matrilineage, which was rare, then the selection was made by a localized segment of the sib. In this case the office passed from one matrilineage to another. The most influential person in selecting a sachem was the oldest woman in the particular matrilineage down which the sib title passed. In the event that it was necessary to displace a sachem before his death, this action could be taken by the sib council of the nation to which the sachem belonged.

The League in council dealt primarily with problems relative to the common good of all member nations; each nation handled its own domestic problems through its sachems. Thus the nine Mohawk sachems were the final authorities on Mohawk internal affairs, and they functioned in the same manner as did the League council as a whole. Furthermore, if a sachem from one tribe visited another in the League, he was accorded the same status that he enjoyed at home.

After the League had been functioning for an unknown length of time, a new office, that of chief, was created. Such a person was called Pine Tree Chief, An Elevated Name, or Brace in the Long House. Chiefs were nonhereditary office holders elected by the sibs of a nation for the lifetime of the individual. There was no set number of chiefs, and they were selected on the basis of such qualifications as oratorical skills or deeds in warfare. The chiefs first served as local leaders and as advisers to the sachems. Later they sat in League councils with the sachems and rivaled the sachems in authority; at this time they were invested by the sachems. According to tradition the creation of the office of chief was the only innovation in League structure after it was founded. In general the League was bound to follow as closely as possible the organization and purposes established at its founding.

Considering the unique nature of the League of the Iroquois in the annals of American Indian political life, it is desirable to consider one version of the League's creation. John N. Hewitt, a Tuscarora who also was an anthropologist, recorded the following version in 1888. An Onondaga shaman named Tododaho used his supernatural powers to further his own ambitions, and he repeatedly prevented other Onondaga leaders from meeting in council to decide what could be done about his tyranny. The leader Hiawatha arrived for one proposed meeting, and when a group of people gathered, Tododaho caused them to knock Hiawatha's heavily pregnant daughter to the ground and she died as a result. Since this was the third of Hiawatha's children to be destroyed by Tododaho, Hiawatha left the tribe. He ventured to the house of a man and was taken in, but he was not admitted to the councils of the leaders. He traveled on to the home of Daganoweda, a Mohawk. Two men who changed themselves into crows went from Daganoweda's settlement to spy on Tododaho. They entered his home in human form and saw that Tododaho had assumed a weird appearance. His head was covered with snakes, his hands were like the claws of turtles, and his feet were like those of a bear. The spies left quickly, again became crows, and returned home to report what they had seen. Daganoweda was determined to go to the shaman to make him human again. He took Hiawatha and some of his people to Tododaho's village, and they sat in council with the leaders of the settlement. They sang the Six Songs, which Daganoweda had composed earlier; on hearing these, Tododaho started slowly to turn into a rational being and soon was transformed into fully human form. The next effort was (Hewitt, 1892, 140) "to work, first, to secure to the nations peace and tranquillity." To gain peace among the Iroquois was proposed, and the message was carried to the tribes. The names of the sachems were recited; the allotment of sachems to the different nations and other specific regulations governing League functioning were set forth. Finally, the consent of all the nations was obtained, and the Tree of the Great Peace, with roots in each direction, was planted among the Onondaga to symbolize the unity of the new League. The question of when the League was founded is open to dispute. Some authorities would place the event as early as around A.D. 1400 and others as late as about 1600; the latter date seems more likely on the basis of present evidence.

The original and guiding purpose of the League was to bring peace to the warring Iroquois tribes. The League structure was designed to handle civil affairs only, and any military operations were implemented outside its framework. If a sachem planned to participate in warfare, it first was necessary for him to resign his office temporarily. A chief customarily was the leader of a raiding party, and each was organized as a small contingent which might join one or more other such units. There was no overall command in a combined expedition; each party leader was responsible for his own force. In warfare the individual was free to act according to his own feelings, and proper behavior could not be dictated. After returning from a raid or war, the temporary war leaders ceased to have authority. Since warfare was a primary focal point in the lives of men, the organizer of a war party could recruit a following readily, for most men sought glory and the accompanying prestige. The Iroquois considered themselves at war with all other Indian tribes with whom they had no alliance; thus there always were potential victims. When war was declared against an enemy tribe by the League as a whole, the warriors were coordinated by Seneca war chiefs, although these men did not necessarily play a part in the direct conflict.

The principal weapon of war was a self bow up to four feet in length with a slight outward curve at the ends. The bow could be strung only with practice and skill since the wood was largely inflexible. The arrows were vaned with two twisted feathers and tipped with flint or antler arrowpoints. About fifteen arrows were carried in a skin quiver which was hung on the back, with the feathered ends of the arrows reaching just above the left shoulder. One form of club used in close combat was about two feet long and was made from a piece of ironwood with a large knot at the end. Another type of club had a slightly curved wooden handle, and set into the convex surface was a sharp, curved antler point which likewise was highly effective in close combat. When not in use, a war club was hung from the owner's belt. The famous tomahawk apparently was not an aboriginal weapon of the Iroquois but was known among the eastern Algonkians from whom the word is derived. The blade was hafted in the manner of a modern hatchet; tomahawks soon were manufactured by Europeans from metal, sometimes with a pipe bowl at the head.

A chief who sought to organize a fighting party war whooped about the village and went to the war post, one of which stood near the center of each settlement. Into it he stuck a red tomahawk adorned with red feathers and then performed a War Dance around it. Any man who wished to join the party participated in the dance. After a band of warriors had been enlisted women prepared food for the trip. The standard fare for war parties was maize, which had been parched twice to dry it thoroughly, ground into flour, mixed with maple sugar, and placed in a bearskin bag. The war parties from various communities might join forces, but each was under the supervision of its originator. While seeking out an enemy, the men moved in a single-file formation. At their nightly camps they marked trees with symbols of the size of their party and its destination. Likewise, at their home settlement just before they departed, they peeled the bark from a large tree and with red paint depicted, for example, the number of canoes and paddlers departing. An animal symbol representative of the group of people they were setting out to conquer was painted on the bows of the canoes. When the party returned, they painted on this tree or one nearby a pictorial account of the venture. In it the canoe paddlers faced the settlement, scalps were represented in black paint, and the number of prisoners was indicated by bindings employed to fetter individual captives.

When a returning war party passed through a League village, its captives were forced to run the gauntlet naked, and according to Cadwallader Colden (1755, v. 1, 9), "The Women are much more cruel than the Men." As the party approached their home village, they sounded a war whoop and danced as they led their captives. At the war post they were welcomed and praised by an elder. A reply was made by the warriors, who narrated their exploits and then performed the War Dance. Repatriation of a captive did not occur except in most extenuating circumstances. A man either was adopted into the tribe or he was tortured to death. The one exception was to free an extremely brave but captured enemy warrior. If the warriors had lost one of their number to an enemy, the Iroquois wife suffering the loss could adopt any male prisoner to take the place of her husband. First, however, he was obliged to run a gauntlet to his new home. The women and children lined up with whips, and the potential adoptee ran between the lines. If he stumbled and fell, he was considered an unworthy person and was killed; if he ran the lines successfully, he was then considered a member of the tribe. It thus would appear that widows had first choice concerning the fate of captives. This fact has been cited as one indication of the importance of women in decision-making. In addition to these observations there are records of women inducing men to go on war parties or restraining them under certain circumstances. All of these factors have led to the generalization that the Iroquois were a matripotestal society, one in which the power and authority of women were great, the nearest known approach to the ideal of a matriarchy. This interpretive stance has been challenged by Cara B. Richards in a review of the earliest historical accounts. She notes that the fate of captives was in the hands of the captor and the council. When a woman disagreed with their decision, she could not take an effective counteraction, for it was only after a prisoner had been released by his captor and the council that the women had any voice in his fate. Later, women obtained jurisdiction over prisoners after the mere formality of their release by the council, a development which clearly is indicative of increased female authority. One factor leading to the increased importance of women in decisions of this sort may have been the instability of community life after the introduction of firearms led to the deaths of more warriors.

It was the general League pattern to assimilate defeated tribes who were related distantly to them. Thus, when they conquered the Erie, Huron, Neutral, and other peoples, they were brought into the League, but not with a voice equal to that of the original Five Nations.

The League nations are famous not only for their complex political structure and its successful implementation, but for their treatment of prisoners. The tortures conceived were diverse and diabolical. A summary of their methods prepared by Nathanial Knowles (1940, 188) gives a good idea of the variations. Among the techniques "were: applying brands, embers, and hot metal to various parts of body; putting hot sand and embers on scalped head; hanging hot hatchets about neck; tearing out hair and beard; firing cords bound around body; mutilating ears, nose, lips, eyes, tongue, and various parts of the body; searing mutilated parts of the body, biting or tearing out nails; twisting fingers off; driving skewers in finger stumps;

pulling sinews out of arms; etc." The usual practice, except for a person slated for possible adoption, was to begin abusing a captive soon after he was taken. Only the Onondaga tortured young and old, male and female; the other nations reserved their tortures for men. The general pattern was to begin the systematic torture of a victim when he arrived in the settlement of the captor. The prisoner was forced to run around inside a longhouse as young men burned him, primarily on the legs, until he fainted. While he was being tortured slowly, he was expected to sing about his lack of fear. After a captive fainted, he was revived and the tortures repeated. Care was taken to see that he did not die from the tortures because he was to mount a platform at dawn. Here he was bound so that he could move about and was tortured more before the entire community. When the captive was very near the point of dying, he was stabbed to death or his head was smashed. Normally the body of a tortured person was cooked and eaten.

The Iroquois world was occupied by a host of invisible spirits. The greatest deity was Hawenneyu, translated as the Ruler or termed the Great Spirit. It was he who created men, other animals, plants, and additional forces for good in nature. The Great Spirit guided indirectly the lives of Indians, but he could not be reached through direct appeal by men. He was capable of counteracting the Evil Spirit by applying his energies, and men passed through life standing between these fraternal deities. Among the lesser supernaturals of good was Heno, the Thunderer, who was capable of bringing rain or exacting vengeance, particularly against witches. Associations of Heno with fertility are found in the prayers offered to him when crops were planted and the thanks expressed after a harvest. Gaoh, the Spirit of the Winds, commanded the winds which could help or harm man. The Three Sisters, the spirits of Maize, Beans, and Squash, were conceived as lovely women and collectively termed Our Life. Everything that aided man had its spiritual associations, including particular plants, fire, and water. Some assumed human form and were assigned specific obligations, and all bore the general name, the Invisible Aids. It was possible to communicate with the lesser spirits for good by burning tobacco, for it was thought that through this medium prayers and special needs were made known to the gods. Men acknowledged their gratitude to the spirits in thanksgiving statements. The Evil Spirit controlled a host of lesser spiritual beings who brought pestilence to men and crops, but these forces were not systematized in detail as were those for good. One organized group of evil supernaturals were the False Faces, who existed only as contorted and evil-appearing faces. They lived in out-of-the-way places, and if they chanced to be seen, their viewer was paralyzed. They were able because of their great powers to send death and destruction to the people.

The religious specialists known as Keepers of the Faith were chosen by male and female elders of the matrisibs. These individuals, with both sexes represented in nearly equal numbers, were expected to serve when requested. Each was given a new name, which was announced at the next general meeting of the nation; this constituted investiture. Such persons were accorded respect by the population but realized no special honors. A person could at his choosing relinquish his obligations as a Keeper of the Faith by again assuming his old name. The primary duty of these specialists was to arrange and conduct the major religious ceremonies. There was no set number of such persons, and all held the same rank. The sachems and chiefs were ex officio Keepers of the Faith. A second function performed by the Keepers of the Faith was to censure antisocial behavior. In the case of a serious transgression they reported the individual to the tribal council, which was a strong form of censure.

During a year, according to Morgan, there were six major religious ceremonies, with the first five quite similar in character. In sequence of occurrence they were the Maple, Planting, Strawberry, Green Maize, Harvest, and New Year's (Midwinter) ceremonies. The first five shared the common feature of public confessions prior to group observances. When confessing, an individual held a string of white wampum as a symbol of sincerity. The assembled throng did not pass judgment on any transgression, but future behavior was to reflect renewed purpose and intent. During the days of ceremonies it was the pattern for the sacred rituals to be held before noon. The religious aspects included speeches by the Keepers of the Faith on the precedent and purpose of the ceremony; offerings of burnt tobacco; prayers; and speeches of thanksgiving. The social festivities included dances and feasting in the afternoon and evening. One of the most popular dances was the Feather Dance, which consisted not only of a dance but accompanying songs of thanksgiving. A specifically designated Thanksgiving Dance was performed at the Green Maize and Harvest ceremonies. When the sap began to flow in the maple trees during the spring, the Keepers of the Faith announced when and where the Maple Ceremony would be held. It was a localized celebration with observances held in diverse settlements. The Planting Ceremony followed the patterning of the Maple, and the purpose of the former was to make the seeds which were planted productive. In the event that rain did not fall, a special ceremony was performed later and addressed to the Thunderer for rain. The Strawberry Ceremony was celebrated with the harvesting of these berries and a feast, in which strawberries mixed with maple sugar were consumed. The Green Maize celebration lasted four days and was held when the first maize of the year was harvested. Inasmuch as maize was the most important staple, it is not surprising that this was an important ceremonial event.

One departure from the usual pattern was that on the third day individuals offered personal speeches of thanks for individual blessings. The final day was devoted to gambling, which was secular, and feasting. The Harvest Ceremony, like the one preceding, was celebrated over four days and was a general thanksgiving for the harvest of all crops.

The New Year's Ceremony usually was held early in February and lasted for seven days. Before the rituals began, individuals who had dreamed went from house to house asking the residents to guess the nature of their dreams. Dreams were regarded as important supernatural signs and were treated seriously. When someone suggested a text and meaning for a dream that seemed reasonable, the dreamer ceased his quest for an interpretation. If the accepted text and its meaning included statements about the future behavior of the dreamer, he was obligated to behave as directed. This account of dream interpretation taken from Morgan may be idealistic. Jesuit missionaries who witnessed the dream procedure in 1656 record it as a violent affair, with the threatened and actual destruction of a great deal of household property by the dreamer until he was satisfied with an interpretation.

The New Year's events were initiated by two Keepers of the Faith disguised in skin robes and cornhusks which hung from their heads, over their bodies, and attached to the arms and ankles. Their skins were painted, and they carried pestles for pounding maize as they visited every household during the morning. In each dwelling they made a formal statement concerning the ceremony and sang a song of thanksgiving. In the afternoon they returned to recite a second speech and sing another song. The day's activities included strangling one or two white dogs which symbolized purity. The body of a sacrificed dog was spotted with red paint and adorned with feathers; white wampum was hung from its neck, and it was suspended from a branch of a pole erected for this purpose. The following day in the morning, again at noon, and in the evening the Keepers of the Faith returned to the houses. Dressed as warriors, they stirred the ashes in the fireplace with a shovel, sprinkled ashes over the hearth, and offered a prayer, followed by a thanksgiving song. The people dressed in their best clothing and visited each house twice during the day. The next two days, the third and fourth, were allotted to dancing and additional visits. This was the time too when groups of boys, accompanied by an old woman carrying a large basket, visited each house. The boys danced for the family, and if they were given presents they went to the next dwelling. If they received nothing, they attempted to steal whatever they could before they moved on; if caught in the theft, they gave the item back without hesitation. After they had visited the houses, they feasted on their take. On the fifth day the white dog or dogs were taken from the poles and placed on a platform in the council house. A speech was made by a Keeper of the Faith concerning the precedent for the sacrifice and expressing thanks to the Great Spirit. A song was sung and the dog's body carried out to be burned in a fire built by the Keepers of the Faith. This ritual was to purge any evil and transfer it to the sacrificed animal, who carried the message of contrition to the Great Spirit. The offering additionally was to reflect the thanks of the people for the rewards of the year. As the dog burned, a Keeper of the Faith recited an invocation three times to gain the attention of the Great Spirit. Other songs were sung and a lengthy speech delivered to the Ruler. While the dog continued to burn, the people gathered at the council house to witness dances. The most important event of the sixth day was the Thanksgiving Dance, and the final day, which was devoted to gambling, ended the ceremony. There is some evidence that although the sacrifice of a white dog occurred among the Iroquois in aboriginal times, it was not associated with the New Year's Ceremony.

The information about ceremonial activities from Morgan's ethnography may be supplemented by Fenton's compilation from historical and ethnographic sources for the Tonawanda Seneca. The most important omission by Morgan appears to be the Green Bean Ceremony, held when the beans ripened in late July or early August. The festivities lasted a single day and were thanksgiving in their purpose.

The most dreaded antisocial actions were performed by witches who were in league with the Evil Spirit. It was possible for anyone to assume the form of an animal, bird, or reptile in his evil doings. Witches were difficult to detect since they could transform themselves into inanimate objects at will. There was thought to have been a society of witches with regular initiations, in which the most important test for a new member was to kill his closest friend by supernatural means. Anyone who saw a witch practicing was free to kill him, and the normal punishment for unconfessed witches was death. It was possible for a council meeting to establish whether someone was a witch; if the accused confessed, he was freed if he promised to reform.

One group organized in order to counteract the Evil Spirit and his emissaries was the famous False Face Society. Participants were persons who had dreamed that they were members, and one left the association by dreaming that he no longer was active. All members were male except for one woman who was the Keeper of the False Faces. She not only kept the ceremonial paraphernalia, but was supposed to be the one person who knew who the members were. A False Face Society probably was present in each community, and the duties of members included curing illness as well as keeping evil spirits at bay. If a person was taken ill with a disease often treated by the society and if he dreamed of the false faces, this was considered to be a sign that he could be cured by False Face Society activities. The False Face Society was most noted for its ability to cure nosebleeds, toothaches, swellings, and eye inflammations. The Keeper of the False Faces was notified when someone desired to be cured, and she assembled the members, each of whom was covered with a face mask and a blanket and carried a rattle made from a turtle shell. There was a ritual sprinkling of the patient with hot ashes, and the members performed a dance, after which they withdrew. Fenton records that another function of the False Face Society members was to clear disease from a village at regular times during the early spring, late fall, and midwinter. Also according to Fenton, there were one-night performances in June and October by the Little Water Medicine Society to renew the sacred medicine bundles.

The false face masks were inspired by mythological beings and creatures seen during dreams. A mask was carved from a living basswood tree and would be one of about a dozen facial types. Some had crooked mouths, others a smile, some a protruding tongue, and so on, as their most distinguishing feature. In color they might be painted black, brown, red, or white. Another type of mask was made from braided and sewn corn husks. These were representative of important farming and hunting deities. Corn husk masks also may be divided into types according to the facial features.

Systematic information about the life cycle of a typical Iroquois is unavailable. Morgan's material on the subject seems to apply best to the 1841-1850 period when he did most of his fieldwork and was corresponding with Ely S. Parker concerning the Iroquois. From Morgan's published descriptions it is clear that by the mid-nineteenth century women dominated family life. However, the early sources discussed and summarized by Cara B. Richards concerning various aspects of mating and marriage support an earlier historic patterning which differs from Morgan's presentation. An account from 1624 states that a person could not marry a cousin on either side of the family, but in 1724 matrisib endogamy was possible when no genealogical ties were traceable; at the time about which Morgan wrote, the matrisibs were exogamous. The choice of a spouse in 1624 ultimately was in the hands of the couple, but by 1724 the mother of a son sought his wife. The young man approved the selection, and further arrangements were made by the parents, with the couple usually following their parents' wishes. By 1850 the couple might be unaware that marriage arrangements for them were being negotiated by the maternal lines. In the ceremony the bride was taken to the home of the groom by her mother and the latter's female friends. The bride gave her mother-in-law corn bread as a symbol of her domestic accomplishments. The mother of the groom in turn offered meat which had been killed on a hunt, and this exchange concluded the formal ceremony. The couple assumed residence with the wife's family and ideally remained in this household.

Before the time of Morgan's field study, there existed plural marriages of a polygynous nature; however, by his time monogamy was observed strictly. In instances of divorce Morgan makes it clear that the children were kept by the mother and were under her general control. The 1624 and 1724 records differ; it appears that during these times a father had considerable voice in the disposition of children after a divorce. It was most common for him to take the older males and for the small males and all females to stay with their mother. The reader should remember that this information on mating and marriage is drawn from scattered accounts for diverse tribes. It may indicate, however, rather dramatic changes taking place in Iroquois society between about 1624 and 1850.

Morgan presents a strong case for the matripotestal nature of Iroquois society, and even stronger evidence might be introduced for a somewhat earlier period, just before 1800. From a description of Mohawk women living along the Grand River in Ontario we gain the following view. All the products of a hunt and a man's labor became the property of women, and a wife allotted money to her husband for his needs (Johnston, 1964, 31); "indeed every possession of the man Except his horse & his rifle belong to the Woman, after Marriage."

The Iroquois clearly distinguished between the activities of men and women. There were no close bonds with members of the opposite sex. Men sought the company of men, and women preferred to associate with other women. The primary duties of women were to care for children; to plant, cultivate, and harvest crops; to collect wild food products, and to prepare foods for consumption. Men by contrast never farmed; they devoted their intellectual and physical energies to hunting, warfare, and politics. The ideals of behavior were set forth in the oral traditions of the people.

Each individual was identified with the totemic group of his mother but additionally possessed a personal totem, or perhaps more aptly a guardian spirit or *oki* comparable to the Algonkian manitou. An oki was acquired in a dream or vision quest and aided the possessor. It was represented by an object in his personal medicine bundle.

The analysis of historical references to Tuscarora personality characteristics by Wallace offers what possibly are general traits for the aboriginal Iroquois. Their "demandingness," which Wallace considered a mask for their extreme dependency, was best exhibited in their expectations from others; they never ceased, it seems, to expect goods and services. The same attitude was reflected in their desire for intoxicants; this appetite apparently knew no limits in early historic times. They blamed the difficulties resulting from intoxication on the white traders or on the rum itself but not on the person drinking it. Another striking characteristic of the Tuscarora and apparently of other Iroquois was the absence of fear of heights. It was observed that they walked over creeks on small poles without hesitancy and could stride along the peak of a gabled roof casually and without any fear.

Wallace also has analyzed early historic records for the form and meaning of Iroquois dreams. He found that the meanings they attached to dreams in some respects were similar to ideas developed by Sigmund Freud. The Iroquois in general believed that dreams expressed the desires from the most inner realm of their soul and that the fulfillment of a dream was essential. Dreams stemmed from inner and symbolic unconscious desires which if frustrated could cause psychosomatic illness. An individual could not always interpret his dream properly, in which case he consulted a shaman versed in such matters. The dreamers most often mentioned in the literature were adolescent boys who embarked on vision quests, warriors who feared torture, and the ill who feared death. Boys seeking spiritual guardians were among those who had dreams of the visitation form, according to the twofold Iroquois dream classification of Wallace. In these dreams the supernaturals communicated with the dreamer, bestowing power such as good fortune in hunting or war or some other inordinate ability. One of the most important powers given was a capacity to predict the future. Symptomatic dreams differed from visitation dreams in being an expression of the desires of one's soul. Wallace (1958, 244) writes, "that the only way of forestalling realization of an evil-fated wish was to fulfill it symbolically. Others were curative of existing disorders, and prophylactic only in the sense of preventing ultimate death if the wish were too long frustrated. The acting out patterns can also be classified according to whether the action required is mundane or sacred and ceremonial." It was under the compulsion of fulfilling a symptomatic dream that men were tortured by their friends, some material object sought even if it meant great hardships, traditional but special ceremonies held, or a new ritual introduced. In summary Wallace's (1958, 247) concluding paragraph is best quoted. "The culture of dreams may be regarded as a useful escape-valve in Iroquois life. In their daily affairs, Iroquois men were brave, active, self-reliant, and autonomous; they cringed to no one and begged for nothing. But no man can balance forever on such a pinnacle of masculinity, where asking and being given are unknown. Iroquois men dreamt; and, without shame, they received the fruits of their dreams and their souls were satisfied."

Diversion in the form of games of chance and skill played an important part in Iroquois religious and social life. The contests were between individuals or teams organized within a community or beyond it, even including different tribes. The teams seem to have been divided along sib lines. These people were avid gamblers, and betting on the outcome of a game was intensive. A man might even gamble away all of his property on a game. The favorite game was lacrosse, played on a field about 450 yards long. The six to eight players on each team carried a crook with netting strung from the curved end to about halfway up the racket; the ball could be moved only with this racket. The object was to drive a deerskin ball from midfield through the opposing team's goal, which consisted of two poles near each other at the field. The rules allowed a variation from five to seven in the number of goals necessary to win a game. Another game was to throw a javelin through a rolling hoop or to throw it farther than an opponent could.

The snow snake game was played mainly by children. The snow snake was a thin, smoothed hickory shaft some six feet in length, with the forward end increased in diameter and slightly upturned. There were up to six players, with three to a side, and each hurled his snow snake across a snow surface. The game was scored according to the distance achieved until the specified number of points had been reached by one side. The snow boat game was based on the snow snake principle. A snow boat, constructed from a solid piece of beech wood, looked like a round-bottomed vessel with an upturned bow. The boat had small feathers at the top of the stern and an oblong central opening in which was placed an arched piece of wood from which rattles hung. On a hillside each player trampled a runway in the snow, iced the depression, and propelled two or three boats down the chute and as far as possible across the snow below.

According to Morgan, in early historic times the dead were buried in a sitting position facing the east. After the burial a captured bird was released from the grave site in order to carry away the spirit. Grave goods left with a man's body included his bow and arrows, his pipe, and food for the trip to the world of the dead. From the dwelling of each man to the home of the Great Spirit was a path, and along this route the soul traveled. At an earlier period bodies were placed on scaffolds where they could decay. The bones later were collected to be deposited in the household of the deceased or in a separate nearby structure. Just before a house and settlement were abandoned or after an unstated number of years the accumulated bones were buried in a mound. The aboriginal mourning period was probably of a year's duration. For one season the soul lingered near the place of burial, and it required a year to reach its final resting

Plate 60 *An aquatint of an Iroquois warrior made in 1787*
(Courtesy of the Library of Congress).

Plate 61
*A Seneca warrior in ceremonial garb
during the early nineteenth century*
(From Morgan, 1904).

Plate 62
Seneca False Face Society mask
(Courtesy of UCLA Museum
of Cultural History).

Plate 63 *Model of an Iroquois village with a longhouse under construction* (Courtesy of the Rochester Museum & Science Center).

Plate 64 *Model of one portion of a Seneca longhouse* (Courtesy of the Rochester Museum & Science Center).

place. At the end of the mourning period the relatives assembled and held a feast to signify the soul's arrival among the dead. After this time the name of the deceased never again was mentioned.

When a woman died, her farmland, along with her material property of a domestic nature, was usually inherited by her children, although it also was possible for her to will them to other persons. A man's property normally was passed to his matrilineage, whose members disposed of his separate dwelling or apartment in a longhouse as well as his other material goods. The members might keep some items by which to remember the deceased. A man too could will his property to his wife or children if he made his desires known before a witness.

The afterlife of an individual was spent in the upperworld of the Great Spirit. Here there was a peaceful existence where sexual desires were unknown and families again lived together. In heaven it was always summer, and the occupants passed their time in games and feasts. Here there were only the spirits of Indians, for whites were not created by the Indian gods. However, there was a partial exception to this rule. The spirit of George Washington existed in a compound just outside the land of the Great Spirit. Washington's heavenly home was built like a fort, and he reportedly walked silently back and forth. The special consideration for this white man resulted from the humanitarian efforts of Washington in behalf of the Iroquois after the American Revolution.

It is necessary to reemphasize that the preceding descriptions of the Iroquois have been drawn largely from Morgan's ethnography, which presents an idealistic view of their lifeway. Then too the information gathered by Morgan was primarily from one group of Seneca long after they had their first contacts with Europeans. Thus what has come to be regarded as typically aboriginal Iroquois is really a view of the acculturated Seneca. At the same time material has been introduced from studies other than the one by Morgan in order to correct errors and to add greater substantive detail. No attempt will be made to follow systematically the later historic changes among the Iroquois. Instead summary remarks will be offered about particular historical events and trends following the American Revolution. Then the scene will shift to the modern Iroquois, and the Mohawk in particular.

Frank G. Speck made a number of comments about the nature of Iroquois material culture which are worth repeating. He observed that of the eighty-three classes of artifacts reported by Morgan for 1841-1850, most still were employed in the early 1940's. The proportions unquestionably differed at the two time periods, but the material forms had remained consistent for at least one hundred years. The change from aboriginal materials to those largely from traders became crystallized by about 1820. The major changes were from deerskin to cloth as clothing material and from porcupine quills to trade beads for decorative patterns on clothing.

As was mentioned earlier the League disintegrated at the time of the American Revolution because the member nations could not agree on a unanimous course of political action. The Seneca were torn in two directions. Some favored neutrality, but most supported the British cause. Among the Seneca leaders was Cornplanter, who received a British commission as a "captain." In order to convince other Iroquois to remain neutral, the rebels laid waste to their villages and farmlands in 1779, and about 1780 Cornplanter and his followers moved to the upper Allegheny River drainage. After the American Revolution the Seneca in general were in the unenviable position of having supported the losers. However, the Americans were searching at this time for an Indian group to counteract the influence of Joseph Brant and his pro-British Mohawk, and they selected Cornplanter and his people. He accepted the responsibility and actively sought supporters for the Americans. In the course of his official travels he went to Philadelphia on a number of occasions and became acquainted with the Quakers. In 1795 the Commonwealth of Pennsylvania granted Cornplanter a fee patent title to three separate plots of land very near the New York State line on the Allegheny River; each about a mile square, one was called Burnt House. Here Cornplanter had soon gathered about him some 400 persons in thirty dwellings. One of the individuals living in the home of Cornplanter was his half-brother, Handsome Lake or Ganiodayo.

In 1798 five Quaker missionaries went to Burnt House, and one of them, Henry Simmons, was selected to live at the settlement and teach the children. In the analysis by Merle H. Deardorff of what occurred at Burnt House during this general time period we have an ethnographic gem in the presentation and interpretation of the Simmons diary and other Quaker writings. We learn that Simmons was asked by Cornplanter about his beliefs, and answers were supplied cautiously. As Deardorff (1951, 90) writes:

Questions about theology and morals had been referred to Simmons, and answered in the Quaker way: Look inside. You have a Light in there that will show you what is good and what is bad. When you know you have done wrong, repent and resolve to do better. Outward forms and books and guides are good; but they are made by men. The Great Spirit himself puts the Inner Light in every man. Look to it. Learn to read and write so that you may discover for yourself whether or not the white man's Book is true. Learn to distinguish good from evil so that you may avoid the pricks of conscience in this world and prosper; and that you may avoid punishment in the next.

The missionary, however, did not note many forms of behavior which were compatible with his beliefs. He particularly was annoyed at the preparations for a "Dancing Frolick," and the council decided to stop them, in part as a result of Simmons' objections. Furthermore, the men returned from Pittsburgh with intoxicants, which they had received in trade for furs, and consumption of these led to a community binge of several weeks' duration. This brought reproval from the Quaker, and the contrite Indians resolved that two chiefs would be appointed to curb drinking. The killing of a witch and dances held for the dead were other distressing events which Simmons witnessed.

At the house of Cornplanter in June 1799, his half-brother Handsome Lake appeared to be near death. On the fifteenth of the month Handsome Lake had a vision, the details of which were recorded by Simmons. In summary, Handsome Lake saw three men carrying different types of bushes with berries attached. The men asked him to eat some of the berries, for by doing so he would live to see berries ripen in the summer. The men told him that the Great Spirit was unhappy about the drunkenness of the people, and said that if Handsome Lake recovered he was not to drink intoxicants. The three men said further that a fourth man would visit him later. When he regained consciousness, he asked Cornplanter to assemble the council, to repeat what had occurred in the vision, and to have each person eat a dried berry; these instructions were followed. Handsome Lake still was very ill, and within a short time he had a vision in which the fourth man, assumed to be the Great Spirit, came to take him because he pitied him in his suffering. When Handsome Lake awoke, he sent for Cornplanter and after talking with him fell into a trance for seven hours. Simmons (Deardorff, 1951, 91) wrote, "His legs and arms were cold, his body warm but breathless." Handsome Lake revealed later that he was led by a guide with a bow and a single arrow who was clothed in a "clear sky colour." Soon he met his dead son and Cornplanter's daughter who recently had died. The girl told of her unhappiness because her father and her brother argued, while the son of Handsome Lake revealed that he was sorry that he did not care for his father better. The guide then stated that sons should treat their fathers well, that Handsome Lake must not drink intoxicants, and that he must give up all dances save the Green Maize Ceremony. The guide pointed toward a river where there were canoes loaded with barrels of whiskey. There was an evil man in charge of the cargo who was (Deardorff, 1951, 91) "going about very busy doing and making all the noise and mischief he could amongst the people." Furthermore, Handsome Lake was told that if all the people agreed, it would be proper to accept whites as teachers. Finally, the guide said that Handsome Lake was to return among the living and he would see no more of these things until he died; in death he would return to this setting if he behaved properly. When Cornplanter heard the second series of revelations, he again called a council meeting to which Henry Simmons was invited. When asked what he thought of the revelations, Simmons cautioned that Handsome Lake may not have reported precisely what he had seen and (Deardorff, 1951, 92), "I told them there had been instances of the same kind amongst white people even of the Quakers, falling into a trance, and saw both the good place, and bad place, and saw many wonderful sights which I did believe."

A White Dog Ceremony was held, in accord with another of the guide's instructions, to prevent illness, and following the Green Maize Ceremony the missionary Simmons left Burnt House. He was replaced by Halliday Jackson, who continued to record events at Cornplanter's village. Handsome Lake preached his doctrine, which came to include the rejection of schools and a return to a subsistence-based economy. In 1802 his cause received American support when Handsome Lake went to Washington, D.C., with other Iroquois and President Thomas Jefferson condoned his teachings. Partly because of this official sanction Handsome Lake became an acknowledged prophet. Cornplanter, however, thought schools for children should be accepted, and he did not agree with Handsome Lake's witch hunting. From the time of his recovery until his death, Handsome Lake visited Seneca communities to influence the behavior of others. By 1807 his fame as a prophet had spread widely among the Iroquois and to other eastern tribes as well. When the War of 1812 began, the Iroquois had learned their lesson, and most of them did not participate. Handsome Lake in particular preached neutrality because of his continuing close ties with the Quakers. In 1815 the prophet moved to Onondaga, and it was here that he died the same year.

As Deardorff has noted, the Handsome Lake revelations, or Gaiwiio (Good Message), came to include not only the revelations but biographical material, prophecy, law, parable, and anecdote. Its members call the entire system the New Religion. It should be noted that the Good Message was not the only basis of the New Religion. Some of the more important changes proposed in the revelation had been initiated before Handsome Lake's series of trances. If only the text of the revelations had survived, it might have been assumed that Handsome Lake was a great innovator, but from the diaries of the Quaker missionaries it is obvious that the revelations were in step with what were recognized and pressing problems at Burnt House. Like all prophets, Handsome Lake is remembered because he was the right man at the right moment in history. Most important, and unlike many other Indian prophets, he was willing to adapt his basic ideas to accommodate Quaker beliefs and even certain material aspects of white culture such as agricultural methods. This flexibility contributed to the improved realities of Iroquois life in his time and unquestionably aided in the long-range survival of the Good Message. Soon after Handsome Lake's death, other Christian missionaries began to proselytize among the Seneca, and the Indians labored in council to establish a uniform approach to religion. The time-honored pattern of unanimity, however, could not be reached, and by 1820 the New Religion was of necessity separate from all others but that of the Quakers. The Good Message was not recorded systematically until 1845, and no single text has become standard. In 1949 the New Religion was taught in ten ceremonial structures, each termed a longhouse, on the meeting circuit of the Six Nations. For most of the preachers four days were required to relate the Good Message, but the range was between three and five days' recitation time. The Tonawanda Longhouse was the Central Fire, and here were kept the most sacred strings of wampum which had belonged to Handsome Lake.

The New Religion includes the following tenets: the prohibition of intoxicants; obedience of children toward their parents and care of aged parents; faithfulness of married couples; reproval of gossiping or boasting; witches should be killed; there is a hell for sinners and heaven awaits persons who have lived good lives or repent having lived evil lives; and the ways of whites may be accepted save for schools. As was noted by Edmund Wilson (1960, 87) the New Religion "has a scope and a coherence which have made it endure as has the teaching of no other Indian prophet, and it is accepted at the present time by at least half the Iroquois world as a source of moral guidance and religious inspiration."

A surviving stronghold of Iroquois culture was found among the descendants of those Indians who had followed Joseph Brant to Canada. The Six Nations Reserve population in 1956 consisted of about 6500 Iroquois, on 72 square miles of land. The reserve was far from homogeneous in its members' approach to life; in fact, great diversity in any facet of the sociocultural system was the norm. Also, since there had been so much intermarriage among the Iroquois tribes, a confusion in descent systems, and other related problems, it was not realistically possible to determine clear tribal identity. The study of the Six Nations Reserve by Annemarie A. Shimony ranks with the *League of the Iroquois* by Morgan and is the second great Iroquois ethnography. To attempt a summary of Shimony's analysis does violence to the wealth of detail in her compilation. Nonetheless, the major aspects of Six Nations Reserve life will be presented briefly with some stress on the New Religion. The study concentrated on the conservative segment of the population, persons who accepted some white material items but rejected rapid assimilation, followed the New Religion, supported the hereditary matrilineal chiefs, and stressed sib as well as moiety ties. These people were most likely to live on the reserve; they might be rich or poor, although the New Religion deemphasized material wealth.

The Six Nations Reserve population lived on homesteads scattered about the reserve on land which belonged to the band, although individual holdings were inherited by members. The stress placed on patrilineal inheritance by the Canadian authorities confused the traditional matrilineal system of the Indians. If a man owned land, it passed to his wife and children unless he made a will to the contrary, and when there were no heirs the land reverted to the band. Individual rights to band membership, like inheritance rights, were calculated in a patrilineal line according to the Canadian authorities but matrilineally by the Iroquois. This led to complications when a Six Nations woman married someone from outside the band. Although the Canadian government normally did not interfere with the decisions of the elected council in determining band membership and was sympathetic with the old system, there always was the possibility that the government might change its policy in the future. Understandably, girls were encouraged to marry band members. The nuclear family as an important social unit was comparatively new to the Indians, and the Canadian emphasis on it robbed the sibs of important functions.

There were no sib landholdings, and the original settlement pattern of localized areas for particular tribes had broken down except that the Cayuga and Mohawk tended to retain geographical sections. A newly married couple on the reserve lived with either the husband's or wife's relatives initially, depending on which side of the family could best accommodate them. Such residence was temporary, and the couple established their own household (neolocal residence) as soon as they were able to do so in economic terms. The combined matrilineal and matrilocal family no longer existed; for some women the family meant the nuclear family and for others, the matrilineage. The matrilineages were important in selecting sachems and chiefs of the sib, and disputes arose over which were the leading lineages with the vested rights. Members of the leading lineages of a sib were most likely to be familiar with their sib ties and as a result were able to establish their political and religious authority. A real difficulty, however, stemmed from the fact that even some conservative families no longer knew their sib affiliations. As would be anticipated, many of the earlier functions of the sibs had been dropped. At the time of Shimony's studies, 1953-1960, the sibs invested the sachems and chiefs; the sibs also could remove them from office. The sibs bestowed names on members as in the past, but this function was of rapidly declining significance. The exogamous nature of the matrisibs continued to be observed by some persons, but others felt it was satisfactory to marry anyone to whom close genealogical ties could not be established.

The New Religion, based mainly on the Good Message of Handsome Lake, had four local congregations, each symbolized by a "fire" and centered at a different longhouse. The "head fire" was at the Tonawanda Longhouse in New York State; here each preacher on the longhouse circuit was invested. Each longhouse had its wampum, which validated the legitimacy of the local organization in the circuit, but the head fire had no jurisdiction over the "home" fires. The rituals of the four longhouses of the Six Nations Reserve varied in the details of their yearly cycle but were essentially the same. The particular longhouse to which a person belonged was determined by matrilineage ties and by its proximity, although all four were within eight miles of each other. Active members wanted to live near their longhouse in order to hear of each event.

A longhouse was in the form of a rectangular wooden building, usually with doors at each end; wood-burning stoves were near the ends and each stove served as the fire for a moiety. Benches were along the walls, and the central area of the room was left open. In fulfilling social and ceremonial obligations as well as maintaining the structure the moieties reciprocated in their activities. Reciprocity was a basic characteristic of the longhouse organization. The moiety alignments were not the same as those reported for earlier historic times, and although three of the longhouses were named for tribes (Cayuga, Seneca, and Onondaga), there was no clear indication that they were affiliated with these respective tribes.

The leaders in a longhouse were the Keepers of the Faith, or deacons, as they more commonly were called by the Six Nation people. Each moiety had a leading male and female Keeper of the Faith, selected on the basis of merit. The Keepers of the Faith were overseers of all longhouse functions; their advice on secular and ceremonial matters was sought, and they tended to represent the longhouse at political functions. With a breakdown of the sib structure the Keepers of the Faith had an increased voice in general community affairs. Some of these offices were inherited in matrilineal families; others, with no fixed number, were selected by deacons because of their abilities or ties with a sachem. One personality trait expected of all these individuals was that they be nonaggressive in dealing with each other and the congregation. The most capable longhouse leaders successfully and without obvious pressures induced members to participate in the longhouse as fully as possible. A second longhouse functionary was the Keeper of the Fire, who was the guardian of the longhouse wampum. His moiety and sib affinities were unimportant, but he had to be a staunch believer in the New Religion. The wampum was highly symbolic of the longhouse traditions, and the people believed that Canadian officials would like to destroy the wampum in order in turn to destroy the longhouses. A third and final category of longhouse leaders was the Speaker, who presented traditional and extemporaneous speeches to the congregation. Such persons were not invested in any formal office, nor were they usually preachers on the longhouse circuit. A speaker was required to have an established talent for public speaking and a knowledge of traditional speeches.

A longhouse clearly served many functions in the members' efforts to resist becoming like other Canadians. The organization had come to fulfill social, medical, economic, and political needs. Social gatherings included softball or lacrosse games, raffles, and dances. Organized social activities sponsored outside the longhouse usually were closed to longhouse members by their own dogma. The longhouse ceremonial round was rich in detail; it was based on the Handsome Lake revelations plus the aboriginal planting and harvest ceremonies, and the old and new means for curing. An important aspect of almost any longhouse function was the recitation of a formal address of thanks to the Great Spirit for the continued life of the persons attending and thanks to the participants for attending. In all longhouse activities the ritual and social language was Iroquois; speaking English was disapproved in any context. To the members, participation in longhouse events gave real purpose to life and at the same time offered a systematic philosophy for living. People were encouraged to remember the teachings of Handsome Lake and to live good lives. At times the younger members were told not to imitate such fashion extremes of whites as high-heeled shoes and low-cut dresses for girls. Neither should one listen to the radio, watch television, or drink intoxicants, for such behavior was not in keeping with the New Religion. Behind it all was the real fear that the longhouse members would become imitations of their white Canadian neighbors. The conflict of values seems often to have led to trauma at the time of death for those individuals who had at some time followed forbidden white ways.

For members of the New Religion and other Iroquois as well there was a deeply rooted focus on death. A person's death could be caused by failure to accept a time-honored view about the spirit world, by showing a lack of respect for plants or animals, or by failing to hold rituals as directed. Furthermore, the dead possessed great power over the living, and to neglect them, especially right after someone had died, was an invitation to disease and death. In general, it was thought that souls resided in a pleasant upper-world or else they suffered punishment. Souls bent on evil could assume animal forms but in ordinary instances were nonmaterial or a light vapor. All of this concern with death and the dead necessitated the proper performance of obligations to the dead. To avert death and illness for the community or the individual the Ceremony for the Dead was held at least once and preferably twice each year.

The sachems represented traditional authority and functioned as the recognized political body until 1924. Sachems were either Christians or adherents of the New Religion. This religious division was very important since the longhouse sachems considered that their Christian counterparts could not legitimately hold office unless invested at a longhouse ceremony, which was comparable to raising up a sachem in the old League. The sachems divided also over whether or not they favored closer rapport with Canadian officials. In 1924 a group of World War I veterans and other more acculturated persons, collectively termed "warriors," sought governmental recognition of an elected council. In a subsequent investigation of Six Nations Reserve affairs the sachems would not present their case to the governmental representatives; thus the government heard only the acculturated faction, which supported elected chiefs. The Canadian government itself favored elected leaders since it received little cooperation from the sachems. An elected council was installed during 1924; the New Religion sachems were locked out of the council house, and Royal Canadian Mounted Police officers enforced the government's decision. The sachems were bitter against the Canadians as well as against their factional opposites. Continuing opposition on the part of the sachems and their supporters was demonstrated by their refusal to accept some forms of Canadian aid such as Family Allowance and Old Age Assistance payments. The elected council clearly did not have widespread support. This was reflected in the election returns; although there were burning issues, from a total population of 7000 only about 600 ballots were cast in typical elections. This reflected the idea of conservatives that to vote constituted recognition of the elected council and the Canadian government's right to validate it. By not voting they expressed their continued opposition.

The ability of the aboriginal Iroquois to work with ease at heights, commented on earlier, continued after contact. Many of the Tuscarora of New

York State who entered the armed services during World War II chose to become paratroopers or to join the air force. Some men over sixty years of age are capable pruners of high trees, painters of roofs, and carpenters working on scaffolds. Jobs of this nature are attractive to them in spite of the dangers involved. Futhermore, the Iroquois seem to prefer living in houses which have two or three floors.

From the studies of modern Mohawk by Morris Freilich, Joseph Mitchell and Fred Voget, we learn a great deal about how the Caughnawaga have come to find a secure place in the economic development of modern Canada and the United States. It will be recalled that some of the Mohawk were attracted to Canada by Jesuit missionaries in the late seventeenth century. They were known as the Praying Indians and came to occupy their present reservation after three short moves before 1719. The land they occupied until 1830 was a mission holding, but in that year it became a reservation. Land was alloted to families, and other ground was held for future generations. The holdings might be leased to anyone but sold or given only to another member of the reservation. The Caughnawaga Reservation extends about eight miles along the St. Lawrence River and is up to four miles in width. In the 1940's the community of Caughnawaga consisted of about fifty homes in addition to an Indian Affairs Branch office, Roman Catholic and United Church of Canada churches, Protestant and Catholic schools, a Catholic hospital, a post office, grocery stores, and gasoline stations. The highway from Montreal to Malone, New York, passed through the reservation, and to attract tourists to his souvenirs one man had a striking advertising display. Before his house he placed a bark-covered tepee, two totem poles, and a sign which read "Stop! & Pow Wow With Me. Chief White Eagle. Indian Medicine Man. *Herbages Indiens*" (Mitchell, 1960, 5). It might be added that the advertising efforts of this enterpriser were not approved by other reservation residents. Some dwellings at Caughnawaga were frame structures; others were a combination of framing and stone masonry, or log cabins. A yard was likely to contain a garage, stable, chicken coop, and privy, as well as fruit trees and an assortment of miscellaneous items. The stable was for a horse, which was needed to carry water from the river and to haul firewood.

Extended families lived together, and the total reservation had nearly 3000 persons. Some 2700 were Roman Catholics, and 250 were Protestants. Fewer than 100 belonged to the New Religion. The Roman Catholics have been losing ground since the 1920's. Some persons have become Protestants, and since World War I small numbers have been attracted to the doctrines of Handsome Lake. A longhouse for the New Religion meetings was constructed on a hillside at the cemetery.

After the move to Caughnawaga in the early 1700's, the economy of the migrants underwent a series of diverse adjustments. The Jesuit priests attempted to teach the men to farm when they arrived at their new home. This activity of course was regarded as work for women, and the men continued to be hunters, who also fought their enemies at every opportunity. Before long more and more men were attracted to the fur trade and served as canoemen or voyageurs for French trading parties, sometimes fighting as they moved through hostile country. After the British controlled the area, the Mohawk continued working in the fur trade until its decline began about 1800. Next, some of the men found employment in the logging industry by rafting timber through rapids and along fast water; this work was as dangerous as being a canoeman or warrior. At about this time some men finally turned to farming, while still others were numbered among the first medicine show Indians, traveling about New England by horse and buggy selling Indian medicinal preparations. Others seem to have performed with circuses during the summer months and returned to the reservation for the winter. Another segment of the population was obsessed by the desire for alcohol; although they found temporary employment in Montreal, much of their time was spent drinking excessively.

In 1886 the Dominion Bridge Company began construction of a cantilever bridge across the St. Lawrence River, using reservation land for a bridge abutment. In obtaining permission to use the land the company agreed to hire reservation Indians, but only for unskilled labor jobs. The Mohawk were unhappy with this arrangement and could not be kept off the bridge structure as the span was being built. Soon it became apparent that they not only were unafraid of heights but were pleased with the new experience. The din of the riveting did not faze them in the least. After pestering the crew foreman, a few men finally were hired, and they turned out to be excellent workers. It appears that three crews were trained on this bridge. In the erection of a bridge of this type precut and drilled beams and girders were hoisted into place with a crane or derrick, temporarily bolted and plumbed, then riveted. The Iroquois were to become members of riveting crews, the most risky as well as the most lucrative jobs.

Afterwards the Caughnawaga Mohawk worked on other bridges and systematically trained more and more riveting crews. By 1907 there were over seventy skilled workers, about half of whom were employed on the Quebec Bridge which spans the St. Lawrence River near Quebec City. On August 29, 1907, "the disaster" occurred; the span fell and ninety-six men, including thirty-five Caughnawaga, were killed. Bridgework now took on a new meaning; obviously dangerous, it became a more attractive form of employment than either timber rafting or performing in circuses. The reservation women had a somewhat different attitude; one of their first moves was to force the gangs to work on many different projects so that a similar disaster could not affect so many families. Since there were relatively few bridge jobs in Canada, some men found employment on other high steel projects. The women also demonstrated that their Christian faith had not been shaken by purchasing a large crucifix of St. Francis Xavier for the church.

About 1926 three or four high steel crews from the reservation went to New York City to work, and three more gangs arrived in 1928. With the construction of Rockefeller Center in the 1930's, seven more gangs arrived in the city. They became members of the Brooklyn local of the International Association of Bridge, Structural, and Ornamental Iron Workers and roomed nearby in the North Gowanus area. By the late 1940's, the North Gowanus locality was occupied by about 125 steel workers and their families. The families lived in Brooklyn, but the men spanned the country, working first on one job and then another. The reason offered for moving about was the overtime wage at distant jobs, but this simply was a rationalization of their desire to wander. They heard of a new and distant job, and before long they had left for it with little or no warning.

North Gowanus consisted mainly of tenements and some factories. The Mohawk lived in the best houses and were within ten blocks of each other. Households were composed of a series of related females and their families, who occupied one or adjacent apartment buildings. The residences were furnished in the manner typical for local whites with the addition of Mohawk artifacts on a wall or mantel. In these homes, where the men frequently were away, many women spent their free time making what have come to be regarded as typically Indian craft items. These were sold at fairs in the New York State area by the most Indian-looking men of the group. Other members of a household were single girls from the reservation. They worked in nearby factories, not infrequently married non-Indians, and were lost to the Iroquois community. The boys raised in these households adjusted well to school life, but they dropped out after fulfilling the minimum state requirements to become workers in high steel. Inasmuch as very little training was necessary, it was not long before a boy could work as an adult in a work gang and earn about $150 a week (ca. 1955).

Social life of the Brooklyn Mohawk centered at a particular bar in the North Gowanus neighborhood. The high steel men dropped by there at the end of the work day; on weekends and in the evening they brought their wives. On the walls of the bar were a reproduction of "Custer's Last Stand," drawings of Iroquois warriors, and steel workers' helmets. According to Freilich (1958, 479), "Periodically, the Indians tear the place apart;

they feel it their right, since it is their home. If outsiders give any sign of attempting to make it their clubroom too, blood flows fast and furious." The combative nature of the individual Mohawk existed still, and examples of bloody fights were not uncommon. They nurtured the element of daring in their jobs and in dealings with other individuals, and their continued use of intoxicants led to other forms of recklessness. Again to quote from Freilich (1958, 478), "Some examples from my field work include driving 90 miles per hour on a winding road at night in the mountains of New York State in an old car while inebriated; accepting a dare to go faster than the speedometer could register and two men having sexual intercourse with a girl while her fiance was asleep beside her."

Ties with Caughnawaga were maintained by the Brooklyn residents. Reservation members came to find work in Brooklyn, and relatives came to visit, especially in any time of crisis. A man might take his family to the reservation for the summer, but he remained with them for only a short time. When a steel worker retired, he was likely to return to the reservation, but his adjustment to the uneventful and sedentary life was difficult. One response was to return to Indians ways to the point of not speaking English and to become deeply involved in reservation politics and social life.

In a search for the reasons behind the striking success of the Mohawk in high steel work, Freilich has made some noteworthy observations. First, he felt that they were behaving in the pattern of warriors, exhibiting no fear of heights as a warrior would in theory not fear the enemy or death. From listening to a conversation about heights among moderately intoxicated Mohawk, he learned that they did in fact fear heights. They concealed their fear in order to prove their courage and to maintain their reputation as being unafraid. Surprisingly, work in high steel was highly compatible with many essential features of the old Mohawk way of life. The men left home to work for extended periods as they left to hunt and fight in aboriginal times. There was danger and possible death in what they did as there was danger of old. When a man returned, he could boast of the tall buildings on which he had worked, just as he once boasted of his skills in combat. The modern steel worker was subject to little authority, and if he was displeased he could quit his job just as he formerly could drop out of a war party. These and other parallels lent support to the traditional status of the male in a nontraditional setting.

After studying conservative persons on the Caughnawaga Reservation, Fred Voget described their way of life in the 1940's. The "native-modified" population, as Voget termed them, felt that they had been forced by the French to become Roman Catholics, and that they had been losing their physical strength and stature, as well as their lands, since they abandoned their old religion, which was conceived in terms of the Good Message of Handsome Lake and his followers. In order to regain their physical strength and political powers of old they felt they had to return to an Indian religion. They considered themselves chosen people and advocated retention of their identity as a means for consolidating and achieving their purposes. Voget (1951, 223) also stressed, "the important historic role of the Iroquois has awakened a national consciousness based on their original autonomy and structured according to the traditional organization of the League of the Five (or Six) Nations." The efforts of these Caughnawaga led to a modern nativistic movement striving for the freedoms of old. This movement was centered in the councils at the Grand River Reserve in Ontario and the Onandaga Reservation in New York State.

The personality characteristics of the modern Tuscarora, as presented by Wallace, may be extended cautiously to the Iroquois in general. The people retained their strong desire for alcohol, but its consumption now was more channeled than in early historic times. When the study of the New York State Tuscarora was made in 1948-1949, the Indians still were prohibited from legally consuming intoxicants, but this restriction had not been successful in the past nor was it at the time of the study. The Indians frequented bars which were known to sell intoxicants to Indians. By drinking mainly in bars they were subject to the authority of the bartender, and there was always the possibility of police intervention if there were disturbances. Furthermore, since they drank away from home, at least one man in a group remained sober to drive the others home. Thus there were regularized controls over the behavior of drunken persons. A counterforce also had developed in the Indians' attitudes toward intoxicants. Some persons rejected alcohol because of traumatic childhood experiences with drunks, and some were reformed middle-aged drinkers. A nearby Baptist Church to which most of the Tuscarora belonged rejected drinking, and there was also a local Temperance Society. These were possible ways out of drinking problems for individuals, and in addition gossip had become an important means for curbing drinking.

Iroquois and white American attitudes were in so many ways fundamentally different that it is little wonder the group failed to understand one another. Whites were in general thrifty, coveting wealth to accumulate more wealth; the Iroquois were generous and wasteful with money and material things. Whites were orderly in keeping house, and their dwellings, which were built by contractors, followed standard plans. Indian houses were untidy, jerrybuilt, and often left unfinished. Whites were time-oriented and considered promptness as a great virtue, but "Indian time" meant being late or not appearing at all. The old Tuscarora demandingness ran wild in their dealings with the state of New York. The state supplied schools, school buses, welfare, road maintenance, and other services. The Indians not only accepted these but expected more and more. Their dependency, to their thinking, was based on obligations of the Federal and state authorities stemming from old injustices which were both real and imagined.

The attempts in recent years by the Iroquois to assert their nationalism have led to diverse protests; for example, most of the United States Iroquois population have refused to vote, although they all have had the right to do so since the passage of the Citizenship Act of 1924. By not voting they indicated that they did not recognize United States political domination over them and in the process reinforced their own identity. During World War I they separately declared war on Germany. In World War II when subject to selective service as a result of the Citizenship Act, some went to jail, or in some other way evaded the draft. The Iroquois in New York State have resisted strongly all efforts by state officials to intervene in their affairs. Justification for the Indian position was based on treaties with the Federal government with the implication of equality in national standing between the Six Nations and the United States. Predictably, the Iroquois have resisted both state and Federal income taxes and have fought efforts to use reserved lands for the St. Lawrence Seaway, the Power Authority of New York State, and the relocation of highways. These disputes usually were complicated by the fact that elected chiefs cooperated with the whites, but the hereditary chiefs did not. The conflict between the Tuscarora and the Power Authority of New York State is a sad example of an effort by the state to obtain about a fifth of the Tuscarora Reservation for a reservoir. The Power Authority was at that time headed and controlled by Robert Moses, who later became chairman of the Triborough Bridge and Tunnel Authority. There was a great advantage in taking Indian lands through the process of eminent domain, for unlike other possible land, that of the Iroquois contained so few improvements that its value was comparatively small. Furthermore, reservation lands were not taxable, and by using them there would be no reduction in the local tax base. The callous immorality of the Power Authority campaign need not be detailed. The outcome was, however, as might be expected. The case was carried to the United States Supreme Court, and the Power Authority won.

The stance of the Iroquois in the United States was similar to that of the Six Nations Reserve residents near Brantford, Ontario. Protests of the conservative and traditionally oriented Six Nations population in Canada stemmed in part from a 1924 decision by the Canadian government to dispose of the hereditary chiefs because of their slow response to change. The leaders were replaced by an "elected" council which was appointed by the Indian Affairs Branch. This new council tried to function as the government of a nation, issuing its own passports "good anywhere in the world." They sought recognition by the League of Nations and the King of England, but without success. Later appeals to the United Nations were equally futile. Revolution broke out on the Six Nations Reserve in 1959 when the government-backed leadership was opposed by some 1300 supporters of the hereditary chiefs. In a meeting attended by about 5000 a proclamation was read doing away with the government-supported political structure, reinstating the hereditary leaders, and creating an Iroquois Police to replace the Royal Canadian Mounted Police officers who had local jurisdiction. Further plans were made to make the reserve self-sufficient economically. A schoolteacher was tried for treason after he wrote to a newspaper that the movement did not have widespread support. The offender was freed when he swore on wampum that he would support the new authorities, under the threat of expulsion from the reserve if he failed in his vow. The Canadian government reasserted itself when R.C.M.P. officers attempted to dislodge the Iroquois Police from the council house. The men were passive until some Iroquois women attacked the Mounties; a general fight followed. The Indians finally submitted, but warrants issued by the police were withdrawn when the lawyer representing the hereditary chiefs assured the Canadian authorities that such violent action would not take place in the future.

In 1958 the very dynamic nationalistic Iroquois leader Mad Bear accepted an invitation to Cuba, where he visited Fidel Castro. Mad Bear and his followers hoped that they could be admitted to the United Nations under Cuban sponsorship. The current emergence of highly nationalistic governments in various parts of the world has given the Iroquois hope, strengthened their position, and contributed to the consolidation of their own nationalism. They want the day to come when the League of the Iroquois or Hodenosaunee again will guide the destiny of its people.

In recent years the St. Lawrence Seaway and Power Authority of New York State has nibbled away at Iroquois lands, but a more bitter dispute involved the Federal government and the Seneca. In order to control flooding of the Ohio River, a series of dams was to be built on the Allegheny River. The Seneca opposed the one which was to be at Kinzua, Pennsylvania, because the reservoir would flood 10,000 acres of their best land at the Allegheny Reservation in New York State and would require the relocation of 130 families. The Seneca involved sought to have an alternate plan accepted which would not involve their lands, but the U.S. Army Corps of Engineers objected because of its greater cost. The Indians attempted to block the project through the courts, but each of the 1957-1959 decisions supported the right of the Federal government to condemn the land involved. The Seneca persistently maintained that a Six Nation treaty assured their lasting right to the land and that the Federal government had no equal or moral right to abrogate it. The treaty was signed in 1794 and stated the following about these and other Iroquois lands, "Now the United States acknowledges all the land within the aforementioned boundaries to be the property of the Seneka nation; and the United States will never claim the same, nor disturb the Seneka nation ..." "Never" is a time past, since the Kinzua Dam was built.

References

Beauchamp, William M. "The Principal Founders of the Iroquois League and its Probable Date," *Proceedings of the New York State Historical Association*, v. 24, 27-36. 1926.

Colden, Cadwallader. *The History of the Five Indian Nations of Canada*. 2 v. London. 1755.

Cory, David M. *Within Two Worlds*. New York. 1956.

Deardorff, Merle H. "The Religion of Handsome Lake: Its Origin and Development," *SI, BAE,* † *Bulletin* 149, 79-107. 1951.

*Fenton, William N. "Problems Arising from the Historic Northeastern Position of the Iroquois," *Essays in Historical Anthropology of North America*. Smithsonian Miscellaneous Collections, v. 100, 159-251. 1940. An excellent study of the Iroquoian tribes from the time of early historic contact until the modern period.

*Fenton, William N. "Tonawanda Longhouse Ceremonies: Ninety Years after Lewis Henry Morgan," *SI, BAE, Bulletin* 128, 140-166. 1941. Included is a detailed summary outline of the Tonawanda Seneca ceremonial calendar which provides comparable detail for each event.

Fenton, William N. "Locality as a Basic Factor in the Development of Iroquois Social Structure," *SI, BAE, Bulletin* 149, 35-54. 1951.

Fenton, William N. "The Concept of Locality and the Program of Iroquois Research," *SI, BAE, Bulletin* 149, 1-12. 1951.

Fenton, William N. "Iroquois Studies at the Mid-Century," *Proceedings of the American Philosophical Society*, v. 95, 296-310. 1951.

Fenton, William N. "Long-Term Trends of Change among the Iroquois," *Cultural Stability and Cultural Change*, 30-35. American Ethnological Society. 1957.

†Smithsonian Institution, Bureau of American Ethnology

Freilich, Morris. "Cultural Persistence among the Modern Iroquois," *Anthropos*, v. 53, 473-483. 1958.

Gridley, Marion E., ed. *Indians of Today*. 3rd ed. Chicago. 1960.

Griffin, James B. "The Iroquois in American Prehistory," *Papers of the Michigan Academy of Science Arts and Letters*, v. 29, 357-374, 1944.

Griffin, James B. "The Northeast Woodlands Area," in *Prehistoric Man in the New World*, Jesse D. Jennings and Edward Norbeck, eds., 223-258. Chicago. 1964.

Hewitt, John N. "Legend of the Founding of the Iroquois League," *American Anthropologist*, v. 5, 131-148. 1892.

Indians of Quebec and the Maritime Provinces. Department of Citizenship and Immigration, Indian Affairs Branch. Ottawa. No date.

Johnston, Charles M. *The Valley of the Six Nations*. Toronto. 1964.

Kinzua Dam (Seneca Indian Relocation). Hearings before the Subcommittee on Indian Affairs of the Committee on Interior and Insular Affairs, House of Representatives, 88th Congress, 1st session. Washington, D.C. 1964.

Knowles, Nathaniel. "The Torture of Captives by the Indians of Eastern North America," *Proceedings of the American Philosophical Society*, v. 82, 151-225. 1940.

Lounsbury, Floyd G. "Iroquois-Cherokee Linguistic Relations," *SI, BAE, Bulletin* 180, 9-17. 1961.

Lydekker, John W. *The Faithful Mohawks*. Cambridge. 1938.

McKenney, Thomas L. and James Hall. *The Indian Tribes of North America*. Edinburgh. 1934.

Martin, Paul S., et al. *Indians Before Columbus*. Chicago. 1947.

*Morgan, Lewis H. *League of the Ho-De-No-Sau-Nee or Iroquois*. 2 v. 1851. (The 1901 and 1904 editions were edited and footnoted by Herbert M. Lloyd and were reproduced in 1954 by the Human Relations Area Files.) The standard Iroquois ethnography and a key Iroquois source; more precisely, a detailed description of one group of Seneca living between 1841 and 1850 and capable of recalling the past.

Mitchell, Joseph. (*see* Wilson, Edmund.)

Parkman, Francis. *A Half-Century of Conflict*. 2 v. Boston. 1892.

Parkman, Francis. *The Conspiracy of Pontiac and The Indian War after the Conquest of Canada*. 2 v. Boston. v. 1, 1901; v. 2, 1902.

Richards, Cara B. "Matriarchy or Mistake: The Role of Iroquois Women through Time," *Cultural Stability and Cultural Change*, 36-45. American Ethnological Society. 1957.

Schoolcraft, Henry R. *Notes on the Iroquois*. New York. 1846.

*Shimony, Annemarie A. *Conservatism among the Iroquois at the Six Nations Reserve*. Yale University Publications in Anthropology, no. 65. 1961. The best comprehensive study of the Iroquois since Morgan's ethnography, the second key Iroquois source, and one of the finest studies of North American Indians.

Speck, Frank G. *The Iroquois*. Cranbrook Institute of Science, Bulletin no. 23. 1955.

Stone, William L. *Life of Joseph Brant-Thayendanegea*. 2 v. New York. 1838.

Thwaites, Reuben G. *Travels and Explorations of the Jesuit Missionaries in New France*. v. 13. 1898.

Voget, Fred. "Acculturation at Caughnawaga: A Note on the Native-Modified Group," *American Anthropologist*, v. 53, 220-231. 1951.

Wallace, Anthony F. C. "Some Psychological Determinants of Culture Change in an Iroquoian Community," *SI, BAE, Bulletin* 149, 55-76. 1951.

Wallace, Anthony F. C. "Dreams and the Wishes of the Soul: A Type of Psychoanalytic Theory among the Seventeenth Century Iroquois," *American Anthropologist*, v. 60, 234-248. 1958.

*Wilson, Edmund. *Apologies to the Iroquois*. (Includes a reprinting of "The Mohawks in High Steel," by Joseph Mitchell.) New York. 1960. The study by Mitchell is the most complete discussion of the history of Iroquois work in high steel and should be consulted in conjunction with the study of the same subject by Morris Freilich. The balance of Wilson's book is a sensitive analysis of the modern scene in New York State and in Ontario, Canada.

Wintemberg, William J. "Distinguishing Characteristics of Algonkian and Iroquoian Cultures," *Annual Report, 1929, National Museum of Canada*, 65-125. 1931.

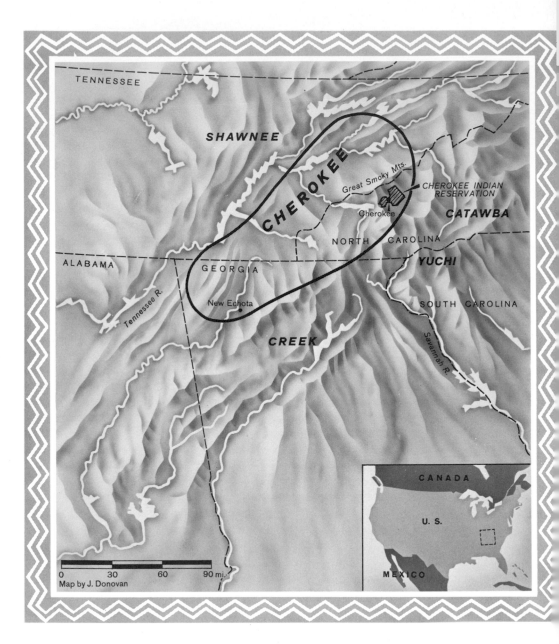

TENNESSEE

SHAWNEE

CHEROKEE

Great Smoky Mts.

CHEROKEE INDIAN
RESERVATION

Cherokee

CATAWBA

NORTH CAROLINA

ALABAMA

GEORGIA

YUCHI

Tennessee R.

New Echota

SOUTH CAROLINA

Savannah R.

CREEK

0   30   60   90 mi.

Map by J. Donovan

CANADA

U. S.

MEXICO

The Eastern Cherokee:

farmers of the southeast

In the early history of the Southeast, four tribes were larger and more influential than any others; these were the Cherokee, Chickasaw, Choctaw, and Creek. Along with the Seminole, who arose as a distinct entity in historic times, they have been termed collectively the Five Civilized Tribes. The largest aboriginal nation in the southeastern United States was the Cherokee; the one with the greatest political influence early in its history was the Creek. The Choctaw soon were divided internally, which dissipated their political effectiveness, while the Chickasaw strength declined early in the historic period. Each of these nations possessed lands which white settlers dearly coveted, and by 1830 the Federal government supported a "Removal Policy" to send these Indians west of the Mississippi River. In implementing the policy the Indians often were driven from their homes and their property seized illegally; thousands died as a result of both calculated cruelties and gross negligence on the part of their white oppressors. Some of the Cherokee, who lived in the southern Appalachian Mountains, refused to leave. They hid in mountainous areas of their homeland, and when it was safe, they re-established themselves in North Carolina, where they have continued to live. These people are described because they successfully resisted removal and because they are the largest aboriginal tribe remaining in the eastern states. Furthermore, they exhibit a vitality that is refreshing, and the numerous studies of quality about them make it possible to plot the changes in their way of life with considerable precision.

Many theories, most of them fanciful, have been advanced to account for the presence of the Cherokee in the Southeast. They usually have been presumed to be recent migrants into the area. While the archaeological record is poor at best, Joffre L. Coe has suggested it indicates that their ancestors had occupied the southeastern area for thousands of years. At the time of early historic contact it has been estimated that they numbered 22,000 persons, but this figure quite likely is an exaggeration, possibly by about one half. Their language belongs to the Iroquoian family and to the Macro-Siouan phylum; thus their closest linguistic relatives are the Iroquois. When first encountered they lived in what is now the eastern portion of Tennessee and western North Carolina as well as in adjacent sectors of Kentucky to the north and Georgia to the south. They occupied the Great Smoky Mountains, and in part because of the rugged nature of the terrain they were divided into four regional groups: the Lower Cherokee of the upper Savannah River; the Overhill of the Tennessee River and its upper drainages; the Middle settlements north of these major divisions; and the Valley Cherokee to the south. The four groups had at least a certain degree of isolation, which was reflected in dialectic differ-

502

ences. The people of concern in this chapter are designated today as the Eastern Cherokee (to distinguish them from the Cherokee in Oklahoma), and they occupy about 57,000 acres in western North Carolina. In 1967 about 4,400 persons lived on these lands, and another 2,100 were listed on the tribal roll.

The expedition led by Hernando de Soto possibly passed through a Cherokee community in 1540, but it was not until the late 1600's that white intrusions became relatively common. Firearms and other trade goods became available about 1700, and shortly thereafter traders settled among them. It was not long before the Cherokee were embroiled in major and minor hostilities with white colonists from the eastern seaboard, and old rivalries with other Indians became intensified. In a series of conflicts with English colonists in 1759-1761 many Middle and Lower settlements were destroyed, and the Cherokee were defeated. Soon thereafter intrusions by white settlers became increasingly common, and the Cherokee were forced to give up large sectors of land. In the American Revolution, they understandably fought on the side of the British, and this led to the repeated destruction of their settlements. Peace was made in 1794, and some of them decided to settle west of the Mississippi River because they felt that whites would never be satisfied in their desire for more land. Most Cherokee remained, however, and became prosperous farmers, even organizing a government modeled after that of the United States. Yet pressures by whites for land never ceased, and by 1839 they all had been forced from their homes. About 1000 escaped to live in the mountains as fugitives; it is the descendants of these persons who emerged as the Eastern Cherokee.

The Cherokee were not described in reasonable detail until the mid-1700's, and by this time they had well-established ties with traders and other whites. Thus there are no aboriginal baseline studies for these people. The Cherokee of reasonably early historic times occupied scattered settlements because relatively level plots of ground suitable for cultivation were scarce. Communities were situated along streams and rivers because these were important for fish, for the game that was attracted to them, and for the performance of religious rituals. A large settlement might encompass 450 acres if that much land was relatively flat, but a typical community was much smaller. A large community or a number of smaller ones were grouped into political aggregates which included from 350 to 600 individuals. When a collectivity of this nature approached the larger number, the tendency was for a segment to bud off and organize as a separate group. In the early 1700's there were about sixty settlements clustered into about thirty-five bands.

As was true of other Indians in the Southeast, most clothing was made of deerskins sewn with sinew thread. The basic garment for a man was a breechclout, and women wore skirts extending from the waist nearly to the knees. These people wore deerskin moccasins and bison skin robes during cold weather or lighter ones made of feathers attached to a fiber base in the summer. Buckskin shirts and cloth boots were early historic additions. The most distinctive characteristic of personal adornment was the manner in which males decorated their ears. A section of the outer border of each ear was cut free, stretched to lengthen it, and then wound with wire to hold the partially detached section in an expanded arc. This practice, which was aboriginal, declined in popularity in the late 1700's when silver nose rings and earrings as well as pendants, armlets, and bracelets of silver became popular. Wealthier individuals wore collar-like bands of clamshell beads around their necks. Youthful warriors were tattooed by pricking the skin with a needle and rubbing bluish coloring into the openings. The designs included flowers, animals, and geometric forms, and were made on the chest or muscular parts of the body. All the hair was plucked from a man's head except for a scalp lock at the back; this was adorned with beads or feathers. The hair of women appears to have been drawn back in a very long bundle held with ribbons.

Men built the rectangular houses by setting poles vertically, weaving twigs between them, and covering the walls inside and out with a coating of clay mixed with grass. These houses had gabled roofs and sometimes were two stories in height. They often were divided into rooms, and in one of these was a fireplace from which the smoke drifted out a hole in the roof. The most prominent furnishings were raised beds made of poles with wooden cross pieces covered with mats and skin blankets. Another type of dwelling was cone-shaped and was termed a "hot house." This form appears to have been used mainly as a bathhouse for purification or as sleeping quarters on cold nights. The most imposing structure was the council house; some of these accommodated as many as 500 persons. A council house was seven-sided, framed with logs, and had a roof supported by concentric circles of interior posts. The entire structure was covered with earth except for a narrow doorway and a smokehole at the center of the roof. Inside there were benches and a central fireplace. It was here that political decisions were made, religious observances held, and social events often took place.

Aboriginally the most important domestic crops appear to have been maize, beans, pumpkins, and tobacco, but they soon began to raise cultigens of European origins, some of which arrived among them before whites appeared. In early historic times, and presumably before, it seems that their harvest of maize could not be depended on to sustain them for the year. When this crop failed, they abandoned their settlements, and families separated to hunt and collect plant products. Even in ordinary times wild plant foods were important dietary items; included were wild potatoes, berries, grapes, persimmons, plums, and various nuts.

Cornbread was an important food, and it was baked by building a fire on a flat hearth stone and then removing the embers. A loaf was placed on the heated stone and covered with a pottery vessel; embers were placed over the bowl, which served as an oven to bake the bread. Meats were fried, roasted, or boiled.

The wild animals important for meat included bison and deer; turkeys, waterfowl, and other birds were also eaten. Large game and birds were killed with self bows strung with bear sinew. The reed arrows were headed with triangular points made of fish scales, bone, or metal which had been cut to shape. Small prey were taken with darts propelled from blowguns which had an effective range of up to sixty feet; a blowgun was about nine feet in length and was made from a reed. Fish were taken with hooks or leisters, and in traps as well as in baskets after they had been frightened into shallow water. Dogs were the only domestic animals owned in aboriginal times; later, some families kept hogs and then horses and other domestic animals of European origin.

The only important conveyance was the dugout canoe. Made from a log which was up to forty feet in length, it was hollowed out by building a fire along one side and chipping out the charred wood. Such a vessel was about two feet in width, straight-sided, flat bottomed, and capable of carrying up to twenty men. Canoes made with wood frames and covered with bark were known but were not important among the Cherokee.

Among their domestic artifacts which have been noted were a wide variety of well-made large and small baskets made from split canes. These probably served as dishes, storage containers, carrying baskets, sifters, and winnowing trays. The Cherokee also made superior pottery in the form of water containers, and other pottery was used for eating and food storage. They also made fine stone pipes adorned with sculptured figures of animals or persons; the long stems of these platform pipes were made from wood.

Eighteenth century Cherokee households usually were comprised of a number of nuclear families related through females (matrilineal extended family). Ideally the household included an elderly couple, their daughters, the daughters' husbands (matrilocal residence), unmarried males born into the household, and the daughters' daughters. The mutual obligations of household members and their relationship with the members of other such units were defined with precision. It was a father who taught his son to hunt, but it was a mother's brother in another household who was a child's disciplinarian. An in-marrying male was respectful toward his in-laws, but was expected to joke with his wife's brothers and brothers-in-law. It was through the jokes of others that one became aware of his erring ways. In-marrying males retained close ties with their natal households and the sibs of their birth, yet a household's members formed the most closely cooperating economic unit in the society.

In social and political terms the persons to whom one traced actual genealogical ties through females (matrilineage) was less important than the larger aggregate of individuals among whom these ties were presumed to have existed (matrisib). Members of the same matrisib in a large village, or in a number of small villages, acted as a collectivity for specific purposes. Seemingly seven different named matrisibs were represented in each village, and members of the same matrisib cooperated closely at the village level. The seven segments of each sib in a settlement allotted lands for cultivation to member households and also regulated marriage. Another major obligation of a sib section was to settle serious disputes with members of another sib. The most serious crime was murder. If someone killed a person in another sib, all of the local members of the murderer's sib were held responsible, and likewise all the males in the dead man's sib were obligated to seek revenge. Preferably the offender himself was killed by members of the sib of the deceased, but one of the murderer's sib mates might be substituted in exacting revenge.

An individual was prohibited from marrying a member of his own sib (sib exogamy) or from taking a spouse from his father's sib. The preferred mate for a man was from his father's father's or mother's father's sib. If a man married and lived in another community, he was recognized as a member of the same sib he belonged to in the settlement of his birth. It was the local sib members who saw to it that a spouse was mourned properly and that men fulfilled familial obligations. Violations led to public whippings by the women of the sib involved. A widow was expected to marry her deceased husband's brother (levirate), and a widower was supposed to take his deceased wife's sister as a spouse (sororate).

The aboriginal Cherokee kinship terminology reportedly was the "Crow system," meaning that the cousin terms were of the Crow type and descent was matrilineal. In this cousin terminology a father's sister's daughter and mother's brother's daughter were termed differently from each other and from sisters or parallel cousins (mother's sister's and father's brother's daughters.) However, a father's sister's daughter was classed with father's sister. The kinship terminology made it possible to distinguish precisely the four matrilineages which were most important to an individual; these were the matrilineages of mother, father, mother's mother, and father's father.

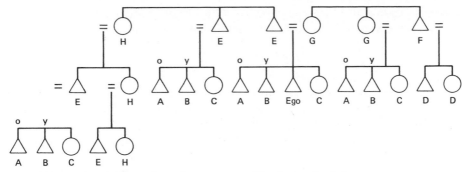

Aboriginal Cherokee kin terms. Each capital letter represents a different term; o indicates older than Ego and y indicates younger than Ego.

The activities of women tended to be much the same throughout the year. They cooked and prepared foods for storage, cared for children and the ill, and fashioned artifacts for domestic use. It was only during the summer months that the obligations of women varied from this routine, for it was then that they planted, tended, and harvested their garden plots. Fred Gearing has described the tempo and texture of eighteenth century Cherokee male life in studied detail and stressed its seasonal variability. In the summer after helping women plant the crops, young men played stickball (lacrosse), sometimes hunted, and constructed or repaired buildings. In the late summer they helped harvest the crops and then devoted three weeks to a series of ceremonies. In the fall and winter younger men hunted and fought and held their own ceremonies.

From an analysis of myths and ethnographic reconstructions eighteenth century Cherokee ideals about adult male behavior emerge with clarity. A good person was one who interacted congenially with others to produce harmonious interpersonal relations. As Gearing (1962, 31) noted, a guiding principle behind behavior was embodied in the negative statement "thou shalt not create disharmony." In their ethos a man studiously avoided face-to-face conflict, he was cautious in his dealings with others, and if overt conflict did arise he withdrew emotionally and physically if at all possible. Conflict was expressed at a distance through gossip and backbiting or more seriously in the use of magic to cast a spell over an adversary. A major means for eliminating personal animosities was a yearly ceremony to expose and purge ill-feelings against other villagers.

In the fall between the harvest ceremony and the rekindling of a sacred fire a white flag was raised above the council house on numerous occasions as a summons for the entire population to assemble there. A small number of elderly men seated themselves near the center of the building, and other men as well as women sat on benches in separate clusters determined by matrisib ties. Older men spoke at length and younger males made their opinions known; women seldom expressed themselves at such a time. A village council sat to consider relations with other Indians or Europeans, to decide questions of war or peace, and to determine trading arrangements. The general council was composed of elderly men called "beloved men" under the leadership of a chief priest, three other priests, plus a secular officer, all of whom lived near the council house. An inner council consisted of seven beloved men, one from each sib section. The matters brought before the council were stated and restated time and again until general support or the clear opposition of the body emerged as the consensus. Deliberations often spanned days or even weeks since all decisions apparently were unanimous. The priests had no power to coerce or compel others to act in a manner they might have considered as fitting; instead, they served as arbitrators who reconciled differences. It appears that the members of each sib discussed together any particular problem to be raised and attempted to present a unified position. The seven sib representatives met with the priests, expressed their feelings, and reported back to their constituents to discuss the matter; they then reassembled as a body to deliberate. If a sib section had maneuvered as much as possible and still could not support the consensus which was emerging, they withdrew from the deliberations in order to avoid open conflict.

A village council served either one large settlement or a cluster of smaller communities, but there was no larger organization which united either a band or the entire nation. Each village was an independent political unit which sought to live in harmonious relations with other such units. Gearing (1962, 83) reasoned that prior to 1730 the Cherokee as a whole comprised a "jural community," meaning that they were united by cultural and social ties. The members of one village might cooperate with those in another, and they appear never to have fought against each other, although they often were at war with adjacent tribes. Some villages were more important than others because of their strategic location, the learning of their priests, or the importance of a secular leader, but no village appears to have been dominated for very long. Conflict between Cherokee villages most likely developed if a man killed someone from another village. This was a matter to be resolved by the members of the sibs involved, and since each sib was represented by fictive brothers in any other village, these ties, and the ideals of proper behavior in times of disputes, were enough to avert open conflict.

During the 1700's warfare was an extremely important focus of Cherokee energies as a direct and an indirect result of contact with whites. When a council had decided to make war, a red flag was raised over the council house, and the war organization began to make its preparations. There were rituals by priests, fasting and dances by warriors, narrations of heroic deeds, and ritual bathing. An oration by the war speaker anticipated the formal departure of a war party. When they ventured forth, they were elaborately painted red and black. In aboriginal times weapons for war included a club with a projection into one end; it either was hand-held or thrown. They also used bows and arrows and spears when fighting. In early historic times the metal tomahawk of European manufacture became popular, but these and aboriginal weapons were replaced by imported knives and firearms as soon as they became available.

In an enemy's domain a war party erected a small post with symbols carved on it to indicate their past exploits; such a sign appears to have been a declaration of war. If the raiders succeeded in an attack, they might make carvings on a tree near the spot to record their victory. There appear to have been two classes of combatants, warriors and chiefs, and some women were famous for their abilities in battle. The leader of a war party had only nominal control over the persons he led, and apparently a warrior could abandon the party at any time except during actual combat. They attacked stealthily and attempted to kill and scalp as many persons as they could; when they withdrew, they took captives if at all possible. Before returning home, the raiders painted the scalps red and tied them to a pole which was paraded at the head of a line of warriors as they entered their village. Captives might be adopted, but more often they were tortured to death slowly by males and females, young and old. Women whose relatives had been killed by members of the victim's tribe were the most persistent torturers.

Political activities in the 1700's were linked to a round of religious observances. In the late fall the first of three important ritual sets was the harvest ceremony. Held in late September when the maize crop had matured, this celebration involved processions in which green boughs were carried and four days of dancing. There were religious dances in the council house as well as social dances in which women participated. Soon after these festivities were completed and when the moon was new, the council house became the center for ritual offerings to a sacred fire. Later a priest led the villagers to a river where each person bathed seven times, and then they all feasted. Within about ten days after the completion of this ceremony, rituals were held in order to negate any ill-feelings that a person might harbor against others. The purpose was for each individual to become ritually pure. It was at this time that the sacred fire in the council house was extinguished and then rekindled. The members of each household lit new fires in their homes from embers of the new sacred fire. The people then bathed in a river, permitted their old clothing to drift away, and put on new garments when they emerged. During the time between these ceremonies the most important political conferences of the year were held.

In 1730 the village council still functioned at the local level as it had in the past, but British colonial administrators had begun viewing the Cherokee as a single political unit rather than as an aggregate of independent villages. Thus, when a raiding party attacked a frontier settlement or interfered with the activities of a white trader, all of the Cherokee were held responsible by the British. In order to avoid unexpected reprisals a tribal political network began to develop among the Cherokee. The first person to emerge with political authority beyond the village level was Moytoy; he was from an Overhill settlement and presumably was a war chief. He was crowned "Emporer" of the Cherokee in 1730 by the British representative Alexander Cuming, who largely was responsible for originating the office. The Overhill settlements long had been influential, and they became more important when the military effectiveness of the Chickasaw declined. This placed the Overhill communities on the French frontier and led to their strategic importance to the British and Cherokee alike. The influence of Moytoy was not acknowledged everywhere among the Cherokee, but his political office was widely recognized as legitimate. A smallpox epidemic of 1738-1739 appears to have killed about half of the people, and as a result the curers, who probably were the war party doctors, lost their position of respect, so much so that they destroyed their ritual equipment. This resulted in even more power being shifted to the political leadership. With the death of Moytoy in 1741 his son Amouskositte succeeded him. Presumably it was he who threatened to destroy a Cherokee village and kill all the inhabitants if they did not kill a man who had murdered a trader. The pressure to take some form of action against the murderer had come originally from the governor of South Carolina, who threatened to cut off trade to the Cherokee. Without arms and ammunition they would not have been able to defend themselves against the French and their Indian allies. Thus, the actions of any village began to be subordinated to the general interests of the entire tribe. In this and other episodes particular individuals began to emerge as spokesmen for the Cherokee, but only in dealing with alien powers. The inability of Amouskositte's successor to prevent raids against frontier settlers led to a war with the English, which lasted from 1759 to 1761. The destruction of Lower and Middle villages forced the Cherokee to sue for peace. By 1753 a priest state was beginning to emerge among them, roughly paralleling the village level

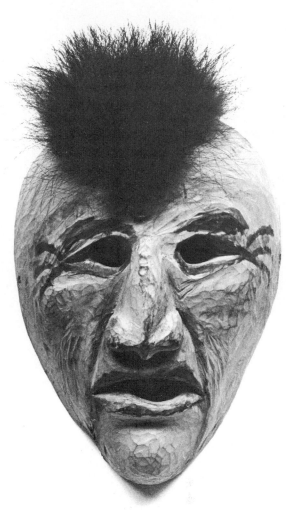

Plate 65
Cherokee Booger Dance masks
(Courtesy of the UCLA Museum
of Cultural History).

The Three Cherokees, came over from the head of the River Savanna to London 1762
& their Interpreter that was Poisoned.

Plate 66 *(Above)   An illustration of three Cherokee*
made during their visit to England in 1762
(Courtesy of the British Museum).

Plate 67 *(Top left)   An Eastern Cherokee cabin in*
North Carolina photographed in 1888
(Courtesy of the Smithsonian Institution National
Anthropological Archives, neg. no. 1000-b).

Plate 68 *(Bottom left)   Elderly Eastern Cherokee women*
photographed in 1900 making pottery
(Courtesy of the Smithsonian Institution National
Anthropological Archives, neg. no. 1034-a-2).

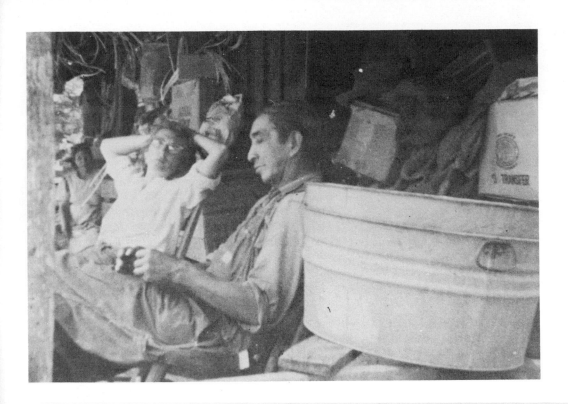

Plate 69 *Eastern Cherokee on the porch of their home in 1959*
(Courtesy of Harriet J. Kupferer).

Plates 70 & 71 *Two Eastern Cherokee houses photographed in 1960*
(Courtesy of Harriet J. Kupferer).

organization. The capital settlement was the residence of the most notable leader and the chief priest. Other leaders from the representative villages met there to deliberate. The major problem was how to prevent warriors from launching raids. The tribal council could punish raiders after the fact but had no institutionalized network to prevent raids. This difficulty became even more acute after 1761 when white settlers boldly began to farm Cherokee lands and retaliatory raids increased.

By 1768 it had been decided to include outstanding warriors among the decision makers at meetings of the tribal council. Heretofore it was only during preparations for conflict and when actually at war that warriors played an integral part in council decisions. Although the tribal council in theory remained opposed to reprisal raids, by integrating the warriors into the tribal political organization, any activities they undertook would be legitimate. The Revolutionary War and the opening of Kentucky to white settlers split the Cherokee into two factions. Most young warriors sided with the British and were armed by them; the old men sought only peace. The raids of the warriors led to the destruction of virtually all Cherokee settlements by American military forces; nonetheless, these people were not destroyed. When their villages were burned, the people sought refuge in the mountains, but after the conflict ended, they returned to re-establish farming communities. Although they were forced to give up land repeatedly, they still held title to about 43,000 square miles in 1800. About half of their land was in Tennessee and the balance in adjacent sectors of Alabama, Georgia, and North Carolina. The Cherokee at this time set out to establish a new way of life which represented a reformulation of their old ways combined with white customs. This intention was reflected in their dealings with Moravian Church missionaries. As Sharlotte N. Williams notes in her historical analysis of formal education among the Eastern Cherokee, the council threatened to expel the Moravians from their mission in northwestern Georgia unless young persons were taken as boarding students and educated. The first school was opened in 1804 at Cherokee insistence. The stress of early formal education was on its usefulness to the people involved, and by 1831 three different groups of missionaries operated schools.

In 1820 the people founded the Cherokee Nation, which was modeled after the government of the United States, and in 1825 a capital was established at New Echota in Georgia. Soon after the founding, the Cherokee leaders were presented with a proposal to make their language a written one. The originator of the system was Sequoya, who was of Cherokee and white ancestry. In 1809 he became impressed with the importance of writing and finally originated a system whereby symbols represented syllables in the Cherokee language. Within a few months after the syllabary was adopted in 1821, thousands of Cherokee had learned to read and write their own language. A print shop was established at New Echota, and the first issue of a newspaper, the *Cherokee Phoenix*, appeared in 1828. By this time the Cherokee were numbered among the "Civilized Tribes." Their population was about 13,500 in addition to nearly 150 white men who had married Cherokee women and about 75 white women who had Cherokee husbands. At this time too they owned nearly 1300 Negro slaves, which indicates that some members of the nation were succeeding in the southern economic system.

In spite of, or more likely because of, the growing affluence of the Cherokee, pressures by whites to obtain all of their land mounted. The discovery of gold in northern Georgia and federal support of a policy to remove all Indians in the eastern United States to land west of the Mississippi River doomed the new Cherokee Nation. Some individuals signed an agreement with Federal agents to move to Oklahoma and give up their lands for $5,000,000. In spite of the fact that this agreement was not made by the leaders of the nation, the Federal government considered it binding on all Cherokee. In 1838 a military force was used to dislodge these people from their lands and make certain that they migrated west. Although some slipped into hiding in the mountains, those people who adopted white ways most successfully were the ones forced to move and live in Indian Territory.

About 1,000 conservative Cherokee escaped to the mountains of North Carolina to hide until 1842. They were befriended by a white man named William H. Thomas, who had been a trader in the area since 1817. He eventually succeeded in establishing their legal right to remain in the locality and became their Indian agent. With the money which they received for their seized property, he bought parcels of land from whites from 1842 to 1861. Since Indians legally could not own land in the state, the plots were held by Thomas in his name. When he was ill and in debt following the Civil War, his creditors claimed all this land as a part of his estate. However, Congress sued the creditors to preserve the land for these Indians, and the matter was settled in favor of the Cherokee in 1874. In order to protect them in the future, the Commissioner of Indian Affairs was made their trustee, and a deed for their holdings was obtained in 1876. During this period when their right to the land was in question, the Cherokee drafted a constitution which provided for a chief and one representative from each settlement. In 1870 this body began to function as the Eastern Band of Cherokee, but it was not incorporated formally until 1889.

After the Cherokee refugees reestablished themselves in North Carolina, they became relatively prosperous farmers with a material culture which was essentially the same as that of nearby white farmers. They differed in other ways, however. Their language still was spoken, their sib organization operative, and many old traditions remained intact. During the Civil War most men fought for the Confederacy, but some joined the Union Army. After the war a further disruption of their lives was a smallpox epidemic, which killed many people. Schools were opened in 1881 by the Society of Friends on a contractual basis with the Federal Government, and this arrangement lasted until 1892. The Quaker emphasis at the day and boarding schools was on practical knowledge, such as farming and domestic arts, but they also taught English and other basic subjects and placed considerable emphasis on religious training. They withdrew their support after their superintendent became embroiled in a dispute about the use of school buildings and refused to give up his post. This individual became the Federal superintendent of the entire reservation until a later controversy forced him to leave this position in 1903. The pattern of formal education under the Federal Government was for a child to attend a day school through the fourth grade and then attend a local boarding school through the ninth grade; his education was completed at a distant boarding school such as the one for Indians in Carlisle, Pennsylvania. The initial Quaker administrators attempted to encourage the Cherokee to become teachers, but they were relatively unsuccessful in this effort as were their later Federal counterparts.

In 1924 the compilation of an Eastern Cherokee tribal roll was ordered, and at that time they numbered about 1900. However, by the early 1930's the population had expanded to some 3000. The sudden increase is explained by the Federal Government's decision to accept persons with one-thirty-second Indian blood as members of the band. This decision was fought to no avail by Cherokee who were pure bloods or had a high percentage of Indian blood. Some whites reportedly became "Five Dollar Indians" by paying this amount as a bribe to have themselves entered on the band roll, and others married a Cherokee or even adopted a Cherokee child for the same purpose. The reason was that such persons were hoping tribal land would be allotted and fee simple titles would be granted.

When William H. Gilbert studied the Eastern Cherokee in 1932, the political units created after removal were continuing to function. The six towns had locally elected officers, and there was also an elected Band Council. The State of North Carolina controlled taxation and the law, the Federal Government had jurisdiction over education and welfare, and the Band Council regulated land usage. The towns not only were political units, but served important economic and social functions. The *gadugi* or Free Labor Companies were not as important as in the past but provided significant services for their members. A typical organization had about a dozen members who annually elected officers from among their membership. The participants contracted their labor as a unit and helped each other in farming and other activities; a member could borrow money from the collective treasury as well. The gadugi had been an important cooperative enterprise in the historic past and apparently had an aboriginal base in the civil organization. Around 1900 as the Free Labor Companies began to hire themselves out to whites with increasing frequency, these organizations were judged as taxable by the State of North Carolina, and this led to their decline.

The aboriginal Cherokee had performed a wide variety of dances, and by the early 1930's most of these were remembered and a comparatively large number still were performed. One of the best known is the Booger Dance. The word "Booger" had the same root as the English word "bogey" meaning goblin, but in its Cherokee context it most closely approximates the idea of a ghost. The masks worn during the dance were designed as caricatures of aliens. Originally the dance may have been performed in order to induce warriors to join war parties and to dilute the harmful effects of the spirits of foreigners. By the 1930's, however, the dance was almost free from religious associations. The masks at that time portrayed Indian enemies; Negroes; Chinese, who were identified with an old Cherokee myth, and whites. The dances were performed by a small number of men and sometimes by a few women, all of whom were disguised. The performers danced in a circle, frightened children, and joked with those adults who stood in a proper joking relationship to them.

The gadugi, the dances, the importance of the matrilineal sibs in regulating marriage, and much of the additional substance of traditional life were waning in importance by the late 1950's. Furthermore, the 1924 decision about who qualified as an Indian contributed to a reformulation of what it meant to be an Eastern Cherokee.

The Eastern Cherokee lands consist of nearly 57,000 acres in western North Carolina adjacent to the Great Smoky Mountain National Park. The Qualla Boundary area with some 44,000 acres is the major reservation; 80 percent of it consists of mountain slopes and the balance is bottom lands, although not the rich bottom lands of nearby areas. Until the turn of the century these holdings were adequate for their subsistence-based agriculture. They also raised cattle and hogs, but stock-fencing laws and then the chestnut blight, which depleted the prime source of food for hogs, put an end to these enterprises by the late 1920's. By this time too the population had increased, and all possible land had been brought under cultivation. This combination of factors brought a crisis in the economy. Eastern Cherokee isolation had been broken by an ever-expanding network of roads, and they were drawn into a cash economy. Most persons maintained gardens for produce, but they also needed wage employment, and there were comparatively few jobs. Thus the standard of living became increasingly depressed. The tourist trade began to emerge around the turn of the present century, but it was not sizeable until after World War II. Tourists then began to arrive in greater and greater numbers, and by the late 1950's over 2,000,000 automobiles passed through the town of Cherokee, North Carolina, each summer.

At this community two major north-south and east-west highways intersected, and in the late 1950's much of the automobile traffic was bound for the Great Smoky Mountain National Park and to see the Cherokee. There were many stores selling souvenirs; each had an official greeter dressed in a feather headdress and other items of Indian clothing. These men might pose for photographs next to a totem pole or tepee for a fee. The number of motels, restaurants, and gas stations was growing rapidly, and all were likely to have Cherokee employees. The largest tourist-oriented enterprise was the Cherokee Historical Association. It sponsored the drama "Unto These Hills," which was performed nearly every day during the summer, and maintained a museum as well as a reconstructed aboriginal village. The Bureau of Indian Affairs maintained an agency center and schools here as well as at other localities. There was a U.S. Public Health Service hospital and a nursing facility. This was no ordinary "reservation" however, because the Eastern Band of Cherokee Indians was a legal entity and owned the land. Some Cherokee family lines had occupied a particular acreage for generations, but they did not own this land as individuals. The Tribal Council dealt with land allotments and reallocations as well as leases of land to non-Indians, which were controlled with particular care and on a short-term basis. Leases to business establishments provided about 80 percent of the money received by the council. One of the major functions of the council was to settle disputes over land; these were made more difficult by the fact that some boundaries were ill-defined.

The core of Eastern Cherokee lands are divided into the townships of old, and within each are settlement clusters located mainly along roads, at the edges of bottom land, and near streams and springs. Except for the houses near highways, dwellings were situated near land that could be cultivated. Most people lived in rectangular frame houses made of milled lumber with tar paper or asphalt base siding and gabled roofs with heavy wooden shingles. The dwellings with high roofs had an upper story of rooms or an attic. The houses most often had from two to four rooms, and linoleum often covered the floors. Electricity was common for lighting, but plumbing was very rare. Wood-burning stoves often served for cooking and heating, while other furnishings included tables, chairs, stools, and bedsteads. The most imposing structures in each township were the schools and churches. Baptist churches were most common; it was estimated that about 75 percent of the people belonged to this denomination. The tendency was for persons to attend services at the most convenient church, although some persons might become part of a distant congregation if the service was held in Cherokee.

In economic terms during the late 1950's a majority of the approximately 700 households depended on subsistence farming for most of their food, and the intermittent wage labor performed during the summer was the major source of cash. Some families relied on welfare payments during at least part of the winter; this also was a characteristic of non-Indian farmers in the region. Very few individuals had full-time jobs which provided their sole income, and conservative families had the most difficulty in making the transition from subsistence farming to a cash economy. In spite of the depressed standard of living for most persons, very few Eastern Cherokee were willing to move away permanently. Most experience outside the area had occurred after World War II and included residence at boarding schools, time spent in the armed service, or temporary jobs elsewhere.

The New Deal for Indians, as for the rest of the country, which began in 1934 was a concerted effort to accept the diversity in cultural and historical background for the different tribes under Federal control. It was a humanistic endeavor to respect the integrity of Indian cultural traditions and to encourage their on-going vitality. An effort was made to teach the Cherokee syllabary in Federal schools, but the program was abandoned due to a lack of interest in it. Attempts to do away with boarding schools were not entirely successful because of the distance between some homes and school facilities. There were, however, some local programs which succeeded. In her study of Eastern Cherokee education which has been followed in these pages, Williams noted that it was not until 1954 that the last boarding school was abandoned and that high school students were accommodated in county schools. With reference to the previous pattern Williams (1971, 44) wrote, " . . . the students were boarded at schools so that their association with Anglo-American cultural phenomena would outweigh their exposure to Cherokee culture in their homes." Further changes included the consolidation of four grade schools as the Cherokee Elementary School in 1962 and the end of the last Indian day school in 1965.

In the 1950's the educational stress continued to be on vocational training with an emphasis on farming skills; academic courses were similar to those in other sectors of rural North Carolina. Since wage labor employment was difficult to obtain and the farms were declining in value, it was difficult for high school students trained in this way to succeed locally. As the tourist business increased and some industries began to move into the area, the employment opportunities expanded, but because the Indians tended to be noncompetitive in terms of white values, they were at a distinct disadvantage in the job market.

In the early 1970's a new direction to Eastern Cherokee education seemed to be emerging through the Headstart and Follow Through programs. The small classes, well-trained staff of teachers, predominately Cherokee teacher aids, and community-wide interest suggested an intensity of concern over education which was far greater than in the recent past. Over 90 percent of the children spoke English at home, and thus there was not the problem for most of them to learn a "school" language. Furthermore, there were physical reminders of their Cherokee heritage such as paintings of Indians along the halls and Indian as well as white dolls with which to play. Classroom instruction included Cherokee culture when appropriate, and instruction in the aboriginal language was initiated in the Follow Through Program.

The Free Labor Companies, although smaller in number, were a source of pride for the Eastern Cherokee in general. Such an organization was most often composed of conservative Indians. One person directed the company, composed of a group of workers, and certain women cooked for the group. Mutual aid was extended in crises, and the members cooperated in farming activities. Unlike the situation in early historic times a Free Labor Company did not embrace all persons in a settlement unit. In its more recent form a company had elected officers and about twenty male members who helped one another plant and harvest maize, chop wood, and repair or build houses. Money for a treasury, from which members might draw funds, accrued from food sales.

Visiting relatives probably was one of the most important activities on a personal level. It was especially common to "drop in" on parents or siblings who lived away from one's home. People often walked to visit or perform errands, but the automobile and truck were of growing importance in facilitating communication. Probably about half of the households owned a car or truck in the late 1950's. Most households owned at least one radio, and newspapers as well as magazines commonly were obtained by subscription. People socialized at box suppers, which were a means of raising funds for Free Labor Companies and also for softball teams. In one sector box suppers were held on a weekly basis during the summer and were attended by about a dozen adults.

Stickball, from which the game of lacrosse is derived, was a popular sport, and each township fielded a stickball team until the 1930's, when they were done away with at the insistence of the Bureau of Indian Affairs. Two reasons appear to have been responsible above all others for the repression. One was that the games were played as battles, which resulted in many injuries, and the other was that spectators were so unruly that disturbances of serious proportions sometimes resulted. Softball games had replaced the stickball contests but did not serve as a direct substitute. The teams were organized by township and attendance was good, but the rivalry and spectator participation was subdued.

Membership in exotic voluntary organizations was not common until an increase in the tourist trade drew persons with business interests into the Chamber of Commerce and Kiwanis Club. Many Eastern Cherokee were members of the Farmer's Cooperative, but it served largely as a marketing institution which required comparatively little interaction among members. Local community clubs had considerable appeal for a wide range of persons with business and farming interests.

Since 1914 the Cherokee Indian Fair had been held on an annual basis in the fall and attracted all the people. In recent years rides and games of chance were provided by a traveling carnival company. The most important dimension of the fair, however, was that fostered by the Fair Association, whose president was the tribal chief. The association's goal was to show progress in terms of farming and business enterprises, and diverse exhibits for which there were competitive prizes figured as important. The fair also featured a stickball game, with twelve players, apparently drawn from the conservative population, on a team. Every player carried a stick which had a small loop and a wire-mesh pocket attached at the end. The object of the game was to carry a small ball across the goal of the opposite team. The ball could be carried in one hand, in the mouth, or in the mesh pocket of the stick. Any means, including the use of the stick, could be employed to obtain the ball; injuries, both purposeful and unintended, were difficult to prevent. In aboriginal times the game was preceded by an elaborate ritual, and at least some teams still observed ritual obligations before a game. In 1959 the Chamber of Commerce began sponsoring weekly games played by teams representing all the townships. The frequency of the encounters led to increased competitiveness, which resulted in some serious injuries to players and spectator involvement recalling the problems of the 1930's.

All of these people spoke English in the late 1950's, but some older persons rarely conversed in it. In spite of the fact that their aboriginal culture had long since disappeared, a large percentage of the population, especially those identified as conservative, spoke Cherokee. In one sector all members of about 40 percent of the households spoke it by preference. Households in which the aboriginal language habitually was used most often were composed of persons who were considered as full-blood Indians or with only a quarter of non-Indian blood. John Gulick reasons that the prevalence of spoken Cherokee among them has been, and will continue to be, sustained as long as such persons marry one another. The persons who had retained their language of old appeared to have done so because it symbolized their Indian identity. The syllabary developed by Sequoyah still was in use, and the Bible printed in it continued to be available. Some of the Free Labor Companies recorded their minutes in the syllabary, but its most important use appears to have been to record the formulas of shamans.

The kinship terminology of old was known only to some of the most elderly Eastern Cherokee in the late 1950's. The majority of persons familiar with the Cherokee terms employed them in such a way that the words were comparable in usage to those employed by English speakers. In other words, the terminological stress of old which made it possible to distinguish relatives according to lineage and sib lines had been modified for bilateral emphasis.

It appears that these people preferred household units to be comprised of a nuclear family (a man, his wife and their children), and most houses were so occupied. A significant number of additional households contained a number of related nuclear families, that is, small extended families. These households often were the nuclear families of siblings, or a nuclear family plus grandchildren. The larger living units tended to occur more often among conservative families, and one reason might have been because they placed a high value on hospitality. These people also tended to be poor and lived together out of necessity. Then too daughters with nonlegitimate children often lived in their parents' households. Yet no clear evidence suggests that large households represented continuity with older residence patterns.

The matrilineal sib organization which was so critical in the regulation of marriage in aboriginal and early historic times had declined. In the early 1950's older people were familiar still with the sib system, and about 80 percent of the marriages were in accord with it. By the mid-1950's the percentage had dropped to 20, and it was not certain that all these marriages had in fact taken sib regulations into conscious concern. "Common law" marriages seemingly were typical, and nonlegitimate offspring were not stigmatized. It is noteworthy that there was a tendency for those young adults with a minimum percentage of Indian blood to marry persons with a greater proportion in order to insure the rights of Eastern Cherokee for their children.

In the 1950's when persons identified as Eastern Cherokee considered their Indianness in abstract terms they expressed a clear dichotomy between "Full-Bloods" and "White Indians." A Full-Blood was biologically Indian, or nearly so, spoke Cherokee, belonged to a Free Labor Company, and subscribed to the traditional Cherokee value system. White Indians had the attitudes and values of whites, spoke English, and had comparatively little Indian blood. This dichotomy was neat, but it did not always appear to be valid even among the Cherokee themselves. A person might be judged an Indian in one context and white in another; clearly there were gradations and contexts to being Indian. This led Robert K. Thomas tentatively to identify four value systems among these people. The conservatives, who possibly numbered about one-fourth of the population, were "true Indians" in blood, language, and behavior. A "Generalized Indian" thought of himself as an Indian, but unlike a conservative he attempted to accommodate the white world. He accepted important values of conservatives and whites alike and thus was not a White Indian. A "rural-White Indian" did not look like an Indian, he had a minimal degree of Indian inheritance, and his general attitudes were those of whites in the rural south. Such persons seldom were active in purely Cherokee institutions but were likely to be members of such white organizations as the Four-H Club. These individuals might interact with Generalized Indians but did not usually function well with conservatives. Finally there were the "Middle Class Indians," the smallest group in numerical terms, who were involved in nonfarming businesses or were office workers. They tended to socialize with non-Indians holding similar jobs.

An insightful contribution by Gulick and his associates to understanding the Eastern Cherokee concerned the values of the conservative segment. The analysis demonstrated that this behavioral system was not an odd assortment of "survivals," but an integrated configuration, termed the "Harmony Ethic." A critical component was the minimization of overt and direct aggression against others in face-to-face situations; the aggression which did occur was expressed indirectly in gossip and sorcery. A high positive value was placed on being generous with other persons in terms of rendering personal services and providing food. Such persons did not assert themselves; they withdrew in the face of potential conflict and made a point of "minding their own business." Given these attitudes there were no well-defined leaders even in situations where they might be expected. For example, the officers in a Free Labor Company worked together as a group rather than in a hierarchical decision-making structure and tended to render decisions which reflected common consent. Because the concept of disagreement ran contrary to this value system, conservatives tended to cast an affirmative vote or did not vote at all.

One of the most overworked and least satisfying words used by anthropologists with reference to historic changes in Indian life is "acculturation." It often is employed with the presumption that total assimilation is the logical end product, yet there is no inherent justification for this assumption in a strict interpretation of the word. In general, acculturation implies the ways in which Indians are becoming more like white Americans, and in certain respects it is more reasonable to use the word "accommodation." With this notation in mind we may consider the Eastern Cherokee further as they have been described by Harriet J. Kupferer, Thomas, and Williams.

The aboriginal Cherokee first accommodated white traders and soon became dependent on them in economic terms. This in part led to their political involvements with the eighteenth century colonists. Both before and after removal marriages with whites not only introduced white "blood" but also made an impact on Eastern Cherokee accommodations because the outsiders literally came into their homes. Before 1880 the general pattern was for persons of mixed blood to identify with the Cherokee, not with whites. When the missionary-teachers and later teachers alone entered the scene, they stressed the development of Anglo-American rather than Cherokee ways in an effort to absorb these Indians into the dominant cultural system. Kupferer reasons that the conservative-modern dichotomy became crystallized as a result of the emphasis formal education gave to white ways and its competition with the Cherokee lifeway. The Harmony Ethic emerged as a result of competition with the Protestant Ethic.

Efforts by the Federal Government in the decade following 1934 to revitalize Eastern Cherokee culture failed, possibly because absorption had come to be accepted as the only possible goal by most persons. The great influx of tourists after World War II brought an increasing awareness of what it was to be an Indian; in practical terms, one of the immediate effects was a market for craft items. Williams feels that these people have an expanding interest in reestablishing their clear identity as Indians and that this is best reflected in the Follow Through Program, particularly by instruction in the Cherokee language. Similarly there is a growing pride in those business enterprises which focus on them as Indians. If efforts to revitalize Cherokee culture continue to expand, the differences between conservative and "modern" Eastern Cherokee should decline, and their lasting identity as a people will become more assured.

References

Bloom, Leonard. "The Acculturation of the Eastern Cherokee: Historical Aspects," *The North Carolina Historical Review*, v. 19, 323-358. 1942.

Coe, Joffre L. "Cherokee Archeology," *SI, BAE* †, *Bulletin* 180, no. 7. 1961.

Cotterill, R. S. *The Southern Indians*. Norman. 1954.

Fogelson, Raymond D., and Paul Kutsche. "Cherokee Economic Cooperatives: The Gadugi," *SI, BAE, Bulletin 180, no. 11. 1961.*

*Gearing, Fred. *Priests and Warriors*, American Anthropological Association, Memoir 93. 1962. This is the major ethnohistorical study about eighteenth century Cherokee political organization. Gearing carefully plots the major changes in political structure and explains why shifts occurred.

*Gilbert, William H. "The Eastern Cherokee," *SI, BAE, Bulletin* 133, 169-413. 1943. In 1932 Gilbert made a field study among these people which focused on an analysis of the kinship terminology, but he also considered diverse aspects of life at that time and presented a brief review of ethnohistorical sources which is very useful.

Gilbert, William H. "Eastern Cherokee Social Organization," in *Social Anthropology of North American Tribes*, Fred Eggan, ed., 283-338. Chicago. 1965.

*Gulick, John. *Cherokee at the Crossroads*. Chapel Hill. 1960. Based on 1956-58 field studies by Gulick and his students, this is the most comprehensive and thoughtful presentation of changing Cherokee life in recent times.

*Kupferer, Harriet J. "The 'Principal People,' 1960," *SI, BAE, Bulletin* 196, no. 78. 1966. In 1959-1960 the author studied the Eastern Cherokee and focused especially on degrees of acculturation as reflected in educational attitudes and health concepts.

Kupferer, Harriet J. "The Isolated Eastern Cherokee," in *The American Indian Today*, Stuart Levine and Nancy O. Lurie, eds., 143-159. 1968.

Speck, Frank G., and Leonard Broom. *Cherokee Dance and Drama*. Berkeley and Los Angeles. 1951.

Swanton, John R. *The Indians of the Southeastern United States. SI, BAE, Bulletin* 137. 1946.

Williams, Sharlotte N. "The Role of Formal Education among the Eastern Cherokee Indians, 1880-1971." M. A. thesis, University of North Carolina at Chapel Hill. 1971.

†Smithsonian Institution, Bureau of American Ethnology.

13

The Natchez:
sophisticated farmers
of the deep south

Along the eastern bank of the lower Mississippi River emerged the most elaborate American Indian cultures to be found north of Mexico. Nowhere else were there similar heights of complexity in social, political, and religious life. The people who best represented this climax of achievements were the Natchez. The word Natchez apparently is derived from a French interpretation of the name for one settlement occupied by these people, a community called Naches. However, the people of this and the associated communities termed themselves the Theloel. They maintained a highly developed class system which stressed rank and birth, they possessed material luxuries of rare elaboration, and they had developed an overriding formalized religious system which gave focus and direction to their sociocultural system. The prime reasons for discussing the Natchez are that they were complex and also were well described for the period of their early contact with Europeans. In addition, they passed through rather well-defined stages of relationships with the French which in many respects are similar to developments between Europeans and other Indian groups in North America. Finally, these people were systematically destroyed by the French, which in some ways illustrates a not unusual approach to dealing with Indians by Europeans.

The Natchez occupied an area on the eastern bank of the Mississippi River along St. Catherine Creek near the present city of Natchez, Mississippi. This was their main area of settlement, but they seem to have controlled adjacent land along the opposite bank of the Mississippi River. The general area of occupancy is within the Austroriparian biotic province. Characteristically, the region is one of pine and hardwood forests, with swamps and marshes numerous in the lowlands. During the French period the Natchez locale along the eastern riverbank was a rolling plain of black soil covered with grasses, hickory forests, and cane thickets in the draws. The settlements were inland from the steep riverbank. Perhaps nine communities existed in the earliest historic period, but five usually are listed by later sources. The population numbered about 3500 at the end of the seventeenth century. In 1720 it was estimated that the Natchez, the refugees absorbed into the community of Grigras, and the Tiou, a dependent people among them, still could assemble about 1200 warriors. By 1731 there were only 300 warriors, and in 1735 among the Chickasaw were some 180 in addition to an unknown number elsewhere. By then the Natchez were a remnant people; however, a few Natchez survived into the present century. Actually by 1731 the old way of life was destroyed, but the account of this destruction is a topic for later consideration.

The language of the Natchez is classed as belonging to the Macro-

530

Algonkian phylum and the Algonkian family, in which Natchez is a distinct language without close ties to any others. It is interesting to note that while the women spoke the same language as the men, women were said (Le Page du Pratz, 1774, 312) to "soften and smooth their words, whereas the speech of the men is more grave and serious." Since the French acquired their knowledge of the language from women, their pronunciation was that of females and was ridiculed by Natchez men and women alike.

The rapid historic decline of Natchez culture was preceded by two or more millenniums of prehistory coursing toward a complex way of life. At the present time the beginnings of man's occupancy of the lower Mississippi River are mysterious even among those who have studied the problem with greatest care and intensity. It would appear that the present alluvial valley surface is not an extremely old configuration, but dates from about 3000 B.C. It is reasoned that if man had lived in the area at that time or previously, his remains would now be deeply buried in the ground or else washed away. One of the oldest excavated sites along the lower Mississippi River drainage is Poverty Point in northeastern Louisiana. The remains from this settlement do not reflect a simple way of life for the inhabitants. The site was occupied around 700 B.C. and includes an artificial mound which is almost seventy feet in height. The mound is aligned closely to the cardinal directions, and the base measures some 640 by 710 feet. To the east a series of six slightly-rounded ridges forms half an octagon measuring some three quarters of a mile across at the outer ridge. About five feet high, the ridges are regularly spaced at 150 foot intervals and are separated by a series of gaps. It may be that the octagon originally was more nearly complete, but the Bayou Macon has cut into the area of the other possible half. About a mile and a half from the octagon is another mound which is essentially the same shape as the one at Poverty Point, and it has been suggested that both of these mounds originally were intended to represent birds. Beneath the ridges at Poverty Point was a thin layer of cultural debris, indicating that the area had been occupied for at least a brief period before the construction of the ridges. No evidence of structural remains was found on the ridges because of surface erosion, but it is probable that the ridges were bases for house structures. Found at the site were hundreds of tons of small, irregularly shaped lumps of fired clay. To say that these clay objects probably were heated in fires and then dropped into vessels in order to cook food is a reasonable assumption; heating stones are common over parts of North America, but stone in any form is rare in this area. A few crude clay figurines were found which seem to have represented females, although the features were not clearly represented. Fiber-tempered pottery was present, but very few sherds were recovered, suggesting that the pottery was not of local manufacture. Steatite vessels, or at least the raw material, were imported from the southern Appalachian region, apparently in large quantities since many fragments were found. Other nonlocal raw materials included red sandstone from northern Mississippi; galena and gray-white chert from the Ozark Mountains; and even copper from the Lake Superior area. All of this implies established routes of trade, but the reuse of flaked stone, the repair of steatite vessels and other patchings suggest that raw materials or artifacts from afar were not abundant. The people made a wide variety of projectile points. Knife blades were chipped of stone, and they had small flint tools made of microblades struck from polyhedral cores. Furthermore, they possessed the technological skills necessary to grind and polish stone, which led to the manufacture of celts, plummet stones, and gorgets. The general cultural complex had affinities with the developmental level termed Archaic, but farming was added and very likely was the basis for their economic system. In summary, the excavators of the site, James A. Ford and Clarence H. Webb, considered that the occupants represented two different classes of people, a lower class stemming from an Archaic background and an upper, ruling class of Ohio River drainage people called Hopewell.

Joseph R. Caldwell has proposed that we recognize what he would term the Gulf Tradition along the northern part of the Gulf of Mexico, with the Natchez of Mississippi and the Timucua of Florida as the best examples reported for early historic times. The tradition was derived from an Archaic base, but received Mississippian influences from the north which were strong or weak, depending on the locality. The Gulf Tradition includes class-stratified societies with retainer sacrifice, elaborate burials, temple mounds and plazas, effigy vessels of pottery, and painted clay vessels. It is proposed by Caldwell that these characteristics had their origins in Mesoamerica and spread northward in a west-to-east direction. The rise of the later Mississippian Tradition is viewed as an integration of the Gulf Tradition with local cultures in the heart of the Southeast. The Mississippian Tradition was based on intensive maize cultivation in the rich bottomlands and gave rise to towns, temple mounds, extended burials, and elaborate ceramic forms. About A.D. 1300 the Southern Cult or Southern Death Cult climaxed from a local base, but with influence from Mesoamerica. Elaborate grave goods made at this time included engraved shell gorgets with representations of the sun, death, and winged serpents. The late prehistoric cultural manifestations of this cult apparently were on a decline in the Southeast by the time the French arrived, but their essence was preserved among the Natchez. What we see in the lower Mississippi River area are long-established traditions of a cultural complexity based on rather intensive farming. The Natchez and closely related peoples with similar cultural foci controlled both sides of the Mississippi River between the junctions of the Arkansas and the Red rivers at the time of historic contact.

History dawned in the lower Mississippi with the arrival of a Spanish expedition under the original command of Hernando de Soto. The party descended the Mississippi River in 1543, and the Natchez attacked the explorers along the lower course of the river. The next contacts known to be with the Natchez took place in 1682 with the visit of the French explorer Sieur de La Salle, who first recorded the name Natchez. In an important study of the course of French and Natchez relationships, Andrew C. Albrecht labeled this as a first phase, one of visiting explorers. The Natchez were gracious hosts to the La Salle party. They provided the French with food and smoked the peace calumet with them, but the Indians were not overawed by the Europeans. La Salle was respectful toward these Indians, for he was well aware that they were the most powerful tribe in the region. Friendly relations temporarily were disrupted when two Frenchmen were killed in 1690, but in 1698 four missionaries sent from French Canada to the lower Mississippi remained briefly among the Natchez. In 1700 one baptized 185 children. In the same year Pierre de Iberville established friendly relations between the Natchez and the French who were penetrating from the lower Mississippi River. De Iberville attempted to wrest political control from the French in Canada in order to establish an independent colony. With the arrival of missionaries and traders from Canada a new phase of contact began, but neither the *coureurs de bois* nor the Roman Catholic missionaries were very successful. As will be understood later, the religious system of the Natchez was so integrated with the social and political life that making Christians of these people was nearly impossible. In addition, the distance between the lower Mississippi River and eastern Canada made trading and mission ties tenuous. A French administration independent of Canada, established by de Iberville, became the most influential force in the lives of the Natchez. During the early 1700's English traders operating from the Carolinas were successful in winning the support of a leading Natchez called Bearded Chief, who apparently controlled the communities of White Apple, Hickory, and Grigras. The settlements of Grand Village, the home of the Great Sun who was the reigning ruler, and Flour were loyal to the French.

The next phase of Natchez relations emerged in 1713 with the establishment of a French trading post in their midst. Antoine Crozat was granted a monopoly on all the trade in Lousiana, with the stipulation that he was to bring slaves from Africa and settlers from France. The post built by Crozat possibly was at Grand Village, but it did not succeed. Intrigue by English traders and Bearded Chief apparently led to its being plundered in 1715. The French now found themselves in a tenuous position: the obvious solution was to subjugate the Natchez and establish military control over the area. In 1716 with a force of no more than fifty men Jean de Bienville tricked the Indians so that he was able to seize and kill those individuals who had plundered the trading post and had killed some Frenchmen. The Natchez agreed to maintain peace with the French and aided in the construction of the stockaded Fort Rosalie, which was built to the west of their villages and overlooked the Mississippi River. For the moment relations temporarily became stabilized, with the Natchez controlling their settlements and the small French garrison representing the outpost of an empire. In 1717 Crozat terminated his monopoly, and soon after this the Western Company of John Law assumed the responsibility for trading and colonizing. It obtained the right to grant lands to private individuals and proceeded to do so. The company attempted to settle the country with a French landed nobility who would bring with them tenants, skilled craftsmen, and slaves. In 1718 the concession holders began to settle the area, and two years later French immigrants were well established. One even owned large tracts of land near Grand Village; the land evidently had been sold to him by the Indians. The French farmers prepared the land for raising tobacco, and Indian-French relationships were quite congenial. In 1718 the particular colonist to whom we are most indebted for our knowledge of the Natchez settled in the area. He was Antoine S. Le Page du Pratz, a Dutchman by birth, who remained in Louisiana until 1734. The French were provided land and food by the Indians, who in turn were offered guns, powder, lead, intoxicants, and cloth; this was highly satisfactory to both parties. Then in 1723 at Fort Rosalie an old Natchez warrior was killed needlessly by a soldier, and his murderer went unpunished by the French commander of the fort. In retaliation the Natchez killed some French settlers. Peace was reestablished within a few days, but a course toward further hostilities had been set. After the peace the French attacked White Apple, demanding and receiving the head of a leader who had been hostile to them. The Natchez could not understand this deception by the French and subsequently avoided contacts with them.

At this crucial period in Natchez-French relations two deaths occurred among the Natchez which quite possibly led to temporary Indian disorganization. In 1725 the younger brother of the Great Sun, Tattooed Serpent, died, and three years later the Great Sun himself died. Thus in 1728 a young and inexperienced Great Sun was in power. In the next year, 1729, a new commander of the Fort Rosalie garrison decided quite arbitrarily that he required the land of White Apple for settlement. When he told the Natchez leader of the community to forfeit the village, the noble refused, and the commander became furious. The Natchez parleyed to decide what course of action should be taken. It was decided that because the French were becoming more numerous, were corrupting the Natchez youth, and were breaking their promises, the French should be destroyed. The Great Sun agreed on this general course of action, and the Natchez sought the aid of neighboring tribes. In spite of an attempt by the leaders to keep their decision from the women, one noblewoman, Tattooed Arm, the mother of the Great Sun, prodded her son into revealing the general plan. She managed to warn the French, but the commander would not take this and other warnings seriously. Finally the Natchez fell upon the French and killed more than 200 persons who were at or near the fort. As an aside it is perhaps noteworthy that the Natchez warriors had such great contempt for the French commander that he was not killed until late in the massacre and then was beaten to death by a commoner who used a wooden war club. The Yazoos, allies and neighbors of the Natchez to the north, killed the small number of French among them but not until after the massacre by the Natchez. Apparently Tattooed Arm, the woman who had warned the French, altered the time of the attack and made the Natchez uprising premature, which angered their allies. The Choctaw were to have aided the Natchez in the attack but could not do so because of its premature nature. They were angry, too, because the Natchez did not share the spoils with them, and so the Choctaw subsequently aided the French against the Natchez. In late January 1730 a French and Choctaw force, estimated between 700 and 1600, attacked the Natchez at two forts they had constructed. A larger French force arrived in mid-February and bombarded the Natchez with cannon fire. Before long, however, the French began to run low on ammunition, and their Choctaw allies talked of withdrawing. By mutual agreement the Natchez released the captives they still held, and the French withdrew to the Mississippi River. Then the Natchez with their loot slipped across the Mississippi River and escaped. They ascended the Red River to the Black River and built a fort at Sicily Island. In 1731 another French and Indian force was sent against the Natchez, and about 400, including the Great Sun, were forced to surrender. John R. Swanton, whose study of Natchez sources is monumental, stressed that these people were not destroyed by the two French campaigns against them; in fact, the French efforts were quite clumsy. What did destroy the Natchez were the numerous skirmishes with other Indians and the illness and death caused by physical exposure in the swamps where they took refuge. Those who

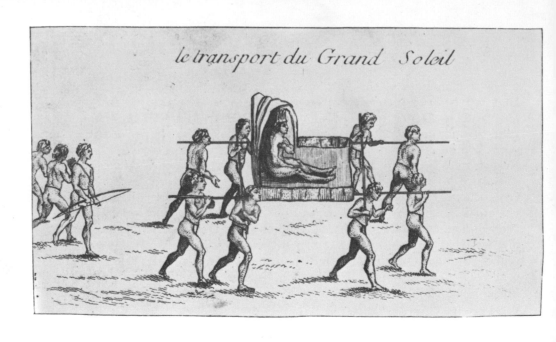

Plates 72 & 73
*The Great Sun of the Natchez being carried on a litter (top),
and Natchez torture methods and a plan of a fort (bottom)*
(From Le Page du Pratz, 1758, v. 2).

Plates 74 & 75

*The burial of Tattooed Serpent, the brother of the Great Sun (left),
and a Natchez dance (right)* (From Le Page du Pratz, 1947).

Plate 76 *Nancy Taylor.*
One of the last Natchez speakers, photographed in 1908
(Courtesy of Smithsonian Institution National
Anthropological Archives, neg. no. SWANTON BOOK IV 180-A).

escaped or were not at the fort, some 180 warriors, eventually joined the Chickasaw, against whom the French turned for having received these refugees. Some of the Natchez did not remain with or join the Chickasaw after their defeat, but lived with the Creek. This group probably included the largest number of survivors. They came to occupy a town near the Coosa River in Alabama, and in 1764 they had about 150 warriors. In 1832 the Natchez and the Creek were displaced to Indian territory in what is now Oklahoma. This migration was made as a result of the removal policy of the Federal government which was designed to move all Indians from the east banks of the Mississippi River to the west of it. To complicate the matter further some of the Natchez who joined the Catawba after their wars with the French later left them and lived with the Cherokee. In 1907 Swanton located some Natchez near Braggs, Oklahoma, in the southwestern part of the Cherokee nation; five of the individuals he found still knew some of the language. In 1934 when Mary R. Haas worked among the Natchez living near Braggs, she found that only two Natchez speakers had survived.

The mythological origins of the Natchez provide particular insight into the type of sociopolitical structure which they developed. According to tradition two individuals entered an already established community southwest of historic Natchez country. The newcomers, a man and his wife, were so bright in appearance that they seemed to have come from the sun. The man said he had noted that the people did not have effective means for governing themselves and that he had come from the sky in order to instruct them. He told the people about the Great Spirit and what they must do to please it. Among the rules of behavior were a series of prohibitions: do not kill except in one's own defense; do not have sexual intercourse with a woman not one's own; do not steal, nor lie, nor become intoxicated. Finally, he said that the people should give freely of what they had to those in need. After hearing these rules of conduct, the people agreed to their wisdom and asked the man to be their leader. He said he would do so only under certain conditions. Among these were that the people must obey him but no other and that they must move to another country to which he would lead them; finally, he set forth the rules for selecting his successor. He said too that they should build a temple in which the leaders could communicate with the Great Spirit. In the temple would be an eternal fire which he would bring from the sun. The people agreed to all of these and other conditions, and the sacred fire was brought from the sun. This man then became the first Great Sun.

It is difficult to state with certainty the precise configuration of structures in a typical Natchez settlement. While a composite reconstruction may not have reality for any particular community, each of the characteristics would have been found in at least one of the five major settlements in the early historic period. The principal settlement, Grand Village, which may have been termed Natchez, was the residence of the Great Sun, and the other villages were nearby. These included Grigras, a community of refugees among the Natchez; Hickory, sometimes termed Walnut; Flour; and White Apple, which has also apparently been called White Earth. It is by no means certain that there were five distinct villages; the designations simply may have been references to neighborhoods about Grand Village. Furthermore, the only physical location identified with reasonable certainty is that of Grand Village. It has been excavated in part and the finds reported on by archaeologists.

In Grand Village there was an open plaza which measured 250 by 300 paces in width and length. At one end was a flat-topped temple mound, and at the opposite end was a similar mound upon which was built the home of the Great Sun. The temple mound at Grand Village was elevated some eight feet and was relatively steep on three sides but sloped gradually on the fourth side. The gentle slope which was the ramp to the top faced the east and the open plaza. The temple probably measured about thirty feet in length and was somewhat less than thirty feet in width. It was constructed of thick cypress logs reaching some ten feet above the top of the mound. Over the logs of the outer walls a layer of mud was plastered, and the structure was topped with a ridged roof having three large wooden figures of birds along the peak. The temple was entered through a rectangular doorway, and the inside was divided into two rooms. In the larger outer room was a perpetual fire, and nearby on a platform was a cane coffin which contained the bones of the most recently deceased Great Sun. The contents of the inner room included two boards to which were attached various unidentified items. It was probably in this room that a wooden box was kept which contained the stone statue of the first Great Sun. Reportedly he turned himself into stone because he feared that if he were buried in the ground his remains would become tainted.

The dwelling of the Great Sun was twenty-five feet wide and forty-five feet long. It was on an earth mound some eight feet in height, whereas all other dwellings were at ground level. Eight were noted to be near the home of the Great Sun and were larger than all the other houses. At the death of a Great Sun his house was burned, and the same mound probably was increased in size and used as a foundation for the home of his successor. The houses in general appear to have been square, rectangular, or less often round. The straight walls were not less than fifteen feet in length. At the four corners the trunks of hickory trees were embedded in the ground; bent over at their tops, they were tied to form a dome. Along the sidewalls similar poles were embedded in the earth, bent, and tied at the top to the four main poles. Along each inner wall a pole was laid, and to this all the other poles were fastened with split cane. On the inner and outer walls was spread a clay and moss plaster, with split cane mats covering the plastered walls. The roof was covered with a mixture of sod and grass, and over the entire structure were cane mats held in place with vines. A rectangular door opening was left, but windows were not included. In the winter a fire was built for warmth, and the smoke filtered out the entrance. It appears that the houses may have been scattered widely. Somewhere near a village were raised platforms on which the bodies of deceased persons were placed. Covering a body was a woven mat smeared with mud; the head of the individual was left uncovered so that food offerings might be placed before it. After the flesh had decayed, the bones were moved to the temple.

To the French who first lived in the locality the Natchez seemed striking in physical appearance. They had the proud air and noble bearing which became the ideal representation of American Indians. Du Pratz described them as five and a half feet or more in height, lean, sinewy, with regular features, coarse black hair, and black eyes. To him these people were "naturals," but to the other French observers they were savages. As infants their foreheads had been flattened by the thongs which held them in their cradleboards. A woman's dark hair hung over her forehead in short bangs; in back her hair was long and was bound with a mulberry thread net that had tassels at the ends. Her ears were pierced, and from each large hole hung an elongated shell ornament. Around her neck she might wear strings of small stones or perforated shell disks. Around a man's head was a band of short hair; a few hairs were allowed to grow long at the crown. Often the young Natchez dandies painted themselves red and wore bracelets of deer ribs bent into circles by steaming and then polished to a high luster. They wore white feathers in their scalp locks and might even carry fans of turkey tail feathers. Furthermore, they wore necklaces of stone beads like those of the women. The people plucked their axillary hair, and the men plucked out their whiskers. The tattoos of these people were impressive in their diversity and complexity. Youthful males and females were tattooed with a line over the bridge of the nose, and some females had vertical lines on their chins. Persons of the nobility and warriors were elaborately tattooed on the body, head, and limbs. The patterns were of serpents, suns, and other undescribed forms. Warriors who had slain an enemy were permitted to tattoo themselves as evidence of their kills, and for a brave deed a man had the right to tattoo a war club on his shoulder, with a sign beneath it to symbolize the people involved in his conquest. The tattooing method was to prick the skin until blood flowed freely and then rub charcoal, red pigment, or blue pigment into the openings. Warriors pierced their earlobes and expanded the holes until they would hold decorative plugs about an inch in diameter.

Natchez clothing was made of either skins or plant fibers. Boys went without any apparel until they were about twelve years old, and the girls were nude until about nine years of age. An older girl's clothing consisted of a short, fringed skirt made from the inner bark threads of the mulberry. Adult women wore a dressed deerskin which fitted about the waist and reached the knees. The skin breechclouts of ordinary men were white, and those of nobles were black. A breechclout was held in place with a belt about the waist. Some upper-class women wore cloaks with a mulberry inner bark netting made on a two-pole frame loom. The netting was covered with overlapping rows of bird feathers. In cold weather a woman wore a cape, probably of skins, which passed under her right armpit and fastened over the left shoulder. As protection against the cold a man wore a poncho-like shirt of dressed deerskins which reached beneath the knees and was sleeved. The leggings of men reached from their thighs to their ankles. Deerskin moccasins were worn only when traveling. In severe weather a bison-skin robe with the hair intact and facing inward was worn. Deerskin garments, which were the most numerous form, were sewn together with sinew; an awl was used to pierce the skins. Class distinctions in dress and adornment included elaborate tattoos for the nobility, the feather-covered mantles of the noblewomen, and black breechclouts of the chiefs. Likewise, infants of the nobility wore two or three pearls about their necks. These were taken from the temple, and when a child was about ten years old, they were returned.

A number of household artifacts were recorded specifically among the Natchez, and others excavated from a historic Natchez site may with assurance be attributed to them. Within the cane-walled dwellings, inhabitable for about twenty years, were household goods usually not found among Indians north of Mexico. The most prominent furnishings were the beds made from poles and cane placed along the sidewalls. Over the bed frame bearskins were placed and a bison skin served as a cover. A log was used as a pillow at the head of the bed. When relaxing during the day, the people either sat on the beds or on short-legged stools made from a solid piece of wood about seven inches high. Pottery vessels were commonly used as containers around the houses. The various forms included shallow bowls with rounded or flat bottoms and necks that were constricted or flared. The vessels were decorated by making incised scrolls or meanders with a sharp implement. Some of the larger containers held up to forty pints and were described as receptacles for bear oil. The forms were manufactured by the coiling process, and the clay was tempered with grit, organic material, or shell fragments in order to prevent its cracking during firing and in later use. The people used wooden mortars and pestles, and they had spoons as well as ladles carved from bison horns. A wide variety of cane basketry included sieves of various grades for sifting maize, containers for small items of adornment, and hampers of cane for maize.

Among the tools and weapons utilized by men were knives made from split sections of hard cane. Axes probably had blades of fine-grained gray stone which was ground to a beveled edge, with a hole drilled through the head for hafting the ax to a wooden handle. To fell a large tree or to remove a section of wood to make a mortar, the wood was charred and then chipped away. The hunting weapons included bows made from locust wood and strung with plant fiber or twisted sinew. Arrow shafts of wood or cane had feathered vanes attached with a glue made from fish, and glue also held the points in place. The arrowpoints varied in form from splinters of bone, garfish scales, and fire-hardened shaft tips to stone points shaped like elongated triangles with notches knapped at the base for hafting. At the end of a cane spear, some six feet in length, was attached a flint spearpoint; spears were used when hunting large game such as bison, bear, or deer.

For water transportation both rafts and canoes have been reported. Rafts were used to carry relatively light loads and were made from bundles of cane which were lashed together. For transporting heavy loads large canoes were made from hollowed-out cypress or poplar logs. The interior of the log was removed by controlled burning, followed by chipping away the charred wood. These dugout canoes were propelled with paddles, measured some forty feet in length, had three-foot beams, and could carry up to twelve tons.

In Natchez subsistence activities farming was of greatest importance, followed by hunting and fishing, which clearly were secondary. The principal crop was maize, and from the two different forms some forty named dishes were prepared in the Natchez area. Soil to be tilled first was cleared of cane, and the ground was broken up with an L-shaped mattock of hickory. The Natchez probably also used a hoe consisting of a bison scapula hafted at right angles to a wooden handle. After the cane had been cut, it was allowed to dry and then set afire. Maize was planted by making holes in the ground by hand and depositing a few grains of corn in each hole. Additional crops included pumpkins and probably beans, while two species of wild grass were cultivated along riverbanks.

Hunting was most important in the fall of the year when deer were taken. The hunter wore a deer disguise, and if the animal was cautious, an imitation of a deer's call was made to attract it closer. Deer sometimes were hunted as a sport by about one hundred men at a time. Once a deer was located, it was surrounded by men who kept the animal running back and forth until it was exhausted. It was then taken alive to the Great Sun, or his representative, who killed the animal and divided the meat among the leaders of the hunt. This particular hunting technique was not an ordinary means for obtaining meat. Bison were taken in winter on the grasslands away from the river. They were approached by wearing a disguise or else by stalking them against the wind. When a kill was made near a settlement, the hunter returned with the choice parts and sent his wife to retrieve the remainder of the animal. The meat either was smoke-dried for future use or was soon cooked. Bear meat was eaten only if lean, but bears were killed when they were fat in order to obtain the oil. These animals were smoked out of their holes in trees, and if a cub was found it was sometimes taken alive to the village and tamed. The only domestic animal of the Natchez was the dog. It was used to tree turkeys so that the birds could be killed with arrows. Fishing was a means of obtaining food which was less important than either farming or hunting. Among the fishing devices were gill nets made from organic fibers and fish arrows made with pointed bone tips, to which wooden floats were attached by a cord. Hooks likewise were used, and the species most often taken were suckers and catfish.

Maize was prepared in many different ways—mixed with beans, smoke-dried, ground into meal, prepared as hominy, or parched. Ground meal was made into cakes that were roasted in ashes, baked, or boiled in water. Salt for seasoning was obtained in trade with the Caddoan-speaking people to the north and west. The Natchez made bread from walnuts and consumed chestnuts as well as acorns, but these were not important dietary items. There were no set mealtimes except for feasts. When an ordinary meal was served, the males, including those who were very young, ate before the females.

The cultivation of tobacco was one of the primary reasons the French settled plantations in the Natchez region. This crop was raised by the Indians in aboriginal times, and the people were described as avid smokers. They smoked pipes of an unknown form and inhaled the smoke. To make the smoke mild, dried leaves from the sumac tree were mixed with the tobacco. Smoking was not merely a pleasant activity; pipes and smoking played an important part in events surrounding war and peace.

Natchez social life was structured primarily around each individual's relationship to the Great Sun. This leader held absolute control over his subjects and was served by the tribe as a whole but particularly by personal retainers and slaves. He was spoken to at a distance of four steps; he was thanked and bowed to no matter what he said, and when leaving his presence a person walked backward. He was saluted whenever seen by ordinary persons, and he could have an individual killed by saying to a retainer, "Go and rid me of that dog," all of which is clear evidence of his exalted position. The administrative offices delegated by the Great Sun included two war chiefs, two leading priests at the temple, two men who dealt with the external affairs of war and peace, one in charge of public works, and four who arranged public feasts. The decisions of the Great Sun were tempered by the amount of influence brought to bear upon him by his near relatives, particularly his brother and mother. He also consulted a council of elders, the leaders of the various villages, and outstanding old warriors.

More printer's ink has been spilled by more persons over the Natchez social system than over that of any other people. The reason is that it appeared from one series of studies that their marriage and descent patterns were unique and difficult, if not impossible, to explain in terms of existing sources. A thoughtful re-evaluation of the original sources by Carol Mason appears to have resolved what sometimes has been termed the Natchez "riddle" or "paradox," and similar conclusions were reached by Elisabeth Tooker. Since the previous debate now seems to have had a spurious basis, no purpose is served by considering the controversy. As Mason reconstructed the system, the Great Sun was at the apex of the social hierarchy, and nearly as important were his siblings, his mother, and other near relatives through females (matrilineage) who, like himself, were members of the Sun matrilineage. All such persons were required to marry individuals from other lineages (matrilineage exogamy). Children of a Sun man belonged to their mother's lineage because of the matrilineal descent system, but since they were indirect issue of the Sun lineage, they were accorded the title of "noble"; they were "honored persons" if their relationship was more distant. Thus, the titles of noble and honored person were ascribed for some persons, but they could be achieved by commoners. An ordinary person could become titled by performing heroic deeds in warfare or by sacrificing his infant at the death of a Sun. Summarily, the Sun matrilineage was the ranking social group and was exogamous.

From the nature of early French attitudes toward the Natchez, it is apparent that they were considered successful warriors under able leadership. Although the Great Sun headed the nation, the Great War Chief at one period was Tattooed Serpent, the brother of the Great Sun and a very powerful individual in his own right. There were lesser war chiefs, probably leaders of different villages, and warriors of three grades: apprentice, ordinary, and true warriors. Most, if not all, men belonged to one of these three categories or were numbered among the old warriors. When hostilities were contemplated, a pole was erected in the ground at the entrance to the house where a decisive meeting was to be held. Attached to the pole was the war calumet, a pipe adorned with red feathers, tufted and tasseled in black, with the black skin from the neck of a buzzard surrounding the pipe itself. The meeting was attended by old warriors, the Great War Chief, lesser war chiefs, and the Great Sun. The grievance against the potential enemy was presented vividly by the Great War Chief. The rationale for aggressive action was real or fabricated; it might be that another people had hunted on Natchez lands, for example. The offense was discussed, but the opinions of the old warriors were decisive. A delegation of warriors led by an old warrior went to the offenders carrying a peace calumet but without gifts so that they could not be considered appeasers. Arriving under these circumstances, they generally were received well and were sent home with gifts as an admission of the wrong done to them. Open conflict seldom erupted if this approach to an offense was taken.

When the Natchez anticipated an attack, they decided, usually in council, to defend themselves rather than to attempt appeasement of the aggressors. They first warned outlying families to join the main group and posted scouts to watch the approaches to their settlements. Another defensive move was to build palisaded fortifications. Forts were rather complex structures built around a tall tree which served as a watchtower. The trunks of trees were stripped of branches and were set in the ground to reach a height of about ten feet. The palisades were arranged in a roughly circular form with an overlap at the ends. Inside were structures to protect the women and children from arrows. The entrance was protected by towers, and in the passage to the outside were placed brambles and thorns. When an attack was imminent, emissaries carrying a peace calumet were sent to enlist the aid of friendly peoples. In the meantime the Great War Chief cited in their council the reasons for defending themselves. He sought the support of older warriors by reminding them of their honor and pointing out the vengeance they could obtain, and for youths there was the hope of glory.

When it had been decided to make war on another people, the warriors hunted and returned with their kills to the dwelling of the Great War Chief. For the three-day ceremony that followed, the bodies of the warriors were painted in different colors. The warrior's only clothing was a breechclout held in place with a belt decorated with rattles; stuck into this belt was a war club. In his left hand a warrior carried a round shield of bison skin and in his right hand a bow. The warriors gathered at a clearing, in the center of which was erected a pole some seven feet in height. To this was attached the war calumet. Around the pole, about eight feet away, were arranged three foods in wooden dishes. At the base of the pole was a large dog which had been roasted for the occasion. One of the dishes contained coarse cornmeal cooked in fat; the coarseness of the meal was a reminder that warriors did not require dainty foods. They also were served deer meat, both roasted and boiled, in order to be swift as a deer. Before the meal the oldest warrior, a man who was no longer able to take part in raids, orated to the assembly. He recounted his deeds of bravery and instructed the party how to go into battle and to fight. Then the old man lit the war calumet and presented it to the Great War Chief to smoke first. All the others smoked in order of rank; the old orator drew on the pipe last and returned it to the pole. The Great War Chief took a piece of the dog meat to eat, and the others followed in succession. By partaking of the roasted dog a warrior demonstrated his willingness to participate in the pending hostilities. As they ate, one young warrior went a short distance away and screamed the death cry. The warriors rushed to him in a group, and after he screamed again, they returned the cry. This episode was carried out twice more during the meal. Later the war drink was brought forth; it was a powerful emetic which caused the drinker to vomit violently. The retching could be heard at a great distance according to one observer. In the next ritual act each man ran in front of the pole of the calumet. This post, carved to look like a man and painted red, represented the enemy, and each warrior uttered a death cry as he struck it. He then told the post of his past deeds of valor. After seasoned warriors had recounted their achievements, each apprentice warrior told what he hoped to accomplish. A war dance then was performed. During the three days of ceremony, dances were held before the temple, along with recitations of personal accomplishments and the singing of death songs. The women prepared food for the men to take on their expedition, and old men refurbished war clubs and incised graphic symbols on a bark tablet. On it a symbol of the sun, representing the Natchez, was set above a figure of a naked man with a war club. An arrow was shown as though about to strike a fleeing woman, near whom was the sign of the enemy nation. Another set of symbols recorded the forthcoming month and the day when an attack would take place in force if this was included in the planning.

A raiding party could include from 20 to 300 warriors. As they approached the enemy's community, they traveled only at night and sent scouts to reconnoiter. The party carried fetishes attached to a long pole which was leaned toward the enemy when they stopped to camp. If any sign were interpreted as an ill omen for the venture, the warriors returned to their villages in spite of their elaborate preparations. Likewise when raiding parties encountered each other unexpectedly they withdrew. An attack was made at daybreak, and the persons to be killed were dispatched as quickly as possible. Women and children were taken alive, as was at least one man if at all possible. The raiders withdrew as quietly as they had arrived, taking their prisoners and leaving behind the inscribed bark, two red-painted arrows crossed and stuck in the ground, and the scalped dead. If the raid had been anticipated and the enemy was prepared for an attack in a palisaded fortification, the Natchez searched for hunting parties to kill. If one of the raiders was killed, his comrades attempted to scalp him, to prevent the enemy from obtaining a Natchez scalp; on their return the Great War Chief would compensate the dead man's family for its loss. The party returned home in honor if they had captured a living enemy man. Back in their own village, they planted two poles in the ground, and on them they lashed a crosspiece near the ground and another somewhat higher than a man's head. The captive was stunned with a blow at the base of the skull by his captor and was then scalped by him. The victim's naked body was tied in spread-eagle fashion on the pole frame. The young persons in the assembled throng gathered canes which were lighted, and the first flaming cane was applied to the captive by his captor. The torturer was free to apply the cane anywhere he chose, and it was most likely to be on the arm with which the victim had best defended himself. The victim was then burned by others as he sang his song of death. Some sacrificial victims were reported to have sung for seventy-two hours without pause before dying. However, not all captive males were dealt with in this manner; if a young woman whose husband had been killed claimed the captive, he was given to her as a husband. Captive women and children had their hair cut short and became the servants of their captors.

Warriors who had distinguished themselves were given new names by the Great War Chief. These denoted particular levels of achievement in warfare. For example, the name or title Great Man Slayer could be claimed by a warrior after he had taken twenty scalps or ten prisoners. A warrior also might tattoo his body to commemorate an achievement or might be elevated in social class.

Natchez religion was a highly formalized system, and specialists devoted all of their time to supernatural matters. These individuals, who were priests in a generic sense, were guardians at the major temple. It was one of these priests who explained their religion to du Pratz. They believed in a Great Spirit who was all-powerful. He created all good things, and he was surrounded by lesser spirits who did his bidding. There existed, too, spirits of evil led by a particularly malignant spirit. However, the Great

Spirit had tied him up forever, and as a result the lesser spirits of evil could do no great harm. The Great Spirit molded the first man from clay, and the figure grew to the proportions of a normal man. Woman probably was created in the same manner, but since man was created first, he was the stronger and more courageous. It was apparently the Great Spirit who sent the first Great Sun among the people, and this man established the line of Suns. Of the Great Sun's eldest daughter's children, the eldest son became the next ruling Great Sun, while her eldest daughter became the mother of the next Great Sun. Thus, the spiritual leadership was passed through a matrilineage to the oldest son.

The reigning Great Sun, the highest authority on earth, combined the qualities of a god and a king. His power and authority over things religious were paramount, and his decisions were very important in secular matters. In this theocratic state, all religious, social, and political control was, in theory, in the hands of this individual. The Great Sun was surrounded by warriors and retainers wherever he went. When he traveled about, he was carried on a litter by eight warriors; in his dwelling he sat on a small wooden throne. The Great Sun was distinguished in his dress from others; for example, his normal headdress was a net covered with black feathers, around which was a red border with white seed beads; hanging from it on the top were long white feathers in front and shorter ones behind. The lesser Suns appear to have worn similar headpieces.

The core of religious life focused on the preservation of a sacred temple fire tended by eight elders; two of them cared for the fire continually and were killed if they permitted the fire to die out. When an ordinary person walked in front of a temple, he put down any load that he might be carrying and extended his arms toward the temple as he wailed loudly. The same type of behavior was followed when he passed before the Great Sun. The Great Sun visited the temple daily to make certain that the fire still burned, and each morning at sunrise he faced the east, bowed to the ground, and wailed three times. A special calumet was brought to him, and he blew smoke first toward the rising sun and then in each of the other cardinal directions. Thus, the Great Sun venerated the sun and was in turn venerated by all other persons in the tribe. What we see is a direct line of continuity into the past functionally linked to the Great Spirit, the Great Suns, and an eternal fire.

The first products of any harvest were taken to the temple by the heads of families. These foods were received by the temple guardians and conveyed to the Great Sun, who was free to distribute them as he chose. Furthermore, seeds to be sown were blessed at the temple before planting. Each of the thirteen months of the calendar was named for the most important food of the prior month, and the beginning of each month was celebrated by a feast in which either the Great Sun or a lesser Sun played a major role. The feast of the first month, corresponding roughly to the month of March, was called Deer, and this marked the beginning of the year. A commemorative celebration was held each year during the month of Deer in honor of a particular event said to have been historically true: the capture of the Great Sun by an enemy party, his liberation by Natchez warriors, and his return home in triumph. Afterwards there were other ritual acts, and gifts were presented to the Great Sun as he sat on his throne.

The month of the Great Corn was ushered in by the most important of all yearly ceremonies, which was for the first fruits of the harvest. This was in the seventh month of the year, and the maize for the feast was sown on virgin soil by the warriors. The warriors cared for the crop and notified the Great Sun when it had been harvested and stored in a granary of cane. The entire village assembled at the cache to receive the Great Sun who arrived on his litter, which was covered with a flower-decked canopy. A new fire was kindled by rubbing sticks together, and the corn was presented to the female Suns and then to all other women. The maize was cooked, and a feast followed additional rituals. After the people had eaten, the warriors recounted their brave deeds, and youths told of their ambitions. In the evening, some two hundred poles of dry cane were lighted around the area, and the men and women danced until morning. One man drummed on a pot covered with a deerskin; around him was a circle of women. An outer circle was composed of men who shook gourd rattles. The women moved in one direction and the men in the opposite direction; as an individual tired he or she was replaced by someone from the audience. The next day a ball game was held. The warriors were divided into two teams, one led by the Great Sun and the other by the Great War Chief. In the hair of the Great Sun's men were white feathers, and the opposite team wore red feathers. The object of the game was to force a ball to one or the other end of the plaza. The winning team was presented with gifts by the captain of the losing team, and the winners were permitted to wear their feather headdresses until the game again was played. After the ball game, a war dance was performed by the warriors. The festivities were not over until the harvested maize had been consumed completely. The two celebrations just described took place at Natchez, the capital settlement. Similar ceremonies, however, took place at the other settlements, and these were led by the different resident Suns.

Religion embraced more than the temple cult, for there were a host of spirits that probably were lesser agents of the Great Spirit. Power existed in the honey locust tree, and under one such tree near the temple was

the wood for the sacred fire. A tree struck by lightning was burned completely by the Indians, and snakes were regarded with terror. The Great
Sun and people of all classes fasted to bring rain. When commoners fasted
on certain days, they smeared black paint on their faces and did not eat
until the sun had set. The position of shamans in the religious hierarchy
is obscure, but they seem to have operated outside the sun-centered theocracy. Shamanistic power was sought by consuming nothing but water for
nine days. In this period of isolation a spirit presented itself to the aspirant,
and from it he learned certain skills such as how to change the weather
or cure illnesses. The spirit aids, which were kept in a small basket,
included such tangible items as plant roots, owl heads, animal teeth, pebbles
or small stones, and hair from a deer. A shaman had very real obligations
to his patient. Were an individual treated by him to die, the shaman might
be killed, but success brought material gain. Among the techniques for
curing and weather changes were fasting, smoking, singing, and dancing.
A shaman could, after rubbing himself with a particular form of root, handle
poisonous snakes without fear. One cure included making an incision at
the locus of an illness and sucking blood from the wound. When the shaman
spit the blood into a container, not only blood was seen but also a foreign
object such as a piece of wood, straw, or leather; the illness was attributed
to this item.

Comparatively little is known about the individual life cycle in Natchez
society, but the available information rounds out their ethnographic sketch.
Soon after a baby was born, it was tied into a cradleboard and strips of
deerskin were bound over its forehead to flatten it. The cradleboard was
placed in a bed beside the baby's mother. Infants were smeared with bear
oil to keep flies from biting them and to make them supple. Strands of
bison wool were bound below a month-old baby's knees and above its ankles,
and these were worn until the child was about five years of age. When
nearly a year old, the infant was encouraged to walk, but it was nursed
until it weaned itself or until the mother again became pregnant. As children grew they came under the influence of the elder male of the family,
who as an extended family head was termed "father" but might be a great-
grandfather or even a great-great-grandfather. Children were considered
to belong to their biological father, and so long as he lived they were responsible to him as well as to the elder male in the extended family, who coun-
selled all families responsible to him. Children who might have fought
with each other feared to do so because of the threat that they would be
sent away from the Natchez to live. Boys were encouraged to exercise and
gradually acquire adult skills from about the age of twelve. The sexual
division of labor was instilled in the youths. Hunting, fishing, fighting,

some farming and the manufacturing of most artifacts were male activities. Carrying home game or fish, most of the farming, preparing food, and manufacturing clothing, baskets, or pottery were female responsibilities, along with the raising of children.

After puberty the young males and females were free to have sexual intercourse. The girls apparently did not bestow sexual favors without material gain, and a potential husband was proud of the amount of property his future mate had accumulated in this way. A man was required to be about twenty-five years old before he married, and a girl appears to have been somewhat younger. Once the couple decided to marry, the man went before the heads of their respective families to be questioned. If no close blood ties existed, and if the pair loved each other, the elders sanctioned the marriage. On the day of the wedding the girl was led by the elder of her family, and followed by the remainder of her family, to the home of the man. Here they were greeted and invited into the house where, after a pause, the elders of both families asked the couple whether they loved each other and were willing to be man and wife. The ideals of domestic harmony were set forth, there was an exchange of vows by the couple, and a gift was made to the bride's father. The bride's mother handed her a laurel branch to hold in one hand and an ear of corn to hold in the other hand. She gave the corn to her husband, and he said, "I am your husband," to which she answered, "I am your wife." Finally the husband told his wife, "There is our bed, keep it tight," which was an injunction against committing adultery. After a special meal the couple and their guests danced from early evening through the night. In this description of a marriage by du Pratz it is not specified whether or not these customs were observed by everyone. The need for such clarification is evident since other descriptions of Natchez marriages vary from this form.

Plural marriages were known, with sororal polygyny being the most common form, although nonsororal polygyny also was practiced. Plural marriages were more common among the nobility than among commoners. A noble with many wives retained only one or two in his house; the others lived at their natal homes where they were visited by him. In the polygynous households the wife who bore the first offspring supervised the other wives. Divorce was extremely rare for most persons, but an upper-class woman married to a common man was free to take other husbands. Furthermore, such a woman could have her husband put to death if he committed adultery. This appears to be a most unusual form of the double standard of morality. Berdaches (transvestites) were reported, but their position in the society is not clear.

From the writings of du Pratz and a few others it is possible to obtain a generalized perspective of the ideals which guided adult life. Complete tribal unity did not exist during the brief historical era, and it may be inferred that a struggle for power was taking place among leading upper-class persons, which would have had an effect on intervillage affairs. In any event, some Natchez communities were friendly to the French while others were hostile, which suggests an absence of overall unity. Under the aegis of the Great Sun and his close relatives there was a conceptually rigid and well-defined hierarchy of sociopolitical control. The distinct impression is that the upper class did not abuse its power and that village harmony was the norm. The people in general were honorable in dealing with each other and with the French. In the story of the acceptance of the first Great Sun it will be recalled that certain specific rules of behavior were stated. These were supported by the guardians of tradition, the temple priests, and the upper class in general.

One of the most vivid descriptions left by du Pratz is that of the funeral ceremonies for the Great War Chief, Tattooed Serpent, the brother of the Great Sun and almost as powerful. When he died the tribe was greatly distressed since each brother had vowed to kill himself at the death of the other. The temple guardians turned to du Pratz, who was influential among the Natchez and a friend of the Great Sun, to avert the leader's potential suicide. Du Pratz and other leading Frenchmen of the area went to the home of the Great Sun and talked with him. The Great Sun was grieved deeply over the death and had to be restrained from committing suicide. At the house of Tattooed Serpent his corpse lay on the bed he had occupied during his life. His face was painted red, and he was clothed in his finest garments, including a feather headdress. Attached to the bed were his weapons, displayed with the peace calumets he had received during his life. From a pole stuck into the ground were forty-six linked pieces of red-painted cane sections representing the number of enemies he had killed. Gathered around the body were his "chancellor," physician, chief domestic, pipe bearer, two wives, some old women, and a volunteer from among the noblewomen, all of whom were to be killed as a part of the funeral ceremony. The next day included a "Dance of Death" and two rehearsals of the deaths of those persons who were to be killed. At about this time the commoner parents of a child strangled their offspring out of respect for Tattooed Serpent; by doing so they were raised to noble standing, and would not be killed when the Great Sun died. Some warriors also had apprehended a common man who had been married to a Sun woman but had fled at her death to avoid being killed. His capture once again slated him for death, but three old women related to him offered themselves to be killed in his place. The man in turn was elevated to the upper class by the women's sacrifice. The activities on the day of the funeral were directed by a "master of ceremonies." The upper part of this man's body was painted red, and about his waist was a tight-fitting garment fringed to the knees with red and white feathers. On his head he wore a crown of red feathers. The red staff that he carried had a crosspiece near the top, and from the upper part of the staff hung black feathers. When this impressively arrayed individual approached the house of the deceased, he was greeted with "hoo" and by wailing indicating death. The procession formed behind the master of ceremonies, who was followed by the oldest warrior carrying the staff from which hung the red cane rings and a war pipe that reflected the honor of the dead man. These men were in turn followed by six temple guardians who carried the body on a litter; then came those who were to be killed, each accompanied by eight relatives who served as executioners. Each of these relatives was subsequently freed from the probability of being killed at the death of the Great Sun and seemingly was raised to the class of noble. The procession circled the house of the deceased three times, and then the litter bearers walked in intersecting circles to the temple. The dead child was thrown repeatedly in the path of the bearers and retrieved by its parents. When the body of Tattooed Serpent was placed in the temple, the sacrificial victims, their hair covered with red paint, were drugged with tobacco and strangled. Within the temple the two wives of Tattooed Serpent and two men were buried in the same grave as the Great War Chief. The other victims were buried elsewhere, and the funeral ended by burning the home in which Tattooed Serpent had lived.

With a great man's death unrolled pomp, pageantry, and human sacrifice; the death of a Sun was a tragic highlight to life. The number of persons killed at the funeral of Tattooed Serpent unquestionably was fewer than would have been considered fitting before the French arrived. For other people to die was of lesser moment, and yet any death was surrounded with further deaths. When an outstanding female Sun died, her husband, a commoner, was strangled by their eldest son. Then the eldest surviving daughter ordered twelve small children killed and placed around the bodies of the deceased couple. In the plaza fourteen platforms were erected, and on each was a man who was to die during the funeral. These men danced before the house of the deceased every fifteen minutes and then returned to their public stations. It was said that after four days the "March of the Bodies" ritual took place. The dead children previously had been placed outside the dead woman's home, and with them were the live victims. The woman was carried out on a litter, and the small bodies were dropped repeatedly before the procession so that by the time the litter reached the temple the corpses of the children were in pieces. After the woman's body was inside the temple, the fourteen victims were strangled, but not before they had received water and wads of tobacco which drugged them into unconsciousness. The living mourned for an important deceased person by weeping for four days. In general, mourners cut their hair but did not paint their faces, and they avoided public gatherings. The temporary grave was on a raised platform. A shelter of branches formed a vault over the body, and there was an opening at the end near the head where food was placed. The mourners grieved at the grave each day at dawn and at sunset for a month. Then after the flesh had decayed, the bones were placed in a basket in a temple.

The custom of executing persons at the death of the Suns and other upper-class individuals may seem barbaric and senseless, but it had very real advantages to the individuals involved. In their belief system one's spirit under such circumstances would accompany the deceased upper-class person to the world of the dead and serve him or her there in perennial happiness. The same future awaited all others who observed the rules of the society during their lifetime. It was thought that a person who had broken the rules of the people would go to a place which was covered with water; naked, he would be bitten by mosquitoes and have only undesirable foods to eat.

It was only a few short years after the dramatic death and burial ceremonies for Tattooed Serpent that the Natchez became extinct as a people. It seems fitting to record a speech which Tattooed Serpent delivered to du Pratz (1774, 40-41) after a war with the French and shortly before the Natchez were destroyed.

> I did not approve, as you know, the war our people made upon the French to avenge the death of their relation, seeing I made them carry the *pipe of peace* to the French. This you well know, as you first smoked in the pipe yourself. Have the French two hearts, a good one to-day, and to-morrow a bad one? As for my brother and me, we have but one heart and one word. Tell me then, if thou art, as thou sayest, my true friend, what thou thinkest of all this, and shut thy mouth to everything else. We know not what to think of the French, who, after having begun the war, granted a peace, and offered it of themselves; and then at the time we were quiet, believing ourselves to be at peace, people come to kill us, without saying a word.
>
> Why ... did the French come into our country? We did not go to seek them: they asked for land of us, because their country was too little for all the men that were in it. We told them they might take

land where they pleased, there was enough for them and for us; that it was good the same sun should enlighten us both, and that we would walk as friends in the same path; and that we would give them of our provisions, assist them to build, and to labour in their fields. We have done so; is not this true? What occasion then had we for Frenchmen? Before they came, did we not live better than we do, seeing we deprive ourselves of a part of our corn, our game, and fish, to give a part to them? In what respect, then, had we occasion for them? Was it for their guns? The bows and arrows which we used, were sufficient to make us live well. Was it for their white, blue, and red blankets? We can do well enough with buffalo skins which are warmer; our women wrought feather-blankets for the winter, and mulberry-mantles for the summer; which indeed were not so beautiful; but our women were more laborious and less vain than they are now. In fine, before the arrival of the French, we lived like men who can be satisfied with what they have; whereas at this day we are like slaves, who are not suffered to do as they please.

References

Albrecht, Andrew C. "The Location of the Historic Natchez Villages,"*Journal of Mississippi History*, v. 6, 67-88. 1944.

Albrecht, Andrew C. "Indian-French Relations at Natchez," *American Anthropologist*, v. 48, 321-354. 1946.

Albrecht, Andrew C. "Ethical Precepts among the Natchez Indians," *Louisiana Historical Quarterly*, v. 31, 569-597. 1948.

Caldwell, Joseph R. *Trend and Tradition in the Prehistory of the Eastern United States*. American Anthropological Association, Memoir 88. 1958.

Ford, James A., and Clarence H. Webb. *Poverty Point, A Late Archaic Site in Louisiana*. Anthropological Papers of the American Museum of Natural History, v. 46, pt. 1. 1956.

Griffin, James B., ed. *Archaeology of Eastern United States*. Chicago. 1952.

Haag, William G. "The Archaic of the Lower Mississippi Valley," *American Antiquity*, v. 26, 317-323. 1961.

Mason, Carol. "Natchez Class Structure," *Ethnohistory*, v. 2, 120-133. 1964.

*Le Page du Pratz, Antoine S. *The History of Louisiana*. Paris. 1758: London. 1774 (reprinted at New Orleans in 1947). Between the years 1718 and 1734 the author lived most of the time near the Natchez, where he owned a plantation. The observations by du Pratz concerning these Indians are the most systematic of all the firsthand accounts. The book is very enjoyable to read and is at the same time highly informative.

Quimby, George I., Jr. "The Natchezan Culture Type," *American Antiquity*, v. 7, 255-275. 1942.

Swanton, John R. *Indian Tribes of Lower Mississippi Valley and Adjacent Coast of the Gulf of Mexico*. Bureau of American Ethnology, Bulletin 43. 1911.

Swanton, John R. *Social Organization and Social Usages of the Indians of the Creek Confederacy*. Bureau of American Ethnology, Annual Report 42. 1928.

Swanton, John R. *The Indians of the Southeastern United States*. Bureau of American Ethnology, Bulletin 137. 1946. Virtually all that is known about Natchez ethnography is in this volume. It is a monumental regional culture history and a key secondary source on the Natchez.

Swanton, John R. *The Indian Tribes of North America*. Bureau of American Ethnology, Bulletin 145. 1953.

Tooker, Elisabeth. "Natchez Social Organization: Fact or Anthropological Fancy?" *Ethnohistory*, v. 10, 358-372. 1963.

Red Man –
White Man

Soon after discovery of the New World, a great debate raged in Spain concerning whether aboriginal Americans were human or only humanlike. The conquistadores argued that Indians were irrational, heretical, and tainted with mortal sin. Irrespective of the manner in which the Spanish had been received by Indians this attitude emerged as the prevailing opinion. It served as justification for treating Indians in a nonhuman manner and for seizing their land or property with impunity. Francisco de Vitoria, a professor at Salamanca and the founder of international law, argued against this thesis. He noted that in Europe even heretics were privileged to own property and could not be punished for sins without a trial. Implicit in Vitoria's arguments was the conception of Indians as human beings. When the exploiters of Indians maintained that the Pope had granted title to all newly discovered lands to the kings of Spain and Portugal, Vitoria countered that the Pope had no power over the aborigines and their land, and that title by discovery could apply only to unoccupied lands. In a papal bull of 1537 Pope Paul III, proclaimed "that the Indians are truly men and that they are not only capable of understanding the Catholic faith, but according to our information, they desire exceedingly to receive it" (Cohen, 1960, 290). Considering Indians as human beings gave the church new millions of immortal souls to be saved, which no doubt was a consideration in the Pope's pronouncement; regardless of his motives, however, the principle of acknowledging Indian humanness and Indian ownership of land served as a guide for colonial governments in all of North America. In the section to follow most of the information has been drawn from the scholarly studies of Roy H. Pearce (1965), Lewis O. Saum (1965), and Edward H. Spicer (1969).

White Attitudes and Policies

Early maritime explorers found the Indian and his ways fascinating because they illustrated what men could be like if stripped of Christian and civilized behavior. The indigenous people were considered as savages who lived more like animals than men; although human in form, they were barely human in their customs. A word often used to describe them was "beasts," and while their land might be attractive, many settlers felt that the Indians were its blight. A brief review of early contacts in diverse areas conveys an overview of Indian-white relations which leads to a greater understanding of the subsequent course of history.

The charter under which Virginia was founded in 1606 provided for

560

bringing God to the savages since adopting Christian ways was equated with becoming civilized. Lands were purchased from the Indians, and settlers were certain that they could live in harmony with the infidels, who soon would be Christianized. Before many years had passed about fifty missionaries had been sent to the colony to work with the Indian children, for it was felt that they would learn more readily than adults. The colonists were convinced that their efforts were succeeding since there were no major outbreaks of hostility. In actuality, the most powerful Indian leader, Powhatan, was waiting and hoping that the colony would fail; however, the English became more confident and firmly entrenched as each year passed. Then suddenly in 1622 Powhatan's successor decided he had waited long enough, and the colonists were attacked. Nearly 350 whites were killed, and the only reason the colony was not destroyed was that a Christian Indian had warned the English at the last moment. To the colonists this massacre was clear evidence of inborn Indian treachery, and the settlers now felt justified in destroying these savages whom they no longer attempted to understand. The Indians in Virginia now were viewed as an impediment to the march of civilization, and within the next fifty years they were deliberately destroyed or displaced.

The "Indian experience" of no two colonies was the same because of the settlers' backgrounds and the nature of the Indians encountered. The Anglicans and Roman Catholics who established Maryland in 1634 protected the local Indians against far more powerful tribes who lived nearby. Here the Indian lands always were obtained by purchase, the aboriginal population was well treated, and Jesuit missionaries largely were responsible for Christianizing efforts. It might be anticipated that the Quaker settlers of Pennsylvania would have been the most successful in making Indians into Christians given their commitment to nonviolence and humanistic tolerance of others. The Quakers stressed the common denominators which united all men and did not seek to identify the differences between themselves and Indians. There was peace and the Quakers offered Indians love, but they won few converts because to the Indian, religion meant comparatively little without ritual and ceremony and the Quaker approach to God was largely devoid of both. The Quakers remained in their position of neutrality when non-Quakers in and beyond Pennsylvania intrigued and fought with Indians in their midst and at their frontiers.

The Pilgrims and Puritans of New England believed that God would guide their affairs with Indians, who were to them descendants of Noah through the Tartars. They had entered the New World from Asia as fallen people in the grip of Satan. When many Indians died in a "wonderful plague" of smallpox, it was God's way of furthering the goals of the settlers.

The Puritans knew that Indian lands were intended for Christian English use and they were purchased only to keep peace. They had no hesitancy in raiding and warring against the Indians or fostering dissensions among them for Puritan advantage. At the same time it was recognized that these savages should be civilized. Some missionaries, such as John Eliot, did concern themselves with Indians, but the number of conversions was few and their successes transient. As savages they stood in opposition to civilized persons, and while they might manifest natural virtues, they seldom were noble. Efforts by these colonists to integrate Indians into transported Western European culture failed for transparent reasons.

The Spanish who first entered the Southwest in 1540 expected to find barbarians or savages and felt a strong obligation to civilize these people. Church and civil authorities alike accepted this as their primary goal after it was realized that the area was not going to yield great riches. The gross patterning of Spanish life was to be introduced to Indians, but this was not regarded as an attempt to replace Indian customs since they were thought to be without meaningful social, political, and religious institutions. The Spanish were to decide what was best for the indigenous population, and the advance agents of their culture usually were Roman Catholic missionaries. These men began to build churches and quarters near established pueblos, instructed certain individuals in Catholic doctrines, and as soon as possible recruited other persons to serve as catechists and other helpers. It usually was the missionaries who were responsible for introducing the structure of civil government, new crops, and novel crafts; the goal was to create self-sufficient Roman Catholic communities. The missionaries in New Mexico usually were accompanied by soldiers who reinforced Spanish authority; in general, the priests here treated Indian transgressions far more harshly than did their counterparts farther to the south. Soon the Eastern Pueblos were paying tribute to the king of Spain, which is a good indication of the program's effectiveness.

Apart from the mission environment Spanish frontiersmen impinged on the Indians of New Mexico through the policy of giving large and small grants of their land to soldiers for services rendered the government. The great encomienda grants in New Mexico did not include any of the large pueblos, but the people who lived in the small communities in the midst of such grants were forced to work these lands for the Spanish, usually with very little or no compensation. Before long Spanish employees of encomenderos married Indians and came to acquire their lands. Abuses in the encomienda system engendered a great deal of hostility in some pueblos, and this eventually led to an abandonment of such grants. Smaller land allotments or "village" grants were made for unoccupied lands, or at times for land near an Indian settlement, and once again intermarriage began to bind the settlers and Indians into a single social matrix. Spanish towns, with Santa Fe as the prime example, formed another culture contact setting, but since Indians were drawn to them only for certain services, their impact was relatively minor.

When the Mexican War for Independence ended in 1821, Indians in the southwestern part of North America were granted the full rights of Mexican citizens. All persons born in Mexico became citizens, irrespective of their culture or race, and efforts were made to incorporate Indians into national life in a meaningful manner. This goal was not achieved in New Mexico, however. Americans began to penetrate New Mexico in the 1840's, and their attitudes contrasted rather strikingly with those that previously had prevailed. The mission settlement had no meaningful place in their plans. They regarded the pueblo-dwellers as moderately "civilized," but most less sedentary Indians were considered "wild." In either case, the Anglo-American policy was designed to push Indians aside, either peacefully or by force, in order to facilitate their thrust westward.

Effective Spanish intrusion into California beginning in 1769 was guided by the same general policies that prevailed in the Southwest, but the indigenous population was quite different. In the Southwest the pueblo peoples were sedentary farmers, and the wandering tribes, such as the Apache, were warlike. Most Californian Indians, except for the farming peoples along the lower Colorado River, were wanderers, moving often in their search for nuts and seeds which were their staples, but they were far from bellicose. A primary purpose of the Spanish colony in California was to Christianize Indians and have them settle at missions which were to be self-sufficient; thus the Indians were very much a part of the economic order. Yet most of the people who were drawn to the missions, either voluntarily or by force, were poorly prepared to adapt to a sedentary life in crowded conditions with a rigid work routine. The experiment rather clearly failed by the time the missions were secularized, beginning in 1834. Souls had been saved, but the cost in human life was great.

It has been seen that Indians in the northeastern states were confronted with white settlers in search of lands to occupy. The indigenous people were a hindrance to progress and were to be displaced by gentle, callous, or cruel means; they had no meaningful place in the colonial order except to the few missionaries. In the Southwest the primary Spanish goal was to civilize Indians, and the development of Spanish farming and ranching establishments was largely a by-product of this effort. The Spaniards penetrated California as a political move because they feared Russian intrusions from the north. Missions were founded in California to save Indian souls, and thus the pattern parallels that in the Southwest. In the northern portions of the continent, the English, French, and Russian ventures were of a different order. Here it was the fur trader, not the settler or missionary, who usually was the most important advance agent of Western civilization. Irrespective of their national origins and the time at which they lived, fur traders viewed Indians very differently than did most other white intruders. The Indian and the trader were joined by economic ties which profited them both. The areas where the fur trade dominated longest were those which were not suitable for large settlements of whites, and thus the Indians' way of life was not disrupted by large groups of intruders. Furthermore, the fur trader and the Indian could maintain their relationship only as long as the Indian trapped and followed the essence of his aboriginal way of life.

Frequently it has been maintained that French traders dealt with Indians more effectively than did their English counterparts. English traders often have been characterized as intolerant of Indian customs as well as haughty and aloof in business or personal contacts. The French by contrast have been depicted as sympathetic and understanding, with an ability to quickly establish good rapport with Indians; in a word the Indians could be friendly with the French but not the English. Saum has studied primary sources by writers of both nationalities and challenges the validity of these stereotypes. The truth appears to be that all parties involved were guided by self-interest which at times made them devious. The French and English vilified each other, and men of both nations were at times difficult. Regardless of their nationality, they could be intolerant or tolerant, cruel or kind, depending on their personalities and experiences with Indians. Another dichotomy often noted between traders does stand as valid; free traders often were unscrupulous when compared with licensed traders and those representing large trading companies.

Unlike the white settler on his farm or the land-hungry pioneer pushing westward, whether into Ohio, Manitoba, or California, the trader lived among Indians and became a part of their way of life. A trader was obligated to be reasonably tolerant of his clientele if only to further his enterprise, and at times his very survival depended on aid from Indians. These were literate and practical men of action, not philosophers; they justifiably had the hearts and heads of merchants. In their judgment some individual Indians and tribes were good while others were bad—it was that simple. They were parsimonious with their praise and often characterized Indians as "scoundrels" and as "rascals," on occasion even as "monsters" or "inhuman." Yet an active and productive Indian was an essential ingredient to a successful trading enterprise, and the Indians as well as the traders appreciated the fact. These generalizations about traders apply to those of English and French origins who were important over most of the continent. A brief summary of the relationship between the Eskimos of Greenland and the Danes was presented in the opening chapter. It remains to discuss the Russian fur trade in brief.

The Russian maritime expedition led by Vitus Bering in 1741 discovered islands in the northern Pacific Ocean, and the men saw but did not reach the North American mainland. The vessel commanded by Bering was wrecked on Bering Island, and from there the survivors sailed back to Kamchatka in 1742. They carried with them the pelts of sea otter, an animal abundant around Bering Island, but only occasionally found along coastal Kamchatka. A host of small-scale expeditions soon set sail to Bering Island in a quest for these luxurious pelts, and within a few years the Aleutian Islands were explored rather thoroughly and the Alaskan mainland along the northern Pacific Ocean was discovered. The men who launched these ventures were *promishleniki,* the Russian counterpart to the French *coureurs des bois;* they were bold and cruel freebooters. The atrocities which the promishleniki committed against the Aleuts and Pacific Eskimos were numerous and sometimes infamous. It was not until the Russian-American Company was founded in 1799 that the most gross transgressions against aboriginal Americans were curbed with a certain degree of effectiveness.

The Russians established themselves on Kodiak Island but soon moved their colonial headquarters to Sitka in southeastern Alaska. Their sphere of dominance extended from the Aleutian Islands to the Gulf of Alaska, but they never effectively controlled southeastern Alaska in general or the vast region north of the Alaska Peninsula. They did not found their first station or redoubt along a Bering Sea drainage until 1818, and they built only two other such establishments in this area before the purchase by the United States. During the latter part of the Russian era the administrators were naval officers, but it was apparently common for ordinary employees to be criminals from Russia who chose to work for the company in Alaska rather than go to jail in Russia. A number of men who held high posts in the company were "creoles," or persons of mixed Russian and aboriginal Siberian or American ancestry, and these men appear to have been much more even-handed in dealing with the fur trade clientele than were their Russian counterparts. One indication of the manner in which the administration viewed the aboriginal people is to consider the words that the commanders-in-chief used in their official correspondence when referring to them. In the Russian-American Company records for the years centering about 1830 the chief colonial administrator referred to the clientele of southwestern Alaska as "savages" more often than by any other term, although together the terms "people" or "natives" were used as often as savages. By and large during the latter part of their period of control the Russians assumed a stern but essentially paternalistic attitude toward the native peoples. They always were anxious to expand the fur trade but not at the expense of drastically altering the economic foundations of the Eskimos and Indians with whom they dealt.

Peoples Destroyed and Displaced

It would be difficult to prove, but it seems likely that after initial historic contact far more Indians were killed by diseases introduced by whites than by bullets. It also appears that more Indians were killed by other Indians than by whites although many such murders unquestionably were abetted by whites. It is probable that every tribe was subjected to at least one major epidemic, and there were precious few Indians whose way of life was not altered dramatically, or even destroyed outright, early in their history.

In the preceding chapters the importance of disease as a disruptive force has been documented for specific peoples, and its influence cannot be underestimated. Diseases which had a long history among Europeans led to biological accommodations among them, yet the same illnesses could be deadly to a virgin population; measles and whooping cough are two examples. Diseases might rage in epidemic proportion among Indians and whites alike, as did malaria. Tuberculosis was a dreaded killer of Indians but was somewhat less frightful among whites.

Examples of tribes destroyed by diseases are not difficult to locate in the literature; two depressing examples will illustrate the speed of the demise. The Massachuset, whose population was estimated at 3000 in 1600, numbered only 500 by 1631 as a result of a terrible epidemic, possibly of smallpox, and soon thereafter smallpox reduced them to a remnant population. By 1663 when John Eliot published a Bible in their language they were practically extinct. The Mandan of North Dakota possibly numbered about 3600 early in their history; an estimate for 1836 was that there were about 1600 individuals, but as the result of a smallpox epidemic during 1837 the tribe was reduced to sixty-one survivors. For the Massachuset there could be no cultural continuity, but the Mandan slowly increased in number from the point of virtual extinction.

Even though disease might not utterly destroy a tribe an epidemic might wipe out so many persons that they were unable to fend off human enemies or effectively sustain their established cultural traditions. After the small-pox epidemics which struck the Pawnee in 1837-1838 they were harassed by their once less powerful enemies. The terrible epidemics in 1838 and 1900-1901 among the Kuskokwim Eskimos left so few adults that it is difficult to understand how their cultural ways could have been perpetuated in any but an attenuated manner. The malaria epidemic which struck the Columbia River Indians and those in the Central Valley of California in the early 1830's had a mortality rate estimated at 75 percent. As a result their population was reduced so severely that when whites arrived in large numbers somewhat later they could not be effective in their resistance.

The extinction of a population unquestionably is tragic, but another result of the contact setting was nearly as sad. Considering the intimate and often religious associations of Indians with their traditional homelands, their displacement to other areas was heartrending. The plight of the Fox in this respect has been documented, but there are other instances involving isolated tribes which are even more distressing. One example will suffice to make the point. In aboriginal times the Delaware occupied present-day New Jersey and adjacent areas, but in the early 1700's the Iroquois came to dominate them politically and sanctioned their displacement by white settlers. Before long many Delaware settled in eastern Ohio, but not with-out wandering largely homeless for some time. By 1820 some lived in Arkansas, and others had ventured on to Texas. Some fifteen years later many of them had settled on a reservation in Kansas, from which they were moved to Oklahoma in 1867. Most of them remain there today, but there are Delaware Indians scattered from eastern Canada to Montana, far from the New Jersey homeland of their historic origins.

The personal and cultural trauma wrought by purposefully displacing a tribe from its home to its remade home is tragic in itself. But to imagine that it became a Federal policy to move all Indians from one vast area to another violates the very principles on which the United States was founded. Yet such was the case, and the drama began to develop with clarity about 1800. One overwhelming argument had been advanced as justifica-tion for assuming control of Indian lands, and it never changed. Indians obstructed progress, whites could utilize land much more effectively than Indians, and thus it was the God-given right of the settlers to obtain and till such ground. Indian displacement became a blanket policy with the Removal Bill of 1830, and it was supported strongly by President Andrew Jackson. New Englanders could deplore this policy elsewhere because they long ago had resolved their Indian "problem." It was the southeastern states and the settlers venturing into the midwest who were considered the wan-ton, immoral destroyers of Indians.

Most surviving tribes with large landholdings in the area east of the Mississippi River were bribed and intimidated into moving westward. By 1831 the states of Alabama, Georgia, and Mississippi had forced the removal of the Choctaw, Chickasaw, and Creek. Fox and Sauk reluctance to forsake their lands led to the Black Hawk War, which was documented previously, and Cherokee resistance to removal likewise has been described. The Cherokee had adopted civilized ways and had become successful farmers, which was highly disconcerting to politicians in Georgia who yearned to bring their productive lands under state control. In 1829 the Georgia legislature passed a law incorporating much of the land of the Cherokee Nation as state holdings. Furthermore, under terms of the act all previous federal legislation and regulations were to be null and void by June of the following year. In addition Indians were prohibited from testifying in court cases involving whites, and prohibitions were established against interference with removal plans. About this time gold was discovered on Cherokee holdings, and the governor declared that all gold-bearing lands belonged to the state. The actions of the Georgia legislature led to the famous *Worcester vs. Georgia* case, which reached the Supreme Court in 1832 when John Marshall was Chief Justice. The court judgment was that the Federal government, not the state of Georgia, was responsible for the Cherokee. This decision led Jackson to make his famous remark, "John Marshall has made his decision, now let him enforce it." Illegal seizures of land and property by whites, conflicting policies of the Indian leaders, intrigue by unscrupulous persons who were both white and Indian, and harassment by state representatives finally led to the 1835 Treaty of Echota and Cherokee removal.

Before the Cherokee treaty leading to their "legal" removal, gross injustices were perpetrated by citizens and representatives of the state of Georgia. Indians were forced from their lands at bayonet point, they were removed in chains without due legal process, they were sold intoxicants in violation of federal regulations, and their movable property often was stolen with impunity. A state law prohibiting a Cherokee from employing a white was used as a pretext for seizing plantations, which then were disposed of to whites by lottery. The Cherokee were required by law to transfer land only to the state. When some families finally were forced to leave Georgia, much of the property that they carried with them was seized and money extorted from them. Food and shelter during the forced migration often was inadequate or nonexistent, and finally cholera struck, along with other diseases. Yet by 1838 when all of these people were to be removed only 2000 Cherokee had been deported; the other 15,000 still believed that somehow they would not be driven from their homeland. But such was not the case. About 7000 troops under General Winfield Scott moved against the Cherokee, who previously had been disarmed. He ordered that within a month's time every Cherokee must be moving westward. Soldiers went from house to house and forced people to leave at once. Often they were unable to take anything with them, and they were impounded in stockades until they could be shipped westward. Their journey to Oklahoma is known to the Cherokee as the Trail of Tears; about 4000 persons died as a direct result of their forced removal. The Cherokee had their own Bataan Death March a long time ago—courtesy of the United States Army.

Treaties

Most of the land in North America was used by Indians when Europeans arrived, but Indians today own and occupy only a very small portion of their original holdings. As is obvious from the preceding chapters most Indian lands were obtained by treaties negotiated with tribes who relinquished land in one area for that in another, often with monetary compensation as added inducement. The treaty arrangements for a number of tribes have been documented, yet it is worthwhile to present a brief overview of the changing status of Indian lands in historical perspective.

In northeastern North America the early Dutch and English administrators in the 1700's held that Indian tribes were sovereign nations and the legitimate claimants to the lands they occupied. Any land acquired from Indians was obtained on a national, not an individual, basis. The pre-Revolutionary War treaties of the British dealt primarily with the question of boundaries and the acquisition of lands from Indians. As early as 1670, during the reign of Charles II, England was concerned that those tribes desiring her protection should receive it. There are treaties and agreements with New England tribes dating from 1664, and by 1755 a bureau was founded to deal with Indian matters. Formal recognition of Indian title to land was to guide policy in both Canada and the United States.

Between the years 1778 and 1871 the United States government negotiated formal treaties with Indian tribes in the same manner as it did with foreign powers. Tribes were viewed by Federal authorities as "dependent nations," and treaties were considered in the same light as other statutes of the United States Congress. In some instances early treaties prohibited U. S. citizens from venturing onto Indian lands without passports, but more often the subordinate position of the Indian nations to the United States is made clear by the provisions. It may come as a surprise that in spite of the hostilities between the Federal government and various tribes, the United States never drew up a formal declaration of war against any hostile Indians.

In spite of the fact that no new treaties have been made with Indians for nearly a century there are still treaty obligations being fulfilled by the Federal Government, and Indian treaties have an important place in the development of Federal Indian law. It is clear that the Federal Government reserved the right to regulate affairs with Indians, and only rarely was this right relinquished to a particular state. Once a treaty was negotiated and ratified, it could not be regarded as invalid owing to fraud, duress, or improper Indian representation. Treaties might be renegotiated by the mutual consent of the Indians and the Federal Government, and a treaty could be superseded by other Congressional action. Hostilities with a tribe could invalidate a treaty, and a treaty could be modified or nullified under other circumstances. It has, however, been a general policy of the government to interpret ambiguities in treaties in favor of the Indians involved and to consider the circumstances under which a treaty was negotiated. At the same time the courts could not interpret a treaty in a manner not intended in the original wording.

Treaties with Indians were negotiated by the President of the United States and were binding when approved by the Indians and two thirds of the U. S. Senate. It is important to note that a treaty could not provide funds for Indians; monetary commitments required separate Congressional action. The subjects dealt with in Indian treaties varied widely, and in all nearly 400 treaties were negotiated. The greatest number, nearly 260, were arranged between 1815 and 1860, during the great westward expansion of white settlers following the War of 1812. The majority of the treaties, 230, involved Indian lands. These concerned the exchange and cession of lands or the establishment of boundaries for Indian lands. A block of 76 treaties called for Indian removal from their lands and resettlement on other lands. As early as 1818 there was a treaty setting aside or reserving lands for specific Indian tribes; however, the majority of the reservations were established much later. Nearly 100 treaties dealt primarily with boundaries between Indian and white lands and affirmed the friendly relations between a tribe and the United States. This was the general nature of most early treaties. Two tribes, the Potawatomi and Chippewa, each negotiated 42 separate treaties, which is a record number.

Most early treaties made no attempt to regulate or control the internal affairs of a tribe. As Federal power over Indians increased, this policy was changed, and treaties came to stipulate certain rules for the behavior of tribal members in their own communities. This shift took place in 1849 in a treaty with the Navajo which included the provision that the Federal Government could (*Federal Indian Law*, 1958, 163) "pass and execute in their territory such laws as may be deemed conducive to the prosperity and happiness of said Indians." By the 1860's the Federal Government made treaties which could be amended unilaterally by Congress. This was an anticipation of the end of treaty-making. By the mid-nineteenth century it was becoming increasingly apparent that treaties with Indian tribes were unrealistic because of the increased Indian dependence on the Federal Government. It was not until 1871, however, that the last treaty was negotiated and ratified by the U.S. Congress. The end of treaty-making came as a result of a dispute between the U.S. Senate and the House of Representatives. The Senate approved treaties, but the House was obliged to appropriate money relative to the treaties. Their failure to agree finally brought an end to the treaty period.

An interesting sidelight in Federal dealings with Indians was the attempt to have Indian representation at the national level. In the first treaty of the United States with Indians, the Delaware in 1778, there was the provision that at a future date this tribe might consolidate with others and form a state, with the Delaware as the leaders. The state was to have Congressional representation, but nothing ever developed from the possibility. In a treaty of 1785 and another of 1830 it was proposed that Indians send a representative to Congress, but again this possibility was never realized.

In the United States, Indians have land rights based on aboriginal possession, treaty, a Congressional act, Executive order, purchase, or by the action of some colony, state, or foreign nation. Indian reservations were created by treaty arrangements before 1871, by acts of Congress after that time, and by Executive orders of the President. In almost every instance the Federal Government retained the title to reservation lands. Treaty reservations were created in some instances in recognition of aboriginal title and in others in exchange for different lands or for the privilege of joining another Indian group on its reservation. Occasionally during the treaty-making era and often thereafter, reservations were established by Congressional action. Such statutory reservations consisted usually of an area of public domain or land purchased by the Federal Government for use by a designated segment of the Indian population. The legality of reservations established by Executive orders was uncertain, but their validity was established in the General Allotment Act of 1887. Reservations were created by Executive order between about 1855 and 1919. The practice, however, met resistance from Congress and was brought to an end except to add some Alaskan reservations. It has happened also that from time to time

Indians have purchased lands with their own funds for their group as a whole; such land has been supervised by the Federal Government. Since virtually all of the territory which is now the United States was held earlier by a European-based power, the rights of Indians under British, Dutch, French, Mexican, Russian, and Spanish rule have been taken into consideration when there was a transfer of sovereignty. In each instance at least some implicit recognition was given to aboriginal rights of occupancy by the Indians.

As Allan G. Harper has noted, the Canadian government was not particularly generous in its treaties with Indians, but the promises which were made have been kept rather faithfully. In general, treaties with Canadian Indians were arranged before the arrival of settlers into a particular area of Indian occupancy, and thus there were no great conflicts between Indians and whites in Canada. The cornerstone of Indian policy was embodied in the "Proclamation of 1763" following the defeat of the French and the establishment of British sovereignty. This proclamation contained the principles which were to guide Indian-white relations: Indians possessed the rights to all lands not formally surrendered; Indians could not grant to whites any lands which had not been surrendered; and land could be surrendered only to the Crown. Between 1781 and 1836, twenty-three treaties were made, and all but one included remunerations to the Indians involved. It was only in the Crown Colony of British Columbia that the governor had control over Indians, and this special condition ceased to exist after Confederation in 1867. In a treaty of 1850 the stipulations of all later treaties were set forth. The major points were that the Crown alone had the right to receive Indian land; reserves were established for Indian use; payment was made for the surrender of land with perpetual annuities to the Indians involved; and Indian rights to hunt and fish on ceded lands were recognized. Between 1871 and 1921 the final eleven treaties were negotiated.

In Canada the earliest significant grant of lands to Indians was made in 1680 by Louis XIV to a band of Iroquois in Quebec. This land still is occupied by the Iroquois. The next major grant of land was to the Six Nations, who were Iroquois, in 1784. They received nearly 700,000 acres for their loyalty to the British during the American Revolution. By 1821 the Six Nations had alienated nearly half of the original grant by selling lands to whites before this practice was prohibited. In the early 1940's there were some 5,500,000 acres of land held in trust by the Dominion government for Indians. Under the Canadian Act of 1870 reserved lands may be held by a particular Indian under an allotment system. This means that the allottee has exclusive rights of use and occupancy. He may pass the land on to heirs or sell it to another Indian of his group, but he does

not receive clear title to the holding. Indians with more land than is necessary for their welfare may surrender some and use the money derived from
the sale for the benefit of the group. Under certain rare conditions an
individual Indian may obtain a clear title to his land; for example, it is
possible if he requests Canadian citizenship or enfranchisement and it is
granted. Title to his land is obtained by receiving the consent of his group
and the Dominion government, but he must pay the band for the land.

As a closing observation about treaties with Indians it must be noted
that they seldom were "negotiated" in any meaningful sense of the term.
Representatives of a particular tribe or tribes were assembled, and a treaty
was offered for their approval. The signers seldom had any realistic opportunity to modify the terms. Then too treaties often were made through
"chiefs" who were sympathetic to the whites, and in certain areas of the
United States it was not uncommon for intoxicants to be distributed freely
at treaty-making sessions. In addition the interpreters often could not or
did not set forth the details of an agreement in true detail or spell out
the implications of what the Indians were losing and what they gained.
A most important final observation along these lines is that most Indians
had no concept of the permanent alienation of land. Since they had never
bought and sold land, their concept was that they were granting whites
the rights to its use. Thus, many such agreements were not "treaties" in
a strict sense of the word's usage.

Administration

The Continental Congress of the United States in 1775 created three
agencies to deal with Indian affairs. These were in the three geographical
areas, the northern, middle, and southern. The commissioners in charge
of the respective areas were instructed to make treaties and to establish
friendly relations with Indians to prevent them from aiding the British.
The general structure of Indian administration remained the same as that
which had existed under British control. The individuals in charge of the
middle department included Benjamin Franklin and Patrick Henry, and
their leadership indicates the importance attached to Indian affairs. In 1786
the administration of Indians was placed under the Secretary of War with
two departments, the north and south, whose administrators were
empowered to grant licenses to trade and live among Indians. With the
adoption of the Constitution of the United States, the War Department
maintained jurisdiction over Indians. The first Congress of 1789 appro-
priated funds for negotiating treaties and placed the governor of a particular

territory in charge of Indian affairs in his area. The following year Congress began licensing traders among Indians; this was an important step toward Federal control. The year 1824 saw the creation of the Bureau of Indian Affairs, which remained under the War Department. Its basic organization was established by a Congressional act in 1834, and the only major alteration occurred in 1849 when the overall control of the Bureau passed from military control into the hands of the newly created Home Department of the Interior. Owing to the flagrant corruption and mismanagement of the Bureau, a Board of Indian Commissioners was created in 1869. Composed of ten outstanding citizens who were appointed without compensation by the President and who reported to him, the Board oversaw the expenditure of funds for Indians and served to advise the Bureau of Indian Affairs. It was abolished in 1933.

In Canada the direction of Indian affairs was delegated to the Commander of the Forces in the British North American Provinces in 1816. In 1830 the management of Indian affairs in Upper Canada passed into civilian control, but that in Lower Canada remained under military jurisdiction. By the Act of Union in 1841 the two Indian Affairs departments were joined into a single Department of Indian Affairs, and in 1860 the Crown Lands Department assumed the responsibility for Indian management. With the Confederation of Canada in 1867 the administration of Indians passed into the hands of the Dominion of Canada. At this time the Department of State directed Indian affairs, but in 1873 with the creation of the Department of the Interior the Indian branch was made a part of this agency. A few years later in 1880 a separate Department of Indian Affairs was founded with a minister who was the Superintendent General of Indian Affairs. The portfolio of this minister always was held by an individual with another ministerial post, usually the Minister of the Interior. In 1936 the Department of Indian Affairs was changed into a branch and placed under the new Department of Mines and Resources. In 1950 the Department of Citizenship and Immigration assumed control of the Indian Affairs Branch.

The Dominion Parliament alone is responsible for legislating for Indians. The general structure for rights and services was framed in the Indian Act of 1876. The administration was to control the management of Indian lands—both the reserves and other lands set aside for use only by Indians —as well as the Indian Trust Fund, an accumulation of money derived mainly from the sale of natural resources on Indian lands. The Indian Act of 1876 recognized also that the Dominion government was responsible for relief, education, health services, and Indian-based agriculture and industry. Finally the Parliament was made responsible for the enfranchisement of Indians to full Canadian citizenship.

The next major revision of Indian policy in Canada, the Indian Act of 1951 with its subsequent revisions, is the legal basis for current policy. The Act sets forth in exact terms the authority and power of the Governor in Council, the Minister and the Minister's field representatives, the superintendents. Robert W. Dunning, in discussing the effects of the Act on the Indians, stresses the power of the superintendent on a reserve and his flexibility in formulating and administering local policy. Among the duties of a reserve superintendent are to consider what nonlegitimates may become members of a band and to screen enfranchisement applicants, in addition to administering welfare, relief, and education on the reserve. He furthermore may accept or veto the nomination of an Indian to a band council.

Treaties and laws referring to both Canadian and United States Indians often made reference to the consumption of intoxicants. In Canada an Indian, unless he was enfranchised, could not buy liquor legally for ordinary consumption until 1951. The Indian Act of 1951 permitted the provinces or territories, with the approval of the Governor in Council, to allow Indians to consume intoxicants in public places. This condition existed over most of Canada until 1958. Between 1958 and 1963 the restriction was lessened in most provinces and territories to permit Indians to buy alcoholic beverages in the same manner as Canadian citizens in general, that is, either in a public place or from a package store. At the same time a band still may elect to prohibit intoxicants on its reserve lands. In the United States the first Federal regulation of intoxicants among Indians originated in 1802. The law was periodically modified to ease enforcement and to cover loopholes. It was not until 1953 that the Federal government repealed this law. Prohibition on any reservation still was possible under local option. Before Indians could consume intoxicants in some states, the state laws against the sale of liquor to Indians had to be changed.

Pan-Indianism

At the time of discovery the range of cultural diversity among American Indians to the north of Mexico was great. They spoke many very different languages, often gained sustenance by contrasting means, and their political structure ranged from virtually nonexistent to highly organized. In comparative terms the European intruders were homogeneous in cultural background, their linguistic diversity was comparatively minor, and their political organization and religious convictions differed only in narrow dimensions. Thus in comparison with the European migrants the Indians living in the New World were fractured and fragmented along many dimensions.

The agents of Western civilization often exploited Indian differences to divide them further still.

Indian tribes in fact as well as in theory were relatively free and independent nations until the end of the War of 1812. Soon thereafter they became "domestic, dependent nations" and lost any realistic control over their destiny. The Removal Act of 1830 was a clear indication of the change in white-Indian relations. The end of treaty-making in the United States in 1871 was another important plateau, but it was the General Allotment (Dawes) Act of 1887 that was to have the strongest effect in changing Indians into white Americans. Under its terms the President was authorized to allot the lands of most reservations to individual Indians. The Indians were to select their acreage, and the Federal Government was to hold a trust title for twenty-five years or longer, during which time the land could not be encumbered. Surplus reservation lands then were to be sold to the government, and the funds derived were held in trust for the tribe, subject to use for education and civilizing the tribe when Congress approved this use. Over the next ten years the General Allotment Act was modified in some of its aspects in order to permit the leasing of allotted lands and to validate claims of descendants from those marriages that were in keeping with tribal customs. Indian education came to be stressed with particular enactments from 1892 to 1897. These provided for schools and virtually forced the attendance of Indian children, while Federal support of church schools was withdrawn. An important supplement was made to the Dawes Act in 1906; it permitted the President to extend the trust period for allotted lands. Again in 1910 the act was revised to resolve problems arising from inheriting allotments, leasing timber lands, and replacing trust patents for reservation lands with others of comparable value. The aim of the Dawes Act and its amendments was to bypass tribal organizations and make land allotments to individual Indians. The act was designed to destroy the tribes by doing away with the land base held in collectivity and at the same time to integrate Indians into the dominant society. Many whites who truly were concerned with Indian welfare felt that the sterile and depressing quality of reservation life should be destroyed and that the means to accomplish this end was to make individual Indians property holders and farmers.

Indian efforts to halt white intrusions or to reject all Euro-American ideas were doomed to failure. Yet from the persistent resistance of many Indians to assimilation arose the Pan-Indian movement, and from it Indianism has crystallized. Many whites feel that they have cast an all-encompassing net over Indians from which they cannot escape and which will lead to total Indian assimilation before many more years have passed. Yet history and present events suggest that there has been and is a great deal more vitality to Indian culture than is admitted by those who predict its imminent doom. By now Indian resistance to white dominance is rooted deeply in their heritage and has manifest itself along both political and religious lines. At times these means for asserting their identity have been combined.

Religious prophets emerged to advocate what Indians must do in order to free themselves of white control, but we know comparatively little about most of these men. One such individual was Neolin, better known as the Delaware Prophet, who emerged in the 1760's. By this time the Delaware and a number of other Algonkian peoples who formerly had lived farther east were in present-day Ohio. They had been displaced by whites but not destroyed, and anticipated a surge of whites into their adopted homeland. Like other contemporary Delaware prophets, Neolin urged his listeners to abandon European customs and return to an aboriginal way of life. God had revealed to him that if Indians once again pursued a simple life, recited certain prayers, and dispelled whites, then the game would return and the purity of Indian ways would prevail. Neolin made a map which charted the way to heaven and the obstacles placed along the way by whites. His message was appealing to many Indians, and he won converts not only among his own people but among other tribes in the Ohio valley. The message of Neolin had special appeal to the Ottawa chief Pontiac, for this religious revelation served as partial justification for political action. He planned a sudden attack against British outposts and a general uprising. A number of forts were taken and their garrisons often massacred, but it was necessary to lay seige to Detroit and the effort to take it failed. Indian dominance was of brief duration since the confederation was organized so loosely that the British soon divided the Indians and were able to reconsolidate their position.

Although the messiahs who advocated a return to aboriginal life failed to achieve their goal, those who sought accommodations with whites sometimes were more successful. Efforts of this nature, often termed revitalization movements, have continued to emerge. Valene L. Smith recorded what appeared to be the beginning of one among the Caribou Eskimos in the late 1960's. The man involved was Tagoona, who was born at Repulse Bay in 1926 of German and Eskimo ancestry. A self-educated man, he became the first ordained Anglican Church minister from the arctic. He spoke Eskimo and English with equal ease and was assigned to serve at Eskimo Point where he was well liked because of his modest manner and appreciation of Eskimo ways. Before long he experienced difficulties with his superiors, however, and was encouraged to sever his church ties at least temporarily. He continued to have sympathetic supporters in several communities, and he recorded messages for those followers. Tagoona received financial aid from distant settlements, and some local families tithed in his behalf. He was fully aware of the Red Power movement, and his personal blend of Christian values and Eskimo ethos made him a potential focal point for the emergence of a new religious force in the north.

Much of the Pan-Indianism background may be traced to the efforts of men such as Pontiac and Handsome Lake, but there were essential non-Indian elements as well. The most important of these was the formal education process imposed on Indians and whites. In government and mission schools on reservations instruction was in English, and it became the language in which members of diverse tribes could communicate. It was the boarding schools, however, which had the most profound influence. None was more famous than the Carlisle School in Pennsylvania. It was founded in 1879 by Richard H. Pratt, a lieutenant in the army at the time, and it was attended by members of far-flung tribes. Pratt's philosophy was remarkably clear. He viewed the boarding school environment as the most useful waystation between the reservation and assimilation. His slogan was, "Kill the Indian and save the man!" Carlisle often is thought of as a college since its football team played many university teams, but it was largely a secondary school which stressed vocational training and the fundamentals of English. Indians who attended Carlisle and other boarding schools often had a difficult time readjusting to reservation life. Although some went "back to the blanket," meaning that they reverted to Indian ways, others were assimilated into the white world, and many worked for the Indian Service.

Christianity also was an important influence on Indians at this time. Missions maintained many schools, and diverse white organizations with Christian backing were concerned with Indian welfare. These included the Women's National Indian Association (founded in 1879), the Indian Rights Association (1882), and the Lake Monhonk conferences (1883), all of which lobbied for Indian justice. At the same time members of these organizations sought to assimilate Indians, and most members had little tolerance of Indian customs. These white activists in Indian affairs supported the principles of the General Allotment Act but deplored the injustices of its administration. As Hazel W. Hertzberg (1971, 22) noted in the best study of this era, "All unwittingly the reformers—the Indians' chief friends in court in the white world—thus helped to break down Indian self-respect and Indian attempts at self-help." Many Indian leaders were Christian, but at the same time they often were unwilling to abandon their Indian heritage. They sought accommodation between white and Indian customs, and their general approach has been a lasting one for those Indians seeking to retain their identity. For many others assimilation into white society was desired and achieved.

Indians of many tribes with differing historical backgrounds have been drawn into the Pan-Indian movement through the peyote cult. The peyote plant, which grows in central Mexico, is a spineless cactus which has a root similar to a carrot or turnip in size and shape. The rounded surface of the plant is cut off and dried. Called the peyote "button," it contains alkaloids which are stimulants and sedatives in varying proportions. When consumed, it produces a wide range of reactions. A common reaction to taking peyote is exhilaration and an inability to sleep for about twelve hours; depression and hallucinations follow, sometimes including visions in color. This nonhabit-forming drug was consumed in Mexico in aboriginal times, but it probably was not widely used in the United States until comparatively recent historic times. It became popular among Indians of the southern Plains between 1850 and 1900 and then spread to other western tribes. Early usage in the Plains appears to have been associated with warfare, and consumption was limited to men. They began using peyote more widely at a time when they were suffering from the dismal aftermath of military defeat, physical displacement, and confinement to reservations. A peyote ceremony was held in a tepee at any time of the year, and ritual equipment included the gourd rattle, eagle bone whistle, and water drum. The Bureau of Indian Affairs, Christian missionaries, and white reformers all were actively opposed to the peyote cult, and its adherents were harassed. In spite of the rigid oppression by whites and some Indians there were about 12,000 members in 1918. Efforts were made in 1916 and again in 1917 to pass a federal law against peyote, but these bills failed. In 1918 as a response to crystallized opposition a group of participants incorporated as the Native American Church in Oklahoma. Although a number of states soon passed laws against the use of peyote (e.g., Kansas, 1920; Arizona, 1923), seven states had chartered Native American Churches by 1925. As members of a formal religious organization, they were afforded far greater protection from persecution than previously. The differences in ritual and belief between the incorporated churches in different states, or with unincorporated congregations, did not stand as barriers in mutual participation in ceremonies.

The peyote service among Plains tribes typically was held in a tepee and lasted all night. Participants sat around a central fire, and peyote buttons were passed for each person to take as many as he chose. A special gourd rattle and drum were used to produce a distinctive musical style. One person after another chanted his sacred song either in English or in his tribal language. Bibles and crosses might be part of the ceremonial equipment. The goals of the ceremony were to achieve physical and spiritual well-being and to promote harmonious relations with others. Brotherly love, self-reliance, and the avoidance of alcohol all were important values held by participants. The psychedelic experience gained through the use of peyote was never an end in itself.

According to Hertzberg the peyote religion was appealing because old tribal religions had lost their meaning and Christian teachings seemed remote from reality. Furthermore, this was an Indian religion that united members of different tribes in a common sense of brotherhood. Peyote often was considered as a powerful medicine for the diseased, and the rituals provided an opportunity for social gatherings. Some Indians such as the Pueblo peoples, Five Civilized Tribes in Oklahoma, and Iroquois largely were uninfluenced by the peyote religion, but it became *the* religion for many Indians by 1934.

The Plains Indian has come to symbolize Indians to whites, and members of the Pan-Indian movement in particular. How is it that Indians in one sector of the country now represent all Indians?

Indians of the Great Plains were seen first by Spanish and then by French and English explorers, yet they were nearly unknown until after the Louisiana Purchase of 1803. In 1821 members of Plains tribes visited Washington, D.C., and none was more popular than Petalesharo, the Pawnee who rescued a Comanche girl from being sacrificed to the Morning Star. In three paintings of him by different artists he wore a flowing feather headdress, and according to John C. Ewers this probably was the first pictorial record of the feather "war bonnet." Many other Indians in the same party of visitors had their portraits painted, and the exhibit of them in Washington long was a popular attraction. The earliest picture of a Plains tepee appeared in 1823, and the first illustration of a Plains Indian on horseback was printed in 1829. This beginning possibly never would have led to the emergence of the Plains tribes in popular fancy were it not for the efforts of Karl Bodmer and George Catlin, who painted Plains Indians in the 1830's. Catlin especially was important, for he not only painted many pictures of Indians but exhibited his Indian Gallery widely in the United States and then in London and Paris. His book *Manners, Customs and Condition of the North American Indians*, published first in 1841, had a wide distribution, and this two-volume work with over 300 engravings was reprinted again and again. To Catlin the noblest Indians clearly were those of the Plains. His paintings and those of Bodmer were copied or modified and also served to inspire other artists to venture west to paint Indians.

The Plains Indian symbol crystallized in Buffalo Bill's Wild West Show, which opened in 1883. It was seen by millions of people in Canada, the United States, and Europe during its run of more than thirty years. William F. Cody or "Buffalo Bill" had been a colorful frontier figure with diverse experiences, and he had become the hero of innumerable dime novels. The show was a reenactment of episodes in Plains life and was highlighted by an Indian attack on a stagecoach, which was rescued at the last moment by cowboys led by Buffalo Bill. Other Wild West shows which imitated the original and Indian medicine shows intensified and spread the Plains Indian image. By the turn of the present century Indians all over the country were beginning to dress as Plains Indians for special occasions.

James H. Howard (1955) made one of the first studies of the modern Pan-Indian movement and identified its roots as being in Oklahoma, especially among the small tribes originally from the East. Howard felt that racial discrimination against Indians was an important factor fostering solidarity among them. Coupled with poverty, apartheid tended to bind Indians of diverse background together. Other contributing considerations were the peyote religion, intermarriage between members of different tribes, the use of English as the common language, and the importance of schools for Indians. Pan-Indianism was identified best with particular traits associated with powwows. The "war dance," which possibly began among the Pawnee, originally had religious associations with a men's war society but became a social dance. Men danced as a group, yet each man performed in his own style to the accompaniment of singers and a drum. Thus no rehearsals were necessary, which made the dance ideal for persons from diverse tribes performing together. A modified Plains Indian scalp dance, the buffalo dance, and stomp dance were likely to be performed; the latter was once a religious dance among tribes in the East. The feather roach headdress, feather shoulder bustle and back bustle of feathers, a choker neckband, and hard sole Plains type moccasins prevailed widely. Indians and whites alike found that the predominately Plains Indian dances were the most exciting and the costuming from this area the most visually appealing.

1934 and Later

The most basic change in Federal Indian policy after the General Allotment Act of 1887 was the Indian Reorganization Act of 1934. The earlier legislation was designed to force individual Indians to become self-sufficient

Plate 77 *(Above)   The first published illustration of a
Plains Indian tepee, which appeared in 1823* (From Ewers, 1965).

Plate 78 *(Top right)   Probably the first published
illustration of a Plains Indian warrior on horseback,
which appeared in 1829* (From Ewers, 1965).

Plate 79 *(Bottom right)   An illustration of a Crow Indian
by George Catlin* (From Ewers, 1965).

farmers with full rights of citizenship and to break away from tribalism and the stagnation of reservation life. Indians received their own special New Deal in 1934. A major provision of the Indian Reorganization Act was to end the alienation of Indian lands through the allotment process. In fifty years of allotments Indians had lost nearly ninety of their 138 million acres of land, and about half of the remaining land was desert. The major means to permit retention of the land base was to extend the period of trust holding. Furthermore, additional land was acquired for Indians, declared exempt from taxes, and placed under Federal control. Indian tribes were encouraged to form chartered corporations, and a revolving credit fund was established to bring viability into the tribal economies of those choosing to incorporate. It also became possible for the Indians to obtain loans to further their education, and preferential hiring was given to Indians in the Bureau of Indian Affairs (B.I.A.). One very important section of the law was that it would apply only to those tribes in which a majority voted to come under its provisions. Initially, 181 tribes accepted, and seventy-seven rejected the Indian Reorganization Act. Fourteen groups came under it because they did not vote, and the Act was extended in 1936 to include Alaskan and Oklahoman peoples without their vote of approval. Since Indians in general had come to distrust the Federal government, the Indian response to this enlightened legislation was not as positive as had been hoped for by its creators. Some tribes favored allotments and were able to obtain clear title to their land in spite of the Indian Reorganization Act.

The policy changes conceived in the late 1930's were hampered by the economic depression and then by World War II. After the war the Federal Government began to divest itself of diverse obligations to Indians much more systematically than ever before. In spite of claims to the contrary the Federal Government clearly is "getting out of the Indian business." Documentation is in order.

1. Indian Claims Commission Act, 1949. This legislation was designed to settle claims by any "identifiable group" of Indians against the United States arising from various inequities including when "fraud, duress, unconscionable consideration, mutual or unilateral mistake" were involved. By 1969 about 300 claims had been heard, of which about half were decided in favor of Indian claimants; nearly one-third of a billion dollars was awarded. In 1969 the award total was $37 million, ranging from $273,250 for the Kickapoo to $8,679,815 for the Blackfoot and Gros Ventre Indians. The general pattern of settlement has been to use a portion of an award for per capita payments to tribal members and to retain most of the money in a tribal trust fund administered by the U.S. Treasury. In recent years Indians have had control over the investment of this money.

2. House Concurrent Resolution 108, 1953. This was a strong expression of congressional sentiment that federal control over Indians should be ended as soon as possible. The advocates of termination argued, just as the supporters of the General Allotment Act had reasoned, that the reservation system has denied the Indian his self-reliance and freedom. It also was felt that the Federal Government could save considerable amounts of money by "buying off" treaty and other obligations. Specific tribes were earmarked for termination in the near future, and subsequent legislation ended federal responsibilities to the Klamath of Oregon, the Menominee of Wisconsin, the Paiutes and Utes of Utah, and some small groups in Oregon and Texas. The results have by and large been disastrous because the people involved were unprepared to assume the responsibilities thrust on them.

3. Relocation program, 1950. In the 1930's efforts were made to encourage Indians to seek employment in urban centers, but the economic conditions were not propitious. In 1952 the B.I.A. began its intensive program to resettle reservation Indians in urban areas. The offices for relocation which have continued to function include those at Chicago, Cleveland, Dallas, Denver, Los Angeles, Oakland, San Francisco, and San Jose. It is estimated that about 100,000 persons, including dependents, had been relocated by 1971; this figure recounts persons who were relocated more than once. The cost of the program in 1967 was about four million dollars. From 1953 to 1957 three out of ten relocated Indians returned home during their first year in a city. Return and repeat rates are not obtainable after 1959 because these statistics had proven too useful to opponents of the program!

4. The transfer of Bureau of Indian Affairs health services to the Department of Health, Education, and Welfare, 1955. Prior to this change Indian health care had been underfunded and generally was deplorable. Money for Indian health care tripled from 1955 to 1966, and the mortality as well as the morbidity rates have declined at a dramatic rate. The status of Indian health is now vastly improved, which very well may be used as an argument for termination in the future.

5. Alaska Native Claims Settlement Act, 1971. Very few reservations were created for aboriginal Alaskans, but encroachment on their lands has increased steadily. Before the state of Alaska could gain control over large portions of land still held by the Federal Government it was mandatory that they settle native claims. As a result of the 1971 settlement some 60,000 Aleuts, Eskimos, and Indians eventually will receive title to some 40 million acres of land and some $960 million from federal appropriations and mineral royalties. Before the bulk of the funds can be distributed it will be necessary to compile a roll of eligible recipients as well as form village corporations. The twelve Alaskan native regional corporations will

function in deciding what land is to be selected and administering the monies involved.

With termination of the Indian Claims Commission in 1973 and the partial implementation of the Alaska Native Claims Settlement Act the same year, the Federal Government will have discharged its last major responsibilities involving land. With its efforts to improve the standard of Indian health and to resettle large numbers of Indians in urban areas, the Federal Government is divesting itself of major involvements in Indian affairs. On December 11, 1971, the U.S. Senate passed a resolution disavowing the termination policy of 1953. Furthermore, in his 1970 message to Congress about Indian affairs President Nixon spoke out against termination. Could it be that the government has had a sincere change of heart about its responsibilities to Indians?

In 1953 when termination of federal responsibilities to Indians in the United States became official policy, two tribes with comparatively large landholdings were singled out as capable of handling their own affairs: They were the Klamath of Oregon and the Menominee of Wisconsin. Thanks to Nancy O. Lurie the course of subsequent events in the Menominee case is documented with care. The Menominee Reservation land was considered as relatively undesirable when the reservation was created in 1854, but the Indians accepted it rather than be forced to move from Wisconsin. It was not divided into individual holdings as a result of the General Allotment Act of 1887, and since they already were organized to govern themselves they were not covered by the Indian Reorganization Act of 1934. The Menominee did file suit in that year against the Federal Government for the mismanagement of their timber lands, and finally in 1951 a U. S. Court of Claims judgment awarded them nearly eight million dollars. Yet the money was held by the Federal Government and required Congressional approval before any dispersement. As unbelievable as it may seem, in order for these people to obtain the money awarded to them by the courts, they were forced to accept termination. When a vote was taken, 169 persons favored the "principle of termination," and five opposed it. This vote represented only 10 percent of those eligible to cast ballots. Some who voted had been led to believe that they were voting for the release of the money due them. Others thought they were voting for the "principle" of termination which would give them bargaining power against unilateral federal action. Many persons appear not to have voted in order to express their negative feelings toward the proposal. In any event the particulars of Menominee termination were considered only after the 1954 public law to terminate them had been passed. Per capita payments were to be made from the money owed as settlement of the timber suit, and the tribal roll was closed after a ninety day period. Thus, a Menominee born after that time was not an "Indian" in terms of federal responsibilities.

With termination tribal assets were consolidated in Menominee Enterprises Incorporated. Jurisdiction over the land was transferred to the State of Wisconsin, and Menominee County was created from the old reservation. The people owned shares in Menominee Enterprises, but they held only "certificates of ownership." A Common Stock & Voting Trust comprised of seven persons, including three whites, voted the shares for most adults and elected the corporation directors. An Assistance Trust held and voted certificates for minors and "incompetents." Thus parents had no control over the rights of their children, and incompetency was established by the Bureau of Indian Affairs, not the courts. Tragedy followed stupidity. The organizational maze could not function, the county soon was deeply in debt, the lumber mill was turned over to the corporation in such poor condition that it was forced to lay off workers, welfare aid to such persons contributed to the impossible strain on county finances, persons who bought their land —as they had been encouraged to do—could not pay their taxes. The corporation was forced to go into partnership with a land developer to sell lots to whites just to expand the tax base on a short-term basis. The whites negatively involved in this charade are a part of our current Indian "affairs."

In 1969 the Minister of Indian Affairs and Northern Development issued a White Paper which set forth a new direction for Indian policy in Canada. In essence the report was a framework to terminate federal responsibilities to Indians on reserves. The proposal met with firm, united opposition from Canadian Indians. They feared that if implemented the proposal would lead to a disaster like that resulting from the termination policy in the United States in the 1950's. Canadian Indians felt strongly that since treaty obligations were "forever" the government had no legal or moral justification for termination. The Prime Minister shelved the White Paper and promised a reevaluation of the question.

In 1968 the Indian population of the United States living on or near existing or former reservations was 452,000. Most of them lived in Arizona (105,900), but other states with large numbers of Indians included New Mexico (74,500), Oklahoma (72,400), Alaska (55,400), and South Dakota (30,000). It also is estimated that the Canadian Indian population numbered about 250,000, and there are approximately 36,000 Greenlanders. The most populous tribe by far was the Navajo (119,500). In 1969 it was estimated that nearly 130,000 Indians lived in urban areas, and of this number about

50,000 were in Los Angeles County. The following statistics about reservations were compiled by Alan L. Sorkin. In 1964 the median income for reservation Indian males in the United States was $1,800; for all U.S. males median income was $6,283. In 1964 median family income ranged from $900 for the Choctaw and Rosebud reservations to $3,600 for the Northern Cheyenne Reservation. The unemployment rate for reservation Indian males in the United States in 1960 was 51.3 percent, compared to 5.4 percent for all males. In 1967, 37.3 percent of reservation Indian males were unemployed, compared to 3.1 percent of all U.S. males. These figures make it abundantly clear that the most depressed living conditions anywhere in the United States are to be found on Indian reservations. Indians who leave reservations for urban areas usually do so for economic reasons.

Since the 1930's the concept of "acculturation" has been dear to the hearts of many anthropologists. It has come to mean the steps by which Indians are gradually absorbed into the dominant sociocultural pattern. With assimilation acculturation is complete. Yet few anthropologists are completely satisfied with the concept because it has failed to define the stages leading to assimilation or to explain the persistence of Indianness in the face of hundreds of years of pressures to negate it. Quite clearly the idea of acculturation does not allow for the lasting quality of Indian identity. By far the most bold and innovative approach to the general problem has been conceived and articulated by Joseph G. Jorgensen.

The central idea of Jorgensen's thesis is that tribes were in fact integrated into economic and political life as soon as they came to be controlled by the United States. He attributes the deplorable conditions under which most Indians live to the economic order imposed on them. Efforts to gauge relative degrees of acculturation fail to recognize that Indians are enmeshed in a political system which essentially is colonial. He identifies the "metropolis" as the center where economic and political power are concentrated; the manipulators of it are able to promote legislation to sustain their goals and insure their growth. Thus, the politically weak rural areas are exploited by the metropolis for its growth, and this applies to the rural areas in which Indians live as well as any others. Indians are subject to the same laws that apply to everyone else and in addition to those imposed by federal control through the Bureau of Indian Affairs.

Continuing to follow Jorgensen's thesis, he noted that most reservations are located in arid and semiarid areas, and it is not possible for the Indians to develop successful large-scale farming enterprises because they usually have inherited small and often scattered plots of ground which cannot be cultivated efficiently. Even if all land were farmed at its maximum productivity, the harvest would seldom be sufficient to provide a reasonable standard of living. Since reservations usually are remote from major markets or industrial developments, there are comparatively few nonfarming jobs available. The economies of rural areas near reservations have declined as farms in other areas have grown larger and technologically sophisticated under the management of large corporations. Of great importance in terms of metropolis control, the large-scale farming enterprises have received far more government aid than have the small farmers. For example, in 1967 65 percent of the federal subsidies to farmers went to the top 10 percent of the producers. It is not surprising that as the economic base for the small rural white farmer has declined disastrously, the position of the Indian farmer has grown desperate. The Bureau of Indian Affairs has attempted to promote industrial development on or near reservations. Between 1962 and 1968 some 10,000 jobs were created, but about half of these have been held by non-Indians. " 'Industrial development' has been mostly talk; development has accrued to industry and not to Indians or Indian-owned and controlled industry" (Jorgensen, 1971, 83). Understandably, with economic conditions so bad on and near reservations, Indians have moved to cities in ever-increasing numbers.

In essence Indians are enveloped in a culture of poverty, and the move from a reservation to a city is to substitute an urban ghetto for a rural one. Since Indian migrants to cities have few skills, little confidence, and a foreign cultural tradition, they are not likely to succeed. Often they make a little money and then return to their reservation. If they remain in urban centers, they usually have the poorest paying jobs and very little job security. The growing body of studies about urban Indian life is very depressing. The unemployment rates among them, the arrest rate for drunkenness, the suicide rate, and so on are incredible (e.g., Waddell and Watson, 1971).

Probably the major difficulty encountered by reservation Indians who move to an urban setting is arrest for intoxication. Some anthropologists write about this "problem" *ad nauseam*, but when Fred W. Gabourie discusses the subject, his insights as a lawyer and an Indian are refreshing. Between 1802 and 1953 Federal laws prohibited Indians from legally purchasing intoxicants. After the latter date, and after the revocation of state laws dealing with the matter, Indians could drink just as anyone else, although some reservations were "dry" by local option. To Indians the right to drink had great symbolic meaning, and often it was interpreted quite literally. When this right was abused on the reservation, the intoxicated person was put to bed by a local policeman or jailed overnight and released more often than booked for drunkenness. Gabourie points out that when reservation and rural Indians visit local towns for relaxation, they usually frequent a "skidrow" because it is only there that Indians are welcome in bars. When these Indians move to distant urban centers, they are attracted to skidrows for the same reason. Even many successful urban Indians visit such sectors of a city to socialize with other Indians. In a city an intoxicated Indian is most likely booked and jailed. The likelihood is that he cannot post bail or does not have enough assets to be a satisfactory risk for a bondsman. A fine cannot be paid in most instances and probation does not suffice; thus a jail sentence is the result. A pilot program in Los Angeles to provide information about the law and legal services has been conducted by a private law firm and has succeeded in greatly reducing the difficulties of urban Indians and also has lowered the arrest rate.

Goodbye, Great White Father-Figure

The heading for this section is taken from the title of an article by George W. Rogers about changing white-Eskimo-Indian relations in Alaska, yet the title applies equally well to American Indians in general. In 1944 a number of progressive Indians formed the National Congress of American Indians (N.C.A.I.) as the first broadly-based and enduring Indian organization whose purpose was political action. About 25,000 Indians served in the armed services during World War II, and when these men returned to civilian life, they were largely unwilling to accept the Indian stereotype. Some decided to form an Indian organization which would speak for Indians, and the N.C.A.I. was the result. The membership fee for whites is twice the amount for Indians, and whites may not vote. The philosophy of the group is that individuals should be able to choose between retaining their identity as Indians or assimilating, but should not be pushed in either direction. They also consider federal obligations to Indians which resulted from treaties and agreements as being permanently binding; thus they strongly oppose any efforts to end these responsibilities. The activities of the organization include aiding local groups in taking effective stands, pooling useful information, and lobbying for Indian causes.

In 1961 a second and more radical organization called the National Indian Youth Council was founded by college-educated Indians. They were highly critical of the N.C.A.I., whose members they regarded as representing wealthy acculturated persons whose Indian identity was more in terms of blood than culture. The newer organization purported to represent the "real Indian," meaning those who were more traditionally oriented. They are adamantly opposed to the B.I.A., which they would like to see abolished and replaced by agencies which would advise and guide Indians, but not control them. They resent the fact that large sums of money designated for Indians are consumed in the bureaucratic structure of the Federal Government.

As Murray L. Wax (1971, 148) has noted, "Despite the emergence of these national pan-Indian political organizations, the political and social interests of most Indians are still tribal or local." He states further, "For most Indians, problems remain tribal and local, the tangle of tribal, state, and federal laws, and of treaty rights, as well as decisions in state courts, mean that these problems must indeed be taken up at the local level." The importance of this observation is beyond question, but at the same time Indians are striving to forge a new broad-scale coalition as a supra-tribe. Red Power has become more than a slogan, especially as Indians in Canada and the United States assemble to discuss common problems and strategies.

An example of the new assertiveness by Indians is illustrated by the recent controversy over wampum belonging to the Iroquois. The Onondaga requested that twenty-six wampum belts purchased by or given to the State of New York in 1898 be returned to the Onondaga. The stated reason for the request was that the sacred belts were necessary in their religious rituals. In 1970 the Assembly of the State of New York approved a bill for the return, but it was killed in a Senate committee. Before the end of the session the Committee on Anthropological Research in Museums of the American Anthropological Association urged the governor of New York to oppose the return of this wampum. They reasoned that since the League of the Iroquois had ceased to function as a political body with the end of the American Revolution, the traditions associated with "reading" the wampum had been forgotten, and the importance of the wampum as religious objects was only partially valid. They wanted the state to retain custody. The greatest concern expressed by the signers was that the return of this wampum would set precedent for the descendants of other once aboriginal peoples to make similar requests. An editorial in *The Indian Historian* expressed the opinion that a majority of non-Indian scholars disagreed with the five signers of the memorial to the governor. In 1971 a bill was passed providing for the return of five wampum belts on the condition that they be appropriately protected in a museum.

The differences among Indians in terms of their cultural backgrounds, histories, and local problems loom large, but they also share many important values and attitudes. These have been well summarized by Lurie. As especially stressed in the chapter about the Eastern Cherokee, the principle of seeking a consensus in decision making is very widely shared, and the abilities of an individual as a speaker are widely appreciated. Orations serve not only as a means to persuade others but indicate the capabilities of the speaker. When a faction is unable to reconcile its position with that of a clearly emerging majority, it tends to withdraw from the deliberations. In dealing with each other on a personal basis the withdrawal technique again is evidenced. If a person such as an intoxicated individual is troublesome, the tendency is to avoid and ignore him as long as possible. Were this to be an impossible means of handling the situation, direct confrontation would be considered as a last resort and in a calculated manner. Not to interfere with the behavior of others is to show respect for them, and this applies to individuals as well as to groups. In general Indians seem not to place a high value on material wealth when compared with white Americans. They might own objects of value but seem to give them away casually, especially if they are admired. This is no doubt a part of the importance attached to being generous in general and sharing one's food, company, and worldly goods with others.

Indians and Anthropologists

American anthropologists have had a deep and abiding interest in American Indians for obvious professional and less obvious personal reasons. Since Indians in the United States and Canada have been quite accessible and usually considerate hosts, they have served as the subjects for thousands of ethnographic studies. A well-established tradition exists in cultural and social anthropology to study people in at least one other society as a part of professional training. In this manner the observer not only gains meaningful cross-cultural experience, but assembles a body of information which hopefully will contribute to a broader understanding of mankind in general. The personal dimension is important because ethnographers often, if not typically, come to feel a great affinity for the people whom they study and as a result empathize with Indians in a way other whites do not. In essence the field study of an ethnographer has two primary goals: to record the activities of others and to employ this information for the solution of theoretical or practical problems. In recent years a growing number of Indians have become resentful of anthropologists, and it is well to ask: What do anthropologists do that displeases Indians?

It would appear that describing Indian life would be a relatively neutral activity. This is the primary business of ethnographers and is important if only for the reason that they describe customs which otherwise would go unrecorded and be lost to history. This fact has been a very real concern for many investigators, especially those who thought that they were witnessing the rapid disappearance of aboriginal ways of life. Some ethnographers became secular crusaders who devoted their lives to recording cultural ways before these were gone forever. Surely this is a worthwhile, if not noble, goal. Field workers around the turn of the present century especially were anxious to obtain aboriginal baseline data from Indians. In some areas the goal could be achieved or approximated, but over most of the continent so much had already happened in the lives of Indians that aboriginal baseline information could not be obtained.

With aboriginal customs as the focal point for ethnographic attention anthropologists stressed behaviors of the past in their reports, especially in those written before 1930. They wrote about breechclouts, feather headdresses, tepees, and so on, unintentionally conveying the impression that these forms continued to prevail. Contemporary Indians often cry "foul" because in their lives and often in the lives of their grandparents such customs were not followed. Thus, ethnographers misrepresented Indians because they froze them in time. No one could deny that this often has been the case. However, it should be noted that by now far more studies have been written about historic changes in Indian life than have appeared about their aboriginal life.

Directly related to this atmosphere of misunderstanding is the fact that aboriginal Indian life often was described in terms of the "ethnographic present." This means that in spite of the fact that an ethnographer realizes the customs he describes are extinct, he reports his information in the present tense. He does so as a technique to convey that these were actual behaviors. Furthermore, information about Indian life twenty or thirty years ago often is described in the ethnographic present just as is information dealing with a far more remote time period, and again this conveys the false impression of changeless societies. This criticism is valid, and considering the vast changes that have occurred among many Indians in the recent past, it clearly distorts contemporary realities.

D'Arcy McNickle suggests that the use of the ethnographic present, and the failure by ethnographers to consider the adaptive changes in Indian lifeways, has led to another unfortunate result. The failure of investigators to stress the vitality of Indian customs as a modern life style has abetted the advocates of Indian assimilation. Acculturation studies have been an important thrust in ethnographic fieldwork since the early 1930's, and most of them indeed have stressed the negative aspects of reservation life. This hardly is a criticism of the Indians involved, however, nor was it intended as a prop for assimilation programs. Instead it often was an expression of dismay about federal programs as they were administered at the time.

Many older Indians are quite sympathetic when an ethnographer arrives to collect information about the past, but younger Indians often have neutral or hostile attitudes toward these efforts. One reason for the dichotomy is that older people see what they regard as the essence of Indian life disappearing, and they are aware that their children or grandchildren have no interest in perpetuating the traditional past. Thus it is very satisfying for an old man or woman to talk about the past to an ethnographer and have him record the conversation. The attitude of many younger Indians about such information is one of disinterest or of shame about old customs. If or when the younger people do want to learn of their past, it is most likely that they will have to rely on the writings of those ethnographers they currently resent.

Possibly a more important question than why Indians object to being studied by anthropologists is: If anthropologists know so much about Indians, why have they not played a greater role as "experts" in guiding culture change? The basic reason is quite straightforward. The guiding principle behind Federal Indian policy in the United States has been assimilation, and the sooner the better. This view runs contrary to the values held by many anthropologists. By training and inclination they find the death of any culture sad and regrettable. At the time the Indian Reorganization Act went into effect, because it was designed to bring vitality back into reservation life, a number of outstanding anthropologists worked for the B.I.A. in efforts to further provisions of the act. However, World War II diverted national attention from this program, and the early 1950's ushered in the termination policy, which found little sympathy among most anthropologists. The B.I.A. always has been in theory committed to a policy of Indian assimilation, but as most bureaucratic organizations it has in fact devoted a great deal of energy to its own expansion. From 1955 to 1968 the number of B.I.A. employees rose from 9500 to 16,000. Furthermore, bureau personnel often regard anthropologists as "Indian lovers" and neither seek nor welcome their advice. Anthropologists in turn have little sympathy with bureau policies in general and have preferred not to become involved in their programs

Anthropologists clearly have served Indians in diverse useful and positive ways. The Fox Project is the example most completely discussed in the text. Anthropologists have worked for the Department of Health, Education, and Welfare in order to improve the effectiveness of health programs; they have given evidence before the Indian Claims Commission in order to validate claims; they have testified in vigorous support of the Native American Church; they often have served as advisors to Indians in economic development programs. Furthermore, anthropologists have played an important role in interpreting Indian behavior to interested whites, both in the classroom and outside of it.

One chapter of *Custer Died for Your Sins* by Vine Deloria, titled "Anthropologists and Other Friends," is a direct attack by an Indian on anthropologists. The text is very clever and often most perceptive. Deloria objects to the use of anthropological data about Indians in order to build theoretical models with Indians as the testing ground. He feels that the models distort what Indians really are. However, models are designed to distill an essence of behavior, not to convey details about reality, and while they may not be beneficial to Indians, neither are they dangerous. Furthermore, he blames anthropologists for many of the ills which beset Indians. The implication is that anthropologists have had a profound influence in plotting the course of federal policies concerning Indians, which is quite doubtful. He also stresses that anthropologists have produced a vast archive of useless information, which is no doubt true insofar as many persons are concerned. Yet these writings exist and may be read or ignored. Deloria also writes, "Why should we continue to be the private zoos for anthropologists?" The answer seems clear. Indians should not accept anthropologists if they are disinclined to do so. If the purpose of a study seems questionable or offensive, the Indians involved have the clear right to refuse their cooperation.

Numerous anthropologists, myself included, are distressed by some of the prevailing criticisms, such as those offered by Deloria. I always have considered anthropologists to be the most sympathetic block of non-Indians interested in Indian customs. At one time some, or possibly many, anthropologists were most interested in seeing old Indian ways preserved, but just as Indians have changed so have anthropologists.

Indians often have been called the "first Americans," to indicate the priority of their residence in North America. Because they were here when whites arrived, Europeans usually attempted to deal with Indians as if they were nations in the European sense. As whites came to dominate Indians in political and economic terms, they reassessed their position and considered Indians as dependent nations and then simply tribes.

The administrative paternalism which evolved recognized the unique status of Indians among American minorities. Indians themselves are increasingly aware that their heritage is important to them, no matter how different it may be from life when whites first arrived among them. Many feel that they are SPECIAL AMERICANS to whom the governments of the United States and Canada have lasting, extraordinary obligations. Many Indians seek not just tolerance of their ways but meaningful financial and moral support in order that their identity may endure so long as the waters shall flow and the sun shall shine. This is their clear right and our abiding obligation because this land indeed was theirs.

References

Cohen, Felix S. *The Legal Conscience*. Lucy K. Cohen, ed., New Haven. 1960.

Cook, S. F. *The Epidemic of 1830-1833 in California and Oregon*, University of California Publications in American Archaeology and Ethnology, v. 43, no. 3. 1955.

Deloria, Vine. *Custer Died for Your Sins*. New York. 1969.

Duran, James A. "Canadian Indian Policy: A Year of Debate," *The Indian Historian*, v. 4, no. 3,34–36. 1971.

Ewers, John C. "The Emergence of the Plains Indian as the Symbol of the North American Indian," *Smithsonian Report for 1964*. 531-544, 1965.

Foreman, Grant. *Indian Removal*. Norman. 1932.

Gabourie, Fred W. *Justice and the Urban American Indian*. (pamphlet), Sherman Oaks, California. nd.

Hagan, William T. *American Indians*. Chicago. 1961.

Harper, Allan G. "Canada's Indian Administration: The Treaty System," *American Indigena*, v. 7, 129-148. 1947.

Hertzberg, Hazel W. *The Search for an American Indian Identity*. Syracuse. 1971.

Howard, James H. "Pan-Indian Culture of Oklahoma," *Scientific Monthly*, v. 81, no. 5, 215-220. 1955.

"The Iroquois Wampum Controversy," *The Indian Historian*, v. 3, no. 2, 4. 1970.

Jorgensen, Joseph G. "Indians and the Metropolis," in *The American Indian in Urban Society*, Jack O. Waddell and O. Michael Watson, eds., 66-113. Boston. 1971.

La Barre, Weston. "Twenty Years of Peyote Studies," *Current Anthropology*, v. 1, 45-60. 1960.

Lurie, Nancy O. "Menominee Termination," *The Indian Historian*, v. 4, no. 4, 33-43, 1971.

Lurie, Nancy O. "The Contemporary American Indian Scene," in *North American Indians in Historical Perspective*, Eleanor S. Leacock and Nancy O. Lurie, eds., 418-480. New York. 1971.

McNickle, D'Arcy. "American Indians Who Never Were," *The Indian Historian*, v. 3, no. 3, 4-7. 1970.

Officer, James E. "The American Indian and Federal Policy," in *The American Indian in Urban Society*, Jack O. Waddell and O. Michael Watson, eds., 8-65. Boston. 1971.

Pearce, Roy H. *The Savages of America*. Baltimore. 1965.

Rogers, George W. "Goodbye, Great White Father-Figure," *Anthropologica*, n.s., nos. 1-2, 279-306. 1971.

Saum, Lewis O. *The Fur Trader and the Indian*. Seattle. 1965.

Sorkin, Alan L. *American Indians and Federal Aid*. Washington, D.C. 1971.

Spicer, Edward H. *Cycles of Conquest*. Tucson. 1962.

Thomas, Robert K. "Pan-Indianism," in *The American Indian Today*, Stuart Levine and Nancy O. Lurie, eds., 128-140. Baltimore. 1970.

Waddell, Jack O., and O. Michael Watson., eds. *The American Indian in Urban Society*. Boston. 1971.

Wallace, Anthony F. C. "New Religions among the Delaware Indians, 1600-1900," *Southwestern Journal of Anthropology*, v. 12, 1-21. 1956.

Wax, Murray L. *Indian Americans*. Englewood Cliffs, New Jersey. 1971.

Bibliography

All items listed here were consulted for more than one chapter.

Brebner, John B. *The Explorers of North America*. London. 1933 (reprinted, New York. 1955).

Dice, Lee R. *Biotic Provinces of North America*. Ann Arbor. 1943.

Driver, Harold E. *Indians of North America*. Chicago. 1961.

Driver, Harold E., and William C. Massey. "Comparative Studies of North American Indians," *Transactions of the American Philosophical Society*, v. 47, pt. 2. 1957.

Hodge, Frederick W., ed. *Handbook of American Indians North of Mexico*. Smithsonian Institution, Bureau of American Ethnology, Bulletin 30, pts. 1, 2. 1907.

Kroeber, Alfred L. *Cultural and Natural Areas of Native North America*. University of California Publications in American Archaeology and Ethnology, v. 38. 1939.

Mooney, James. "The Aboriginal Population of America North of Mexico," *Smithsonian Miscellaneous Collections*, v. 80, no. 7. 1928.

Murdock, George P. *Ethnographic Bibliography of North America*. New Haven. 1960.

Swanton, John R. *The Indian Tribes of North America*. Smithsonian Institution, Bureau of American Ethnology, Bulletin 145. 1953.

Tax, Sol. *The North American Indians, 1950 Distribution of Descendants of the Aboriginal Population of Alaska, Canada, and the United States* (map). 1960.

U. S. Indian Population (1962) and Land (1963). United States Department of the Interior. Bureau of Indian Affairs. 1963.

Name Index

General Index

605